D0552383

Lisbon

timeout.com/lisbon

Penguin Books

PENGUIN BOOKS

Published by the Penguin Group
Penguin Books Ltd, 27 Wrights Lane, London W8 5TZ, England
Penguin Books USA Inc., 375 Hudson Street, New York, New York 10014, USA
Penguin Books Australia Ltd, Ringwood, Victoria, Australia
Penguin Books Canada Ltd, 10 Alcorn Avenue, Toronto, Ontario, Canada M4V 3B2
Penguin Books (NZ) Ltd, 182-190 Wairau Road, Auckland 10, New Zealand

Penguin Books Ltd, Registered Offices: Harmondsworth, Middlesex, England

First published 1999
Second edition 2001
10 9 8 7 6 5 4 3 2 1

Colour reprographics by Icon, Crown House, 56-58 Southwark Street, London SE1,
and Precise Litho, 34-35 Great Sutton Street, London EC1
Printed and bound by Cayfosa-Quebecor, Ctra. de Caldes, Km 3 08 130 Sta, Perpètua de Mogoda, Barcelona, Spain

Edited and designed by
Time Out Guides Limited
Universal House
251 Tottenham Court Road
London W1T 7AB
Tel + 44 (0) 20 7813 3000
Fax + 44 (0) 20 7813 6001
Email guides@timeout.com
www.timeout.com

Editorial

Editor Alison Roberts
Deputy Editor Rosamund Sales
Proofreader Rachel Sawyer
Indexer Marion Moisey

Editorial Director Peter Fiennes
Series Editor Ruth Jarvis
Managing Editor Dave Rimmer
Deputy Series Editor Jonathan Cox
Editorial Assistant Jenny Noden

Design

Art Director John Oakey
Art Editor Mandy Martin
Senior Designer Scott Moore
Designers Benjamin de Lotz, Lucy Grant
Scanning/Imaging Dan Conway
Picture Editor Kerri Miles
Deputy Picture Editor Olivia Duncan-Jones
Picture Researcher Cecile Borra
Ad Make-up Glen Impey

Advertising

Group Commercial Director Lesley Gill
Sales Director Mark Phillips
International Sales Co-ordinator Ross Canadé
Advertisement Sales (Lisbon) João Carvalho
Advertising Assistant Catherine Shepherd

Administration

Publisher Tony Elliott
Managing Director Mike Hardwick
Financial Director Kevin Ellis
Marketing Director Christine Cort
Marketing Manager Mandy Martinez
Group General Manager Nichola Coulthard
Production Manager Mark Lamond
Production Controller Samantha Furniss
Accountant Sarah Bostock

Features in this guide were written and researched by:

Introduction Alison Roberts. **History** Brad Cherry, Simon Kuin, Alison Roberts. **Lisbon Today** Alison Roberts. **Architecture** Dave Rimmer, Anthony Smith. **Ethnic Lisbon** Gareth Chetwynd, Alison Roberts. **Accommodation** Rupert Eden. **Sightseeing** Brad Cherry, Dave Rimmer, Alison Roberts. **Museums** Alison Roberts. **Restaurants** Claire Davies, Simon Kuin, Dave Rimmer, Alison Roberts, Anthony Smith, Tomas Tranaeus. **Cafés** Dave Rimmer, Alison Roberts. **Bars** Jared Hawkey, Dave Rimmer, Alison Roberts, Alvaro Soto, Tomas Tranaeus. **Shops & Services** Claire Davies. **By Season** Alison Roberts. **Children** Barry Hatton. **Film** Martin Dale. **Galleries** Ruth Rosengarten. **Gay & Lesbian** Jonathan Weightman. **Music: Classical** Ivan Moody. **Music: Fado** Gonçalo Macedo, Peter Wise. **Music: Roots, Rock & Jazz** David Hardisty, Alison Roberts. **Nightlife** Jared Hawkey, Alison Roberts, Alvaro Soto. **Performing Arts** Alix McAlister, Alison Roberts. **Sport & Fitness** Claire Davies, Rupert Eden, Kevin Rose, Filipe Rufino. **Getting Started** Manuela Braga, Alison Roberts. **Beaches** Gareth Chetwynd, Alvaro Soto. **Around Lisbon** Christina Lamb, Alison Roberts. **The Alentejo** Dave Rimmer, Alison Roberts. **The Algarve** Len Port. **Coimbra** Alison Roberts. **Oporto** Dave Rimmer, Alison Roberts. **Directory** José Feitor, Sandy Gageiro, Alison Roberts, Kevin Rose, Peter Wise.

Maps by JS Graphics, 17 Beadles Lane, Old Oxted, Surrey RH8 9JG.

Photography by Hadley Kincade except: page 7 AKG London; page 11, 15, 20 Mary Evans Picture Library; page 12 Art Archive; page 22, 23 Hulton Getty; page 24 Associated Press; page 188 BFI; page 179 Alvaro Soto;page 205 Museu da Cidade de Lisboa; page 251, 252, 254, 257, 259, 263 Images Colour Library; page 243, 244, 245, 247 World Pictures; page 244 Junta de Turismo da Costa do Estoril.
The following photographs were supplied by the featured establishments: pages 189, 203.

Contents

Introduction

Many of the world's cities can be said to be full of contradictions, but Lisbon's claim is probably better than most. Here, medieval alleys where sitting tenants on controlled rents pay the equivalent of £20 a month can be found not much more than a mile away from gleaming office buildings where a shortage of good properties has pushed rents up to levels higher than those in Madrid.

Black-clad widows who wouldn't look out of place in a remote hill village potter around the *bairros populares*, the city's older quarters, rarely going further afield than the nearest market. On summer nights, you might find the same streets crammed with groups of young people with drinks in their hands, generating the kind of atmosphere that in most European cities only comes with an organised street festival. There may not be more going on in Lisbon than there is in other European cities, but it can feel that way because it's more concentrated.

After years languishing under the world's longest-lasting dictatorship (which won it an entry in the *Guinness Book of Records*), surviving the turbulent aftermath of the 1974 Revolution with a stable parliamentary democracy, and consolidating its membership of the European Union, the country is undergoing something of a renaissance. The arts world is buzzing, despite a chronic lack of funding in what is still one of the poorest countries in western Europe. The success of Expo 98 has given the Portuguese the confidence to think big, most recently by successfully bidding to host the Euro 2004 football championship finals.

And renaissance it is for a people long in the habit of basking in the reflected glory of their forebears. In fact, projects on this scale haven't been undertaken since Portuguese caravels set out from Lisbon to 'discover' the rest of the world more than five centuries ago.

Modernity may have its price, not least appalling traffic jams, but thankfully it hasn't ironed out all Lisbon's quirks. There are still lots of hidden corners waiting to be explored, Take the city's African live music venues, frequented not only by immigrants but by some of the hundreds of thousands of ethnic Portuguese *retornados* who 'returned' to Lisbon in the 1970s after Portugal's colonies gained independence.

Lisbon's long experience of contact with other cultures, in the form of exploitation, exchange, or a messy combination of the two, has marked it deeply. Seen as a backwater for much of the last century, it was once a world city – perhaps the first of the kind – and is finally becoming one again.

ABOUT THE TIME OUT CITY GUIDES

The *Time Out Lisbon Guide* is one of an expanding series of *Time Out* City Guides, now numbering over 30, produced by the people behind London and New York's successful listings magazines. Our guides are all written and updated by resident experts who have striven to provide you with all the most up-to-date information you'll need to explore the city or read up on its background, whether you're a local or a first-time visitor.

THE LOWDOWN ON THE LISTINGS

Above all, we've tried to make this book as useful as possible. Addresses, telephone numbers, websites, transport information, opening times, admission prices and credit card details are all included in our listings, which were all checked and correct as we went to press. However, in Lisbon, small shops and bars may not keep precise opening hours, sometimes close earlier or later than stated according to the level of trade and may close for as much as a month at a time, especially in summer. Performing arts events also may start a little later than scheduled. Cafés and bars open and close with startling rapidity. While every effort has been made to ensure the accuracy of the information in this guide, the publishers cannot accept responsibility for any errors it may contain.

PRICES AND PAYMENT

We have noted where venues such as shops, hotels and restaurants accept the following credit cards: American Express (**AmEx**), Diners Club (**DC**), MasterCard (**MC**) and Visa (**V**). Many businesses also accept other cards, including Switch, Delta and JCB. In addition, some shops, restaurants and attractions take travellers' cheques issued by major financial institutions.

There is an online version of this guide, as well as weekly events listings for over 30 international cities, at www.timeout.com.

THE LIE OF THE LAND AND MAPS

We have divided Lisbon by area, covering the places that are likely to be of most interest to visitors. Our Sightseeing chapters cover central Lisbon, areas east and west of Baixa, the city's western waterfront, São Bento and beyond, northern Lisbon, Caminho do Oriente and some parts of the city south of the River Tagus. But bear in mind that some shops, bars, clubs, restaurants or cafés may lie outside these zones. For each entry, we have given a map reference, indicating the page and square on which an address will be found on our maps at the back of the book.

TELEPHONE NUMBERS

There are now no city codes in Portugal; Lisbon numbers all start with 21, but these digits form part of the number. (If you want to call an old seven-digit number, adding 21 onto the front should work; this replaces the old city code, 01.) To dial another part of Portugal from Lisbon, simply dial the number, which invariably starts with 2. The country code for Portugal is 351

ESSENTIAL INFORMATION

For all the practical information you might need for visiting the city, including emergency phone numbers and details of local transport, turn to the **Directory** chapter at the back of the guide. It starts on page 268.

LET US KNOW WHAT YOU THINK

We hope you enjoy the *Time Out Lisbon Guide*, and we'd like to know what you think of it. We welcome tips for any places that you consider we should include in future editions and take note of your criticism of our choices. There's a reader's reply card at the back of this book, or email us on lisbonguide@timeout.com.

The euro

As of midnight on 28 February 2002, the escudo will cease to be legal tender, its place taken by the euro. Below is a guide to equivalent values of the euro and escudo. For more information, see p282.

E1 = 200.482 escudos
E2 = 400.965 escudos
E5 = 1,002.41 escudos
E10 = 2,004.82 escudos
E25 = 5,012.05 escudos
E50 = 10,024.1 escudos
E100 = 20,048.2 escudos
E250 = 50,120.5 escudos

100$00 = E0.50
500$00 = E2.49
1,000$00 = E4.99
5,000$00 = E24.94
10,000$00 = E49.88
50,000$00 = E249.40
100,000$00 = E498.80
250,000$00 = E1,246.99

ROLEX

Rolex Day-Date. Chronometer in 18 ct gold.

In Context

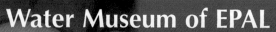

Water Museum of EPAL

The 1990 European Counsel Museum Award

WATER RESERVOIR OF MÃE D'ÁGUA OF AMOREIRAS

This reservoir was constructed in 1764 to store and distribute the water flowing from the Águas Livres Aqueduct.

Due to its beauty and splendour, the Mãe d'Água site is used for cultural events, such as art exhibitions, concerts, ballet and theatre, allowing access for the visitors to the panoramic terrace overlooking the city of Lisbon.

THE PATRIARCHAL RESERVOIR

Built between 1860 and 1864, the reservoir has become very important in the water distribution of downtown Lisbon.

Due to its location and inner beauty, the EPAL and the 94 Lisbon Society established a programme to rebuild this space and was later honoured with the "Eugénio dos Santos" Architecture Municipal Award.

The Reservoir was rebuild and since then has been the stage of several cultural activities, in particular, ballet and fashion events and also photograph and sculpture exhibitions.

Rua do Alviela, no 12   1170-012 Lisbon
Tel: 21 8100215

BARBADINHOS STEAM ELEVATORY STATION

The Barbadinhos Steam Elevatory Station, inaugurated in 1880, was constructed within the walls of the Barbadinhos Convent (property of the Italian order that lived there until 1739). The station was built to distribute the water coming from the river Alviela, being then consumed in Lisbon.

The Steam Elevatory Station is an eyewitness example of a 19th century industrial installation considered to be an unique case for industrial archaeology.

It includes a Permanent exhibition and a temporary exhibition room.

THE ÀGUAS LIVRES AQUEDUCT

Proposed in 1732 by the Portuguese King João V, this Lisbon "ex-libris" is considered to be one of the most remarkable hydraulic engineering achievements of all time and one the most rare and complex water supply systems of the 18th century.

EPAL has put into effect a dynamic programme and promoted the Unlimited Water Aqueduct by permitting guided tours for visitors.

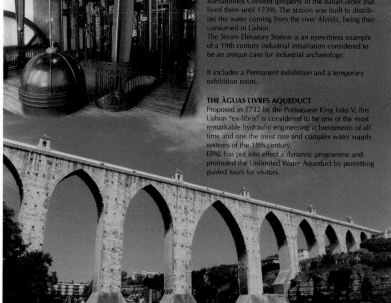

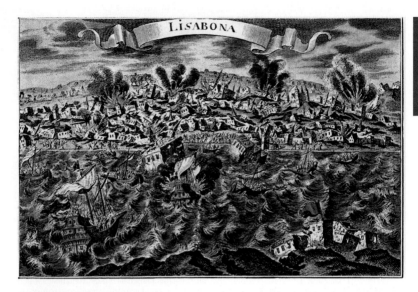

History

From the Romans to the 1974 Revolution and its aftermath.

Before reaching Lisbon, the Tagus broadens out into an estuary that is one of the world's largest natural harbours, before narrowing into a bottleneck and emptying into the Atlantic. On the northern bank numerous fresh-water streams empty into the river from the surrounding hills. The south bank land is flatter, with marshes and inlets that from prehistory until the industrial age were famed for rich oyster beds and fisheries; a wide network of salt pans can still be seen outside the towns of Alcochete and Montijo. Lisbon grew up on and around the north bank's most prominent hill, above a section of riverbank where the current runs fastest and deepest. The city owes its eminence not just to the opening to the sea, but also to the Tagus river, the longest water course in the Iberian peninsula, draining a basin stretching beyond Madrid and Toledo.

One widely held tradition has it that Ulysses visited this estuary and founded the city, and that Lisbon is a corruption of his name. Others point to the Phoenicians, whose term 'Alis Ubbo' – 'peaceful harbour' – eventually mutated to Olisipo, and then to Lisbon. Legend aside,

this region has been populated for millennia. Nomadic hunting societies left their mark in the area, while later prehistoric agricultural populations settled on small tributaries of the Tagus. The estuary also harboured various primitive shell-gathering cultures.

The Lisbon area was a crossroads of late Bronze Age trade and from the eighth to the sixth centuries BC was touched by Phoenicians extending their Atlantic trade up from Cadiz in Spain. They were often seeking gold – then easily found in the sands of the Tagus estuary.

THE ROMANS

The Roman presence in the Iberian peninsula dates to the Second Punic War in the late third century BC, which ended half a century of Carthaginian domination. Putting down restive locals proved altogether more difficult, however, and the Pax Romana was only established across the entire peninsula after two hard-fought centuries. One chieftain – Viriatus – gained renown as a leader of the resistance between 147 and 139 BC, harrying Roman legions from his redoubt in the Serra da Estrela. His tribe, the Lusitani, gave its name to the Roman province of

The **Castelo de São Jorge** was built by the Moors on Roman foundations. *See p9.*

Lusitania, whose borders encompassed most of present-day Portugal. (The prefix 'Luso' is still used to mean 'Portuguese'.)

Lisbon fell to the Romans in 138 BC and was occupied by the governor Decimus Junius Brutus. He fortified the emergent city, though it's not clear where he built his walls. Lisbon was made a district capital under the provincial capital Mérida, in what is now Spain. By the third decade BC the city was renamed Felicitas Julia Olisipo after Julius Caesar, then an Iberian peninsula commander. The Roman city grew quickly, spreading down from today's Castelo de São Jorge (*see p79*) to the Tagus in the south and, in the west, along the inlet that then ran all the way up to what is now Rossio – in those days the site of a hippodrome.

The most notable Roman remain in Lisbon is the Teatro Romano, an amphitheatre built during the reign of the Emperor Augustus; it was rediscovered in 1798, just up from where the Sé Cathedral now stands. It is covered by an iron shed, only half-excavated, although you can make out rows of stone seats. The Forum was probably near a Roman arch that stood by the present-day Largo da Madalena. On Rua da Conceição is the entrance to a catacomb of vaulted cellars under part of the Baixa. There are varous theories as to their purpose: perhaps conserving fish or as the foundations for a waterfront temple.

TRADING PLACES
For four centuries Olisipo remained a prosperous Roman city governing a district that extended northwards towards present-day Torres Vedras and Alenquer, with the main road passing through the northern suburb of

Sacavém and southward to Olisipo along the valley of Chelas. Rich farmland was dotted with large estates known as 'villae', remains of which have been found near the airport and in various sites around Cascais. Waterfront activity centred on the fish conservation industry and on maritime commerce with the rest of the empire. Excavated tombstones show that many citizens bore Greek surnames, evidence of trade links with the eastern Mediterranean.

'Roman rule in the Iberian peninsula came to a crashing end in the year 409.'

Christianity was established by the middle of the fourth century. There is a persistent legend of three Christians – Verissimus, Maximus and Julia – martyred during the persecution by the Emperor Diocletian. The beach where they were executed was named Santos, and it was to them that the first Portuguese king addressed his prayers before conquering Lisbon.

Roman rule in the Iberian peninsula came to a crashing end in the year 409 when hordes of Suevi, Alans and Vandals swept over the Pyrenees. The Suevi took much of the north; the Alans settled between the Douro and Tagus; and the Vandals split up, one group heading up to Galicia, the other south. Lisbon fell to the Alans, a people of Iranian origin, although they have left few traces. In 418, the Romans called in the Visigoths to kick out the other tribes. The Alans were forced to join with the Vandals in the south (in Vandalusia, later Andalusia), before both groups were kicked across into North Africa.

The Visigoths set up their own kingdom, ruled from Toledo, which came to dominate most of the peninsula. Their only serious rivals were the Suevi, based in Braga, who continued to rule much of northern Portugal.

Olisipo seems to have got along rather independently with intervals in Suevi hands, before finally falling to the Visigoths in 469. Elsewhere, the last Suevi domains were absorbed in 585, and for most of the next century the Visigoths ruled the Iberian peninsula.

MOORISH LISBON

In 711, the armies of Islam disembarked in southern Spain and within five short years had conquered most of the peninsula. They arrived in Lisbon in 714. The scattered remnants of Iberian Christendom regrouped in the mountains of northern Spain and began what became known as the Reconquista. By the mid-800s, much of northern Portugal was once again in Christian hands, with raiding parties making occasional forays as far south as the Tagus.

The Christian area around Oporto became known as Portucale, the 'gateway to Cale', a county of the Kingdom of Leon. Lisbon, however, remained in Muslim hands for three more centuries. The Moorish traveller Al-Idrisi in his *Geography* wrote of the city now called Al-Uxbuna: 'This lovely city is defended by a ring of walls and a powerful castle'. The castle was built over the earlier Roman fortification where the Castelo now stands. The Moorish siege walls – Cerca Moura – enclosed about 15 hectares/38 acres. They ran down from the Castelo to the present-day Portas do Sol, where one tower now houses the Cerca Moura café (*see p143*). From there the line of the walls can be traced down the steps, through Alfama to the riverfront, and over to Largo da Madalena where the Roman arch was now used as the main city gate.

LABYRINTHINE LISBON

However, much of the city stood outside the walls, such as the Alfama district tumbling down towards the river. Its labyrinthine street pattern dates back to this period, while its name (Al-Hama, 'hot springs') refers to the abundance of water – later medieval fountains on Largo do Chafariz de Dentro and Chafariz d'el Rei are still in use.

Moorish Lisbon at its ninth-century height had a population of nearly 30,000, making it a major city of Al-Andalus. The main mosque – situated where the cloisters of the present-day Sé now stand – was the centre of the city's life. Immigrants, from Yemeni Arabs to newly converted Moroccan Berbers, had flooded in from North Africa and Arabia, and Arabic became the predominant language. As so-called Peoples of the Book, the native Christian and Jewish populations stayed on and were allowed to practise their own religions. Christians were known as Mozarabs, and had their own bishops. After centuries of such religious tolerance, one third of the city's 15,000 population was Christian when the city fell to Portuguese and crusader forces in 1147, and most were massacred along with everyone else. Muslims would have to wait eight more centuries for permission to build a place of worship – the new Lisbon Mosque was inaugurated near the Praça de Espanha in 1985.

THE RECONQUEST

The Christian reconquest of Lisbon was led by Afonso Henriques. After the death of his father, Henrique, who had ruled Portucale and Galicia, Afonso Henriques wrestled control of Portucale from his mother Teresa in 1128. In 1139, he won an impressive victory over the Moors at Ourique; a year later he proclaimed Portugal a kingdom, and himself king. Though the Portuguese claim 1140 as the year their nation was founded, the Pope only gave his approval in 1179 (in exchange for 1,000 gold coins).

> **'For centuries Lisbon had been a provincial outpost. Now it was the political and business capital of a new nation.'**

Aided by a passing army of crusaders from northern Europe, in summer 1147 Afonso Henriques attacked Lisbon. After a three-month siege chronicled by English crusader Osberne, on St Crispin's Day, 25 October 1147, the combined Christian force was led over the top by a soldier called Martim Moniz. (The walls of the Metro station named after him are decorated with crusader-style figures.) The army breached the walls on the slope by the present-day Escadinhas de São Crispim, just below the Castelo, and soon crusaders were running amok through the city in an orgy of plunder and bloodletting.

During subsequent raids against the Moors further south, Afonso Henriques heard of a cliffside shrine in the Algarve where relics of St Vincent were supposedly kept hidden, guarded by flocks of ravens. A first land expedition to what is now called Cabo São Vicente, near Sagres, failed to come up with the goods, but a second sea expedition retrieved the remains. According to the legend, the boat bearing the saint's corpse, still circled by ravens, reached Lisbon in September 1173. Since that day the image of a boat and ravens has been the symbol of the city of Lisbon, although reverence for St Vincent, the city's official patron saint, has been supplanted by the more popular midsummer celebrations in honour of the Lisbon-born St Anthony of Padua. *See chapter* **By Season**.

LISBON BECOMES CAPITAL

The last Moorish bastions in the Algarve fell in 1249 and Lisbon soon established itself as the capital of the new kingdom, replacing Coimbra. The city was still concentrated within the old Moorish walls, and the royal palace located in the castle. The Sé Cathedral (*see p78*) was built on the site of the Moorish mosque soon after the city was conquered, and Afonso Henriques appointed Gilbert of Hastings as bishop. The Sé joined other houses of worship such as the primitive chapels of Santos and St Gens (nowadays Senhora do Monte). Moors and Jews were allowed to stay on but only outside the city walls – in Mouraria behind the castle and Judiarias in Alfama and the Baixa.

For centuries Lisbon had been a provincial outpost on the frontiers of Islam or Christianity; now it was political and business capital of a new nation. Maritime commerce picked up as Portuguese ships plied northern trade routes as far as the Baltic, and south into the Mediterranean. Overland trade increased sporadically, depending on the shifting state of relations with neighbouring Castile and Leon, and with Muslim Andalusia.

Medieval Portugal reached its height during the reign of Dom Dinis (1279-1325), a brilliant administrator and poet who set himself up in one of Europe's most intellectually dazzling troubadour courts. Besides founding the University of Lisbon in 1290 (it eventually moved to Coimbra), Dinis also planted pine forests along the coast to protect against erosion, and built castles to defend against Castilians and Moors. Portugal's borders were formalised in the 1297 Treaty of Alcanices with Castile and survive almost unchanged until this day.

By the late 13th century, the city's population had swollen to over 14,000 and the walls were expanded to enclose 60 hectares/150 acres. The commercial centre moved downhill into the Baixa, with the diagonal Rua Nova (now disappeared) as the main street. The river inlet that earlier stretched up to Rossio was now dry, though still subject to occasional flooding. Rossio was a busy open-air marketplace.

The decades following the death of Dinis, in 1325, were decidedly grimmer than the period of his enlightened reign. In Lisbon there were several earthquakes. The first, in 1321,

knocked down part of the Sé. In 1337, the earth shook on Christmas Day. Another serious quake occurred in 1344, again damaging the Sé. The city took a further drubbing in 1356, when tremors set the church bells ringing all by themselves. And the Black Death devastated the city in 1348 and 1349.

THESE CITY WALLS

Despite quakes and persistent grain shortages, Lisbon would soon once more outgrow its walls, creeping up the hills north and west of Rossio. When a Castilian raiding party laid waste to much of extramural Lisbon in 1373, torching a large part of the Baixa, Dom Fernando I had new walls built. The Cerca Fernandina was 5.35 kilometres/three miles long with 77 towers and 38 gates (16 landward, 22 facing the Tagus) and enclosed Rossio, the entire Baixa and part of today's Chiado, along with nearly 50,000 residents. The Portas de Santa Catarina stood where two churches now face each other in Largo do Chiado. Downhill, on the left side of Rua do Alecrim, remnants of these walls can still be seen.

When Fernando died in 1383, war broke out between supporters of his widow Leonor Teles and João, master of the Aviz Military Order. Leonor sought support in Castille. When the two sides met in 1385 at Aljubarrota, a vastly outnumbered Portuguese force, assisted by English archers, trounced the invaders. The battle cemented Portuguese independence. João I was hailed as king and thus founded Portugal's second ruling house – the Avis dynasty. In gratitude he ordered the construction of the magnificent monastery of Batalha. And partly as thanks for the English archers, he signed the Treaty of Windsor, an alliance with England still valid today. Meanwhile, in Lisbon, João's right-hand man Nun'Álvares Pereira set about building the Convento do Carmo (*see p85*). Its roofless ruins on Largo do Carmo bear witness to the destructive power of the earthquake four centuries later.

THE DISCOVERIES

Portugal's first maritime foray was the 1415 conquest of Ceuta on the North African coast. Among those who took part in the assault were a young royal prince named Henriques, son of Dom João I and the English princess Philippa of Lancaster. In Portuguese Henriques is known as the Infante Dom Henriques and in English as Prince Henry the Navigator. After Ceuta, Henry began training and funding mariners. In 1415 and 1416 expeditions sailed to the Canary Islands; Madeira was 'discovered' around 1419; the Azores in the 1430s. Ships were also dispatched to explore the African coast. The physical and psychological barrier of Cape Bojador – people thought they'd fall off the edge of the world – was overcome and charted by Gil Eanes in 1434.

What prompted this sudden burst of activity? João I had taken over a country with a sense of identity forged in battle, but which could not expand on the Iberian peninsula. So Portugal went to sea, driven by greed, adventure and religious fervour – Prince Henry was a master of the Order of Christ, the successor to the Knights Templar and a powerful religious-military society dedicated to attacking Islam. The Portuguese took on the Moors in North Africa. After Ceuta fell in 1415, Alcacer-Ceguer followed in 1458, and Arzila and Tangier in 1471.

Madeira and the Azores had by now been settled and a brisk trade soon grew up between Lisbon and these latest additions to what was now known as the 'Kingdom of Portugal, the Algarve and the Ocean Seas and Beyond in Africa'. Prince Henry died in 1460, but his enterprise carried on, and by the mid-1470s Portuguese squadrons were active in the Gulf of Guinea and had crossed the equator.

Trade with Asia in the 15th century was controlled by Venice, Genoa and Cairo, and there was no way around them without achieving the unachievable and sailing around Africa. After Prince Henry, the next royal to take an interest in exploration was Prince – and later King – Dom João II, nicknamed the Perfect Prince, of whom it has been said that if he hadn't been born, Machiavelli would have invented him. João II's first priority was the elimination of rivals. He had the Duke of Braganza publicly beheaded in Évora and the next year personally stabbed to death his brother-in-law, the Duke of Viseu. Meanwhile, he masterminded Portugal's policy of expansion and trade.

Sailing under the king's orders, a Portuguese navigator named Diogo Cão reached the Zaire river in 1482 and later explored the coast as far south as Angola. Bartholomew Dias rounded the Cape of Good Hope in 1488 and reported to João II that Africa was indeed circumnavigable. In 1497 Vasco da Gama set out from Restelo

(later renamed Belém) with a fleet of three caravels and one supply ship. Rounding the Cape in November, he sailed up the East African coast and across to India, putting in at Calicut on 20 May 1498. The door was now open for Portuguese domination of the Indian Ocean trade.

Portugal's one serious rival in the first century of maritime expansion was Spain. The 1479 Treaty of Alcaçovas was the two countries' first attempt to divide the world between them. So when Christopher Columbus returned from his 1492 voyage to America, the Portuguese were at pains to point out that the lands he had claimed for Spain actually lay within the Portuguese sphere of influence. The 1494 Treaty of Tordesillas divided the world between the two along a line drawn 370 leagues west of Cape Verde. Portugal could take anything to the east – which included much of present-day Brazil – with the exception of the Canary Islands (already ruled by Spain).

ROUTES TO RICHES

In Lisbon, the reigning monarch was Dom Manuel I, nicknamed the Fortunate because he took the throne in 1495, just before Portugal won the India lottery jackpot, which he greedily controlled through a series of royal monopolies. The wealth of Africa, the Azores and Madeira was beginning to enrich Lisbon merchants. After Vasco da Gama returned from India with his first cargo of spices, the city was soon overwhelmed by the 'vapours of India', an irresistible force that drew young and old alike out and over the seas. Many never returned, victims of shipwreck, piracy, tropical disease, combat or, far too often, quarrelling over the easy plunder.

The capital had a population of 40,000 at the end of the 15th century, and it was growing west along the river, with convents and palaces springing up between Santos and Belém. The influx of Asian riches soon made Lisbon the richest city in Europe. Traders in silks and spices, moneychangers and booksellers jostled

Prince Henry launched a thousand ships.

An unattributed 16th-century Portuguese school painting depicts caravels setting sail.

for space along the Rua Nova in the Baixa. The opulence was unrivalled – as was the depravity that accompanied it. The atmosphere was caricatured by Gil Vicente in his play *Auto da Índia*, depicting a Lisbon wife at play while her husband was in the Indies.

King Manuel now moved his royal residence down from the Castelo to a waterfront palace on the Terreiro do Paço, as Praça do Comércio is still sometimes known. The new palace was next to the Ribeira dos Naus, the shipyards that outfitted the fleets. From his new digs Manuel could keep an eye on the wealth flowing in, much of it into his own pockets. He spent part of it in building two important monuments: the Torre de Belém (*see p94*) to guard the harbour entrance, and the Mosteiro dos Jerónimos (*see p95*) to thank God for all this newfound wealth. Both are masterpieces of the Portuguese late-Gothic style known as Manueline, replete with numerous oriental and maritime motifs.

In 1492, Ferdinand and Isabel of Spain had expelled all non-Christians after conquering Moorish Granada. Portugal at first welcomed fugitive Jews, but in 1496 expelled all Moors and Jews who refused baptism. Those who stayed on soon formed a sub-class of so-called New Christians. In 1506 thousands of Jews were massacred in a Lisbon-wide riot that lasted for days, and a plume of smoke rose above Rossio as bodies were burnt. After this, Jews fled to North Africa and northern Europe, notably the Low Countries.

Lisbon's population grew in fits and starts through the 16th century, to 72,000 in 1527 – another plague year. The city certainly had its glories – Damião de Góis described seven of its buildings as wonders of the world, among them the Palácio de Estaus and Hospital de Todos-os-Santos on Rossio. (None survived the 1755 earthquake.) But other travellers complained of the stench of rotting bodies in the Poço dos Negros and Poço dos Mouros, large pits into which were cast slaves' corpses. Crime was rampant. One Portuguese adventurer walked all the way back from India, braving countless dangers en route, only to be robbed at daggerpoint before the gates of the royal palace.

EMPIRE IN ASIA

The Indian Ocean, traversed by Roman, Arab, Indian and Chinese merchants, had for centuries been surrounded by prosperous cities and states. In many places standards of living and literacy were more advanced than in western Europe and the various religions who lived and traded on its shores were generally tolerant of each other. The Portuguese rolled in like fundamentalist terrorists, armed with bronze cannon – unknown in the region – and willing to use calculated,

The Discoveries glorified under Salazar – the **Padrão dos Descobrimentos**.

cold-blooded violence on a scale for which locals were completely unprepared.

On Vasco da Gama's second visit to Calicut he bombarded the city for three days, cutting off the ears, noses and hands of prisoners before burning them alive. Elsewhere he took a ship of 700 Muslim pilgrims, sank it with all passengers on board, and then sent out longboats to spear survivors in the water. Other Muslim prisoners were hauled up in the rigging and used for crossbow practice.

Thus did the Portuguese cow the Indian Ocean. Hormuz and the Persian Gulf came under Portuguese domination in 1507. In 1510, Viceroy Afonso de Albuquerque conquered Goa, which soon became the sumptuous seat of the 'pepper empire', based on the monopoly of the spice trade. In 1511 the Portuguese conquered Malacca and opened the way to the Far East. Soon fleets of caravels reached the Spice Islands (Moluccas) and Timor, and by 1513 were trading with China. When Manuel I died in 1521 his extravagant title had now become: King of Portugal and the Algarve, of the Ocean Seas and Beyond, and of Africa, Lord of Guinea and of the Conquest, Navigation, and Commerce of Ethiopia, Arabia, Persia and India.

In 1542, Portuguese ships reached Japan and, in 1557, gained the right to administer the small enclave of Macao on the southern coast of China. The poet Luís Vaz de Camões spent time here as well as in Africa, Goa and the East Indies during his 17 years of travel. At one point he almost lost his epic poem, *The Lusiads*, in a shipwreck in the South China Sea, but made it ashore on the Mekong Delta and later completed his manuscript. Published in 1572, it chronicles Vasco da Gama's first voyage to India.

Inspired by the origins of empire, Camões lived to see that empire end. The young, heirless and foolhardy Dom Sebastião I led a disastrous expedition to Morocco in 1578, where he perished along with much of the Portuguese nobility. Camões died two years later and, by 1582, Philip II of Spain had successfully claimed the Portuguese crown and put an end to the golden age of the Discoveries.

SPANISH RULE

Philip II backed his claim to the vacant Portuguese crown with an armed force that landed outside Lisbon and routed the Portuguese forces in a brief battle in the Alcântara district. Crowned Philip I of Portugal in 1581, he ruled until 1598, instituting reforms that brought Portugal's bureaucracy into line with the more modern Spanish administration. With the Iberian peninsula unified, the Habsburg Philip switched his attentions overseas. In 1588, he assembled a fleet of 130 ships and 27,000 men in Lisbon harbour and sent it northwards against England. The supposedly invincible Spanish Armada lost to both the elements and the English, scuttling Spain's ambitions of global domination.

That wasn't Lisbon's only brush with Spain's number one maritime enemy. In 1587, Sir Francis Drake had harried shipping off the coast near Lisbon. In 1589, he returned to land a force at Peniche and marched southwards. Unable to take Lisbon, he sailed back to England just three weeks later. Meanwhile in the city, construction of the Igreja de São Vicente de Fora started in 1590, King Philip bringing in his own personal architect, Juan de Herrera of Escorial fame, to help with the project.

The Inquisition had been established in Lisbon in 1537. In 1570 the religious court took up residence in the Estaus Palace in Rossio, on the site of the present-day Teatro Nacional Dona Maria II. Soon after the Spanish takeover, the Inquisition requested more funds to expand its overcrowded dungeons. Sentences were carried out in the famous *autos-da-fé*, public shows that began with processions from the Igreja de São Domingos (*see p73*) and ended with the condemned being burned at the stake in Rossio or Terreiro do Paço.

Although the country was relatively stable under the Philippine dynasty, the Portuguese soon chafed under Spanish rule – especially when Philip IV (III of Portugal) began appointing Spanish nobles to positions supposedly reserved for Portuguese and ignoring the welfare of Portuguese overseas possessions in favour of protecting Spanish ones. On 1 December 1640, a group of noble conspirators overpowered the Spanish authorities in Lisbon and proclaimed the Duke of Braganza as Dom João IV of Portugal. A nasty war of secession followed, but in 1668 Spain once again recognised Portugal's independence within its traditional borders. It also regained its overseas possessions, with the exceptions of Ceuta in North Africa and Ceylon and Malacca in Asia.

Portugal, seeking support against Spain, in 1661 arranged a marriage between Catherine of Braganza and England's King Charles II, ceding to England as part of her dowry the ports of Bombay and Tangier. Catherine is credited with

Dom Sebastião. Foolhardy.

introducing the English to tea. She is also the queen after whom the New York borough of Queens was named. A replica of her statue there now stands on the Tagus waterfront north of the Parque das Nações.

PORTUGUESE BAROQUE

In 1699 large quantities of gold were discovered in Brazil, and Portuguese coffers were soon once more overflowing with riches. The new exuberance had been prefigured by the reconstruction of the Igreja do Loreto in Chiado, the church of the city's Italian community, finished in 1663 after a dozen years of work and richly decorated with marble imported from Genoa. Meanwhile, the reconstruction of the Panteão Nacional de Santa Engrácia (*see p81*) was begun in 1681. Major delays dogged the project; the dome was only capped more than two-and-a-half centuries later, in 1966.

Brazilian gold funded construction projects around the country, the flagship being the massive monastery-palace complex started by Dom João V in 1717 at Mafra, northwest of Lisbon (*see p248*). Its bell carillon is still the largest in the world.

Elsewhere, artisans created baroque masterpieces of gold-gilt work around Lisbon – among them altarpieces in the churches of Madre de Deus (in what is now the Museu Nacional do Azulejo, *see p109*), Santa Catarina and São Roque (*see p88*). Ornate private carriages from this period can be seen at the Museu dos Coches (*see p110*). The 1730s also saw construction of the Aqueduto das Águas Livres (*see p98*), a major feat of engineering that is still standing.

But Lisbon was still mostly a medieval city of narrow lanes huddled along the shore of the Tagus. Private carriages were now commonplace for the rich and the combination of these with the narrow streets made for traffic nightmares. It was in this period that the Bairro Alto first became a centre for entertainment, as popular theatres opened to stage farces and comedies for plebeians. The aristocrats had to wait until 1750 before Dom José I built a makeshift opera house at his palace on Terreiro do Paço. By 1755 the city's population was nearly 190,000.

THE EARTHQUAKE AND AFTER

On 1 November 1755, Lisbon was struck by a devastating earthquake that was felt as far away as North Africa. It was All Saints Day at the time of morning mass and the churches were packed, while at home candles had been lit in memory of the dead. The earth shook for six minutes as the roofs and domes of churches collapsed onto screaming crowds. Houses caved in and panic-stricken citizens racing down to the river were met by a tidal wave that engulfed

You'll be the first up on the wall…

So you say you want a revolution? Then take tram 15 towards Belém and look out for an explosion of violent red and screaming yellow on a wall on Avenida 24 de Julho, just a paintbrush's throw from the trendy clubs of Alcântara. Here, larger-than-life workers sport bulging muscles, framed by old-style communist flags.

The mural is a reminder of a waning form of political propaganda in what was once a capital of the European left. It will delight connoisseurs of Marxist iconography, painted as it is by the die-hard Maoists of the Partido Comunista dos Trabalhadores Portugueses – Movimento Revolucionário do Proletariado Português. The PCTP-MRPP (as it is, thankfully, always abbreviated) is one of a myriad splinter movements that emerged in the wake of the 1974 Revolution, and for over 25 years it has been responsible for most of the revolutionary murals in Lisbon. Easily recognisable, PCTP-MRPP works are predominantly yellow and red, full of heroism, and usually allude to specific issues ('European Union out of Portugal' is a favoured theme).

The Alcântara mural, in a realist style that apes that used during China's Cultural Revolution, tells the history of the party itself, referring to its martyrs and 'Great Educator' Arnaldo Matos. It was painted just a few years ago; since Mao's teachings lack enough appeal to win the PCTP-MRPP a seat in parliament, this is how the party marks its presence on the political landscape.

In the 1970s, revolutionary murals were widespread in Lisbon and the industrial areas on the south bank, as the democratisation of artistic expression and sense of freedom after 48 years of censorship triggered an explosion of colour and slogans. It all started on 10 June 1974, when 48 painters of various artistic styles were invited to paint the exterior of Belém's Mercado do Povo (Popular Market). The mural was completed in a day, in an energetic celebration of the end of dictatorship. (It was destroyed in a fire years later.)

Most of the murals of the period were the work of political parties, each with a distinct style: neo-realism for Communists, naïf for the far left, soft tones for Socialists, orange for Social Democrats, and 'Chinese-style' yellow and red for Maoists. Most of these works have disappeared or faded to the point of being unrecognisable. More common today are the stencilled gags of the recently formed Bloco de Esquerda (Left Block), such as a black sheep mocking the electorate's herd instinct.

So has Portuguese mural art died a silent death? Not quite, but today's causes are different. In August 1999, when the Indonesian army and local militia terrorised civilians in the former Portuguese colony of East Timor after they voted massively for independence, ordinary Portuguese found their voice, mounting huge demonstrations in Lisbon and Oporto. Artists took the cause to heart and painted a mural near the US Embassy (Avenida das Forças Armadas, in Sete Rios), urging intervention in Timor. The mural is a little lost amid the chaos of motorway flyovers, but worth a visit. Lisbon's walls still have a story to tell.

Timor mural

much of the lower part of the city. On the rocky hillsides buildings collapsed, and in the Baixa even foundations disappeared in the rubble. When the first shocks were over, a dry north-east wind stirred up a fire that lasted for days.

Dom José I's chief minister, Sebastião José de Carvalho e Melo, threw himself into recovery work. Seen by some as an enlightened despot, by others as high-handed and dictatorial, he is known today as the Marquês de Pombal, a title awarded in 1769. The dust had barely settled after the earthquake when Pombal implemented the policy of 'bury the dead, feed the living'. Teams worked through the rubble searching for bodies, while tax duties on food were dropped and grain requisitioned to store up for winter. As a result no one starved and no major epidemics followed the disaster.

Rocky hillside neighbourhoods had suffered the least damage; the Baixa had been hit by the triple scourge of earthquake, tidal wave and fire. Pombal opted to build a new city on top of the old. The plan, drawn up by Eugénio dos Santos and Carlos Mardel, was closely based on the grid scheme of a military encampment. Streets in the Baixa were earmarked for distinct trades, and the old medieval maze was overlain by straight roads and right-angled corners. Anything still standing was razed and the rubble used as landfill to reduce the dangers of flooding; the Baixa, after all, was built over an old river inlet.

'Pombal's authoritarian approach brought results but also earned him enemies.'

The open space at the top of the grid – Rossio – saw its boundaries evened out into a regular rectangle, and a new main street, Rua Augusta, cut wide down to the riverside Terreiro do Paço, now renamed Praça do Comércio. Here, the rebirth of Lisbon was celebrated in 1775, 20 years after the disaster. The equestrian statue of Dom José I was unveiled in the centre of the incomplete square; makeshift wooden façades filled in the unfinished spaces on the east side.

Pombal's influence was not confined to the Baixa. Under his rule small factories opened near the Mãe de Água (*see p98*), the aqueduct terminus above Largo do Rato. Streets here are still named after the factories once housed in their low buildings.

Pombal's authoritarian approach brought results but also earned him enemies. He cowed the aristocracy after rounding up and executing nobles accused of involvement in a 1758 plot to kill the king. The following year he expelled the powerful Jesuit order from Portugal. He ended discrimination against 'New Christians' – the descendants of Jews and Moors – and in the colonies granted Brazilian Indians freedom from slavery. And he issued decree after decree to better organise Portuguese commerce. Among his accomplishments were the 1756 delimitation of the Port Wine Region in northern Portugal.

When Dom José I died in 1777 he left power in the hands of his daughter, crowned Dona Maria I. No admirer of the Marquês, she removed Pombal from power and shifted away from the English alliance, favouring links with the French monarchy. This policy had to be reversed after the French revolution in 1789. The queen's fragile health degenerated into insanity in 1791 and power was transferred to the prince regent, later Dom João I.

SOCIAL REFORM

The new power in Lisbon was the superintendent of police, or 'intendente', Diogo Inácio de Pina Manique. Increasingly in court favour from the 1780s to 1803, he was a social reformer who both waged war against urban crime and worked to alleviate social ills. He was instrumental in founding the Casa Pia charity in 1780, which still attends to orphans and the homeless today. That year Pina Manique brought in Lisbon's first widespread street-lighting scheme. He also oversaw the paving of streets, laying of sewers and rubbish collection. Even prostitutes were subject to regular health inspections. At the other end of the social scale, Pina Manique saw to the construction of the Teatro Nacional de São Carlos in 1793, and greened the city with 40,000 trees in 1799. It's a sad irony that the square named after him, the Largo do Intendente off Avenida Almirante Reis, is now the squalid centre for much of the red-light lowlife that Pina Manique worked to stamp out.

For her part, before going bonkers, Dona Maria I did leave Lisbon one important legacy, the Basílica da Estrela, built between 1779 and 1789. Another major monument was more the passion of her husband, the prince-consort Pedro, who oversaw construction of the Palácio de Queluz (*see p247*) outside Lisbon, often called the Portuguese Versailles.

In 1801, Lisbon's population stood at around 170,000 and the Baixa was thriving. Construction of yet another royal palace started in 1802 in Ajuda, above Belém, replacing the burnt-down wooden palace that housed the monarchy after the earthquake. But political turbulence interrupted the work and the Palácio da Ajuda (*see p95*) was never completed.

THE PENINSULAR WARS

In 1801 France and Spain joined in alliance and invaded Portugal. Their armies wrought havoc in the Alentejo and after a brief campaign Portugal was forced into submission, ceding to Spain the small town of Olivenza near Badajoz – still a bone of contention between the two countries.

The next few years saw the rise of Napoleon in France. Portugal tried to keep a low profile while maintaining trade links with England, but in 1806 Napoleon decreed a continental embargo on all commerce with England. Portugal was faced with an unhappy choice: give in to French demands and watch Britain take over their overseas possessions; or stand up to Napoleon and be invaded. Napoleon gave the Portuguese until September 1807 to declare war on England, or else. Portugal stalled, France invaded, and the royal family caught the last boat to Brazil, where they stayed for 14 years. Many others followed their less than valiant example and in Lisbon 11,000 passports were issued in short order.

The French invaded Portugal three times. The first time, in 1808, a British force led by General Arthur Wellesley (later Lord Wellington) sent the French packing after the decisive battles of Roliça and Vimeiro. And they packed plenty, much to the dismay of the Portuguese, who were shut out from the truce talks: Marshal Junot's forces were allowed to take everything they had plundered. The next year the French were back under Marshal Soult, but were soon ejected by joint Portuguese and British forces. In summer 1810, Marshal Masséna tried once again, and after some initial setbacks the French forces were soon marching towards Lisbon. Wellington stopped them with fortifications (the Torres Vedras Lines) stretching north of Lisbon from the Tagus to the sea. After a phoney war lasting several months the French fled. By 1814, they had been pushed back to Toulouse.

LIBERALS AND ABSOLUTISTS

The Peninsular Wars left Portugal a wreck. The countryside had been ravaged by both armies and by the 'guerilla fighters' – small bands of partisans who fought the French in both Portugal and Spain. Lisbon stagnated. The population dipped to near 150,000 and would not regain its turn-of-the-century peak until almost 1860. The wars were followed by a British regency (read, occupation) under Marshal Beresford. Over in Brazil, Dom João VI was loth to trade the comforts of court life in Rio de Janeiro for his devastated homeland.

Under the British, unrest was never far from the surface, especially as new ideas took root in Europe – words such as 'liberal' and 'constitution' had come into the dissident political vocabulary. In 1820, Beresford went to Brazil to try to coax the King home. In his absence, a revolution overthrew the British regency and installed a liberal government. Elections were held in 1820 and the Cortes, or parliament, drafted a new constitution. When it was passed in March 1821, Lisbon was lit up in celebration. The Papal Núncio neglected to hang a light in his window, which was promptly stoned.

João VI now returned, bringing his court of several thousand, and swore allegiance to the new constitution. Crown Prince Pedro, more inclined to Brazilian interests, stayed behind. In 1822, when the new Lisbon Cortes appeared ready to strip Brazil of its status as a kingdom on a par with Portugal, Brazil declared independence with Pedro as its emperor. Portugal lost her largest colony and source of overseas income, and her crown prince.

Conflicts between the constitutionalist Liberals and those favouring a return to absolutist monarchy were mirrored by a split in the royal family. The Absolutists were led by Prince Miguel. The Liberals championed his brother Pedro, whom they proclaimed Dom Pedro IV when João VI died in 1826. Pedro, content as mere Emperor of Brazil, abdicated the Portuguese throne in favour of his seven-year-old daughter. When she was crowned Dona Maria II in February 1828, Miguel responded by returning from exile and declaring himself king. So Pedro abdicated the Brazilian throne and returned to Portugal to head a Liberal counter-revolt.

The war between the two brothers lasted from 1832 to 1834, when Miguel was finally forced into permanent exile. Lisbon was captured on 24 July 1833 by a Liberal army that had marched north from the Algarve. Pedro took over as regent for the now 13-year-old Maria II. He died only months later but oversaw one lasting reform: the 1834 abolition of religious orders. Lisbon, for centuries famous as a city of convents and monasteries, saw monks and nuns turned out from their cloisters, which were annexed by public and private institutions. Parliament set up in the vacated Mosteiro de São Bento, renamed the Palácio da Assembléia da República (see p96). The Mosteiro da Graça, the Paulite monastery next to the Igreja de Santa Catarina, and the Convento do Carmo all became barracks, and remain so today.

In 1836 Maria II married Ferdinand of Saxe-Coburg Gotha, who set about building the fantasy Palácio da Pena on a misty hilltop near Sintra (see p245).

CONSTITUTIONAL MONARCHY

Back in Lisbon, the era was tinged with both fado music and military uprisings. Maria Severa Onofriana, the prostitute known as 'A Severa', kept a notorious house of fado in Mouraria, matching her alluring soprano voice with a string of lovers, among them the bullfighting Count of Vimioso. She died in 1846, at the age of 26. See p205 **Marialvismo**.

Meanwhile, the city had witnessed a series of military revolts. The bloodiest was on 13 March 1838, when government troops fought rebellious national guardsmen in Rossio. Rossio itself underwent a major facelift in the following years. Black and white cobblestone paving was laid out in 1840 and, in 1846, the new Teatro Nacional (see p224) was inaugurated by Dona Maria II. The driving force behind its construction had been the romantic poet and playwright Almeida Garrett, one of many intellectuals who had spent long periods in exile.

The city they returned to was not always a healthy one. In 1833, a cholera epidemic killed more than 13,000 people in Lisbon; the disease returned in 1856 and killed 3,000. The 1857 yellow fever epidemic killed 6,000 people, this at a time when the city's population numbered only 170,000.

By the mid-19th century, renewed political stability made possible a major building programme. In the Baixa, the finishing touches were put to the street grid, with the grand arch on Praça do Comércio completed in 1873. Railways had arrived in the 1850s; by the next decade Lisbon had rail links from Santa Apolónia station to Oporto and Madrid. And by the 1890s trains were steaming out of the neo-Manueline Rossio station towards Sintra. Prosperity meant bigger and better public entertainment: the Coliseu dos Recreios opened in 1890 and the Campo Pequeno bullring in 1892.

During Pombaline reconstruction a green space had been opened in the area to the north-west of Rossio. The Passeio Público, as it was called, wasn't much of a success in its first few decades – the idea of both sexes strolling together in a public garden still grated on the prevailing conservative mindset. In the 1830s it was remodelled as a Romantic Age garden and became popular with the emergent bourgeoisie. In the 1880s it was extended once again, becoming the wide, tree-lined Avenida da Liberdade (*see p75*). On its southern end, at Praça dos Restauradores, a monument was raised to the 1640 restoration of the country's independence. The Avenida was topped by a park later named after King Edward VII.

LEADING LIGHTS

In the 1870s, a group of writers known as the 'Cenáculo' dominated literary Lisbon. Among them were Teófilo Braga, author and storyteller, later president of the Republic; Oliveira Martins, the historian whose pan-Iberian vision shaped (some say warped) generations of future historians; and Eça de Queiroz, one of the most brilliant novelists of the age, whose novels *The Maias* and *Cousin Bazílio* paint an unrivalled vision of 19th-century Lisbon life.

Politically, many of these leading lights were inclined towards republicanism. Opposition to monarchy gained impetus after the government gave in to the British Ultimatum of 1890, in which Britain demanded Portugal withdraw its claim to large parts of south-central Africa.

In 1905, Dom Carlos I appointed João Franco as chief minister. Franco stepped up censorship and persecution of Republicans, but only inflamed the situation. On 1 February 1908 Dom Carlos, accompanied by his wife Amélia and the princes Luís Filipe and Manuel, was returning from a visit to the Alentejo. They crossed the Tagus by boat and were met with carriages and horse guards at the Praça do Comércio. Their procession had reached the

Rossio rail station. Neo-Manueline nostalgia in the age of steam.

north-west corner of the square when a black-cloaked figure circled behind the carriage and opened fire with a rifle. Another conspirator, waving a pistol, ran out from the arcade by what is now a post office. At least one more was spotted firing from the statue of José I. The horse guards rampaged, killing two of the assassins and several bystanders. But it was too late: the king and crown prince were both dead.

> **'The old regime was gone but rival factions failed to agree on the framework of the new republic.'**

The young Manuel (he was 18) assumed the throne, but only lasted two and a half years until the Republican revolution of 4-5 October 1910. Warships that had joined the rebellion shelled the Palácio das Necessidades residence of Dom Manuel II. He got the message, fleeing to Ericeira outside Lisbon and then into permanent exile. Leaders of the revolt gathered at the Câmara Municipal (City Hall) and proclaimed Portugal a republic.

EARLY REPUBLIC
In Lisbon, the urban projects of the late monarchy ground to a halt during the confusion of the First Republic, only to start

Regicide in the Praça do Comércio.

up again infused with the 'imperial' style of the 1930s and 1940s. The population grew slowly and steadily: from about 300,000 in 1890 to nearly 550,000 when the military took over in 1926. The first funiculars had been introduced in 1884, using the water gravity system – a tram would fill a tank of water at the top of the hill, and that weight on the downhill run would provide enough counterweight to pull up another car from the bottom. Electrification began in 1901, and the city was soon filled with electrical trams, known as *eléctricos* in Portuguese.

The provisional government that came in on 5 October 1910 took power on a groundswell of optimism that was soon betrayed. The old regime was gone but rival factions failed to agree on the framework of the new republic, leading to a weak constitution and chronically unstable governments, punctuated by a succession of revolts. Governments came and went, but a persistent concern was hanging on to Portugal's possessions in Africa, which led to its entering World War I on the side of the Allies. The Portuguese Expeditionary Force was more or less wiped out in the April 1918 battle of La Lys on the Western Front.

On 5 December 1917, an army major named Sidónio Pais led a successful military revolt that ushered in what many consider to be Europe's first fascist government. His forces took the heights around Parque Eduardo VII and set about bombarding the government ministries in Praça do Comércio into submission. Loyalist troops mounted a three-pronged attack northwards and the two sides met in the Largo do Rato; hundreds of soldiers died in the brief but bloody skirmish and Sidónio emerged the victor. His brief regime saw mass demonstrations in its favour, mass arrests of opposition leaders and heavy censorship.

In time-honoured style, Sidónio made himself the centre of attention in numerous carefully staged parades. However, his increasingly chaotic governance soon led allies to abandon him, and he was assassinated in December 1918 at Rossio station.

Sidónio's death left the country vulnerable, as competing local powers threatened to rip it apart. In January 1919, the monarchy was proclaimed in the north; it took a month before republican forces could enter Oporto to quell the rebellion. In Lisbon, the National Republican Guard (GNR) had been armed to the point that it often had the final say in government. On 19 October 1921, remembered as the Noite Sangrenta or 'bloody night', members of the GNR and the navy, egged on by various factions, took part in a revolt that led to the massacre of several leading politicians, including Prime Minister António Granjo.

The next government – the 31st since 1910 – lasted barely two weeks; 45 republican governments would fall before the military definitively took over in 1926.

Political upheavals aside, the First Republic was the backdrop for a lively cultural and intellectual life. In 1915, the only two issues of the magazine *Orfeu* were published, introducing the poets Fernando Pessoa and Mário de Sá Carneiro and the painter José de Almeida Negreiros. The moving picture had also arrived: in 1924, the Tivoli cinema opened on the Avenida da Liberdade; in 1928, the Teatro Municipal de São Luis in the Chiado was inaugurated as a cinema with a screening of Fritz Lang's *Metropolis*.

SALAZAR'S ESTADO NOVO

This cultural awakening was stifled by the Estado Novo, the 'New State' regime that came to power in the May 1926 coup d'etat, led by Marshal Gomes da Costa. Two years later a conservative Coimbra professor, Oliveira Salazar, was named finance minister, a position he accepted on condition he be granted absolute control over the country's finances. In 1932, Salazar became prime minister and effectively dictator of Portugal for most of the next four decades, backed by the infamous PIDE political police.

The Estado Novo regime has often been called a dictatorship without a dictator, as Salazar imposed authoritarian rule while avoiding the personality cult prevalent elsewhere in Europe. The regime faced major opposition in the early 1930s; Salazar clamped down hard on the left while playing right-wing rivals off against each other.

By the end of the decade, the Estado Novo was firmly established and confident enough to mount the 1940 Exhibition of the Portuguese World, aimed at glorifying Portuguese achievements while not mentioning World War II. The Belém district is the legacy of this first Lisbon Expo: the Museu de Arte Popular (*see p109*); the reflecting pools near the Padrão dos Descobrimentos (*see p94*); and the grandiose Praça do Império. In northern Europe, France had fallen and the Battle of Britain raged in the skies over southern England, but in Lisbon the Portuguese trooped through pavilions showcasing the glorious legacy of Portuguese colonialism in Africa and Asia. Not only did the exhibition ignore the war, it also neglected homegrown miseries such as the conditions of the rural and industrial workers who supported the whole imperial edifice.

UNEASY NEUTRALITY

World War II had broken out in 1939 and Portugal was once again playing a balancing act between two belligerent sides. On the one hand, the country still maintained treaty links with England dating back 650 years; on the other, government sympathies were clearly with Germany. In the balance again were Portugal's colonies. When the threat of an Axis invasion evaporated in 1940, the country settled into an uneasy neutrality, providing essential tungsten for the Nazi war effort, while lending Azores air bases to the Allies. The British and German ambassadors carefully avoided each other at receptions, while Sintra airport was the only one in Europe with scheduled weekly flights to both London and Berlin.

In Lisbon, the cafés were now crowded with an influx of refugees from a crumbling Europe. Their staid regulars were somewhat taken aback by the new clientele, many of whom were women, and most of whom were Jews. Among those who passed through Lisbon during the war were the King of Romania and the royal family of Denmark, who hopped a wartime boat from Lisbon to the United States. In January 1941 Laurence Olivier and Vivien Leigh stopped off in Lisbon on their way to London. It is no accident that the film *Casablanca* was originally meant to be set in Lisbon and remained as the final hoped-for destination in the finished film. The city didn't spell good fortune for film actor Leslie Howard, however, who died in June 1943 when his flight from Lisbon to London was shot down by German fighters over the Bay of Biscay. The French flyer and writer Antoine de Saint Exupéry whiled away the time at the Estoril Casino in December 1940 while awaiting passage to America, eventually making it to New York in the company of refugee film director Jean Renoir. Another budding writer inspired by the casino's wheel of fate was Ian Fleming, who got some ideas for his character James Bond from watching Yugoslav spy Darko Popov at the gaming tables.

The Allied victory in 1945 put Portugal in a tricky position: it was a right-wing dictatorship celebrating the victory of democracy – and communism – over its more natural allies. The Cold War came to the rescue, however, and after some cosmetic concessions to the opposition, Portugal landed firmly on the side of the West in 1949, becaming one of the founding members of Nato. Salazar had a nasty scare in 1958 when opposition candidate General Humberto Delgado garnered impressive support in show elections for the presidency. Delgado was soon forced into exile (he was assassinated by the

PIDE political police in 1965) and the regime settled into a policy of inward-looking repression, bent on maintaining Portugal's colonies at any cost. Violent incidents in the African colonies in 1960 and 1961 soon led to a full-blown colonial war – a situation only resolved after the 1974 Revolution.

While the rest of the West went bust to boom through the 1950s and 1960s, Salazar obstinately kept Portugal closed to outside influences. Lisbon maintained a reputation as one of the cleanest cities in Europe, and one where you could stand in the middle of Avenida da Liberdade at rush hour and hold a conversation without worrying too much about oncoming traffic. In older neighbourhoods like Alfama, extreme poverty was rampant; keeping everything in order were the police, who could fine citizens for cursing out loud or hanging laundry that dripped.

THE THREE FS

Those who could, emigrated. Those who couldn't hunkered down and swallowed the three F's promoted by the regime: Fátima, Football and Fado.

Fátima. In 1917 the Virgin Mary supposedly appeared to three shepherd children near the town of Fátima, north of Lisbon. At first the church had doubts, but the regime soon picked up the cult, building an enormous shrine at Fátima, a major pilgrimage destination on the 13th of each month from May to October.

Football. Portuguese football newspapers still far outsell other dailies. The top two teams in Lisbon are and have always been Benfica and Sporting. Benfica reached the heavenly heights

The discreet **Dr Salazar**.

of European football in the 1960s thanks to the peerless Eusébio.

Fado. The 1950s and 1960s were a golden age; fado houses lined the streets of old Lisbon, especially the Bairro Alto, where customers lined up to hear the likes of Amália Rodrigues (*see p207* **Amália**). Meanwhile, down on Praça de Alegria, the **Hot Clube** (*see p211*) turned Lisbon onto jazz; the Cais do Sodré quarter remained the centre for red-light nightlife.

Various major public works projects were undertaken by the Estado Novo. Not least of these was the bridge over the Tagus (first called the Ponte Salazar, changed to the Ponte 25 de Abril after the Revolution) that linked Lisbon to the south bank suburb of Almada and its newly completed statue of Cristo Rei, put up in 1958 in thanks for keeping Portugal out of World War II. The Metro was inaugurated in 1959, and has since expanded to four lines. The city spread outwards, filling in the Avenidas Novas north of Praça Duque de Saldanha. The art nouveau buildings that had characterised the Avenida da República began falling to the wrecking ball, to be replaced by concrete office blocks – a process that continues today.

REVOLUTION AND AFTER

In 1968, Salazar was incapacitated by a stroke after a deck chair collapsed beneath him at the São Julião da Barra fortress in Oeiras. He lingered on as an invalid for two more years before dying in 1970. No one had the heart to tell him that President Américo Tomás had replaced him as prime minister with the reformist Marcello Caetano; government ministers went on holding sham meetings at Salazar's bedside to spare him the truth.

All eyes were now on Caetano, who soon proved unable to unravel the complicated legacy of the Estado Novo while dealing with the colonial question. Student demonstrations had been commonplace throughout the 1960s, but now the army joined the general discontent. On 25 April 1974, the regime was overthrown in a revolution led by the military in a plan masterminded by Otelo Saraiva de Carvalho. Caetano and the remnants of his regime, holed up in the National Guards barracks on Largo do Carmo, were forced to surrender after a young captain named Salgueiro Maia threatened them with tanks, supported by a cheering populace. The only bloodshed came when crowds massed outside the PIDE headquarters in the Chiado. Shots were fired from inside the building, killing three men in the street. A plaque marks the place on Rua António Cardoso.

General António Spínola presided over a newly named Junta de Salvação Nacional and

Jubilant marchers fill the Avenida da Liberdade in the wake of the April 1974 coup.

on 1 May hundreds of thousands turned out for demonstrations on Avenida Almirante Reis to show their support for the Revolução dos Cravos – 'Revolution of the Carnations' – so-called after citizens began stuffing soldiers' rifle barrels with the red flowers.

Spinola was out by September 1974 and for the next 14 months right and left, military and civilians, tussled for power. Fading murals from this time, peppered with hammers and sickles and the alphabet-soup of political party initials, can still be seen throughout Lisbon (*see p16* **You'll be the first up on the wall**). After the 'hot summer' of 1975, when the far left, led by Communist Party leader Álvaro Cunhal, seemed to be gaining the upper hand, the country settled down to being a parliamentary democracy. The period since November 1975 can roughly be divided into before and after Portugal's 1986 entry into the European Union.

In the immediate aftermath of the 1974 Revolution, Portugal divested itself of its overseas colonies, provoking a mass exodus of Portuguese citizens from the newly independent countries. Almost overnight hundreds of thousands of *retornados*, as these white returnees were called, flooded in, at a time when the economy was a post-revolutionary shambles. More recently, the latest wave of African immigrants has been prompted by economic or political motives. Many have found low-paid, insecure work in construction, and homes in the shanty towns that have ringed the city for decades.

AGE OF THE AUTOMOBILE

In the early 1980s, the city's image at its best was one of genteel decay. Money was still scarce, public works at a standstill, and many still emigrated to better, high-paying jobs in northern Europe or North America. But, after 1986, governments began to provide the stability needed for sustained economic development. Money flowed back in and Lisbon braced itself for the advent of consumer society and the age of the automobile. Mass shopping culture only really arrived with the opening of the Amoreiras shopping centre in 1986. The Colombo mega-mall in Benfica, opened in 1997, is on a scale to make even an American suburbanite blanch.

Meanwhile, the once quiet streets of Lisbon are clogged with a loud new generation of motor vehicles. Their arrival drastically changed the feel of the city; the number of cars on its roads has grown enormously in the past two decades and the city is now ringed by a tangle of motorways and bypasses. The Ponte 25 de Abril is notorious for rush-hour traffic jams, not noticeably eased by the recent inauguration of a rail service hanging from the road carriageway. A new bridge, the Ponte Vasco da Gama, opened in 1998, but has drained off little more than some weekend traffic flow to points south. There are now plans to build another bridge, probably a rail link. Meanwhile, there has been an explosion of road-dependent bedroom communities on the outskirts of the capital, away from the nearer, more train-dependent dormitory suburbs. But in the old city at least, a few more streets are barred to traffic each year and paved over in black and white cobbles.

On 25 August 1988, a devastating fire broke out in the Chiado district, ripping the heart out of Lisbon's shopping district and sounding the death knell for the outdoor café culture of the Rua do Carmo. (The esplanade platforms had prevented fire trucks from reaching the blaze.) Renowned Oporto architect Álvaro Siza Vieira was called in to oversee reconstruction, and in the face of competing interests and a sloth-like city administration, his vision has been triumphantly realised in a revitalised Chiado.

More notable redevelopment has taken place on the waterfront, where parks, promenades and marinas have emerged from Belém eastwards to Santa Apolónia train station. Still farther upriver, the decade's major happening was the 1998 Expo, held on a huge swathe of riverfront that had been an industrial wasteland. Expo's stated purpose was to mark the 500th anniversary of the discovery of the sea route to India by Vasco da Gama, while its theme was the world's oceans. To that end, the hallmark of the event was the Oceanário – a giant aquarium (*see p103*). Just two weeks after its closure on 30 September 1998, Expo reopened as Parque das Nações, a fully integrated city district that promises to be an important pole of development for years to come (*see p102*). It is now home to several government departments and has been the site of major events such as the national end-of-

The 1988 fire ripped the heart out of the Chiado, Lisbon's fashionable shopping district.

A tale of two countries

Relations between parents and children can be troubled, especially when an unruly adolescent outgrows his father as Brazil has Portugal. Like Britain, another former imperial power since eclipsed by its most successful colony, Portugal has long had a bit of a complex about its brash colonial offspring.

In 2000 both countries marked in their own way the 500th anniversary of the landing by Portuguese mariner Pedro Álvares Cabral on the coast of what is now Bahia. In Brazil, the official ceremonies were overshadowed by protests by indigenous peoples angrily pointing out that they had little to celebrate. Meanwhile, it was forcefully brought home to the Portuguese just how irrelevant their country now is to most Brazilians, as roving TV reporters failed to find more than a handful who knew anything about modern Portugal. And many Portuguese were genuinely hurt when veteran Brazilian singer Caetano Veloso, who is almost equally revered in both countries, railed against the crimes of imperialism.

Perhaps it's no bad thing if a few illusions are shattered, though. Carnival, football and soap operas still dominate Portuguese images of Brazil, but in recent years the relationship between the two countries has become altogether more complex as windy rhetoric about fraternity has been replaced by firm economic ties. Since Portugal joined the EU, the flood of emigrants to Brazil has slowed to a trickle, while there are ever more Brazilians of all professions in Portugal, sharing in its new-found prosperity. Meanwhile, Portuguese business has rediscovered Brazil. The size of Portugal's investments there multiplied by 20 in the four years leading up to 2000, as an EU-subsidy-fuelled boom and a burgeoning stock market provided companies with the capital to set sail for new horizons. Despite its tiny size, the former imperial power is now the third largest investor in what was once its largest colony.

Brazilian President Fernando Henrique Cardoso remarked on this astonishing change during his state visit to mark the anniversary of Cabral's voyage. 'Now, when Brazil looks at Portugal, it sees Europe,' he said. 'It sees Portugal not only as a cradle of civilisation but also as an opportunity for growth and trade.' His comments were all the more striking for coming on a history-drenched day. He and his host, Prime Minister António Guterres, saw off a fleet of 40 sailing ships and yachts – including a replica of the *Boa Esperança*, the tiny caravel that carried Cabral to Brazil – that were aiming to repeat the feat.

During Cardoso's visit, both men highlighted the way the two countries were working together in East Timor, another former Portuguese colony, as a symbol of their down-to-earth approach. Perhaps Brazil and Portugal really are now ready to rise above past family quarrels and tensions and develop a healthy adult relationship.

millennium celebrations. Another legacy of Expo is Portugal's new-found confidence in its ability to organise big happenings; hence its (successful) bid to host the 2004 European football championships.

'The most striking moment was a one-minute silence to demand international intervention in East Timor.'

On the political front, Portugal's entry into the European monetary union on 1 January 2000 and the subsequent successful EU presidency stint underscored its European identity. But although 1999 saw Portugal hand over its last colony, Macao, to China, the country's historical legacy is still deeply felt by ordinary citizens. Proof of that were the popular demonstrations in the summer and autumn of 1999 in support of the long-suffering East Timorese, who were being massacred by Indonesian-backed militias. The most striking moment of that agitated time in Lisbon was a nationwide one minute's silence to demand international intervention in Timor. Drivers halted their cars and clambered out to mark the moment, across town offices and factories stopped work, and broadcasters fell silent. Later, once a multinational force had pacified the troubled territory, there were joyous popular gatherings in Lisbon to acclaim Timorese heroes Xanana Gusmão and Bishop Carlos Ximenes Belo.

> ▶ For more on the development of Lisbon and its buildings, *see chapter* **Architecture**.

Key events

218-202BC Second Punic War starts Roman dominance of the Iberian peninsula.
138BC Lisbon falls to the Romans and is occupied by the Roman governor Decimus Junius Brutus.
Third decade BC City renamed Felicitas Julia Olisipo after Julius Caesar, then an Iberian peninsula commander.
409 Roman rule in the Iberian peninsula ends as the Suevi, Alans and Vandals sweep over the Pyrenees.
418 Romans call in Visigoths to kick out the other tribes.
714 Armies of Islam arrive in Lisbon.
1139 Moors defeated in Battle of Ourique.
1140 Alfonso Henriques proclaims Portugal a kingdom, with himself as king.
1147 Lisbon falls to Christian forces led by Afonso.
1279-1325 Portugal ruled by Dom Dinis.
1290 University of Lisbon founded.
1297 Dinis formalises Treaty of Alcanices with Castile.
1321 First of three earthquakes in 45 years.
1348-1349 Black Death devastates the city.
1367-83 Reign of Dom Fernando I.
1373 Castilian raiding party wastes extramural Lisbon.
1383 Civil war between supporters of Fernando's widow, Leonor Teles, and João, master of the Aviz Military Order.
1385 Battle of Aljubarrota. João I hailed as king. Beginning of the Avis dynasty.
1386 Portugal signs the Treaty of Windsor with England.
1415 Portugal conquers Ceuta on the African coast.
1419 Madeira 'discovered'.
1430s Azores 'discovered'.
1457 Cape Verde 'discovered'.
1497 Vasco da Gama discovers maritime route to India.
1506 Thousands of Jews massacred in a Lisbon-wide riot.
1537 The Inquisition established in Lisbon.
1557 Portugal granted right to administer Macao.
1572 Camões's *The Lusiads* published.
1581 Philip II of Spain crowned Philip I of Portugal.
1588 The Armada sails to England from Lisbon harbour.
1640 Conspirators overpower Spanish authorities in Lisbon and proclaim the Duke of Braganza as Dom João IV.

1661 Catherine of Braganza marries King Charles II.
1699 Gold discovered in Brazil.
1777 Dom José I dies. His daughter crowned Dona Maria I.
1791 Dona Maria I goes bonkers. Power transferred to the prince regent and later Dom João I.
1807 France invades Portugal and the royal family catch the last boat to Brazil.
1808 Start of the Peninsular Wars.
1810 French forces stopped with the aid of the Torres Vedras Lines.
1814 British and Portuguese forces push French back to Toulouse.
1820 Revolution overthrows British regency. New constitution passed in March 1821.
1832-1834 The War of the Two Brothers.
1834 Religious orders abolished in Portugal.
1838 In another military revolt, government troops fight rebellious national guardsmen in Rossio.
1884 First funiculars introduced to Lisbon.
1901 Start of electrification in Lisbon.
1910 Republican revolution.
1916 Portugal enters World War I on the side of the Allies.
1917 The Virgin Mary appears to three shepherd children near the town of Fátima.
1917 Army major Sidónio seizes power; later seen as Europe's first fascist leader.
1918 Portuguese Expeditionary Force wiped out in the battle of La Lys.
1921 *Noite Sangrenta* (Bloody Night) – GNR and army revolt, leading to the massacre of several politicians, including Prime Minister António Granjo.
1926 Coup d'etat, led by Marshal Gomes da Costa.
1932 António de Oliveira Salazar becomes prime minister.
1940 Exhibition of the Portuguese World.
1959 Lisbon's Metro inaugurated.
1961 Start of African colonial wars.
1966 Panteão Nacional Santa Engrácia finally completed after a mere 285 years.
1968 Salazar incapacitated by a stroke after a deck chair collapses beneath him.
1970 Salazar dies.
1974 Regime overthrown in a revolution masterminded by Otelo Saraiva de Carvalho.
1986 Portugal joins the European Union.
1988 Fire devastates the Chiado.
1998 Lisbon Expo.

Lisbon Today

The capital of a nation obsessed by the past is learning to look ahead.

For a city drenched in history, whose people were long told by their rulers to think in terms of centuries rather than years, the past decade has been one of breathtaking change. Ten years ago, the dominant impressions of visitors might have included endless avenues of dilapidated 1950s buildings; fusty shop window displays; and the old-fashioned politeness and reserve of lisboetas themselves.

Now, like as not, a trip to Lisbon will involve visits to both historical monuments and shiny new cultural centres; the city offers a retail experience little different, in kind if not in scale, from any other European capital; and its nightlife is among the most vibrant in the continent. In particular, the development of the riverfront has meant that a city that was long *de costas viradas para o rio* – with its back turned on the river – is finally taking full advantage of one of its main assets.

Yet despite the changes Lisbon retains an old-world charm recognised not only by visitors inured to different ways of life, but by lisboetas

themselves. Despite global financial markets and cheap foreign travel, Lisbon really does move to a slower rhythm than Madrid, let alone London.

If you understand Portuguese, you might overhear a black-clad widow in the village-like Alfama tell her neighbour that she 'hasn't been to Lisbon' (meaning the Baixa, half a mile away) for a month. And in what other European capital would the mayor himself, speaking at a ceremony attended by the media, proudly highlight the fact that lisboetas have a lackadaisical sense of time compared to residents of other European capitals? Hardly the words of a man with his eye fixed on footloose global investors, surely – yet Mayor João Soares is as hard-nosed as they come and has an acute sense of which side the city's bread is buttered. It's just that he's also a lisboeta and speaks from the heart.

ANNUS MIRABILIS

Yet despite – or perhaps because of – such sentimental attitudes, investment has been flowing in. Much if it, of course, is from the

European Union; Portugal has benefited hugely from subsidies designed to help it catch up with the rest of the EU in terms of infrastructure. Where a decade ago the country had just one motorway – between Lisbon and Oporto – there are now dozens, and a direct road link from Lisbon to Madrid was completed in 2000.

In the city itself, the Expo 98 world's fair, staged on reclaimed industrial land in Lisbon's neglected eastern hinterland at a site now called Parque das Nações, and the projects associated with it, gave Lisbon its biggest makeover since the 1755 earthquake. Three years on, a survey showed that more than half the Portuguese people still feel 'personally proud' of Expo's success and the way it showed that Portugal could organise such a high-profile event.

That year, 1998, really was an *annus mirabilis* for tourism, with a 14 per cent leap in visitor numbers. While the marketing of the event in some countries, notably the UK, left much to be desired, arguably the most important achievement was the surge in the number of Spanish visitors coming to Lisbon. Many liked it enough to come back. Every Easter, the streets of Lisbon ring with the sound of castellano as *nuestros hermanos*, as the Portuguese half ironically call their Spanish 'brothers', take advantage of the longest of their long weekends.

'Portugal and Spain are finally getting acquainted.'

That irony is often barely perceptible, but it is there. *Nem bom vento, nem bom casamento*, is an oft-used Portuguese saying: neither a good wind nor a good marriage comes from Spain – a reference to past dynastic trickery. Historical memories run deep, and the Portuguese are proud to be the only nation in the peninsula that has remained free of the clutches of Castile for almost all of the past 800 years, making Portugal's borders the oldest in Europe.

But these fellow EU members, who for centuries lived with their backs turned to each other, are finally getting acquainted, and not just at the human level of tourism. Spain now rivals giant Germany as Portugal's biggest trading partner, from a standing start.

Fears that Expo 98 would mark the peak for Lisbon in terms of tourism have turned out to be unfounded; the number of overnight visitors actually rose slightly in 1999, the crunch year. Hotel occupation rates have held up, despite ever-increasing capacity. The numbers look set to keep rising, and the tourism authorities have set a target of 2.5 million overnight visitors for 2002, requiring nine per cent annual growth.

Lisbon has also emerged as a favoured stopping-off point for round-the-world cruises. In the past, ships steamed on to destinations perceived as more glamorous, but the number of passengers docking in Lisbon jumped by one fifth in 2000.

'For the first time in 500 years, Portugal doesn't have to look backwards for self-validation.'

So for once, perhaps for the first time in 500 years, Portugal doesn't have to look sadly back to the Discoveries for self-validation. For one thing, this football-mad country now has 2004 to look forward to: the European football championship finals are to be held at various venues around in the country in the summer of that year, and a slew of new stadia are being built to host them, and others renovated.

More visitors, of course, means more strain on the city's already juddering infastructure. The street plans selected by Marquês de Pombal after the 1755 earthquake may have been the ultimate in rational urban planning at the time, but they were not designed to take lorries and tourist buses. Not to mention older *bairros* whose pot-holed, narrow streets are lined with cars parked on pavements.

Traffic jams have become an inseparable part of life in Lisbon. In the morning they're so bad that some office workers drive into town at 6am in order to find a parking spot, nap in their car for a couple of hours and then head for a café for a bite before arriving at work some time between 9am and 10am. The evening rush hour starts as early as 5pm but jams on most exit roads don't ease until after 8pm. A trip to an outlying suburb can take as little as ten minutes on the motorway at midday, but an hour at night.

The traffic chaos is partly caused by a distaste for public transport on the part of some newly prosperous individuals but, to be fair to drivers, transport links remain grossly inadequate. Lack of investment is one obvious reason, but the fact that Lisbon is on the bend of the River Tagus anyway limits the potential for new surface links – whether road or rail. Hence plans to construct a new rail link across the river, just a few years after the construction of the Ponte Vasco da Gama road link.

Meanwhile, there are plans to build a new airport serving Lisbon, with a capaity of 25 million passengers a year (compared to the current facility's 2000 tally of 10 million). The project at Ota, to the north-east of the

Towering aspirations: **Parque das Nações**.

city, will cost an estimated 400 billion escudos (£1.3 billion). It's due to open by 2010.

The demand is certainly there, as the city's economy has boomed in recent years. Consumer spending in Portugal as a whole has soared, with household saving rates almost halving in ten years, from among the highest in western Europe to among the lowest. But Lisbon and the Tagus valley, with a combined population of about 2.5 million, account for 45 per cent of the country's purchasing power, and lisboetas have very visibly discovered the joys – and perils – of consumerism. The city's malls are jam-packed at weekends, while debt has soared. In paticular, the fall of lending rates to record lows in the wake of Portugal's qualification for European monetary union triggered a house-buying spree.

'The truth is, thousands of lisboetas are in debt up to their eyeballs.'

WORRYING SIGNS

But all this isn't built on the firmest of foundations. Weekending visitors are unlikely to pick up on this, but the number of cars on

Lisbon's normally traffic-choked streets eases noticeably about a week before the end of the month, just before public and many private sector employees get their pay packets. The truth is, thousands of lisboetas are in debt up to their eyeballs after going for the most expensive car their budget could (barely) cover – so much so that by the end of the month they can't afford any petrol to put in it.

These finely balanced calculations could soon be upset; the economy is already cooling rapidly. After oustripping the EU average for three years, growth in gross domestic product in 2001 is expected to be the laggard, at less than three per cent.

Slower growth hasn't yet translated into higher joblessness: Portugal's is among the lowest in the EU at six per cent (one quarter the level in Spain), partly because wages are so low. There are already signs, though, that the long construction boom that has sucked in so many thousands of foreign workers is faltering, and that has prompted the Socialist government to tighten both the immigration rules themselves and their enforcement (*see p42* **Eastern exposure**).

And, at a time when the EU is preparing to take in new, poorer members from eastern Europe, where wages are lower, the situation does indeed pose some risks. Portugal is already having to struggle to attract foreign investment of the kind it appeared effortlessly to pull in ten years ago.

The winding down of EU subsidies is also a potential problem, and here Lisbon's past gains are the whole country's loss. From 2000, Portugal gets less EU funds because GDP per head in Lisbon and the Tagus valley nudged its way over the level of 75 per cent of the EU average. That means it no longer qualifies for Objective One status, in other words, top dosh.

'Portugal's governments have only themselves to blame for fostering lopsided development.'

The fact is, Portugal's governments have only themselves to blame for fostering the kind of lopsided development that has meant both unmanageable traffic snarls in the capital and rural depopulation in the interior; dizzy growth in consumer spending and the widest gap between rich and poor in the EU. It's not hard to find symbolic contrasts in Lisbon that sum up this gap, such as the shanty town shacks in the shadow of the gleaming glass tower that houses the Lisbon Stock Exchange.

Officials now acknowlege this and, chivvied by Brussels bureaucrats, are developing more regionally balanced policies. Whether they're more sensible is another matter; the massive Alqueva dam project, designed to regenerate large swathes of the Alentejo while flooding other swathes of it, is already attracting criticism from environmentalists.

The environment is likely to become more of an issue in Lisbon itself, too, as a better informed and more prosperous population think more in terms of quality of life. True, there are members of parliament that answer to the name of Greens. But they're generally viewed as lapdogs of the Partido Comunista Português, with which they form an electoral alliance and whose support base is very much old economy: active and retired manufacturing workers and public sector employees. Fresh ideas are more likely to come from the free-thinking Bloco Esquerda, or Left Block, which gave the ruling Socialist Party a fright in the 1999 general election by winning two seats in Lisbon.

Slower growth and lower EU subsidies will also make it even harder for a government that doesn't have a majority to hack away at the thorny problems in its own back yard. The national health service, which takes a larger share of national income than its counterparts in several richer EU countries, but offers poorer quality healthcare, is in the grip of vested interests: the frequent complaints are justified.

Despite tentative attempts at reforms, the educational system is not yet up to the job of preparing the nation's kids for life in the 21st century. But the biggest scandal of all is the legal system. Again and again the public sees high-profile cases, often involving fraud, *arquivado* – shelved, never to be resumed – because the constitutional deadline for judgement has passed. Yet in many, if not most, cases, delays result from the system's own inefficiency and inflexibility. Only as recently as 2001 did the governnment introduce legislation to allow court hearings to go ahead if one witness failed to turn up.

Small wonder, then, that Portugal has the highest proportion of its population locked up, the bulk of them remand prisoners. Aids is not choosy about its victims, however, and Aids is the biggest killer in Portugal's jails.

The degree of contempt with which many Portuguese now view the legal system was spectacularly illustrated in early 2001. When a litigant whose libel case against state television company RTP had dragged on for a decade entered its headquarters on Avenida 5 de Outobro carrying a briefcase that he said was full of explosives, shut himself into a toilet and threatened to blow up the building, there was a wave of public sympathy for him. Or, at least, that was the impression given when, after a tense few hours, he gave himself up, only to be cheered by onlookers as he was led away.

RIVAL CAMPS

Other Portuguese institutions are under more metaphorical siege, but some are better than others in maintaining their power. Though congregations are at record lows, the Catholic Church's continued influence was evident in the campaign for the 1998 referendum on legalising abortion. People who had winked at relatives or friends having an illegal abortion, and even some women who had themselves had one, thought twice before voting in defiance of the Church. The result was a turnout of less than one third in the country's first ever referendum, despite fierce debate.

Freemasonry remains a counterweights to the Church, particularly in Lisbon. Its role throughout the past two centuries as an anti-clerical and progressive force means that some leading masons such as Lisbon mayor João Soares are proud to declare their allegiance, although most are more discreet.

There are many such historical continuities just below the surface in Lisbon. Even young people, who have travel opportunities their parents never had except as economic migrants, see themselves as modern Europeans and eagerly adopt emblematic technologies such as mobile phones and the internet, still identify strongly with the concept of *saudade* (*see p31* **Saudade**), famously one of the defining aspects of the Portuguese character.

They also retain the highly developed sense of history that was drummed into their parents by Salazar's henchmen, whom it suited to have a backward-looking people. One result of this lingering sense of the Portuguese man's burden in Africa was that, in the run-up to the country's joining the European Union in 1986, there was heart-felt debate in some quarters about whether its future really lay with the continent to the north and east rather than with the one to the south.

The past few years have provided the opportunity to indulge such sentiments to the full, with an orgy of anniversaries relating to the Age of Discoveries five centuries ago. Expo 98 itself, whose theme was the oceans, was partly a tribute to Vasco da Gama, who discovered the sea route to India in 1498.

In 2000, Portugal and Brazil jointly marked the 500th anniversary of the landing of Pedro Álvares Cabral in what is now South America (*see p25* **A tale of two countries**) and in 2001 there will be more opportunities for wallowing in the country's Golden Age glories as the Mosteiro dos Jerónimos (*see p95*) celebrates its 500th birthday.

All this commemoration certainly encourages lisboetas to take the long view, as the mayor so aptly noted. The flexible attitude to time applies to lisboetas' social life, too. If you say goodbye to a group of Portuguese friends after a night our, allow plenty of time. First comes the initial round of farewell *beijinhos* – little kisses, a phrase that's also used in on the phone, in letters and in emails – then more chat, then some more *beijinhos*, then more chat and then, maybe, the final round of *beijinhos*.

'Such Portuguese vagueness can be both irritating and endearing at the same time.'

Such Portuguese vagueness can be both irritating and endearing at the same time. If you're in the right mood, and especially if you're on holiday, you should be able to view with humour the apparent inability of many Portuguese to give a straight answer to a request for directions or similar, even if it's just to say they don't know. Even in a tourist office, you can have half a dozen people running up and down, all looking things up but no-one coming up with the right answer. Truth is evidently an evasive concept in Portugal.

One endearingly vague trait that visitors will certainly be thankful hasn't gone out of style is the way Lisbon bartenders measure out – or rather fail to measure – spirits. In general they just pour until they feel like stopping, which may be a couple of fingers or more up the glass.

And of course, another unchanging element in the Lisbon package is the light, which can be quite breathtaking, especially viewed from one of the city's many *miradouros* – look-out points – or from a vantage point on the south of the river. At dusk on a fine day, a yellow-pink light caresses the buildings, making the city look – well, timeless.

Saudade

Portuguese possesses a beautifully evocative word whose meaning English fails to capture in translation. To feel *saudade* for a place, person or just about anything no longer in reach is to suffer an intense yearning or nostalgia that weighs heavily on the heart.

Fado, that melancholy national art, is replete with references to the *saudades* endured by this nation of hardy seafarers and emigrants. It shines a light into the soul of a nation where the sentimental fatalism of an Atlantic temperament seems to be in constant conflict with a sunnier Mediterranean side.

So what is it all about? For many long centuries seafaring and fishing have been key aspects of national life. *Saudade* is what the villagers feel when their menfolk have been long days at sea. Or perhaps it better describes the yearning of those men for their hearths, the comforting arms of their women and a stiff fish stew.

Saudade is what the emigrant feels for his home town or city as whole decades of separation slip by. Since the time voyagers first rounded the Cape of Good Hope, millions of Portuguese have resettled, seeking riches and a better life. Until recently, economic hardship at home meant that a move to northern Europe or across the Atlantic was the clearest path to a better life, and the currency sent back by emigrants is still a tangible element of the balance of payments. Again, women did not always accompany their men abroad, and some spent whole lifetimes seeing little of their loved ones before retirement.

But the men usually did come back, and that was because they were in the grip of *saudade*. Like the Spanish, many Portuguese believe their village, town or city is the most blessed patch of earth on the planet, and none of the finery of Paris or the nightlife of London's would deter them from saving their pounds or francs ready for the day when they will settle in a fine house in their home town.

But all this is changing. You are unlikely these days to find many black-clad fishwives sending a heart-rending fado out across the waves. Portugal recently became a net recipient of immigrants for the first time, and young Lisboetas are not so keen to leave their beautiful city at the first opportunity. But there are still 4.5 million Portuguese living abroad, and *saudade* and the sea are still defining features of the national character.

Take a trip along the coast and, whatever the weather, you'll notice people of all ages parked up and gazing in silence at the waves. Some Portuguese gene seems to compel them to do this, and *saudade* is its name.

Architecture

From Moorish patios to post-modern glass towers.

Architecturally speaking, Lisbon is both a silk purse and a sow's ear, as a view from any of the city's many *miradouros* – lookout points – will reveal. If you climb up the limestone ramparts of the **Castelo de São Jorge** (*see p79*), the city's oldest extant edifice (the Moors began its construction in 719), and swing your gaze east to west from the river up toward the newer parts of town, the passage of architectural history – with all its glories and horrors – hits you in the face.

On the slopes surrounding the Castelo, the labyrinthine, souk-like streets of the Alfama and Mouraria display a dilapidated Moorish heritage. Their square, whitewashed houses, built round generous patios with few windows to the narrow streets, set the tone for popular Portuguese architecture for centuries. Thick walls and tiny windows to keep out the heat and sun were the norm for house construction until very recently.

West of the Alfama, the twin towers of the **Romanesque Sé Catedral** (*see p78*), built over the ruins of the mosque obliterated by

reconquering crusaders in the 12th century, are solid reminders of the early days of Portugal's Christian kingdom. In the streets below the Sé, the ornate, neo-Gothic portal of the **Igreja da Conceição Velha** (*see p78*) is just one of many reminders of the glorious Discoveries era. Just beyond are the arcades of **Praça do Comércio**, the beautifully symmetrical three-sided square where the geometrically laid-out Baixa opens out to the Tagus estuary. From Rossio at the Baixa's upper end, the broad Avenida da Liberdade cleaves north, linking the old town centre with more modern districts where the only real surprise on the skyline is the sheer size and bad taste of many buildings thrown up in the property boom of the last 15 years.

ROMAN AND MOORISH

Although the origins of Lisbon are lost in the mists of legend and history, the architectural remains of its days as a Roman provincial city can still be seen as Roman ruins that dot the city centre in subterranean (but sometimes visitable) pockets. The **Teatro Romano on Rua de São Mamede** (*see p77*), built in 57BC and dedicated to Nero, is one of these. But the earliest roots of urbanism that can still be felt in the modern city are undoubtedly those planted during Moorish rule from the eighth to the 12th century. Limited by the Cerca Moura, the Moorish siege wall that skirts the castle, Alfama and Mouraria were the core of the city. Latticed window shutters, put in place to shield women from the glances of passers-by, can still be seen on some Alfama houses today, and the quarter retains something of the feel of Tangier, Tunis or other North African port cities.

Popular architecture has not changed much over the centuries, with the traditional *casa portuguesa* being one of simple lines, classical proportions, whitewashed walls and terracotta-tiled roofs turned up at the corners like the pagoda temples Portuguese seafarers found on voyages to the Far East.

THE MANUELINE STYLE

It was in the 15th century, the era of the Discoveries, that Portuguese architecture made its first real quantum leap. Dom Manuel I, known as the Fortunate, began putting to use the riches gained from the sea route to the Indies. Palaces and churches were built and royal architects, such as Francisco de Arruda, devised a new, late-Gothic style that has become Portugal's own – the Manueline style. Named for the king, the style featured extravagant forms of windows

and portals and glorious seafaring imagery. Walls are plain and portals heavily decorated with ropes, anchors, flora and fauna of the seas and other maritime motifs, plus the king's seal (a sphere with bands to represent the equator and tropics) and the true cross – the Vera Cruz. Ropes appear in the ribs of the vaulting, the arches of the portals, tops of supporting columns and window frames. The seal appears in doors and windows and in the boss (ornamental carving) at the intersection of ribs.

Although the 1755 earthquake devastated much of the city, several important Manueline structures remain intact. Marking Lisbon city limits on the western riverfront is the **Torre de Belém** (*see p94*), star of a hundred guidebook covers, and the **Mosteiro dos Jerónimos** (*see p95*), with its spectacular cloister and nave. At the eastern edge of the city, the Madre de Deus church, now part of the **Museu Nacional do Azulejo** (*see p109*), is another example. Local limestone known as lioz was (and still is for many large-scale projects) the favoured construction material, lending a light, airy look that belies the buildings' actual dimensions.

REIGN FROM SPAIN

At that time, Manuel dreamed of uniting Portugal and Spain through marriage to the Spanish Infanta and of ruling the peninsula himself. As it turned out, the opposite happened and, a mere two generations later, Philip II of Spain ascended to the Portuguese throne as

The **Torre de Belém**: Manueline star of a hundred guidebook covers.

Calçada à portuguesa – leaving no stone unhewn

Though you'll probably have to peer under a parked car or two to get a good look at much of it, the ubiquitous *calçada à portuguesa* (Portuguese paving) is one of the endearing hallmarks of Lisbon's streets, squares and parks. *Calcário* (limestone), hewn into tiny blocks, decorates walkways with traditional and modern designs, street numbers and business logos as well as the eight-pointed star, a superstitious symbol to protect against further earthquakes and the like.

It was after the completion of Rossio Square in 1849, with its distinctive wave design, that the authorities decreed that all Lisbon's streets were to be paved in this way. Quarries were opened, artists brought in, and, at the profession's peak, there were around 200 skilled *calceteiros* (pavers) hammering away in the city's employ.

Creditably, bearing in mind that every stone is still cut and laid by hand, the city has not done away with *calçada* in the face of the inevitable cost pressures. As well as featuring in prestigious recent developments such as the 1998 Expo and ultra-modern mall Centro Colombo (see p175), it continues to be laid as the standard cladding for pavements and squares all over the city.

But priorities have changed: cheap and fast now wins out over skilled and precise. On today's streets, untrained manual labour, including a fair number of immigrants, do the majority of this back-breaking work and some fine examples of old *calçada* have been lost to less than careful public repair work. These days, as few as 20 or so people possess the full panoply of traditional skills, most of them master *calceteiros* now well into retirement. Part of Lisbon's heritage and identity *calçada à portuguesa* may be, but connoisseurs lament that before long the true craft will be no more than part of its history.

Philip I, bringing a more monumental, mannerist style to Lisbon's buildings. Sombre almost to the point of monastical on the outside but dripping with gold on the inside, many of Lisbon's grandiose churches date from this era. Still intact and visitable are the **Igreja de São Vicente da Fora** (*see p82*), the **Igreja de São Roque** (*see p88*), the Mercês church on Largo do Chiado and the Convento do Beato on Alameda do Beato out east in Xabregas. **São Vicente de Fora**, in Alfama, is typical of the epoch. Designed by Spaniard Juan Herrera and Italian Filipo Terzi, the church was built on the site of an original 12th-century place of worship. White and imposing from afar, it is typical of the mannerist style of the Counter-Reformation, rich in ideology and imagery. No

expense was spared on the impressive façade and twin bell towers that were to serve as models for Portuguese architects during the next two centuries. The interior still houses some of Lisbon's most original and elaborate panels of *azulejos* (tiles). Also in this period, the first attempts at organised settlement were made. In 1580, the Bairro Alto or 'Upper Town' (*see p86*), was laid out on a grid of streets considered at the time to be wide and regular, although judged by today's standards they are huddled and maze-like.

THE RESTORATION

Following the restoration of the Portuguese dynasty in 1640, a rather sober style known as the Estilo Chão (Flat or Plain Style) developed, featuring horizontally organised façades wedged between massive stone corner pillars. The façades' simple balconies were topped with stone balustrades or plain iron railings. Most of the surviving downtown palaces from this period are in this style. Larger country houses and city palaces also began to appear mimicking the French U-style, though many of these open-ended courtyards have since been closed to restore the Portuguese patio tradition. Several of these palaces still exist, some still surrounded, as they were then, by a maze of narrow streets and stairs flanked by tall, narrow houses with tiny doors and windows. The Palácio Galveias, next to the neo-Moorish Campo Pequeno bullring, now hosts exhibitions and is easily accessible, as is the **Palácio dos Marquêses de Fronteira** (*see p101*) in Benfica's Largo de São Domingos. The sober lines apart, however, this was a period in which artistry and engineering flourished: the vertiginous **Aqueduto das Águas Livres** (*see p98*) was completed, elaborate wood carving and sculpture became de rigueur in royal, church and public interiors, and the habit of tiling façades with intricately painted blue and white *azulejos* became increasingly popular.

Under Dom João V, known as the Magnificent, the baroque came to town in the form of palaces such as the Paço de Bemposta (off the Campo Martíres da Pátria), today a military academy, the **Igreja da Graça** (on Largo da Graça, *see p82*) or the Palácio das Necessidades (on Largo das Necessidades), today's Foreign Ministry. The source of inspiration for many of these Lisbon buildings was the palatial convent of Mafra, north-west of Lisbon (*see p248*). This was designed by João Frederico Ludivice, Architect of the Realm for 43 years, whose imposing urban residence opposite the upper station of the Elevador da Glória now houses the Solar do Vinho do Porto. This, then, was the urban mix of Lisbon that was smashed and washed away by the 1755 earthquake and ensuing fires and tidal wave.

POMBALINE RECONSTRUCTION

On the morning of 1 November two powerful tremors shook Lisbon to its foundations. Over 20 churches, the royal palace and dozens of other noble dwellings, plus two-thirds of Lisbon's medieval housing, collapsed into a pile of rubble. The all-powerful minister of Dom José I, the Marquês de Pombal, tried to impose modernity on Lisbon in the shape of a completely rebuilt town centre. Still known today as the Baixa Pombalina, the lower town's rectilinear grid of streets seems immediately at odds with the chaotic nature of the rest of Lisbon's cityscape.

In his effort to try to impose some sort of logical order, Pombal forbade building outside city limits immediately after the quake, and did not allow building inside them until the new city plan was concluded in detail. To complete this task in the remarkably short time of seven months, Pombal drafted in the country's brightest three architects – Manuel da Maia, Carlos Mardel and Eugénio dos Santos. They came up with a plan to rebuild the Baixa on a grid of seven streets running north-south and eight streets running east-west over an area of some 200,000 square metres. The Terreiro do Paço (Palace Square) was renamed Praça do Comércio (although both names are nowadays used interchangeably) and various streets on the grid were christened for the trades that would operate on them.

> **'Lisbon, as if mindful of its North African roots, was none too impressed by this attempt to tame it in northern European style.'**

Pombaline style is characterised by very plain classic features with little or no exterior decoration. Façades were given a glossy finish obtained by pressing the fresh stucco with tin plates – a process called *estanhado*, now forgotten – but even the palaces were plain on the outside. Most of the mainly four-storey houses were constructed around a flexible structure of stone corner pillars, with criss-crossed wooden joists stuffed with brick, stone and plaster to form the walls. This gaiola, or cage, system aimed to make buildings more earthquake-proof. Another innovation was to raise the walls separating houses to a level higher than the roof joists, thus serving as a firewall. Fully equipped with modern sanitation, the rectangular blocks formed by these houses were the state of the art in urban planning at the time.

But Lisbon, as if mindful of its North African roots, was none too impressed by this attempt to tame it in northern European style. As soon as Pombal fell from grace, the city turned its back on the Baixa's order and discipline and resumed its haphazard growth over seven hills to become the sprawling urban puzzle that it is today. After Dom José's death, his daughter became Dona Maria I. A pious woman, she was responsible for the construction of two of Lisbon's most beautiful churches – the **Basílica da Estrela** (*see p98*) and the **Igreja da Memória** in Ajuda (*see p95*). The Basílica, on the 28 tram line, is monumental. Its exterior

The **Eden** – a skeleton of its former self.

is well balanced in white stone, topped by an impressive and ornate dome that, when illuminated, dominates the western skyline at night. The interior is covered in a finely crafted profusion of pink and black marble.

The Igreja da Memória bears more than a passing resemblance to the Basílica but it is much smaller and more intimate. Like the Basílica, it is mostly the work of Mateus Vicente, a pupil of Frederico Ludovice, the architect responsible for the Mafra convent. Also of note from this epoch are the **Teatro Nacional de São Carlos** of 1792 (*see p202*), inspired by Milan's La Scala and perhaps Lisbon's first neo-classical building, and the Palácio da Ajuda, the royal palace that now houses the Ministry of Culture.

STAGNATION AND INDUSTRY

Portugal entered the 19th century plagued by Napoleonic invasions, the flight of the royal family to Brazil and the ensuing struggle for the crown between liberals and autocrats. During the first half of the century, urban planning virtually stagnated. However, several projects started in that period still mark the city centre today. The **Teatro Nacional Dona Maria II** (*see p224*) was built to flank the northern end of Rossio and the Passeio Público – a promenade with gardens and artificial lakes that was later developed into today's Avenida da Liberdade. The closure of religious orders in 1834 saw a massive number of convents and monasteries handed over to civil and military authorities. The industrial revolution, although arriving late in Portugal, heralded a new age of

engineering (and a romantic wave of nostalgia) that bequeathed the neo-Manueline Rossio station and the Elevador da Santa Justa, designed by Eiffel disciple Raul Mesnier du Ponsard. The **Campo Pequeno** bullring (*see p99*) and the **Casa do Alentejo** (*see p127*) reflect a retro-Moorish trend in the late 1800s.

At the turn of the century, a new generation of architects were beginning to make their mark, both through art nouveau houses constructed for wealthy industrialists, and through Vilas, residential complexes built in working-class quarters that often housed both employer and employees. The Graça district (*see p82*) is particularly rich in this type of Vila and several – Vila Berta, with its wrought-iron balconies, and Vila Sousa on Largo da Graça, tiled in a distinctive turquoise – are today still very much part of the district's make-up.

ESTADO NOVO

In the first two or three decades of the 20th century, Portugal's first shaky experiment with democracy produced a number of interesting projects: the first district of social housing in Arco do Cego, today dwarfed by the gigantic headquarters of the state-owned Caixa Geral de Depósitos; the Bairro Azul, an attempt to modernise and, at the same time, beautify residential areas; and the Parque Mayer – a cluster of variety theatres just off the Avenida da Liberdade that included the ultra-modern Teatro Capitólio, built from 1925 to 1931, and the first building in Portugal to house an escalator.

'It would be too simplistic to write off all Salazar-era architecture as politically warped and therefore invalid.'

With the rise of Salazar's authoritarian regime, architecture took on a pseudo-fascist look. Large monumental buildings, such as the Palácio da Justiça at the top of Parque Eduardo VII or the **Biblioteca Nacional** at Campo Grande (*see p110*), symbolised the power and durability of the regime. As in Italy, this did not immediately mean the death of modernism, as shown by buildings such as the Eden theatre on Praça dos Restauradores – whose skeleton is preserved as the Orion Eden aparthotel – and the Instituto Superior Técnico, the first university campus in Portugal, designed as an 'acropolis' of technical learning by architect Profirio Pardal Monteiro.

Under Salazar's Estado Novo, modernism was also countered by the Portuguese Modern Traditional style. Reflecting folksy nationalistic

Where did you get that tile?

The ornamental element that most delights visitors to Lisbon is undoubtedly the *azulejo*, or tile. They are everywhere: from church interiors to Metro stations, from butchers' shops to public fountains, from palaces to ordinary house façades. There is a Museu Nacional do Azulejo housed in the former Madre de Deus convent (see p109), but sometimes it seems as if the whole of Lisbon is one big tile museum.

Azulejos take their name from either *zulej*, the Persian word for 'blue', or *az-zuleycha*, Arabic for 'polished stone', and the tradition indisputably has its roots in the Iberian peninsula's deep-rooted Moorish culture. It was in the 14th century that Islamic-style tiles produced by *mudéjar* (local Moorish) artists in Seville – the main production centre throughout the 15th century – started entering the country in large numbers. Sintra's Palácio Nacional (see p247) has some fine examples. The *azulejo* craze only really took off in the 16th century, though, after majolica techniques came over from Italy. After the *mudéjars* were expelled from Spain, several *azulejo* factories were established in Portugal, and set to work producing majolica-influenced tiles – flat and glazed with painted designs, rather than with designs in relief as previously. They were used mostly for churches and cloisters, such as the Igreja de São Roque (see p88), and depicted biblical landscapes or popular saints. Panels of St Anthony in various poses can be seen all over Lisbon.

The fashion for such 'tile tapestries' grew during the 17th century. Splendid examples survive in the Igreja São Vicente da Fora (see p82) and the Palácio dos Marquêses de Fronteira in Benfica (see p101), where the Sala das Batalhas – full of panels representing battles of the Restoration – has been called 'the Sistine Chapel of tilework'.

The first mass production began in 1767 when the Marquês de Pombal set up the Real Fábrica do Rato to churn out pieces needed for the post-earthquake reconstruction of Lisbon. Tilework from this period, when it began to establish itself on façades as well as interiors, is in a more restrained, neo-classical style.

The fashion for tiles declined in the early 19th century with the Peninsular Wars and the removal of the court to Brazil. The Real

Fábrica closed in 1835, a year after the dissolution of the monasteries. But with the arrival of the industrial age, *azulejos* staged a comeback as ornaments for guilds and factories. Examples from this period include the 1865 façade of the Fábrica Viúva Lamego on Largo do Intendente (see p170), where tiles can still be purchased today, or the house on Rua da Trindade opposite Largo Rafael Bordalo Pinheiro, depicting Progress and Science. The three firms from this period still in existence, which nowadays export most of their output to northern Europe, stick rigidly to the old techniques.

The craft has not stood still, though. In Lapa, Campo de Ourique, the Bairro Alto, parts of Baixa and around Saldanha, colourful art nouveau *azulejos* frame doors, windows and balconies. Artists such as Rafael Bordal Pinheiro and Jorge Colaço created lavish façades and interiors for residential and commercial buildings. Today, *azulejos* by contemporary artists can be seen in many Metro stations (see p104 **Underground art**), or purchased at specialist shops. All too often, though, mass-produced tiles are slapped on to façades as a splash of colour or to protect them against rain. For all their artistic potential, on some new buildings they can be the very height of tack.

values, this was characterised by the use of romantic touches in modern apartment buildings, houses and public works. Small square windows with heavy plain frames, high tiled roofs and buttresses pretending to prop up walls are the most common marks. Galleries with round arches and, sometimes, bas-relief sculptures grace some of these pieces. The Igreja da Nossa Senhora da Fátima on the Avenida da Berna and the twin-towered Igreja São João de Deus on Praça de Londres are outstanding examples.

By 1940 things had taken an ever more nationalistic turn and a site in Belém was set aside to build the Exposião do Mundo Português, the Exhibition of the Portuguese World. The work of the self-proclaimed Modernist Generation of architects, the exhibition was centred around the overtly chauvinistic Padrão dos Descobrimentos, Monument to the Discoveries, which proudly displayed giant statues of Henry the Navigator and his brave courtiers, mapmakers and sailors advancing along a plinth towards unknown seas. The building that houses the **Museu Nacional de Arte Popular** (*see p109*) was also part of the Exhibition, while the monumental fountain on Alameda Dom Afonso Henriques, with decorative Tagus nymphs and mythical creatures out of Camões's Lusiads, likewise stems from this period.

It would be too simplistic, however, to write off all Salazar-era architecture as politically warped and therefore invalid. This epoch also saw the construction of Pardal Monteiro's impressively modernist **Gare Marítima de Alcântara** (1943), with its bas-reliefs by José de Almada Negreiros. The regime's hyperactive Minister of Public Works, Duarte Pacheco, was a visionary, albeit reputedly as despotic as the Marquês de Pombal. Under his auspices, three large residential neighbourhoods were conceived – Alvalade, Restelo and Olivais. The first dual-carriage highway was started and Lisbon was promoted as the Capital do Império. But by the 1960s, Portugal could no longer shut itself off from international architectural and urban trends: the first Metro line was opened in 1960; the Ponte Salazar (now the Ponte 25 de Abril) was inaugurated in 1966; and the understated, South Bank-like **Fundação Calouste Gulbenkian** (*see p110*) was completed in 1969.

MODERN TIMES

In the two and a half decades since the 1974 Revolution restored democracy, much harm – and more recently, much good – has been done to the city's urban structure. Following the Revolution, a wave of chaotic, clandestine

construction washed over the capital. Strange, corrugated-iron shanty towns sprang up all round the town and whole new dormitory suburbs were built, largely illegally. To make matters worse, Portugal's 1986 entry into the European Community generated wealth at a time of virtually nil public awareness of urban planning. During the 1980s, Mayor Nuno Kruz Abecassis permitted the wholesale rape of some of the city's most historic zones. On Largo de Martim Moniz, a huge, postmodern shopping mall was built onto the back of one of the city's oldest, tiniest chapels. Architect Tomás Taveira seemed to have free rein to do whatever he liked, which was mainly building pink and smoked-glass towers. One set, the **Amoreiras** shopping centre (*see p175*), juts out from an old hilltop district; another, the Banco Nacional Ultramarino headquarters on the corner of Avenida 5 de Outubro and Avenida de Berna, is in the form of the lute-like Portuguese guitar. Taveira's defenders claim his sense of humour 'saves' these buildings. Others point out that, as with taste, there are no rules for humour and many Lisboetas fail to see the joke.

'The most important urban project of recent years was undoubtedly Expo 98.'

In 1992, Portugal took over the presidency of the EU and built the **Centro Cultural de Belém** (*see p192*) to house the closing summit. Built by Vittorio Gregotti and Manuel Salgado just opposite the Mosteiro dos Jerónimos, the block-like limestone structure caused no end of controversy when opened. But the murmuring died away after a few years and this functional, beautiful building inspired by traditional Moorish forms – housing exhibitions, shops, restaurants, cafés and concert halls – is now a favourite spot for Lisboetas to spend weekend afternoons.

In August 1988, a terrible fire swept through the historic Chiado district, leaving the heart of Lisbon's café culture in charred ruins. The reconstruction project was handed to Portugal's best-known architect, Álvaro Siza Vieira – Oporto born and bred and until then with little exposure in the capital. Known as an architectural purist, Siza fought to preserve the Chiado's historic appearance. Eighteen out of 20 façades were propped up and their gutted insides reworked and rebuilt. The project's triumphant finale was the reopening of the former **Armazéns do Chiado** department store (*see p175*) as a human-scale shopping centre and luxury hotel. Siza came under some criticism for failing to provide the new buildings with garages, which many shopkeepers complain has led to a commercial desertification of the area, but the underground park being built under Largo do Chiado should help.

The most important urban project of recent years, though, was undoubtedly Expo 98, which involved rehabilitating a riverside stretch polluted with oil refineries, munitions factories, a slaughterhouse and other such buildings. Despite much doom and gloom, Expo was actually ready on time and many observers agreed that its main and lasting attraction was the architecture. The highlights were Peter Chermayev's **Oceanarium** (*see p103*); a huge

UFO-like Pavilhão Multiusos (since renamed **Pavilhão Atlântico**, *see p102*) by Regino Cruz; Siza's Bauhaus-like **Pavilhão de Portugal** (*see p103*) with its massive concave concrete canopy ; and the jewel in the crown – Santiago Calatrava's imaginative **Gare do Oriente** (*see p103*). Although not officially part of Expo but built in conjunction or as a result of it were the 17-kilometre (10.5-mile) **Ponte Vasco da Gama**, providing a second link between Lisbon and the south bank of the Tagus, and the expanded and beautifully decorated **Metro** network, which has tile panels by some of Portugal's and the world's best artists.

Álvaro Siza Vieira's **Pavilhão de Portugal**.

Ethnic Lisbon

Lisbon's cultural mix is becoming ever more diverse.

Take a walk around Rossio or Praça da Figueira, and you will notice groups of Africans milling around, engaged in easy but businesslike conversation. Those colourfully robed gents gathered around the steps of the Teatro Nacional Dona Maria II and the women selling ground nuts and palm oil from the pavement are from Guinea Bissau. Nearby, groups of younger Guineans and Angolans hang out, many waiting to make contact with the subcontractors who supply the booming construction industry with 'flexible' immigrant labour.

A short walk across Martim Moniz – itself something of an immigrant haunt since the construction upheaval in Rossio – leads to Rua do Benformoso, a street lined with shops run by Gujarati Indians. The nearby Centro Comercial Mouraria (*see p166* **Mouraria – centro comercial or centro cultural?**) is a honeycomb of African and Asian shops selling groceries, textiles, CDs, haircare products and tons of imported tack. In the basement, a

multiracial horde chat at bars, savouring cold beers and snacks ranging from Indian dal to Angolan *moamba*. And before Lent each year a downtown carnival parade – in which each Portuguese-speaking nation displays its dance, costume and music – provides another window onto some of these worlds.

That the capital of a former colonial power has a strong 'ethnic' flavour is no surprise. But there is something deeper at work here. More than half a millennium of contact with the tropics has created a familiarity and brought a sense of romance that the Portuguese strive to maintain: the sights, sounds and scents of Africa, Brazil and Asia hang in the air along Lisbon's docksides and up its palm-lined avenues and squares.

Like their Spanish cousins, the Portuguese are a mix of European, North African, Jew and Gypsy. But the long contact with Africa's languid tropics seems to have added something to the national psyche, making facile comparisons with Spain evaporate on arrival.

Go to one of Lisbon's many African nightclubs or dance halls and you will see brown and pink faces enjoying the close sensual dancing that prevails in these convivial dens. Look closer at the white Portuguese, and you may think you can spot that faraway look that identifies someone as one of the ten per cent or so who lived in Africa before war-weary Portugal withdrew from its colonies in the 1970s.

The can-do dynamism of these *retornados* has driven them to prominent positions in business and the professions, and their lives bear little relation to those of the African immigrants who now perform the city's menial tasks. But when night falls, both sets head for the same restaurants or clubs. And when talk turns to Africa, many *retornados* speak with the same wistful longing as the Angolan cleaner forced to leave her war-torn homeland or the Cape Verdean construction worker who sings a *morna*, laced with what in creole is called *sodade*.

'Many Africans continue to live in shanty towns on the city's outskirts.'

Windows into Lisbon's immigrant communities open wider at night: at Cape Verdean dance halls, where elegant bohemians dance cheek to cheek; at cavernous African nightclubs, where Angolan DJs create mutant brands of zouk and afro-techno; and at bars where Brazilian bands drive the Portuguese to delirium. But immigrants, and especially Africans, have also played a vital role in the process of modernisation that has changed the face of the city. In recent years, as works such as the Colombo mall and Expo 98 hurried to completion, over half the estimated 70,000 workers employed in Lisbon's construction industry were African. Since then they've been joined by Pakistanis and thousands of east Europeans (*see p42* **Eastern exposure**).

During this boom many formerly illegal workers were issued residence permits, as industry's needs outweighed immigration fears. But this did not change industry practices of keeping employees off the books or dodging social security payments, leaving them doubly vulnerable to a downturn in the job market. Provision of services such as housing and education in the European Union's second poorest country is also lacking. And there is little encouragement for parents to naturalise their children, so many second-generation Africans have grown up as foreigners in their own country, further reducing their access to education and housing. Many Africans continue

to live in shanty towns on the city's outskirts (*see p101* **Shanty town shame**). Despite the communal warmth of these neighbourhoods, the poverty in places such as Quinta do Mocho or parts of Amadora can be shocking.

The Portuguese take pride in their self-image as a tolerant nation, and many see racism as something that exists only in countries like Britain, France and Germany. They feel their own experience as emigrants has made them less prone to discrimination. There is even a debate about whether racism even exists here. This stems partly from the idea that the colonising Portuguese proved their colour blindness by interbreeding with the natives, rather than standing aloof like the puritanical British.

This is disingenuous – it was expediency rather than ethics that encouraged interracial relations – and certainly unhelpful today. Any African will tell you that racism exists in Portugal and the problem could get worse when the construction boom finally peters out. The anger of younger Afro-Portuguese can already be sensed in a growing rap scene.

OUT OF AFRICA

The African presence in Portugal stretches back to the 16th century, providing a mixture of non-Caucasian genes found even in far-flung villages. Lisbon's Africans now number almost

The **Mouraria** shopping centre: immigrant haunt. *See p40.*

Workers takes a hard-earned break.

200,000, although the figure is distorted by definitions of nationality. The influx in modern times began in the 1960s, when immigration policy was relaxed to offset the haemorrhage of Portuguese workers to northern Europe. The first community to fill this gap came from Cape Verde, where poverty and drought prompted several waves of emigration. The community is better integrated than more recent arrivals, and the one best represented in the trades and professions – reflecting the time when Cape

Verdeans served as clerks, administrators and mariners throughout the empire. It is also more racially mixed, and does not concentrate together as visibly as other African groups.

The **Associação de Cabo Verde** community centre, on the eighth floor at Duque de Palmela 2 (21 353 1932), in the heart of the business district around Praça Marquês de Pombal, is a great place to enjoy a long, lively lunch of inexpensive Cape Verdean dishes. Open between noon and 3pm on weekdays, on

Eastern exposure

Stroll past one of Lisbon's many construction sites and you'll notice more than a sprinkling of sandy-haired, light-eyed workers in among the otherwise black and brown workforce. These men, who make up the latest wave of immigration in Portugal, have unwittingly triggered a revolution in government policy.

It was in 1999 that Ukrainians, Russians, Romanians and Moldovans started first to trickle, then to flood across Europe and into Portugal. Unlike most of the tens of thousands of Africans who did the grunt work on the infrastructure projects of recent years, these new arrivals didn't speak a word of Portuguese. As they move around the city in little knots, the far-off look in their eyes is testament both to brutally long working hours (seven-day weeks are common as they strive to earn as much cash as possible for families back home) and to their lack of connection with the host culture.

Official figures put the number of illegal immigrants in Portugal in mid-2000 at about

30,000, against 210,000 legal immigrants. But the figure is based on the number of requests for legalisation lodged since 1996; unofficial estimates are much higher. *Público* newspaper recently put the number of east Europeans in Portugal at 50,000. They come to Portugal not for sun and good red wine, but because they hear that there is plenty of work and – crucially – that the authorities don't bother you.

For a long time, Portugal was notably more tolerant on this issue than many European Union countries. Periodic amnesties for illegal immigrants provided some protection against the excesses of unscrupulous employers, as well as attracting more hopefuls from countries with an efficient grapevine, such as Pakistan and India. The relaxed attitude was reflected lower down the chain of authority. The police did little to expose paperless migrants, while labour inspectors stuck to their job of ensuring workplace safety, turning a blind eye to other

In Context

Tuesdays and Thursdays it has live music; incongruously, couples dance for a spell before filing back to their offices for the afternoon.

There are Cape Verdean dancehalls, restaurants and bars scattered around town, such as **B.Leza** (*see p212*), **Enclave** (*see p213*) and the speakeasy-style restaurant **Cachupa**, upstairs at Rua do Poço dos Negros 73 (no phone), which serves up Cape Verde's national dish of the same name until dawn in a distinctly shady atmosphere. *See chapters* **Restaurants** and **Nightlife**.

Immigration from Angola and Mozambique began in the late 1970s, when these countries slid into civil war. Many Angolans came here as refugees, and traumatic stories are told with a philosophical shrug of the shoulder. They look wistfully to their rich but sadly screwed homeland, and most insist they will go home one day.

Particularly painful are the hardships suffered by the students whose grants dried up with the chaos back home. Many Portuguese professionals now go about their business in offices built and cleaned by hands trained for doctoring or accounting. Angolans are at their most visible in large modern nightclubs such as **Mussulu** (*see p222*). Their capacity for partying is admirable and their contribution to the city's cultural scene is at least as strong as that of Cape Verde.

Lisbon's Mozambicans tend to be better off and higher qualified and many have returned home in recent years, encouraged by signs of stability. By contrast, conflict and economic pressures have brought growing numbers from Guinea Bissau and São Tomé. There is also now an increasing number of immigrants from the Democratic Republic of Congo, adding their resonant French and flashy dressing to the Lisbon streets.

In recent years, African festivals have proliferated. Some sense of unity was provided for a time by Portuguese state radio station RDP Africa, which used to organise a hugely successful African cultural day in May. Now, though, the various communities are back to doing their own thing.

BRAZILIAN LISBON

Brazil is all around you in Lisbon. From bohemian Bairro Alto bars to swanky dockside restaurants, and at countless beach bars, people sip Caipirinhas and listen to Brazilian music. Five-star hotels offer Brazilian *picanha* beef cuts and *feijoada*, the bean and pork stew first dreamed up by plantation slaves. Families cluster round TVs to watch the latest Brazilian soap opera. And every summer, groups of Brazilians gather at chosen spots for their own ritual of football, samba, cold beer and barbecue.

infractions. Trade unions have been understanding, too. In one case in Oporto, a contractor was found to be paying illegal eastern European workers well below the minimum wage. The construction workers' union first approached the company and ensured that the migrants were replaced by union members. But it then went on to find the foreigners jobs with another firm working on the Oporto metro, help them secure work permits and enrol them in the union.

This kind of win-win approach works when labour is short. But with east Europeans earning wages far below what Portuguese would accept (as little as £2 an hour, minus the cut taken by the agent who found them the job) and signs that the construction boom may be ending, the political warning signs started to flash. In the summer of 2000, the government tabled a measure very different from the amnesties implemented in the past. For the first time, temporary residence permits for foreign workers were envisaged, triggering accusations from the left that the government wanted a cheap, 'disposable' labour force.

January of 2001 saw another new departure, with the setting up of a committee that is to draft Portugal's first-ever overall immigration policy. The government is quite open about the fact that its aim is 'to make legal immigration more flexible in line with the needs of the labour market'. It wants to combat clandestine immigration but also 'socially degrading phenomena related to it' – a praiseworthy aim, given the exploitative practices of many employers.

But there's a contradiction at the heart of another of the government's stated aims: 'to move to a rational management of migratory flows, while promoting the harmonious integration of immigrants so as to avoid situations of racism and xenophobia'. The clinical language disguises the fact that the measure approved in 2000 provides only for temporary work permits of one year, extendable to no more than five years. What kind of integration can that offer a non-Portuguese speaker toiling long hours to make the most of his brief stay in Portugal, one might wonder.

The **Associação de Cabo Verde**. See p42.

The cultural influence exerted by Brazilians far outweighs their numbers, estimated at around 25,000. It is less than a decade since Portugal started taking in more Brazilians than the other way round, but the South Americans are already more integrated than their African cousins. This is partly racial; after all, many are here because of immigration advantages afforded by their Portuguese descent.

> ## 'Some Portuguese harbour an image of Brazilians as untrustworthy tricksters, but there's more that unites than divides them.'

Brazilians have also moved to fill gaps in the job market. In recent years a wave of Brazilian talent shook up the sleepy Portuguese advertising sector. Others found work in information technology, while less qualified immigrants provided yet more muscle for the construction industry.

But there has been friction. When highly specialised Brazilians threatened to dominate private dentistry, local professionals used legal technicalities to challenge their qualifications. Some Portuguese harbour an image of Brazilians as untrustworthy tricksters, or worry about being swamped by brazen new world culture. But there is more that unites than divides them, as evidenced by enthusiastic Portuguese support for Brazil's football team.

The **Casa do Brasil** (Rua São Pedro de Alcântara 63/or 1, Bairro Alto, 1250, 21 347 1580), is a community centre and library that provides information on jobs and legal advice for Brazilians living in Lisbon. It also hosts Friday night dance parties. Other Brazilian venues include **Chafarica**, **Bruxa Bar** and **Gasoiil** (for all, *see p213*).

PASSAGE FROM INDIA

Like Africa, India has a special place in the Portuguese collective consciousness. Any local will tell you that Vasco da Gama was the first European to find the maritime route to India. It was only after a brief conflict with the vast Indian army in 1962 that Portugal could be persuaded that its presence in Goa was over. Long before the transition to independence, some Goans (and natives of Daman and Diu, two Portuguese-run enclaves further north) went to Mozambique, where many prospered in business. The Portuguese withdrawal from Mozambique, and the subsequent civil war, prompted most to head for Portugal. They now form a large part of Lisbon's Indian community.

The Navaratri festival (*see p182*), usually falling in September or October, is the community's main annual event, preceding the Diwali new year celebrations. It takes place at the Hindu Community Centre and Temple on Alameda Mahatma Gandhi in Lumiar. Word of the Lisbon bash has spread to Indian communities overseas, and it is growing in scale. The nine-day festival (open to non-Hindus for an admission fee of around 500$00) features traditional dancing, songs and music to evoke the goddess Amba and her eight sisters.

The migration from Mozambique also explains Lisbon's small Ismaili community, whose spiritual leader, the Aga Kahn, visited to open the stunning new community centre in Laranjeiras. More recently there has been an influx from the Punjab and Bangladesh (and Pakistan), again meeting demand for labour in the construction sector.

EAST TIMOR

A low-profile presence for years, in the shape of refugees from the brutal Indonesian occupation of their homeland, Lisbon's handful of Timorese found themselves centre-stage in the summer of 1999. Twenty-three years after the invasion, negotiations between Indonesia and Portugal led to a referendum on independence. But after voters plumped overwhelming to sever links with Jakarta, pro-Indonesian militias went on the rampage. The Portuguese, who had been hoping fervently that this unfinished colonial business would have a happy ending, first watched in horror and then mobilised on an unprecedented scale alongside the Timorese. Huge demonstrations and other initiatives to demand international intervention helped stiffen the Portuguese government's resolve in pressing the Timorese case in international fora.

Lisbon's Timorese community is small and plays little role in wider economic or political life, but the city is a good place to learn more about the culture of the world's newest country. Those interested should head for **Espaço por Timor** (Rua de São Bento 182/4, 21 396 1546), the nerve centre for campaigning during the occupation, right opposite parliament in São Bento. It has a community centre and library, and organises presentations and debates.

Accommodation

Accommodation

From palaces to pensões, there's plenty to choose from, both in town and out on the coast – at prices still lower than elsewhere in western Europe.

The number of visitors to Lisbon has soared in recent years, largely thanks to major events like Expo 98. For a time, accommodation had trouble keeping pace, but now, thanks partly to foreign investment, Lisbon has lots of new hotels, and there are more on the way before the 2004 European football championship finals. Mayor João Soares has encouraged business and the government to convert crumbling palaces and state buildings into mid-sized luxury hotels and a dozen such schemes are in the pipeline (none expected to open before 2003). Even now, though, Lisbon has what it takes to cater to the well-heeled as well as the mid-market tourists that were long its speciality.

Our categories range from Deluxe through Expensive and Moderate to Budget. A single room in a Deluxe hotel, taking summer 2001 prices, will cost upwards of 30,000$00; an Expensive one 20,000$00-30,000$00; a Moderate one 10,000$00-20,000$00 and a Budget hotel 3,000$00-10,000$00. You can still find cheap hotels in Lisbon (usually designated *pensões*) or

but prices have crept up as more downmarket places have been forced to upgrade their facilities; many of the seedier establishments have gone out of business. That shouldn't alarm those on a shoestring; prices are still cheap compared with the rest of Europe, and after the inflation caused by Expo many rates have fallen or been held steady. In many lower-priced hotels it is also worth haggling, as prices are sometimes negotiable. This practice is not recommended in fancier establishments, but even these can be beaten down if you book in advance. Discounts may be available if you book as a group or company, or even through a local travel agent such as **Halcon Viajes** (Rua Domingos Sequeira 74C, 21 395 9099), a Spanish-owned outfit that can secure discounts of up to 50 per cent in low season.

In general, even budget accommodation is clean, partly because the authorities are strict. Some places also have surprising features for their price category: the **Pensão Portuense** (*see p62*) and **Residencial Marisela** (*see p65*)

Lapa Palace – living in the Lapa luxury. *See p50.*

both offer breakfast in your room, and the Marisela also has a basketball court, of all things. Another cost-saving option is the aparthotel. We list two: the **Clube do Lago** (*see p51*) in Estoril and the **Orion Eden** (*see p53*) on Praça dos Restauradores. Both offer self-catering apartments that can be rented weekly. More permanent accommodation is harder to come by; the best apartments are found by word of mouth. If you are not well connected, check the ads in *Diário de Notícias*, *Correo de Manha* or the weekly classifieds rag *Ocasião*.

Prices tend to soar in summer, particularly on the Cascais-Estoril coast. We recommend that you book at least two weeks in advance in July and August, particularly if you want to be near a beach. In Lisbon, rates at many business-oriented hotels won't change much – in fact prices may actually fall in July and August because fewer tour groups are in town. Rates can vary a lot within a hotel, depending on the size of the room, the view and whether there's an en-suite bathroom. It is worth inquiring to avoid being automatically directed to the most expensive rooms.

Each of our price categories is sub-divided into areas corresponding with those used elsewhere in this guide. The vast majority of hotels are clustered downtown, between Praça do Comércio down by the river and Parque Eduardo VII at Praça Marquês de Pombal. In between are Rossio, with its cafés, fountains, flower stalls (and seemingly endless construction), Praça dos Restauradores, and Avenida da Liberdade, Lisbon's Champs-Elysées. Along and around this tree-lined avenue, you will find many of Lisbon's upmarket hotels as well as a host of mid-range and budget options.

Unless otherwise stated, breakfast is included in the price of the hotels listed. Most will serve a continental breakfast, perhaps with fruit. A buffet breakfast in an upmarket hotel is sure to include cooked food such as bacon and eggs as well as cold meats, cereals, breads and fruit.

All hotels listed have telephones in rooms unless otherwise stated (or, with budget hotels, if we say there's a payphone). Most allow an internet connection from your room if you are using a portable computer, but if you are coming from the UK you will need an adaptor. It's rare for hotels to offer their own internet access, and where they do, there's a fixed fee per minute. Surprisingly, some of the most expensive hotels in the city either provide no internet access in their business centres or have slow or faulty connections.

The coastal resorts towards Cascais (reached by train from Cais do Sodré station) offer an interesting alternative to Lisbon. This coast has wonderful beaches and all kinds of hotels but can get very busy in the summer. If you want to get off the tourist trail go right through Cascais and onto the Guincho coast road, where you will find quieter places to stay.

Booking

Direcção-Geral do Turismo

Avenida António Augusto de Aguiar 86, Saldanha, 1929 (21 357 5015/fax 21 848 9070/www.dgturismo.pt). Metro Parque. **Open** 9am-8pm Mon-Fri; closed Sat, Sun. **Map** p308 E1.
Provides help with finding accommodation and on-the-spot bookings but has no advance reservation service. Also has a long list of hotels, but these are not categorised.
Branch: Lisbon Airport (21 849 4323).

Empresa Nacional de Turismo (Enatur)/Pousadas de Portugal

Avenida Santa Joana a Princesa 10-A, Alvalade, 1700 (21 844 2000/reservations 21 844 2001/www.pousadas.pt). Metro Alvalade. **Open** 9.30am-1pm, 2.30-6.30pm Mon-Fri; closed Sat, Sun. **No credit cards. Map** p305 N2.
State-run agency that handles bookings for pousadas all over Portugal. Also provides online booking service for more upmarket hotels around Lisbon.

Hotel Reservation Service

Rua de Santa Marta 37-1, Avenida, 1100 (21 314 1562). Metro Avenida. **Open** 9am-1pm, 2-8pm. Mon-Fri; closed Sat, Sun. **Map** p308 E7.
A private 24-hour advance booking service offering useful price information and advice on good places to stay in Lisbon.

Associação Portuguesa de Pousadas de Juventude (Youth Hostels Association)

Avenida Duque de Ávila 137, Saldanha, 1000 (21 359 6000/www.sejuventude.pt). Metro Saldanha. **Open** 9am-7.30pm Mon-Fri; closed Sat, Sun. **Map** p304 L5.
General information for young travellers, including how and where to find discounts. Helpful staff provide advice on Portugal's youth hostels and an advance booking service. Use of internet, reference library, photocopier and so on.

Deluxe

Rossio & Restauradores

Avenida Palace

Rua 1 de Dezembro 123, 1200-359 (21 346 0151/fax 21 342 2884/www.hotel-avenida-palace.pt). Metro Restauradores. **Rates** 34,000$00 single; 38,000$00 double; 44,000$00 triple; 55,000$00-80,000$00 suite. *Low season* 26,000$00 single; 32,000$00 double; 38,000$00 triple; 48,000$00-75,000$00 suite. **Credit** AmEx, DC, MC, V. **Map** p310 L9.

Local designers Lucien Donnat and João Chichorro have attempted to redecorate and furnish the interior of this Lisbon landmark in a blend of Louis XV, Louis XVI, Dona Maria, Dom José and classic Imperial styles. So many styles together have created an uncomfortable clutter of period furniture and confused colour co-ordination: opulence rather than good taste. Bedroom furnishings and marble bathrooms are similarly luxurious, but again not very relaxing. The bedrooms are surprisingly soundproof considering the busy location next to Rossio rail station. Staff are not very friendly and have surprisingly little knowledge of true customer service for a hotel of this stature.

Hotel services *Air-conditioning. Babysitting. Bar. Conference facilities. Currency exchange. Fax. Laundry. Lift. Parking (free). TV lounge.* **Room services** *Hairdryer. Minibar. Radio. Room service (24hr). TV: satellite.*

Avenida de Liberdade & Marquês de Pombal

Hotel Altis

Rua Castilho 11, Avenida da Liberdade, 1269-072 (21 310 6000/fax 21 310 6262). Metro Avenida. **Rates** 33,000$00 single; 37,000$00 double; 41,000$00 triple; 60,000$00-90,000$00 suite. **Credit** AmEx, DC, MC, V. **Map** p307 K7.

This hotel attracts a mix of business travellers and tourists and has a very popular conference centre. Well located halfway between the gay hangouts of Principe Real and the shops and businesses on Avenida Liberdade, the Altis has all the modern comforts of five stars at a competitive price. On the top floor the Grill Dom Fernando offers fine traditional Portuguese cuisine and panoramic views over Lisbon and the Tagus, and the Girassol Restaurant serves a buffet. There is a small heated indoor pool with snack bar and a well-equipped gym.

Hotel services *Air-conditioning. Babysitting. Bars (2). Beauty salon. Car park (1,200$00). Car rental. Conference facilities. Currency exchange. Fax. Fitness centre. Laundry. Lift. Restaurants (2). Sauna. Secretarial service. Shops. Swimming pool. Turkish bath.* **Room services** *Hairdryer. Radio. Room service (24hr). Safe. Telephone. TV: satellite.*

Hotel NH Liberdade

Avenida da Liberdade 180B, 1250-146 (21 351 4060/fax 21 314 3674/www.nh-hoteles.com). Metro Avenida. **Rates** 32,900$00 single; 34,900$00 double. **Credit** AmEx, DC, MC, V. **Map** p307 E7.

A welcome first opening in Portugal for the NH chain, which has recently been expanding rapidly across Spain. The hotel caters mainly towards corporate clients, but is just as welcoming to tourists. Its rooftop terrace and swimming pool have a fine view and the superb buffet restaurant and cosy top-floor coffee shop put it firmly on the local accomodation map. The spacious rooms are more like mini-apartments, with separate lounge and kitchenette decorated in a stylish matt black. Young,

The best Hotels

Estalagem do Muchaxo
To check out the talent on the beach from your room. See p61.

As Janelas Verdes
For hiding out in a secluded garden. See p50.

Hotel Eduardo VII
To drink caipirinhas on a rooftop. See p54.

Pensão York House
To write your next best-seller. See p55.

Lapa Palace Hotel
For a champagne breakfast. See p50.

Pensão Portuense
For a cheap breakfast in bed. See p62.

Albergaria Senhora do Monte
For romantic rooftop views. See p51.

Hotel Quinta da Marinha
To go riding after a round of golf. See p55.

Residencial Marisela
To pretend you're Michael Jordan. See p65.

Casa de São Mamede
To run into a nun. See p60.

Bar with a view – **Senhora do Monte**.

friendly and multilingual staff greet you at reception and are cool and casual, making you feel instantly welcome and comfortable.

Hotel services *Bar. Buffet restaurant. Business centre. Cloakroom. Coffee shop. Convention rooms (2). Currency exchange. Fax. Internet. Laundry. Lift. Parking (free). Swimming pool.* **Room Services** *Air conditioning. Hair dryer. Kitchenette. Minibar. Pets allowed. Playstation. Radio. Room service (noon-3pm, 7-11pm daily). Safe. Telephone. TV: cable/pay movies.*

Hotel Sheraton Lisboa

Rua Latino Coelho 1, Marquês de Pombal, 1069-025 (21 312 0000/fax 21 354 7164/ sheraton.lisboa@sheraton.com). Metro Picoas. **Rates** 43,000$00-53,000$00 single; 41,000$00-65,000$00 double; 95,000$00-155,000$00 suites; 8,000$00-11,000$00 extra bed. **Credit** AmEx, DC, JCB, MC, V. **Map** p307 L6.

A popular choice with foreign business travellers, with all the conveniences available for mobile office work and a number of small private conference rooms. Rooms are modern and luxurious and interior comfort compensates for a rather ugly concrete exterior. A top-floor restaurant and bar has stunning views of the city and river, and a panoramic banqueting room is available for receptions and conferences. Staff can be a little offhand if you're not wearing a suit.

Hotel services *Barber. Bars (2). Beauty salon. Business centre. Car park (2,000$00). Conference and banqueting facilities for up to 520. Currency exchange. Disabled: access. Fax. Fitness centre. Health club. Laundry. Lift. No-smoking rooms. Restaurants (2). Sauna. Shops. Swimming pool.* **Room services** *Air-conditioning. Hairdryer. Minibar. Radio. Room service (24hr). Safe. Telephone. TV: satellite/cable.*

Hotel Tivoli Lisboa

Avenida da Liberdade 185, 1250-141 (21 319 8900/fax 21 319 8950/htlisboa@mail.telepac.pt). Metro Avenida. **Rates** 42,000$00 single; 46,000$00 double; 66,000$00-82,500$00 suite. **Credit** AmEx, DC, MC, V. **Map** p307 L8.

Situated halfway down Avenida de Liberdade, this large 1950s hotel has become a city landmark. It attracts a wide range of clients: businesspeople, honeymooners, families and tour groups. The lobby is huge and scattered with clusters of comfy chairs and constant waiter service. The hotel has an excellent rooftop grill restaurant with great views of the city. There is also a very private oval swimming pool with tennis court at the back of the hotel. In the summer you can order food and drink at the poolside. Staff are charming and attentive and rooms quiet and spacious.

Hotel services *Air-conditioning. Babysitting. Bars (3). Barber. Beauty salon. Car park (2,000$00). Conference and banqueting facilities. Currency exchange. Fax. Gym. Internet. Lift. Restaurants (2). Shops. Swimming pool. Tennis court.* **Room services** *Hairdryer. Minibar. Radio. Room service (24hr). Safe. Telephone. TV: satellite.*

Lapa

As Janelas Verdes

Rua das Janelas Verdes 47, Lapa, 1200-690 (21 396 8143/fax 21 396 8144/jverdes@heritage.pt). Tram 25/bus 27, 40, 49, 60. **Rates** 20,500$00-37,800$00 single; 31,900$00-37,000$00 double; 43,200$00-53,400$00 triple. *Low season* 23,300$00-28,800$00 single; 24,700$00-30,500$00 double; 30,900$00-38,100$00 triple. **Credit** AmEx, DC, MC, V. **Map** p306 C10.

Once the home of the late Portuguese novelist Eça de Queiroz, this late 18th-century mansion, said to have inspired his magical novels *O Ramalhete* and *Os Maias*, has been transformed into a charming private hotel. The memory of Queiroz is still very much alive and evident in the form of books and paintings. All rooms are sunny and comfortable and there is a small garden with an ivy-covered patio where you can relax away from the noise of the city. Just next door is the National Art Museum.

Hotel services *Air-conditioning. Babysitting. Bar. Car park (1,800$00). Currency exchange. Garden. No-smoking rooms.* **Room services** *Hairdryer. Room service (24hr). Safe. TV: cable.*

Lapa Palace Hotel

Rua do Pau da Bandeira 4, Lapa, 1249-021 (21 394 9494/fax 21 395 0665/www.orient-expresshotels.com) Tram 15, 28/bus 27. **Rates** 65,000$00 single; 70,000$00 double; 130,000$00 single/double suite. *Low season* 50,000$00 single; 55,000$00 double; 95,000$00 single/double suite. **Credit** AmEx, DC, MC, V. **Map** p306 H9.

Set in tranquil gardens with views onto the Tagus, this former aristocratic residence is one of Lisbon's classiest hotels, now owned by the Orient Express group. The interior is positively opulent and the hotel offers excellent facilities for those who enjoy beauty therapy or exercise as well as fine, if expensive (around 10,000$00 a head), Italian food at the Cipriani restaurant. Rooms are truly superb, each with a terrace or balcony. The Lapa serves an amazing buffet spread at breakfast; there's even chilled champagne. Recommended.

Hotel services *Babysitting. Bars (2). Breakfast room. Car park (free). Conference and banqueting facilities. Currency exchange. Disabled: access. Fax. Fitness centre. Gym. Internet. Laundry. Lift. Restaurants (2). Sauna. Shops. Solarium. Swimming pools (2).* **Room services** *Air-conditioning. Hairdryer. Minibar. Radio. Room service (24hr). Safe. Telephone. TV: cable/VCR.*

Rato & Amoreiras

Hotel Ritz Four Seasons

Rua Rodrigo da Fonseca 88, Rato, 1099-039 (21 381 1400/fax 21 383 1783/www.fourseasons.com). Metro Rato. **Rates** excluding breakfast 52,000$00-80,000$00 single; 57,000$00-85,000$00 double; 120,000$00 one-bedroom suite; 500,000$00 penthouse. **Credit** AmEx, DC, JCB, MC, V. **Map** p307 D6.

Since its recent take-over by the Four Seasons chain, the Ritz has undergone a much-needed facelift and seen major improvements in service and catering – the hotel offers the most impressive customer service in Lisbon. Located near the main business district, the Ritz is a popular choice for those wanting to forego traffic complications. A museum-worthy art collection adorns the lounge and lobby areas. The busy Varanda restaurant is one of the best in the city, attracting many outside clients. It adjoins an outdoor pool that overlooks Parque Eduardo VII and central Lisbon. The huge penthouse fitness centre has breathtaking views. Recommended.

Hotel services *Air-conditioning. Bar. Barber. Beauty salon. Business centre. Car park (free). Complimentary shoe shine. Complimentary newspaper. Conference and banqueting facilities. Currency exchange. Disabled: access. Fax. Fitness centre. Internet. Laundry. Lift. No-smoking rooms. Pets allowed. Restaurant. Shops. Snackbar.* **Room services** *Hairdryer. Minibar. Radio. Room service (24hr). Safe. TV: satellite/in-house movies.*

West of Baixa

Lisboa Regency

Rua Nova do Almada 114, Chiado, 1200-290 (21 325 6100/fax 21 325 6161). Metro Baixa-Chiado/28 tram. **Rates** 26,000$00-37,000$00 single; 28,000$00-40,000$00 double; 41,000$00-52,000$00 suite. *Low season* 22,000$00-32,000$00 single; 24,000$00-35,000$00 double; 46,000$00-62,000$00 suite; 11,000$00 extra bed. **Credit** AmEx, DC, MC, V. **Map** p310 L9.

At the bottom of Rua Garrett in Chiado, the Regency is one of the best-located hotels in terms of accessibility and view, although its bid to join the wave of 'design' hotels falls a bit flat. Nevertheless, it's comfortable and has an upbeat atmosphere. There's a fantastic buffet breakfast in the main dining room, which also serves lunch or dinner. Suites are particularly good value - roomy and light with touches of luxury such as fresh flowers and bath salts.

Hotel services *Babysitting. Bar. Business centre. Currency exchange. Disabled: access. Fax. Laundry. Lift. No-smoking rooms. Restaurant.* **Room services** *Air-conditioning. Hairdryer. Internet. Minibar. Room service. Safe. TV: satellite/web.*

Cascais & Estoril Coast

Clube do Lago

Avenida do Lago 4, 2765-420 Monte Estoril (21 464 7597/fax 214647599) Train to Monte Estoril from Cais de Sodré. **Rates** 30,000$00-46,000$00 single; 25,000$00 double; 30,000$00-40,000$00 suite. *Low season* 12,500$00 single; 14,000$00 double; 20,000$00-30,000$00 suite. **Credit** AmEx, DC, MC, V.

This swish health club-cum-aparthotel is the best bargain on the Estoril coast and one of the most comfortable hotels in the area. Prices may seem high, but split it between a group of friends and you'll find it cheap. Nowhere in Lisbon compares in terms of facilities and price. Indoor and outdoor pools, gym, Jacuzzi, Turkish bath, sauna, solarium, squash and tennis courts, indoor and poolside bar, games room and restaurant makes it paradise for anyone who likes to both have a good time and stay in shape. The mini-apartments are very spacious, all with kitchenette, terrace and sofabeds. A huge buffet breakfast is served in the restaurant, which also has a charcoal grill and à la carte menu. Understandably, some guests have become resident and rooms and suites can be rented for extended periods at reduced rates. Recommended.

Hotel services *Air-conditioning. Bar (2). Beauty salon. Billiards. Car park (free). Conference facilities. Currency exchange. Fax. Health Club. Internet. Jacuzzi. Lift. Massage. Restaurant. Sauna. Scottish bath. Shops. Solarium. Squash. Swimming pool (2). Tennis court. Turkish bath.* **Room services** *Fully equipped kitchen. Radio. Safe. Telephone. TV: satellite.*

Estalagem Senhora da Guia

Estrada do Guincho, 2750-642 Cascais (21 486 9239/fax 21 486 9227/www.senhoradaguia.com) Train to Cascais from Cais de Sodré/405 bus. **Rates** 33,000$00-36,000$00 single; 38,000$00-40,000$00 double; 45,000$00-53,000$00 suite. *Low season* 19,000$00-21,000$00 single; 21,000$00-23,000$00 double; 31,000$00-41,000$00 suite. **Credit** AmEx, DC, MC, V.

You feel you are in a luxurious private home with fantastic sea views when you stay in this guesthouse. The interiors have an old English flavour, with antique furniture everywhere. But all 39 rooms have the modern amenities and services expected of a five-star hotel; what's different is the personal touch. There are special rates for guests at a number of local golf courses, and beaches are within easy reach. Staff offer to organise just about any local activity for children or adults such as tennis tournaments, barbecues, helicopter rides or sailing.

Hotel services *Air-conditioning. Babysitting. Bar (2). Business centre. Car park (free). Car rental. Conference facilities (up to 60 people). Currency exchange. Internet. Laundry. Restaurant. Swimming pool.* **Room services** *Hairdryer. Minibar. Radio. Room service (8am-11pm daily). Safe. TV: satellite. Valet.*

Hotel Albatroz

Rua Frederico Arouca 100, 2750-353 Cascais (21 484 7380/fax 21 484 4827/www.albatrozhotel.pt). Train from Cais do Sodré to Cascais. **Rates** excluding breakfast 34,000$00-55,000$00 single; 40,000$00-60,000$00 double; 70,000$00-80,000$00 suite. *Low season* 25,000$00-40,000$00 single; 30,000$00-45,000$00 double; 45,000$00-50,000$00 suite. **Breakfast** 2,250$00 per head. **Credit** AmEx, DC, MC, V.

No longer part of the Lapa Palace group, the Albatroz now seems less of a link in a chain. The interior has had a complete facelift; it now has a relaxed, oriental flavour that makes you just want

Pestana
HOTELS & RESORTS

is...

CARLTON MADEIRA HOTEL

CARLTON RIO ATLANTICA

CARLTON PARK HOTEL

DOM JOÃO II HOTEL

PALMS HOTEL

VILLAGE HOTEL

ATLANTIC GARDENS HOTEL

ATLANTIC GARDENS SUITE HOTEL

ATLANTIC BAY HOTEL

INBOCA LODGE

KAVUMA CARLTON HOTEL

BAZARUTO LODGE

CARLTON ALVOR HOTEL

DELFIM HOTEL

LEVANTE HOTEL

PORTO CARLTON HOTEL

MIRAMAR HOTEL

CARLTON PALACE HOTEL

Beautiful when lit up – **Hotel Albatroz**. *See p51.*

to sit on the floor and meditate. There's a stylish
mosaic oval pool looking onto Cascais harbour,
which is beautiful when lit up at night. Also check
out the Villa Cascais, the hotel's smaller sister down
the road, which shares the pool, is cheaper and has
a great restaurant (21 486 3410).
Hotel services *Air-conditioning. Bar. Business
centre. Car park (free). Complementary newspaper.
Conference and banqueting facilities. Currency
exchange. Disabled: access. Fax. Internet.
Restaurant. Shops.* **Room services** *Hairdryer.
Minibar. Radio. Room service (24hr). Safe.
Telephone. TV: cable.*

Hotel Estoril Sol

*Parque Palmela, 2754-504 Cascais (21 483
9000/fax 21 483 2280/hotel@estorilsol.pt). Train to
Cascais or Monte Estoril from Cais de Sodré.* **Rates**
39,200$00 single; 43,000$00 double; 80,000$00 suite.
Low season 37,000$00 single; 41,000$00 double;
75,600$00 suite; 9,400$00-8,900$00 extra bed.
Credit AmEx, DC, MC, V.
In its heyday this was a favourite haunt of such
celebs as Rod Stewart and Phil Collins, but it went
sharply downhill in the early '90s. It's now recov-
ering somewhat. The building is an ugly concrete
tower block; inside a strange combination of old-
style luxury and holiday-camp atmosphere prevails. Rooms have stunning views across Cascais
harbour and the hotel has a tunnel connecting it
directly to the beach and the seafront promenade.
The hotel has both a family and 18-to-30 atmosphere in summer; it's popular with British and
German holidaymakers, so get up early to reserve
your poolside spot.
Hotel services *Air-conditioning. Babysitting. Bars
(3). Barber. Beauty salon. Car park (free). Car rental.
Conference and banqueting facilities. Currency
exchange. Fax. Gym. Lift. Restaurants (2). Sauna.
Shops. Swimming pool.* **Room services** *Hairdryer.
Minibar. Radio. Room service (24hr). Internet. Safe.
Telephone. TV: satellite.*

Rossio & Restauradores

Hotel Metrópole

*Praça Dom Pedro IV (Rossio) 30,1100-200 (21 321
9030/fax 21 346 9166/www.almeidahotels.com)
Metro Restauradores.* **Rates** 26,200$00 single;
28,400$00 double; 5,000$00 extra bed. *Low season*
22,100$00 single; 24,200$00 double; 7,000$00 extra
bed. **Credit** AmEx, DC, JCB, MC, V. **Map** p310 L9.
Located in Rossio, right above Café Nicola (*see p140*),
the Hotel Metrópole combines art nouveau with modern comfort. The charming interior is a throwback to
the 1920s, with individually decorated rooms containing original furniture. Bathrooms are spacious
and decorated in white marble. A stylish bar looks
across to São Jorge Castle and onto Rossio; it was
from these windows that communist revolutionaries
addressed the masses during the 1974 Revolution.
Traffic outside can be noisy during the day, but
rooms are quiet at night. Recommended.
Hotel services *Air-conditioning. Babysitting. Bar.
Conference room. Childrenís room. Currency
exchange. Disabled: 1 room. Fax. TV Lounge. Pets
allowed.* **Room services** *Radio. Room service (24
hr). Safe. TV: satellite.*

Orion Eden

*Praça dos Restauradores 24, Rossio, 1250-187 (21
321 6600/fax 21 321 6666) Metro Restauradores.*
Rates excluding breakfast 27,700$00 single/double;
30,800$00 3-4 people. *Low season* 22,000$00 single/
double; 30,800$00 3-4 people. Deposit of 30,000$00 on
arrival. **Credit** AmEx, DC, MC, V. **Map** p310 L9.
The Orion Eden is an aparthotel popular with business travellers for its central location and reasonable
price. Named after the Eden cinema that once occupied the building, the hotel retains most of the art
deco façade. All the 134 air-conditioned apartments
are simply decorated, comfortable, soundproof and

Hotel Veneza – over-the-top ornate.

have a fully equipped kitchen. There's a fantastic swimming pool on a roof terrace, complete with bar and patio, where breakfast can be taken, and amazing panoramic views across Lisbon.
Hotel services *Air-conditioning. Conference facilities. Disabled: access to 3 apartments. Fax. Laundry. Lift. Meeting rooms. Pets accepted. Solarium. Swimming pool.* **Room services** *Dishwasher. Equipped kitchenette. Fridge. Hairdryer. Microwave. Oven. Radio. Safe. TV: satellite.*

Avenida da Liberdade & Marquês de Pombal

Hotel Eduardo VII

Avenida Fontes Pereira de Melo 5, Marquês de Pombal, 1069-114 (21 356 8822/fax 21 356 8833/hoteleduardoiv@mail.telepac.pt). Metro Marquês de Pombal. Rates 17,300$00 single; 19,700$00 double; 24,600$00 triple; 7,000$00 extra bed. *Low season* 12,900$00 single; 15,200$00 double; 18,900$00 triple; 5,000$00 extra bed. **Credit** AmEx, DC, MC, V. **Map** p307 D6.
Part of the Best Western group, the Eduardo VII is right by the leafy Parque Eduardo VII. The views from the rooftop bar and restaurant are a major attraction, pulling in many non-guests eager to try out the renowned Portuguese and Brazilian cuisine. Service is outstanding but unfussy and you get a real sense of luxury at a very reasonable price. Guests get a 20 per cent discount at the restaurant and bar and access to a local golf course. Recommended.
Hotel services *Air-conditioning. Babysitting. Car park (2,200$00). Conference facilities. Currency exchange. Golf course access. Fax. Laundry. TV lounge.* **Room services** *Minibar. Room service (24hr). Safe. TV: satellite/cable/pay. Valet service.*

Hotel Lisboa

Rua Barata Salgueiro 5, Avenida da Liberdade, 1166-069 (21 355 4131/fax 21 355 4139/hotlis@ip.pt). Metro Avenida. **Rates** 16,800$00 single; 20,000$00 double. **Credit** AmEx, MC, V. **Map** p307 E7.
This newly refurbished hotel has been tastefully decorated but is one among many; it seems geared solely to businesspeople. Rooms have all the basic services and double glazing cuts out traffic noise from the Avenida da Liberdade. Staff seem a little clueless as to what the hotel offers. All told, not the best value for money in the area.
Hotel services *Air-conditioning. Bar. Fax. Laundry. Lift. Parking (free).* **Room services** *Hairdryer. Radio. Room service (9am-midnight daily). Safe. TV: satellite.*

Hotel Lisboa Plaza

Travessa do Salitre 7, Avenida da Liberdade, 1269-066 (21 321 8218/fax 21 347 1630/plaza.hotels@heritage.pt). Metro Avenida. **Rates** excluding breakfast 28,200$00-34,900$00 single; 31,300$00-38,800$00 double; 39,000$00-48,300$00 triple; 49,000$00-54,400$00 suite. *Low season* 23,300$00-28,800$00 single; 24,700$00-30,500$00 double; 31,900$00-36,000$00 triple; 30,900$00-46,200$00 suite. **Credit** AmEx, DC, JCB, MC, V. **Map** p307 L8.
Opened in the early 1950s, this grand hotel was designed in bold neoclassical style by architect Lucinio Cruz. Graça Viterbo, one of Portugal's best known interior designers was let loose on the foyer, and a cream-coloured marble floor now blends with the soft pastels of the carpets and furniture. The spacious rooms are also in Viterbo's style, with comfortable furnishings and light, airy bathrooms. A massive breakfast is served in the restaurant, which also has a very good à la carte menu. Prices have risen lately but still compare well to nearby rivals.
Hotel services *Air-conditioning. Babysitting. Bar. Car park (1,800$00). Conference facilities. Currency exchange. Fax. Laundry. Lift. No-smoking floor. Restaurant.* **Room services** *Disabled: 3 rooms. Hairdryer. Minibar. Radio. Room service (24hr). Safe. TV: satellite.*

Hotel Veneza

Avenida da Liberdade 189, 1250-141 (21 352 2618/fax 21 352 6678/www.3khoteis.com). Metro Avenida. **Rates** excluding breakfast 22,000$00 single; 27,000$00 double. Breakfast 750$00. **Credit** AmEx, DC, MC, V. **Map** p307 E7.
The decor in this hotel is fabulous and totally over-the-top ornate. A stained-glass window above the entrance leads to a colourful mural of Lisbon that goes up the elegant spiral staircase. Thankfully, the spacious rooms are not quite so kitsch, but all follow a certain colour motif with curtains matching the bedclothes. Staff are friendly, but the hotel has few services compared to some of its competitors.
Hotel services *Air-conditioning. Bar. Car park (1,400$00). Currency exchange. Fax. Laundry. Lift. Safe. TV lounge.* **Room services** *Minibar. Pets allowed. Room service (7pm-midnight). TV: satellite.*

East of Baixa

Albergaria Senhora do Monte

Calçada do Monte 39, Graça, 1170-250 (21 886 6002/fax 21 887 7783). Tram 28. **Rates** 19,000$00 single; 21,000$00 double; 29,000$00-35,000$00 triple. *Low season* 15,000$00 single; 18,000$00 double; 22,500$00-27,500$00 triple. **Credit** AmEx, DC, MC, V. **Map** p308 G8.

Set on one of Lisbon's seven hills, with the old town at its feet and looking out onto the castle and the river beyond, the Albergaria Senhorra do Monte hotel is totally removed from the bustle of the city. It's a great place for romantic rooftop views – if you don't mind skimping a little on modern facilities. All the rooms are simple though recently redecorated in pink pastels and white. The panoramic bar (open to non-guests) serves drinks and light snacks all day and a modest breakfast can be taken onto the terrace. The pricier air-conditioned rooms have balconies with truly stunning views, but if you want a room with a view, make sure you ask when you reserve. Not the handiest place for going out downtown, and maybe a little overpriced, but if you like long romantic walks, and quiet relaxation, this is the place for you.
Hotel services *Air-conditioning. Babysitting. Bar. Fax. Safe. TV room.* **Room services** *Room service (7.30am-5pm daily). Safe. TV: satellite.*

Lapa

Pensão York House

Rua das Janelas Verdes 32-1, Lapa, 1200-691 (21 396 2785/fax 21 397 2793/yorkhouse@mail. telepac.pt). Tram 25/bus 27. **Rates** 15,000$00-29,000$00 single; 32,500$00 double; 39,000$00 triple; duplex 42,000$00. *Low season* 10,000$00-22,000$00 double; 24,000$00 double; 29,000$00 triple; 33,000$00 duplex. **Credit** AmEx, DC, JCB, MC, V. **Map** p306 J10.

With Graham Greene and John le Carré among past guests, there can't be many better places to find literary inspiration tahn York House. Behind a pink-painted wall at the top of an flight of stairs you discover a courtyard filled with flowers, trees and plants. Around it are 36 rooms, a dining room and bar installed within the 17th-century structure. Comfortably solid furnishing gives the air of a country retreat, but cool corridors and ecclesiastical artefacts betray a more pious past – until 1834 this was a Carmelite convent. The hotel got its unusually anglicised name in 1880, when a pair of Yorkshire ladies rented the property and turned it into a guesthouse. These days the rooms vary enormously, from cramped and over-furnished to huge and opulent. The restaurant serves tasty Portuguese dishes and in the summer you can eat outside in the courtyard. It's advisable to book well in advance during the high season.
Hotel services *Babysitting. Bar. Fax. Laundry. Restaurant. Safe.* **Room services** *TV: satellite.*

Parque das Nações

Hotel Meliá Confort Oriente

Avenida Dom João II, 1990-083 (21 893 0000/fax 21 893 0099/www.solmelia.es). Metro Oriente. **Rates** 18,400$00 single; 20,400$00 double; 5,200$00 extra bed. **Credit** AmEx, DC, MC, V.

This brand new hotel is right by the former Expo 98 site, a few minutes from Lisbon airport. A 10-minute train ride from the futuristic Oriente train station takes you to central Lisbon, but the service does not run after midnight. Rooms have stunning view of the river, the Expo site and the Vasco da Gama bridge. They're comfortable and come with a small kitchenette and plenty of modern facilities.
Hotel services *Air-conditioning. Babysitting. Bar. Car park (1,200$00). Conference rooms. Currency exchange. Disabled: 3 rooms. Fax. Laundry. Lift. No-smoking floor. Restaurant/coffeeshop.* **Room services** *Hairdryer. Internet. Kitchenette. Minibar. Radio. Room service (10.30am-10.30pm daily). Safe. TV: satellite/pay.*

Cascais & Estoril Coast

Hotel Quinta da Marinha

Quinta da Marinha, 2750-715 Cascais (21 486 0100/fax 214869488/www.quinta-da-marinha.com) Train to Cascais from Cais de Sodré/401 bus. **Rates** 28,500$00 single; 30,000$00 double; 40,000$00 suite; 40,000$00-90,000$00 villas. **Credit** AmEx, DC, MC, V.

Set within the grounds of the Quinta da Marinha resort, this newish hotel is surrounded by one of the best golf courses in Portugal and is only 500 yards/450m from the sea. Guests have access to a host of facilities: three outdoor pools, six tennis courts and a four-mile, 18-hole golf course (5,000$00 a day). If you prefer horse riding, there are stables within five minutes' walk. The hotel has 200 rooms on three levels and hundreds of palm trees and ferns are carefully nurtured along passages and around the foyer. A good place for peace and quiet.
Hotel services *Air-conditioning. Bar (2). Business centre. Car park (free). Conference and banqueting facilities. Currency exchange. Disabled: access. Fax. Fitness centre. 18-hole golf course. Hairdresser. Internet. Massage. Restaurant. Sauna. Shops. Swimming pools (5) Tennis courts (6) Turkish bath.* **Room services** *Hairdryer. Minibar. Radio. Room service (24hr). Safe. Shuttle bus. Telephone. TV: satellite.*

Vila Galé

Avenida Marginal Apt 49, 2766-901 Estoril (21 464 8400/fax 21 464 8432/galeestoril@vilagale.pt). Train to Estoril from Cais do Sodré. **Rates** 26,600$00 single; 30,750$00 double; 5,100$00 extra bed. *Low season* 15,100$00 single; 18,550$00 double; 4,170$00 extra bed. **Credit** AmEx, DC, MC, V.

A good alternative to some of the more expensive hotels in the area as it's right opposite Estoril train station and beachside bars and restaurants. The terrace pool with sea views also makes it a great place to relax; a health club offers a Turkish bath, Jacuzzi and gym. The hotel's newly refurbished interior is pleasingly simple and the cosy bar beyond the main entrance sets a relaxing tone; the O Divino restaurant serves fine traditional Portuguese cuisine. **Hotel services** *Air-conditioning. Babysitting. Bar. Beauty salon. Billiards. Internet kiosk. Car park (750$00). Conference facilities. Currency exchange. Disabled: facilities. Fax. Health Club. Lift. Restaurant. Swimming pool.* **Room services** *Hair dryer. Radio. Room service (24hr, 800$00). Safe (360$00). Telephone. TV: satellite/Akai guestlink/pay TV.*

Moderate

Rossio & Restauradores

Hotel Internacional

Rua da Betesga 3, Rossio, 1100-090 (21 346 1913/ fax 21 347 8635). Metro Rossio. **Rates** 10,500$00 single; 12,500$00 double; 14,500$00 triple. *Low season* 10,000$00 single; 11,000$00 double; 14,000$00 triple. **Credit** AmEx, DC, JCB, MC, V. **Map** p310 F9.
Centrally located halfway between Praça da Figueira and Rossio square, this hotel has an attractive old façade, but the interior has been refurbished and modernised with a modest bar and lounge area and plain and simple furnishings. Bedrooms are light and roomy with comfortable beds and come with decent-sized en-suite bathrooms; those on the top floor have great views of the castle. Although slightly lacking in character and exposed to traffic noise, this is a reasonably priced central base. **Hotel services** *Bar. Fax. Laundry. Lift. TV lounge.* **Room services** *Air-conditioning. Safe. Telephone. TV: satellite.*

Hotel Mundial

Rua Dom Duarte 4, Rossio, 1100-198 (21 884 2000/fax 21884 2110/www.hotel-mundial.pt). *Metro Rossio/12, 28 tram.* **Rates** 18,850$00 single; 21,700$00 double; 5,000$00 extra bed. *Low season* 15,300$00 single; 19,200$00 double; 4,000$00 extra bed. *July, Aug* 17,700$00 single; 20,400$00 double; 4,800$00 extra bed. **Credit** AmEx, DC, MC, V. **Map** p311 F9.
Opened in 1958, the Mundial has undergone extensive renovation including a new rooftop grill with its own garden and panoramic views across Lisbon; the food is also excellent. All rooms have decent views and are very quiet, thanks to double-glazing, but many are not large enough and have odd dimensions because of the curvature of the hotel. A newly built coffee shop is a good place to hang out or read. All-round good value for money. **Hotel services** *Air-conditioning. Babysitting. Bar. Car park (free). Coffee shop. Conference and banqueting facilities. Currency exchange. Fax. Laundry. Lift. Restaurant and rooftop terrace with weekly grills. Shops. Reading lounge.* **Room services** *Hairdryer. Minibar. Room service (24hr). Safe. Telephone. TV: satellite/pay.*

The spies who stayed in the sun

HOTEL PALÁCIO

Ever felt like donning a tux and pretending you were in a Bond movie? Well, the Hotel Palácio Estoril is one of the best places to unleash World War II spy fantasies. During the war, when Portugal stayed neutral, it was a centre for Allied intelligence operations. At the height of the conflict, a network operated in the hotel, supposedly using concierges to glean information on agents from both sides.

This network extended to the Hotel Parque opposite, the main meeting point for Nazi agents. When the Parque was demolished after the war the true extent of covert activity was revealed: dozens of bugging devices and yards of wire were found in the walls.

Real-life spy stories inspired novelist Ian Fleming, who stayed at the Palácio and wrote at least one best-seller there. It later served as a setting for the 1970 James Bond film *On Her Majesty's Secret Service*. More recently Robert Wilson's *A Small Death in Lisbon* used the hotel's wartime past to reconstruct a not-so-neutral Portugal, the plot revolving around tungsten exports to Germany.

Hotel Portugal

Rua João das Regras 4, Rossio, 1100-294 (21 887 7581/fax 21 886 7343) Metro Rossio/12, 28 tram.
Rates 11,000$00 single; 13,500$00 double; 27,500$00 triple. *Low season* 9,000$00 single; 11,000$00 double; 14,000$00 triple. **Credit** AmEx, DC, MC, V.
Map p311 F9.
This central hotel has simple services and is run by friendly and efficient staff. All rooms come with clean, roomy bathrooms. A simple continental breakfast is served in an elegant breakfast room. Reasonably priced, considering the location and the evident investment in refurbishment of the bedrooms.
b *Bar. Safe. TV lounge.* **Room services** *Air-conditioning. TV: satellite.*

Hotel Suíço Atlântico

Rua da Glória 3-19, Restauradores, 1250-114 (21 346 1713/fax 21 346 9013/h.suico.atlantico @portugal-info.net) Metro Restauradores. **Rates** 11,000$00 single; 14,000$00 double; 16,500$00 triple; 18,000$00 four-person. *Low season* 8,100$00 single; 10,200$00 double; 12,600$00 triple; 14,400$00 four-person. **Credit** AmEx, DC, MC, V.
Map p310 L8.
Located next to where the Elevador da Glória goes up to Bairro Alto, the Hotel Suíço Atlântico is only five minutes' walk from the central Praça dos Restauradores square and the main tourist information centre: ideally situated for shopping and sightseeing. There is a pleasant TV lounge off the main foyer next to the pub-like Taverna bar. The

surrounding area can get a little noisy and seedy at night but the hotel itself is quiet. Rooms could be a little brighter and cleaner – as could the staff.
Hotel services *Bar. Currency exchange. Fax. Lift. Pets admitted.* **Room services** *Safe. TV: satellite.*

Avenida da Liberdade/Marquês de Pombal

Hotel Dom Carlos

Avenida Duque de Loulé 121, Marquês de Pombal, 1050-089 (21 351 2590/fax 21352 0728/ hdcarlos@mail.telepac.pt) Metro Marquês de Pombal.
Rates 18,000$00 single; 21,600$00 double. *Low season* 12,000$00 single; 14,500$00 double; 18,000$00 suite. **Credit** AmEx, DC, MC, V. **Map** p307 E6.
Owned by the same chain as the nearby Hotel Presidente (*see p59*), the Dom Carlos shares some of the same features but is generally more welcoming and comfortable. The location, right next to Marquês de Pombal square, makes it busier, but it is surprisingly secluded and overlooks a small, leafy park. Rooms are newly decorated, very comfortable and soundproof; most are also spacious with bright en-suite marble bathrooms. A smart conference room (capacity 50) provides state-of-the-art audio-visual facilities. The cosy, dimly lit bar is a good place for a meal or a drink in the evening; it is transformed into a brightly lit breakfast room in the morning.

Portugal's neutrality also made the Palácio a favourite haunt for deposed royals from around Europe, including ex-king Umberto of Italy, the Count of Paris (pretender to the French throne), Don Juan of Bourbon y Battenberg (who would have been king of Spain but for Franco), and real royals from Norway, Monaco and Luxembourg and Japan.

Set on the palm tree-lined Estoril coast, the hotel looks onto Estoril's famous casino. There's a statue of the hotel's designer, Fausto Cardoso de Figueiredo, in the casino gardens. In his hand Figueiredo holds the ambitious plans he drew up for the whole Estoril/Cascais coast; he was essentially responsible for transforming the area into a playground for the rich and famous during and after the war, and there are plans to transform the area once more into a playboy's paradise by pouring money into restoration projects using Figueiredo's vision as a blueprint.

The Hotel Palácio itself has a real 1940s elegance, with restoration work on its lavish interior extending to the hotel's bedrooms and suites. For the equivalent of £100, you can enjoy marble halls, high stucco ceilings graced

with crystal chandeliers and the chance to rub shoulders with misplaced bluebloods. The feeling is one of pure pampered luxury, yet service is friendly and there's none of the stuffiness often found in hotels of this standard. This may not be the most modern hotel in the Lisbon area but it does have a great atmosphere and is geared towards couples and families rather than businessmen – although it would be a plausible place for international crime bosses to gather.

Hotel Palacio Estoril

Rua do Parque, 2769-504 Estoril (464 8000/fax 468 4867/palacioestoril@mail. telepac.pt). Train from Cais de Sodré/bus 498.
Rates 40,000$00 single; 45,000$00 double; 65,000$00 suite. *Low season* 25,000$00 single; 30,000$00 double; 40,000$00 suite.
Credit AmEx, DC, JCB, MC, V.
Hotel services *Air-conditioning. Babysitting. Bar. Café. Car park (free). Conference facilities. Currency exchange. Fax. Laundry. Massage/beauty parlour. Pets accepted. Restaurant. Swimming pool.* **Room Services** *Hairdryer. Minibar. Radio. Room service. Safe. Telephone. Trouserpress. TV.*

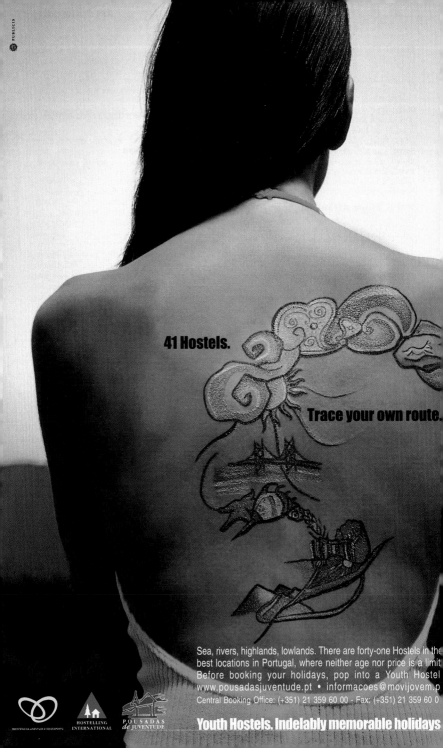

Hotel services *Babysitting. Bar. Conference facilities. Currency exchange. Fax. Laundry. Lift. Snack bar.* **Room services** *Air-conditioning. Hairdryer. Minibar. Radio. Room service (24hr, 20% service charge). Safe. TV: satellite.*

Hotel Ibis

Rua Barata Salgueiro 53, Avenida da Liberdade, 1250-043 (21 330 0630/fax 21 330 0631/ www.ibishotel.com). Metro Avenida. **Rates** excluding breakfast 10,100$00 single/double. **Breakfast** 800$00. Credit AmEx, MC, V. **Map** p307 K7.

This new branch of the French chain offers creature comforts at a modest price in a central location, five minutes from either the Bairro Alto or Avenida da Liberdade. While aimed at the business market, it has a relaxed atmosphere, with a small bar and comfy seating off the main foyer. Rooms are reasonably spacious, although you never quite escape that hotel-chain airport atmosphere.
Hotel services *Air-conditioning. Bar. Car rental. Currency exchange. Fax. Laundry. Lift.* **Room services** *Hairdryer. Radio. Safe. TV: pay/ satellite.*

Hotel Jorge V

Rua Mouzinho da Silveira 3, Marquês de Pombal, 1250-165 (21 356 2525/fax 21 315 0319/ info@hoteljorgev.com). Metro Marquês de Pombal. **Rates** 13,000$00 single; 16,000$00 double; 19,000$00 triple; 24,000$00 suite; 3,000$00 extra bed. **Credit** AmEx, DC, MC, V. **Map** p307 K7.

Run by friendly manager João Silva, the Jorge V offers modern services and 49 rooms, some with balconies and views. All have clean en-suite bathrooms but could be more spacious. There is a garish TV lounge with a small bar adjoining that serves light snacks, but it lacks atmosphere and won't detain you long. Try not to leave valuables in your room as there have been some recent complaints of robbery.
Hotel services *Air-conditioning. Babysitting. Bar. Currency exchange. Fax. Lift. No smoking floors.* **Room services** *Hairdryer. Minibar. Safe. TV: satellite/cable/pay.*

Hotel Madrid

Rua do Conde Redondo 24, Marquês de Pombal, 1150-106 (21 319 1760/fax 21 315 7575/ www.3khoteis.com) Metro Marquês de Pombal. **Rates** 18,500$00 single; 21,000$00 double. **Credit** AmEx, DC, MC, V. **Map** p307 E7.

Part of the Spanish 3K chain, this new hotel is well situated just off the Avenida da Liberdade. Its simple but stylish furnishings may lack historical charm but provide a clean, uncluttered environment. Staff are attentive and the bar area is open until the early hours, although it's not the kind of place you'd want to stay all night. Rooms are well-lit and spacious, with modern fittings and comfy beds; all have en-suite bathrooms with shower. Good place for young business travellers and very good value.
Hotel services *Bar. Conference facilities (200). Car rental. Currency exchange. Dry-cleaning. Fax. Laundry. Parking.* **Room services** *Air-conditioning. Hairdryer. Minibar. Radio. Room service (24hr). Safe. Shoeshine. TV: satellite.*

Hotel Miraparque

Avenida Sidónio Pais 12, Marquês de Pombal, 1050-214 (21 352 4286/fax 21 357 8920). Metro Parque. **Rates** 12,800$00 single; 16,000$00 double; 18,000$00 triple. **Credit** AmEx, DC, MC, V. **Map** p307 E6.

The recently renovated Hotel Miraparque is in a central yet quiet location overlooking the Parque Eduardo VII. Rooms are a bit cramped and plainly furnished but a friendly atmosphere and helpful staff make up for any style shortcomings. A fairly featureless restaurant serves the usual local cuisine.
Hotel services *Air-conditioning. Babysitting. Bar. Currency exchange. Fax. Laundry. Lift. Meeting room. Restaurant.* **Room services** *Laundry. Minibar. Pets allowed. Radio. Room service (7am-midnight). Safe. TV: satellite.*

Hotel Presidente

Rua Alexandre Herculano 13, Marquês de Pombal, 1150-005 (21 317 3570/fax 21 352 0272/ hpresidente@mail.telepac.pt) Metro Marquês de Pombal. **Rates** 16,800$00 single; 19,500$00 double. *Low season* 11,000$00 single; 13,200$00 double. **Credit** AmEx, DC, MC, V. **Map** p307 E7.

This very reasonably priced, central hotel has been refurbished recently. It's both luxurious and cosy and the staff are a well-trained, friendly bunch. Rooms are very comfortable and tastefully simple although not very spacious despite having verandahs looking onto the Avenida. The bar area is a bit too much like an airport lounge – the buffet breakfast is also served here.
Hotel services *Bar. Babysitting. Conference facilities. Currency exchange. Fax. Laundry. Lift.* **Room services** *Air-conditioning. Hairdryer. Minibar. Radio. Room service (24hr, 20% service charge). Safe. TV: satellite.*

Residencial Astoria

Rua Braamcamp 10B, Marquês de Pombal 1250-050 (21 386 1317/fax 21 386 0491). Metro Marquês de Pombal. **Rates** 10,000$00 single; 12,500$00 double. 15,00$00 triple; 16,500$00 four-person. **Credit** AmEx, MC, V. **Map** p307 K7.

This family-run guesthouse has built up a good reputation for friendliness and comfort. All rooms have private bathrooms and are surprisingly quiet for somewhere so close to Marquês de Pombal. Good value if you're lookig for somewhere central, but if you're using a car, parking can be a problem.
Hotel services *Laundry. Fax.* **Room services** *Air-conditioning. TV: satellite.*

Residencial Dom Sancho I

Avenida da Liberdade 202, Avenida da Liberdade, 1250-147 (21 354 8648/fax 21 354 8042). Metro Avenida. **Rates** 9,500$00 single; 12,500$00 double; 3,000$00 extra bed. **Credit** AmEx, MC, V. **Map** p307 E7.

A good, centrally located guesthouse, which is impeccably run by its friendly manager, José Martins. Seems to offer all the services of a top-notch hotel at a reasonable price, although the decor of the bedrooms is a bit old-fashioned. A

Sé Guesthouse – charm and cosiness on a budget.

comfortable option for those who can't afford the Tivoli and Sofitel hotels opposite.
Hotel services *Air-conditioning. Babysitting. Bar. Currency exchange. Small pets allowed. Tobacconist. TV/video lounge.* **Room services** *Safe. TV: satellite.*

East of Baixa

Sé Guesthouse

Rua de São João da Praça 97-1, Alfama, 1100-301 (21 886 4400). Tram 28, 12/bus 37. **Rates** 13,000$00 single; 17,000$00 double. *Low season* 8,000-12,000$00 single/double. **Credit** AmEx, V. **Map** p308 M10.
Named after the neighbouring Sé, a medieval cathedral, this charmingly simple guesthouse is run by a family from Mozambique who have created a friendly, welcoming atmosphere. The rooms are clean, although bathrooms are shared. A generous continental breakfast is included in the price.
Hotel services *Library. TV lounge.*

West of Baixa

Casa de São Mamede

Rua da Escola Politécnica 159, Príncipe Real 1250-100 (21 396 3166/fax 21 395 1896). Metro Rato. **Rates** 13,000$00 single; 15,000$00 double; 16,000$00 triple. *Low season* 10,000$00 single; 13,000$00 double; 14,000$00 triple. **No credit cards. Map** p307 K8.
Rather austere, old-fashioned hostel with lots of religious paintings and crosses. It feels like a nunnery and strict house rules apply: no noise after midnight and guests are expected to be on their best behaviour. Rooms are big and reasonably comfortable with decent bathrooms, and a basic breakfast is served. If you're looking for calm and spiritual soul-searching, it's ideal. If you're openly gay and planning to stagger in at 4am after a bar crawl, it isn't.
Hotel services *Fax. TV lounge.*

Hotel Borges

Rua Garrett 108, Chiado, 1200-205 (21 346 1951/fax 21 342 6617). Metro Baixa-Chiado/28 tram. **Rates** 9,500$00 single; 10,500$00 double; 13,000$00 triple; 15,000$00 four. *Low season* 8,500$00 single; 9,500$00 double; 12,000$00 triple; 14,000$00 four. **Credit** AmEx, DC, MC, V. **Map** p310 L9.
In the middle of Chiado, the Borges is one of Lisbon's oldest hotels. It has seen better days, but provides a decent breakfast and comfortable rooms, some of which look out onto Rua Garret, Chiado's main pedestrian thoroughfare. The owners have recently restored the façade and made minimal changes on the inside in a bid to maintain the elegant, if faded, appearance. Restaurant service is only available for group bookings.
Hotel services *Currency exchange. Laundry. Lift. Safe. TV room.* **Room services** *Room service (7.30am-5pm daily). Safe.*

Cascais & Estoril Coast

Casa da Pergola

Avenida Valborn 13, 2750-508 Cascais (21 484 0040/fax 21 483 4791/www.ciberguia.pt/casa-da-pergola). Train from Cais do Sodré to Cascais. **Rates** 18,000$00-20,000$00 double. *Low season* 13,500$00-16,500$00 double. **No credit cards.**
This homely, family-run hostel is an architectural gem – covered in rare Portuguese handpainted tiles and bougainvillea, but there's no sign of a pergola. The inside is a treasure-trove of antiques; each room has its own decor and beautiful paintings covering the walls. The more expensive rooms have a huge terrace where meals can be served; all have large bathrooms. A traditional English tea is served each day, complete with scones and clotted cream. The young, mainly Brazilian staff are friendly and efficient.
Hotel services *Air-conditioning. Laundry. TV room.* **Room services** *TV. Room service (8am-10pm).*

Estalagem do Farol

*Avenida Rei Humberto II de Italia 7, 2750
Cascais (21 483 0173/fax 21484 1447). Train
to Cascais from Cais de Sodré.* **Rates** 8,000$00-
16,200$00 single; 10,000$00-17,200$00. *Low season*
6,000$00-8,000$00 single; 10,200$00-12,200$00.
No credit cards.

A great place for young travellers to get to know
Cascais and the beach-lined coast north towards
Guincho, this hotel is right next to the marina and
walking distance from the town centre. The adjacent
Coconuts nightclub closes at 6am; unless you are
clubbing yourself, you may find it noisy. The hotel
has a rather kitsch interior with a trendy bar serving up cocktails and snacks that can be taken out to
the pool. It has spectacular views of the sea, as do
most of the more expensive rooms. A new wing was
being added in early 2001 and refurbishments are
planned, which will no doubt push up prices; visit
while it's still a bargain.

Hotel services *Air-conditioning. Bar. Car park
(free).* **Room services** *Telephone. TV: satellite.*

Estalagem do Muchaxo

*Praia do Guincho, 2750-642, Cascais (21 487
0221/fax 21 487 0444/muchaxo@ip.pt). Train
to Cascais from Cais do Sodré/405, 415 bus.*
Rates 14,000$00-21,000$00 double without view;
20,000$00-26,000$00 double with view. *Low season*
8,000$00-14,000$00 double without view; 10,000$00-
17,000$00 double with view. **Credit** AmEx, DC,
JCB, MC, V.

This atmospheric converted fort overlooks the
huge Guincho beach, where international windsurfing championships are held. Rooms are basic
and comfortable with fantastic sea views from the
more expensive ones. There's a salt-water pool out
back with its own bar. The charismatic owner has
recently installed an internet corner and is offering
to hire out mountain bikes so guests can cycle
along special tracks to Cascais. In the high season
there is also an hourly bus service into town – the
journey takes around 15 minutes. The hotel has its
own lobster bed and an excellent seafood restaurant that compares favourably to come of the
expensive eateries that line the coast road.

Hotel services *Air-conditioning. Babysitting.
Bar. Car park (free). Currency exchange. Laundry.
Restaurant.* **Room services** *Minibar. Radio.
TV: satellite.*

Hotel Inglaterra

*Rua do Porto 1, 2765-271 Estoril (21 468 4461/fax
21 468 2108/hotelinglaterra@mail.telepac.pt). Train
from Cais do Sodré to Estoril/498 bus.* **Rates**
excluding breakfast 15,600$00-18,500$00 single;
20,000$00-24,100$00 double; 32,650$00 suite. *Low
season* 12,000$00- 14,000$00 single; 15,000$00-
20,000$00 double; 23,300$00 suite. Breakfast
1,000$00. **Credit** AmEx, JCB, MC, V.

Beautiful converted mansion set on a hill with
superb views to Cascais harbour and the Sintra hills.
Breakfast can be served on your private terrace or
by the pool, which has its own coffee bar. The young

and friendly staff put you at ease, and you definitely get your money's worth considering the spacious
rooms and generous continental or cooked breakfast, served with great coffee. Business facilities are
available, including internet access and conference
and banqueting facilities. Recommended.

Hotel services *Bar. Coffee shop. Conference
facilities. Currency exchange. Internet. Fax. Laundry.
Lift. Car park. Restaurant. Swimming pool.* **Room
services** *Air-conditioning. Minibar. Safe. Room
service (8am-midnight daily) TV: satellite/cable.*

Hotel Lido

*Rua do Alentejo 12, 2765-188 Estoril (21 468
4098/fax 21 468 3665/hotellido@mail.telepac.pt).
Train from Cais do Sodré to Estoril.* **Rates** 17,500$00-
22,500$00 single; 19,500$00-22,500$00 double. *Low
season* 8,500$00 single; 12,500$00 double; 15,000$00-
20,000$00 suite. **Credit** DC, MC, V.

Very handy for Estoril beach, with a particularly private pool with bar service, light snacks and plenty
of room to sunbathe. The Lido has a good reputation for customer service and is small enough to feel
intimate. Rooms have en-suite bathrooms and the
more expensive ones have sea views. The restaurant
has panoramic views of the sea and serves excellent,
if pricey, seafood dishes. On the sixth floor a conference room seats 120 – also with harbour views.
Overall, very good value for money.

Hotel services *Bars (2). Currency exchange. Fax.
Laundry. Lift. Car park. Restaurant. Solarium.
Swimming pool.* **Room services** *Air-conditioning.
TV: satellite.*

Tone it down at the **São Mamede**. *See p60.*

Residencial Solar Dom Carlos

Rua Latino Coelho 8, 2750-408 Cascais (21 482 8115/fax 21 486 5155). Train from Cais do Sodré to Cascais. **Rates** 8,000$00 single; 12,000$00 double; 15,000$00 triple. *Low season* 5,000$00 single; 7,000$00 double; 9,000$00 triple. **Credit** AmEx, DC, JCB, MC, V.

Housed in a former royal residence, this clean, family-run hostel has atmosphere but is not a place you would want to spend all day. No matter: it's close to the centre of Cascais and ideal for backpackers and those bent on local nightlife. A basic continental breakfast is served in the slightly faded dining room, plastered with badly restored, garish frescoes depicting cherubs on clouds. Large, cool rooms have old-fashioned furniture and most have decent-sized bathrooms. The manager is chatty and speaks good English – ask him to show you the 17th-century chapel hidden behind the building. The secluded garden beside the chapel is open to guests.
Hotel Services *Currency exchange. Fax. Laundry. TV room.* **Room services** *Minibar. Room service (24hr). TV/satellite.*

Budget

Baixa

Pensão Portuense

Rua das Portas de Santo Antão 151-153, Baixa, 1150-167 (21 346 4197/fax 21 342 4239). Metro Restauradores. **Rates** 7,000$00 single; 9,500$00 double; 14,500$00 triple. *Low season* 6,000$00 single; 9,500$00 double; 11,500$00 triple. **Credit** MC, V. **Map** p310 F9.

First-floor hostel owned by an upbeat, helpful family who run the place very efficiently. Rooms are well furnished and comfortable and have clean, modern bathrooms with decent high-pressure showers. There are enterprising touches not often seen in this price category such as room service and internet access. A generous and fresh continental breakfast can be served in your room, as well as other snacks. Prices are low for what you get and the place has a good vibe. Recommended.
Hotel services *Currency exchange. Fax. Internet. Laundry. Lift. Safe.* **Room services** *Room service (8am-midnight daily). TV: satellite.*

Pensão Prata

Rua da Prata 71-73, Baixa 1100-414 (21 346 8908). Bus 9, 28, 39, 46. **Rates** excluding breakfast 4,000$00 single; 6,000$00 double. **No credit cards.** **Map** p310 M10.

Handy for Santa Apolónia train station (although the walk is a bit of a strain if you're carrying a backpack) and close to ferries across the Tagus. The decent-sized rooms have showers, sink and bidet; toilets are just outside the rooms. The owners, Carlos and his son, both speak English and are very helpful. Breakfast is not included, but there are plenty of good eating places nearby (*see chapter* **Cafés**). Recommended.

Residencial Duas Nações

Rua da Vitória 41, Baixa, 1100-150 (21 346 0710/fax 21 347 0206) Metro Baixa-Chiado/28 tram. **Rates** 4,000$00-7,000$00 single; 5,000$00-9,000$00 double; 11,000$00 triple; 15,000$00 four-person.* *Low season* 3,500$00-6,000$00 single; 4,500$00-7,500$00 double; 9,000$00 triple. **Credit** AmEx, DC, MC, V. **Map** p311 M9.

One of the best cheap bargains left in the Baixa. Rooms are simple and comfortable; the more expensive ones have private bathrooms with showers. Try and avoid rooms along Rua Augusta, which can be noisy; the rest are pretty quiet. You can order a basic continental breakfast in bed. The modest bar at the back can get quite animated in the summer.
Hotel services *Air-conditioning. Fax. Laundry. Lift. TV lounge.* **Room services** *Safe.*

Rossio & Restauradores

Pensão Campos

Rua Jardim do Regedor 24-3, Restauradores, 1150 (tel/fax 21 346 2864). Metro Restauradores. **Rates** excluding breakfast 4,000$00-6,500$00 single; 5,000$00-7,500$00 double. **Credit** AmEx, V. **Map** p310 L9.

Currently closed, but due to reopen in autumn 2001, this hostel is on a charming narrow street lined with balconies and offers nine spacious and clean rooms with showers and private WC in an intimate atmosphere. The Santos family run the place like clockwork and are particularly friendly. Breakfast not included.
Hotel services *Laundry. Lift. Safe. TV lounge.* **Branch:** Estrela do Chiado, Rua Garret 29-4E, Chiado, 1100-135 (21 342 6110).

Pensão Coimbra e Madrid

Praça da Figueira 3, Rossio, 1100-240 (21 342 1760/fax 21 342 3264). Metro Rossio/15 tram. **Rates** 5,000$00-7,000$00 single; 8,000$00-10,000$00 double; 12,000$00 triple. *Low season* 4,000$00-5,000$00 single; 6,000$00-8,000$00 double; 10,000$00 triple. **No credit cards. Map** p310 M9.

Lively and fun place to stay. Attracts a young crowd, mostly backpackers and interrailers, who mingle or watch videos in the comfy TV lounge. Centrally located but not centrally heated, so could be chilly out of season. All rooms have phones and most share corridor bathrooms; excellent rooftop views.
Hotel services *Fax. Payphone. TV: satellite lounge with bar.*

Pensão Ibérica

Praça da Figueira 10-2, Rossio, 1100-085 (21 886 5781/fax 21 886 7412). Metro Rossio/12, 15 tram. **Rates** 4,000$00-8,000$00 single; 6,000$00-10,000$00 double; 10,000$00-14,000$00 triple. **No credit cards. Map** p311 M9.

Great hostel looking onto Praça da Figueira. Inside the decoration has an African motif, and the friendly family that runs it is from Mozambique. A generous buffet breakfast is served in an airy breakfast room and bedrooms have en-suite bathrooms and are bright and very clean. Good value for money.
Room services *TV: satellite.*

Pensão Praça da Figueira

Travessa Nova de São Domingos 9-3E, Rossio,
1100-372 (tel/fax 21 342 4323). Metro Rossio/12,
15 tram. **Rates** 4,500$00 single; 9,000$00 double.
Credit AmEx, DC, JCB, MC, V. **Map** p310 M9.
Still the best value for money of the hostels overlooking Praça da Figueira, especially after the recent
refurbishment. The rooms are large and simply decorated with decent views; all have showers. Friendly
and upbeat atmosphere with excellent service.
Hotel services *Air-conditioning. Fax. Laundry.*
Safe. TV/video lounge. **Room services**
TV: satellite.

Residencial Florescente

Rua das Portas de Santo Antão 99, Restauradores,
1150-266 (21 342 6609/fax 21 342 7733). Metro
Restauradores. **Rates** excluding breakfast 5,000$00
single; 8,000$00 double; 10,000$00 triple; 12,000$00
suite (sleeps 5). **Credit** AmEx, DC, MC, V.
Map p310 L8.
On first sight this recently refurbished hostel with
a lovely typical Portuguese façade seems more like
a posh hotel. It is in fact a well run and comfortable
guesthouse – if you want a private bathroom and
shower you will be paying for one of the more expensive rooms. Cosy atmosphere, and with only 20
rooms the place never gets too busy.
Hotel services *Air-conditioning. Fax. Laundry.*
Room services *TV: satellite.*
Branch: Flor da Baixa, Rua das Portas de Santo
Antão 81-2, Baixa, 1150 (21 342 3153).

Eyrie – **Ninho das Águias.** *See p64.*

Avenida de Liberdade & Marquês de Pombal

Pensão Residencial 13 da Sorte

Rua do Salitre 13, Avenida da Liberdade, 1250-198
(21 353 1851/fax 21 395 6946). Metro Marquês de
Pombal. **Rates** 7,000$00 single; 8,500$00 double;
10,000$00 triple. **Credit** MC, V. **Map** p307 L8.
With 21 rooms strung out on five floors, this hostel
never feels crowded. The clean and simple rooms
each have a bathroom with shower and views of the
Avenida. The friendly owners have gone to some
lengths to make the place attractive with pretty curtains and fresh flowers, seeking to convince guests
at the 'Lucky 13' that it is not an unlucky number.
Good value for money.
Hotel services *Bar. Fax. Safe.* **Room services**
TV: satellite.

Pensão Residencial Horizonte

Avenida António Augusto de Aguiar 42, Marquês de
Pombal, 1050-017 (21 353 9526/fax 21 353 8474).
Metro Rotunda or Saldanha. **Rates** 7,800$00 single;
9,900$00 double; 12,000$00 triple. **Credit** AmEx, DC,
MC, V. **Map** p307 E6.
This newly refurbished *pensão* is a popular choice
for young businesspeople on a budget. Very com-
petitive, given its location and comforts, compared
to local rivals. Each room has private bathroom and
is modern and well decorated. The lobby has a bar.
Its nearby sister pensão is more expensive, with
more services and comfort.
Hotel Services *Bar, Fax, laundry.* **Room**
services *Air-conditioning. TV: satellite.*
Branch: Hotel Nacional, Rua Castilho (Marquês de
Pombal) 34, 1250-070 (21 355 4433/fax 21356 1122).

Residencial Dom José

Avenida Duque de Loulé 79, Marques de Pombal,
1050-088 Baixa (21 354 6568/fax 21 352 6537).
Metro Marquês de Pombal. **Rates** 5,000$00
single; 6,000$00 double. **No credit cards.**
Map p307 E6.
This is about as basic as it gets in Lisbon. Double
rooms have private bathrooms and cheaper rooms
share. The hostel is reasonably clean but there is
not much atmosphere and the manager is a bit
matron-like. The central location is a bonus, but
busy traffic outside and poor soundproofing is a
nuisance if your room looks onto the street. Don't
be tricked by the pink neon sign on the bottom floor
pointing up to the next. There are two more signs
that eventually entice you up to the third floor.
Hotel Services *Payphone. Fax. TV room.*

Residencial Dublin

Rua de Santa Marta 45, Marquês de Pombal, 1150-
293 (21 355 5489/fax 21 354 3365). Metro
Avenida. **Rates** 7,500$00 single, 8,000$00 double;
12,000$00 triple. **No credit cards. Map** p307 E7.
Bottom of the range hostel ideal for shoestring travellers. Rooms are basic, but bathrooms are clean and
with showers. Staff speak good English and are

helpful, but the place is a little dingy and lacks atmosphere. There are plenty of bars and seafood restaurants in the vicinity, but the area can get quite noisy at night. Women travelling alone should be aware of nearby red-light establishments, although this should not affect your stay at the hostel itself. **Hotel services** *Fax. Payphone. TV room.*

East of Baixa

Pensão Residencial Ninho das Águias

Costa do Castelo 74, Castelo, 1100-150 (21 885 4070) Tram 12/bus 37. **Rates** excluding breakfast 5,000$00 single; 6,500$00 double. **No credit cards**. **Map** p311 M9.

The best view on a budget, far from both traffic and nightlife. Nestling below the castle, this beautiful turreted guesthouse offers simple lodgings with five-star views. It's a fair walk up from Baixa through cobbled streets, then a further climb up a spiral staircase to a precipitous patio. At the top of another spiral stairway is an octagonal tower with rickety seats where you can admire the view on three sides. Try and get room 12 on the northern corner to feel really on top of the world. The rooms are clean but spartan; most share bathrooms with other guests.

Hotel services *Payphone. No breakfast.*

Pensão São João da Praça

Rua São João da Praça 97-2, Alfama, 1100-519 (tel/fax 21 886 2591). Tram 12, 28/bus 37. **Rates** single/double 8,500$00-10,000$00. Low season single/double 5,000$00-8,500$00. **Credit** MC, V. **Map** p311 N10.

Beautifully situated family-run guesthouse by the Sé cathedral, with great views. Nicely decorated, decent-sized, light rooms with private bathrooms. Very good service at reasonable rates and spotlessly clean. Full of charm.

Hotel services *Fax. Laundry. Restaurant. Safe. TV room.* **Room services** *TV.*

West of Baixa

Pensão Globo

Rua da Teixeira 37, Bairro Alto, 1200-459 (21 346 2279). Metro Baixa-Chiado/28 tram/44, 45 bus. **Rates** excluding breakfast 3,000$00-4,000$00 single; 5,000$00-7,000$00 double; 8,000$00 triple. **No credit cards. Map** p310 L9.

One of the best choices for all-round value and proximity to some of Lisbon's trendiest restaurants and clubs, this friendly, well-run guesthouse is tucked away on a quiet street, avoiding nightlife mayhem. More expensive rooms have en-suite bathrooms with showers; cheaper interior rooms are windowless and share facilities. Rooms are clean without services. There's no breakfast, but plenty of cafés nearby.

Hotel services *Bar. Payphone. TV room. Laundry.*

Pensão Londres

Rua Dom Pedro V 53, Bairro Alto 1250-092 (21 346 2203/fax 21346 5682 www.desenvolve.com/ londres). **Rates** 5,200$00-8,500$00 single; 7,200$00-11,500$00 double. **No credit cards**. **Map** p310 L8.

This basic guesthouse has rooms on four floors. The more expensive have their own bathroom, TV and phone. It occupies a good location at the Principe Real end of Bairro Alto, which is not too noisy, despite being within easy walking distance of the nightlife. Try to get a room with a view across Lisbon; the alternative is one of the street behind. Staff can seem somewhat monosyllabic and taken aback when you arrive, but soon remember they are supposed to be running a hostel.

Hotel services *Fax. TV lounge. Laundry. Payphone.* **Room services** *TV: satellite.*

Residencial Alegria

Praça da Alegria 12, Avenida da Liberdade, 1250-004 (21 347 5522/fax 21 347 8070). Metro Avenida. **Rates** 5,000-10,000$00 single; 10,000-12,000$00 double. **Credit** AmEx, MC, V. **Map** p307 L8.

Charming guesthouse overlooking the tree-lined Alegria 'happiness' square. Rooms vary from the small, single and windowless to roomy doubles overlooking the square. Some have large, bright bathrooms; others share. Not all rooms have TV. Little service but reception will take calls and messages. Not best value for money in the area.

Hotel services *Currency exchange. Fax. Laundry. Payphone. TV lounge.* **Room services** *TV: satellite.*

Residencial Camões

Travessa do Poço da Cidade 38, Bairro Alto, 1200-334 (21 346 7510/fax 21 346 4048). Metro Baixa-Chiado/28 tram. **Rates** 8,000$00 single; 12,000$00 double; 15,000$00 triple. **No credit cards**. **Map** p310 L9.

Popular with backpackers, the Residencial Camões is a well-placed guesthouse with large, comfortable, clean rooms, each with a shower cubicle. The chirpy family that run it speak good English. The main drawback is likely to be noise from the streets below at weekends, but the double glazing does combat this to a certain extent. Recommended.

Hotel Services *Payphone. TV: cable lounge.*

Residencial Santa Catarina

Rua Dr Luis de Almeida e Albuquerque 6, Santa Catarina, 1200-154 (21 346 6106/fax 21 347 7227) Metro Baixa-Chiado/28 tram. **Rates** 7,000$00 single; 10,800$00 double; 14,000$00 triple. **Credit** AmEx, MC, V. **Map** p310 K9.

This quiet, family-run guesthouse is a short walk away from the bars and restaurants of the Bairro Alto. The romantic and panoramic Miradouro de Santa Catarina is also just down the road. Rooms are clean, with private bathrooms, and some have fantastic views of the Tagus.

Hotel services *Currency exchange. Fax. Laundry. Safe. TV lounge.*

Northern Lisbon

Pensão Residencial Estrela dos Santos

Avenida Almirante Reis 53, Anjos, 1150-011 (21 317 1030/fax 21 315 1397/estrela_dos_santos@ mail.pt). Metro Anjos. **Rates** 6,500$00 single; 10,500$00 double. **No credit cards. Map** p308 G7.
Modern, homely, family-run guesthouse with ten spacious rooms, all with private bathrooms. Nice location right next to Anjos metro station, which means you can be in the centre of Lisbon in ten minutes. Traffic can get a bit noisy.
Hotel services *Fax.* **Room Services** *TV: satellite/cable.*

Pensão do Sul

Avenida Almirante Reis 34, Anjos, 1100-018 (21 814 7253/fax 21 813 6297). Metro Anjos/28 tram. **Rates** excluding breakfast 5,000$00-7,500$00 single; 7,500$00-10,000$00 double; 10,000$00-15,000$00 triple. **No credit cards. Map** p308 G7.
This decent, well-run hostel compares favourably to other budget options in the area. Interior decor is austere but the comfortable and large rooms, most with en-suite bathroom and shower, make up for this. The house-proud family that run the place really try to please guests. Breakfast is not included but there are plenty of good cafes on this street. The smaller sister hostel provides less for the same price.
Hotel services *Fax. Payphone. TV room.*
Room services *TV: cable.*
Branch: Praça Dom Pedro IV (Rossio) 59-2E, Baixa, 1100 (21 342 2511).

Pousada de Juventude

Rua Andrade Corvo 46, Saldanha, 1050-009 (21 353 2696/fax 21 353 7541). Metro Picoas/1, 36, 44, 45 bus. **Rates** 2,900$00 single; 6,500$00 double. *Low season* 2,000$00 single; 5,000$00 double. **Credit** MC, V. **Map** p307 L6.
The more central of Lisbon's two youth hostels, this is cheap, well run and clean. There is a conference room equipped with simultaneous translation booths and good facilities for the disabled, but no internet access. Rooms are basic but comfortable and some have their own bathrooms. Lunch and dinner (both 950$00) are served in the campus-like canteen. The decent bar serves drinks on a large sunbathing patio in the high season. Note that this is probably not the best place for nighthawks as reception closes at midnight.
Services *Bar. Disabled: access. Entertainment room. Lockers. Self-service canteen. TV/video lounge.*

Residencial Marisela

Rua Filipe Folque 19, Saldanha, 1050-111 (21 353 3205/fax 21 316 0423). Metro Picoas/Saldanha. **Rates** 5,500$00 single; 6,500$00 double; 10,000$00 triple. **Credit** AmEx, MC, V. **Map** p304 L5.
A little out of the centre, but with good transport links, this unusual guesthouse has an enterprising feature: an outdoor basketball court built in the interior patio. Good atmosphere and well run by Dona Marisela and her extended family. Reasonable price considering it includes a decent breakfast and a private WC with most rooms.
Hotel services *Basketball. Fax, Internet. Payphone. TV room.* **Room services** *Room service (7.30am-midnight daily).*

Peace and quiet in the boisterous Bairro Alto – **Pensão Globo**. *See p64.*

Residencial Saldanha

Avenida da República 17, Saldanha 1050-185 (21 354 6429/fax 21 354 6552/www.residencialsaldanha. pt). Metro Saldanha. **Rates** excluding breakfast 4,000$00-6,000$00 single; 6,000$00-8,000$00 double; 1,000$00 extra bed. **Breakfast** 500$00. **Credit** AmEx, DC, MC, V. **Map** p304 M5.
Residencial Saldanha is a plush guesthouse with reasonable rates. All rooms are modern and attractively decorated with spacious, light bathrooms. Brilliant service; the friendly young staff know how to look after guests. Advanced booking available online. A little removed from the centre but the metro is nearby. Recommended.
Hotel services *Air-conditioning.* **Room services** *Radio. TV: cable.*

Parque das Nações

Casa da Juventude

Rua de Moscavide 47-101, 1998 (21 892 0890/ fax 21 892 0891). Metro Oriente. 2,100$00 single; 5,100$00 double. *Low season* 1,700$00 single; 4,300$00 double. **Credit** MC, V.
A comfortable, modern youth hostel at the Parque das Nações, the former Expo site. Everything is laid on, from internet access to shared cooking facilities. As in other government-sponsored youth hostels in Portugal, the atmosphere is one of strict order bordering on religious obedience. Breakfast is served at 8.30am every morning and the hostel closes its doors at midnight (although the doors are not actually locked). It's out on a bit of a limb if you're planning to sample Lisbon nightlife, though there's no shortage of bars in the Parque das Nações.
Hotel services *Disabled: access/showers. Games room. Kitchen. Lockers. Self-service restaurant. TV room.*

Cascais & Estoril Coast

Pensão Costa

Rua de Olivença 2, 2765-262 Estoril (21 468 1699). Train from Cais do Sodré to Estoril. **Rates** excluding breakfast 6,000$00-7,000$00 double; 8,000$00-9,000$00 triple; 12,000$00-15,000$00 four-person. *Low season* 4,500$00 double ; 6,000$00 triple ; 8,000$00 four-person. **No credit cards.**
This guesthouse offers the minimum in creature comforts, but it seems churlish to complain when you're just a stone's throw from Estoril beach and a short walk from the casino.
Hotel services *Safe. TV lounge.*

Pensão Pica Pau

Rua Dom Afonso Henriques 48, 2765-185 Estoril (21 466 7140/fax 21 467 0664/albert@mail. telepac.pt). Train from Cais do Sodré to Estoril. **Rates** 6,000$00-10,000$00 single; 8,0000$00-15,0000$00 double, 10,500$00-19,200$00 triple; 13,000$000$00-24,000$00 four-person.
Credit AmEx, DC, JCB, MC, V.

The Pica Pau (literally 'woodpecker') is small, friendly guesthouse with lots of character, a short walk from the pleasant Estoril beaches. Although it has been refurbished recently, rooms are a little cramped and only the few that look out onto the small pool can claim to have a view. A large bar area near the entrance comes to life at night when cocktails are served but is a little dingy in the morning when it's used as a refectory in which to serve the basic continental breakfast.
Hotel services *Air-conditioning. Bar. Central heating. Safe. Swimming pool. Restaurant. TV room.* **Room services** *TV: satellite.*

Pousada da Juventude da Catalazete

Estrada Marginal, Oeiras, 2780 (21 443 0638). Lisbon train to Oeiras, halfway between Lisbon and Cascais. 15min walk from the railway station, but signposted. **Rates** 2,100$00 single; 4,300$00 double. *Low season* 1,700$00 single; 4,300$00 double. **Credit** V.
The location is a little unfortunate; it overlooks the rather dirty Oeiras beach, but this is a good little hostel nonetheless.
Hotel services *Bar. Cooking facilities.*

Camping

Lisboa Camping

Estrada da Circunvalação, Parque de Monsanto, 1400-041 (21 762 3100/fax 21 762 3106). Bus 14, 50, 43. **Rates** 800$00 per tent; 800$00 per person; 10,000$00-15,000$00 bungalow.
Credit AmEx, MC, V.
A very pleasant campsite with a full compliment of modern facilities, within easy reach of Lisbon. Busy in summer, it attracts a mostly Portuguese crowd, although you will see foreign tourists. Service could be better judging by the amount of litter under the pine trees. A brand new bar serves alcohol and hot snacks.
Services *Bar. Basketball. Mini-golf. Laundry. Restaurant. Tennis court. Supermarket. Swimming pool. TV lounge.*

Camping Orbitur-Guincho

Estrada da Areia, 2750-053 Cascais (21 487 0450/fax 21 487 2167/info@orbitur.pt). Train from Cais do Sodré to Cascais/405, 415 bus. **Rates** 7,000$00-12,000$00 bungalow; 600$00-1,000$00 camping pitch fee; 800$00 per person.
Credit AmEx, DC, MC, V.
Great situation in pine woods, just ten minutes' walk from Guincho beach and five kilometres from Cascais, makes this a popular hangout for surfers. Plenty of facilities, including a tennis court, minimarket and post office and a decent snack bar. Can get very busy in the high season but the crowd usually provides a good party atmosphere. Rates may change in May 2001.
Services *Currency exchange. Disabled: facilities. Snackbar. Laundry (self-service). Mini-market. Post Office. Showers. Snack bar. Tennis.*

Accommodation

Sightseeing

Introduction

From grand river vistas and Manueline monuments to labyrinths of alleyways
and funny old funiculars – there's something around every corner on the slopes
of Lisbon's seven hills.

Most people arrive in Lisbon by air these days, and flight paths usually sweep over the city centre. The view from the right side of the plane takes in the great curve of the River Tagus and the breadth of its estuary, with the tangle of city-centre streets below. But, traditionally, visitors would arrive by water – whether on a cruise ship or one of the ferries that cross the Tagus from the south to dock at the Cais do Sodré or Praça do Comércio terminals.

Trains coming into the city of Lisbon from the Algarve still terminate at Barreiro on the south side of the Tagus, where passengers step onto a ferry. There are few more spectacular entrances to a major European city. The ferry arcs across the vast Tagus estuary, the 'peaceful harbour' – 'Alis-Ubbo' in Phoenician – from which Lisbon probably earned its name. The mouth of the Iberian peninsula's longest river, this is one of the world's largest natural harbours. Soon after the ferry sails forth, the Ponte 25 de Abril, comparable in size and design to San Francisco's Golden Gate bridge, looms into view, spanning the river to

the west, presided over by the statue of Cristo Rei ('Christ the King') at its southern foot. Far to the east, the new Ponte Vasco da Gama also traverses the estuary, its white suspension cables looking, at this remove, like delicate white threads.

Ahead lies Lisbon. The ferry heads for the flat 18th-century heart of the city – the Baixa, fronted by the Praça do Comércio, which opens out on to the water. From here, the city scrambles up on to seven hills. Rising above the clutter of terracotta rooftops, the skyline is dominated by the Castelo de São Jorge, with white-domed churches to the east and west – Panteão Nacional de Santa Engrácia just below the Castelo, and the Basilica da Estrela way over to the west.

Outside the ferry terminal, the grand expanse of the Praça do Comércio serves as Lisbon's welcome mat. The front door of the city is the Arco Triunfal on the square's northern side, topped with the royal coat of arms and leading into Rua Augusta, the thoroughfare of the Baixa beyond.

Central Lisbon

The Baixa still bustles, but big business has moved up the Avenida.

The Baixa

Lisbon's traditional downtown, the Baixa is currently in a state of transition. Once the retail heart of the city, as well as home to many banks and government ministries, it's still a busy commercial district but no longer the true centre of things. Rent control means that here old-fashioned shops are able to survive where they would have perished in most comparable cities, while new businesses mostly locate in out-of-centre malls. There are streets where trades have clustered for centuries: jewellers linger on Rua do Ouro (also marked on some maps by its old name, Rua Aurea); Rua dos Sapateiros is still a 'street of shoemakers'; Rua dos Fanqueiros is home to textile merchants and fabric shops, just as it has always been.

Or at least since the mid-18th century. Before that time the Baixa was the heart of medieval Lisbon, a labyrinthine tangle of narrow streets spread across the low ground between the Castelo and the Chiado. Then as now, the poles were the two squares: the Terreiro do Paço on the waterfront, remade as the **Praça do Comércio** but still sometimes known by its old name; and the **Rossio** at its upper end where the low ground splits into two valleys. The centre of commerce was then the Rua Nova, which cut east-west across the lower end of the modern grid. The largest of Lisbon's medieval Jewish quarters, the Judiaria Grande, occupied a big chunk of the Baixa, centred around the main synagogue that stood in the vicinity of present-day Rua dos Fanqueiros between Rua da Conceição and Rua de São Nicolau.

The 1755 earthquake put paid to all that. Charged with the job of reconstruction, the Marquês de Pombal decided to clear the old maze of streets, which had in any case been reduced to rubble. The new plan was based on a military encampment, whereby each street had a specific function. The orderly rows still stand as Pombal planned them, though some of the Baixa took the next century to finish – the **Arco Triunfal** (Triumphal Arch) capping Rua Augusta was finally completed in 1873. That's Glory atop the arch, holding wreaths above the heads of Genius and Bravery. Below them are Viriatus, Nun'Álvares Pereira, Vasco da Gama and the Marquês de Pombal; the Tagus is the River God on the left, the Douro is on the right.

The **Praça do Comércio** – centrepiece of Pomabline reconstruction.

There is talk of letting the public see the workings of the arch's clock, but for now there's no way inside.

The rectilinear grid that resulted from all this meticulous planning retains nothing of medieval Lisbon, yet has accumulated its own patina of history in over two centuries of existence. The waterfront Praça do Comércio was the centrepiece of Pombaline reconstruction, replacing the old Terreiro do Paço and 16th-century royal palace. The Marquis wanted a majestic square that would rival anything of its kind in Europe, and more or less got what he wanted. Architects Carlos Mardel and Eugênio dos Santos designed the square with one side open to the river and the other three for government ministries. The centrepiece is Joaquim Machado de Castro's 14-metre high equestrian statue of Dom José I, monarch at the time of the earthquake. Long condemned to be a car park, the centre of the square was paved over and pedestrianised a few years ago and was once again used as a public gathering place, and even at times as an outdoor sculpture gallery. Traffic still rushes around the edges, though, severing the square from the river. There is talk of a tunnel to relieve this problem, but the project was put back after a corner of the Praça do Comércio

collapsed in mid-2000 during work to extend the Metro to Santa Apolónia rail station.

Rush-hour crowds pour on and off buses, trams and ferries all week – this is the entry point into the city for many inhabitants of the southern suburbs. On summer weekends, crowds move through in the opposite direction, as half of Lisbon decamps to the beach. On Sunday mornings the eastern arcade hosts a collectors' market with stalls specialising in stamps, coins, medals, phone cards, books and comics. On the square's north-east corner, the **Café Martinho da Arcada** (*see p140*) has been open since 1782. Lisbon's iconic poet Fernando Pessoa was a regular here in the 1920s and 1930s, and supposedly wrote Mensagem at one of the corner tables.

Lisbon's **Câmara Municipal** (city hall) sits at the west end of the Baixa on the Praça do Município. Originally built in 1867, it was recently renovated following a 1996 fire that mysteriously broke out in the department of financial records. As part of the renovation, a whole new top floor was added, lined with marble and full of masonic symbolism echoing the emblems in the original downstairs rooms. If you want a peep inside, ask at the desk about the regular piano and violin recitals held in the Sala de Arquivos on Thursday evenings. The Câmara's grand balcony was the site for the proclamation of the Portuguese Republic on 5 October 1910, and the square is thus the setting for annual Republic Day celebrations.

What appears to be a church across Rua do Comércio from the Câmara Municipal is really the back end of the **Banco de Portugal**, which uses the main portal as a gateway to its garage. The Rua do Arsenal links the Praça do Município with the Cais do Sodré waterfront district, and is principally famous for the smell of *bacalhau* (salt cod) emanating from its storefronts. Banco de Portugal is just one of many government and banking institutions that inhabit the lower Baixa. Many of the streets are now pedestrianised, notably the main drag, **Rua Augusta**. The bottom end by the arch has a few raggedy stalls that locals call the 'Mercado dos Hippies'. On and around Rua Augusta are outdoor cafés, buskers, shops and fast-food joints. There are many places to eat, though few that we'd especially recommend. **Paris** on Rua dos Sapateiros (*see p127*) is something of an institution. The workaday lunch crowd head for the cluster of cheap Portuguese restaurants on Rua dos Correeiros or even more obscure eateries (*see p138* **Where the eats have no name**). At night the Baixa is pretty dead, and utterly devoid of bars. Late strollers on the Rua Augusta are the only sign of life.

The **Baixa** – post-quake rationalisation.

The **Arco Triunfal** – part of the original Baixa plan but completed a century later. *See p69.*

Many businesses hereabouts still have appealing old signage and neon. Some of the button shops and haberdashers near the tram 28 stops on Rua da Conceição have beautifully dilapidated art nouveau storefronts. Between the tram tracks near the junction with Rua da Prata, a rectangular manhole cover marks the way down to some Roman tanks, often erroneously referred to as 'baths'. Some archaeologists have declared the complex part of the city's ancient fish conservation industry, while others reckon it to be the base of a Roman temple. The tanks are in any case usually flooded and rarely open to the public. Those interested in Roman Lisbon should instead step into the **Núcleo Arqueológico** (*see below*) behind the Banco Comercial Português on Rua dos Correeiros.

The tallest landmark in the Baixa is the **Elevador de Santa Justa** (*see below*, not built by Eiffel as most guidebooks and natives will tell you). This was the 19th-century solution to the problem of getting up to the Chiado without breaking into a sweat. Nowadays the series of escalators in Baixa-Chiado Metro station do the job just as well, but they're underground. There are vague plans for another *elevador* on the other side of the Baixa, carrying pedestrians up and across to the Castelo de São Jorge, but when artists' impressions showed the spindly construction slicing across vistas of the castle, a furious debate broke out and there were calls for a referendum.

Elevador de Santa Justa

Rua do Ouro, Baixa, 1100 (21 342 7944). Metro Baixa-Chiado. **Open** 9am-7pm daily; until later on busy days. **Tickets** 175$00. **No credit cards.** **Map** p310 L9.

The industrial-age iron tracery of the Santa Justa lift – sometimes called the Elevador do Carmo – is one of Lisbon's most beloved landmarks. The 45m (147ft) tall elevator was designed and built by Portuguese-born Eiffel disciple Raul Mesnier de Ponsard, and officially opened in August 1901, linking the downtown Rua do Ouro with the square next to the Carmo Church up above. A 15-metre viaduct bridges the Rua do Carmo and is supposed to link the tower to terra firma next to the old Carmo Church. Unfortunately the viaduct has been closed in recent years as engineers try to find a way to shore up the buildings on the hillside, some of which are in danger of collapsing. At the top of the Santa Justa lift a café offers 360° views out over the rooftops of the Baixa. The Elevador is officially part of Lisbon's public transport system; the ride up costs the equivalent of a bus or tram ticket, and passes are valid.

Núcleo Arqueológico da Rua dos Correeiros

Rua dos Correeiros 9, Baixa, 1100 (21 321 1000). Metro Baixa-Chiado/tram 28. **Guided tours** 3pm, 4pm, 5pm Thur; 10am, 11am, noon, 3pm, 4pm, 5pm Sat. **Admission** free. **Map** p310 M10.

Tucked into the back of the Banco Comercial Português, the Archaeological Centre offers a glimpse of what's lurking below pavement level in the Baixa. In Roman times this was a river beach. The locals made sauces with fish and shellfish bits mixed with salt, spices and herbs. The ingredients were then put in tanks and left to rot over time into a suitably tasty decomposition. When Banco Comercial Português wanted to redo its Rua Augusta head office in 1991, construction teams dug into the ancient fish conservation complex. The experts were called in and the centre opened to the public in 1995. On display are artefacts found during the last round of digging, some ancient walls and a holding tank, along with an intact section of Roman mosaic floor.

Rossio

Rossio has for centuries been the crossroads of downtown Lisbon. Anyone moving around the city will pass through here at least once a day. It's also a central meeting point. Of its cafés, **Café Nicola** (*see p140*) has the most historical resonance, here in one form or another since the late 18th century. **Casa Suíça** (*see p140*) across the square is gossip central for mid-afternoon matrons. Meanwhile, Africans cluster around the steps of the **Teatro Nacional Dona Maria II** (*see p224*), catching up with news from Cape Verde or Angola – clustering in this area because the nearby **Igreja de São Domingos** traditionally had a black priest. Businessmen peruse the paper during a lunchtime street shoeshine. Shopworkers fortify themselves with a nip of *ginjinha*, the cough syrup-like brandy made from morello cherries that is served from various stand-up bars in the area (*see p153* **Popping the cherry**). Crowds of commuters queue for buses, tourists mill about everywhere browsing at kiosks selling foreign-language newspapers, and the square's central taxi rank is one of Lisbon's busiest – although it's moved around the corner into

Largo de São Domingos since Rossio descended into construction site chaos.

Supposedly built on the site of the Roman hippodrome, medieval Rossio was the open marketplace at the top end of town. Pombal intended his new, more rectangular version to be secondary to the Praça do Comércio. But by virtue of geography – this really is the city's crossroads, from which routes stretch in every direction – Rossio increased in importance as the city expanded. Its official name, Praça Dom Pedro IV, is something you'll only read on maps or the occasional business card. It has been called the Rossio since the Middle Ages, and Rossio it remains today.

Dom Pedro IV is the chap on top of the square's 23-metre (75-foot) central column. Or at least, that's who the bronze statue nominally represents. Historical rumour has it that the figure is actually a likeness of Emperor Maximilian of Mexico. In 1870, the ship bearing his statue happened to be docked at Lisbon, en route from Marseille to Mexico, when word came that Maximilian had been assassinated. By chance Portugal had just ordered a statue of Pedro IV from the same French sculptor, Elias David, and so a deal was struck. The figures

Busking in the **Rua Augusta**. *See p70*.

Pizzas and paperbacks in
the Largo do São Domingos.

around the base represent Justice, Wisdom,
Courage and Restraint.

Restraint was not always Rossio's hallmark.
Where the Teatro Nacional now stands was
once the site of a royal palace. It was taken over
by the Inquisition and many an *auto-da-fé*
(public show with an execution as its
centrepiece) ended with the condemned being
burned at the stake in the centre of the square.
In the 1506 anti-Jewish riots a column of smoke
was said to rise up from Rossio for days, as a
pyre consumed the bodies of the victims.

Next door to Rossio lies the **Praça da
Figueira**, its smaller sibling. Here the statue is
of Dom João I, erected in 1971. Every
Portuguese city has a central square where
people sell seeds to feed the pigeons and this is
Lisbon's – at least it was before it was dug up
to build yet another underground car park. Less
gracious than Rossio, Praça da Figueira is
ringed with small and mostly undistinguished
shops. One curious exception is the **Hospital
das Bonecas** (*see p175*), a doll's hospital on
the square's north side. At night the population
runs from kids on skateboards to ageing
downmarket whores; and on winter days the
homeless warm themselves in the hot air
steaming from Metro vents.

The **Rua das Portas de Santo Antão** is a
pedestrian-only street leading up from behind
the Teatro Nacional. It's full of tourist-trap
outdoor restaurants where touts attempt to
lure in passers-by and signs advertise such
delights as tripe or pig's ear salad. If you have

to stop and eat here, try the grilled fowl at
Bonjardim (*see p127*) – more commonly
known as Rei dos Frangos, 'King of Chickens'.
Otherwise there's a bewildering range of
seafood at the 1950s-style **Solmar** beerhall
(*see p131*) on the ground floor of the Ateneu
Comercial de Lisboa – location of Lisbon's most
central public swimming pool. One discreet
doorway marks the **Casa do Alentejo** (*see
p129*), home away from home for Alentejanos in
Lisbon. Inside it's part neo-Moorish surprise,
part stodgy old club. The restaurant is open to
the public, serving specialities such as *carne de
porco alentejano* – pork chunks with clams.

Portas de Santo Antão is also the location
of the enormous **Coliseo dos Recreios**, the
Lisbon Coliseum, opened in 1890 and these
days a concert venue. A side entrance in the
building leads into the Sociedade de Geografia
at number 100, which contains the **Museu
Etnográfico** (*see p111*). The further away
from Rossio, the fewer businesses there are. The
road eventually arrives at the bottom end of the
Elevador da Lavra, a funicular hoisting
passengers up to the Campo de Santana district.
But if you ignore that and keep walking, after a
few minutes the road turns into Rua de São
José – lined with eateries serving local office
workers that provide a cheap, non-touristy
lunch option.

Igreja de São Domingos

*Largo de São Domingos, Baixa, 1150 (21 342
8275). Metro Rossio/tram 15.* **Open** *7.30am-6.45pm
daily.* **Map** *p310 M9.*

Quinta da Regaleira

Sintra / Portugal

A romantic journey to the worlds of Art, Nature and the Portuguese Mythical Tradition.

Including unique places of hermeticism and freemasonry initiation.

Phone: 351 21 910 66 50

Fax: 351 21 924 47 25

Email: regaleira@mail.telepac.pt

Open 10am-6pm daily

Guided Visits

The Estate is only five minute's walk from the Old Quarter of Sintra

A succession of catastrophes has laid waste to this Dominican church over the centuries, since it was founded by Dom Sancho II in 1242. Most notable were the earthquakes of 1531 and 1755 and the fire of 1959. It was recently renovated and reopened in 1997. The high altar was completed in 1748 to the designs of Ludovice, architect of the monastery of Mafra. The Dominicans were at the centre of the Inquisition, which was based across the square, and *autos-da-fé* often included a procession from here.

Restauradores & Avenida da Liberdade

The Avenida da Liberdade began as an extension of the Passeio Público, a late 18th-century garden promenade. This busy 90-metre-wide boulevard on the Champs-Elysées model was completed in 1886, forming an axis that connects the 18th-century downtown with the new areas that were to be built in the 19th century. Previously the river had been the central focus of the city; now Lisbon began to expand inland to the north. Carrying several lanes of traffic between the Praça dos Restauradores and the Praça Marquês de Pombal roundabout, it has been spruced up a bit in recent years and is home to new office blocks, big hotels and upmarket fashion shops.

At the bottom end of the Avenida, just to the north-west of Rossio, the neo-Manueline façade opposite the Teatro Nacional is **Rossio station**, completed in 1892 and terminus of the Sintra line. Built against the hillside, the main hall and platforms, recently renovated, are up on the top floor.

The obelisk in **Praça dos Restauradores** commemorates the 1 December 1640 restoration of independence from Spain, inscribed with dates that recall decisive battles in the subsequent 28 years of war. The Eden cinema on this square was once one of Lisbon's most outstanding art deco landmarks, but now stands tastefully disfigured as an aparthotel that saves face, if not grace, by keeping the old cinema's monumental staircase. Next door, the Palácio Foz housed a notorious nightclub in the 1920s, and later the Ministry of Propaganda. It is now home to Lisbon's main **Turismo** or tourist office and also temporarily to the **Cinemateca Portuguesa** (*see p190*), with its programme of Portuguese and international classics and art movies. The central post office is across the square, as is the ABEP kiosk selling tickets for most cinemas, theatres, bullfights and other sports and cultural events.

On the tree-lined lower end of the Avenida, there is often music and cheek-to-cheek dancing outside some cafés on the shady median walkways. This stretch is also a tolerated prostitution zone, spilling out from the discreet red-light district around Praça da Alegria – also

Sightseeing

The best *Miradouros* (look-out points)

Castelo de São Jorge
To take a crash course in Lisbon's tortuous topography. *See p79.*

Miradouro de Santa Luzia
For romantic views of Alfama and the river, framed by grapevine-draped trellises. *See p80.*

Jardim de São Pedro de Alcântara
For even more romantic views – of the castle across the Baixa. *See p88.*

Esplanada da Igreja da Graça
For a west-facing vantage point to see the sun set over the city. *See p82* and *p143.*

The rooftop bar of the Albergaria Senhora do Monte
For a refreshing beer after climbing the highest of Lisbon's seven hills. *See p55* and *p82.*

The Boca do Vento elevator in Almada
Lisbon from a completely different perspective – from the other side of the river. *See p105.*

Esplanada do Adamastor
For a late-afternoon drink with river views before hitting the Bairro Alto – or a late-night drink afterwards. *See p89, p153.*

The roof of the Igreja de São Vicente
For a stunning panorama of the river sweeping round behind Lisbon to the east. *See p82.*

Any ferry on the River Tagus
Better than your average commuter journey. *See p105.*

Torre Vasco da Gama
For an overview of the new face of Lisbon – the Parque das Nações – and the stunning Vasco da Gama bridge. *See p103.*

Casting off the Spanish yoke. *See p75.*

home to the **Hot Clube**, Lisbon's most
venerable jazz venue (*see p211*). A few blocks
north on the west side, two art deco pillars
mark the entrance to **Parque Mayer**, a
decaying 1920s entertainment complex of
restaurants and theatres that is home to
Portuguese revista – revue theatre – but is set
to be demolished at any time now.

By Avenida Metro station, the São Jorge
cinema, completed in 1950 to a design by
Fernando Silva, was the last of Lisbon's big
old movie theatres. It closed at the end of 2000,
although there's talk of turning it into a film
museum. With the São Jorge gone, there's now
little life on the Avenida at night; this is a
daytime boulevard where tourists mix with
office workers, and where the **Hotel Tivoli
Lisboa** (*see p50*) still puts on afternoon tea for
the old folks. Opposite is the neo-classical
former **Tivoli Cinema**, built in 1924 by the
architect Raul Lino and today used for
concerts and shows. The kiosk in front, one of
the most striking of its type, was installed in
1925 by the owners of the Diário de Notícias,
whose modernist editorial offices (1936) stand
further to the north. But this end of the
Avenida is pretty quiet any time of day or
night. The excellent **Livraria Buchholz**
bookshop (*see p157*) is on Rua Duque de
Palmela. Cakes can be had at the **Confeitaria
Marquês de Pombal** (*see p141*).

Marquês de Pombal & Parque Eduardo VII

At the head of the Avenida stands the
enormous column from which the statue of
the Marquês de Pombal lords it over Lisbon's
worst traffic headache – the Praça Marquês
de Pombal roundabout, at rush hour a
seething, honking, bad-tempered mass of cars.
The statue represents the dictatorial Marquês
in the bronze company of a lion, serenely
overlooking the distant Baixa that he
imposed upon the city.

Behind him is the **Parque Eduardo VII**,
laid out in the late 19th century as the natural
extension of the Avenida da Liberdade axis,
and later named after the British King Edward
VII during his 1903 visit to Portugal. The
formal layout of the gardens precludes mass
use of the lawns and greenery – it's really not a
very friendly space – although the **Estufa Fria**
gardens and greenhouse (*see p76*) on the west
side of the park provide some of Lisbon's most
welcome and romantic shade.

Two fascist pillars at the park's upper end
now enclose a mysterious pile of stones –
purportedly a sculpture by João Cutileiro – that
somehow supposedly commemorates the 1974
Revolution. A pond garden in the upper eastern
corner has the **Cafeteria Botequim do Rei**
(*see p141*), a pleasant outdoor esplanade. At
night this part of the park is a gay cruising area
and rent boys, many feeding heroin habits,
solicit passing traffic on the Avenida Sidónio
Pais. Down by the Marquês de Pombal end,
gypsy fortune tellers lurk in ambush, leaping
out to offer palm readings.

Many of Lisbon's bigger hotels loom around
the edges of the park, among them the **Ritz**
(*see p50*), **Hotel Altis** (*see p49*), **Hotel
Miraparque** (*see p59*) and the **Hotel
Eduardo VII** (*see p54*).

Estufa Fria

*Parque Eduardo VII, 1070 (21 388 2278). Metro
Marquês de Pombal, Parque.* **Open** *Summer* 9am-
5.30pm daily. *Winter* 9am-4.30pm daily. **Admission**
215$00; free under-10s. **No credit cards.**
Map p307 K6.

This greenhouse garden on the north-west side of
Parque Eduardo VII was completed in 1930. The
promenade on the pond leads into three greenhouse
areas: the Estufa Quente, or hothouse, for plants
needing a lot of hot air and humidity; the Estufa
Fria itself, a cool greenhouse; and the Estufa Doce,
the 'sweet' greenhouse, for plants that like dry
conditions. Together they make up one of Lisbon's
favourite romantic gardens, with ponds, statues
and water cascades providing the backdrop for
a shady stroll.

East of Baixa

Traces of Lisbon's Roman, Moorish and medieval heritage abound in the area where it was founded, and which takes in its oldest and most colourful *bairro*.

Sé

Lisbon's most picturesque tram ride – the number 28 east from the Baixa and eventually up to Graça – leads past the **Igreja de Santo António** (*below*) and the12th-century **Sé Catedral** (*see p78*), skirting the hill below the Castelo on a street that changes names so many times locals find it easier to refer to it simply as 'Rua do Eléctrico da Sé' – 'the street of the tram of the cathedral'.

Unlike neighbouring Alfama, which kept its pre-earthquake street pattern, the neighbourhood around the Sé was extensively modified, giving way to wider streets and elegant 19th-century houses. A number of these buildings on the 'Rua do Eléctrico da Sé' house interesting antique shops. Also of interest is the innocuous-looking building labelled the Insituto de Reinserção Social (Institute of Social Placement), which once housed the dungeons of the Salazarist secret police.

The **Teatro Romano**, Lisbon's Roman amphitheatre, was begun during the reign of the Emperor Augustus and rebuilt under Nero

in AD57. It can now be found fenced off and under a shed on Rua de São Mamede (visits by appointment only – call 21 886 0343). It is rather difficult to discern the lie of the place, especially since a 19th-century residential building stands obstinately in the middle of what was once presumably centre stage.

If you follow any one of the narrow alleys that run downhill from the right of the Sé, you'll pop out on to the **Campo das Cebolas** ('field of the onions'). This is a big open square near the river full of souvenir shops, whose main attraction is the **Casa dos Bicos** (*see p78*) and its peculiar spiky façade. Turning east along Rua da Alfândega brings into view the medieval stone façade of the **Igreja da Conceição-a-Velha** (*see p78*).

Igreja de Santo António

Largo de Santo António da Sé, 1100 (21 886 9145).
Tram 12, 28/bus 37. **Open** 8-12.30pm, 3-7pm daily, with 30-45min breaks at 11am and 5pm for mass. **Map** p311 M10.

This small baroque church opened its doors to worshippers in 1787, 20 years after construction began. It replaced an earlier structure destroyed in the 1755

The 12th-century **Sé** – built on the site of what was the city's main mosque. *See p78*.

earthquake and stands on the spot where Fernando Bulhões, otherwise known as St Anthony of Padua, was born around 1190. He later travelled on to Morocco and, after being shipwrecked, to Italy, where he died in Padua in 1231. Mass marriages for those too poor to afford individual ceremonies, known as 'St Anthony's weddings', are held here during the mid-June St Anthony's day celebrations, and a late 18th-century painting by Pedro Alexandrino de Carvalho depicts the famous Sermon of St Anthony to the Fishes. The church also has a fund-raising candle machine. Rather than pay a few coins for the privilege of lighting a real candle, you pop a coin into a box to light up an electric one. A door next to the entrance opens into the small Museu Antoniano (see p111).

Sé Catedral

Largo da Sé, 1100 (21 886 6752). Tram 12, 28/bus 37. **Open** *Church* 9am-7pm Tue-Sat; 9am-5pm Mon, Sun. *Cloisters, treasury* 10am-5pm Mon-Sat; closed Sun. **Admission** *Cloisters* 100$00. *Treasury* 500$00. **No credit cards. Map** p311 M10.

The Lisbon Cathedral, known as the Sé, was built in the 12th century on the site of the city's main mosque, which had occupied the area of today's cathedral cloisters. Recent excavations have uncovered a section of Roman road and remains from the period of Visigothic occupation, as well as parts of the former Mosque wall. The Sé was erected under the supervision of Gilbert of Hastings, the Englishman named bishop of Lisbon after the city was conquered in 1147. Enlarged in subsequent centuries, most facelifts were made necessary by earthquake damage, particularly after the great quake of 1755 and the fire that followed: the south tower collapsed and the interior chancel, chapels and high altar all suffered significant damage. The Sé's current appearance is the result of restoration work completed in 1930 that removed many baroque trappings. The rose window was reconstructed at this time from fragments of the original. In the original Romanesque scheme the Sé was laid out in the form of a Latin cross, with three naves. Gothic cloisters were added during the reign of Dom Dinis (early 14th century). The Sé once housed the relics of St Vincent, patron saint of Lisbon, but his urn was destroyed in the 1755 earthquake. The treasury houses artefacts and vestments connected to the cathedral, but the dig going on in the neighbouring cloisters, which has turned up remnants of the mosque that formerly stood here, is in many ways more engaging.

Casa dos Bicos

Rua dos Bacalhoeiros, Campo das Cebolas, Sé, 1100, (21 881 0900). Tram 18. **Open** 9.30am-5.30pm Mon-Fri; closed Sat, Sun. **Admission** free. **Map** p311 M10.

Recognisable in illustrations dating back over four centuries, the Casa dos Bicos owes its name to the extravagant façade of pyramidal spikes (*bico* meaning beak or point) arranged in a gridwork pattern.

It was built around 1523 by the merchant Brás de Albuquerque, who wanted a home down near Dom Manuel's new riverfront palace, and also used it as a shop and warehouse. The top two floors fell in during the 1755 earthquake, and were only pasted on again when major renovation work was completed in 1983. Among items discovered under the earth at that time were Roman-era fish conservation tanks, Moorish paving and part of an old medieval tower. The ground floor is used as a temporary exhibition space, so it's sometimes possible to look inside.

Igreja da Conceição-a-Velha

Rua da Alfândega, Sé, 1100 (21 887 0202). Tram 18. **Open** 8am-6pm Mon-Fri; 8am-1pm Sat; 10am-2pm Sun (for mass). **Map** p311 M10.

The edifice originally housed a church built in 1534 and dedicated to Nossa Senhora da Misericórdia (Our Lady of Mercy), who can be seen above the portal sheltering various notables under her cape (among them Dom Manuel and João III's wife Queen Leonor, founder of Lisbon's main house of charity, the Casa da Misericórdia). The 1755 earthquake demolished the building, leaving only the stone Manueline-style façade. In 1770, the church reopened to house the congregation of Nossa Senhora da Conceição-a-Velha, whose original house of worship, a converted synagogue in the Baixa, had been flattened by the quake. The relatively simple post-earthquake interior has only one nave and contains an image of Our Lady of Restelo, donated to the earlier Conceição Church by Prince Henry the Navigator.

Castelo

Lisbon began on the hill of the Castelo, with an Iron Age settlement that was later occupied successively by Romans, Visigoths and Moors; all of whom added their own fortifications. Some of the oldest segments, thought to be of Roman origin, are at the entrance near the 37 bus stop. These are the outer walls, enclosing both the **Castelo de São Jorge** (*see p79*) itself and the small *intramuros* ('within the walls') neighbourhood. (A walkway is planned around these outer walls that will soon offer fine views in every possible direction.) To your left is the Goan-run **Arco do Castelo** restaurant (*see p135*), a spicy stopping-off point; and round the corner is the Tasquinha, a good lunch option with a pretty esplanade.

From here the way in is through the Arco de São Jorge, where on the left a niche houses an image of St George, the castle's – and also Portugal's – dragon-killing patron. You are now inside the castle walls, and fair game for the frenzy of souvenir shops and postcard palaces that guard the entrance into the Castelo proper.

The Moorish **Castelo de São Jorge.**

Off to the right, narrow streets lead into an increasingly upmarket neighbourhood. The number of older residents living in rent-controlled flats is dwindling, while newcomers pay fortunes for renovated flats in the calm castle air. At the north-east corner of the neighbourhood the **Igreja da Santa Cruz do Castelo** stands on shady Largo de Santa Cruz do Castelo and contains a statue of St George. The original church was built atop a mosque right after the 1147 conquest of Lisbon; the present post-earthquake version dates from 1776. Nearby on Rua Santa Cruz da Castelo, the **Antiga Casa do Castelo** (*see p170*) sells tiles and interesting artisanal souvenirs.

The open square just past the entrance to the Castelo proper serves as a veranda overlooking the city. This is a favoured photo spot for weddings, and on spring Saturdays the procession of brides, grooms and relatives seems never-ending. The cannons sticking out over the parapet are a reminder of the castle's original purpose. These are the outer walls, raised above the orange and lemon gardens of the houses below. Further in, several gardens lead to the inner walls that contain the heart of the medieval castle, a series of open courtyards and ramparted walkways. What remains of the Palácio de Alcáçovas, where medieval kings lived, is a separate stone building now housing a restaurant.

Just below the entrance to the castle on the Chão da Feira is an unusual little corner urinal, much photographed by tourists despite a very characteristic odour. The Palácio Belmonte, just through the archway around the corner, was renovated with the help of city council funds but

has not yet opened as the top-class hotel it was intended to become. Here, the tunnel through to the Pátio de Dom Fradique is still a public passageway. Take it: the quiet patio is surrounded by old houses; the view here is west towards the white dome of the Panteão Nacional de Santa Engrácia. The bottom entrance to the patio opens on to the Rua dos Cegos – the 'Street of the Blind' – whence streets lead down into the Alfama and Mouraria.

The street circling just below and around the castle is called Costa do Castelo for much of its length, and rewards walkers with occasional views out over the city. One of Lisbon's most romantic little hotels – the **Pensão Residencial Ninho das Águias** (*see p64*) – pokes its octagonal tower up above the narrow street and offers the city's best view on a budget. At the junction of Calçada Marquês de Tancos, which leads down to the Baixa, an esplanade pit-stop called **Costa do Castelo** (*see p152*) offers drinks on the terrace and Mozambican food. Up the street the bar-restaurant called **Chapitô**, or big top (*see p152*), has spectacular views out over the old city and is often filled with a young circus-artsy crowd – this is the patio of Lisbon's circus school (*see p225*). The nearby staircase, Escadinhas de São Crispim, follows the course of the old Moorish siege wall down to the neighbourhood of the Sé.

Castelo de São Jorge

Castelo, 1100 (21 887 7244). Tram 12, 38/bus 37. **Open** *Apr-Sept* 9am-9pm daily; *Oct-Mar* 9am-6pm daily. *Câmara Oscura* open 10am-1pm, 2-5.30pm Mon, Wed-Sun (last entry 12.30pm and 5pm); closed Tue. **Admission** free. **Map** p311 M9.

The Castelo hilltop was fortified even before the arrival of the Roman legions; in later centuries the castle walls were strengthened by the Visigoths and Moors before falling to Portugal's first king, Afonso Henriques, in 1147. His statue stands in the open square just past the main castle gate. The Castelo has gone through numerous transformations. From the 14th to the 16th centuries Portuguese kings resided in the Palácio de Alcaçovas, the remains of which now house the Casa do Leão restaurant and, round the back, a multimedia exhibit on Lisbon's history called Olissiponia (*see p113*). In the 1930s a major renovation removed a number of government offices and a firehouse, thus baring the walls, which were then topped off with some new authentic-looking battlements. More recently, a cosmetic clean prior to Expo 98 spruced up the castle walls and gardens, and gave the 'intramuros' neighbourhood a much-needed facelift. The battlements have ten towers, which can be climbed, plus a steep staircase leading down to the outlying Torre de São Lourenço. In one of the castle's inner towers is the Cámara Oscura, in which you can scan the streets below the castle walls, spying on unwitting pedestrians.

Alfama

A beautiful *miradouro* (look-out point) on the 12 and 28 tram lines introduces visitors to Alfama. The **Miradouro de Santa Luzia**, just before Largo das Portas do Sol, has a rose garden, wading pool and grapevine trellises that combine to provide one of Lisbon's most relaxing views over Alfama and the Tagus river harbour. On the south wall of the nearby small church are two tile panels: one depicts the pre-earthquake Terreiro do Paço (Praça do Comércio); the other is of Christians storming the Castelo in 1147. Another twist of the road up the hill leads to the Largo das Portas do Sol (Sun Gate Square) graced by a statue of Lisbon's patron St Vincent bearing the city's symbol, a boat with two ravens. On the southern side of the square, the former city palace of the Visconde de Azurara is now occupied by the **Museu-Escola de Artes Decorativas** (*see p111*) while the adjacent **Cerca Moura** café (*see p143*) is housed in an old stone tower that was once part of the Moorish siege wall. The esplanade overlooks a vast expanse of red Alfama roofs where TV antennas sprout like weeds. In the foreground below local kids scramble about in enthusiastic games of football; over the next hill, the white marble churches of São Vicente and Santa Engrácia mark the western boundary of Alfama.

Running down the south-eastern slope of the hill topped by the Castelo, Alfama is Lisbon's oldest bairro or quarter. It's an appealing warren of narrow streets and blind alleys, stooping archways and twisting staircases.

Some of the buildings around here stand on foundations dating back to the Visigoths, but the street pattern is Moorish (as is the local style of latticed window shutter) even though no Arabic houses remain. Canaries twitter from cages hung outside small windows. Washing flutters everywhere. Children chase each other down the street as grown-ups chatter outside tiny shops and cafés, many of them little more than holes in the wall.

The most densely populated of Lisbon neighbourhoods, Alfama is still a community. The poor linger on in tiny rent-controlled apartments, though rooftop flats with a view are much sought-after by wealthier newcomers. It looks cheerful and postcard-perfect in summer, and the city, aware of the area's attractiveness to visitors, subsidises the maintenance of façades. But many houses are still in dire need of renovation, being draughty and cold in winter.

The name Alfama likely comes from the Arabic 'Al-Hama' meaning springs or fountains. Most of this well-watered neighbourhood stood outside the Moorish city walls, which from the Portas do Sol descended along Rua Norberto

Alfama – Lisbon's oldest *bairro*.

Araújo and Rua da Adiça down to the river. The fountain on Largo do Chafariz de Dentro has been in use since medieval times. Another fountain, the Chafariz d'el-Rei on the nearby Rua Cais de Santarém, has also been in use for more than seven centuries. In the 17th and 18th centuries the taps here were segregated: blacks used the tap on one side, whites the other.

The narrow Rua de São Pedro is a fishmarket on weekday mornings. Here you can tune into the singsong patter of the fishwives (much of which would be unprintable in Portuguese) while dodging trays of slippery squid. At the end of the street the Largo de São Rafael opens on to a remaining portion of the Moorish siege wall, complete with a private lemon-tree garden on top. Below this, a small side street is called the Rua da Judiaria, in medieval times home to Alfama's Jewish community (other, larger Judiarias existed in the medieval Baixa).

The Largo de São Miguel is a sloping square centred around a palm tree and fronted by the white façade of the **Igreja de São Miguel** – like so many old Lisbon buildings a post-earthquake reconstruction of an earlier church. The narrow Rua de São Miguel leads off from the church; it's a main street of sorts, with its grocery stands, butchers and tiny tascas where the buzzing of flies is drowned by televisions tuned to the football. Don't be daunted by the tiny alleys off the Rua de São Miguel: they lead up into wondrous networks of staircases, patios, streets and gardens.

What's missing in Alfama is the sound of motor vehicles. They can't get in here – something that is likely to act as a brake on gentrification. Early morning rush hour in Alfama is accompanied by the sound of birds singing and footsteps scurrying off to work. Where Alfama meets the traffic is down on the Largo do Chafariz de Dentro where tourist buses stop and decant their camera-toting contents into the bottom of the district. On summer evenings crowds head into Alfama looking for an outside table and a dinner of grilled sardines and red wine. A number of fado houses crowd the bottom end of the neighbourhood. The **Parreirinha de Alfama** (see p208) on Beco do Espírito Santo is one of the city's most renowned such institutions.

A good way to get an intimate look at Alfama is to step up (past the Mestre André restaurant on Rua dos Remédios) to the Igreja de Santo Estevão, whose veranda-cum-*miradouro* provides yet another view over red roofs and the harbour. You can see grape vines growing in back lots of some houses. From here streets lead up to the Igreja de São Vicente de Fora, which lends its name to Lisbon's smallest parish, and the neighbourhood of Graça.

But the best way to get to know Alfama is simply to wander around and let yourself get a little lost; something visitors will in fact find almost impossible to avoid doing. Be a little watchful, though, as it's one of the areas where pickpockets operate.

São Vicente de Fora

Between the **Igreja de São Vicente de Fora** (see p82) and the white dome of the **Panteão Nacional de Santa Engrácia** (below) lies the sloping hillside space known as the Campo de Santa Clara. Here, from dawn until early afternoon on Tuesdays and Saturdays, the **Feira da Ladra** flea market (see p171) is held. The name means 'thieves' market' and this is more of a car-boot sale than open-air auction house, but bargains can be had in bric-a-brac and tiles if you're early enough.

Panteão Nacional de Santa Engrácia
Campo de Santa Clara, Alfama, 1100 (21 888 1529). Tram 28. **Open** 10am-1pm, 2-5.30pm Tue-Fri, Sun; 10am-7pm Sat; closed Mon. **Admission** 400$00; 200$00 over-65s, 5-25s; free under-5s. **No credit cards. Map** p308 N9.

The dome of this church was finally completed in 1966, a mere 285 years after construction began in 1681. It's on the site of an earlier church, which was torn down after being desecrated by a robbery in 1630. A Jew was blamed for this and executed, but was later exonerated. Before dying he is supposed to have prophesied that the new church would never be completed because of the conviction of an innocent man. The first attempt at a new Santa Engrácia duly collapsed, in 1681, and work continued from a new plan in 1682. The Lisbon expression 'a job like Santa Engrácia' refers to a job that takes forever to get done. The plan by master stonemason João Antunes bears many similarities to Peruzzi's plans for St Peter's in Rome. Marble in various colours dominates the interior.

In 1916, the Republican government decided that the still roofless Santa Engrácia would become the national Pantheon, a temple to honour dead Portuguese heroes. Among the notables since laid to rest here are former Portuguese presidents Teófilo Braga, Sidónio Pais and Óscar Carmona, as well as the writers Almeida Garrett and Guerra Junqueiro; another tomb contains the mortal remains of General Humberto Delgado, an opposition leader assassinated by the Salazarist secret police in 1962. The remains of Amália, Portugal's most famous fado diva (see p207 **Amália**), are to join them in a few years, after parliament voted to transfer them from Prazeres Cemetery in recognition of her iconic status. Visitors may take a lift to the roof under the dome, which offers views out over the Tagus river harbour and the Alfama district.

The **Panteão Nacional** – completed in a mere 285 years. *See p81.*

Igreja de São Vicente de Fora

Largo de São Vicente, Alfama, 1100 (21 882 4400/cloisters 21 888 5652). Tram 28. **Open** *Church* 9am-6pm Tue-Sun; closed Mon. *Cloisters* 10am-6pm Tue-Sun; closed Mon. **Admission** cloisters 500$00; 250$00 concessions; under-12s free. **No credit cards. Map** p311 N9.

Portugal's first king, Afonso Henriques, laid the foundation stone for the first church of St Vincent in 1147, barely a month after taking Lisbon from the Moors. He was fulfilling a vow to construct Christian houses of worship on the sites where Portuguese soldiers and northern European Crusaders lay buried. In 1580, Portugal's then ruler King Philip II of Spain decided to start from scratch and brought in his own personal architect Juan Herrera (builder of the Escorial outside Madrid) who, accompanied by the Italian architect Filippo Terzi, would design a new Igreja de São Vicente more in the Italian mannerist style. The church was inaugurated in 1629, but severely damaged in the 1755 earthquake, when the main dome and roof collapsed on a crowded house of worshippers. The cloisters are richly decorated with early 18th-century tile panels, some of which illustrate the fables of La Fontaine. Inside you'll also find the royal pantheon of the Braganza family, the last dynasty to rule Portugal. Particularly moving is the weeping woman kneeling before the twin tombs of Dom Carlos I and Crown Prince Luís Filipe, both cut down by assassins' bullets in 1908.

Graça

Whereas Alfama has the feel of a busy village, Graça, up on the hill above São Vicente, is more like a small town. Activity centres around the busy Largo da Graça and the tram 28 stop. Off to the west of it is the Esplanada da Igreja da Graça, an open-air café with one of Lisbon's best sunset views. The **Igreja da Graça** (*see below*), itself is one of Lisbon's oldest churches, originally built in 1271 though substantially enlarged in the mid-16th century. The attached former monastery has been a barracks since religious orders were dissolved in 1834. Until quite recently the scrubby wasteland on the slope below leading down towards Mouraria was used to breed rabbits to feed the soldiers. From the esplanade you could watch Portuguese squaddies scuttling around the undergrowth trying to catch them for the cooking pot.

In the late 19th century, many vacant lots in Graça were developed as worker housing. One major project, the Vila Sousa, is the block tiled in turquoise opposite the Igreja da Graça. Over on the west side of the Largo da Graça, off the Travessa da Pereira, you can walk along the front of the Vila Berta, another project of that era. *See chapter* **Architecture**.

The small promontory above Graça (follow Rua Damsceno Monteiro from the main square, and then haul up the Calçada do Monte) is the highest of Lisbon's seven central hills. It is topped by the chapel of **Senhora do Monte**, once called the Chapel of São Gens. The *miradouro* here is a favourite for lovers and perhaps the best place in town to catch the sunset, offering a panoramic view across the Castelo and central Lisbon. In front of the chapel is a glass-encased image of the Virgin. Inside, the chapel contains the stone chair of St Gens, a legendary bishop martyred during Roman times. A good sitdown on the saintly seat is supposed to ease the pangs of childbirth, and the chair was thus popular with Portuguese queens over the centuries.

Igreja da Graça

Largo da Graça, Graça, 1170 (21 887 3943). Tram 28. **Open** 9.30am-noon, 3-7.30pm Mon-Sat; 9.30am-12.30pm, 6-8pm Sun. **Map** p311 N9.

The original monastery of Graça was built in 1271, and completed with an image of Nossa Senhora da Graça, washed up in the waters of Cascais that same year. Renovated in the mid-16th century, most of the church came tumbling down in the 1755 earthquake. The later renovation reduced three naves to one, and removed much austere marble in favour of more flamboyant rococo decoration. During Lent the church hosts the Senhor dos Passos procession: the images of Christ and the Virgin are taken on a tour of the surrounding neighbourhood, as they have since the mid-16th century. The old monastery complex was turned over to the military when religious orders were abolished in 1834.

Mouraria & Martim Moniz

Mouraria is the district wedged on the hillside between the north side of the Castelo and Graça. Moors driven from their homes within the city walls in 1147 were allowed to settle here by Portugal's first king, Afonso Henriques. In the 12th and 13th centuries two mosques were still functioning; a 1471 Muslim petition to the king mentions that the Mouraria was enclosed by walls and that residents locked the gates at night. Twenty-five years later all non-Christians were either forcibly converted or expelled from the country. In the 19th century, Mouraria was known for its prostitutes, seedy *tascas* and fado houses. One street, the Rua de Capelão, is known as the most famous street in fado due to the mid-19th century fado house run by the notorious Maria de Severa (*see p205* **Marialvismo**).

Nowadays Mouraria is a bit scruffy, though no less typically lisboeta than its neighbour Alfama on the other side of the hill. The main street here is the Rua dos Cavaleiros/Calçada do Santo André, which follows the course of the 12 tram. The bottom of the neighbourhood has been taken over by Indian-run discount stores and the multi-ethnic Centro Comercial Mouraria bustles with Chinese, African and Indian shops and businesses (*see p166* **Mouraria – centro comercial or centro culrural?**).

Mouraria also spreads southward along the west slope of the castle. On Rua de São Lourenço the alleys and open square seem a world away from the busy Baixa just down the steps. If you follow this street south, it changes its name no less than four times and leads past several low-priced African restaurants including the Mozambican **Cantinho do Aziz** (*see p131*) and the Cape Verdean Restaurante **São Cristovão** (*see p132*) to the white **Igreja de São Cristovão**. The locals celebrate the now-decanonised St Christopher's day in mid-October, when you can line your car or bike up after Sunday Mass and have it blessed by the priest. Behind the church is a small square, the Largo da Achada, with surviving examples of pre-earthquake houses.

Mouraria meets the Baixa at Martim Moniz, the open square at the bottom of the Rua da Palma. This was originally the heart of Mouraria, but in the 1950s and 1960s old byways, squares and churches were bulldozed in the name of urban renewal. For more than three decades Martim Moniz was a maze of rubble and temporary sheds put up to house

displaced shopkeepers. The 1980s brought a first taste of things to come when an out-of-scale shopping centre was tacked on to the back of the old Socorro church. A few years later another glassy emporium went up on the other side of the square. The most recent city administration was not to be outdone, and while paving the square added lots of strange metal kiosks that remain mostly unoccupied two years on. It also allowed planning permission for the ugly annexe of the Hotel Mundial (*see p56*) at the south end. Citizens now worriedly eye the remaining empty lots around the square: what will they build next?

Running north of Martim Moniz towards the airport, the Rua da Palma/Avenida Almirante Reis provides downtown Lisbon with its workaday axis, a contrast to the glitzier Avenida da Liberdade. At this end it's a down-at-heel shopping district and notably devoid of landmarks save for the red-light district on and around the Largo do Intendente: a round-the-clock precinct of sleaze featuring dodgy bars, ageing whores and fairly regular stabbings. One saving grace is **Ramiro's** restaurant opposite (*see p131*), which has the fastest waiters in the west serving the finest shrimps in garlic. The tiled façade of the **Fábrica Viúva Lamego** (*see p170*) is also worth a look.

Campo de Santana

Rising in the fork between the two Avenidas, Almirante Reis and da Liberdade, is Campo de Santana, a mixed bag of a neighbourhood with assorted fado houses, Lisbon's **Centro Comunitário Gay e Lésbico** (*see p197*) and an uncommon number of hospitals. An appropriate location, then, for the statue of Sousa Martins, which stands on the square outside the Faculdade de Medicina.

José Thomaz de Sousa Martins was entirely secular in his outlook, but gained great favour among the poor for his even-handed approach to curing the sick. He died in 1897 and grateful locals have since made him a religious cult hero. His statue here is a shrine for many who keep candles burning in memory of the good doctor. The numerous stone plaques around the base of the statue base have been left in thanks for miracle cures attributed to the divine aid of the deceased medic.

The **Jardim de Torel**, a small park on Rua de Júlio de Andrade, offers good views over the Avenida da Liberdade to the Bairro Alto opposite. Film buffs may recognise the house at Júlio Andrade 7; it was used in the film of Isabel Allende's *The House of Spirits*. The Lavra funicular descends to Largo da Anunciada off the Avenida da Liberdade.

Sightseeing

West of Baixa

The Chiado has risen from the ashes, while the Bairro Alto is as hot as ever.

Chiado

Neighbourhood of theatres and cafés, of fashion shops and venerable booksellers, the Chiado was once the centre of Lisbon's intellectual life, the **Rua Garrett** its most fashionable street. Much of what remained from its 19th- and early 20th-century golden days went up in smoke when the August 1988 fire swallowed the intersection of Rua Garrett and Rua do Carmo, reducing two major department stores to ruins. Reconstruction was overseen by the renowned Oporto architect Alvaro Siza Vieira, who kept the original urban tracery while carving out two new patios: one linking the Rua do Carmo to the Largo do Carmo, the other a courtyard off Rua Garrett. Reconstruction of the Chiado took far longer than it should, but a whiff of former grandeur still remains.

The ascent from Rossio up the **Rua do Carmo** and then along Rua Garrett is reasonably gentle and leads into the heart of the quarter. On the way, as the road passes under the viaduct of the **Elevador da Santa Justa**, modern fashion shops such as **Ana Salazar** (*see p163*), **Gardenia** (*see p159*) and **Zara** (*see p161*) rub shoulders with anachronisms such as the **Luvaria Ulisses** (*see p165*), a tiny, ancient glove shop. The **Livraria Bertrand** (*see p157*) is Lisbon's oldest bookshop and the **Café A Brasileira** (*see p143*) favourite meeting points. Once a haunt of writer Fernando Pessoa, whose bronze likeness has a permanent seat on the terrace, today it services both tourists and locals, who collect here before a night out in the Bairro Alto.

A Brasileira stands on the Largo do Chiado, though there's not much Largo left now the upper passage from the Baixa-Chiado Metro station emerges into the centre of it.

Downhill towards the river, the **Museu do Chiado** (*see p193*), which was redesigned in 1994 by French architect Jean Michel Wilmotte, houses a collection of Portuguese art from the 19th and 20th centuries. The nearby **Teatro Nacional de São Carlos** (*see p202*) was built in 1793 and modelled after La Scala in Milan. The **Teatro Municipal de São Luíz** (*see p224*) is more notable for the ironwork fire escapes that lace its plain back façade on Rua Duque de Bragança, right by the outside tables of the excellent **Café no Chiado** (*see p143*).

Shopfront in **Chiado**.

Up on the other side of Rua Garrett, the **Largo do Carmo** is one of Lisbon's prettiest squares, fronted by the simple façade of the ruined **Convento do Carmo** (*see below*), which stands next to the headquarters of the paramilitary GNR, the National Republican Guard. Uniformed minions brandishing swords still stand guard outside the building, scene of one of the most memorable moments of the 1974 Revolution in Portugal as the last refuge of the last ancien régime Prime Minister Marcello Caetano. A flagstone on the square commemorates the event.

Convento do Carmo

Largo do Carmo, Chiado, 1100 (21 346 0473). Metro Baixa-Chiado/tram 28. **Map** p310 L9.
The Gothic lines of the Church of Our Lady of Mount Carmel went up on the orders of Nun'Álvares Pereira, who was indispensable in helping Dom João I consolidate the rule of Portugal's second dynasty, the House of Avis. Pereira, known as the Consdestável, or Constable, founded the church and

neighbouring convent to fulfil a pledge made before a crucial battle, and was adamant in his choice of location – despite the nearby precipice and various false construction starts after foundations caved in. During the 1755 earthquake the roof collapsed on a crowd of All Saints Day worshippers, leaving the structure close to collapse with only the walls and some vault ribbing still standing. Said by many to be the most beautiful church in Lisbon, it has been maintained thus ever since, and now a grassy lawn grows in the open air under what was once the central nave. The Museu Arqueológico, a ragbag of finds from around Europe, inhabits the back end of the church, but has been closed since Metro tunnelling once again brought the walls to the point of collapse. As of early 2001, no date had been set for its reopening.

Bairro Alto

When Dom Manuel I moved his residence down from the castle to the waterfront in the early 1500s, the axis of Lisbon's development shifted slightly westward: harbour activity expanded along the area now known as the Cais do Sodré, while up the hill the level ground outside the Fernandine walls was divided into regular lots and sold off to aristocrats and the emerging merchant class. The Jesuits soon set themselves up at the top of the hill in the **Igreja de São Roque** (*see p88*) and the quarter became known as the Bairro Alto de São Roque (upper neighbourhood of St Roch). Wealthy merchants gradually gave way to small shopkeepers and craftsmen. For a while there were many print shops and newspaper offices, and both Rua de O Século and Rua do Diário de Notícias are named after daily papers that once had their editorial offices on these streets. Today only the sports dailies *O Bola* and *Record* have their offices around here – the latter above the bar **Portas Largas** (*see p151*), which is thus often referred to as 'Record'.

Though maps may refer to a larger area as the Bairro Alto, the quarter is essentially bounded by Rua de O Século to the west, Rua Dom Pedro V to the north, Rua de São Pedro de Alcântara and Rua da Misericórdia to the east and Rua do Loreto to the south. The geometric layout between these streets predates the Baixa. The Bairro Alto was the first district in Lisbon to have straight and regular streets. Straight and regular by the standards of the time, that is. In many ways it's as maze-like as the city centre's other old quarters, just in a more rectilinear fashion and with enough kinks and dead ends that even locals sometimes get confused as to what's on which street – especially after a long session in this neighbourhood of determined nightlife.

The ruined **Convento do Carmo**. *See p85.*

During the day the Bairro Alto is relatively quiet. Kids play ball in the streets while old ladies shop and chat and hang out the laundry. Interesting shops are dotted about. The neighbourhood is home to many of the more alternative fashion outlets, such as **la** on Rua da Atalaia (*see p163*) or **Agência 117** and **Eldorado** on Rua do Norte (for both, *see p159*), where you can complete the look with a tattoo or a piercing at **Bad Bones** (*see p176*). There are also many second-hand bookstores, little specialist record shops and a couple of art supplies places on Rua da Rosa. But still, it's mainly a residential area and by day streets rarely bustle.

At night it's another story. On a weekend, thousands of revellers cram into these narrow streets, hopping from bar to bar or collecting at certain nexus points, such as on Rua do Diário de Notícias outside **Cafédiário** and **Café Suave** (for both, *see p148*), or at the junction of Rua da Atalaia and Travessa da Queimada outside Portas Largas and the original Bairro Alto club **Frágil** (*see p217*). The area is also full of restaurants, varying from traditional and cheapish Portuguese *tascas* to purveyors of sophisticated cosmopolitan cuisine. **Primavera** (*see p127*) on Travessa da Espera, **Casa Nostra** (*see p136*) on Travessa Poço da Cidade and **Pap' Açorda** (*see p122*) or **Hell's Kitchen** (*see p135*) on Rua da Atalaia are among those we recommend, but round here you can find food to suit any taste or budget.

The Bairro Alto also has Lisbon's largest collection of fado houses – 20 or so – which have been in this quarter since long before all the more fashionable bars and clubs began opening up in the early 1980s. **Café Luso** (*see p206*) on Travessa da Queimada is Lisbon's oldest fado house, **Adega Machado** (*see p205*) nearby on Rua do Norte is almost as venerable, while **Tasca do Chico** (*see p208*) on Rua Diário de Notícias is a cheaper and more informal venue. All of these places are after the tourist trade – the biggest magnet for tour groups is **O Forcado** on Rua da Rosa (*see p206*) – but Portuguese visit them too. And sometimes, as the Bairro Alto begins to close down around 2am, rising above the clatter and chatter still emanating from the scores of bars and clubs, you'll hear someone singing fado on the street – a lament for the end of the night.

There are three open spaces on the southern and western edges of the Bairro Alto. The first is the **Praça Luís de Camões** at the south end of the neighbourhood, a square ringed with umbrella pines and adjoining the Largo do Chiado to the east. A monumental statue designed by Vítor Bastos was unveiled in 1867 in its centre; it represents the 16th-century epic poet Luís de Camões, standing on a pedestal ringed by smaller statues of classical Portuguese authors. But Camões has had to take a hike as work to build yet another underground car park under the square named after him drags on.

Up Rua da Misericórdia and in front of the Igreja de São Roque is the **Largo de Trindade Coelho**, although lisboetas prefer to call it the Largo da Misericórdia, after the Santa Casa da Misericórdia charity institution whose head offices are on the square. (This also explains the bronze statue of a lottery ticket seller – Misericórdia has the monopoly on the lottery.) This end of the Bairro Alto is where all the antiquarian and second-hand bookshops cluster. There are two on the south side of the square, a couple more on the Rua da Misericórdia just down from the McDonald's, and more still on the Rua Nova da Trindade, where there is also the **Teatro da Trindade** (*see p224*) and the **Cervejaria Trindade** (No.20C, 21 321 9316), a beerhall built into the walls of a former monastery that has fabulous *azulejos* but overpriced food. A scenic staircase, the Calçada do Duque, leads down from Largo da Misericórdia to Rossio, passing a few cheap restaurants and still more bookshops.

In the **Igreja de São Roque**. *See p88.*

Sightseeing

The third open space bounding the Bairro Alto is the **Jardim de São Pedro de Alcântara**, a garden *miradouro* (look-out point) laid out in the early 19th century and offering splendid views out over the Avenida da Liberdade business district, the Baixa, Castelo and river. The **Casa do Brasil** (*see p44*), on the first floor above **Harry's Bar** (*see p199*), overlooks this small park and everyone runs out here to dance around whenever Brazil win a football game.

The **Elevador da Glória** funicular has been whisking passengers down and up the steep Calçada da Glória between Jardim de São Pedro de Alcântara and Largo dos Restauradores since 1885. The proud-to-be-fit churn up the hill on leg power alone; those who tire can hitch a handhold on the back of the car and literally get pulled up. The **Solar do Vinho do Porto** (*see p151*) is opposite its upper terminal point. Its building was once known as the Palácio Ludovice, after the architect of Mafra, who built it as his city residence in 1747 at a time when Bairro Alto was the in neighbourhood for the wealthy.

The building is organised around an inner courtyard and takes up an entire city block at the top of the Elevador da Glória. The port wine people moved in in 1944.

The street running north up the side of the park is named after the still active nunnery of **São Pedro de Alcantara** at its upper end. The doors are barred to visitors but it's worth having a look at the blue-tile depiction of St Peter receiving his stigmata, on the wall by the entrance.

Igreja de São Roque

Largo de Trindade Coelho, Bairro Alto, 1200 (21 323 5000). Metro Restauradores then Elevador da Glória. **Open** noon-5pm daily. **Map** p310 L9.

The Igreja de São Roque was built by the Jesuits on the site of an earlier chapel dedicated to São Roque (St Rock). Most of the single-nave structure was built between 1565 and 1573, though it remained roofless for almost another decade. The ceiling is a wonder of sorts. The original architect had planned a vaulted roof, but in 1582 a decision was made to flatroof the space in wood, and sturdy timber was brought in from Prussia to complete the job, which was then richly painted. The most opulent of the side chapels is the one dedicated to St John the Baptist, built in Rome and shipped to Lisbon in 1749 after being personally blessed by the Pope. The paintings in the inner sacristy are often open to viewing and are well worth a visit.

Príncipe Real

Rua Dom Pedro V leads north to the Praça do Príncipe Real. There are antique and book shops along here, and the **Pavilhão Chinês** (*see p152*), the bar with the best interior decor of any Lisbon drinking establishment, designed by Duarte Pinto Coelho. In some ways Príncipe Real is little more than a continuation of the Bairro Alto, especially for the gay and lesbian community, many of whose bars and clubs are in this quarter on the streets below the park. Bars such as **Max** (*see p199*) are on Rua de São Marçal; the **Bric-à-Bar** disco (*see p199*) is on Rua Cecílio de Sousa and **Finalmente** (*see p199*) on Rua da Palmeira – all within easy cruising distance of each other. **Katedral** (Rua Manuel Bernardes 52, 21 395 8793), one of the few Lisbon bars for lesbians, is also nearby.

The **Praça do Príncipe Real** is one of Lisbon's most romantic garden settings. It was laid out as a small park in 1860, with lots of exotic imported greenery. On sunny afternoons knots of old men play cards at one end, while lovers curl up on benches under the century-old cedar tree, bent out horizontally to provide some of the capital's most renowned shade. Its **Esplanada do Príncipe Real** café provides pleasant respite from urbanity, though the service is notoriously gruff.

Playing hard in the **Praça do Príncipe Real**.

The **Elevador da Bica** snails its way up from near Cais do Sodré to the Bairro Alto.

Praça do Príncipe Real is ringed by pastel-painted buildings, the most notable of which is the Arabesque palace at No.26, built in the late 19th century as the Palácio Ribeiro da Cunha and today housing a university department. The slightly older mansion next door nowadays stores the riches of the Banco de Portugal. The streets between Príncipe Real and the Tagus are a gridiron of 19th-century townhouses, home to, among other things, the British Council and Library on Rua de São Marçal. Eça de Queiros' novel *Cousin Bazílio* portrays the life of a bored, upper-class, 19th-century housewife living in this neighbourhood.

Rua da Escola Politécnica is home to the **Museu da História Natural** (*see p116*) and its outdoor aisleway lined with enormous spindly palm trees. Follow them in – they lead to the **Jardim Botânico** (*below*), where for a small fee you can get away from it all by taking a bench seat under your choice of exotic plant.

Rua de O Século runs south from Praça do Príncipe Real to Calçada do Combro. This is a quiet street, home to Portugal's constitutional court, art galleries and a dance conservatory built into the boyhood home palace of the Marquês de Pombal. The open square opposite, backed by the Século Fountain, is the May setting for the Manóbras de Maio fashion show.

Jardim Botânico da Faculdade de Ciências

Rua da Escola Politécnica, Príncipe Real, 1200 (21 396 8180). Metro Rato/15, 58, 100 bus. **Open** *Winter* 9.30am-6pm Mon-Fri; 10am-6pm Sat, Sun. *Summer* 9.30am-8pm Mon-Fri; 10am-8pm Sat, Sun. **Admission** 250$00; 50$00-125$00 concessions. **No credit cards. Map** p307 K8.

The four hectares of shaded walkways of the Botanical Garden were laid out between 1858 and 1878 and contain nearly 10,000 plants. Highlights include large numbers of cycads, palm-ferns that have been around since the time of the dinosaurs. The back entrance on Rua da Alegria is closed at weekends.

Bica

The Bica funicular snails its way up a steep street between the Cais do Sodré waterfront and the lower end of the Bairro Alto, beginning its journey in a yellow building marked 'Ascensor da Bica' on Rua de São Paulo. It climbs through one of old Lisbon's quirkiest neighbourhoods, an area where fashionable restaurants and bars such as **WIP** and **Baliza** (for both, *p153*) fit in neatly with taverns and tatty grocers. The lie of the land here was formed when a landslide swept away much of an earlier Bica during an earthquake in 1598. Topping out the neighbourhood is the **Santa Catarina miradouro**, where the kiosk often serves drinks deep into a summer night. Lots of people gather here to drink and admire the dawn view over the Tagus, or lie out on the lawn under the statue of the Adamastor – the mythical beast who guarded the Cape of Good Hope in Camões's *Lusiads*.

If you like to wash away your sins in gold-gilt, head over to **Igreja de Santa Catarina** on Calçada do Combro. The original building dates to 1647, though it was remodelled after the 1755 earthquake. The adjoining monastery is now a National Guard barracks, and there is an interesting military library upstairs, but the main church is still in use and contains gold-giltwork dating back to the late 17th century, as well as a ceiling that is a masterpiece of 18th-century rococo painting.

Western Waterfront

Lisbon no longer turns its back to the riverbank from where the caravels set sail.

The railway lines and avenues running alongside the Tagus, plus all the warehouses and other paraphernalia of the docks, used to provide a barrier between the rest of Lisbon and the river. The city and the port each went about their own business, back to back. No longer.

In the past decade Lisbon has woken up to its waterfront, with much new development concentrating along the river, aided by improved waste water treatment that has taken the edge off the odour of the Tagus. In bygone centuries this bit of riverbank was the site of shipyards that outfitted the caravels of the maritime Discoveries. Today's riverfront is hopping with bars, restaurants, skateboarders, gyms and joggers, especially in the western part of town.

The 1966 **Ponte 25 de Abril**. *See p106.*

Cais do Sodré

Immediately west of the Praça do Comércio is a garden walk along the river to the Cais do Sodré boat, Metro and train station. Much of the garden, however, has been torn up to make way for the construction of a traffic tunnel under the Praça and the dust and dump trucks look to be ubiquitous for a while to come. The giant red concrete ring and sculpture set on a remaining patch of lawn were erected to mark Lisbon's term as Europe's cultural capital in 1994.

At rush hour it's overrun by commuters heading every which way (the summertime rush is to the beaches). It's the end of the line for many buses, for trains on the Cascais line and on the Lisbon Metro's green line. It's also the boat terminal for ferries to Cacilhas. Cais do Sodré has a very port-like red-light neighbourhood just in from the river where there is still a sniff of Querelle de Brest-style seedy sailor nightlife. Many clubs still bear the names of old ports-of-call such as **Jamaica** (*see p215*), Copenhagen or Hamburg, while the prostitutes that loll about the Praça de São Paulo are a reminder of Cais do Sodré's whorier heyday. *See also p220* **Red-light routes**.

But the flipside is a slew of trendier bars, among them two new Irish pubs that have joined the old **British Bar** (*see p153*) – a fixture since before World War II. A number of restaurants in this area are famed for their seafood – **Porta de Abrigo** (*see p129*) – and shoppers looking for that extra oilskin may find

it in the various local ships' chandlers. The **Mercado da Ribeira** (*see p171*), built in 1882, is a market hall on Avenida 24 de Julho; its bar opens early and is a famous early morning gathering spot for late-night revellers to sip hot chocolate in winter while waiting for the first train home on the Cascais line. A little later, the first stallholders are unpacking fruit and veg, and in the afternoons the place is transformed into a blaze of colour when the flower sellers take over.

Santos

The nightlife continues westward along **Avenida 24 de Julho** in the neighbourhood of Santos, and more particularly in the string of nightclubs such as the somewhat kooky **Kremlin** (*see p219*) and the upper-krust **Kapital** (*see p218*). (K is a letter that traditionally never existed in Portuguese, being rendered usually as qu. But the times, as they say, are a-changing.) Fast-food stops stay open late here to take care of the disco crowd, serving up traditional Portuguese fare such as *caldo verde* (cabbage soup with a slice of sausage) and *pão com chouriço* (sausage bread served straight from the brick oven), or Big Macs galore opposite the towering steel cage-like building of the Design and Architecture faculty at the bottom of Avenida Dom Carlos I.

During the day, Avenida 24 de Julho is pretty empty and bleary, but at night the clubbing crowds are often out on the street until sunrise and beyond (*see chapter* **Nightlife**). This area was named after three saintly Christian siblings – Verissimus, Maxima and Julia – who according to legend were martyred on the beach by the Romans in the early fourth century. The only hint left of that beach is the short Escadinhas da Praia – Staircase of the Beach – now home to a Renault factory showroom on one side, and a couple of clubs, one of which is **Kremlin** (*see p219*), on the other.

Santos is also home to various crumbling old monasteries and nunneries, and there are tales of secret tunnels used by enterprising young monks in search of lonely nuns. One old palace up on Rua de Santos-o-Velho now houses the French Embassy but was once a royal palace; legend has it that this is the place where Christopher Columbus was introduced to his future wife.

The main drag in Santos is the **Rua das Janelas Verdes** – Street of the Green Windows – which leads up to the old Alvor, or Janelas Verdes, Palace, now housing the **Museu Nacional de Arte Antiga** (*see p109*). Highlights of its collection include a famous tryptych by Hieronymus Bosch and the Polyptych of St Vincent, the enigmatic late 15th-century masterpiece of Portuguese painting. The museum has its own garden and restaurant in the back with a view over the port neighbourhood.

This is the preferred place to snack for many visiting artists and writers, including Antonio Tabucchi, while Graham Greene was once a patron of the **Pensão York House** (*see p55*) nearby. You'll need a museum ticket to get into the garden (unless it's before 2pm on Sunday, when entry is free), so give yourself time to visit the museum and then relax a bit outdoors. It costs nothing to sit in the garden in front of the main entrance and watch the cruise and cargo ships line up at the quay below.

Alcântara & Docas

Further west, the Alcântara district marks the end of Avenida 24 de Julho. Here, in the shadow of the Ponte 25 de Abril, many nightclubs and restaurants have been carved out of old warehouses, while up on the hill, commanding a splendid view, are the pink walls of the Palácio das Necessidades, a former palace housing the Foreign Ministry.

Across the train tracks and under the Ponte 25 de Abril are the Docas de Santo Amaro, a yachting marina complete with outdoor esplanades and indoor bars with a variety of music and muzak: certainly not a quiet place to

Friendly fishwives at the **Mercado da Ribeira**. *See p90 and p171.*

spend the night in a boat, but it can be entertaining if you're not kipping in a berth. **Salsa Latina**, in the west wing of the beautiful modernist ocean-liner terminal, the **Gare Marítima de Alcântara** (*see below*), is the place for late-night Latin dancing, while other bars on the promenade nearby blast music out on to the water. **Zeno** (*see p133*) is a good place to sample Brazilian food, while **Doca 6** (*see p125*) takes care of seekers of quality Portuguese fare. Much of the rest is conveyor-belt cuisine and if you hate crowds, don't venture down here on weekend nights. To the north is the 16th-century **Igreja de Santo Amaro** (*see p92*).

Gare Marítima de Alcântara

Doca de Alcântara Norte, Alcântara, 1350. Bus 20, 51. **Map** p306 G10.
The sleek modernist lines of the Alcântara maritime terminal went up in the 1940s, designed by architect Porfírio Pardal Monteiro. The idea was to provide Lisbon with a state-of-the-art receiving station for passenger ships, and to that end the interior was decorated with enormous murals by the painter Almada Negreiros. One focuses on Lisbon daily life, particularly on the waterfront; the theme of another is the legend of Dom Fuas Roupinho, a medieval knight and naval hero who almost followed an evil hart over a foggy cliff in the seaside town of Nazaré. The Virgin Mary appeared just in time to warn him back.

Igreja de Santo Amaro

Rua 1 de Maio (à Calçada de Santo Amaro), 1300. Tram 15, 18/bus 22, 42, 60. Open 11am Sun (for mass). **Map** p303 E10.
This round church was built in 1549. Its early 17th-century polychrome tile panels recount the life of St Amaro. Other 18th-century panels tell the story of the church. Legend has it that the original chapel was founded by a grateful group of Galician sailors who were saved from shipwreck just offshore from here. This perhaps accounts for the ship-shaped layout of the church courtyard, with its sweeping views over the Tagus and the Ponte 25 de Abril. Until recent decades the church was a centre of worship for the large Galician community in Lisbon. St Amaro is also the patron saint of the handicapped, and this chapel contains replicas of arms and legs turned over to the saint's care in the hope of obtaining a miracle cure.

Belém

Belém by itself could be called a museum. The rather eclectic 'collection' includes a wide range of monuments, from the Manueline, late-gothic Torre de Belém to the fascistoid Padrão dos Descobrimentos, from the Mosteiro dos Jerónimos, a temple to God, to the Centro Cultural de Belém, a temple to culture. Tourists troop through on foot, on buses, or pour out of trams.

On Sundays, lisboetas crowd the open lawns and promenades along the river, lunch at the many outdoor esplanades, gorge themselves on creamy Belém custard tarts or flock to exhibits at the Centro Cultural.

The area was once separate from the city of Lisbon and bore the name Restelo, changed to Belém (Bethlehem) in the early 16th century by Dom Manuel I. Once a prime anchorage spot, the history of Belém is neatly intertwined with the glory days of the Portuguese Discoveries. In 1415, the first overseas expedition left Restelo beach on the way to conquer Ceuta in Morocco. In March 1493, Christopher Colombus stopped in on his way back to Spain after discovering the Americas and, in 1497, Vasco da Gama departed with a fleet of caravels to discover a maritime route to India.

That scene is recorded in the 16th-century epic poem *The Lusiads* by Luís de Camões, when an old man in the crowd stepped out in a vain attempt to warn da Gama's fleet back.

Also, in 1588, during Spanish rule, Belém was the assembly point for the mighty Spanish Armada sent out against protestant England.

So, take a walk through history, starting at the **Torre de Belém** (*see p94*), a curious little fortress put up between 1514 and 1520, and today one of Lisbon's most recognisable symbols.

Padrão dos Descobrimentos. *See p94.*

Set in stone – Belém's map of the world charts the sequence of Portuguese Discoveries.

Nearby and almost under the adjacent road overpass is a newly erected inverted 'V' of a monument that pays homage to Portugal's dead in the African colonial wars that were this country's Vietnam, raging through the 1960s and ending only with the 1974 Revolution and the toppling of the old regime and empire.

In 1940, to divert attention from the maelstrom of World War II raging all around neutral Portugal, the Salazar regime put on a show called the Exhibition of the Portuguese World, dolling up the Belém waterfront district and levelling out the grandiose Praça do Império that fronts the Mosteiro dos Jerónimos (Jerónimos Monastery). Remaining from the show are the reflecting pools, the **Museu Nacional de Arte Popular** (*see p109*), and the building that houses a branch of the archetypal Portuguese beer hall, **Portugália** (*see p131*). The monolithic **Padrão dos Descobrimentos** (Monument to the Discoveries, *see p94*) on the marina depicts a heroic Prince Henry the Navigator leading a troupe of Portuguese discoverers out into the unknown. Following the sun's course, the huge, sword-like shadow of the monument's cross-section traces the Portuguese explorers' progress around a marble map of the world on the square below. Vital dates, such as Vasco da Gama's rounding of the Cape of Good Hope in 1498 and Pedro Álvares Cabral's landing in Brazil in 1500, are marked.

Inland, across the gardens, the **Mosteiro dos Jerónimos** (*see p95*) is one of Portugal's most emblematic and beautiful landmarks, containing the tombs of Vasco da Gama and Luís de Camões, both laid to rest here in the 19th century. The longer wing of Jerónimos facing the Praça do Império was actually built

in the 19th century and now houses, in the middle, the **Museu Nacional de Arqueológia** (*see p109*), and at the far end, the **Museu da Marinha** (*see p112*).

The modern complex facing the Praça do Império is the **Centro Cultural de Belém**, or CCB (*see p192*), put up as a showpiece for Portugal's 1992 presidency of the European Union. Originally controversial for its cost and proximity to the emblematic Jerónimos, the centre, with its striking modern architecture, has since settled into its role as host of numerous cultural events and congresses. Since 1999, it has housed the excellent **Museu do Design** (*see p114* **Designs on you**). The CCB is a favourite with visitors, who can see important travelling exhibits, listen to jazz, buy books and records, or idle away afternoons in the upstairs olive garden overlooking the river. The garden and the inside terrace bar are frequent concert venues.

One block-long section of the old residential Belém survives amid all the monumentality. The houses along the **Rua de Belém** were once right up against the riverfront, which has since retreated to the other side of the train tracks. Its **Antiga Casa de Pastéis de Belém** (*see p146* **Tarts with tradition**) is a local mecca that has been serving its speciality pastéis de Belém, a creamy custard tart-like concoction topped with cinnamon and sugar, since 1837; the place is absolutely mobbed at weekends. Just west of the pastry shop, a small alley on the right leads into a small square with a strange column. The five bands on the pillory stand for the five members of the aristocratic Távora family who were executed here in 1759, condemned by the Marquês de Pombal for complicity in an assassination attempt against

The elegant **Jardim Botânico de Ajuda**.

Dom José I. The Marchioness of Távora was decapitated; her husband and sons tortured and their bones crushed. Salt was spread on their surrounding property so nothing would ever grow there; today the pillory stands forgotten, and weeds peek up from among the cobbles.

Still on Rua de Belém, between the pastry shop and the monastery is the entrance to the **Jardim do Ultramarino**, tropical gardens with long lawns and ponds and several hundred exotic species of lush outgrowth. Leading off from the road is the shady Praça Afonso de Albuquerque, named after the fiery Indian Ocean governor who established Portugal's pepper empire in the early years of the 16th century. The salmon-coloured palace above one side of the square is the official residence of the president of Portugal, and below is the **Museu Nacional dos Coches** (*see p110*), reputed to be the biggest and best of its kind in the world. In the heights above the Belém district is the **Palácio da Ajuda** (*see p95*), begun in the year 1802 and still incomplete. Nowadays, it houses the Culture Ministry and has a section that opens as a museum. Once, in the late 19th century, it was the preferred residence of the monarchy. Nearby on the Calçada da Ajuda, and well worth a visit, are the **Igreja da Memória** (*see p95*) and another botanical garden, the **Jardim Botânico da Ajuda**.

Beyond Ajuda is the enormous pine forest of **Monsanto**, set aside as a park in the 1930s, when over a million trees were planted over the rocky and sparsely populated hillsides. Monsanto is known as the 'lung' of Lisbon, freshening the west wind as it breezes into the city; indeed, the park comprises nearly an eighth of the total area of the city. On the map, so much green space looks inviting. But don't be fooled. It's not. Despite a few pockets of civilisation, such as the old tennis club and the newer **Alto da Serafina** adventure playground (*see p185*), Monsanto is best-known as a favourite haunt for prostitutes and drug dealers and locals will warn you not to stop your car there at night, nor wind down your windows. There's the well fenced-off Lisboa Camping (*see p65*) at one end, though, and at the top there's a pleasant belvedere and recreation area.

Torre de Belém

Praça da Torre de São Vicente de Belém, Belém, 1400 (monastery phone 21 362 0034). Train from Cais do Sodré to Belém/15 tram/27, 28, 43, 49, 51 bus. **Open** *Winter* 10am-5pm daily. *Summer* 10am-6.30pm daily. **Admission** 600$00; 300$00 concessions; free under-15s. **No credit cards. Map** p303 A20.
The Tower of Belém was put up to guard the river entrance into Lisbon harbour. Built on the orders of Dom Manuel the Fortunate (*see p11*), it incorporates many stonework motifs of the maritime Discoveries, among them twisted rope and the Catholic Crosses of Christ. Other sculptures depict St Vincent, patron saint of Lisbon, and – under the north-west watchtower – an exotic rhinoceros that is said to have inspired Dürer's drawing of the beast. The tower was originally some distance from the riverbank; it is now easily accessible by wooden walkway from a green park and reflecting pool.

Padrão dos Descobrimentos

Avenida de Brasília (opposite Praça do Império), Belém, 1400 (21 303 1950). Train from Cais do Sodré to Belém/15 tram/27, 28, 43, 49, 51 bus. **Open** *July, Aug* 9am-7pm Tue-Sun; closed Mon. *Sept-June* 9am-5pm Tue-Sun; closed Mon. **Admission** 360$00; 180$00 concessions; free under-13s. **No credit cards. Map** p303 B10.
The original temporary Monument to the Discoveries was put up to mark the 1940 Exhibition of the Portuguese World that was responsible for remaking so much of the Belém district. The permanent stone Salazarist glorification of the Discoveries only opened to the public in 1960. From the side, it is in the form of a tall oblong marker; at the base sculpted figures of discoverers line a stylised prow jutting out over the Tagus. At their head stands Prince Henry the Navigator. Viewed head on, the monument appears to be a giant sword-cum-cross with the point embedded in the riverbank just where the entrance opens to the minute museum space inside. A lift carries visitors to the top for views of the marina, though the lip of the concrete balustrade is too tall for most children to look over.

Mosteiro dos Jerónimos

Praça do Império, Belém, 1400 (21 362 0034).
Train from Cais do Sodré to Belém/15 tram/27, 28,
43, 49, 51 bus. **Open** *Winter* 10am-5pm daily.
Summer 10am-6.30pm daily. **Admission** *Cloisters*
600$00; 300$00 concessions; free under-14s.
No credit cards. Map p303 B10.

The Jerónimos Monastery is the major masterpiece
of Manueline architecture, the very Portuguese twist
to the late Gothic. Construction of the church and
cloisters for the Hieronymite religious order was
begun in 1502 on the orders of Dom Manuel I, in
thanks for the divine favour bestowed on the
Portuguese Discoveries. The site had previously
housed a chapel dedicated half a century earlier by
Prince Henry the Navigator. The monastery was
intended to provide a commemoration of Portugal's
maritime prowess, and master architect Diogo de
Boytac was set to work. The original entrance to the
church faced west, though it is now obscured by the
19th-century extension housing the Museu Nacional
de Arqueológia (*see p109*). The sculptural relief of the
south lateral entrance, however, continues to capti-
vate visitors. The hierarchic pile of stonework saints
is topped by the image of St Mary of Bethlehem
(Belém), patron saint of the church and monastery.
Immediately inside the church are the stone tombs of
Vasco da Gama and Luís de Camões. Jerónimos is
famous for the almost mystic quality of light that
sweeps into the nave during the day. A visit during
a choir performance is enough to make even the most
wicked long for heavenly redemption. The exquisite
cloisters were designed by Boytac and completed by
João de Castilho and are often the setting for outdoor
concerts, theatre performances and other gala events.

Igreja da Memória

Calçada do Galvão, Ajuda, 1300 (21 363 5295).
Bus 27, 29. **Open** 3-7pm Mon-Sat; 10-11am Sun (for
mass). **Map** p303 B9.

The neo-classical Church of the Memory was built
on the exact spot where Dom José I survived an
assassination attempt on 3 September 1758. The
suspected conspirators of the Távora family were
brutally put to death in Belém four months later. The
church was designed by Italian architect Giovanni
Carlo Bibienna, who died a few months after
construction began, and took more than two decades
to complete. More recently, restoration work has
been carried out to repair damage from a lightning
strike in 1985.

Palácio da Ajuda

*Largo da Ajuda, Ajuda, 1300 (21 363 7095). Tram
18/27, 32, 42, 60 bus.* **Open** 10am-5pm Mon,Tue,
Thur-Sun; closed Wed. **Admission** 600$00; 300$00
concessions; free under-14s; free for all Sun until
2pm. **No credit cards. Map** p303 D8.

Where's the rest of this palace? Construction began
in 1802 but was interrupted in 1807 when the royal
family high-tailed it to Brazil to escape the approaching French armies. The next half-century would see
work occasionally resumed in fits and starts, but it
was never really finished and looks sawn in half as
you approach it from the Calçada da Ajuda.
Nevertheless it did serve as a royal residence in
the late 19th century and is now classified as a
national monument with some palace wings open as
a museum, while others house the Ministry of
Culture. Highlight of any tour is a visit to the throne
room used by Dom Luís I.

Piles of stonework saints on a towering Manueline pile – the **Mosteiro dos Jerónimos**.

São Bento & Beyond

Parliament, the African inner city and swathes of well-to-do Lisbon.

São Bento

The neighbourhood in front of the Palácio de São Bento, the massive old Benedictine monastery that now houses the Portuguese parliament, takes its name from the building. Perhaps the best approach to this pile is from the narrow Travessa da Arrochela, a typical old Lisbon street with neighbours gossiping at windows and laundry hanging out to dry, and, capping the view at the bottom of the street, the enormous pediment and columns of the **Palácio da Assembléia da República**, as it's also known.

The broad Avenida Carlos I leads down towards the Tagus and the neighbourhood of Santos, and is gathering some strength as a nightlife district, both geographically and culturally about halfway between the Bairro Alto and the Docas. The excellent **Casa do México** (*see p137*) restaurant is in a basement below the somewhat preppy **Café República** (Avenida Dom Carlos I 140A, 21 395 8370). Late-night steaks can be had at the **Café de São Bento** (*see p130*) opposite parliament.

The area around the busy Rua do Poço dos Negros ('well of negroes') to the east of Avenida Dom Carlos I is a quarter that in the 16th century often reeked with the smell of rotting bodies – African slaves were dumped in a depository at the bottom of the hill after fulfilling their useful terms of service. It's now a lively residential area served by assorted seedy *tascas* and cheap restaurants. There's an African feel as well, especially in the early hours when hungry nighthawks troop into the semi-legal Cape Verdean kitchen called **Cachupa** on the upper floor of Rua do Poço dos Negros 73. Almost opposite, the **Indo-Africa** restaurant is owned by Cape Verdean singer Bana, who often sings for his guests. Live music from Cape Verde is also a nightly event at the splendid **B.Leza** (*see p212*) on nearby Rua da Boavista, ironically located in a former slaveowner's palace.

Tucked between the parliament and the river is one of Lisbon's most enduring old traditional neighbourhoods – **Madragoa**. Traditionally home to fado singers and fishwives, in former centuries it housed a colony of African fishermen; their waterfront irreverence contrasted with the holy orders housed in the many nearby houses of religion. The rail line

and Avenida 24 de Julho have since cut the neighbourhood off from the river and the religious orders were expelled in 1834. What remains of Madragoa are narrow little alleys, home to several quality restaurants. For fresh fish there's the **Varina de Madragoa** (*see p129*). Belgian beer and mussels can be had at **A Travessa** (*see p132*).

Palácio da Assembléia da República

Largo das Cortes at Rua de São Bento, 1200 (21 391 9000). Tram 28/6, 27, 49, 100 bus. **Open** no tourist visits but you can watch parliament when in session: from 3pm Wed, Thur; from 10am Fri. **Admission** free. **Map** p307 K9

The imposing façade of the São Bento palace seems as if it ought to face out to more than just a huddle of red-roofed neighbourhoods kept at bay by the stone lions of parliament. Portugal's national assembly is housed in the former convent of São Bento (St Benedict), which was turned over to parliament in 1834 when religious orders were abolished in Portugal. Major renovation work since then has left little evidence of the original late 16th-century structure; it is now noteworthy for some of the artwork contained therein, especially the upstairs historic murals painted between 1920 and 1926 by Rafael Bordalo Pinheiro. The house and gardens behind the São Bento palace are the official residence of the prime minister.

Lapa, Estrela, Campo de Ourique, Rato & Amoreiras

West of São Bento the neighbourhoods are more well-to-do. Lapa, on a hillside facing south over the river, is home to much of Lisbon's diplomatic community. A walk along Rua do Sacramento, Rua do Caetano or Rua de São Domingos provides a view of how Lisbon life can be lived in the lap of diplomatic luxury.

Estrela is the neighbourhood around the late 18th-century **Basílica da Estrela**. Tram 28 passes by here, on the west end of its run up and down the hills of old Lisbon. The **Jardim da Estrela** opposite the church comes replete with swan pond and playground, making it a popular stop for parents with children. On the other side of Rua de São Jorge, the **Cemitério Inglês** contains the mortal remains of Henry Fielding, among others. The area has various other features of relevance to the British expat

On guard for democracy at the **Assembléia da República**. *See p96.*

community. **Estrela Hall** (*see p225*) on Rua Saraiva de Carvalho is home to the English-language theatre group, the Lisbon Players. Around the corner is the Hospital Inglês.

Campo de Ourique is a middle-class district above Estrela that was laid out earlier this century on a grid pattern. The poet Fernando Pessoa was an early fixture in the neighbourhood; his house on Rua Coelho da Rocha is now the **Casa Fernando Pessoa** (*see p192*). At the far west end of the neighbourhood is the enormous municipal cemetery called **Prazeres** – pleasures – with a veritable city of the dead spread out beneath

the lonely cypresses. Today, Campo de Ourique is staunchly bourgeois – it has a high concentration of interior decoration stores and an indoor market with better quality fruit and veg than those in poorer areas (*see p171*).

A pile of pastel postmodernism marks the north end of Campo de Ourique and the beginning of the Amoreiras/Campolide business district. Architect Tomás Taveira boasted in the mid-1980s that his intention with the **Amoreiras** towers, *see p175* – which look like giant Liquorice Allsorts with smoked glass instead of liquorice – was to provide a skyline counterbalance to the Castelo de São Jorge.

Most critical and popular opinion would seem to indicate that he was unsuccessful, but the towers are still there and Amoreiras remains one of the capital's most popular malls.

Just down the Rua das Amoreiras, and just above the busy Largo do Rato, one can escape from all that reflecting glass and ostentatious marble and take a shady seat in the delightful **Jardim das Amoreiras**, located under the arches at the end of the **Aqueduto das Águas Livres** before it terminates in the **Mãe de Água**. The kiosk café serves light lunches. Across the street is the **Fundação Arpad Szenes-Vieira da Silva** (*see p193*), housed in the former Royal Silk and Textile Workshop and exhibiting a permanent collection of the work of Portuguese modernist painter Maria Helena Vieira da Silva and her Hungarian husband Arpad Szenes. The surrounding neighbourhood was set up as an industrial park in the late 18th century, which is why so many of the streets are named after factories, such as Travessa da Fábrica dos Pentes (Comb Factory Way) or Travessa da Fábrica de Seda (Silk Factory Way).

Aqueduto das Águas Livres

Contact the Museu de Água (21 813 5522/fax 21 812 9134) for information on group tours. **Map** p306 H6.
Lisbon's aqueduct spans the valley of Alcântara. Best views are from Campolide train station or roads leading south to Ponte 25 de Abril. Lisbon's aqueduct was built to supply the expanding 18th-century capital with fresh water. Construction began in 1731 and by 1748 the first water was flowing down the line from the main source 58km (36 miles) to the north-west. At the time of construction, the scale of the project was only rivalled by the building of the massive palace and church complex at Mafra (*see p248*). The main span of the aqueduct is nearly 940m (3,133ft) long and bridges the valley of Alcântara on a series of 35 arches, the largest of which rises over 64m (213ft) from the ground. When built they were the tallest stone arches in the world. And they were built to last: the 1755 earthquake that devastated much of Lisbon left the aqueduct unscathed.

Basílica da Estrela

Praça da Estrela, Estrela, 1200 (21 396 0915). Tram 25, 28/13, 14, 20, 22, 27, 28, 32, 38, 40, 43, 49, 60 bus. **Open** 7.30am-1pm, 3.30-8pm daily. **Map** p306 J8.
The ornate white dome of the Basilica da Estrela is one of Lisbon's most beloved landmarks. It was built on the orders of Dona Maria I of Portugal, to fulfil a promise over the birth of a male heir to the throne. Construction lasted ten years, from 1779 to 1789, with statues wrought by artists from the Portuguese Mafra School. Dedicated to the cult of the Sacred Heart of Jesus Christ, the church is richly decorated inside with Portuguese marble, although many of the paintings are by Italian masters.

Cemitério Inglês

Rua de São Jorge à Estrela, Estrela, 1250 (21 390 6248). Tram 25, 28/9, 20, 22, 27, 38 bus. **Open** knock loudly at the gates from 9am-5pm Mon-Sat; 9am-1pm Sun. **Map** p306 J8.
Across the street from the top end of the Jardim da Estrela a tall wall encloses the English Cemetery, which dates back to a 1654 agreement between Dom João IV and Oliver Cromwell over the need for an English protestant burial ground in Lisbon. Intentions were only made good seven decades later, and the first customer officially laid to eternal rest in 1729. The cemetery was originally shared with Lisbon's Dutch community; also, a small Jewish cemetery is hidden behind a wall on the west side of the property. Among those under earth in the English burial ground is 18th-century novelist Henry Fielding, who came to Lisbon to improve his health and promptly died.

Jardim da Estrela

Praça da Estrela, Estrela, 1200 (21 397 4818). Tram 25, 28/13, 14, 20, 22, 27, 28, 32, 38, 40, 43, 49, 60 bus. **Open** 7am-midnight daily. **Map** p306 J8.
Also known as the Jardim Guerra Junqueiro, the Gardens of Estrela were laid out in 1842 across the street from the Basílica. The bandstand near the top end of the park once graced the old public promenade that became the Avenida da Liberdade, and was moved to its present location in the 1930s. The garden is also home to a large play area for children, making it a favourite afternoon hangout for mums and dads, nannies, toddlers and prams. The café on the swan pond esplanade serves as a pit-stop for parents with children.

Mãe de Água

Jardim das Amoreiras (near Largo do Rato), Rato, 1250 (21 325 1646). Metro Rato/bus 6, 9, 15, 20, 22, 27, 38, 49, 58, 74. **Open** 10am-6pm Mon-Sat; closed Sun. **Admission** 400$00; 200$00 concessions; free under-12s. **Map** p307 K7.
The Aqueduto das Águas Livres ends at the Mãe de Água (Mother of Water), a large stone building that looms behind the Socialist Party headquarters on Largo do Rato. Construction began in 1745 and work carried on until 1834. The original architect was Carlos Mardel, who was later much used by the Marquês de Pombal in the post-earthquake reconstruction of Lisbon. Inside, the central tank has the capacity for 5,500 cubic metres of water, and the cool stone interior has all the feel of an eerie grotto. Water arriving tumbles into the central pool over a fantastic sculpture at one end of the space. The walkways around the tank are nowadays used for art exhibitions and a floating platform is often used for performances or exhibitions. Upstairs, visitors can peer down the rectilinear aqueduct passage, or climb up to the roof, an open flat space that offers spectacular views out over this part of the city.

Northern Lisbon

Business, bullfights, Benfica, and one of Lisbon's top cultural institutions.

Alameda Dom Afonso Henriques – bombastic, but still impressive when lit up at night.

Saldanha & Avenidas novas

Much of Lisbon's day-to-day business life takes place in the *Avenidas novas*, or new avenues, off the **Avenida da República**, once a showcase for art nouveau buildings but now dominated by modern office architecture. Indeed, many lisboetas find it hard to grasp what foreigners find so beautiful about their city, because for most of them life consists of the commute from concrete blocks in the dormitory suburbs to downtown concrete office blocks like these.

Yet bits of an older, gentler city remain: **Pastelaria Versailles** (*see p146*) at the start of the Avenida near Praça Duque de Saldanha retains its bourgeois appeal; **Galeto** (*see p130*) opposite is decorated in fine 1960s cafeteria style; the **Clube dos Empresários** at No.38 is a fine art nouveau building, now a businessmen's club.

About midway up the Avenida da República, ringed by brick-red cupolas, is the Campo

Pequeno bullring (*see p230* **No death in the afternoon**), built in 1892. A less bloodthirsty spectacle can be found further up at the Feira Popular (*see p185*), a fun-fair with rides ranging from a water splash to the Casa do Terror, where the usual robotic dummies are superseded by actors in costume wielding scary props. The Feira has lots of cheap traditional restaurants and stands selling candy floss. It's a great place for a low-budget date.

Avenida da República forges north to Campo Grande, home to the **Museu da Cidade** (*see p111*). A few blocks east, the Avenida da Roma cuts through Alvalade, one of Lisbon's more chi-chi residential areas. It is lined with upmarket shops and at weekends is often full of large dogs walking their owners. A good place to watch them is **Café Mexicana** (*see p146*) on **Avenida Guerra Junqueiro**, which links Avenida da Roma with **Alameda Dom Afonso Henriques** and its bombastic Salazar-era fountain.

Avenida Guerra Junqueiro – a good place for people-watching. *See p99.*

Praça de Espanha, Sete Rios & Benfica

To the west, the Praça de Espanha is one of Lisbon's most infamous traffic nightmares at rush hour; the grassy middle lawn now sports an aqueduct arch that used to constrict traffic further downtown. On one side the Palácio de Palhavão now houses the Spanish Embassy, behind which peeks the tower of the Lisbon mosque, put up in the 1980s. Opposite the Embassy are the gardens of the **Fundação Calouste Gulbenkian** (*see p108*), one of Lisbon's most important cultural institutions, which has pleasant gardens and an amphitheatre to boot. The Foundation's museum collection includes some dazzling Lalique jewellery, bequeathed by Calouste Gulbenkian, an Armenian oil magnate who took refuge in Lisbon during World War II (*see p203* **Gulbenkian's tuneful legacy**). The **Centro de Arte Moderna** (*see p192*) on the premises showcases modern painting, while the outdoor amphitheatre is often used for summer theatre or jazz performances.

Opposite, beyond a pair of dilapidated theatre buildings that have interesting repertoires – the **Teatro Aberto** and the **Teatro da Comuna** (for both, *see p225*) – is a ramshackle market with tent-like stalls that sell everything from plastic buckets to imitation CK T-shirts to car radios of dubious provenance.

With its whiff of souk or bazaar, it's known locally as the Centro Comercial do Céu-Aberto – the Mall of the Open Skies. Just beyond Praça de Espanha is the **Jardim Zoológico de Lisboa** (*see p185*) in the neighbourhood of Sete Rios. And while the zoo does host the usual assortment of lions and elephants, along with a dolphin show, an extra relaxing attraction are the well-organised gardens and esplanades.

Behind Sete Rios, with its sprawl of bank headquarters and airport-style hotels, is Benfica, home to the famous football club, a massive shopping mall and hundreds of thousands of commuters. The once quiet, almost rural suburb has turned into a concrete dormitory city over the past few decades. Old jewels still shine through, though, such as the **Palácio dos Marquêses da Fronteira** (*see p101*), famed for its gardens and for its old wall panels of *azulejos* (tiles) that depict exotic African hunting scenes.

The new Benfica, and indeed, the new consumption-oriented Lisbon, can best be viewed in the **Centro Colombo** (*see p175*), a mega-mega mall billed as one of the largest such temples in Europe. Despite moans and groans from traditionalists, the mall's anchor stores such as Habitat, French multimedia chain Fnac and a sprawling hypermarket pull in the crowds daily.

Across from the Colombo centre is one of Lisbon's most revered shrines, **Estádio da Luz** (*see p228*), the home of Benfica football club, until recently a perennial powerhouse on the European stage and a constant candidate in the three-way tug of war with FC Porto and Sporting Lisbon for the Portuguese league title.

Palácio dos Marquêses da Fronteira

Largo de São Domingos de Benfica 1, Benfica, 1500 (21 778 2023). Metro Parque Zoológico then 10mins walk/70 bus. **Guided tours** *House & gardens* June-Sept 10.30am, 11am, 11.30am, noon, Mon-Sat; closed Sun. Oct-May 11am, noon, Mon-Sat; closed Sun. *Gardens* 11am, noon Mon-Sat; closed Sun. **Admission** *Palace & gardens* 1,000$00 Mon-Fri; 1,500$00 Sat. **Gardens** 400$00 Mon-Fri; 500$00 Sat. **No credit cards**.

At the foot of the Monsanto Forest park, the idyllic setting of this palace is a sharp contrast to the concrete jungle of Benfica sprawled across the way. (It's a real obstacle course trying to get here by public transport, so best to take a taxi.) St Francis Xavier supposedly read Mass in the chapel here before leaving for India in 1541. The palace itself was mostly put up in the 1670s, then rebuilt in the late 18th century after the 1755 earthquake. The Sala das Batalhas is still decorated with 16th-century *azulejos* depicting battles against Spain during the restoration war (1640-68), while the rest of the complex of noble halls, patios and gardens is a living museum of baroque statuary. The coat of arms of the Mascarenhas family – responsible for all the luxury – hangs above the main entrance. Guided tours last approximately one hour; be sure to arrive a few minutes early.

Shanty town shame

One of the most shameful legacies of the Salazar regime and the odd mix of feudalism and capitalism that it fostered are Lisbon's shanty towns. These *barracas* have dotted the city's periphery for decades, and are still home to a population far larger than officials would care to admit. There's even one a stone's throw from the glass tower that houses the stock exchange, pictured right.

Some of these *bairros de lata*, as they are sometimes evocatively known (*lata* means tin) are hastily thrown-up slums of metal-roofed shacks and dirt 'streets'. Others are more permanent, with running water and electricity. Many are true labyrinths, with alleys barely a metre wide leading into networks of tunnels and yards where even the police fear to tread.

The city council began tackling the problem in the 1980s by building numerous apartment blocks for the poor. But many of these badly built projects have only perpetuated the despair. The monoliths at Chelas, in eastern Lisbon, are a breeding ground for crime. The situation is similar in parts of Almada, south of the river, and in Amadora, to the west.

In 1997 the film *Ossos* (*Bones*), directed by Pedro Costa and a winner at the Venice Film Festival, depicted the material and spiritual poverty of daily life of a Lisbon slum in winter. It was shot in Bairro das Fontainhas in northern Lisbon, a notorious neighbourhood that is home to immigrants from Portugal's former African colonies who have mixed with the local *arraia-miuda*, the poor who have always lived this way.

The most infamous slum is Casal Ventoso, which emerged as a drugs hypermarket in the

1990s, partly because of its fairly central location behind Campo de Ourique. Social workers who serve the area's shifting population of addicts estimate that as many as 5,000 pass through every day. Junkies crowd the main square on Rua Maria Pia, or crouch to shoot up behind a long wall – known locally as the *Muro das Lamentações* (Wailing Wall) – that is visible from the road. The filth here is overwhelming, overdoses common and life very cheap indeed.

A start has now been made on demolishing the worst of Casal Ventoso's shacks and transferring their long-suffering residents to newly built blocks a few hundred metres away at the bottom of the Alcântara valley. The project is the most visible sign yet that the authorities are committed to tackling one of the city's most shameful problems. Meanwhile, new legislation coming into force in mid-2001, which abolishes prison sentences for the mere use of drugs (as opposed to trafficking), should assist medical and social workers to help those thousands of addicts.

Caminho do Oriente

Long forgotten by planners, eastern Lisbon now offers some major attractions for visitors.

In the mid-19th century, the romantic writer Almeida Garrett described the low hills above the eastern Lisbon waterfront as being full of gardens and fruit orchards. The districts of Chelas, Xabregas and Marvila were pleasant garden getaways within easy reach of urban Lisbon. Indeed, the valley of Chelas has a history that rivals Lisbon's. Legend has it that Chelas is a corruption of Achilles, and that it

was here that the Greek warrior disguised himself as a woman to avoid combat at Troy. To no avail. Odysseus discovered his hideaway in Chelas, near where today's Oriente Metro line briefly emerges into the open between Olaias and Bela Vista stations.

The railway that links Lisbon with Madrid and Oporto radically altered the face of eastern Lisbon. By the 1860s, trains were chugging up

Parque das Nações

Few would have thought it possible. In 1990 the area around Cabo Ruivo was an industrial wasteland of near-derelict warehouses, the municipal abattoir, a munitions factory, an oil refinery and dozens of oil tanks. Gone was the area's heyday, when the Companhia dos Diamantes on Avenida Marechal Gomes da Costa oversaw Africa's diamond trade, and Pan-American Clipper seaplanes docked on the Olivais quay – in front of where the ultra-modern Oceanário aquarium now stands.

By the mid-1990s, a site measuring 330 hectares (815 acres) had been levelled as armies of bulldozers and workers wrought the transformation, readying the area for Expo 98's opening on 22 May 1998. The four-month-long World's Fair introduced lisboetas to a different city, one looking east over the Mar de Palha or Sea of Straw – so named either because bales used to be shipped over from Alcochete and Montijo, or because of how the surface shimmers on sunny days.

Expo closed its doors on 30 September 1998, reopening as an urban district dubbed Parque das Nações (Park of Nations), though development of office and residential areas continues. The centrepiece was and is the **Oceanário**, one of the world's largest aquariums, by the Olivais dock. Opposite, the **Pavilhão de Portugal**, designed by Álvaro Siza Vieira for Expo, now houses the Council of Ministers. The rather uncomfortably concave cement canopy hanging over its ceremonial plaza weighs 1,400 tonnes and measures 50 by 67 metres (167 by 223 feet).

The futuristic beetle-shaped building next door is the **Pavilhão Atlântico** (see p210), designed by architect Regino Cruz and built around a wood framework like an old caravel. It hosts now events ranging from Tennis Masters championships to rock concerts.

However, perhaps the most pleasant legacy of Expo has been the open space along the Tagus. The garden promenades extend north from the Oceanário through a larger park to the new Ponte Vasco da Gama and beyond. The Tagus is up to ten kilometres (six miles) wide here, and this is the only place in town where you can relax by the river without the noise of passing trains or cars. Lisboetas appreciate this; at weekends they flock here in their hundreds, filling the many cafés and restaurants. By night lines of bars and clubs cater mainly for young out-of-towners who don't want the hassle of driving across town.

The **Oceanário** – the world's second largest.

and down a line paralleling the river, leaving in their wake a belt of smokestack industries and warehouses along a working harbour. In from the water, the contrasts can be disconcerting. There are still small farm plots – it's not unknown for cars to have to stop to let a flock of sheep cross the road – though the narrow stone-walled country lanes, or *azinhagas*, are as likely to end in concrete blocks of social housing. Crumbling palaces sit next to industrial tank farms. High-rise apartment blocks look out to the river on one side and to tin-roof slums on the other. This is the 'forgotten' side of Lisbon, facing the Mar de Palha – the inland 'Sea of Straw' – where the river is so wide that morning mist often obscures the other side, but its waters glow with a golden hue at sunset. This is supposed to be the home of the Tágides, the river nymphs described by Luis de Camões in *The Lusiads*.

In early 1998, a broad new highway was built down by the river to link Praça do Comércio with the Expo world's fair that was about to open. The road was given the ringing name of Caminho do Oriente (Road of the Orient) – redolent of Portugal's seafaring golden age, celebrated by Camões. It provides a fast link to the now renamed Parque das Nações (Park of Nations) and the Gare do Oriente rail station, as well as access to the main sights in this area.

Santa Apolónia

The Santa Apolónia rail station is the doormat to Alfama and the end of the line on Portuguese and European rail networks stretching to

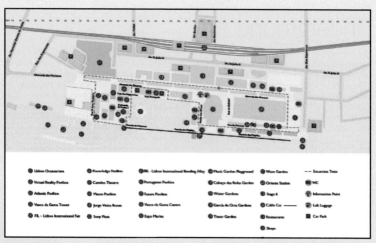

Oceanário

Esplanada Dom Carlos I, Doca Olivais, Expo site, 1998 (21 891 7006). Metro Oriente. **Open** 10am-6pm daily. **Admission** 1,700$00; 900$00 concessions. **Credit** AmEx, V.

The world's second-largest aquarium (the biggest is in Osaka), Lisbon's Oceanário was designed by the American specialist architect Peter Chermayeff. Four holding tanks representing the Antarctic, Indian, Pacific and Atlantic Oceans are ranged around an enormous central tank. There are observation decks on two levels and around every curve in the corridor. Many of the fish on view in the main tank, ranging from hammerhead sharks to rays and schools of smaller fish, would never be found together in the natural environment, but their presence together here is downright dazzling. As in a zoo, you begin to feel sorry for the creatures.

Torre Vasco da Gama

Avenida Pinto Ribeiro, Expo site, 1998 (21 896 9867). Metro Oriente. **Open** 10am-8pm daily. **Admission** 500$00; 250$00 concessions; free under-5s. **No credit cards**. Another Expo landmark, the Vasco da Gama tower is now Lisbon's tallest building, rising 80 metres above the ground. The upmarket Restaurante Panorâmico at the top (21 893 9550) provides spectacular views over the city and the Tagus estuary, although it doesn't rotate as originally planned.

Oporto, Madrid, Paris and beyond. Long the main rail gate of arrival into the city, it has lost some of that status to the monumental new Gare do Oriente rail station up the line near the former Expo site, now known as Parque das Nações. Santa Apolónia was built in the 1860s on the Cais dos Soldados – the Quay of the Soldiers – where troops departed on their way to Africa and India, Timor and Macao. Fittingly, the Museu Militar (see p112) stands opposite the station headhouse. In the last century there was no road to the right of the station; ships would tie up directly alongside the tracks. Nowadays, the port warehouses that sprang up on landfill across the way have been cleared and a new cruise ship terminal installed along with a string of restaurants and nightclubs such as the new **Lux** (see p222) on a waterfront now open to the public.

Old warehouse and monument spaces along the waterfront behind Santa Apolónia are being turned over to other uses. The **Museu d'Água Manuel da Maia** (see p115) is located in an old pumping station back on Rua do Alviela. In 1980, the **Museu Nacional do Azulejo** (National Tile Museum, see p109), took up residence in one of the city's most Manueline landmarks, the 16th-century Convento da Madre de Deus. This once stood on the waterfront but is now separated from the river by a bewildering assortment of streets, overpasses, railways, cranes and shipping containers. The Convento do Beato upriver was built in the 16th century. In the mid-19th century it was annexed to the Nacional biscuit factory but is now being restored and is occasionally used as a venue for special events, such as an annual antiques fair.

Underground art

The concept of underground art took on a whole new meaning in the second half of the 1990s in Lisbon, with the opening of a slew of new and refurbished Metro stations packed platform to platform with panels of tiles by leading Portuguese and international artists. Though controversial for its cost, the Arte no Metro programme has definitely brightened up commuters' lives. What used to be a dull ride along two miserable lines dotted with look-alike, fade-to-grey stations, is now a sort of guided tour through an underground museum.

The traveller can choose among various styles: minimalist, baroque or post-modern. At the deep **Baixa-Chiado** station, the only ornament added to the super-clean lines of Álvaro Siza Vieira's architectural project are discreet gold patterns placed above the main entrance tunnel by designer Ângelo de Souza.

Eduardo Nery's 'deconstructions' of traditional Portuguese blue-and-white *azulejo* art grace the walls at **Campo Grande**. There are bullfighting scenes at **Campo Pequeno** and philosophical quotations on a blue background at **Parque**. At bustling commuter rail station **Cais do Sodré**, António Da Costa's rabbit from *Alice in Wonderland* announces 'I'm late', while José de Guimarães has stamped his inimitable style on **Carnide** with neon and stone renditions of colourful, wobbly animal forms.

A 1997 announcement by the government that Arte no Metro was to be suspended drew protests from prominent figures such as former President Mário Soares and Simonetta Luz Afonso, leading light of Lisbon 1994 European Capital of Culture, who pointed out that the art was only a drop in the ocean of the project's total cost. What was really expensive was – surprise, surprise – the tunnelling.

The government gave in and the programme was back on track. When Expo 98 prompted an extension of the Metro network, it included five stunning new stations. The awesome **Gare do Oriente** was designed above ground by Spanish architect Santiago Calatrava and decked out below ground with huge panels by renowned international artists such as Hundertwasser and Erró. Love-him-or-hate-him Portuguese architect Tomás Taveira went back to the monumental 1980s in the cavernous new station at **Olaias**. With time, the Metro may be recognised as one of Lisbon's best museums.

South of the River

The best views of Lisbon are arguably those you have to cross the river for.

Ferry 'cross the Tagus.

Ferries criss-cross the Tagus between Lisbon and the south bank suburbs of Trafaria, Porto Brandão, Cacilhas, Seixal, Barreiro, Montijo and Alcochete. These boats are the equivalent of commuter trains in other cities and are packed at rush hours, but a trip across the Tagus and back at off-peak hours is an indispensable part of any visit to Lisbon, if only for the view of the capital on the return journey. The railway terminus for trains south of Lisbon is next to the ferry station in Barreiro, but the bulk of commuter traffic docks in **Cacilhas**, about ten minutes by boat from the ferry stations at Praça do Comércio and Cais do Sodré. This terminal serves **Almada**, a burgeoning independent metropolis whose energetic cultural policy includes staging Portugal's most important theatre festival (*see p225*). But in summer, the crowds piling off in Cacilhas are headed for the express buses to the Costa da Caparica and its beaches. Near the quay are some moderately priced seafood restaurants. Further west along the river on the Cais do Ginjal, a river beach and esplanade mark the restaurants **Atira-te ao Rio** (*see p132*) and Ponto Final, with their view of the Lisbon skyline across the Tagus. An alternative theatre festival is staged each winter in an old warehouse on this quay (*see p225*).

Up on top of the cliff is the oldest part of Almada. The view from the *miradouro* behind the Câmara Municipal (City Hall) is one of the region's most rewarding. In 2000 the Boca do Vento elevator opened here; it whisks you to the top, providing even better views. The nearby statue of **Cristo Rei**, arms outspread, guards the southern anchorage of the Ponte 25 de Abril.

Visitors crossing into eastern Lisbon on the Ponte Vasco da Gama pass over an extensive area of old salt pans near Alcochete. This is the beginning of the **Reserva Natural do Estuário do Tejo**, an enormous green space covering much of the marshland at the north end of the Mar de Palha. It's a birdwatcher's paradise and home to hundreds of species. Besides kingfishers, herons and other waders, there is also one of Europe's largest colonies of pink flamingos, who spend their summers in mud flats within easy sight of eastern Lisbon.

Santuário de Cristo Rei

(21 275 1000). Ferry to Cacilhas from Terreiro do Paço or Cais do Sodré, then bus 101. **Open** 9.30am-6pm daily (last entry 5.45pm). **Admission** 300$00; free under-8s. **No credit cards**.
This stiff echo of Rio de Janeiro's statue of Christ the Redeemer gazes across at the city, a rather windswept observation deck at its feet. Worth the trip, if only for the weird sensation of looking down on the Ponte 25 de Abril, which towers over everything on the north side of the river.

Cristo Rei – gazing across at Lisbon.

Bridging loans

Lisbon dominates one of the world's largest natural harbours, formed by the estuary of the Tagus river (Rio Tejo in Portuguese). The Iberian peninsula's longest river empties into an inland sea over ten kilometres (six miles) wide between Sacavém and Alcochete, and more than 20 kilometres (12 miles) long from Ponta da Erva to Alcântara in Lisbon, whence it narrows into a bottleneck before meeting the Atlantic Ocean. The widest part, off eastern Lisbon, is called the Mar de Palha – Sea of Straw – the mirror that gives that special glow to the city on the right bank. It is supposed to be the home of the Tágides, the river nymphs in Luís de Camões' epic *The Lusiads*.

The EU-financed **Ponte Vasco da Gama**.

Fine natural harbour it may be, but the width of the Tagus is an inconvenience when it comes to communications in a modern city. When the Ponte Salazar opened in 1966 the planners confidently predicted that it would carry all cross-river traffic well into the next century. The new bridge was the culmination of more than a century of dreaming and scheming. With a main span of 1,013 metres (3,323 feet), it was the longest suspension bridge in Europe, its two towers rising 190.5 metres (635 feet) above the level of the water. Its four lanes were more than enough to handle all foreseeable traffic. In 1970, they took more than six million motor vehicles across the river between Lisbon and Almada.

But by the mid-1990s the Ponte 25 de Abril (as it was renamed after the 1974 Revolution) was Lisbon's most infamous traffic bugbear, with rush-hour bridge jams lasting for hours, to say nothing of the summer slog to the Caparica beaches and the Algarve. Each year, more than 50 million motorists were squeezing onto the bridge, which had now been widened to five lanes. A new span was needed.

This time planners chose eastern Lisbon. The new bridge was to traverse the Tagus between Sacavém and Montijo, with a view to linking up with the new motorways to Spain. But there was an outcry over this choice of route, as studies had favoured a link further downriver to serve the teeming south bank suburbs. Public outrage came to a head in 1994 when the government announced plans to raise tolls on the old bridge to help pay for the new one. Almada commuters flipped and there were violent incidents at the toll gates as they mounted a noisy blockade. These

buzinhão ('big honk') protests were also significant in that they represented democratic Portugal's first single-issue civic movement.

Construction of the Ponte Vasco da Gama went ahead nonetheless, and despite objections from environmentalists concerned at the impact on water-bird habitats near Montijo. Designed by a team headed by Jean Vassord, built by an international consortium, and financed by a mix of EU, national and private grants and loans, the 17.2 kilometres (10.5 miles) of bridge and viaduct – 11 kilometres (seven miles) over water – opened in March 1998. This one mammoth project accounted for one percent of Portugal's annual gross domestic product. Meanwhile, the Ponte 25 de Abril got a facelift. A sixth traffic lane was added and then in 1999 a rail track that had been part of the bridge's original design but never built. The new railway line links Entrecampos in northern Lisbon with commuter settlements around Almada.

It was soon clear, though, that more than one new bridge was needed. While the Ponte Vasco da Gama is a popular choice with south-bound holidaymakers, it has done nothing to solve beach-related jams. With car ownership and use still on the rise in the city, traffic on the Ponte 25 de Abril has not eased significantly.

At the same time, Lisbon still lacks a direct rail link to the south, and after some dithering the government resolved that this was the priority. The plan is for a new rail-only bridge to link the Santa Apolónia-Gare do Oriente axis with Barreiro. The project is to have a similar public-private funding mix to the Ponte Vasco da Gama, although the authorities hope that this project will prove to be less controversial than last time around.

Museums

Some of Lisbon's institutions could do with a shake-up, but there are plenty of treasures to be unearthed.

Few come to Lisbon with museums in mind, save possibly for the Gulbenkian – the only exhibit in town with an international reputation. That doesn't mean to say the rest aren't worth a visit. Many of Lisbon's museums, both state-run and private, are housed in former palaces or other distinguished buildings, so a visit is often worthwhile even if the contents are unimpressive. And when a fine collection combines with a stunning setting, such as in the **Museu Nacional do Azulejo** (Tile Museum) or the **Museu-Escola de Artes Decorativas** (Museum of Applied Arts), visitors can find themselves spending far longer than anticipated. Most of the major institutions are run by the Portuguese Institute of Museums, the IPM. They have fairly standard prices, discounts and opening times, and often stock the same standard range of souvenirs – tiles, scarves, tiles, ceramics and still more tiles. They are closed on national holidays unless otherwise stated. While most larger museums have English translations of explanatory text, most smaller ones do not. There are rarely free leaflets about the contents of particular

exhibits, and staff are often surly or ill-informed. Presentation can also leave much to be desired. Exhibits are often locked away behind dusty panes of glass, with nothing more than scientific labels to identify them. **The Museu da Ciência** (Science Museum), with its imaginative hands-on approach, and **Olissiponia**, with its multimedia exhibit, might have dropped in from another planet. Guided tours are rarely available except when pre-booked for tour groups, although the definition of a group can sometimes be negotiated down to a party of five or so.

The Lisboa Card sold by the tourism department of the City Council (21 031 2800/ www.atl-turismolisboa.pt) gives free access to 16 museums plus nine palaces and other monuments, as well as unlimited use of the Metro, trams and buses. It also guarantees reduced entry prices to a number of other museums and sights. A one-day card costs 2,200$00 for adults and 880$00 for children aged five to 11. Two-day and three-day cards are also available. The Lisboa Card can be bought at the airport information desk, Santa

The **Museu Nacional de Arte Antiga** offers an overview of Portuguese art. *See p109.*

Miles of tiles at the **Museu Nacional do Azulejo**. *See p109.*

Apolónia rail station, the tourist office in
Palácio Foz (Praça dos Restauradores, 21 346
3314), several upmarket hotels downtown, at
the Museu Nacional de Arte Antiga, and at
other tourist hangouts including the Mosteiro
dos Jerónimos (*see p95*), the Castelo de São
Jorge (*see p79*) and the Zoo (*see p185*). We've
organised museums according to theme, but
it's worth noting that some are clustered
geographically. Belém is home to the **Museu
da Marinha** (Naval Museum), **Museu
Nacional de Arqueologia** (National
Archaeological Museum), **Museu Nacional
de Arte Popular** (National Folk Art Museum)
and the **Museu Nacional dos Coches**
(National Coach Museum), as well as sundry
other sights. The **Museu Calouste
Gulbenkian** (Gulbenkian Museum),
Planetário Calouste Gulbenkian
(Planetarium) and **Museu de Arte Moderna**
(Museum of Modern Art, *see p192*) are clumped
on the foundation's campus.

The downtown **Cinemateca** (*see p190*)
has the legal status of museum but is best
known as the city's only art-house cinema. For
Casa Fernando Pessoa, a museum dedicated
to poetry, and to Pessoa in particular, *see p192*.

Information on temporary exhibitions is
published in the main daily newspapers, as well
as in the free monthly guide *Agenda Cultural*,
available in tourist offices and hotels.

National institutions

Biblioteca Nacional

*Campo Grande 83, Campo Grande, 1700 (21
798 2000). Metro Campo Grande.* **Open** *Summer*
9.30am-5.30pm Mon-Sat; closed Sun. *Winter* 9.30am-
7.30pm Mon-Sat; closed Sun. **Admission** free.
Map p305 L2.

Portugal's main copyright library, which receives
two copies of every book printed in the country, is
open to the public. Bring identification and fill in a
form stating what you want to consult. There is also
some gallery space, housing three or four themed
exhibitions a year – predominantly of items from the
library's own collections, but sometimes including
treasures from institutions around the country.

Museu Calouste Gulbenkian

*Avenida de Berna 45, Praça de Espanha, 1050
(21 782 3000). Metro São Sebastião.* **Open** 10am-
5pm Tue-Sun; closed Mon. *Library* 9.30am-5.30pm
Mon-Fri; closed Sat, Sun. Permanent collection
closed for renovation; to re-open late July 2001.
Admission 500$00; free concessions.
Credit MC, V. **Map** p305 L4.

It is difficult to know where to start in this, one of
the world's great museums, whose exhibits date
from 2000 BC to the early 20th century. From the
ancient world there are Egyptian scarabs, Greco-
Roman jewellery and a larger-than-life Assyrian
bas-relief in alabaster of a warrior from the ninth
century BC. But the sections that stand out are those

on Islamic and oriental art: two rooms full of carpets, robes, tapestries, tiles and glassware, mainly from 16th- and 17th-century Persia, Turkey, Syria and India, plus porcelain, jade, paintings and lacquered boxes from China and Japan. Squeezed in among the Islamic art are artefacts from Christian Armenia – a nod to the founder's origins. In the section on European art there are medieval illuminated manuscripts and ivory and wood diptychs to pore over. Further on is some fine Italian majolica ware, three enormous 16th-century Italian tapestries showing cherubs playing in leafy glades, and a tastefully presented selection of mainly 18th-century French furniture and silverware. Among artists represented by significant paintings are Domenico Ghirlandaio, Roger van der Weyden and Jan Gossaert, Rubens, Hals and Rembrandt, Gainsborough, Manet and Corot. Save time for the end of your visit; the glass and metal fantasies of French art nouveau jeweller René Lalique displayed in the last room will take your breath away. Until July 2001 the main collection is out of bounds because the whole building is being refurbished, but there is usually at least one temporary exhibition. Downstairs is an undistinguished café and the Gulbenkian Library, which contains more than 60,000 books. The downstairs cloakroom is the one to use if you intend to stay on until after 5pm; the one upstairs closes early.

Museu Nacional de Arqueológia

Praça do Império, Belém, 1400 (21 362 0000).
Tram 15/bus 27, 28, 29, 43, 49, 51/train from Cais do Sodré to Belém. **Open** 2-6pm Tue; 10am-6pm Wed-Sun. **Admission** 350$00; 175$00 concessions; free under-14s; free 10am-2pm Sun and holidays. **Credit** AmEx, MC, V. **Map** p303 B10.

Although housed in the same wing of the Mosteiro dos Jerónimos for more than a hundred years, the Archaeological Museum has only existed in its current form since 1990, and seems in an almost constant state of upheaval. When the permanent collection – rather than the odd temporary exhibition – is again on view (no date has been set), visitors with a smattering of Portuguese or who buy one of the decent selection of books in English at the shop can get a sense of the country's pre-history through to Roman times. There is also an impressive collection of Egyptian artefacts. A specialised library is accessible on request (open 10am-noon, 2-5pm Tue-Fri). Surliest staff in town.

Museu Nacional de Arte Antiga

Rua das Janelas Verdes, Santos, 1200 (21 391 2800). Metro Cais do Sodré/tram 18. **Open** 2-6pm Tue; 10am-6pm Wed-Sun; closed Mon. **Admission** 600$00; 250$00 concessions; free under-14s; free Sun 10am-2 pm. **Credit** V. **Map** p306 H10.

Lisbon's largest national museum, the National Museum of Ancient Art can be a frustrating place to visit, with whole wings closed off for renovation. Also, you'll have to ask for a leaflet – they're kept well hidden. That said, this 17th-century palace is the only place that offers a comprehensive view of Portuguese art from the 12th to the early 19th centuries, complemented by pieces from cultures that influenced it. These include Flemish Renaissance paintings, Chinese porcelain, Indian furniture and African carvings. Some of the most fascinating exhibits are products of the stylistic mix fostered by the 15th- and 16th-century 'Discoveries' and empire, such as Indo-Portuguese cabinets with legs in the shape of snarling tigers or topless women. Among the museum's treasures are two Japanese lacquer screens depicting the landing of the Portuguese 'longnoses' on the island in the 1540s, a snapshot of a key moment for both cultures. The museum shop is one of the best in Lisbon, with plenty of books in English, along with the usual tiles and pottery. The café and terrace out back is an calm oasis for the foot-weary.

Museu Nacional de Arte Popular

Avenida de Brasília, Belém, 1400 (21 301 1282). Tram 15/bus 27, 28, 29, 43, 49, 51/train from Cais do Sodré to Belém. **Open** 10am-12.30pm, 2-5pm Tue-Sun. **Admission** 350$00; 175$00 concessions. **No credit cards**. **Map** p303 B10.

The years have taken their toll on this grey, featureless building constructed for the 1940 celebrations that marked the 300th anniversary of Portugal regaining independence from Spain. The contents of the National Folk Art Museum are worthwhile, though: five rooms containing a bizarre but rich assortment of folk art, clothing, tools and toys, musical instruments, fabrics and furniture from the surprisingly diverse regions of this small country. Captioning varies from poor to non-existent, although you can rely on the staff to be well-informed and helpful if you can vault the language barrier. The room on Trás-os-Montes, in the north-east corner of Portugal, contains items redolent of the pagan past: masks, bagpipes and a dummy wearing a kilt-like costume used by men for a dance performed only in the town Miranda do Douro. It also contains some shag carpets that wouldn't look out of place in a British house of the 1950s. The shop sells 'genuine certified handicraft pieces' from around Portugal.

Museu Nacional do Azulejo

Rua da Madre de Deus 4, Madre de Deus, 1900 (21 814 7747). Bus 17, 42, 104, 105. **Open** 2-6pm Tue; 10am-6pm Wed-Sun; closed Mon. Last entrance 5.30pm. **Admission** 450$00. **No credit cards**. **Map** p308 P8.

A favourite with tour groups, the Tile Museum, housed in the former Madre de Deus convent, charts the development of the art of Portuguese ceramic tiles from the 15th century onwards. The convent itself is a treat, including a tiled mural depicting Lisbon before the 1755 earthquake, a tiny Manueline cloister, and a barrel-vaulted church where the warm gilt baroque ornamentation of the altar contrasts with the cool blue of the tiled walls. The museum shop, not surprisingly, has superior tiles.

Sightseeing

Museu Nacional dos Coches

Praça Afonso do Albuquerque, Belém, 1400 (21 361 0850). Train from Cais do Sodré to Belém/tram 15, 18. **Open** 10am-5.30pm Tue-Sun; closed Mon. **Admission** 600$00; 300$00 concessions; free under-14s. **Credit** AmEx, MC, V. **Map** p303 C10.

Lisbon's Coach Museum is back in Belém after extensive renovation work on the 18th-century former royal riding hall (commissioned by Dom João V in 1726) that has been its home since 1902. It claims to have the world's largest and most valuable collection of horse-drawn coaches – 45 of them. The oldest is an early 17th-century coach used by the conquering Philip II (Philip III of Spain) – outwardly austere so as not to incite resentment among his new subjects, but plush inside. The art of coach-making reached its height in three Italian baroque confections used for an embassy sent to Pope Clement XI by Dom João V, where even the wheels are elaborately carved. A teeming group of gilded figures on the tailgate of one vehicle shows Lisbon crowned by Fame and Abundance and a dragon trampling the Muslim crescent. Coach-makers went to extraordinary lengths to make their efforts stand out: the cherubs on the early 18th-century crown coach used in an embassy to Louis XIV of France even have bats' wings.

Museu Nacional de Etnologia

Avenida da Ilha da Madeira, Alto do Restelo, 1400 (21 304 1160). Bus 27, 28, 29, 32, 43, 49, 51. **Open** *Museum* 2-6pm Tue; 10am-6pm Wed-Sun; closed Mon. *Library* 9.30am-5.30pm Mon-Fri; closed Sat, Sun. **Admission** 600$00; 300$00 concessions; free under-14s. **Credit** V. **Map** p303 B8.

Sadly, most of the National Museum of Ethnology's vast collection of items from the former colonies and rural Portugal is in storage. They pop up in its temporary exhibitions, though, which are thoroughly researched and well arranged, and often include video material. A permanent show on rural Portugal is also open to visits (guided if pre-booked) at 3pm on Tuesday and at 11am and 3pm from Wednesday to Friday. Staff are helpful and knowledgeable. The shop has books in English and French. There is a minimalist café (coffee and snacks), so trek down the hill to Belém for something more substantial.

History

Biblioteca-Museu República e Resistência

Estrada de Benfica 419, Benfica, 1500 (21 774 2402/3/recorded info 21 790 1127). Metro Alto dos Moínhos. **Open** 10am-6pm Mon-Fri; 11am-5pm Sat. **Admission** free.

This archive on the history of Portuguese republicanism and resistance to fascism is crammed into a late 19th-century building that was constructed by entrepreneur Francisco Grandela to house his workers. As well as providing a home for 5,000 books dating from the 1870s to the present day, including the archives of trade unions and social organisations, the museum regularly puts on seminars, exhibitions and films, and organises guided tours to sites in Lisbon connected with its favoured themes.

Casa-Museu José Anastácio Gonçalves

Avenida 5 de Outobro 8, Saldanha, 1050 (21 354 0823). Metro Picoas. **Open** 2-6pm Tue; 10am-6pm Wed-Sun; closed Mon. **Admission** 400$00; 200$00 concessions; free under-14s. **No credit cards.** **Map** p304 L5.

One of Lisbon's most underrated museums. Originally commissioned by painter José Malhoa, whose atelier was upstairs, and decked out largely in art nouveau style, the house was later bought by Dr Gonçalves. An enthusiastic art collector, he favoured landscapes and portraits by his chum Silva Porto, by Mário Augusto and by Bordalo Pinheiro. He also amassed a collection of Chinese porcelain from the Ming and Transition periods that rivals even the Gulbenkian. There's a fine selection of 18th- and 19th-century English, French and Portuguese furniture, too.

Gilded glory – **Museu Nacional dos Coches.**

Museu Antoniano

*Largo de Santo António da Sé 24, Alfama, 1100
(21 886 0447). Tram 12, 28/bus 37.* **Open** 10am-
1pm, 2-6pm Tue-Sat; closed Mon, Sun. **Admission**
185$00; free concessions. **No credit cards**.
Map p311 M10.

Saint Vincent is Lisbon's patron saint, but lisboetas
prefer the Lisbon-born Anthony of Padua, patron
saint of lovers and lost objects, perhaps because
the annual festival in his name gives them an extra
day off in June. The Museum of Anthony, right
next to a church that supposedly stands on the site
where the saint was born in 1195, contains icono-
graphic sculptures, paintings and the like, as well
as biographical documents. Some of the exhibits
are truly bizarre, such as soft furnishings or col-
lages representing the saint.

Museu da Cera

*Passeio Marítima de Alcântara, Armazém 2,
Alcântara 1350 (21 397 9095). Tram 15, 18/bus
14, 20, 28, 32, 38, 43.* **Open** 11am-7pm Tue-Sun;
closed Mon. **Admission** 800$00; 600$00 concessions.
No credit cards. Map p306 G10.

The Waxworks Museum takes you on a canter
through Portugal's history from mythical King
Viriato to the 1974 Revolution and beyond. The
scenes from the Inquisition could easily traumatise
young children, though. Visitors who recognise
Portugal's leading politicians will be amused by the
flattering slim-line versions of Prime Minister
António Guterres, former President Mário Soares
and his son João Soares. The mock-up of a fado bar
contains an improbable mixture of showbiz characters listening to Portugal's late fado diva, Amália –
Picasso sits at a table next to Laurel and Hardy, for
instance. The guided tour ends with a blatantly commercial display of china from the factory founded
by Bordalo Pinheiro (*see p112,* Museu Rafael
Bordalo Pinheiro), one of the Portuguese artists represented in the museum – and, believe it or not, this
china shop has a bull in it, albeit a wax one. It is
engaged in a struggle with *forcados* – the amateurs
who wrestle bulls with their bare hands in the fights
staged at Campo Pequeno.

Museu da Cidade

*Campo Grande 245, Campo Grande, 1700 (21 759
1617). Metro Campo Grande.* **Open** 10am-1pm,
2-6pm Tue-Sun; closed Mon. **Admission** 375$00;
free under-18s; free Sun. **No credit cards.**
Map p403 L1.

It was only in 1962 that the city council took over
the 18th-century Pimenta Palace with a view to
founding a City Museum to chart Lisbon's development. While some of the displays are skimpy, they
cover the ground as best they can, starting with the
Stone Age and working through Roman times to the
Visigoths and Moors. Further on, there is a reminder
of the long-standing links between Portugal and
Britain in the form of a bust of Dona Beatriz, the ille-
gitimate daughter of Dom João I who married the
fifth Earl of Arundel. One of the most pored-over

exhibits is a large scale model of Lisbon before the
1755 earthquake. The palace kitchens, which are
covered in tiles, are well worth seeing, as is the formal garden with its peacocks. The displays have
Portuguese text only, although there is a badly
translated English leaflet on the museum's history.

Museu-Escola de Artes Decorativas

*Largo das Portas do Sol 2, Castelo, 1000 (21 888
1991). Tram 12, 28/bus 37.* **Open** 10am-5pm Tue-
Sun; closed Mon. **Admission** 800$00; 400$00
concessions; free under-12s. **Credit** AmEx,
MC, V. **Map** p311 N9.

Banker Ricardo do Espírito Santo Silva – admirer of
Salazar, lover of Amália, and builder of the Ritz
Hotel – was also one of the foremost collectors of
Portuguese applied arts. In 1947, he bought the 17th-
century former palace of the Duke of Azurara and
created the Museum of Applied Arts as a home for
his priceless collection. The range of 16th- to 19th-
century Portuguese, French and English furniture
is the most important in Portugal, and presented as
far as possible in reconstructions of the original
rooms. Tapestries, silverware, porcelain, antique
books and tiles make up most of the rest of the
exhibits. The library is open 1-6pm on weekdays;
the shop sells coffee-table books in English and
items produced in the school-cum-workshop set up
by the founder. It recently expanded to take over the
whole of the neighbouring building and currently
has a staff of about 100, variously skilled in 21
different crafts (the Ritz's suites were originally
fitted out by their predecessors). The museum has a
café with terrace.

Museu Etnográfico

*Rua das Portas de Santo Antão 100, Baixa, 1150
(21 342 5068). Metro Restauradores.* **Pre-booked
guided tours** 11am and 3pm, Tue, Thur.
Admission free. **Map** p310 L8.

The somewhat antiquated Ethnographical
Museum, founded in 1892 in the Sociedade de
Geografia, is a monument to colonial plunder. Glass
cases are overcrowded with textiles, masks, wood-
en sculptures and ceramics from Portugal's former
dominions in Africa and elsewhere. There's little
context on offer, but the museum itself is an interesting example of colonial-era attitudes to the non-
European world. The building – built on the cusp
of the 20th century – is also of interest, particularly the main hall, with its painted wooden galleries.
It's being renovated, and will offer guided tours
only until work is complete.

Museu Maçónico Português

*Rua do Grémio Lusitano 25, Bairra Alto, 1200
(21 342 4506). Metro Restauradores then Elevador
da Glória/bus 58, 100.* **Open** 3-6pm Mon-Fri; closed
Sat, Sun. By appointment only. **Admission** free.
Map p310 L9.

Freemasonry has played a prominent role in
Portuguese history, providing an anticlerical counterweight to the power of the Church and, later, a

non-Marxist pole of thought on the left. Masons took a leading role in events such as the 1820 revolution against absolutist monarchy and have always been well represented in the upper echelons of the army. As a result, the influence of freemasonry is not criticised by those on the left as it is in Britain. The Museum of Portuguese Freemasonry provides a good introduction.

Museu da Marinha

Praça do Império, Belém, 1400 (21 362 0019).
Tram 15/bus 27, 28, 29, 43, 49, 51/train from Cais
do Sodré to Belém. **Open** *Museum* 10am-6pm Tue-
Sun; closed Mon. *Library* 10am-1pm, 2-5pm Mon-Fri.
Closed Sat, Sun **Admission** 500$00; 200$00
concessions; free under-10s. **No credit cards**.
Map p303 B10.

The Naval Museum curators suggest you allow one and a half hours for a complete visit to this enormous collection in the Mosteiro dos Jerónimos. Owned by the Defence Ministry, the display starts with scale models of every type of Portuguese boat, and ends with a hangar full of gilded royal barges – the maritime equivalent of the Museu Nacional dos Coches (*see p110*). Along the way are maps, navigational instruments and crypto-fascist statues and murals from the Salazar years of heroising the country's maritime history. The library (entrance next to Jerónimos church) holds 10,000 books on maritime affairs and general history. Its photographic archive, which includes some negatives from the mid-19th century, is open by appointment only. There's a spacious café by the exit and the attached shop is excellent for scarves and cufflinks with nautical motifs, ships in bottles and reproductions of old maps. No tiles, unusually. An English leaflet is available for 600$00.

Museu Militar

Largo do Museu do Artilharia, Santa Apolónia,
1100 (21 884 2569). Bus 9, 28, 39, 46. **Open** 10am-
5pm Tue-Sun; closed Mon. **Admission** 400$00;
200$00 concessions; free under-18s, over-65s;
free Wed. **No credit cards**. **Map** p308 N9.

A former 17th-century weapons factory provides a highly appropriate setting for the Military Museum. Tiles and paintings on walls and ceilings depict real or imagined battles. The tour begins upstairs, with the first two rooms on the right of the main staircase devoted to the Napoleonic invasions, before a display on World War I. Note the traditional ridged helmet used by the Portuguese until they realised it wouldn't stop bullets and switched to the smooth British model. A series of rooms with elaborately carved and gilded decoration leads on to a comprehensive display of Portuguese arms from prehistory to the 20th century. Downstairs is a vast selection of cannons and a mind-boggling variety of weaponry captured from Portugal's adversaries during the colonial wars of the 1960s and 1970s. Exhibits have Portuguese text only, but there is a useful three-page English leaflet.

Barge your way into the **Museu da Marinha**.

Museu Rafael Bordalo Pinheiro

Campo Grande 382, Campo Grande, 1700 (21 759
0816). Metro Campo Grande. **Open** 10am-1pm,
2-6pm Tue-Sun; closed Mon. **Admission** 265$00;
free concessions. **No credit cards**. **Map** p304 L1.

Portuguese architect and artist Bordalo Pinheiro (1846-1905) had his own ceramics factory in Caldas da Rainha, where he produced colourful and fantastic designs. Examples here include a pig's head on a platter, lobsters in baskets, and frogs sitting on plates or climbing up vases and poles. Among the Toby jug-like caricatures downstairs and cartoons upstairs are many of Zé Povinho, the archetypal Portuguese peasant – a character created by the artist and whose earthy common sense he contrasted with the venality of politicians.

Museu de São Roque

Largo Trindade Coelho, Bairro Alto, 1200 (21 323 5380/1). Metro Restauradores then Elevador da Glória/bus 58, 100. **Open** 10am-5pm Tue-Sun; closed Mon. **Admission** 200$00; free students, over-65s, under-12s; free Sun. **No credit cards. Map** p310 L9.

The baroque church of São Roque is the most sumptuous in Lisbon, designed for the Jesuits by Filippo Terzi. Note the chapel of John the Baptist, fourth on the left, where lavish use of ivory, gold and lapis lazuli attests to Portugal's colonial wealth and extravagance. Built in Italy and blessed by the Pope in 1742, it was dismantled five years later and transported to Lisbon. It took four years to reassemble, not least because of the mosaic above the altar. The museum, renovated in 1998, contains items from the chapel, including Italian goldsmiths' work, paintings and vestments.

Olissiponia – Centro de Interpretação da Cidade de Lisboa

Castelo de São Jorge, Sala Ogival, 1100 (21 887 7244). Bus 37/tram 12, 28. **Open** *Mar-Oct* 10am-6pm Mon, Tue, Thur-Sun; closed Wed. *Nov-Feb* 10am-5pm Mon, Tue, Thur-Sun; closed Wed. **Admission** 600$00; 300$00 concessions; free under-14s. **No credit cards. Map** p311 M9.

A new departure among Lisbon institutions, opened in mid-1998, this self-styled 'multimedia exhibition' occupies three cave-like rooms in the castle. The centre, named after Roman Lisbon, offers a rapid overview of the city's history that is accessible to non-Portuguese speakers, from prehistoric origins to the thrillingly named 1994 Municipal Guidance Plan and beyond. The media used are projected images – using a 3m (10ft) video wall – and narration triggered by infra-red sensors installed in visitors' headphones (the profusion of pillars makes the quality of the reception highly variable). The video-wall sequence has some impressive touches, including a simulation of the 1755 earthquake that depicts, among other things, the collapse of the Carmo church and the tidal wave in Lisbon harbour. It also has plenty of lavish costumes and, unusually for a Portuguese museum, a depiction of slavery.

Children

There are some decent pickings at **Parque das Nações** (*see p184*) and at the **Museu das Crianças** in Belém (*see p184*). But the way that the **Toy Museum** in Sintra is laid out, kids are likely to enjoy it less than adults.

Museu do Brinquedo (Toy Museum)

Rua Visconde de Monserrate, 2710 Sintra (21 910 6016/www.museu-do-brinquedo.pt). Train from Restauradores to Sintra. **Open** 10am-6pm Tue-Sun; closed Mon. **Admission** 500$00; 300$00 children. **No credit cards.**

The small, well-organised Toy Museum houses a huge collection of toys from around the world: dolls, model planes and cars, tin soldiers and dolls' houses.

Costume

Museu do Traje

Largo Júlio Castilho 2, Estrada do Lumiar, 1600 (21 759 0318). Bus 1, 3, 7, 36. **Open** 10am-6pm Tue-Sun; closed Mon. **Admission** 600$00 (includes admission to Theatre Museum); 300$00 concessions; free under-14s. **Credit** AmEx, MC, V.

Although it has no permanent collection on show, the Costume Museum is worth a visit just to poke your head into the rooms of the former Palácio do Actualmente. Walls are decorated with garlands and musical instruments in pastel colours, and topped by moulded relief ceilings. Most original wall tiles are still in place, depicting fruit, flowers and pastoral scenes. If you are lucky, you may also catch one of the temporary exhibitions of various aspects of Portuguese costume from medieval times to the present, which can run for more than a year. The museum has a shop with textiles and some jewellery by contemporary artists. The palace is set in the Monteiro-Mor Park, a sprawling wooded area dotted with statues and grottoes, now surrounded by a dreary suburb. Behind the palace is an upmarket restaurant and terrace with a view of the park.

Literature

Museu João de Deus

Avenida Álvares Cabral 69, Estrela, 1250 (21 396 0854). Bus 9, 20, 27, 38. **Open** 10am-noon, 2-5pm Mon-Fri. **Admission** free. **Map** p306 J8.

There is not much for the casual visitor in this memorial to the poet-pedagogue apart from the art nouveau building itself, which also houses the kindergarten association founded in his name. If you are in the area, though, step in to see a painting by José Malhoa in the office to the right of the lobby, and another by Rodrigo Soares in the office on the left. Inside, in the conference room, there are cartoons and a vase by the multi-talented Portuguese artist Bordalo Pinheiro.

Music

Casa de Fado e da Guitarra Portuguesa

Edifício do Recinto da Praia, Largo do Chafariz do Dentro 1, Alfama 1100 (21 882 3470/www. planeta.clix.pt/casadofado). Bus 25, 28, 35, 39, 40, 59, 90, 107, 206, 216. **Open** 10am-6pm Mon, Wed-Sun; closed Tue. **Admission** 450$00; 225$00 concessions; free under-14s. **No credit cards. Map** p311 N10.

One of Lisbon's newest museums, in a former warehouse at the bottom of Alfama – appropriately enough, given the theme – the House of Fado and the Portuguese Guitar puts on temporary exhibitions about fado, the quintessential Lisbon music, and the lute-like instrument used in it (*see p204*). The shop has a decent selection of recordings and other '*típico*' souvenirs.

Sightseeing

Designs on you

Who would have thought that history-obsessed Portugal could have one of the world's leading museums of 20th-century design? Some critics even maintain that this private collection is the best in Europe – certainly as far as presentation goes.

The Design Museum opened in the summer of 1999 in the Centro Cultural de Belém, a massive modern pile across from the 16th-century Jerónimos monastery, whose brash confidence echoes that of Portugal's Golden Age. It contains more than 600 items: from the angular lines of a 1952 laminated wood and metal storage unit by American Charles Eames to the soft red form of a 1990 rose armchair by Japan's Masanori Umeda; from a slimline 1950 Henning Koppel silver jug to a bulbous 1996 Tom Dixon standard lamp.

These treasures were amassed by Francisco Capelo, the media executive who also brought together the contents of the Sintra Museu de Arte Moderna (see p193). But the new museum, though wide-ranging, is no mere laundry list of styles. Aside from the fact that it arose from the taste of one man, its arrangement is predicated on some controversial choices.

The sequence is chronological, but it starts in 1937 because, Capelo says, that was the year of the Paris International Exhibition where designers first applied traditional approaches to new materials. The exhibits

are divided into three main sections – luxury, pop and cool – and items that jointly illustrate major changes are placed side by side. For example, a 1963 chair by Grete Jalk that (literally) stretches laminated plywood to the limit squats next to Joe Colombo's plastic and rubber creation of a year later: the same play of forms, but in a more flexible material.

Capelo sees the museum as one in a series that, since the opening in 1929 of MOMA in New York, has elevated everyday objects to the status of art. All the pieces were collected with a future museum in mind. Capelo has in the past railed against the fact that the practice – common in the US – of creating a private collection for later donation to a public institution is rare in Portugal, despite the professed patriotism of the country's elite. For him, the Design Museum is a dream realised – a way to help overcome the legacy of a benighted dictatorship that

Museu da Música

Alto dos Moinhos Metro station, Benfica, 1500 (21 778 8074). Metro Alto dos Moinhos.
Open 1.30-8pm Tue-Sat; closed Mon, Sun.
Admission 300$00; 150$00 concessions; free under-14s. **No credit cards.**
Another relatively new state museum, containing some 700 musical instruments and related documents. The collection comprises instruments dating from the 16th to 20th centuries, including Portuguese guitars and an outstanding selection of baroque harpsichords. The museum shop has a good range of books about music, along with scores and classical music CDs, as well as miniature instruments, ties and scarfs with musical motifs.

Theatre

Museu da Marioneta

Convento das Bernardas, Rua da Esperança, Santos, 1200 (21 383 9130). Tram 15, 18. To re-open in June 2001. Map p306 J9.

Founded by puppet-maker Helena Vaz and the late composer José Alberto Gil in 1981, the Puppet Museum is a labour of love for its curators. The 800 marionettes have moved from their former home in Mouraria to new premises, which include a theatre, and are due to open in June 2001. Most of the puppets were used in performances by the São Lourenço company at the Teatro da Ópera. For some years, they also came out for children's shows and tours abroad. But the company has also gone out every year to tour the countryside, reviving the tradition of Portugal's itinerant puppeteers. The oldest exhibits are a couple of battered figures used by the Nepomucenos family, one of the most famous old companies, which folded its tents in 1948 after over 150 years after a family row. Also has puppets from Indonesia, India and China.

Museu do Teatro

Estrada do Lumiar 10, Lumiar, 1600 (21 757 2547). Bus 1, 3, 7, 36. **Open** 2-6pm Tue; 10am-6pm Wed-Sun; closed Mon. **Admission** 600$00 (includes admission to Costume Museum); 300$00 concessions; free under-14s. **Credit** AmEx, MC, V.

closed Portugal off from supposedly corrupting foreign influences.

Capelo is not alone in believing that the museum can give an impetus to design in a country that in a dizzyingly short time has changed from a predominantly agricultural to an industrial, even post-industrial, economy. If the public have direct access to the works that determined the shape of the everyday objects around them, he calculates, it could help counter the lack of taste and sophistication that tends to characterise the output of Portuguese factories. As for students, to pore over a photograph of a seminal piece is one thing; to feel its density and volume another.

Portuguese design is hampered by the small size of the market. There are now young designers producing more functional, less self-absorbed work, while economic growth, European influences, and high-profile cultural events have boosted the visibility of design. But industry remains resistant, prompting some to argue that the museum should do more to showcase successes and institute an active curatorial policy, or even commission work itself.

Capelo, at any rate, is not letting the grass grow under his feet. He has plans for a Fashion Museum, again based on his own collection. Whenever it emerges, it is sure to be presented in a more inspiring way than the existing, rather fusty, Costume Museum (see p113).

Museu do Design

Centro Cultural de Belém, Praça do Império, Belém 1400 (21 361 2400). Tram 15/bus 27, 28, 29, 43, 49, 51/train from Cais do Sodré to Belém. **Open** 11am-8pm daily. **Admission** 500$00; 100$00-250$00 concessions. **Credit** AmEx, MC, V. **Map** p303 B10.

At the other end of the Palácio do Actualmente from the Museu do Traje (*see p113*), but a more recent arrival on the Lisbon museum scene. It was only in 1985, after several false starts, that Portugal got its first exhibition space devoted entirely to theatre. Thanks to private donations, it now has more than 300,000 items, including costumes, stage designs, manuscripts and 100,000 photographs. Attached is a library and a workshop where textiles and papers are restored. There is a pleasant café behind the exhibitions annexe, with a shaded terrace from which to contemplate the overgrown formal garden.

Science & industry

There are several institutions in central Lisbon and in Belém catering to scientific interests, including the **Planetarium** (*see p184*). When it comes to children, though, the science-based shows at **Parque das Nações** (*see p184*) are a good option.

Museu d'Água Manuel da Maia

Rua do Alviela 12, Santa Apolónia, 1170 (21 813 5522). Bus 35, 104, 107. **Open** 10am-6pm Mon-Sat; closed Sun. **Admission** 400$00; 200$00 concessions; free under-12s. **No credit cards**. **Map** p308 O9.

Like the Museu da Electricidade (*see p116*), the award-winning Water Museum and its contents are important parts of Portugal's industrial archaeology. Housed in the first main pumping station to serve Lisbon, it is dominated by four huge steam engines from the 1880s, which were used as pumps. One is set in motion every month or two. The rest of the building contains traces from the history of Lisbon's water supply from Roman times to the present, gathered by state-run water company, EPAL, which owns the museum.

Museu da Ciência

Rua da Escola Politécnica 56-58, Príncipe Real, 1200 (21 396 1521). Metro Rato/bus 6, 9, 30, 49. **Open** 10am-5pm Mon-Fri; 3-6pm Sat; closed Sun. **Admission** free. **Map** p307 K8.

The Science Museum was founded by the University of Lisbon in 1985 with the aim of making science more accessible. It stands out among the city's institutions for the interactive, child-friendly nature of its permanent exhibition, which is accessible to most visitors whatever their language. Phenomena such as momentum, centripetal force, the properties of a vacuum, the course of a pendulum and the speed of sound are demonstrated in entertaining and practical ways. The museum also has a collection of antique scientific instruments, and organises temporary exhibitions, lectures and courses. It recently opened a plane-tarium, which holds sessions Tuesdays, Wednesdays and Thursdays, usually at 10am or noon. They're for school groups, but you can book yourself in if there's space. Once a month, the day after the new moon, the planetarium also has a special hour-long session (normally at 6pm), followed by an observation of the night sky with the museum's telescope.

Museu da Electricidade

Avenida de Brasília, Belém, 1300 (21 363 1646). Tram 15/bus 27, 28, 29, 43, 49, 51/train from Cais do Sodré to Belém. **Open** 10am-12.30pm, 2-5.30pm Tue-Fri, Sun; 10am-8pm Sat; closed Mon.
Admission 300$00; 150$00 concessions; free under-12s. **No credit cards. Map** p303 D10.

Although highly visible, this cathedral-like former power station by the river is tricky to get to. It's easiest on foot, crossing the footbridge by Belém rail station and walking along the river bank to the entrance. The Central Tejo, or Tagus power plant, supplied Lisbon and the surrounding region for more than 30 years from 1918, before being relegated to the status of back-up. Its boilers and generators, many dating from the 1930s, were last called on in 1972. The Electricity Museum opened in 1990. Visitors can wander at will among the giant machines, but the building itself is the main attraction for fans of industrial architecture, with its tall arched windows, red-brick façade and pilasters, pediments and cornices. It makes a dramatic backdrop for the art shows occasionally held here. The museum café near the riverside entrance has home-cooked meals and cakes. An English booklet is 200$00.

Museu da Farmácia

Rua Marechal Saldanha 1, Santa Catarina, 1200 (21 340 0600). Tram 28 then Elevador da Bica. **Open** 9.30am-12.30pm, 2-6pm Mon-Fri; closed Sat, Sun.
Admission free. **Map** p310 K9.

The history of pharmacy in Portugal is shown here through the reconstruction of pharmacies of past times, including a medieval apothecary's shop and the 18th-century Barbosa pharmacy. The Pharmaceutical Museum is the place to see arcane alchemical instruments, along with flasks of secret remedies, 17th-century china vessels, ornate old flask labels and all manner of 19th-century pharmaceutical paraphernalia.

Museu de Historia Natural

Rua da Escola Politécnica 56-58, Príncipe Real, 1250 (21 396 1521/2/23). Metro Rato/bus 58. **Open** 10am-1pm, 2-5pm Mon-Fri; closed Sat, Sun. *Garden* Apr-Oct 9am-8pm Mon-Fri; 10am-6pm Sat, Sun. Nov-Mar 9am-6pm Mon-Fri; 10am-6pm Sat, Sun.
Admission *Museum* free. *Garden* 200$00, 100$00 concessions. **No credit cards. Map** p307 K8.

The idea of this institution, based in Lisbon's technical university, was to create several small museums to organise exhibitions and courses of a 'historical and interactive' nature, tailored especially to schools. But only the Museu da Ciência (*see p115*) is an outright success. The tiny Museu Bocage (open 10am-1pm, 2-4pm Mon-Fri), upstairs through the door on the immediate right of the lobby, has an odd zoological assortment: models of marine mammals, stuffed wolves, and an impressive collection of seashells. Although there are empty rooms, there is no money to expand and the museum may not continue long in its current form. Back downstairs is the Museu e Laboratório Mineralógico e Geológico, a well-presented collection of minerals from Portugal and Brazil. To the left of the building is the entrance to the Jardim Botânico (*see p89*), which contains a library with space for temporary exhibitions.

Museu do Instituto Geológico e Mineiro

Rua da Academia das Ciências 19, Príncipe Real, 1200 (21 346 3915). Metro Rato/tram 28/bus 49, 58. **Open** 9am-5pm Mon-Fri; closed Sat, Sun.
Admission 250$00; 150$00 concessions; free under-7s. **No credit cards. Map** p307 K8.

Entering the Museum of the Geological and Mineralogical Institute is like stepping back in time, not just because of its contents, but also because of their presentation in overcrowded glass cases with mottled labels. These are only in Portuguese, but the head conservationist is helpful and speaks excellent English. The lack of space lends the place a certain charm: you can easily trip over a giant ammonite or dinosaur bone. The largest – an Apatosaurus femur – is in the far left-hand corner of the room devoted to fossils. More than 95 per cent of exhibits are from Portugal, making this the country's most complete geological and palaeontological collection. The spoils include items from Cabo Espichel, the headland near Setúbal where dinosaur footprints can still be seen.

Museu das Telecomunicações

Rua do Instituto Industrial 16, Santos, 1200 (21 393 5107). Metro Cais do Sodré/tram 18. **Open** 10am-6pm Mon-Fri; 2-6pm Sat; closed Sun. **Admission** 500$00; 250$00 concessions; free under-12s.
No credit cards. Map p307 K10.

This combined post and telecommunications museum, which used to be opposite the prestigious Teatro do Trindade, has found its new home in a decidedly more downmarket neighbourhood. Its collection of models includes old mail coaches and modern delivery vans, and telephone and other telecommunications equipment from several decades.

Eat, Drink, Shop

Restaurants

From lightly grilled fish to hearty meat stews, from African *moamba* to Tibetan *momo*, Lisbon's restaurants have something for most tastes.

It's entrecôte or leave at the **Brasserie de l'Entrecôte**. *See p121.*

Lisbon's gourmets make a meal of the fact that their city was the last western European capital to hold out against those awful American fast-food chains. Burgers? Shmurgers! We can do very well on our own fast food, thank you very much! We've got… erm, well… we've got brown breadcrumbed things fried in different shapes and forms so we know what's inside: prawn supreme in semicircles, minced beef in rolls, or chicken in cones. Not bad snacks, actually, and still very much part of the daily diet, but no bastion against the Golden Arches, which are now firmly implanted on many a Lisbon Largo. It's impossible to resist globalisation, sigh the gloomier epicureans, predicting the demise of Portuguese cuisine as they know it.

Well, the good news is that, despite the boom in food habits foreign, lunch and dinner are still very much alive here and observed daily from 1pm to 3pm and 8pm to midnight.

MAKING A MEAL OF IT

Menus are an appetising mix of the fruits of the nearby sea and the culinary traditions of a poor but honest farming hinterland. The best food in Lisbon is simple, honest fare but wherever you go, even in modest *tascas* with

paper tablecloths and chipped white crockery, certain rituals are observed. That means that any combination of cheese, olives, *chouriço* (sausage) and/or fish paste are placed on the table first, with bread. (You pay for what you eat, whether you ordered it or not.)

Main courses are usually accompanied by potatoes or rice, greens or salad, though in more modest eateries, meat and two veg sometimes means meat and two carbohydrates, your steak snuggling up to rice and chips. In traditional places, the antiquated starter, fish course, meat course, dessert routine is de rigueur. It won't necessarily break the bank, but it might bust your belt, as nouvelle helpings haven't had a chance of breaking through here. If you are a vegetarian, bad luck (*see p126* **Veggie vexation**).

Things are very different for fish lovers. If it's not *bacalhau* (*see p125* **Good cod!**), fish is usually sprinkled with coarse salt and grilled, and is as good here as in the best restaurants in any European capital. Generally speaking, the oilier fish give a juicier result. The emblematic Portuguese sardine (*sardinha*) is one of the best, of course, but *dourada* and *sargo* (types of bream) also do well on the grill. Otherwise you may be offered fish that is fried in batter, boiled or oven-baked.

There is a wide and intriguing array of shellfish on offer. The most memorable for many is the *amêijoa*, a type of clam typically cooked with olive oil, garlic and fresh coriander, as *amêijoas à Bulhão Pato*. Crabs of several different kinds and two kinds of lobster are usually available in *marisquieras* (shellfish restaurants). In the warmer months, *lulas* (small squid) are also common, prepared in myriad ways: from grilling to inclusion in a stew.

For diehard carnivores – or on Mondays when lisboetas steer clear of fish because the fleet stays home on Sundays – dishes such as game pie, steak in Madeira sauce topped with a fried egg, or *feijoada* (bean stew with an all too identifiable pig's ear thrown in) are sure to be made according to the chef's mother's recipe.

At present, Portugal's count of BSE cases is the second highest in the EU (though still far behind Britain), so beef may be off your list. In most cases, that's no great loss, since although Portuguese beef has improved in recent years, it is often tough and lacking in flavour.

Pork, though, is generally tasty, particularly ribs (*entrecosto*) and the lean strips of boneless pork known as *febras*. Roast suckling pig (*leitão assado*) is a speciality of the Bairrada region, but widely available elsewhere. The free-range *porco preto* or black pig yields delicious meat. Look for *costoletas* (chops) or loin (*lombo*).

Lamb is usually excellent. The most common dish is plain grilled *costoletas*, but rich stews (*ensopado*) may also feature. Kid (*cabrito*) is a speciality and can be delicious roasted, but the animal has to be terribly young. Rabbit (*coelho*) is also common on menus; as with pork, the meat is often marinated, with tasty results.

If you still have any room after your *feijoada*, Portugal offers some of the gooeyest desserts you'll ever come across. You may be put off when, even in quite fancy restaurants, you are handed a lurid brochure from Olá, the local version of the ubiquitous Unilever. But if it's local colour you want, don't despair; somewhere in it is glued a list of the house desserts, which may include such exotica as *baba de camelo* (camel drool) and *barriga de freira* (nun's belly).

DRINK UP

To wash all this down, lisboetas tend to prefer wine, of which Portugal produces a lot and exports very little. As in most wine-producing countries, this is due to a mix of quality and chauvinism. A good red is easier to find than a good white, or perhaps it's fairer to say that a bad red is even harder to find than a bad white. Portugal remains best known for its port, but there are also many fine table wines, as well as a rising number of more fancily bottled and overpriced mediocrities.

Up north, many port producers in the Douro region now also make table wines, among them some of Portugal's most characterful reds. The Dão region has returned to prominence in recent years and now has a few top producers, some of whom make excellent whites too. The Bairrada region makes both elegant and powerful reds from the thick-skinned Baga grape.

The Ribatejo and Oeste regions just north of Lisbon also produce some very drinkable wines, while to the south, Palmela is where the red Periquita grape made its name. Inland, the vast Alentejo region has been plagued by drought in recent years, but many smaller new producers

The best Restaurants

To put on weight
The **Casa da Comida** (*see p121*), where cream wins out over calorie counting.

For cigar conoisseurs
The **Nariz de Vinho Tinto** (*see p122*), whose cigar menu rivals its wine list.

To see and be seen
Bica do Sapato (*see 121*).

For discreet smooching
The wooden booths at the **Antiga Casa de Pasto Estrela da Sé** (*see p127*).

For the widest range of cheap Portuguese delicacies
Stop do Bairro (*see p129*), off the beaten tourist track in Campo de Ourique.

For homesick Brits
Trifle and bread and butter pudding at **Malmequer Bemmequer** (*see p129*).

To be thankful you're not an octopus
Porto de Abrigo (*see p129*).

For a cross-river view of Lisbon
Atira-te ao Rio (*see p132*).

To be serenaded by a famous singer (if you're lucky)
Águas do Bengo (*see p131*), owned by Angolan musician Waldemar Bastos.

To be serenaded by the owner's mates (most nights)
Restaurante São Cristovão (*see p131*).

Eat, Drink, Shop

RESTAURANTE
Palácio Nacional da Pena

Located in one of the aisles of the Palácio, this space within Sintra's spirit of romanticism is the ideal place for a business dinner or lunch, dinner by candlelight or a thematic dinner.

From 17 h to 18 h you can come to remind XIX century teas. The restaurant can seat about 100 people. Close at Monday.

Palácio Nacional da Pena • 2710 - 609 Sintra
Tel I Fax: +351 21 923 12 08
comercial@gruposilvacarvalho.pt

Grupo Silva Carvalho
Catering Company

www.gruposilvacarvalho.pt

15 Km through marginal road, that leads you from Lisbon to Cascais, you'll find Praia Caffé witch is situated on the Torre beach in Oeiras.

Fresh fish and seafood are always present in most of the proposals, witch you can choose to eat inside enjoying the magnificent view or out side listening to the sea. The cuisine is mostly international.

If the weather allows you may last you visit a little more, doing some beach sports.

Terrace

CAFFE

Praia da Torre r/c inferior 2780 Oeiras
Tel.214418230/26

Restaurant

Paula Marques design

have managed to make some of Portugal's most approachable fruity reds.

Vinho Verde – 'green wine' – from Minho in the north, is light, prickly and ideal for summer.

If you are a stickler for etiquette, the only exception to the fish/white, meat/red rule is that *bacalhau* is accompanied with red. House wine usually comes in the bottle, unless it's bought in bulk, in which case it's served in jugs (*jarros*). Draught beer (*cerveja*) is a popular alternative to accompany seafood.

If you order water, you will invariably be asked earnestly whether you want it *com ou sem gás* (sparkling or still), and *fresca ou natural*. This last query is confusing to the uninitiated, suggesting that the water might not be natural. Don't panic – it relates to whether it is served cold or at room temperature.

THE WORLD ON YOUR PLATE

Being a port city and one-time capital of the seafaring discoverers has daubed Lisbon with a streak of the old spice brush. There are Indian, Chinese and African food joints aplenty and they are usually cheap and cheerful. Brazilian cuisine is also plentiful, just as cheerful but not so cheap. Good Italian, Mexican, French and Belgian food is also to be had, not to mention the odd sushi bar and the all-day Irish breakfast at **O'Gilins Irish Pub** (*see chapter* **Bars**). And you can always nip round the corner for a quarter pounder with cheese, relish and fries.

LISTINGS

We've organised Portuguese restaurants by price-band. Budget is anything where you have a choice of main courses under 1,500$00, mid-range where they rise to about 2,500$00, and top-range anything upwards of that. Other restaurants have been categorised by cuisine and we've also separated out a few *cervejarias* – beerhalls that serve seafood and steaks.

Portuguese

Top-range

Alcântara Café

Rua Maria Luísa Holstein 15, Alcântara, 1300 (21 363 7176). Tram 15, 18. **Open** 8pm-1am daily. **Main courses** 2,950$00-7,500$00. **Credit** AmEx, DC, MC, V.

An eating-out landmark since it opened in the mid-1980s, the Alcântara Café still sets standards for dining in style. A former docks warehouse, this cavernous, postmodern restaurant would be equally at ease in a trendy zone of New York, as would the elegant and attentive staff. The decor – faux-classique steel pillars and yards of red velvet – by António Pinto remains unaltered, effortlessly withstanding the test of time. Some say the menu has

stagnated; conversely, quality remains high. Try the goat's cheese salad, shrimps in lemon sauce, and finally wild berry mille feuilles. Sophisticated, nouvelle style; old-fashioned, generous portions.

Bica do Sapato

Avenida Infante Dom Henrique, Armazém B, 1100 (21 881 0320). Bus 9, 12, 25A, 28, 46, 59, 81, 82, 90. **Open** 12.30-2.30pm, 8-11.30pm daily. **Main courses** 2,900$00-6,700$00. **Credit** AmEx, DC, MC, V. **Map** p308 O9.

Drop-dead trendy joint that is famously part-owned by John Malkovich. But you're about a hundred times more likely to see his business partner, Lisbon nightlife guru and Lux owner Manuel Reis, who often stands at the bar welcoming guests. The large space is boxed off into three eateries: the café-bar, the main restaurant and, upstairs, the sushi bar. The food in the restaurant is outstanding – as are the river views from the esplanade – but the service at times fails to keep up. The head chef, Joaquim Figueiredo (who made his name at the Café da Lapa), offers delicacies ranging from entrecôte to lobster, through crab ravioli in gazpacho sauce, and fillet of moonfish with oysters, spinach and baked tomato. Upstairs, the sushi is excellent, but the waiters are little help if you're perplexed by the menu.

Brasserie de l'Entrecôte

Rua do Alecrim 117-121, Chiado, 1200 (21347 3616). Metro Baixa-Chiado/28 tram. **Open** 12.30-3pm, 8pm-midnight Mon-Sat; 12.30-3pm, 8-11pm Sun. **Set menu** (salad and steak) 2,580$00. **Credit** AmEx, MC, V. **Map** p310 L9.

Lisbon's only convincing attempt at a brasserie has been taken over by Portugália, purveyor of seafood and steak to the masses (*see p131*), but there's been no discernible change in style or substance. The choice is simple – entrecôte or leave. The beef, however, is top-notch and the creamy sauce poured over it truly delicious. If there's no history of heart disease in the family, then the dessert trolley (not included in the set price) is a must and there's no lack of choice – chocolate walnut cake, cheesecakes and mousses abound.

Casa da Comida

Travessa das Amoreiras, Amoreiras, 1250 (21 388 5376/21 385 9386). Metro Rato/bus 22, 27, 38. **Open** 1-3pm Mon-Fri; 8-11pm Sat; closed Sun. **Main courses** 3,500$00-12,000$00. **Credit** AmEx, DC, MC, V. **Map** p 307 K7.

Not for nothing is the Casa da Comida the restaurant of choice for Lisbon gourmets: owner Jorge Vale's mastery of the cream sauce is total and no matter what you choose, every forkful will be delicious, though not for the calorie-shy. A stickler for detail, Jorge, or his savvy maîtresse d'Ana Silveira, receives guests in the lounge before whisking them off to culinary nirvana at one of the tables around the jewel of a courtyard. The style is shamelessly upper-crust, as are the prices, but you will not find a more sophisticated table in the city. Recommended.

Eat, Drink, Shop

Cipriani

Hotel Lapa Palace, Rua do Pau de Bandeira 4, Lapa, 1200 (21 394 9403/21 395 0005). **Open** 12.30-3pm, 7.30-10pm daily. **Main courses** 3,500$00-8,500$00. **Credit** AmEx, DC, MC, V. **Map** p306 H9.

A contender for the most expensive restaurant in Lisbon, and one of the very few places that would take the trouble to fly in white truffles and prepare them properly for diners' delectation. The restaurant is part of the classy Lapa Palace (*see p50*) and was relaunched in 2000 after the Orient Express group took over the hotel. Since then, chefs Franco Luise and Fernando Martinez have turned out impeccable food for impeccably turned-out hotel guests and upper-crust Lisbon foodies. The regular menu is a mix of cordon bleu and posh Portuguese: foie gras with red wine; risotto mantecato with quail; game terrine with creamy apple sauce; and golden bream baked in salt and seaweed. If you're in a group of six or more and want pampering, reserve your table and ask to be picked up: a luxury car will swing by and you'll be plied with champagne on the way over.

Nariz de Vinho Tinto

Rua do Conde 75, Lapa, 1200 (21395 3035). Tram 25. **Open** 12.30-3pm, 8-11.30pm daily. **Main courses** 2,000$00-3,500$00. **Credit** AmEx, MC, V. **Map** p306 H9.

It's only been open a few years, but Nariz de Vinho Tinto is already established on the serious restaurant circuit. Here food, wine and cigars (there's an extensive menu) are treated with respect. Unsurprising, really, since owner José Matos Cristovão is editor of *Epicuro* magazine. The menu is varied, the wine list exhaustive and the quality high. You can even choose which olive oil you want to go with your food. An oaky-nosed restaurant with a rounded, ticklish bouquet.

Pap' Açorda

Rua da Atalaia 57, Bairro Alto, 1200 (21 346 4811). Metro Baixa-Chiado/28 tram. **Open** 12.30-2.30pm, 8-11.30pm Tue-Sat; closed Mon, Sun. **Main courses** 2,100$00-7,500$00. **Credit** AmEx, DC, MC, V. **Map** p310 L9.

When you walk into this Bairro Alto evergreen, you can get the feeling that every eye is upon you – this is because you've entered one of Lisbon's hippest restaurants. So if you want to see and be seen, push open the heavy door, sidestep the velvet curtain and fabulous flower arrangements, and run the gauntlet along the bar, where owners Fernando and Zé make sure everything runs like clockwork. Try the *açorda* (a bread and garlic mixture, like a tasty, runny stuffing) with prawns that gives the place its name. Portuguese cooking at its most successful.

Porto de Santa Maria

Estrada do Guincho, 2750 Cascais (21 487 1036). Train to Cascais then taxi. **Open** 12.15-3.30pm, 7-10.30pm Tue-Sun; closed Mon. **Main courses** 10,000$00-20,000$00. **Credit** AmEx, DC, MC, V.

Up there vying for the 'most expensive restaurant in Portugal' label, the Porto de Santa Maria is definitely among the country's best. Perched on the rocky coast of Guincho, some 40-minutes' drive from Lisbon, it's the place to go for the best fish and seafood money can buy. The tiny shrimps fresh from the bay of nearby Cascais are excellent boiled, while the sea bass baked either in a crust of salt or inside a huge loaf of bread is delicious and visually impressive. Airy, classical decor by Francis and Gabriela Leon completes the picture. Worth a ride out to Guincho, if you're willing to pay for quality.

Tavares Rico

Rua da Misericórdia 35, Bairro Alto, 1200 (21 342 1112). Metro Baixa-Chiado/28 tram. **Open** 12.30-3pm, 7.30-10.30pm Mon-Fri; 7.30-10.30pm Sun; closed Sat. **Main courses** 3,800$00-4,800$00. **Credit** AmEx, DC, MC, V. **Map** p310 L9.

Dating from 1784, Tavares Rico ('rich Tavares') is the oldest restaurant in Lisbon and looks it. The interior is beautifully kitted out in carved, gilded wood to create the air of a princeling's palace or a baroque vestry. Fortunately, the trams that used to run by the front door, shaking the mirrors and chandeliers inside, have been replaced by a quieter bus service. The food is good, but for the money, you can certainly find better. It is an experience, though, so if you're feeling flush and you hear Catherine Deneuve is in town, you might want to book a table. The first floor above is set aside for a low-budget self-service canteen called Tavares Pobre ('poor Tavares').

Via Graça

Rua Damasceno Monteiro 9B, Graça, 1170 (21 887 0830). Tram 28. **Open** 12.30-3.30pm, 7.30-11pm Mon-Fri; 7.30-11pm Sat; closed Sun. **Main courses** 1,750$00-8,800$00. **Credit** AmEx, DC, MC, V. **Map** p311 N8.

Via Graça offers one of the best views in Lisbon, attentive but not pushy service, and fine Portuguese and European food. Tuck into game stew with chestnuts, and slurp a good Alentejo red, while gazing at the illuminated ramparts of the castle or the chaotic city streets below. Take a taxi to get here, as this place is a bit removed from all public transport apart from the arthritic 28 tram. Recommended.

XL

Calçada da Estrela 57-63, Estrela, 1200 (21 395 6118). Tram 28/6, 13, 39, 49, 100 bus. **Open** 8pm-midnight Mon-Wed; 8pm-2am Thur-Sat; closed Sun. **Main courses** 1,900$00-3,250$00. **Credit** AmEx, MC, V. **Map** p306 J9.

A favourite haunt of Lisbon's golden youth (and the more silvery middle-aged), XL built its reputation on steaks and deep-fried potato peelings. One move to bigger premises later and its principal strengths continue to be – steaks and deep-fried potato peelings. Stick with that or the excellent soufflés and you'll be fine. A good place to spot local politicians (it's opposite parliament), TV personalities and soccer stars, if you have nothing better to do.

Eat, Drink, Shop

Understated luxury at **Via Graça**. *See p122.*

Mid-range

O Acontecimento

Rua das Trinas 129, Lapa, 1200 (21 397 7138).
Tram 28 to Estrela then 10min walk. **Open** 8pm-
midnight Mon-Sat; closed Sun. **Main courses**
1,850$00-2,950$00. **Credit** AmEx, DC, MC, V.
Map p3106 J9.
Some members of the Portuguese journalists' club
in which this restaurant is housed may not like the
way the place has been taken over, but you have to
hand it to the Catalans who now run it. Since they
came in, gourmets have flocked to taste house specialities such as onion tart, salmon with brie and
home-made ices in unusual flavours such as honey
with pine kernels. Food is served by multinational
staff in a warren of azulejo-lined rooms with quirky
decorative touches (the lampshades are made from
buckets, colanders and cake tins). The main
drawback is the MOR music, and the threat of a
conservatory being built over the delightful back
patio – presumably to pack in yet more customers.

Bistro XXI

Avenida João XXI, Campo Pequeno, 1000 (21 888
2646/cervejaria 21 796 1842). Metro Campo
Pequeno. **Open** noon-3.30pm, 7pm-12.30am daily.
Set menu 3,500$00. **Map** p305 M4.
Olivier da Costa is the son of prominent Lisbon chef
Michel, and this stylish new venture near the Campo
Pequeno bullring deserves as much success as the
family's past ventures. The style is French and the
set menu includes a dozen or so hot and cold
starters: fried Camembert with fruit jelly; Polish
salad; sautéed aubergine in tomato sauce; fried

mushrooms with ham… they all arrive on your table
in quick succession on pretty pastel-coloured plates.
Then there's a choice of three hearty meat dishes
(this is not a place for vegetarians). Service is ultra-
efficient and the restaurant cosy. It's pricier than da
Costa's old place near the castle, but staggeringly
good value all the same. The only drawback is the
limited wine list. The *cervejaria* downstairs has an
à la carte menu, but it's not a patch on the bistro.

Charcutaria

Rua do Alecrim 47A, Chiado, 1200 (213423845).
Metro Baixa-Chiado/28 tram. **Open** noon-3pm, 8-
11pm Mon-Fri; 7-11pm Sat; closed Sun. **Main**
courses 1,950$00-3,000$00. **Credit** AmEx, DC, MC,
V. **Map** p 310 L9.
A spin-off from a long-established restaurant in
Campo de Ourique, this is better placed to catch
passing trade. The theme is the same, though: solid
Portuguese staples, mostly from the Alentejo,
presented with flair in light, pleasant surroundings.
As so often, greater sophistication means a
decrease in the size of the portions, but you're
unlikely to go home hungry. Follow a starter –
tomatada (a tasty tomato paste) or *empadas* (meat
pies) – with a hearty dish of *arroz de lebre* (hare
rice), *cabrito assado* (roast kid) or a *porok* dish from
the Alentejo. To finish, split one of the achingly
sweet desserts.

Coelho da Rocha

Rua Coelho da Rocha 104, Campo de Ourique, 1300
(21 390 0831). Tram 28 then 5min walk. **Open**
12.30-3pm, 7.30-11.30pm Mon-Sat; closed Sun. **Main**
courses 1,500$00-2,700$00. **Credit** AmEx,MC, V.
Map p306 H8.

Traditional recipes and top-quality ingredients are the secret of this restaurant's success. It has built a faithful customer base – held in thrall by dishes such as *amêijoas à Bulhão Pato*, baked fish or game stew. Some make a special trip on Tuesdays for the *arroz de cabidela* (rice with giblets) – a lot tastier than it sounds. The place is somewhat formal; service is correct rather than friendly. Wine is not sold by the glass, but there are several affordable half bottles.

Çuciadadi de Barrancú

Rua de Misericórdia 74, Chiado, 1200 Lisboa (21 347 8166). Metro Baixa-Chiado, tram 28. **Open** noon-2am Mon-Fri; 8am-2am Sat; closed Sun. Closed last wk of Aug. **Main courses** 1,500$00-3,000$00. **Credit** AmEx, MC, V. **Map** p310 L9.

The tongue-twisting name is neither Catalan nor Romanian, but Barranquenho, a sibilant dialect spoken in the Alentejo border town of Barrancos. Its people fiercely defend local traditions, including the annual lethal bullfights. The menu of the so-called 'Barrancos Society' is meat-oriented, though it does include gazpacho and *pimentada* (mixed grilled peppers). For a meaty snack, try *presunto de bolota* (cured ham from pigs fed on acorns, or *variedade de enchidos* (mixed sausages). To go with it, a bottle of Alentejo red is probably the best bet; the house wine is sweet, fizzy and best avoided. There is Sevillana dancing after 10.30pm on Tuesdays and Thursdays.

Doca 6

Doca de Santo Amaro, Armazém 6, Docas, 1350 (21 395 7905). Tram 15, 17, 18/train from Cais do Sodré to Alcântara-Mar/20, 22, 38 bus. **Open** 12.30-3pm, 7.30pm-midnight Mon-Fri; 12.30-3.30pm, 7.30pm-midnight Sat, Sun. **Main courses** 1,900$00-3,200$00. **Credit** AmEx, MC, V.

This is one of only two eateries in the Docas that is really worth recommending. The food is mainly standard fare, gentrified a bit, but Doca 6 scores with its mini-lunch menu, served out of doors on the dockside, in the shadow of the Ponte 25 de Abril. Octopus salad and the Portuguese classic *arroz de pato* (oven-baked duck risotto) are the musts.

Espaço Lisboa

Rua da Cozinha Económica 16, Alcântara, 1300 (21 361 0212). Tram 15, 18. **Open** 8pm-2am Mon, Wed-Sun; closed Tue. **Main courses** 1,900$00-3,900$00. **Credit** AmEx, DC, MC, V.

This homage to Lisbon teeters on the edge of kitsch, but if you're in Alcântara it's worth stopping by to see the latest creation by António Pinto, designer of the Alcântara Café (*see p121*). Tables are laid out in a mock-up of a Lisbon square, bordered by *típico* shops and stalls. There's a grocer's (where you fetch your starters), a newspaper kiosk, a coffee museum and a bar. As for the food, it's nothing special, not always as hot as it should be, and rather overpriced, but you will get by if you stick with well-known standards such as *bacalhau com natas* or steak.

Good cod !

Bacalhau (dried and salted cod) is on every typical menu, in every supermarket, is consumed in vast quantities on Christmas Eve and is the core ingredient in so many recipes that you can eat it a different way each day of the year – or so the locals claim. In short, it's the national dish and it's everywhere.

Restaurants specialising in Portuguese fare, from chic to basic, will generally have a *bacalhau* option on offer and you'll find the *pastel de bacalhau* (a sort of deep-fried fishcake) in the savoury snack selection of just about any *pastelaria*.

Should you want to make any of the hundreds of recipes yourself, *bacalhau* pieces are available in neat little packets from the freezer of the local supermarket, but hey, why do it the easy way when there's a tradition to be celebrated? The dedicated prefer to buy it dried and salted and then laboriously set about reversing the process by soaking it for a day or two before throwing it in the cooking pot. Tradition it may be, but a glimpse and a whiff of one of these shrivelled carcasses in its untreated state may well put you off; mouth-watering they ain't.

If you're still tempted to bring such a thing into your home, you'll find them piled high in the open doorways of delis such as **Manteigueria Silva** (see p167) and the cluster of stores along the Rua do Arsenal.

The Portuguese love affair with *bacalhau* goes back five hundred years, though these days it's mostly imported from Norway and fishing crisis after fishing crisis means that the national favourite is becoming increasingly difficult for ordinary citizens to afford.

Eat, Drink, Shop

Veggie vexation

Os Tibetanos' heavenly patio. *See p136.*

Lisbon is no friend to vegetarians. The fish is fantastic and the meat can be marvellous, but the typical menu otherwise contains only cheese, an omelette and a salad. The cheeses are excellent, but rarely will the salad amount to anything more imaginative than tomato, lettuce and a few onion rings or grated carrot. Some soups are made without meat stock, but beware the innocent-sounding *caldo verde* – a chunk of *chouriço* (smoked sausage) lurks in this green broth.

And, it's not just that there's nothing to eat; you're up against pretty implacable attitudes. Lisboetas see vegetarianism as a challenge. ('Come on, is a squid really any more intelligent than a carrot?'). Fellow diners may make sniggering jokes, pretending to hide their steak from your view. Asking if the kitchen can make something meatless seems to short-circuit most chefs' imagination. Even in upmarket places you're likely to get a plate of boiled veg, bereft of sauce or sparkle.

Sparkle is also lacking in Lisbon's specialist vegetarian restaurants, most of which might as well offer a free hair shirt with every order. If you don't eat meat or fish, the philosophy goes, then you're not allowed to

enjoy yourself. Expect dessicated tofu rissoles, rice without spice, bland vegetables, worthy salads. Vegans won't starve, but they will be forced to concede that if this is what Portuguese think vegetarians want to eat, it's not surprising they're seen as bonkers.

Most fully vegetarian places are cheap self-service canteens, more for lunch than dinner. The downstairs diner at the **Celeiro** health-food supermarket (see p169) is the biggest and most central. **A Colmeia** (Rua da Emenda 110, Chiado; 347 0500; open noon-7pm Mon-Fri; 12.30-2.30pm Sat), an airy upstairs dining room near Largo do Chiado, offers vegetarian and macrobiotic daily specials.

Over in Estefânia, **Espiral** (Praça Ilha do Faial 14, Estefânia; 357 3585; open 9am-10.30pm daily) has a downstairs restaurant with vegetarian, macrobiotic and 'Chinese' choices, an upstairs snack bar serving salads and veggie versions of those breadcrumbed things, plus a health-food shop and bookstore. As elsewhere, fare is acceptable rather than mouth-watering.

The café at the Gulbenkian's **Centro de Arte Moderna** (*see p192*) has a salad buffet, plus good cakes and fruit salads – the best self-service lunch in town.

For a decent dinner, try **Os Tibetanos** just off the Avenida da Liberdade (the only purely vegetarian place that makes our main listings; *see p136*), or any of the Italian or Indian restaurants. **Hell's Kitchen** in the Bairro Alto offers vegetarian choices (*see p135*), and **Blues Café** (*see p135*) is another option, though not if you're the impulsive type. Its menu has no vegetarian dishes, but if you phone ahead (a day if possible) the cook promises to rustle up something rather more interesting than boiled vegetables. But the *Time Out Lisbon Guide* Golden Cucumber for Tastiest Vegetarian Treats goes to the **São Caetano** in Lapa (*see p135*).

Mercado de Santa Clara

Campo Santa Clara, Graça, 1200 (21 887 3986). Tram 28/12 bus. **Open** 12.30-2.30pm, 8-10.30pm Tue-Sun; closed Mon. **Main courses** 1,850$00-2,550$00. **Credit** AmEx, DC, MC, V. **Map** p308 N9.
Above the market hall at the centre of Tuesday's and Saturday's Feira da Ladra flea market (*see p171*), this restaurant has a stunning view of the gleaming white dome of the neighbouring Panteão Nacional de Santa Engrácia. Carlos Braz Lopes, a gourmet who runs culinary courses in his

Cozinhomania cooks' shop across town, makes sure the menu is up to scratch. On Sunday nights there's a Portuguese *feijoada* buffet that packs the place out, so if you want to try these beans, you'd better reserve.

Paris

Rua dos Sapateiros 126, Baixa, 1200 (21 346 9797). Metro Baixa-Chiado/12, 28 tram. **Open** noon-3pm, 7-10pm daily. **Main courses** 1,500$00-3,000$00. **Credit** AmEx, MC, V. **Map** p310 M9.

In a street that seems to be full of tourist traps, Paris is an exception. First opened in 1958, its generous portions and varied Portuguese menu have made it an institution of the Baixa. The decor hasn't changed much since the place opened, either.

Poleiro

Rua de Entrecampos 30A, Entrecampos, 1700 (21 797 6265). Metro Entrecampos. **Open** noon-3pm, 7.15-11pm Mon-Fri; noon-3pm Sat; closed Sun. **Main courses** 2,300$00-2,950$00. **Credit** MC, V. **Map** p305 M3.

An Aladdin's cave of Portuguese cuisine. If there's no room out front, pass through to the second room or on to the third. The maze-like feel creates a cosy atmosphere, making this a good place during the winter. Food is also heartwarming – nothing fancy but prepared and cooked with care. Start with fried aubergines, and then move on to a dark, delicious cuttlefish risotto or fried kid with coriander *açorda*.

Primavera

Travessa da Espera 34, Bairro Alto, 1200 (21 342 0477). Metro Baixa-Chiado/28 tram. **Open** noon-3pm, 7-11pm Mon-Sat; closed Sun. **Main courses** 1,300$00-5,000$00. **No credit cards. Map** p310 L9.

If you want good, honest Portuguese food, look no further. A Primavera do Jerónimo, usually shortened to Primavera, has it all: grilled fish, *bacalhau* dishes aplenty, clams in white wine, game, delicately grilled liver and other meaty concoctions from the north. The kitchen, on full view from the minute, tiled dining room, is impressively spotless, its hanging pans and pots polished to a shine. If he's in a good mood, Senhor Manuel might show you the portrait of Josephine Baker hanging above the table where she used to eat. The proverbs inscribed on the *azulejos* make good talking points. Recommended.

Book ahead for **A Tasquinha d'Adelaide**.

A Tasquinha d'Adelaide

Rua do Patrocínio 70-74, Campo de Ourique, 1350 (21 396 2239). Tram 25, 28/9 bus. **Open** 8.30pm-2am Mon-Sat; closed Sun. **Main courses** 2,300$00-3,000$00. **Credit** AmEx, DC, MC, V. **Map** p306 H8.

Tasquinha means little tavern, which already gives you a clue about this place. Tucked away on a side street in Campo de Ourique, it can seat just 24 guests at a time. So reserve and be punctual, as there's fierce competition for the privilege of tasting the culinary arts of painter-cook Maria Adelaide Miranda and her architect husband Pedro. Lots of good, hearty oven-baked stuff like leg of lamb or *pernil à patroa* (ham shank cooked the boss's way). Nibbles include *morcela assada*, a delicious toasted black pudding, and *pão de milho*, corn bread. Recommended.

Budget

Antiga Casa de Pasto Estrela da Sé

Largo de Santo António da Sé 4, Sé, 1100 (21 887 0455). Tram 28. **Open** noon-3pm, 7-10pm Mon-Fri; closed Sat, Sun. **Main courses** 990$00-2,200$00. **No credit cards. Map** p311 M10.

Once an age-old tradition in Lisbon, the *casas de pasto*, cheap restaurants with simple, make-the-most-of-the-ingredients-you've-got food, have all but died out. Opposite the Sé and the Igreja de Santo António, the Estrela da Sé is a good place to go and sin after visiting these holy places. The food is simple and good, but the best feature is the curtained wooden booths that enclose the tables. Dating from the prudish 19th century, they allowed at least a modicum of amorous activity at the table.

Bonjardim

Travessa de Santo Antão 11-12, Restauradores, 1150 (21 342 4389/7424). Metro Restauradores. **Open** noon-11.30pm daily. **Main courses** 950$00-1,780$00. **Credit** AmEx, DC, MC, V. **Map** p310 L8.

Although its subtitle 'Rei dos Frangos' is a bit of a joke in translation, the 'King of Chickens is a Lisbon favourite for a quick, cheap meal. Chicken grilled over charcoal is ordered by the bird and comes accompanied by chips, mixed salad and the ubiquitous (and thankfully optional) hot piri-piri sauce. The owners aim for quick turnover, so service is fast, verging on brusque. The restaurant has two buildings, one either side of the street; upstairs in the southern building is the more 'Lisbon' option.

Casa do Alentejo

Rua das Portas de Santo Antão 58, Baixa, 1150 (21 346 9231). Metro Restauradores. **Open** noon-3pm, 7-10pm daily. **Main courses** 1,500$00-1,800$00. **Credit** MC, V. **Map** p310 M9.

Lunch in grand old style and at yesterday's prices in this fabulous old arabesque building just behind Restauradores. First climb the stairs to the interior courtyard with its Moorish gallery, then up to one of the tall dining rooms tiled with fabulous blue and white azulejos. The food is predictable and not that great, really, but this is a true Lisbon experience.

Time Out

'THE GREATEST LONDON AUTHORITY'

Coutada

*Rua da Bempostinha 18, Campo de Santana, 1150
(21 885 2054). Bus 100.* **Open** noon-3pm, 7-10pm
Mon-Sat; closed Sun. **Main courses** 1,100$00-
1,905$00. **Credit** AmEx, MC, V. **Map** p307 M7.
A small neighbourhood restaurant that specialises
in skewering meat, fish, prawns and squid in various combinations, grilling them over charcoal and
then serving them hanging vertically over your
plate. The result is delicious and inexpensive. For
the brave, there is also usually *arroz de cabidela*, rice
cooked with giblets and blood.

Fidalgo

*Rua da Barroca 27, Bairro Alto, 1200 (21 342 2900).
Metro Baixa-Chiado/28 tram.* **Open** noon-3pm, 7-
11pm Mon-Sat; closed Sun. **Main courses** 1,100$00-
1,750$00. **Credit** AmEx, MC, V. **Map** p310 L9.
Fidalgo is a tasca at heart that's grown up into a
more sophisticated restaurant. Here you'll find the
usual Portuguese fish and meat dishes, usually well
prepared. The cook sometimes displays an urge to
get modern, with fads such as ostrich steaks appearing on the menu only to disappear after a week or
so. The desserts are deliciously different for Lisbon:
profiteroles, wild berry tart and other things that
don't contain eggs, almonds and sugar.

Malmequer Bemmequer

*Rua de São Miguel 23-25, Alfama 1100 (21 887
6535).* **Open** 7.30-10pm Tue; noon-3pm, 7.30-10pm
Wed-Sun; closed Mon. **Main courses** 1,380$00-
1,850$00. **Credit** AmEx, MC, V. **Map** p311 N10.
Slap bang in front of the church of São Miguel
(ground zero for June's Santo António festivities) this
is inevitably a bit of a tourist trap. But the food is
tasty and wins points for presentation. The *barbecue dos diabos* (chicken and veal with cayenne pepper) is a favourite with regulars, but other meat
dishes and the grilled fish are also reliable. There are
also desserts for homesick Brits: trifle and bread and
butter pudding, listed as 'English pudding'.

Porto de Abrigo

*Rua dos Remolares 16-18, Cais do Sodré, 1200 (21
346 0873). Metro Cais do Sodré/25 tram/13, 60,
104 bus.* **Open** 12.30-3pm, 7-10.30pm Mon-Fri;
12.30-3.30pm, 7-10.30pm Sat; closed Sun. **Main
courses** 800$00-1,600$00. **No credit cards.**
Map p310 L10.
A safe, sheltered harbour for everyone – unless you
happen to be an octopus, in which case you'll be mer-
cilessly thrown into a pot with rice and a secret cock-
tail of condiments and served up to diners as *arroz
de polvo*. The duck baked with olive sauce is also
worth trying. Behind the Mercado da Ribeira, Porto
de Abrigo is a piece of ungentrified docklands.

1° de Maio

*Rua da Atalaia 8, Bairro Alto, 1200 (21 342 6840).
Metro Baixa-Chiado/28 tram.* **Open** noon-3pm, 7-
10.30pm Mon-Fri; 7-10.30pm Sat; closed Sun. **Main
courses** 1,300$00-2,500$00. **Credit** AmEx, MC, V.
Map p310 L9.

Tile style – **Casa do Alentejo**. *See p127.*

The queue outside the saloon-style swing doors at
about 8.30pm every week night testifies to the popularity of this Bairro Alto classic. The usual honest
mix of grilled fish and meat dishes is served rapidly and with a smile, at reasonable prices. A safe bet.

Stop do Bairro

*Rua Tenente Ferreira Durão 55A, Campo de
Ourique, 1300 (21 388 8856). Tram 28 then 5min
walk.* **Open** noon-3.30pm, 7-10.30pm Tue-Sun; closed
Mon. **Main courses** 950$00-1,900$00. **Credit**
AmEx, MC, V. **Map** p306 H7.
Though famed locally for turning out top-notch
Portuguese dishes at low prices for the last 20 years,
Stop do Bairro is an unpretentious place – walls
are decked with slogans of the 'You don't have to
be mad…' variety. The menu takes in *iscas à
portuguesa* (fried liver), *arroz de tamboril* (monkfish
rice), *leitão assado à angolana* (spicy roast suckling
pig with orange), and – from the Azores – *coelho recheado* (stuffed rabbit). Helpings are generous but
save some room; most of the desserts are eggy and
a challenge even to the gluttonous. The wine list is
impressive for this price bracket, from a drinkable
house Leziria at 650$00 and a 120,000$00 Barca
Velha. Recommended.

Varina de Madragoa

*Rua das Madres 34-36, Madragoa, 1200 (21 396
5533). Bus 6, 13, 49.* **Open** 12.30-3.30pm, 7.30-
11.30pm Tue-Fri, Sun; 7.30-11.30pm Sat; closed Mon.
Main courses 1,300$00-2,500$00. **Credit** AmEx, V.
Map p306 J9.
If you are in Madragoa, the 'fishwife' is as good a
place to eat as any. The fish is normally fresh and
good, but there is meat and a famous *bacalhau à
varina* also. Good solid food and portions.

Late-night eats

Particularly around the Docas and the Avenida 24 de Julho, there are lots of stands selling sandwiches, burgers, *bifanas* (braised pork steaks) and *pão com chouriço* (smoked-sausage roll), but first check how clean they look. See p219 **Meals on wheels**.

There are also plenty of places where you can sit down to snack or dine until late. In addition to those reviewed here, try **Massima Culpa** (see p136), **Alcântara Café** (see p121), **Café no Chiado** (see p143), **A Tasquinha d'Adelaide** (see p127), **Portugália** (see p131), **Solmar** (see p131), **A Picanha** (see p132), **Porcao** (see p133), **Os Tibetanos** (see p136) and **Stravaganza** (see p136), all of which serve food until 2am or so. So do quite a few bars and cafés, such as **Costa do Castelo** (see p152) and, in the Docas, **Esplanada Doca de Santo** (see p145), which does a mean *açorda de gambas,* served with panache – in a loaf of bread. The most atmospheric option is the semi-legal Cape Verdean kitchen known as **Cachupa** upstairs at Rua Poço dos Negros 73 (no phone) in São Bento. It's open all night at weekends, but can sometimes be a bit heavy.

Acinox

Largo dos Santos 1A, Santos, 1200 (no phone). Tram 25. **Open** 6pm-6am daily. **Main courses** 650$00-1,00$00. **No credit cards. Map** p306 J9.
Strategically situated between Cais do Sodré and the clubs of Avenida 24 de Julho, this simple canteen with a pleasant esplanade serves the *comida forte* ('strong food') traditionally favoured by Lisbon night-owls: soup, bean-based dishes, *bifanas* and *pão com chouriço.*

Café de São Bento

Rua de São Bento 212, São Bento, 1200 (21 395 2911). Tram 28. **Open** 6pm-2am daily. **Main courses** 2,650$00-3,150$00. **Credit** AmEx, MC, V. **Map** p307 K9.
This pub proclaims itself 'Primus Inter Bares' on a brass plaque out front, a pun on its status as a watering hole for politicians and staff from parliament, over the road. Contrary to plush, wood-panelled appearances, it's a relative newcomer, founded in 1982. Steaks are the thing to eat here. They're not cheap, but then you are paying for all that wood panelling and upholstery.

Galeto

Avenida da República 14, Saldanha, 1050 (21 356 0269). Metro Saldanha. **Open** *Snack bar* 7.30am-3am daily. *Restaurant* noon-4pm daily. **Main courses** *Snack bar* 1,490$00-2,850$00 before 11.30pm; 1,640$00-3,140$00 after 11.30pm. **Credit** MC, V. **Map** p305 M5.
A slice of 1960s nostalgia, with its wood panelling, complex system of curving formica-topped bars, and PVC-covered stools, Galeto has a special place in lisboetas' hearts. It's a reliable place for a post-film, post-club, post-anything snack or meal, with an impressively varied menu. It also does a decent breakfast for 490$00 (or 540$00 after 11.30pm if that's when you want it), weekly specials and a great range of triple-decker sandwiches. Galeto is also good for people watching; it attracts an incredible variety of fauna, from leather-clad young couples to moustachioed middle-aged singletons who look as though they might be plotting their next novel.

A Merendinha

Avenida 24 de Julho 54G, Santos, 1200 (21 397 2726). Tram 15, 18. **Open** 7pm-6.45am Mon-Thur, Sun; 7pm-8am Fri, Sat. **Main courses** 700$00-1,000$00. **No credit cards. Map** p307 K10.
The leading purveyor of early-morning *caldo verde* and *pão com chouriço* to bleary-eyed revellers. Its huge medieval-looking ovens and stone arches lend the place charm, despite the rather McDonald's-like counter and illuminated price list, which also has staples such as rolls and coffee.

Snob

Rua do Século 178, Príncipe Real, 1200 (21 346 3723). Metro Rato/15, 58, 100 bus. **Open** 4.30pm-3.30am daily. **Main courses** 1,100$00-2,050$00. **Credit** AmEx, DC, MC, V. **Map** p310 L9.
Snob has been Lisbon's definitive journalists' bar for over 30 years. A pub-like atmosphere with leather seats, wood panelling and lots of corners for story-swapping make it a favourite hang-out for reporters and editors after they have put their papers to bed. Menu standards are the famed steak in Madeira sauce topped with a fried egg, or jumbo sausages German-style. There's normally also a dish of the day. Great for late steak, even if you don't care who broke the embargo on the PM's speech.

Cervejarias

Lisbon's *cervejarias* are bustling beer halls that specialise in surf and turf. Bright and brassy, these eateries are also usually open quite late. They're a good place for a snack while drinking in the atmosphere and, of course, the beer.

Portugália

Avenida Almirante Reis 117, Chile, 1150 (21 314 0002). Metro Arroios. **Open** 10am-1.30am daily. **Main courses** 1,300$00-6,500$00. **Credit** AmEx, MC, V. **Map** p308 N6.

The archetypal Lisbon beer hall. The building has recently been renovated and very nice it looks too, but the fare hasn't changed for decades. Decent seafood at decent prices and a city-famous but over-rated steak. Determined to embrace modernity, the owners have branched out into the Colombo shopping centre (*see p175*) and onto the Tagus waterfront, but only the original is really worth a visit.

Ramiro

Avenida Almirante Reis 1, Intendente, 1100 (21 885 1024). Metro Intendente/28 tram/7, 8 bus. **Open** 11.30am-12.30am Mon, Wed-Sun; closed Tue. **Main courses** 1,200$00-5,000$00. **Credit** AmEx, MC, V. **Map** p307 M8.

Senhor Ramiro is what lisboetas call a *cromo*, which roughly translates as 'a card'. A native of Galicia in northern Spain, he came to Lisbon to start up this once tiny *marisqueira* in a then dubious part of town. The fame of his *gambas a ajillo* (prawns toasted in garlic and olive oil) quickly spread, and soon Ramiro bought the shop next door, then the next shop and the next. Today, despite the extensions, you often still have to queue for a table. But the *gambas* are sublime and, as Ramiro only hires the fastest waiters in the West, service is rapid.

Solmar

Rua das Portas de Santo Antão 106, Baixa, 1100 (21 342 3371). Metro Restauradores. **Open** 7am-11.30pm daily. **Main courses** 1,500$00-4,000$00. **Credit** AmEx, DC, MC, V. **Map** p310 M9.

An old, architecturally impressive beerhall just off the Avenida da Liberdade that is still anchored in the 1950s. Fantastic neon lighting, kitsch pebble-dashed

Portugália – a Lisbon institution.

walls and a wondrous station-style clock. The kitchen closes at 10pm, but even after that you still have a bewildering choice of seafood to munch on until the early hours. A bit of a tourist trap, but a real eye-filler.

African

Águas do Bengo

Rua da Teixera 1, Bairro Alto, 1200 (21 347 7516). Metro Restauradores then Elevador da Glória. **Open** 8-11pm Mon-Sat; closed Sun. **Main courses** 1,400$00-2,700$00. **No credit cards.** **Map** p310 L9.

Owned by famous Angolan musician Waldemar Bastos and run by his dynamic wife Lauriana, this cosy place behind the Solar do Vinho do Porto is one of surprisingly few African restaurants in this part of town. It offers Angolan classics such as *mufete*, an African river fish served with banana and beans, and *moamba*, a creamy chicken stew. There are several vegetable side dishes and even a vegetarian main course, containing beans, manioc flour, banana and okra. Bastos himself is frequently on tour, but sometimes drops by to play.

Cantinho do Aziz

Rua São Lourenço 3-5, Mouraria, 1100 (21 887 6472). Metro Martim Moniz/12, 17, 28 tram. **Open** noon-4.30pm, 7-11.30pm Mon-Sat; closed Sun. **Main courses** 800$00-2,000$00. **No credit cards.** **Map** p311 M9.

For a real taste of Africa in Lisbon, you could do far worse than stopping off at Aziz. Although this tiny restaurant's Mozambican founder died a few years ago, his widow Farida and their teenage sons have stared adversity in the face and seen it off, much to the regulars' relief. On tables decked with paper tablecloths, mismatched cutlery and Duralex beakers, tasty meals are served, accompanied by local gossip and the latest episode of Brazilian *telenovelas* blaring on TV. Try the spicy grilled chicken (*frango à Zambeziana*) or *matapa*, a sort of African pesto served with rice.

Restaurante São Cristovão

Rua de São Cristovão 28-30, Castelo, 1100 (21 888 5578). Metro Rossio/28 tram. **Open** 11am-3pm, 7.30pm-midnight Mon-Sat; 11am-3pm Sun. **Main courses** 750$00-1,100$00. **Credit** MC, V. **Map** p311 M9.

This tiny *tasca* is better known locally as Tia – Auntie's Place. Maria do Livramento – Mento for short – is an effervescent character whose non-stop chatter and bravado will either charm or unnerve first-time guests. As she cooks and serves Cape Verdean specialities, members of her extended family enter and depart. The food is passable – the *cachupa* has more bones than meat – but all that is forgivable because of the vibe, especially if you're lucky enough to pick a night when friends roll up for an impromptu jam session. If doubts linger, Mento's *ponche* (a honey-based spirit) will set you right.

Belgian

A Travessa

Travessa das Inglesinhas 28, São Bento, 1200 (21 390 2034). Tram 28. **Open** noon-3pm, 8pm-midnight Mon-Fri; 8pm-midnight Sat; closed Sun. **Main courses** 2,000$00-3,800$00. **Credit** MC, V. **Map** p306 J9.

Saturday night is *moules* night in this self-described 'Luso-Belgian' restaurant in Madragoa. If you don't like mussels, there's always a meat option, and plenty of Portuguese dishes. But whatever and whenever you eat, it's usually cooked with flair. Service is correct, the wine list exhaustive and the decor very Belgian: sturdy wooden furniture with red and white checked tablecloths.

Brazilian

Atira-te ao Rio

Cais do Ginjal 69-70, Cacilhas, 2800 (21 275 1380). Ferry from Cais do Sodré or Praça do Comercio to Cacilhas. **Open** 1-4pm, 8pm-midnight Tue-Sun; closed Mon. **Main courses** 2,000$00-2,700$00. **Credit** AmEx.

This Spanish-owned eaterie serves Brazilian food on the south bank of the Tagus, so you can munch your *muqueca* while gazing across at Lisbon by night. Funky and relaxed, the mood is actually better than the food, and there's a long walk once you get off the ferry. But for a spot of tropical dreaming, Atira-te is hard to beat, and now it's open all

year round. For late-night revellers, there's a river taxi back to Lisbon. *Feijoada* buffet only for lunch on Saturday.

Comida de Santo

Calçada Engenheiro Miguel Pais 39, Príncipe Real, 1200 (21 396 3339). Metro Rato. **Open** 12.30-3.30pm, 7.30pm-1am daily. **Main courses** 2,000$00-2,680$00. **Credit** AmEx, DC, MC, V. **Map** p307 K8.

Good, hearty Brazilian food served in good, hearty Brazilian surroundings: papier mâché toucans, greenery and other tropical tat – this is one of the first and most enduring Brazilian restaurants in Lisbon. Its standard *feijoadas*, *vatapás* and *muquecas* are as good as any in town, but the real secret of Comida de Santo's success is its cosy atmosphere.

A Picanha

Rua das Janelas Verdes 96, Lapa, 1200 (21 397 5401). Tram 25/27, 40, 49, 60 bus. **Open** 7.30pm-midnight daily. **Set meal** (Picanha) 2,500$00. **No credit cards**. **Map** p306 J10.

If you believe meat is murder, then this is a canteen for serial killers. *Picanha* is that famed Brazilian speciality: a large lump of beef doused in garlic, grilled and hauled round tables where succulent slices are shaved off and piled onto customers' plates. Here, the carving and gnashing of teeth is done against a backdrop of antique *azulejos*. The waiters are wits, if you understand Brazilian Portuguese. If you don't, you might think you do after a couple of *caipirinhas*.

What's on the menu?

Portuguese tourist menus have their share of mirth-making mistranslations and spelling mistakes. Beyond the odd chuckle, though, they can create uncertainty – is 'sulking pig' suckling pig or something more sinister?'– leading nervous visitors to stick to a linguistically and gastronomically unchallenging diet of grilled chicken and omelettes with processed cheese. Most restaurants, of course, don't translate their menus into any kind of English anyway.

However, all is not lost. A typical Portuguese restaurant will store its fresh produce in glass-fronted cold counters, allowing guests to see for themselves what's available and to judge how fresh it is. Some restaurants even have a fridge built into a window niche, so that potential guests can check the wares from outside. The only restaurants that don't display their produce in this way are the very cheap or the untypically modern or posh. In the latter, you can always ask to see a fish or cut of meat before ordering.

Basics

alho garlic; **almoço** lunch; **azeite** olive oil; **azeitona** olive; **coentro** coriander; **conta** bill; **dose** portion; **ementa** menu; **entrada** starter; **jantar** dinner; **lanche** snack; **lista da vinhos** wine list; **manteiga** butter; **meia-** half-; **ovo** egg; **pão** bread; **petisco** nibble; **piri-piri** chilli; **sal** salt; **salsa** parsley, **sandes** sandwich.

Cooking styles & techniques

açorda bread soaked with olive oil, garlic, herbs and egg; **assado** roasted; **caril** curry; **cebolada** cooked with onions; **bem passado** well done; **na brasa** charcoal grilled; **caseiro** homemade; **churrasco** barbecue; **cozido** boiled; **espetada** skewer; **estufado** braised; **forno** oven; **frito** fried; **gratinado** baked with cheese on top; **grelhado** grilled; **guarnecido** garnished; **guisado** braised; **mal passado** rare; **massa** pastry/pasta; **médio** medium rare; **molho** sauce; **no forno** oven-baked; **picante** spicy; **quente** hot/warm; **recheado** stuffed; **salteado** sautéd.

Porcão

Avenida da Cintura do Porto, Cais de Santos, Docas, 1200 (21 397 5368). Tram 15, 18. **Open** *Restaurant* 12.30-3.30pm, 8pm-12.30am daily. *Bar* 12.30-3.30pm, 8pm-2am daily. **Set menu** 4,250$00. **Credit** AmEx, DC, MC, V. **Map** p307 K10.

Another offering from Zeno (*see below*), whose Brazilian dockside restaurant is a Lisbon classic. Here, in a converted warehouse along the river, Rio designer Hélio Pellegrino created a colourful, airy space where shoals of fish swim around the walls in mosaic panels, with a pleasant enclosed garden. The Porcão concept, a hit in Brazil, mixes *rodízio* with sushi: 14 types of meat sliced off skewers at your table, and fish served at the salad bar. Live music and generous portions are also trademarks. Pricey for Lisbon, but then this is Europe.

Zeno

Doca Santo Amaro, Armazém 15, Docas, 1300 (21 397 3948). Tram 15, 17, 18/14, 28, 32, 48 bus. **Open** noon-4.30pm, 8pm-1.30am Mon-Sat; 8pm-1.30am Sun. **Main courses** 2,600$00-3,700$00. **Credit** AmEx, MC, V.

The best things about this place in the Docas are the *caipirinhas*, fried manioc root, Brazilian sausage, salads, live music and the attractive customised dinner service. Owner Zeno, a jovial Brazilian, is usually on hand and service is friendly. On Saturdays, there's a good *feijoada* (Brazilian black-bean stew with pork); the rest of the menu is a bit sauce-heavy. Good for dockside drinks and snacks at sunset.

Be a big pig at **Porcão**.

Chinese

Fu Le

Rua do Sacramanto a Alcântara 30, Alcântara, 1350 (21 397 5960). Tram 15, 18. **Open** noon-3pm, 7-11pm daily. **Set lunch** 700$00-880$00. **Main courses** 690$00-1,830$00. **No credit cards.** **Map** p306 G10.

Tucked away next to the flyover that spans Avenida Infante Santo, this little gem of a place is popular with employees of the nearby Foreign Ministry. It has a wide range of cheap dishes made with really fresh ingredients – the vegetable spring rolls are especially tasty. If you hit it off with the staff they may offer you free shots of their rice-based firewater, tinged green by the dead lizard sprawled inside the bottle.

Sopas/ensopados (soups/stews)

Caldo verde shredded kale in potato broth; **canja** chicken broth; **cozido à portuguesa** stew of meats, sausages and cabbage; **feijoada** bean stew made with meat, seafood or snails.

Marisco (shellfish)

amêijoa clam; **camarão** shrimp; **gamba** prawn; **lagosta/lavagante** spiny/Norway lobster; **mexilhão** mussel; **ostra** oyster; **perceve** goose-necked barnacle; **sapateira** crab; **vieira** scallop

Peixe (fish)

atum tuna; **bacalhau** salted cod (...**a brás** shredded, fried with potato and scrambled egg; ...**a Gomes Sá** shredded, fried with onion and served with boiled potato, egg and black olives; ...**com natas** shredded, baked with cream and potato; ...**cozido com grão** boiled, served with chick peas, potato and greens); **besugo** sea bream; **cação** dogfish; **caldeirada** fish stew; **cantaril** redfish; **carapau** horse mackerel; **cataplana** a copper pan for steaming fish; **cavala** mackerel; **cherne** large grouper; **choco** cuttlefish; **corvina** croaker; **dourada** gilthead bream; **enguia** eel; **espadarte** swordfish; **garoupa** grouper; **imperador** cardinal fish; **joaquinzinho** whitebait; **linguado** sole; **lula** squid; **pargo** rosy sea bream; **pastel de bacalhau** deep-fried cod croquettes; **peixe espada** scabbard fish; **peixe-galo** John Dory; **pescada** hake; **polvo** octopus; **pregado** turbot; **raia** skate/ray; **robalo** sea bass; **salmão** salmon; **salmonete** red mullet; **sardinha** sardine; **sargo** white bream; **solha** plaice; **tamboril** angler fish/ monkfish; **truta** trout.

Carne (meat)

bifana slice of braised pork; **bife** steak (not necessarily beef); **bitoque** slice of fried beef, served with chips and fried egg; **borrego** lamb; **cabrito** kid; **caracois** snails; **chouriço** smoked sausage; **costoleta** chop; **dobrada** tripe; **entrecosto** pork rib; **entremeada** pork-belly; **febras** boned slices of pork; **fiambre** uncured ham; **fígado** liver; **ganso de vitela** topside of veal; **iscas** sliced liver; **leitão** suckling pig; **língua** tongue; **linguiça** spiced sausage; **lombinhos** tender pieces of meat; ▶

Hua Ta Li

Rua dos Bacalhoeiros 109-115, Alfama, 1100 (21 887 9170). Tram 15, 18, 28. **Open** noon-3.30pm, 6.30-11pm daily. **Main courses** 750$00-1,950$00. **No credit cards. Map** p311 M10.

It might be in the Alfama, but this busy eaterie hard by Praça do Comércio has the feel of the real McCoy – or is that the real Chen? This could be Shanghai, were it not for all those pesky western clients. A lot of care goes into preparing and serving food here, right down to the fresh garnishes. The decor may be a bit plasticky, but the waiters are abundant and fast, the portions generous, and you can take away your leftovers. Children's high chairs available.

Lon Xiang

Rua Bernardo Lima 48, Estefânia, 1150 (21 314 0726). Metro Marquês de Pombal/Picoas. **Open** 11am-3pm, 5.30pm-2.30am daily. **Main courses** 600$00-1,200$00. **No credit cards. Map** p307 L6.

Another ultra-authentic Chinese eaterie that has built up a reputation largely by word of mouth. A cavernous place, it attracts plenty of local Chinese customers, plus lunchtime trade from local offices and business diners from the many hotels in the area. The waiters' Portuguese (let alone English) is limited, but they couldn't be more friendly – and the food is delicious. They will also happily wrap food for you to take away. Seafood is the speciality, but the menu has all the most popular Chinese dishes. Some aren't even on the menu, so ask after the daily special.

German

Cervejaria Alemã

Rua do Alecrim 23, Cais do Sodré, 1200 (21 342 2916). Metro Cais do Sodré. **Open** noon-3pm, 7-11pm Mon-Sat; closed Sun. **Main courses** 1,500$00-3,500$00. **Credit** AmEx, MC, V. **Map** p310 L10.

A 'German beerhall': small and wood-lined, with lights just a little too bright, and offering *Eisbein*, *Wienerschnitzel*, *Sauerkraut* and other less-than-delicate delicacies from Mitteleuropa. The chef also does a mean Brazilian *picanha* along with some Portuguese standards. Bavarian Weissbier is served just as Herr Doktor ordered in a tall glass with a twist of lemon.

Indian

Arco do Castelo

Rua Chão da Feira 25, Castelo, 1100 (21 887 6598). Tram 12, 28 then 5min walk/37 bus. **Open** 12.30pm-midnight Mon-Sat; 7.30pm-midnight Sun. **Average** 13,000$00-17,000$00. **Credit** AmEx, MC, V. **Map** p311 M9.

From the check tablecloths and bottle-lined walls you might think this tiny place was a cheap Italian, but in fact it's one of the few genuinely Goan restaurants around. Its menu only runs to two pages, but offers *balchão de porco* (pork loin in an intense gravy containing dried shrimp), and *sarapatel*, in a hot ginger sauce. Booking is essential for dinner.

▶ ## What's on the menu? (continued)

lombo loin; **medalhões** medallions; **mãozinha** trotter/hock; **morcela** blood sausage; **paio** cured sausage; **peito** breast; **perna** leg; **porco** pork; **prego** slice of beef, grilled; **presunto** cured ham; **posta** thick slice of meat (or fish); **rins** kidneys; **rojões** pork cubes, marinated and fried; **salpicão** spiced sausage; **salsicha** sausage; **toucinho** lard; **tripas** tripe; **vaca** cow/beef; **vazia** prime cut of beef; **veado** venison; **vitela** veal.

Aves e caça (poultry & game)

cabidela chicken with giblets; **codorniz** quail; **coelho** rabbit; **faisão** pheasant; **frango** chicken; **galinha** broiler chicken; **ganso** goose; **javali** wild boar; **pato** duck; **perdiz** partridge; **perú** turkey.

Arroz, massa e feijão (rice, pasta & beans)

arroz rice; **esparguetes** spaghetti; **favas** broad beans; **feijão(ões)** bean(s); **grão** chick peas; **lentilhas** lentils.

Legumes (vegetables)

agriões watercress; **alface** lettuce; **batata (doce)** (sweet) potato; **cebola** onion; **cenoura** carrot; **cogumelo** mushroom; **couve** cabbage; **ervilhas** peas; **hortaliça** mixed vegetables; **espargos** asparagus; **esparregado** spinach purée; **espinafres** spinach; **grelos** tender greens; **pepino** cucumber; **pimenta** pepper.

Fruta (fruit)

ananás pineapple; **cereja** cherry; **laranja** orange; **limão** lemon; **maçã** apple; **maracujá** passion-fruit; **melancia** watermelon; **melão** cantaloupe; **meloa** melon; **morango** strawberry; **pêssego** peach; **uva** grape.

Sobremesa (dessert)

arroz doce rice pudding; **baba de camelo** dessert of yolks and sugar; **barriga de freira** dessert of breadcrumbs, sugar, egg and nuts; **bolo** cake; **gelado** ice cream; **leite creme** custard; **pudim** caramel pudding; **toucinho do céu** dessert of almonds, eggs and sugar.

Queijo (cheese)

queijo de ovelha sheep's cheese; **queijo fresco** cottage cheese; **requeijão** ricotta-type cheese.

Delhi Palace

Rua da Padaria, 18-20, Sé, 1100 (21 888 4203).
Tram 12, 28/37 bus. **Open** noon-3.30pm, 6.30pm-
midnight daily. **Main courses** 1,190$00-2,790$00.
Credit AmEx, MC, V. **Map** p311 M10.

Trying to offer something for everyone is a risky
business but this little place makes a decent fist of
Indian and Italian specialities. The friendly crew that
run it are from the Punjab, but the cook spent eight
years working in an Italian restaurant. The pizzas
are nothing special, although there is a decent range
of pasta dishes. But it's the other half of the cook's
repertoire that is worth writing home to north India
about. The ingredients are excellent, the sauces thick
and they don't spare the spices. Vegetarians are well
served: the pakoras are bursting with freshness, and
there's a good range of dahls, a rich vegetable korma
with dried fruits and nuts, and half a dozen salads.
Takeaways available. Recommended.

Haweli Tandoori

Travessa do Monte 14, Graça, 1170 (21 886 7713).
Tram 28. **Open** 11.30am-3.30pm, 7-11.30pm Mon,
Wed-Sun; closed Tue. **Main courses** 700$00-
3,000$00. **No credit cards**. **Map** p311 N8.

Pull back the weirdly flimsy door, shield your eyes
from the bright neon light reflecting off the gaudy
brown and orange wall tiles and prepare yourself
for some of the best Indian food around. Hamini and
his brothers are originally from Portuguese India
and their menu has the fragrant coconut flavour of
Goa. Try their *chamuças* (samosas), dahl tarka,
prawn curry Goan style and Kashmir chicken, mop-
ping up the sauce with a stuffed nan. Vegetarians
are also well catered for. It's usually packed in the
evening and there's often a queue at the door.

Maharaja

Rua do Cardal a São José 21/3, Avenida da
Liberdade, 1150 (21 346 9300). Metro Avenida.
Open noon-3pm, 7-11pm Tue-Sun; closed Mon. **Main**
courses 950$00-2,600$00. **Credit** AmEx, MC, V.
Map p307 L8.

A favourite with British expats, this place has built
up its clientele by word of mouth – and it has had
to, since you could hardly stumble across it. (It's in
an alley parallel to the Avenida, two blocks east –
from the metro station, walk up Rua das Pretas, then
it's first left, first right, first left.) This red-plush den
can seem gloomy when you first enter, but the food
brightens the whole place up. The cook is from New
Delhi, and turns out delicious tandoori and mughlai
dishes with nice decorative touches.

International

Blues Café

Rua da Cintura do Porto, Armazém H, Nave 3,
Docas, 1300 (21 395 7085). Tram 15, 18. **Open**
Restaurant 8.30pm-12.30am Mon-Sat; closed Sun. *Bar*
8.30pm-3am Mon-Thur; 8.30pm-4.30am Fri; 8.30pm-
5am Sat; closed Sun. **Main courses** 2,500$00-
3,500$00. **Credit** AmEx, DC, MC, V. **Map** p306 G10.

When in Graça, head for the **Haweli**.

Even Cajun food has made its way onto the Lisbon
nosh list. This cavernous dockside restaurant-cum-
bar, known locally as 'O Blues', is teeming at weekends, but can be a relaxing place to dine during the
week. The efforts at jambalaya and filigumbo are
about as Louisiana as Karen Carpenter and the
restaurant's owner is Dutch, but you gotta give 'em
a hand for trying. On a good night, the live music
(Mondays and Thursdays) is not too bad, either.

Hell's Kitchen

Rua da Atalaia 176, Bairro Alto, 1200 (21 342
2822). Metro Baixa-Chiado/28 tram. **Open**
8pm-midnight Tue-Sun; closed Mon. **Main**
courses 1,150$00-1,650$00. **No credit cards**.
Map p310 L9.

This small, welcoming restaurant is like the world
music section of a Virgin Megastore: chilli, curries,
moussaka, lasagne and houmous with pitta all pop
up on the eclectic menu chalked up on the wall. The
tabletops covered with newspaper cuttings make for
an informal setting – more Berlin than Bairro Alto.
The service is as friendly and as polyglot as the
menu and there are several vegetarian choices. Hell's
Kitchen is on one of the busiest streets in the area,
which makes it a tough place to get a table.

São Caetano

Rua de São Caetano à Lapa 27-31, Lapa 1200
(21 397 4792). Tram 28 then 10min walk. **Open**
8pm-midnight Tue-Sat; closed Mon, Sun. **Main**
courses 1,500$00. **Credit** AmEx, DC, MC, V.
Map p306 H9.

From its location in the swish diplomatic district of
Lapa you might expect this cosy yet sophisticated
place to be quite pricey, but in fact it's a bargain.
It's also a boon for Lisbon's long-suffering vegetarians, thanks to its meat-free menu. Main courses include a couple of fish/seafood options; the rest
are vegetable-only dishes, from pasta to curry.
Ingredients are chosen with care and the food is
presented with panache. Portions are dainty compared to your average tasca, but eat a main course
plus either starter or dessert and you'll come away
well fed without breaking the bank. The wine list
is short but good and the house wine a safe bet.
Chatty owner Maxine is usually on hand to see to
customers' needs.

Eat, Drink, Shop

We're jamming – **São Cristovão**. *See p131.*

Os Tibetanos
Rua do Salitre 117, Rato, 1200 (21 314 2038).
Metro Avenida. **Open** *Buddhist centre* 10am-noon,
4-7.30pm Mon-Fri; closed Sat, Sun. *Restaurant* noon-
3.30pm, 7.30-9.30pm Mon-Fri; closed Sat, Sun. **Main
courses** 1,500$00-2,000$00. **No credit cards**.
Map p307 L8.
The best strictly vegetarian dinner option in Lisbon
– in fact, the only strictly vegetarian dinner option
in Lisbon – is attached to a Buddhist centre and
offers everything from Tibetan *momo* to fake
steaks and tofu sausages. There's a lunchtime dish
of the day for 1,300$00, and French cider if you
don't fancy one of the many teas on offer. The
indoor seating is rather cramped, and unless you
book a table on the patio, festooned with Buddhist
pennants, it is not the best place to relax over a long
sociable meal. Still, there's no competition. No
smoking indoors or out.

Italian

Casanova
*Cais da Pedra, Armazém B, Loja 7, Santa Apolónia,
1250 Lisboa (21 887 7532). Bus 25A, 28, 39, 59,
81, 82.* **Open** 6pm-2am Tue; 12.30pm-2am Wed-Sun;
closed Mon. **Main courses** 1,150$00-1,900$00.
Credit AmEx, MC, V. **Map** p308 O9.
An offshoot of Casa Nostra (*see below*), this place
opened in mid-2000 on a dockside made fashionable
by the nightclub Lux. Thanks to the city's only
wood-fired oven, Casanova rapidly established itself
as *the* place for pizza: from a simple napoletana to
the Casanova – laden with cherry tomatoes, rocket
and mozzarella. If you're a mozzarella fanatic, come
on Friday night or Saturday, after the stuff arrives
from Italy. There isn't much else to choose from, bar-
ring some predictable starters and pasta dishes.
Desserts are limited to pannacotta, tiramisu and the
like. But while not particularly cheap, this place is
certainly cheerful. The waiters are young, linguisti-
cally-challenged but helpful Italians who seem to be

shipped in with the mozzarella. Chaos is held in
check by means of red bulbs dangling above the
tables that diners can switch on to summon the nearest attendant. Reservations are not accepted, but
turnover on the large shared tables is fairly fast.

Casa Nostra
*Travessa Poço da Cidade 60, Bairro Alto, 1200 (21
342 5931). Metro Baixa-Chiado/28 tram.* **Open**
12.30-2.30pm, 8-11pm Tue-Fri, Sun; 8-11pm Sat;
closed Mon. **Main courses** 1,000$00-2,800$00.
Credit AmEx, DC, MC, V. **Map** p310 L9.
The only place for designer pasta with that touch of
authenticity. Owner Maria Paola is a veritable gen-
eralissima in the kitchen and it shows. The pasta is
fresh, the risotto is just so, the aubergines are grilled
to a T and, thankfully, the dishes are not overloaded
with cream. If you book, ask for a table in the front
room. Designed by architect Manuel Graça Dias, its
peppermint green and white decor makes just the
right backdrop for pesto and pistachio.

Massima Culpa
*Rua da Atalaia 35-37, Bairro Alto, 1200 (21 342
0121). Metro Baixa-Chiado/28 tram.* **Open** 8pm-
1.30am Tue-Sun; closed Mon. **Main courses**
1,500$00-3,400$00. **Credit** AmEx, DC, MC, V.
Map p310 L9.
A general prejudice runs in the veins of Italophile
Bairro Altistas – either you eat at Massima Culpa or
at Casa Nostra (*above*). The *Time Out Lisbon Guide*
favours Casa Nostra, but if you steer clear of the
'cleverer' pasta concoctions at Massima Culpa, you'll
get a decent meal here, too. With nondescript beige
decor and low background music, this restaurant's
biggest trump is that it's open until 2am, but there
are some nights when the service is so slow that the
long hours are a necessity, not a luxury.

Mezza Luna
*Rua da Artilheria Um 16, Marquês de Pombal, 1250
(21 387 9944). Metro Marquês.* **Open** 12.30-3pm,
7.30-11pm daily. **Main courses** 1,600$00-4,200$00.
Credit AmEx, DC, MC, V. **Map** p307 K7.
A relatively recent Italian immigrant to Lisbon,
Mezza Luna is more formal than the Bairro Alto
eateries. It's a lunchtime haunt of businessmen
working in the area, while in the evening well-
heeled couples predominate. The food is delicious
and well-presented, and there's a healthy emphasis
on doing interesting things with vegetables. The
mixed veg plate is a treat for those fed up of
scrawny salads, as is the aubergine grilled with
goat's cheese. Recommended.

Stravaganza
*Rua do Grémio Lusitano 18-26, Bairro Alto, 1200
(21 346 8868). Metro Baixa-Chiado/28 tram.* **Open**
7pm-12.30am Mon-Sat; closed Sun. **Main courses**
1,800$00-3,400$00. **Credit** AmEx, DC, MC, V.
Map p310 L9.
This newest of the Bairro Alto's Italian restaurants
is trying hard to please. Two small rooms are
decked in post-modern powder blue and dusty yel-

Restaurants by area

Alcântara & Docas

Alcântara Café (Top-range p121); **Blues Café** (International p135); **Doca 6** (Mid-range p125); **Espaço Lisboa** (Mid-range p125); **Fu Le** (Chinese p133); **Tapadinha** (Russian p138); **Zeno** (Brazilian p133).

Alfama, Castelo, Graça, Mouraria & Campo de Santana

Antiga Casa de Pasto Estrela da Sé (Budget p127); **Arco do Castelo** (Indian p134); **Cantinho do Aziz** (African p131); **Coutada** (Budget p128); **Delhi Palace** (Indian p135); **Haweli Tandoori** (Indian p135); **Hua Ta Li** (Chinese p134); **Malmequer Bemmequer** (Budget p129); **Mercado de Santa Clara** (Mid-range p126); **Restaurante São Cristovão** (African p131); **Via Graça** (Top-range p122); **La Valentina** (Mexican p138).

Avenida de Liberdade & Marquês de Pombal

Maharaja (Indian p135); **Mezza Luna** (Italian p136); **Os Tibetanos** (International p136).

Bairro Alto & Príncipe Real

1° de Maio (Budget p129); **Águas do Bengo** (African p131); **Casa Nostra** (Italian p136); **Comida de Santo** (Brazilian p132); **Fidalgo** (Budget p129); **Hell's Kitchen** (International p135); **Massima Culpa** (Italian p136); **Novo Bonsai** (Japanese p137); **Pap'Açorda** (Top-range p122); **Snob** (Late-night p130); **Stravaganza** (Italian p136); **Tavares Rico** (Top-range p122).

Baixa, Rossio & Restauradores

Bonjardim (Budget p127); **Casa do Alentejo** (Budget p127); **Paris** (Mid-range p126); **Solmar** (Cervejarias p130).

Cais do Sodré & Santos

Acinox (Late-night p130); **Cervejaria Alemã** (German p134); **A Merendinha** (Late-night p130); **Porcão** (Brazilian p133); **Varina de Madragoa** (Budget p129).

Chiado

Brasserie de l'Entrecôte (Top-range p137); **Charcutaria** (Mid-range p123); **Çuciadadi de Barrancú** (Mid-range p125); **Español** (Spanish p138).

Greater Lisbon: Cascais

Porto de Santa Maria (Top-range p122).

Lapa

O Acontecimento (Mid-range p123); **A Picanha** (Brazilian p132); **São Caetano** (International p135).

Northern Lisbon

Bistro XXI (Mid-range p123); **Galeto** (Late p130); **Lon Xiang** (Chinese p134); **Portugália** (Cervejarias p130); **Ramiro** (Cervejarias p131).

Santa Apolónia

Bica do Sapato (Top-range p121); **Casanova** (Italian p136).

São Bento, Estrela & Campo de Ourique

Café de São Bento (Late-night p130); **Casa da Comida** (Top-range p121); **Casa do México** (Mexican p137); **Coelho da Rocha** (Mid-range p123); **Stop do Bairro** (Budget p129); **A Tasquinha d'Adelaide** (Mid-range p127); **A Travessa** (Belgian p132); **XL** (Top-range p122).

South of the river

Atira-te ao Rio (Brazilian p132).

Eat, Drink, Shop

low. The pizza – including three varieties of calzone – is more successful than the pasta, but the salads are excellent and the *funghi trifolati sa crostini di pane* starter, with three different kinds of mushroom, alone makes it worth a visit. Lasagne and pizzas only after 11.30pm.

This old Bairro Alto fixture has recovered from a disastrous tenure and is now run by a Luso-Japanese family. Sit on cushions around low tables in screened-off booths for an intimate dining experience. The sushi's good, the tempura's better, and service is charming.

Japanese

Novo Bonsai

Rua da Rosa 244-245, Bairro Alto, 1200 (21 346 2515). Bus 15, 100. **Open** 7.30-10.30pm Mon, Sat; 12.30-2pm, 7.30-10.30pm Tue-Fri; closed Sun. **Main courses** 3,000$00-3,300$00. **Credit** AmEx, DC, MC, V. **Map** p310 L9.

Mexican

Casa do México

Avenida Dom Carlos I 140, São Bento, 1200 (21 396 5500). Tram 28. **Open** 8-11.30pm Mon-Wed; 8pm-12.30am Thur-Sat; closed Sun. **Main courses** 1,800$00-4,200$00. **Credit** MC, V. **Map** p 307 K9.

Where the eats have no name

Where do lisboetas lunch? That might seem a silly question, what with the profusion of snack bars in this city, but there's more to this than meets the eye. If you track enough office workers on their lunch hour, sooner or later one will disappear into a doorway that turns out to lead to a bustling yet unpublicised eaterie.

Most operate as a canteen rather than a restaurant: you line up at the counter, tray in hand, for a limited menu of good, cheap and filling food. **António Estrela** (Praça Marquês de Pombal 1-CV-F, 1250, 21 352 5220) is one such place, hidden in the basement of a downtown office building. It's a favourite hangout of journalists from the nearby *Expresso* newspaper.

For posher nosh (though still on a self-service basis), head for Lapa, home to embassies and upmarket service companies. At the discreetly signposted **A Coentrada** (Rua de São Domingos à Lapa 100, 1200,

21 397 0749), besuited regulars practise their would-be upper class accents over a bowl of soup or a wedge of quiche at tables set out in a plastic tent in a back courtyard.

The **Paulino da Estefânia** (Rua da Ilha Terceira 21, Estefânia, 21 3142104) is in a working-class neighbourhood near the Instituto Superior Técnico. Here, college students and staff mix with locals, attracted by the cheap food and wine. Here it's waiter service rather than trays; the working-class customers like to be treated like lords.

And one of the best cheap eateries in the Baixa doesn't have a single sign to indicate its existence. **Restaurante Caxemira** (Rua Condes do Monsanto 4-1D, 21 886 5486), on the first floor of a building just off Praça da Figueira, is run by members of the family that owns the Haweli Tandoori in Graça (see p135). It offers some of the best Indian food in town at 900$00-1,750$00 for a main course. Just don't tell anyone, will you?

When they opened this comfortable and brightly coloured basement restaurant in São Bento, Cristina and Isabel Jorge Carvalho declared war on 'the whole Tex-Mex thing' and got a Mexican chef to come over and train their staff. The result is good and as genuinely Mexican as you'll find anywhere in Europe: lots of beans and meat with salsa negra *'para los tradicionales'*, plus Tex-Mex choices *'para los gringos'*. The walls are decked out in sunny orange and green adobe, and even the chairs are multicoloured. There are no mariachis, but after a couple of Margaritas you could swear you were in Mexico. Recommended.

La Valentina

Rua dos Bacalhoeiros 4 A-C, Alfama, 1100 (21 886 9860). **Open** *Restaurant* noon-4pm, 8pm-midnight Tue-Sun; closed Mon. *Bar* noon-4pm, 8pm-midnight Tue-Thur; noon-4pm, 8pm-2am Fri, Sat; closed Mon. **Main courses** 2000$00-3,600$000. **Credit** AmEx, MC, V. **Map** p311 M10.

One of Expo's many legacies to the city, La Valentina moved downtown when the party ended, and the owners have created a brightly-coloured slice of Mexicana in one of Lisbon's scruffiest *bairros*. The 'alta cocina mexicana' it offers doesn't come cheap and, at 1,000$00, nor do the Margaritas. But, to be fair, some ingredients are flown in from Mexico and the food is tasty. Try the *camarones del patron*, (shrimps in a fresh orange juice sauce), or *camarones cuitlacoche*, the biggest seller at Expo. Perhaps unwisely, the owners have also tried to cater to local tastes by inventing a *bacalhau* dish.

Russian

Tapadinha

Calçada da Tapada 41A, Alcântara, 1350 (21 364 0482). Tram 15, 17, 18/train from Cais do Sodré to Alcântara-Mar/20, 22, 38 bus. **Open** noon-3pm, 8pm-2am Tue-Sun; closed Mon. **Main courses** 1,500$00-2,400$00. **No credit cards. Map** p306 G9.

The food here sometimes seems as if it's still being cooked with Soviet ingredients by pre-Glasnost chefs. Blinis, when available, are sometimes sweet, the salads pickled. The decor is black and would-be retro Socialist realist. Still, it's a good place to go in a group; there's a definite atmosphere and the vodka is *'nastoyashchaya'* (genuinski) Moskovskaya and Stoli.

Spanish

Español

Calçada Nova de São Francisco 2, Chiado, 1200 (21 347 0895). Metro Baixa-Chiado/28 tram. **Open** noon-3.30pm Mon-Wed; noon-3.30pm, 8pm-1am Thu-Sat; closed Sun. **Tapas** 950$00-1,400$00. **Main courses** 1,850$00-2,850$00. **Credit** MC, V. **Map** p310 L9.

Tapas is not a Portuguese tradition but that doesn't mean there's no market for it in Lisbon. If location counts for anything, this newly-opened tapas bar should do well. The decor is cool, the service friendly, and the *pinchos* (mini-tapas) excellent. There's a reasonable range of more substantial fare, from tortilla through Spanish black pudding to entrecôte. Vegetarians beware the *salada de pimentos* – it contains a lump of *bacalhau*.

Eat, Drink, Shop

Cafés

Come on in – the coffee's lovely.

Anyone familiar with the habits of the Portuguese won't be surprised to learn that they spend more time and money in cafés than other western Europeans. In fact, according to one recent survey, they spend most of their free time in cafés and restaurants – despite also being the nation that complains most of not having enough of it.

Coffee-serving establishments are everywhere in Lisbon, ranging from workaday *pastelarias* (pastry shops), through *esplanadas* on the main avenues and the fading reminders of the bourgeois café society of the 19th and early 20th centuries. So the image of hard-pressed wage slaves frittering away in cafés what little leisure time they have is not too difficult to swallow. Few lisboetas start the day without caffeine, usually in the form of a turbo-charged *bica* with a bag or two of sugar stirred in. The first thing many office workers do when they arrive in the morning is head back out for the nearest *pastelaria* or *confeitaria* (a slightly classier cake shop) – all in the interests of productivity when they do start work, of course.

In a country where people work the longest hours in the EU, it's no mystery why coffee is so popular. But it's not a recent phenomenon. Portugal, as colonial ruler of the world's largest producer of the stuff, long had access to fine coffee and the time to develop an amazing variety of ways to serve it (*see p141* **Caffeine complications**).

Thought to have been introduced to Brazil in 1720, the rubiacea plant fanned out across the colony in a few decades. Once it found its ideal climatic home in the highlands of Rio de Janeiro state, output soared, as did the slave population. By the mid-19th century Brazil accounted for most world output.

In Lisbon, the growth of empire and the rise of the bourgeoisie was mirrored in the development of the Chiado. The district's reputation as a centre for artistic and political brain-storming rests on two establishments, only one of which survives: **Café A Brasileira**. The other, Café Marrare, was founded by the Italian Antonio Marrare before 1818. 'Lisbon was the Chiado, and the Chiado was Café Marrare,' enthused historian Júlio Castilho, thus dismissing the rival **Martinho da Arcada**, which still exists down on Praça

do Comércio. Marrare owed its brief success – it closed in 1866 – partly to the intellectual ferment following the 1834 ban on religious orders and the spread of freemasonry, Romanticism and Liberalism, and partly to its location between parliament in São Bento and the ministries on Praça do Comércio. Café A Brasileira's fame came only in the 1920s and 1930s, when literary types such as Fernando Pessoa and José Pacheco could be found at one table, politicians at another, and actors from Teatro da Trindade at a third.

With the rise of mass politics, the Chiado was doomed long before the 1988 fire. Rossio's larger cafés had popular appeal and a constant stream of customers from the new rail station. To cope with the numbers, the system of pre-payment was developed – if you see a *pré-pagamento* sign, it means that you go to the till first, pay for what you want, and then take the receipt to the serving counter. In the 1940s, as the rest of Europe was at war, Rossio's cafés flourished. Twenty years later most were gone, but **Café Nicola** and **Casa Suiça** survive.

The heyday of the grand establishments is past, but today Lisbon has more places to drink coffee than ever, including some internet cafés (*see chapter* **Directory**). Concentrations of *esplanadas* can be found on Avenida da Liberdade and in Chiado, but most cafés are much of a muchness, purveying cakes that might as well come from some central factory charged with supplying the city's daily ration of sugar and animal fat. It's worth seeking out those that are a bit special.

The best known Portuguese pastry is the *pastél de nata*, or custard tart, which reaches its acme in Belém (*see p146* **Tarts with tradition**). But there are many others: among full-scale cakes, the big sellers are *bolo rei*, a light fruit cake eaten at Christmas, Easter and any other time people can find an excuse, and *pão de ló*, a fluffy but bland sponge whose main selling point seems to be that it has a hole in the middle. Bite-size specialities include *bolos de arroz* or rice-flour cakes, *queijadas* or cottage-cheese tarts (especially rife in Sintra), *sonhos* ('dreams'), essentially jam-free doughnuts, and *broas de mel*, honey-flavoured cornbread with a pleasant nutty taste but the consistency of lead shot.

Casa Suiça.

Baixa

Café Martinho da Arcada

Praça do Comércio 3, 1100 (21 887 9259). Metro Baixa-Chiado/tram 15, 18, 25, 28. **Open** 7am-10pm Mon-Sat; closed Sun. **Credit** AmEx, DC, MC, V. **Map** p311 M10.

This café and adjacent restaurant have a long history and were one of Pessoa's favourite haunts, but today are almost as famous for their *pastéis de nata*, which you can eat standing up at the wood-panelled counter or sitting at one of the marble-topped tables. Coffee is 80$00 at the counter or 150$00 outside if you can handle the traffic noise and exhaust fumes.

Pastelaria Atinel

Cais da Alfândega, Terreiro do Paço boat station, 1100 (21 887 7419). Metro Baixa-Chiado/tram 15, 18, 25, 28. **Open** *Esplanade* 10am-8pm daily. *Café* 10am-10pm daily. **No credit cards. Map** p311 M10.

Sitting on the dock of the bay, watching the tide of commuters pouring in and out of the ferry station: although the esplanade has a good view of the river, this is not a peaceful spot. Every 10 or 15 minutes a siren warns that the ferry gate is closing. But it's great for people-watching and has a vast range of pastries. Coffee on the terrace costs 130$00. If you want a full meal, there's a menu of Portuguese standards.

Rossio

Café Nicola

Praça Dom Pedro IV (Rossio) 24/25, 1100 (21 346 0579). Metro Rossio/tram 12, 15. **Open** *Café* 8am-10pm Mon-Fri; 9am-5pm Sat; closed Sun. *Esplanade* 9am-10pm Mon-Fri; closed Sat, Sun. *Restaurant* noon-8pm Mon-Sat; closed Sun. **Credit** AmEx, DC, MC, V. **Map** p310 L9.

In its current incarnation Nicola has been here since 1929, but it's on the site of an early 18th-century café where extemporising poet Manuel Maria Barbosa do Bocage held court (his statue is toasted nightly). In the 20th century, it was a centre for political intrigue, boosting the caffeine intake of police officers assigned to keep tabs on would-be agitators. Nicola emerged from a lengthy renovation in mid-1998 in all its marble, steel and glass splendour – a surprise after the stone pillars that frame the entrance. The paintings are 1935 originals by Fernando Santos. Although best known as a café, Nicola has an extensive menu and a downstairs restaurant where steak is a speciality. Coffee is 80$00 at the bar, 100$00 at the tables inside, and 200$00 outside (although the esplanade will be closed for most of 2001 because of construction work in the neighbourhood). The branch round the back sells 25 varieties of coffee beans by the bag, and you can sip a *bica* (120$00) while you make up your mind.

Branch: Nicola Gourmet, Rua 1° de Dezembro 12, 1100 (21 342 9172).

Casa Suiça

Praça Dom Pedro IV (Rossio) 96-104, 1100 (21 321 4090/suica@mail.telepac.pt). Metro Rossio/tram 12, 15. **Map** p310 M9. **Open** 7am-10pm daily. **No credit cards.**

Another recently renovated Lisbon favourite, Suiça now boasts hyperactive automatic doors and a plasticky decor, but the pastries are as good as ever. There are also sandwiches, salads, fruit yoghurts and shakes for the more health-conscious, and a large if predictable lunch and dinner menu. A *bica* costs 100$00 at the counter, 160$00 in the tearoom and 220$00 on the terraces on Rossio and Praça da Figueira.

Confeitaria Nacional

Praça da Figueira 18B/C, 1100 (21 342 4470). Metro Rossio/tram 12, 15. **Open** *8am-8pm Mon-Fri; 8am-2pm Sat; closed Sun.* **No credit cards.** **Map** *p310 M9.*
The plaque boasting 'over 100 years of existence' is itself an antique; Nacional was founded in 1829 and retains its glass cases and painted panelling. With fast, pleasant service, it's a good place to buy biscuits or cakes to take away. There is also a sit-down café.

Bela Ipanema

Avenida da Liberdade 169, 1250 (21 357 2316). Metro Avenida. **Open** *7am-midnight Mon-Sat; closed Sun.* **Credit** *AmEx, DC, MC, V.* **Map** *p306 L8.*
The consummate snack bar: spacious counters, a large indoor seating space, and an esplanade on the Avenida. Fruit juices, shakes and sundaes are a speciality, but there's also an enormous selection of meals and snacks; the soups are always a good bet.

Cafeteria Botequim do Rei

Alameda Cardeal Cerejeira, Parque Eduardo VII, 1250 (no phone). Metro Parque or São Sebastião. **Open** *10am-8pm Tue-Sun; closed Mon.* **Credit** *AmEx, DC, MC, V.* **Map** *p307 K6.*

Although a bit of a haul to get here, it's worth it for the breeze, the trees and the sound of crickets on a summer evening. Popular with bourgeois families, businessmen and their young mistresses, intellectuals and stray dogs, the esplanade is a fine place to while away a warm afternoon with a book or watch the geese on the small ornamental lake. Coffee costs 100$00 on the terrace. There is also a restaurant inside.

Confeitaria Marquês de Pombal

Avenida Liberdade 244 A/B, 1250 (21 356 2362). Metro Marquês de Pombal. **Open** *7am-9pm Mon-Fri; 9am-9pm Sat; closed Sun.* **Credit** *AmEx, MC, V.* **Map** *p307 L7.*
A modern pastelaria on an industrial scale, packed at peak times. The ice-cream parlour is to the right as you enter; for the *pastelaria* head upstairs after taking a token from the woman at the till. The waiter takes your order and notes your number. The bill will be waiting at the till. As well as the usual sugary, eggy confections, there is a variety of breads and chunky, un-iced cakes. Coffee is 80$00 at the counter, 100$00 at table.

Pastelaria São Roque

Rua de São José 60, 1250 (21 322 4358). Metro Avenida. **Open** *7am-7pm daily.* **No credit cards.** **Map** *p307 L8.*

Caffeine complications

So you thought you could just walk in and order a coffee? How naïve. Okay, you could say '*um café, por favor*', but brace yourself for a tiny dose of a potent, bitter brew that, drunk neat, can disable taste buds for hours. Anyway, it's a bit unimaginative just to ask for coffee when you can test the staff's patience while also showing your appreciation of the finer points of Portuguese culture.

For a milky coffee, served in a glass, ask for '*um galão*', but tack on the words '*da máquina*' (from the machine) or the coffee may come from a tankful that's been standing around for an hour. The nearest thing to a cappuccino is *uma meia da leite* (half of milk). To make sure it's strong and hot, say you want it *da máquina com leite quente* (with hot milk).

Most Portuguese don't bother with additives like milk. They opt for a standard *bica* (Lisbon waiters' slang – you order *um café* unless you're tacking on an adjective) or a *duplo* (double) if they're gasping, and offset the bitterness with heaps of sugar. If on a diet they might cut it with a drop (*um pingo*) of milk instead, ordering *um café*

pingado. The other way round – a few drops of coffee in milk – is a *garoto* (literally 'young boy'). Women can amuse themselves by ordering a *garoto claro* or *garoto escuro* (light or dark boy).

If a *bica* doesn't do it for you any more, try *uma italiana* – effectively a thimbleful of hot coffee essence. Or get finicky and order *uma bica cheia/curta* (a weaker/stronger *bica*). Wimps order *um carioca*, a diluted *bica* and not to be confused with *um carioca de limão* – lemon rind in hot water. For a different kind of boost, try *um café com cheirinho* – 'with a whiff' of *aguardente* (grap mash distillate). A decaf is *um descafeinado*.

The really tough customers refuse to accept a cup from on top of the coffee machine, where crockery is left to dry. If they want piping hot coffee but fret about burning their lips (don't you just hate that?) they order *uma bica escaldada numa chávena fria* ('in a cold cup').

To be a real pain in the neck, you could order *uma bica descafeinada pingada escaldada numa chávena fria*. But perhaps that's taking things just a little too far.

Café no Chiado.

If you're hungry and don't mind standing up, it's worth the detour off Liberdade to this tiny *pastelaria*. It serves fresh bread and cinnamon cakes – *bolos de canela* – to a stream of regulars. (Peak times, such as lunch or the I've-just-got-to-work-Christ-I-need-a-coffee hour are best avoided.) How the staff manage to get so much done in such a small space is a mystery. Sandwich fillings are absurdly generous. Excellent home-made soups. A *bica* costs 75$00.

Alfama & Graça

Cerca Moura
Largo das Portas do Sol 4, Alfama, 1100 (21 887 4859). Tram 28. **Open** 9am-2am daily. **Credit** AmEx, DC, MC, V. **Map** p311 N9.
In summer, this esplanade is stiff with tourists gazing at the unrivalled view of Alfama and the river. Despite the crowds, it's ideal for a light snack as it serves toasted sandwiches, baguettes and savouries well into the night. The esplanade closes early if it gets cold or looks like rain, but then you can decamp to the cosy, cave-like bar built into the original Moorish town walls, after which the café is named.

Esplanada da Igreja da Graça
Largo da Graça, Graça, 1100 (21 742 7508). Tram 28. **Open** 11am-2am daily. **No credit cards.** **Map** p311 N9.
More of a locals' hangout than Cerca Moura (*above*), this place fills quickly on sunny afternoons as people gather to soak up one of Lisbon's best views,

particularly magnificent at sunset. While toasted sandwiches and fresh lemonade are reliably excellent, service varies from indifferent to laughable and music veers from Spanish pop to house. A good place to start a conversation on a weekend afternoon; on Friday and Saturday nights it tends to be full of canoodling teenagers. A *bica* costs 180$00.

Chiado

Café A Brasileira
Rua Garrett 120, 1200 (21 346 9541). Metro Baixa-Chiado/tram 28. **Open** 8am-2am daily. **Credit** AmEx, V. **Map** p310 L9.
When A Brasileira opened in 1905, customers got a free *bica* when they bought a bag of coffee beans. These days a coffee on the esplanade of Lisbon's most famous café costs 200$00. At the counter inside, it's just 80$00 and you can prop up the bar and gawp at the magnificent carved and panelled wood interior. At its 1920s peak, this place seemed single-handedly responsible for the saying that, while Coimbra studied and Oporto worked, Lisbon talked and made revolution. Nowadays intrigue has given way to tourists taking each other's pictures by the statue of Fernando Pessoa outside, while it's something of a gay hangout at night.

Café no Chiado
Largo do Picadeiro 11/12, 1200 (21 342 4517). Metro Baixa-Chiado/tram 28. **Open** 10am-2am Mon-Sat; closed Sun. **Credit** AmEx, MC, V. **Map** p310 L9.
Civilised yet informal, this is a lunch favourite with less straight-laced business or media types, offering steaks, salads and quiches, and some mean desserts. Other attractions are the impressive range of Portuguese and foreign newspapers and the esplanade – more peaceful than Café A Brasileira (*above*) around the corner, except when tram 28 rattles past. Coffee is 100$00 at the bar; 120$00 outside.

Café Rosso
Rua Ivens 53-61, 1200 (21 347 1524). Metro Baixa-Chiado/tram 28. **Open** 8am-2am daily. **No credit cards.** **Map** p310 L9.
This all-day courtyard café is an oasis of calm in one of the busiest parts of Lisbon. It's a useful meeting place whether you're out shopping or clubbing, and whether you're gay or straight. There's another entrance from Rua Garrett.

Leitaria Academia
Largo do Carmo 1-3, 1200 (21 346 9092). Metro Baixa-Chiado/tram 28. **Open** 7am-midnight daily. **No credit cards.** **Map** p310 L9.
Although not completely traffic-free, the Largo do Carmo is the site for one of Lisbon's more peaceful esplanades (summer only) and catches the sun for much of the day. The menu includes standard Portuguese fare, sandwiches and tasty orange and coconut cakes, but staff don't mind if you sit and nurse a beer or coffee (120$00 outside).

Café Mexicana. See p146.

Pastelaria Bénard

Rua Garrett 104, 1200 (21 347 3133). Metro Baixa-Chiado/tram 28. **Open** *8am-midnight Mon-Sat; closed Sun.* **Credit** AmEx, DC, MC, V. **Map** p310 L9.

Coffee and cakes of a reliably high quality are served here, in one of Lisbon's longest-established tearooms. The off-hand staff certainly act as though they've seen it all. Croissants, cakes by the slice and fruit tarts are among the attractions. A coffee is 85$00 at the bar, 150$00 on the terrace, where meals are also served. Tends to catch the Café A Brasileira overspill.

Bairro Alto & Príncipe Real

Pao de Canela

Praça das Flores 27, Príncipe Real, 1200 (21 397 2220). Metro Rato/100 bus. **Open** *7.30am-8pm daily.* **Credit** MC, V. **Map** p307 K8.

This rather modish new café in a cute square down from the Jardim do Príncipe Real has that rare commodity – an esplanade not marred by traffic fumes. And, darling, it's *the* place to go at weekends these days. Coffee costs 85$00 at the counter, 100$00 at inside tables, 150$00 outside. There are quiches and cakes, too.

Pastelaria-Padaria São Roque

Rua Dom Pedro V 57, Bairro Alto, 1200 (no phone). Metro Restauradores then Elevador da Glória. **Open** *7am-7.30pm Mon-Sat; closed Sun.* **No credit cards.** **Map** p310 L8.

Truly a 'cathedral to bread', as proclaimed by the *azulejos* behind the counter. The street-corner position of this magnificent old bakery and pastry shop makes the pillared and painted, marbled and tiled interior all the more impressive. Glazed tiles depict sheaves of wheat and ears of maize are painted on the panels higher up. A *bica* costs 70$00.

São Bento & beyond

Simples Pecados

Rua de Santa Amaro 6A, São Bento, 1200 (21 396 2969). Tram 28, bus 6, 49. **Open** *8.30am-8pm Mon-Fri; 10am-6pm Sun; closed Sat.* **No credit cards.** **Map** p307 K8.

Tea and scones, anyone? Although lisboetas set in their ways can find the usual savoury snacks here, there is also a good range of cakes, teas and infusions. These, as well as a coffee at 80$00, are value for money; the pretentiously named *provencettas* – a slice of bread with a smidgeon of something on top – are not. Still, the bright decor is cheerful, and the snug back room offers comfy sofas and music.

Lapa

O Chá da Lapa

Rua do Olival 8/10, 1200 (21 390 0888). Tram 25. **Open** *9am-8pm daily.* **Credit** DC, MC, V. **Map** p306 H10.

'Tea of Lapa' is a bit of a misnomer, since the menu only stretches to Earl Grey and English Breakfast, but this place is very much in the salôn de chá tradition – calm and genteel with attentive staff serving impeccably turned-out ladies. Mouth-watering quiches, tarts, biscuits, and cakes, all made on the premises. Coffee is 150$00.

Sítio do Pica-pau

Rua dos Remédios 61, 1200 (21 397 8267). Tram 25. **Open** *8am-5.30pm Mon-Fri; closed Sat, Sun.* **No credit cards.** **Map** p306 J9.

On one of Lisbon's prettiest terraces, at the bottom of steps leading up to one of Lapa's steeply sloping streets. It serves lunches, but the rest of the time it's a great place for a quiet beer, or for coffee (100$00 on the terrace).

Campo de Ourique

Jamaica
*Rua Ferreira Borges 92B, 1300 (21 371 4191).
Tram 28, then 5mins walk.* **Open** 7.30am-11pm
Mon-Fri; 9am-midnight Sat; closed Sun. **No credit
cards. Map** p306 J7.
A welcome departure from the bog-standard Lisbon
café, this bustling modern outlet is one of the few
places that sells the heavenly (and hellishly expensive) Blue Mountain coffee, both by the cup and by
the kilo. It also offers a range of teas and coffee- and
chocolate-based concoctions, most containing cream
and some containing alcohol. The solid nourishment
is less original: just the usual *salgados* and croissants.

Lomar
*Rua Tomás de Anunciação 72/Rua Correia Teles
23B, 1350 (21 385 8417). Tram 28, then 5mins
walk.* **Open** 7.30am-8pm Mon-Fri; 7.30am-4pm Sat;
closed Sun. **No credit cards. Map** p306 H7.
A bright, stylish neighbourhood *pastelaria* that
attracts a mixture of local *tias* (literally aunts, but
translatable as ladies who lunch), students, and
louche estate-agent types. They come in for a chat
over coffee (80$00 at the counter, 90$00 at the tables)
and for the cakes and savouries – such as the tasty
tuna and chicken pasties – which are all made on the
premises. The place can be a bit smoky, though.

Panificação Mecânica
*Rua Silva Carvalho 209/23, Campo de Ourique,
1250 (21 381 2260). Metro Rato.* **Open** 7am-8pm
Mon-Sat; closed Sun. **No credit cards.**
Map p306 J7.
Chandeliers, tiles depicting ears of wheat, coloured
enamel pillars, painted ceilings and wall mirrors
make this probably Lisbon's most over-the-top *pastelaria*. A stone's throw from the Amoreiras shopping
mall, it has supplied the middle class of Campo de
Ourique with top-notch bread and cakes for more
than 100 years; it also sells cheeses and ice-cream.

Rato

As Vicentinhas
*Rua do São Bento 700, 1200 (21 388 7040). Metro
Rato.* **Open** 4-7pm Mon-Sat; closed Sun. **No credit
cards. Map** p307 K8.
This tearoom, coupled with religious knick-knack
shop, has been here for about 30 years. Stepping
from noisy, filthy Rato into this hushed, whitewashed space is like entering another world. The
tiny, genteel Vicentinhas – a group of women
dedicated to good works and the 'promotion of
Christian and cultural education' among the sick –
who run the place talk and move at a different
rhythm from the rest of Lisbon. There's no menu,
so hope that the ageing waitress can remember
which teas are in stock. There's no such problem
with the home-made cakes, which are displayed in
all their sticky glory.

Western waterfront

Esplanada Doca de Santo
*Doca de Santo Amaro, Alcântara, 1350 (21 396
3522/35). Train from Cais do Sodré to Alcântara
Mar/tram 15, 18.* **Open** 12.30pm-4am daily. **No
credit cards.**
The largest esplanade in the docks, set back a
little at the start of the main boardwalk. It's well
staffed, so service is usually quick compared to
most of its rivals. There is a good range of salads
on the extensive menu, but many come just to sip
one of the gorgeously thick fruit shakes at
450$00-600$00. A *bica* costs 200$00, 250$00 after
midnight.

Guarda Rio
*Cais do Sodré, 1200 (21 347 1395). Metro Cais do
Sodré/tram 15, 18.* **Open** 10am-2am daily. **Credit**
AmEx, DC. **Map** p310 L10.
Bizarre Russian-style wooden hut behind Cais do
Sodré station, with soft drinks, cocktails, snacks and
meals. Its small esplanade is right on the river, so its
a good place to escape the heat and dust of the city.

Leitaria Caneças
*Rua Bernardino da Costa 36, Cais do Sodré, 1200
(21 342 3748). Metro Cais do Sodré/tram 15, 18.*
Open 6am-8pm Mon-Fri; 6am-2pm Sat; closed Sun.
No credit cards. Map p310 L10.
Bakery, pastry shop and stand-up café famous for
its bread and cakes. It passes a crucial test for a
pastelaria: the ability to make *sonhos* that don't sit
in your stomach for three hours. During rush hour
it's packed with commuters from the nearby Cais do
Sodré station, getting their caffeine fix at 70$00 a
shot. It also serves savoury snacks.

Belém

This being a touristy area, there are plenty of
cafés besides the **Antiga Confeitaria de
Belém** (*see p146* **Tarts with tradition**), itself
something of a tourist destination.

Cafetaria Quadrante
*Centro Cultural de Belém, Praça do Império,
1400 (21 361 2400). Train from Cais do Sodré
to Belém/tram 15.* **Open** 10am-10pm daily.
Credit AmEx, DC, MC, V. **Map** p303 B10.
The main draw here is the spacious terrace next to
the Jardim das Oliveiras – a miniature landscaped
area with olive trees, running water and a river view.
As well as the café, which offers a wide range of
drinks, ice-cream and snacks indoors, there's a self-
service restaurant for lunch and dinner. The notice
banning study at meal times is a testament to this
café's popularity with students. Coffee is 110$00.

Milk Bar Evasione
*Avenida Brasília, 1300 (21 362 4232). Train from
Cais do Sodré to Belém/tram 15.* **Open** *Summer* 9am-
midnight daily. *Winter* 9am-8pm Tue-Sun; closed Mon.
Credit AmEx, MC, V. **Map** pD10.

Tarts with tradition

Every lisboeta knows a *pasteleria* or two that make good *pastéis de nata,* or custard tarts, but all agree that the very best are the unique Pastéis de Belém, produced solely by the Antiga Confeitaria de Belém. What makes them different? Well, only three people can answer that question.

Once it was monasteries that made all of Portugal's sweet specialities. Monks used egg whites to refine the impurities from wine, and then had to do something with all the leftover egg yolks. With the dissolution of the monasteries in 1834, many formerly secret pastry recipes came onto the market as monks and nuns suddenly had to earn a living. One of the most renowned recipes was that of the cream pastries made by the Hieronymite monks at the Mosteiro dos Jerónimos. In 1837, an entrepreneur named Domingos Rafael Alvés not only acquired the recipe, but had the foresight to keep it secret – a secrecy that has been maintained to this day. The company now has nine shareholders, but only three bakers know precisely what goes into a Pastél de Belém. When one retires another is chosen to take his place.

Every morning at 7am at least two of the three shut themselves into the Oficina do Segredo (Secret Workshop) and prepare the cream and dough. Until about 20 years ago the dough-roller was powered by hand – the crank was on the other side of a thick wall and the secret bakers had to yell through to get it turning. Nowadays it's mechanised.

Once the mixes are prepared they are wheeled out to the baking hall, where groups of women thumb-knead cubes of dough into baking trays. Other bakers gloop in the filling and it all goes into one of three electric ovens – another recent concession to technology – each of which can bake 1,800 tarts an hour.

On an average weekday 10,000 Pasteis de Belém are sold; at weekends the figure rises to over 20,000. Customers with time to spare scoff their pastries in rooms decorated with tiles depicting Belém in the early 17th century. Others take them away in special paper tubes that can transport half a dozen.

The place is absolutely mobbed winter and summer, rain or shine. A compulsory stop on any tourist visit to Belém, it's no less a favourite feeding ground for lisboetas, who chat away while wolfing down the city's top sweet-tooth addiction, usually topped with a sprinkle of sugar and cinnamon. Now, after more than a century and a half of success, there is talk of a branch being opened for the first time, although it is not clear whether the new premises would be in Lisbon, Oporto or abroad, where *pastéis de nata* are becoming more popular.

Antiga Confeitaria de Belém
Rua de Belém 84-92, 1300 (21 363 7423). Train from Cais do Sodré to Belém/tram 15. **Open** 8am-midnight daily. **No credit cards**. **Map** p303 C10.

A wonderful unobstructed view of the river from one of Lisbon's largest esplanades. The price of drinks is pegged accordingly: a coffee costs 250$00. If you come from Lisbon by car, be sure to cross the railway via the Alcântara flyover, or you'll have to drive miles to Algés before you can turn around.

Northern Lisbon

Café Mexicana
Avenida Guerra Junqueiro 30C, 1000 (21 848 6117). Metro Alameda. **Open** 8am-midnight daily. **Credit** AmEx, DC, MC, V. **Map** p305 N5.

Favoured by local middle-class kids, Mexicana never has a quiet moment. It's particularly convenient for a drink or meal after a visit to one of the nearby cinemas, as it serves soups, sandwiches, steaks and fish dishes in the wood-panelled 1960s dining room right up until closing time. There are also plenty of croissants, fruit slices and cakes, plus counters selling meats, sausages and cheeses during the day. A *bica* costs 85$00 at the counter, 155$00 outside.

Pastelaria Versailles
Avenida República 15A, 1050 (21 354 6340). Metro Saldanha. **Open** 7.30am-10pm daily. **Credit** AmEx, MC, V. **Map** p305 M5.

A great place for afternoon tea or late-night hot chocolate surrounded by chandeliers, carved wooden display cases and stained glass. There is a huge selection of cakes, pastries, meringues and sweets, but be warned: the specials usually involve great gloops of whipped cream and disappear by early afternoon.

Bars

Cosy or cool, gritty or glitzy: there's plenty of choice if you know where to look.

In these diversified times, bars that are just that – places to drink in, not eat or dance – are a bit of a threatened species in Lisbon as elsewhere. That said, there are still clusters in Bairro Alto and around Cais do Sodré. Plenty of cafés and restaurants double up as bars. And dotted around Lisbon are a fair number of holes in the wall where grizzled men congregate around a barrel of wine (*see p149* **Going, going…**).

Lisbon's bar culture is indebted to Luís Pinto Coelho, who opened and decorated several bars here in the 1970s. His most famous is **Pavilhão Chinês**; he also created **Procópio** and **Paródia**. But the undisputed doyens of Lisbon bardom, dating from the 1920s, are **Bar Americano** and **British Bar**, which face each

other on a street near Cais do Sodré. During the zipped-up Salazar years, this old-fashioned harbour area was the only place visiting foreigners could find late drinking and lowlife. The lowlife remains, mainly in Rua Nova de Carvalho, where prostitutes solicit on the street and sex bars are named for faraway port cities. Most of the bars were turned into discos after the Revolution and have wonderfully tacky '70s decor. **Jamaica** (*see p217*) is by far the most successful, **Texas** probably the least reformed.

Up the hill, the Bairro Alto was for most of the 19th century an area of cheap whorehouses and fado places (*see chapter* **Fado**). The fado is still there, though increasingly tourist-oriented. But by the 1990s the district teemed with small, cosy or cool and generally noisy bars, opening late to take over where local restaurants left off. For all their hipness, none were designer bars; most were decorated on limited budgets and redone with the help of regulars paid in beer.

In this rectilinear maze, there are venues on every block, meeting the needs of gays and Africans, goths and rastas, artists in black and skateboarders – all are Bairro Altistas. Local residents may campaign, police may brandish decibel meters, and gloomsters may warn of the area's imminent death as shinier venues open on Avenida 24 de Julho and in the Docas – docks – of Alcântara. But bar life in Bairro Alto goes on – somewhat subdued, perhaps matured. It still has lots of what it was always best for: small bars where people meet over a beer and talk, rather than shout through the din and darkness.

As for the beer, the two main brands, Sagres and Super Bock, are virtually indistinguishable in taste, though with different brand pitches: Sagres has a struggling working-class image while Super Bock is assertively upwardly mobile. They are normally available either bottled/canned or on draught – the latter as an *imperial*, 20cl served in a tall glass. Anyone who thinks ordering such a puny amount of beer compromises their masculinity or that it won't quench their thirst should ask for a *caneca* – a glass tankard that holds half a litre. Sagres also makes a dark beer (*preta*) that is not quite stout, but tasty none the less. Foreign beers, licence-brewed locally or imported, are also widely available.

The best Bars

For feeling you're where it's at
The patch of Rua Diário de Notícias between **Café Suave** and **Cafédiário** (for both, see p148) at 1am.

For a laid-back early evening drink
Clube da Esquina (see p149) – a groovy venue.

For cheap tequila cocktails
And cheap tacos, too – **Mezcaloco** (see p151).

For a bit of rough charm
Estádio (see p149), as unpretentious as it gets.

For sipping a vintage port you'd never buy a whole bottle of
The **Solar do Vinho do Porto** (see p151).

For a slice of Lisbon kitsch that's not overrun by tourists
Procópio and **Paródia** (for both, see p154), the less well-known siblings of **Pavilhão Chinês** (see p152).

For travelling back in time
The **British Bar** (see p153), not only because of its clock.

Eat, Drink, Shop

The sociable **Clube da Esquina**. *See p148*.

At even the tiniest bars, you can usually also get snacks such as *tostas mistas* (ham and cheese toasted sandwiches), *bifanas* (braised pork steak, served in a roll) or *chouriço assado* (smoked sausage, grilled, often by being doused with alcohol and set alight before you).

Bairro Alto

Bairro
Travessa dos Inglesinhos 50, 1200 (21 347 1001). Metro Baixa-Chiado. **Open** 4pm-4am daily. **Credit** MC. **Map** p310 L9.
Opened in late 2000 in a former club praised for its cleverly angular interior design, Bairro is still in an experimental phase. The initial idea of regular live music has been ditched and a resident poet performs on Wednesdays; the rest of the time you'll hear funk and house. The drinks prices are pretty cheeky, but that means this is one of the few places in the Bairro Alto where teenagers aren't the dominant form of life by 3am. Also a good afternoon pit stop.

B'Artis
Rua do Diário de Notícias 95/97, 1200 (21 342 4795). Metro Baixa-Chiado/28 tram. **Open** 8.30pm-4am daily. **No credit cards. Map** p310 L9.
Cosy, smoky, jazz-driven bar, filled with wooden furniture, stone-topped tables, old posters, figurines and glass cases full of books. It's hard to get a table after midnight but there are stools and standing room at the back. Staff can get testy on busy nights. Famed for its chicken toasties, served until late.

Cafédiário
Rua do Diário de Notícias 3, 1200 (21 342 2434). Metro Baixa-Chiado/28 tram. **Open** 10pm-2am Mon-Thur; 10pm-4am Fri, Sat; closed Sun. **No credit cards. Map** p310 L9.
This small single-room bar is painted in blocks of lively colour, lending it a Central American feel. It's a quiet place to meet friends, and early evenings are popular with older couples and professionals. Busier nights see the owner fire things up with danceable African and Brazilian imports. At its best in summer, when the pavement between it and Café Suave fills up. Authentic Mojitos and interesting nibbles.

Café Suave
Rua do Diário de Notícias 6, 1200 (21 342 2793). Metro Baixa-Chiado/28 tram. **Open** 10pm-2am daily. **No credit cards. Map** p310 L9.
Long and lime green, with high-tech light fittings and dull furniture, this unlikely contender is one of Bairro Alto's most popular summer drinking spots. At the weekend the street outside heaves as its customers mix with those from Cafédiário opposite. DJ Lucky's groovy tunes are a good reason to patronise this modest bar, the great Caipirinhas another.

Capela
Rua da Atalaia 45, 1200 (21 347 0072). Metro Baixa-Chiado/28 tram. **Open** 8pm-4am daily. **Credit** AmEx, DC, MC, V. **Map** p310 L9.
This small, atmospheric bar is the principal haunt of Lisbon's artier bohos, off-beat insomniacs and the aesthetic end of the city's tiny music scene. With a bar in front and a few tables in the back it can get overcrowded and smoky at weekends. The insider atmosphere can also be offputting. But the staff are sweethearts and know how to socialise as well as party. DJs Fernando Fadigas and Nuno Rosa select a refined line in electro, warm, organic-sounding dub house and edgy electronica for an excellent sound system. At its best deep on a weekday night.

Catacumbas Jazz Bar
Travessa Água da Flor 43, 1200 (21 346 3969). Metro Restauradores then Elevador da Glória/28 tram/100 bus. **Open** 9pm-4am Mon-Sat; closed Sun & Aug (usually). **No credit cards. Map** p310 L9.
A real jazz lovers' bar. On week nights any would-be musicians can play the house piano (ask permission from Manel, the bespectacled waiter) and there are jazz or blues performances every other Thursday from 11pm to 2am; minimum spend 500$00.

Clandestino
Rua da Barroca 99, 1200 (21 346 8194). Metro Baixa-Chiado/28 tram. **Open** 10pm-4am Mon-Sat; closed Sun. **No credit cards. Map** p310 L9.
This basement-like bar serving up rock and alternative music is a Bairro Alto classic, though not exactly trendy nowadays. It won fame in the early 1990s, when most bars closed at 2am while it stayed open until 6am. The walls are covered with graffitti – you're welcome to write your own thoughts if you can find a space. Snacks served until late.

Clube da Esquina

Rua da Barroca 30-32, 1200 (21 342 7149). Metro Baixa-Chiado/28 tram. **Open** 8pm-2am daily. **No credit cards.** **Map** p310 L9.

A groovy, welcoming bar that's a bit of a squeeze on busy weekends, with a small bar counter and a few sociable tables. Although one owner is a hip hop scenester, it's a chilled-out assortment of up- and downtempo beats, reggae, jazzy funk and dub that draws a diverse and amiable mix.

Di Vino

Rua da Atalaia 160, 1200 (21 346 5988). Metro Baixa-Chiado/100 bus/28 tram. **Open** 9.30pm-4am Mon-Sat; closed Sun & 2wks Aug. **No credit cards.** **Map** p310 L9.

A cosy place, with candlelit tables and jazz and world music to soothe your senses. There's a good range of snacks such as salads, soups and *chouriço assado*. Wine lovers are well served, too: there are 50 different varieties on offer, eight sold by the glass.

Estádio

Rua São Pedro de Alcântara 11, 1200 (21 42 2716). Metro Restauradores then Elevador da Glória. **Open** 1pm-2am daily. **No credit cards.** **Map** p310 L9.

There's no name outside but you can recognise this bar by the paintings of Roman-style stadia – *estádios*. A cheap and pleasingly scruffy bar with rudimentary snacks, a snowy television and the tackiest juke-box in Lisbon, full of fado and the odd 1970s pop tune. Young bohos mix with garrulous

Going, going...

Although beer is gaining ground in Lisbon bars, wine is the traditional tipple, particularly for the working classes. One of the traditional shrines to wine is the *tasca*, a simple tavern where a glass of rough but drinkable plonk from the barrel sells for the price of a lollipop.

There are cheap eateries scattered across Lisbon that younger people especially refer to as *tascas*, but which are licensed as 'snack bars'. These are authentically Portuguese – they often have blaring televisions and middle-aged male regulars debating Benfica's latest crisis. But they lack the rough-and-ready flavour of the real *tascas*, of which precious few remain.

Although *tascas* had existed in Lisbon since the early 1900s, it was during the Spanish Civil War that they flourished. Refugees, mainly *galegos* from Galícia in north-western Spain, settled in Lisbon and opened shops designated *establecimentos de carvoeria e vinho* (coal and wine stores). On one side you could buy coal, oil, salt and vinegar; on the other you could drink wine – then the staple drink, since only the better-off could afford beer.

Workers from nearby construction sites would bring their *marmitas* (food pots) and the owner would heat them, provided they drank the house wine. It was served in *copos 3* (a 'number three glass', holding a tenth of a litre) or *penaltys* (a taller glass twice the volume), both still used today. Genuine *tascas* had the barrels in full view and counter, tables and walls in marble.

The 1974 Revolution and its aftermath altered much in Portugal, including eating and drinking habits. Most *tascas* disappeared

as the *galegos* sold up to go home or retire, and buyers turned them into more profitable bars or restaurants.

A handful have survived, though, little altered from the 1930s. Here you can swill cheap wine and fill your belly for the price of a starter in a posh restaurant. *Tascas* are still places where workers go to eat; customers are predominantly male and etiquette isn't a main feature.

Two former *tascas* in the Bairro Alto, now bars but still with their old marble counters, are **Portas Largas** (see p151), which also has the original tables, and **Di Vino** (see p149). But to see a genuine *tasca*, head for **A Provinciana** (Travessa do Forno 23-25, 21 346 4704), in an alley off the Rua das Portas de Santo Antão, where a glass of wine costs as little as 40$00. It's open 8am to 9pm every day except Sunday and sells main courses from 550$00.

Then there's **Valente e Vaqueiro** (Travessa da Madalena 2, 21 886 7849, closed Sun, closed Aug), just off Rua da Madalena. Known locally as '*a tasquinha do galego*', for obvious reasons, it was used for some scenes in *A Caixa* (*The Box*), a film by Manoel de Oliveira (see p188 **Manoel de Oliveira – the auteur's auteur**).

At the stadium – **Estádio**. *See p149.*

old geezers around formica-topped tables, served by a famously gruff old waiter who's actually a sweetie at heart.

Lisboa Bar
Rua da Atalaia 196-198, 1200 (21 347 1412).
Metro Baixa-Chiado/28 tram. **Open** 7pm-4am Mon-Sat; closed Sun. **Credit** AmEx, MC, V. **Map** p310 L9.
Unpretentious, welcoming bar at the unfashionable end of Rua da Atalaia, serving beer and snacks until late. The black-and-white tiled interior is covered with graffiti and festooned with international football scarves – this is a stopping place for travellers. Unusually for a Bairro Alto bar, it's used by locals, and is a downtown home for outer Lisbon types who see cheap beer and a friendly vibe as more important than in-crowd cred. The music is light: jazz, Brazilian and recent releases; the mini-club downstairs attracts a younger crowd with trance music.

Luso Café
Travessa da Queimada 10 (21 342 2281). Metro Baixa-Chiado/28 tram. **Open** 7pm-2am Mon-Sat; closed Sun. **No credit cards. Map** p310 L9.
A recent spin-off from ultra-trad fado venue Café Luso next door (*see p206*). The decor is modern, with furniture that is more stylish than comfortable. But it makes a change from its scruffy competitors, and the selection of mainly jazz CDs is played low to ease conversation. Lots of wines are sold by the glass, along with what passes for tapas in Portugal: cured ham, *chouriço* and cheese. Staff know their cocktails, too.

Majong
Rua da Atalaia 3, 1200 (12 342 1039). Metro Baixa-Chiado/28 tram. **Open** 7pm-4am daily. **No credit cards. Map** p310 L9.
Utilitarian chic, exposed ironwork, low-tech halogen lighting and a somewhat incestuous atmosphere are the features of this busy corner watering hole favoured by the self-consciously avant-garde: artists, up-and-coming actresses and unemployed bohemians. A new bar has been carved out of one wall to create more space, but after 11pm the place can still get rather crowded and aggressive. The table football adds to the air of chaos, but the owner's dad is a soothing presence.

Mezcaloco
Travessa da Água da Flor 20, 1200 (21 343 1863).
Metro Baixa Chiado/100 bus/28 tram. **Open** 9pm-4am daily. **No credit cards. Map** p310 L9.
Don't be misled by the kids hanging outside, lured by the cheap beer; this bar is ideal for those who like tequila-based cocktails. Although the tacos are not the real thing, they're not far off and improve when a Mexican takes over in the kitchen every now and then. The music is Latin, mainly Mexican.

Páginas Tantas
Rua do Diário de Notícias 85, 1200 (21 346 5495).
Metro Baixa-Chiado/28 tram. **Open** 9pm-4am Tue-Sun; closed Mon. **No credit cards. Map** p310 L9.
This spacious bar is a good post-prandial destination if you want to wind down rather than rage. Trad jazz is played at talkable volume, though the videos shown on one wall are an irritation. It's supposedly a journalists' hangout – hence the name 'so many pages' – but is very mixed. Tends to get smoky so head for the lower part if that bothers you.

Portas Largas
Rua da Atalaia 105, 1200 (21 346 6379). Metro Baixa-Chiado/100 bus/28 tram. **Open** May-Oct 7pm-4am daily. *Nov-Apr* 8pm-3.30am daily. **No credit cards. Map** p310 L9.
A key Bairro Alto bar, not least by virtue of its location opposite Frágil; on summer nights the street outside is packed. Nominally gay, it's actually very mixed, particularly early on; blonde tourists beware! The decor is the same as when the place was a scruffy old *tasca* before the in-crowd moved in (*see p151* **Going, going…**) – it has the old marble tables, a peanut-littered floor and fado blasting away. When not full it's really quite dull, and at times like these the cosy inner bar is the best bet. Also known as 'Record' after the sports newspaper offices upstairs, with its highly visible sign. Excellent Caipirinhas.

Solar do Vinho do Porto
Rua de São Pedro de Alcântara 45, 1250 (21 347 5707/www.ivp.pt). Metro Restauradores then Elevador da Glória. **Open** 2pm-midnight Mon-Sat; closed Sun. **Credit** AmEx, DC, MC, V. **Map** p310 L9.
The Port Wine Institute is a cool, dimly lit haven on the ground floor of the São Pedro de Alcântara Palace, which was built in 1747. Waiters will serve your choice of port from the 200 or so on the menu, ranging from 200$00 per glass to 3,810$00 for a 40-year-old vintage. You can also buy one or two bottles, but for larger quantities go to the supermarket.
Branch: Lisbon airport (21 847 0728).

Targus
Rua do Diário de Notícias 40B (21 347 7039).
Metro Baixa-Chiado/28 tram. **Open** noon-2am Mon-Fri; 8pm-2am Sat, Sun. **No credit cards. Map** p310 L9.
On paper it doesn't sound good: unsuccessful post-modern decor, dodgy art exhibitions, triangular bar stools that are easy to fall off, higher-than-average

Eat, Drink, Shop

For oenophiles it's got to be **Enoteca**.

mishmash. There are two large courtyards, one of them containing a table football table and a pinball machine, and there are three pool tables in the building itself. Staff are almost painfully attentive, and customers of the well-heeled, well-behaved type.

Pavilhão Chinês
Rua Dom Pedro V 89, Príncipe Real, 1200 (21 342 4729). Metro Baixa-Chiado/28 tram. **Open** 6pm-2am Mon-Sat, 9pm-2am Sun. **Credit** AmEx, MC, V. **Map** p310 L8.
Undoubtedly Lisbon's best bar decor, courtesy of Luís Pinto Coelho. A network of interconnecting rooms is lined with floor-to-ceiling glass cases stuffed with toy battleships, eastern European army officers' hats and other grim ornaments. This museum of kitsch is not cheap and the crowd who can afford the prices lend a fairly dreary atmosphere, but it's worth a look and the back room is an atmospherically Bond-style setting for a frame of pool.

prices. It's still a success, though, largely due to the enthusiasm and savvy of Guinea-Bissauan owner Hernâni, manager of a dozen local bands, who's often to be found here selecting the night's tunes from his collection of soul, jazz-funk and bossa nova. With a discerning multi-ethnic crowd, it's known as a journalists' bar but casts a much wider net.

Os Três Pastorinhos
Rua da Barroca 111-113, 1200 (21 346 4301). Metro Baixa-Chiado/100 bus/28 tram. **Open** Summer 9pm-4am Mon-Sat; closed Sun. Winter 9pm-4am Tue-Sat; closed Mon, Sun. **Credit** AmEx, MC, V. **Map** p310 L9.
Once an institution where the original Bairro Alto generation could feel they were in touch with things. It's now basically a bar, but divided into two sections: the front part with low music and an intimate atmosphere; and the back, where the sound is louder and there's still scope for a bit of hip movement. The selection is jazz, rare groove, soul and reggae.

Príncipe Real & São Bento

Enoteca-Chafariz do Vinho
Chafariz da Mãe d'Água, below Príncipe Real, 1200 (21 342 2079). Metro Avenida. **Open** 6pm-2am Tue-Sun; closed Mon. **Credit** MC, V. **Map** p307 L8.
Lisbon's only wine bar does a good job in both promoting the best Portuguese wines and ports and offering an extensive range of foreign wines. Small wonder, given that its owner is João Paulo Martins, Portugal's most influential wine writer. Housed in a monumental old public water reservoir, with a new grey metal mezzanine and pleasant terrace on the steps outside, this is easily the best place in town to taste wine. Some are available by the glass, and interesting snacks are served. Recommended.

Foxtrot
Travessa de Santa Teresa 28, São Bento, 1200 (21 395 2697/2703). Metro Rato. **Open** 6pm-2am Mon-Thur; 6pm-3am Fri, Sat; 9pm-2am Sun. **Credit** MC, V. **Map** p307 K8.
A warren of a bar full of old prints, faded oriental carpets, bronze statuettes and other knick-knacks. Though the name indicates a 1920s theme, it's a

Alfama, Sé, Castelo & Graça

See also **Cerca Moura** and **Esplanada da Igreja da Graça** (for both, *see p143*).

Costa do Castelo
Calçada Marquês de Tancos 1, Castelo, 1100 (21 888 4636). Metro Rossio/37 bus. **Open** *Bar* 1pm-2am Tue-Sun; closed Mon. *Restaurant* 8pm-midnight Tue-Sun; closed Mon. **No credit cards.** **Map** p311 M9.
Costa do Castelo is a bit of a hybrid. Drinks are served on a pretty terrace, marred only by the ungainly metal furniture, while dinner (main courses from 1,400$00) is rustled up inside. The place now has a Uruguayan chef, but African dishes still put in an appearance.

Divina Comédia
Largo de São Martinho 6-7, Sé, 1100 (21 887 5599). Tram 12, 28. **Open** 6pm-2am Tue-Thur, Sun; 6pm-3am Fri, Sat; closed Mon. **Credit** AmEx, MC, V. **Map** p311 M10.
Restaurant-bar in the heart of old Lisbon, just up from the Sé. It has a menu of Portuguese standards, a decent range of wines and spirits and a shady esplanade, but the main attraction for footie fans is its wide-screen TV.

Chapitô
Costa do Castelo 7, Castelo, 1100 (21 886 7334). Metro Rossio/12, 28 tram/37 bus. **Open** 7.30pm-2am Tue-Fri; 1pm-2am Sat, Sun; closed Mon. **Main courses** 1,700$00-3,800$00. **No credit cards.** **Map** p311 F9.
After a couple of years' break, the bar and restaurant attached to the Chapitô circus school (*see p225*) has been reopened. Now visitors can not only enjoy one of the best views in Lisbon from the terrace bar – of Praça do Comércio and the river – but tuck into a truly international menu. At lunchtime there's a choice of snacks, at night full meals. The restaurant – Restô do Chapitô – is closed for lunch from Tuesday to Friday.

Popping the cherry

Could this be the world's most localised drinking phenomenon? Around the north-eastern end of Rossio are a few tiny bars that survive almost entirely by selling a drink that is hardly available anywhere else – a sticky cherry liqueur called *ginjinha*. Opening early and closing at midnight, these bars never lack custom – partly because they're in one of the most touristy parts of Lisbon, partly because *ginjinha*, which many older folks still make at home, reminds sentimental Portuguese of their grandmothers.

The biggest-selling brand is Ginja Sem Rival, which comes with or without whole cherries (*com* or *sem*). But Ginja Espinheira, showcased in **A Ginjinha** at Largo de São Domingos 8 (open 7am-midnight), makes for stiff competition. A fixture since 1840, it also serves home-made lemonade and Eduardino, a herbal liqueur.

A few yards away, at Rua das Portas de Santo Antão 7, another miniscule bar with an ancient frontage (open 9am-midnight) serves Ginja Sem Rival and Eduardino, as well as *aguardente* and port. Further up, at No.61, is **Ginginha Popular** (7am-midnight). There are also *ginjinha* bars at Travessa da Ribeira 24 near Cais do Sodré, and at Largo de Trindade Coelho 17 in Bairro Alto.

Though there are some attractive bottles of *ginjinha* – the most nicely presented is Ginja Sem Rival with cherries, but the finest is Ginginha de Alcobaço, a lighter-coloured, less alcoholic *ginjinha* sold in a conical bottle – don't be fooled into thinking that they'd make a lovely souvenir. Face the facts – once you've got the stuff home, it'll only gather dust in the drinks cabinet. Try it in Rossio, where it belongs, then leave it there.

Santa Catarina & Bica

Baliza
Rua da Bica de Duarte Belo 51A, Bica, 1200 (21 347 8719). Metro Baixa-Chiado/28 tram. **Open** 1pm-2am Mon-Fri; 4pm-2am Sat; closed Sun. **No credit cards. Map** p310 L9.
This cool café-bar is peaceful by day, and draws an intimate gay/straight clientele by night. On busy weekends, the street outside is a scene of light flirtation. Baliza was once an old-style football *tasca* – – its name means 'goal'. With its friendly staff, wild-berry vodkas and great *tostas*, it scores highly.

Esplanada do Adamastor
Largo do Adamastor, Santa Catarina, 1200 (no phone). Metro Baixa-Chiado/28 tram. **Open** 10am-4am daily. **No credit cards. Map** p307 K9.
An ideal pit stop between the Bairro Alto and the Avenida 24 de Julho, where people lounge about the terrace imbibing drinks served from a late-night kiosk and enjoying stunning views of the river.

WIP
Rua da Bica de Duarte Belo 42, Bica, 1200 (no phone). Metro Baixa-Chiado/28 tram. **Open** 8am-2am Mon-Sat; closed Sun. **No credit cards. Map** p310 L9.
No name outside, WIP is halfway down the Elevador da Bica and part of the three-in-one enterprise (bar meets clothes store meets hair salon) that until recently was all across the road. It's a long, stylishly lit space, with original marble-lined walls and a bar counter for serious drinking. Shiny happy people from media, fashion and design mix with Bairro Alto bohos around glass-topped tables, served by staff with razor-sharp haircuts, while DJs play

house, breakbeat, reggae, jazzy grooves and UK garage. Early on it can feel cliquey, but it definitely has charm. A club is planned for next door.

Cais do Sodré

British Bar
Rua Bernardino Costa 52, 1200 (21 342 2367). Metro Cais do Sodré/15, 18 tram. **Open** 8am-2am Mon-Sat; closed Sun. **No credit cards. Map** p310 L10.
Not very British, despite a slightly wood-panelled pub atmosphere and Guinness on tap (plus Stella and Leffe). But this Lisbon institution has withstood trends better than the Bar Americano opposite, not having been overrun by tourists and had its prices jacked up. What has changed is the opening times, which were limited, and the speed of the staff, which was slow. Has a famous anticlockwise clock.

Lounge Café
Rua da Moeda 1-o, 1200 (no phone). Metro Cais do Sodré/25 tram. **Open** 4pm-2am Tue-Sun; closed Mon. **No credit cards. Map** p307 K9.
Tucked away at the bottom of Elevador da Bica is this unpretentious bar with a beery atmosphere. During the week it's a meeting place for jaded intellectuals and young naifs; the giant magic mushroom sprayed outside is more an image statement from the weekend crowd of cinéastes and artists than the work of any identifiable psychedelic contingent. Inside are a few tables over which talented DJs spin disco, breakbeat and retro-German electro next to a lumpy sofa, but there's never much dancing. Loose and undergroundish but not as cool as it thinks it is.

Eat, Drink, Shop

O'Gilins

Rua dos Remolares 8, 1200 (21 342 1899). Metro Cais do Sodré/15, 18 tram. **Open** 11am-2pm daily. **No credit cards. Map** p310 L10.

Better than your usual identikit overseas Irish pub, O'Gilins is done out in solid pine wood and adorned with reminders of the Republican cause. It has a long bar along with ample seating, and attracts a mix of Portuguese and assorted expats. There's live music (usually involving fiddles) on Friday and Saturday nights from 11pm. There are also jam sessions on Mondays from 10.30pm. A hearty Irish breakfast can be had until 5pm on Sundays; during the week, lunch is served from noon to 3pm and snacks are available at all times.

Santos & Avenida 24 de Julho

Fluid

Avenida Dom Carlos I 67, Santos, 1200 (no phone). Metro Cais do Sodré/25 tram/74 bus. **Open** 10pm-4am daily. **No credit cards. Map** p307 K10.

A squeaky-clean, pre-club bar with DJs every night. Entering Fluid is like being dropped into a giant glass of fizz. It's not just the brightly lit bubble mural or the cheerful bar staff that give the place its spark. It's more the fact that, despite the wannabe furniture (lava lamps, 1960s mobiles and retro-kitsch seating), dancing is somehow contagious.

Gringo's

Avenida 24 de Julho 116-118, Santos, 1200 (21 396 0911). Tram 15, 18, 25/14, 20, 28, 32, 38, 40, 43 bus. **Open** 10pm-5am Mon-Sat; closed Sun. **Credit** AmEx, MC, V. **Map** p306 J10.

A biker's bar with no grebos. In fact the Bloody Devils MC, who gather at weekends, are quite an approachable bunch. It's at its busiest on Saturdays, when various levels of enthusiasm roar up, unsaddle and nip in. A pool table is the icing on the three-storey wedding-cake interior full of Americana.

Pérola de Santos

Calçada Ribeiro Santos 25, Santos, 1200 (21 390 0024). Metro Cais do Sodré/25 tram/74 bus. **Open** 10pm-4am Tue-Sun; closed Mon. **No credit cards. Map** p306 J10.

Pleasant bar on a lively corner that's unusually relaxed for the area. Wooden tables in the candlelit back room are complemented by a small bar out front, a few tables outside, annually changing decor and fine nibbles. A place to meet friends rather than strangers, it's patronised by well-heeled revellers headed for nearby Kapital (*see p218*).

Docas & Alcântara

Doca Louca

Doca de Santo Amaro, Docas, 1350 (21 396 1520). Tram 15, 18. **Open** 9pm-4am Tue-Sun; closed Mon. **No credit cards.**

This tiny metal booth on the left as you enter the Docas is utterly unfashionable but offers drinks and snacks at sensible prices and is as good a people-watching spot as anywhere in the area.

Havana

Doca de Santo Amaro 5, Alcântara, 1350 (21 397 9893). Tram 15, 18. **Open** noon-3am Mon-Wed, Sun; noon-6pm Thur-Sat. **Credit** AmEx, MC, V.

Havana does its best to recreate that imaginary world of cane furniture and rum cocktails that is the Cuban theme bar. The huge curved staircases are pleasing to the eye, at least, and the Latin music offers a respite from the house and techno that dominates the rest of Docas. Reasonable food is served until about midnight.

Campo de Ourique & Amoreiras

Paródia

Rua do Patrocinio 26B, Campo de Ourique, 1350 (21 396 4724). Tram 28. **Open** 6pm-2am Mon-Fri; 10pm-2am Sat; closed Sun. **Credit** V. **Map** p306 H8.

One of several bars opened and designed by Luís Pinto Coelho, collector extraordinaire of junk, curios and art. It's all plush sofas, framed caricatures on the walls and knick-knacks, not to mention a musty smell, lack of windows and seedy boudoir atmosphere. But Paródia, opened in the mid-'70s and named after a satirical weekly published a century ago by artist and writer Rafael Bordalo Pinheiro, is friendlier and cosier than Procópio. Ring the bell to get in.

Procópio

Alto de São Francisco 21A, Amoreiras, 1250 (21 385 2851). Metro Rato. **Open** 6pm-3am Mon-Fri; 9pm-3am Sat; closed Sun. **Credit** MC, V. **Map** p307 K7.

Older version of Paródia, now run by designer Pinto Coelho's ex-wife Alice while he retains his master-piece, Pavilhão Chinês. When Procópio opened in the early '70s, left-wing intellectuals met in its dark, red plush interior and dreamed red dreams. Today the plush is stained and worn, clients are mainly furtive couples, and staff like a straight order. Worth seeing for its Wild-West-brothel-meets-musty-museum feel, though. It's just off Rua João Penha, near the Jardim das Amoreiras. Ring the bell to get in.

Northern Lisbon

Metro e Meio

Avenida 5 de Outubro 174, Campo Pequeno, 1050 (21 797 5997). Metro Campo Pequeno. **Open** noon-3pm, 5.30pm-2am Mon-Fri; noon-3pm, 10pm-2am Sat; closed Sun. **Credit** MC, V. **Map** p305 L4.

A real slice of '70s nostalgia, this, once you're past the witty façade: a section of a giant tape measure, in keeping with the name ('one and a half metres'). The decor has changed little since the place opened in 1974 and the music is not much more adventurous. Reasonably priced cocktails in a relaxed ambience.

Shops & Services

Quaint traditions co-exist with the globalised shopping experience – just make sure you have the right change.

Shopping in Portugal tends to inhabit one of two extremes. Lease laws allowing shopkeepers to continue on tiny rents mean that traditional shops are still to be found pursuing the same trade they've followed for generations, and newfangled changes are observed with a certain detached amusement. On the other hand, asking a local where to shop will probably elicit a proud recommendation for one of the large, glitzy edge-of-town shopping centres that have sprung up in the last decade.

Mercearias (grocers), *tabacarias* (tobacconists) and other specialist shops are to be found squeezed into cramped spaces behind open doorways throughout the city and, for those with time to browse, a wander through the traditional retail area of the **Baixa** (*see pp69-71*) will reveal some amazing old shops. Rua da Conceição is still bursting at the seams with colourful haberdashers, some with beautiful art nouveau storefronts, offering a kaleidoscope of buttons, ribbons, tassels, lace, sequins and feather boas as well as button-, belt- and buckle-covering services. There is also any number of excellent cobblers hidden away in tiny rooms amid piles of shoes. Herbalists sell miracle teas for every ailment and you can still get a haircut, shave, shoeshine, manicure and pedicure at the barber's or hairdresser's.

Along with quaint, traditional shops come quaint traditions, not least closing up for lunch or at some other random time when the owner pops out to see a man about a dog. A '*volto já*' (back soon) sign hanging inside the door may or may not mean what it says, and it's not unusual for some family businesses to shut up shop for a month or so in the summer. In shopping centres and larger shops most of the quirks have been ironed out of the retail experience. On the other hand, Portuguese shopkeepers can be admirably patient when dealing with silly foreigners who don't speak the lingo, and volunteering the correct change (*troco*) will make you friends almost anywhere.

It's not all nostalgia and bygone days in the city centre. The rebirth of the **Chiado** district (*see p85*), now largely restored after being ravaged by fire in 1988, has brought with it an influx of modern retailers, which rub shoulders with surviving traditional stores such as Luvaria Ulisses (*see p165*). Former grand department

Silver and jewels on offer in the Baixa.

stores Armazéns do Chiado (*see p175*) and Edifício Grandela have been refurbished as shopping centres and offer the sort of shops and extended opening hours that previously required a trip out of the centre.

Shopping in Lisbon is as much a social occasion as a functional one and nowhere is this more evident than in the **Bairro Alto** (*see pp86-88*), where the distinction is so blurred it's almost non-existent. Here, the shopping experience has been reinvented, with many boutiques opening mid-afternoon and continuing well into the night. Bars sell clothes, hairdressers serve beer and even some of the tiniest shops have DJs.

Further afield, hop off tram 28 at well-to-do **Campo de Ourique** (*see p97*) and you'll find the streets are lined not only with trees, but also with an abundance of upmarket boutiques, children's clothes shops and stores selling furnishings and household goods. These are interspersed with cafés and traditional shops and services and there's plenty of fresh produce to be had at the local covered market (*see p171*).

Eat, Drink, Shop

Both antique and bric-a-brac shops congregate in Rua de São Bento, Rua Dom Pedro V, Rua do Alecrim and around the Sé and Castelo. There's a good cluster of junk shops around the **Feira da Ladra** (*see p171*). For antique tiles, pay a visit to **Solar** (*see p170*).

Antiguidades Doll's

Rua de São Bento 250-254, São Bento, 1200-821 (21 397 8151). Metro Rato/tram 28. **Open** 10.30am-1pm, 3-7pm Mon; 10.30am-7pm Tue-Fri; 10.30am-3pm Sat; closed Sun. **Credit** AmEx, DC, MC, V. **Map** p307 K8.

As the name suggests, old dolls and a few other antique toys. There's also Portuguese furniture from the 17th to 19th centuries and Indo-Portuguese art.

Galeria da Arcada

Rua Dom Pedro V 56, Porta A, Bairro Alto, 1250-094 (21 346 8518). Metro Restauradores then Elevador da Glória. **Open** 10.30am-1pm, 3-7pm Mon-Sat; closed Sun. **Credit** AmEx, DC, MC, V. **Map** p310 L8.

An impressive collection of 15th- to 19th-century religious carvings, primarily Portuguese, from tiny crucifixes to a life-size depiction of the Annunciation. None comes cheap.

Mayer

Rua do Loreto 18, Chiado, 1200-242 (21 342 2881). Metro Baixa-Chiado/tram 28. **Open** 10am-1pm, 3-7pm Mon-Fri; closed Sat, Sun. **No credit cards.** **Map** p310 L9.

Mayer buys and sells old jewellery, cameras and other oddities. An original 1930s camera costs around 20,000$00.

O Velho Sapateiro

Travessa da Queimada 46, Bairro Alto, 1200-365 (21 347 0626). Metro Baixa-Chiado/tram 28. **Open** noon-8pm Mon-Fri; noon-7pm Sat; closed Sun. Closed 15 days in June. **No credit cards.** **Map** p310 L9.

Delightful Danish-owned shop selling an eclectic mix of bric a brac: old rouge boxes, cigarette tins, key rings, cameras, clocks, pill boxes, penknives and games.

Casa Varela

Rua da Rosa 321-325, Bairro Alto, 1200-386 (21 342 8205). Metro Restauradores then Elevador da Glória. **Open** 10am-1pm, 3-7pm Mon, Wed; 9.30am-1pm, 3-7pm Tue-Fri; 10am-1pm Sat; closed Sun. **No credit cards.** **Map** p310 L9.

Large collection of artists' supplies, including paints, pencils and drawing materials, specialist paper, brushes and easels. If you can't find what you're looking for here, try Casa Ferreira down the road at No.185.
Branch: Avenida de Madrid 28B, Areeiro, 1000-196 (21 848 4396).

Papelaria Fernandes

Rua Áurea (Rua do Ouro) 145, Baixa, 1100-060 (21 322 4830). Metro Baixa-Chiado. **Open** 9am-7pm Mon-Fri; 9am-1pm Sat; closed Sun. **Credit** AmEx, MC, V. **Map** p310 L9.

Primarily a stationer's selling office essentials, cards and wrapping paper, but with a decent range of art supplies and a copy centre upstairs. The Inforloja branch round the corner at No.91 Rua da Vitória has computer and printer accessories.
Branches: throughout the city.

BdMania

Rua das Flores 65-71, Chiado, 1200-194 (21 346 1208/bdmania@bdmania.pt). Metro Baixa-Chiado/tram 28. **Open** 11am-7.30pm Mon-Sat; closed Sun. **Credit** AmEx, MC, V. **Map** p310 L9.

Specialises in imported comics from the USA, France, Spain and Belgium, with related merchandise including posters, models, books and T-shirts.

Fnac

Armazéns do Chiado, Rua do Carmo, Chiado, 1200-094 (21 322 1800/www.fnac.pt). Metro Baixa-Chiado/tram 28. **Open** 10am-11pm daily. **Credit** AmEx, DC, MC, V. **Map** p310 L9.

Very good range of Portuguese lit in translation, plus lots of English-, French- and Spanish-language books. The music department has Portuguese, fado, Brazilian, African, jazz, classical and world music as well as pop and rock. There's also a well-stocked computer accessories department, camera and audio-visual equipment, a concert box office and a café offering a programme of films and recitals.
Branches: Centro Colombo, *see p175* (21 711 4200), CascaiShopping, Est Nacional 9, Alcabideche 2765 (21 469 9000).

Ler Devagar

Rua de São Boaventura 115-119, Bairro Alto, 1200-408 (21 324 1000/www.lerdevagar.com). Metro Restauradores then Elevador da Glória. **Open** noon-midnight Mon-Wed; noon-2am Thur-Sat. **Credit** AmEx, MC, V. **Map** p310 L8.

The English-language section has political and social science titles as well as literature. Jazz recitals, piano concerts, art exhibitions and literary discussions take place here, there's a small bar and it's open late.
Branch: **Culturgest**, Edifício Caixa Geral de Depósitos, Rua do Arco do Cego, Campo Pequeno, 1000-021 (21 849 1569).

Livraria Barata

Avenida de Roma 11A, Campo Pequeno, 1049-047 (21 842 8350/barata@ip.pt). Metro Areeiro. **Open** 9am-11pm Mon-Sat; closed Sun. **Credit** AmEx, MC, V. **Map** p305 N4.

Portuguese literature, academic and business titles, glossy coffee-table books and some English lit with a bias towards Penguin classics. There is an excellent selection of magazines downstairs, too, and a good-sized children's department.

Branches: Rua Tomás da Anunciação 68B, Campo de Ourique, 1350-330 (21 383 9000); Instituto Superior de Agronomia (specialist agriculture), Tapada da Ajuda, Ajuda, 1349-018 (21 363 8161); Instituto Superior Técnico (specialist engineering, sciences and IT), Avenida Rovisco Pais, Alameda, 1049-001 (21 841 7853).

Livraria Bertrand

Rua Garrett 73-75, Chiado, 1200-203 (21 342 1941/ www.bertrand.pt). Metro Baixa-Chiado/ tram 28. **Open** 9am-8pm Mon-Thur; 9am-10pm Fri, Sat; 2-7pm Sun. **Credit** AmEx, DC, MC, V. **Map** p310 L9.
Founded in 1732, this is Portugal's oldest bookshop. Apart from local literature, it stocks a reasonable selection of English novels, as well as guidebooks and foreign magazines.
Branches: throughout the city.

Livraria Britânica

Rua de São Marçal 83, Príncipe Real, 1200-420 (21 342 8472). Metro Rato. **Open** *Sept-May* 9.30am-7pm Mon-Fri; 9.30am-1pm Sat; closed Sun. *June-Aug* 9.30am-7pm Mon-Fri; closed Sat, Sun. **Credit** AmEx, MC, V. **Map** p307 K8.
Exclusively English-language bookshop, specialising in study books. It also has an excellent range of novels, classics, children's books, bestsellers and recent releases. Will order from the US and UK.

Livraria Buchholz

Rua Duque de Palmela 4, Avenida da Liberdade, 1250-098 (21 317 0580/www.buchholz.pt). Metro Marquês de Pombal. **Open** *Sept-May* 9am-6pm Mon-Fri; 9am-1pm Sat; closed Sun. *June-Aug* 9am-6pm Mon-Fri; closed Sat, Sun. **Credit** AmEx, MC, V. **Map** p307 L7.

German-founded generalist bookstore covering everything from astronomy to sociology. There are French, Italian, German, Spanish, Russian and English sections. There's also gay literature, classical and traditional music.

Livraria Linhares

Praça da Alegria 43, Avenida da Liberdade,1250-004 (21 324 1070). Metro Avenida. **Open** 10am-7pm Mon-Sat; closed Sun. **Credit** MC, V. **Map** p307 L8.
Art, design, photography and architecture books and Pantone technical colour guides. Around the corner, the branch specialises in imported comics.
Branch: Rua de Santo António da Glória 90, Avenida da Liberdade, 1250-218 (21 347 9164).

Press & periodicals

Tema

Avenida da Liberdade 9, 1250-139 (21 342 0140/belmiro@mail.telepac.pt). Metro Restauradores. **Open** 9am-9pm daily. **Credit** AmEx (Colombo branch only), MC, V. **Map** p310 L8.
Tunnel of a shop offering one of city's best selections of foreign newspapers and magazines, including specialist titles and trade mags. Will also do orders.
Branch: Centro Colombo, *see p175* (21 716 6890).

Second-hand & antiquarian

Loja da Colecções

Rua da Misericórdia 145-147, Bairro Alto, 1200-272 (21 346 3057). Metro Baixa-Chiado/tram 28. **Open** 10am-1pm, 2.30-7pm Mon-Fri; 10am-1pm Sat; closed Sun. **Credit** AmEx, MC, V. **Map** p310 L9.

More candles than you can handle at **Caza das Vellas Loreto**. *See p158.*

Eat, Drink, Shop

The English-speaking owner specialises in old Portuguese comics and children's books. There are also other books, prints and boxes of old movie star photos, ancient postcards and old board games stacked up on Singer sewing-machine tables.

O Manuscrito Histórico

Calçada do Sacramento 50, Chiado, 1200-394 (21 346 4283). Metro Baixa-Chiado/tram 28. **Open** 10am-1pm, 2-7.30pm Mon-Fri; 9am-1pm, 2-6pm Sat; closed Sun. **No credit cards. Map** p310 L9.
Old books, maps and prints dating back to the 16th century. Specialises in European manuscripts.

Computers

Suprides Computadores

Rua do Patrocinio 67E, Campo de Ourique, 1350-229 (21 395 4466/www.suprides.com). Tram 25, 28/bus 9, 13. **Open** 10am-1pm, 2.30-9pm Mon-Fri; 10am-1pm Sat; closed Sun. **No credit cards. Map** p306 H8.
Reputable computer supplier. English-speaking technicians offer PC repairs as well as sales of hardware and related accessories.

'Tou Aqui, 'Tou Aí

Rua Sabino de Sousa 71A, Arroios, 1900-398 (21 814 1640). Metro Olaias. **Open** 9am-1pm, 2-6pm Mon-Fri; closed Sat, Sun. **No credit cards. Map** p308 O6.
Mac specialists offering repairs, upgrades and sales by English-speaking technicians who know their stuff but are usually extremely busy.

Costume hire

Guarda-Roupa Anahory

Rua da Madalena 85, Baixa, 1100-319 (21 887 2046). Metro Baixa-Chiado/tram 12, 28. **Open** 10am-1pm, 2-7pm Mon-Fri; closed Sat, Sun. Closed Aug. **No credit cards. Map** p311 M10.
You can rent carnival outfits, formal wear and period costumes from here (the shop opens on the Saturday before carnival). The full range is kept in a warehouse, so call ahead; and if what you need is not in stock, staff can make it up with enough notice. A tuxedo or gladiator's costume costs 15,000$00 a day.

Design & household goods

A visit to any shopping centre will throw up a whole list of Portuguese and international chains full of ideas for jazzing up your home. Several (including Colombo and Amoreiras, *see p175*) have a branch of **Intério** for Italian designer cookware and Villeroy & Boch porcelain, crystal and cutlery. Failing that there's always **Habitat**. For second-hand furniture and equipment, your best bet is to look in *Ocasião*, a weekly publication containing about 50 pages of classifieds. It comes out on Thursdays and costs 290$00.

Atlantis Crystal

Centro Colombo, Avenida Lusíada, Benfica, 1500-392 (21 711 1054). Metro Colégio Militar-Luz. **Open** 10am-midnight daily. **Credit** AmEx, DC, MC, V.
Finely crafted, handmade Portuguese lead crystal in all shapes and sizes, from copies of 18th-century goblets to modern glassware. A Chiado branch is planned and there are concessions in some department stores such as Pollux (see p159).
Branches: throughout the city.

Casa Alegre

Rua Ivens 58, Chiado, 1200-227 (21 347 5833). Metro Baixa-Chiado/tram 28. **Open** 9.30am-7.30pm Mon-Sat; closed Sun. **Credit** AmEx, DC, MC, V. **Map** p310 L9.
Part of the Vista Alegre group (*see p159*), but stocking trendier, cheaper lines than the original, classier brand. There is a colourful range of modern, affordable Portuguese-made ceramics, along with good value glassware and kitchenware.
Branches: Centro Colombo, *see p175* (21 716 4479); Centro Vasco da Gama, *see p176* (21 895 5603); Oeiras Parque Shopping Centre, Avenida António Macedo, Paço de Arcos, 2750-560, Oeiras (21 441 7456); CascaiShopping, Est Nacional 9, Alcabideche 2765 (21 469 2382).

Caza das Vellas Loreto

Rua do Loreto 53-55, Chiado, 1200-241 (21 342 5387). Metro Baixa-Chiado/tram 28. **Open** 9am-7pm Mon-Fri; 9am-1pm Sat; closed Sun. **No credit cards. Map** p310 L9.
An atmospheric and pungent little shop, this 'house of candles' has been in the family since 1789. Everything is still made on the premises and the friendly owners offer their own aromatic range, including *chá verde* (green tea).

Depósito da Marinha Grande. *See p159.*

Cutipol

Rua do Alecrim 113-115, Chiado, 1200-016 (21 322 5075/www.cutipol.pt). Metro Baixa-Chiado/tram 28. **Open** *Jan-Oct* 2-7pm Mon; 10am-7pm Tue-Fri; 10am-1pm Sat; closed Sun. *Nov, Dec* 2-7pm Mon; 10am-7pm Tue-Sat; closed Sun. **Credit** AmEx, MC, V. **Map** p310 L9.

Well-known Portuguese cutlery maker, selling a beautiful collection of both machine-produced and gold-trimmed, handmade pieces, in stainless steel or silver. Also sells other household goods.
Branches: Alameda Duque de Palmela – Loja 3, CascaiShopping, Est Nacional 9, Alcabideche 2765 (21 483 8913).

Depósito da Marinha Grande

Rua de São Bento 418-426, São Bento, 1200-822 (21 396 3096/dep.marinha.grande@mail.telepac.pt). Metro Rato/tram 28. **Open** 9am-1pm Mon-Fri; 9am-1pm Sat; closed Sun. **Credit** AmEx, MC, V. **Map** p307 K8.

Thousands of pieces of hand-blown glasswork in copies of old, unusual designs. Prices are very reasonable, with large goblets in a range of colours selling for just under 3,000$00.
Branches: Rua de São Bento 234, São Bento (21 396 3234); Centro Colombo, *see p175* (21 716 3120).

Pollux

Rua dos Fanqueiros 276, Baixa, 1149-031 (21 881 1200). Metro Rossio. **Open** 10am-7pm Mon-Sat; closed Sun. **Credit** AmEx, DC, MC, V. **Map** p311 M9.

Known as Pollux Bollocks by local expats, this nine-storey department store is jammed full of things you never knew you needed – from crockery through carpets and bathroom rails to camping gas.

Tom-Tom Shop

Rua do Século 4A-E and 19, Bairro Alto, 1200-435 (21 347 9733). Metro Baixa-Chiado/tram 28. **Open** 11am-8pm Mon-Fri; 11am-7pm Sat; closed Sun. **Credit** AmEx, MC, V. **Map** p307 K9.

Stylish homeware, designer kitchenware and a good selection of lights, teapots, picture frames, door knobs and lots of cheap gift possibilities.

Vista Alegre

Largo do Chiado 18-22, Chiado, 1200-108 (21 324 2920/ www.vistaalegre.pt). Metro Baixa-Chiado/tram 28. **Open** 9.30am-7pm Mon-Sat; closed Sun. **Credit** AmEx, DC, MC, V. **Map** p310 L9.

The best-known Portuguese porcelain manufacturer, stocking a wide range of crockery, vases, plates and bowls. The range includes traditional designs, oriental-inspired styles and modern classics.
Branches: throughout the city.

Dry cleaners & laundries

Most *lavandarias* offer both *limpeza a seco* (dry cleaning) and *roupa branca* (general laundry, literally translated as white clothes, and often defined to include only high-volume items). Dry cleaning costs between 400$00 and 1,000$00 per item; laundry costs around 500$00 per kilo. The ubiquitous **5 á Sec**, with branches throughout the city (including one at Rua dos Correeiros 105-107), offers all the regular services.

Lava Neve

Rua da Alegria 37-39, Avenida da Liberdade, 1250-005 (21 346 6195). Metro Avenida. **Open** 10am-1pm, 3-7pm Mon-Fri; 10am-noon Sat; closed Sun. **No credit cards.** **Map** p307 L8.

Both DIY or service washes cost 800$00 for a wash or 1,400$00 for wash and tumble dry, including detergent. Ironing and dry cleaning services are also offered.

Fashion

For the average Portuguese about town, the conservative almost always wins out over the flamboyant. But a fair number of Portuguese designers are trying to change all that (*see p162* **Portuguese by design**) and a browse around the boutiques in Bairro Alto and Chiado will throw up some interesting creations. For club-and streetwear, Bairro Alto is again your best bet, but beware poor quality imports sold with a hefty mark-up. International label junkies should check out Avenida da Liberdade.

Agência 117

Rua do Norte 117, Bairro Alto, 1200-285 (21 346 1270). Metro Baixa-Chiado/tram 28. **Open** 2pm-midnight Mon-Sat; closed Sun. **Credit** AmEx, MC, V. **Map** p310 L9.

Shiny, lycra hot pants, sexy slip dresses, cut-off T-shirts and assorted 1970s-inspired clothes. There's also a hairdresser's and a tiny bar.

Eldorado

Rua do Norte 23-25, Bairro Alto, 1200-283 (21 342 3935). Metro Baixa-Chiado/tram 28. **Open** 1-9pm Mon-Fri; 3-9pm Sat; closed Sun. **Credit** AmEx, MC, V. **Map** p310 L9.

One of Lisbon's first alternative clothes shops, selling new and second-hand retro gear, mostly imported from London. Emphasis is on the 1960s and 1970s, but there are also Adidas tops, leather jackets, hats and bags. There's a music section, too.
Branch: Amoreiras, *see p175* (21 383 1836).

Gardénia

Rua Nova do Almada 96, Chiado, 1200-290 (21 322 4800/www.gardenia.pt). Metro Baixa-Chiado/tram 28. **Open** *Jan-Nov* 10.30am-8.30pm daily. *Dec* 10.30am-8.30pm Mon-Sat; 1-7.30pm Sun. **Credit** AmEx, DC, MC, V. **Map** p310 L9.

Excellent collection of original clothes and accessories from Portuguese designer Nuno Gama and mens- and womenswear from Luís Buchinho, plus international names such as Basi and Paul Smith. The Rua Garrett branch has outrageous platforms and a good line in cowboy boots.
Branches: Rua Garrett 54, Chiado, 1200-204 (21 342 1207); Centro Vasco da Gama, *see p176* (21 895 5887).

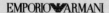

Gloves galore – **Luvaria Ulisses**. *See p165.*

Godzilla

Rua dos Douradores 120, Baixa, 1100-207 (21 886 9845). Metro Rossio. **Open** 11am-7pm Mon-Sat; closed Sun. **Credit** MC, V. **Map** p311 M9.
Tight, skimpy tops, wide trousers and other assorted urban streetwear in subdued colours. Jumpers, shirts and sporty sweats from Boxfresh, Combo and Mambo, and shoes from Fly London.

Iznougud

Centro Comercial Portugália, Avenida Almirante Reis 113, Arroios, 1150-014 (21 352 2807). Metro Arroios/Anjos. **Open** 11am-2pm, 3-7pm Mon-Sat; closed Sun. **No credit cards. Map** p308 N6.
Clothes from designer Katty Xiomara can be found here alongside adventurous in-house creations and imported streetwear. A second shop tucked away in the corner of the same shopping centre has reduced-price items and a rack of second-hand gear.

Nunes Corrêa

Rua Augusta 250, Baixa, 1100-056 (21 324 0930/nunescorreia@ip.pt). Metro Baixa-Chiado/ tram 28. **Open** 10am-7pm Mon-Sat; closed Sun. **Credit** AmEx, DC, MC, V. **Map** p311 M9.
The founder of the store, Jacinto Nunes Corrêa, was tailor to the royal family in the late 19th century. The shop is now one of several tailors in the Baixa continuing the tradition of made-to-measure suits; delivery takes around a month. Ready-to-wear names such as Armani and Gant, sportswear, and an exclusive range of shoes made by a sister company, are also available.

A Outra Face da Lua

Rua do Norte 86, Bairro Alto, 1200-287 (21 347 1570). Metro Baixa-Chiado/tram 28. **Open** 3pm-midnight Mon-Sat; closed Sun. **Credit** AmEx, MC, V. **Map** p310 L9.

Flower-power minis, wide-collared polyester shirts and other retro gear. The shop also stocks smart products, dope-smoking paraphernalia, assorted other toys and gadgets, a temporary tattoo service and lots of different teas.

Por-fi-ri-os

Rua Vitória 63, Baixa, 1100-618 (21 322 4960). Metro Baixa-Chiado/tram 28. **Open** 10am-2pm, 3-7pm Mon, Sat; 10am-7pm Tue-Fri; closed Sun. **Credit** AmEx, DC, MC, V. **Map** p311 M9.
Warren of a place made up of lots of different rooms interconnected by stairs and tunnels. The shop began by selling stockings in 1941 before changing to ready-to-wear clothes in the 1960s, when the façade and interior were reworked into the trademark monochrome. There's an odd combination of budget clubwear, lingerie, childrenswear, menswear, hats and handbags. The clothes are designed in a small backroom on site.

Zara

Rua Garrett 1-9, Chiado, 1200-203 (21 347 1823). Metro Baixa-Chiado/tram 28. **Open** 10am-8pm Mon-Sat; closed Sun. **Credit** AmEx, DC, MC, V. **Map** p310 L9.
Queen of cheap, disposable fashion, Zara's cool, spacious stores are filled with wearable mens-, womens- and childrenswear and benefit from frequent stock changes.
Branches: throughout the city.

Jewellery & accessories

With three streets named after the trade (and still home to the relevant shops), the Baixa is the place to head if you're looking for jewellery and silverware. Other accessories are not far away, with hats at **Azevedo Rua** in Rossio and gloves at **Luvaria Ulisses** in the nearby Chiado.

Araújos

Rua Áurea (Rua do Ouro) 261, Baixa, 1100-062 (21 346 7810). Metro Rossio. **Open** 10am-1pm, 3-7pm Mon; 9.30am-1pm, 3-7pm Tue-Fri; 10am-1pm Sat; closed Sun. **Credit** AmEx, MC, V. **Map** p310 L9..
On the Street of Gold, an established jeweller with unusual gold and silver pieces, some of them copies of old designs. There's also handmade filigree.

Azevedo Rua

Praça Dom Pedro IV (Rossio) 69, 72-73, 1100-202 (21 342 7511). Metro Rossio. **Open** 9am-7pm Mon-Fri; 9am-1pm Sat; closed Sun. **Credit** AmEx, MC, V. **Map** p310 L9.
Rossio used to be home to a whole community of hatters, though only this, founded in 1886, remains. Black, rabbitskin feltro hats, such as those worn by Portuguese horsemen, or the type favoured by Fernando Pessoa, are stacked up to the ceiling in the original wooden cabinets. There's also a large range of berets, Panama hats and bowlers.

Eat, Drink, Shop

Portuguese by design

Portuguese fashion design has a short history, despite centuries of a made-to-measure trade and the long-standing status of swathes of northern Portugal as a producer of textiles and ready-to-wear clothing for international retailers.

Generally acknowledged pioneer of Portuguese fashion Ana Salazar launched her own-label collection in the early 1980s, though she was making fashion statements long before. During the last years of the Salazar regime, she was jazzing things up with clothing imported from London and sold in her shop, Maçã. In the heady days of the '70s, Maçã (now closed) and **Por-fi-ri-os** (see p161) were among the 'in' places for cool, revolutionary threads.

With a backdrop of post-revolutionary fervour and an emerging nightlife scene, the Bairro Alto became a hub for young designers. These days, it continues to be a favoured location, together with neighbouring Chiado.

But it's only in the last couple of decades that an infrastructure has emerged. Design schools have opened and regular catwalk events feature up-and-coming talent as well as top names. In recent years an assault on the international scene has begun, engulfed in a plethora of media attention, prompting comments such as: 'In Portugal, fashion is in fashion.'

Recent shows in places such as São Paulo, New York and Paris have seen the participation of some of the names listed below, including Oporto-based brands such as Inspiro, Bruno Belloni, Maconde and Jotex, and designer duo **João Tomé** and **Francisco Pontes**. At their Lisbon atelier (Rua da Bela Vista à Lapa 21-1º, Lapa, 1200-612 21 390 2490, visits by appointment only), Tomé and Pontes sell adventurous ready-to-wear designs as well as haute couture in the form of urban casuals with a streetwear touch, for men and women. Another pair of designers, **Manuel Alves** and **José Manuel Gonçalves**, produce haute couture for men and women and a ready-to-wear collection for women: flowing skirts and little black numbers with chic suits, blouses, shoes and accessories (Rua das Flores 105-1º D, Bairro Alto, 1200-194, 21 347 5137).

Several Portuguese designers, and a fair number of foreign ones resident in Lisbon, have opened boutiques or ateliers in the city. Some, such as **Luís Buchinho** and **Nuno Gama** are represented in **Gardénia** (see p159), while others, such as **Katty Xiomara**, sell in **Iznougud** (see p161). Bear in mind, though, that imported designs predominate in both these shops.

Jewellery from established and new designers is to be found in gallery outlets and you might also catch some interesting pieces in temporary shows around town.

Aleksandar Protich

Rua da Rosa 112, Bairro Alto, 1200-389 (21 346 9855/protich@oninet.pt). Metro Baixa-Chiado/tram 28. **Open** *2-9pm Mon-Sat; closed Sun.* **Credit** *AmEx.* **Map** *p310 L9.*
Characterful atelier housed in a former butcher's shop. Distinctive skirts and tops with quirky contrasting stitching are lined up on rows of meat hooks together with slinky dresses; try them on in what used to be the fridge. If you're daring, let this Belgrade-born designer come up with a tailor-made novelty.

Prime cuts from **Aleksander Protich**.

Ana Salazar

Rua do Carmo 87, Chiado, 1200-093 (21 347 2289/www.anasalazar.pt). Metro Baixa-Chiado. **Open** 10am-7pm Mon-Sat; closed Sun. **Credit** AmEx, MC, V. **Map** p310 L9.
From the 'first lady' of Portuguese fashion, collections for men and women: suits, jackets and dresses with unusual finishing touches. The shop also stocks shoes, handbags and other accessories.
Branch: Avenida de Roma 16, Areeiro, 1000-265 (21 848 6799).

Fashion Gallery Atelier Kolovrat

Rua do Salitre 169-169A, Rato, 1250-199 (21 387 4536). Metro Rato. **Open** 11am-7pm Mon-Fri; 2-5pm Sat; closed Sun. **Credit** AmEx, MC, V. **Map** p306 K8.
Art meets fashion in this Croatian-owned 'space', where designers can work, exhibit and sell their latest creations. Whether you'd walk down the street in any of them is another matter. Not for the faint-hearted.

Fátima Lopes

Rua da Atalaia 36, Bairro Alto, 1200-049 (21 324 0546). Metro Baixa-Chiado/tram 28. **Open** 11am-4am Tue-Sat; closed Sun, Mon. **Credit** AmEx, MC, V. **Map** p310 L9.
Mens- and womenswear to be noticed in from this extrovert designer, who lives upstairs. Bold colours, figure-hugging leathers and a new angle on pinstripes. The space also houses a model agency, atelier, bar and club that's open until late.
Branch: Avenida de Roma 44 D/E, Campo Pequeno, 1700-348 (21 849 5986).

José António Tenente

Travessa do Carmo 8, Chiado, 1200-095 (21 342 2560). Metro Baixa-Chiado/tram 28. **Open** 10.30am-7.30pm Mon-Sat; closed Sun. **Credit** AmEx, DC, MC, V. **Map** p310 L9.
Portuguese designer stocking more conservative lines than most of the Bairro Alto boutiques. Trendy men's and women's suits, plus cotton shirts, urbane shoes, bags and accessories.

la

Rua da Atalaia 96, Bairro Alto, 1200-043 (21 346 1815). Metro Baixa-Chiado/tram 28. **Open** 2-8pm Mon-Fri; 5-9pm Sat; closed Sun. **Credit** AmEx, MC, V. **Map** p310 L9.
Distinctive, colourful, long knitted dresses, skirts and tops and some leather minis and jackets by Portuguese designer Lena Aires.

Extrovert threads from **Fátima Lopes**.

Maria Gambina

Rua Pinheiro Chagas 4, Saldanha, 1050-177 (21 315 5510). Metro Saldanha. **Open** 10.30am-2pm, 3-7pm Mon-Fri; 10.30am-2pm Sat; closed Sun. **Credit** AmEx, DC, MC, V. **Map** p304 L5.
A kaleidoscope of colourful sporty trousers and flowing skirts coupled with unusual sweaters, waterproof tops and trainers from this Oporto-based designer.

Jewellery

Contacto Directo

Doca de Santos, Rua da Cintura do Porto de Lisboa, Cais do Sodré, 1200-109 (21 392 9673/www.azul.net/cd). Metro Cais do Sodré. **Open** 10am-1pm, 2-7pm Mon-Fri; 2-6pm Sat; closed Sun. **No credit cards**. **Map** p307 K10.
Attached to a jewellery school, this gallery offers unusual contemporary works from students and teachers: school director Filomeno Pereira de Sousa and other designers such as Sílvio Alexandre and Maria João Clara. Also hosts conferences, workshops and temporary exhibitions.

Pedra Dura

Edifício Monumental, Avenida Fontes Pereira de Melo 51, Saldanha, 1050-120. Metro Saldanha. **Open** 10am-11pm daily. **Credit** AmEx, MC, V. **Map** p304 L5.
Stocks good-value, interesting jewellery by Portuguese designers including Claudia André and José Valerio, with some international names also represented. The in-town branch was due to open as this guide went to press.
Branch: Oeiras Parque Shopping Centre, Avenida António Macedo, Paço de Arcos, 2750-560, Oeiras (21 441 6515).

timeout.com

The World's Living Guide

Casa Batalha

Armazéns do Chiado, Rua do Carmo, Chiado, 1200-094 (21 342 7313). Metro Baixa-Chiado/tram 28. **Open** 10am-11pm daily. **Credit** AmEx, DC, MC, V. **Map** p310 L9.

This family-run *bijutaria* (costume jeweller) offers a chic range of costume jewellery, hats and scarves as well as a colourful array of sequins and beads. Also a personalised face-lift service for tired evening wear and handbags.
Branches: Amoreiras, *see p175* (21 383 1891); Centro Colombo, *see p175* (21 716 3862); Galerias Saldanha, *see p176* (21 315 2079); Centro Vasco da Gama, *see p176* (21 895 5601); CascaiShopping, Est Nacional 9, Alcabideche 2765 Est Nacional 9, Alcabideche 2765 (21 460 2455).

Luvaria Ulisses

Rua do Carmo 87A, Chiado, 1200-093 (21 342 0295). Metro Baixa-Chiado/tram 28. **Open** 9.30am-7pm Mon-Sat; closed Sun. **Credit** AmEx, DC, MC, V. **Map** p310 L9.

Rows of drawers contain exquisite gloves indexed by size, colour and material, available in quarter sizes. There are leather, satin, lace, crocheted and sporting varieties, lined with fur, cashmere, cotton or silk. A pair of regular kidskin gloves cost from 6,000$00. They come with a simple guarantee: a free, unlimited repair service.

Ourivesaria Aliança

Rua Garrett 50, Chiado, 1200-204 (21 342 3419). Metro Baixa-Chiado/tram 28. **Open** 3-7pm Mon; 9am-1pm, 3-7pm Tue-Fri; 9am-1pm Sat; closed Sun. **No credit cards. Map** p310 L9.

Worth a visit for the elaborate, gilded room, decorated in the style of Louis XV. There's a nice selection of silver trinkets, pendants, watches, cufflinks and pillboxes, some of them second-hand.

Test your new trainers' boogieability at **Sneakers Delight**.

Shoes

Making shoes is one of Portugal's traditional industries, and it shows in the abundance of shoe shops throughout the city. Prices are generally competitive, but watch out for quality if they seem too cheap to be true. Larger chains are also well-represented in the shopping centres and, for a more funky approach, try the Rua Garrett branch of **Gardénia** (*see p159*) and the boutiques in the Bairro Alto.

ML

Avenida Guerra Junqueiro 8B, Alameda, 1000-167 (21 848 6925). Metro Alameda. **Open** 10am-7pm Mon-Sat; closed Sun. **Credit** AmEx, DC, MC, V. **Map** 306 N5.

Stylish footwear including, unusually for Portugal, some up to size 41 for women and 46 for men. Portuguese-made brands include J MacGill & Co, whose upmarket range is on show at tailor's Nunes Corrêa (*see p161*), owned by the same company.
Branches: Galerias Saldanha, *see p176* (21 355 1542); Colombo Shopping Centre, *see p175* (21 712 0310); Oeiras Parque Shopping Centre, Avenida António Macedo, Paço de Arcos, 2750-560, Oeiras (21 446 1878).

Pablo Fuster

Amoreiras, Avenida Engenheiro Duarte Pacheco, 1070-103 (21 385 6886) . **Open** 10am-11pm daily. **Credit** AmEx, DC, MC, V. **Map** p306 J7.

Spanish designer-Portuguese manufacturer combo. Beautifully designed shoes, including flamboyant stilettos, sexy mules and a few everyday shoes up to size 40. Men's shoes are more conservative.
Branches: Centro Colombo, *see p175* (21 716 3421); Monumental Shopping Centre, Avenida Fontes Pereira de Melo 51, Saldanha, 1050-120 (21 315 4343); Centro Vasco da Gama, *see p176* (21 895 1207).

Seaside

Rua Augusta 248, Baixa, 1100-056 (21 347 6233). Metro Baixa-Chiado/tram 28. **Open** 9.30am-7.30pm Mon-Fri; 9.30am-7pm Sat; closed Sun. **No credit cards. Map** p310 M9.

At the cheaper end of the scale, functional men's and women's styles. Most are made in Portugal (don't be fooled by the English- and Italian-sounding brand names), though some are imported from Spain.
Branches: Praça da Figueira 14A, Baixa, 1100-241 (21 887 3826); Rua dos Fanqueiros 273, Baixa, 1100-230 (21 885 0980); Avenida Almirante Reis 10A, Intendente, 1150-017 (21 885 0069); Praça de Londres 7B, Areeiro, 1000-192 (21 849 4303).

Sneakers Delight

Rua do Norte 30-32, Bairro Alto, 1200-286 (21 347 9976/www.sneakersdelight.com). Metro Baixa-Chiado/tram 28. **Open** 2-10pm Mon-Sat; closed Sun. **Credit** AmEx, MC, V. **Map** p310 L9.

With the same Dutch owner as Outra Face da Lua up the road (*see p161*), this shop specialises in, well, sneakers. After 7pm at weekends a DJ will help you test the boogiebility of the footwear on offer.

Mouraria – centro comercial or centro cultural?

A short walk or an even shorter metro ride from the Praça da Figueira, in a district once settled by Moors who had been booted outside the city walls, is the Centro Comercial Mouraria. Proximity aside, a simple extension of old-world Baixa it isn't, with its eclectic mix of African, Indian and Chinese shops and cafés. The dingy pile that houses it contrasts sharply with the city's sparkling new shopping centres, but behind the unpromising aesthetics of the place is a bustling market and multi-ethnic melting pot.

Members of the city's various immigrant communities come here to work, shop, have their hair done or simply relax. It's by far the best place to stock up on ethnic ingredients and specialist products difficult to unearth elsewhere in Lisbon.

There's rice by the sack, all shades of chillis and spices, couscous and palm oil, an array of fresh produce and imported sauces and, for the sweet-toothed, home-made cakes. There's also a concentration of salons and shops specialising in African hair care.

Rows of shops sell cheap clothing, accessories, watches and any amount of plastic tack at bargain prices. Of course, for this stuff, a meander through any part of central Lisbon should do the trick; gypsies, immigrants and Portuguese alike buy here and re-sell on street corners by day and in the city's watering holes by night. When the centre is at its busiest, the floor disappears under a flurry of cardboard boxes and plastic wrapping as street traders rummage for merchandise and stagger out under the weight of overstuffed black bin bags.

Stivali

Rua Castilho 71C, Marquês de Pombal, 1250-068 (21 386 0944). Metro Marquês de Pombal. **Open** Feb-Sept 2-7pm Mon; 10am-7pm Tue-Fri; 10am-2pm Sat; closed Sun. Oct-Jan 2-7pm Mon; 10am-7pm Tue-Fri; 10am-7pm Sat; closed Sun. **Credit** AmEx, DC, MC, V. **Map** p306 K7.

Stylish Italian imports, mostly women's but a few men's styles too.

Branch: Avenida João XXI 11C, Areeiro, 1000-298 (21 848 5118).

Florists

Flores da Romeira Roma

Avenida de Roma 50C, Campo Pequeno, 1700-348 (21 848 8289). Metro Roma. **Open** 8am-midnight daily. **Credit** AmEx, DC, MC, V. **Map** p305 N4.

A veritable warehouse of cut flowers and potted plants. Credit cards can only be used in the shop; for telephone orders, payment by cash or cheque will be collected first. Helpful staff speak English, are with Interflora and deliver until 11pm seven days a week.

Horto do Campo Grande

Campo Grande 171, Campo Grande, 1700-090 (21 782 6660/www.hortodocampogrande.com). Metro Campo Grande. **Open** 9am-7pm daily. **Credit** V. **Map** p304 L1.

Enormous garden centre selling all manner of flora, from bonsai trees to seven-metre-high palms and giant cacti. The florist does Interflora and the centre offers gardening services and plant rental.

Pequeno Jardim

Rua Garrett 61, Chiado, 1200-203 (21 342 2426). Metro Baixa-Chiado/tram 28. **Open** 8am-7pm Mon-Sat; 9am-1pm Sun. **No credit cards. Map** p310 L9.

Tiny and friendly flower shop, with Interflora.

Food & drink

There's a *mercearia* (grocer) on every other corner and any number of *padarias* (bakeries) and *talhos* (butchers), so you generally don't have to walk too far to buy life's essentials. At the other extreme are the hypermarkets which offer all these things and more and have been successfully luring away customers.

Portuguese delis

Charcutaria Brasil

Rua Alexandre Herculano 90, Rato, 1250-012 (21 388 5644). Metro Rato. **Open** 8am-9pm Mon-Fri; 8am-2pm Sat; closed Sun. **No credit cards. Map** p307 K7.

Portuguese wines, cheeses, ham, sausages and other local deli produce. A takeaway counter features spit-roasted chickens and typical dishes. During the hunting season you may encounter hares and pheasants, complete with fur or feathers.

A Diplomata

Avenida João XXI 24A/B, Areeiro, 1000-302 (21 848 1260). Metro Areeiro. **Open** 9.30am-7.30pm Mon-Fri; 9.30am-1pm Sat; closed Sun. **No credit cards. Map** p305 N4.

Open from 9am to 8pm, Monday to Saturday, with most businesses conforming roughly to the same hours, the Centro Comercial Mouraria could be described as something of a social, as well as a shopping, centre. Expect to find several generations tucking into lunch outside their shops, groups of guys playing cards around formica tables and small children fast asleep on the stock.

Centro Comercial Mouraria

Centro Comercial Mouraria, Martim Moniz, 1100-364. Metro Martim Moniz/ tram 12, 28. **Map** p311 M9.

Discoteca Ópus 222

Level 1 (21 887 8348). **Open** 10am-7.30pm Mon-Sat; closed Sun. **Credit** AmEx, MC, V.
Specialist in African music genres such as zouk, kizomba, funaná and mornas.

Nita Cash & Carry

Level -1 (21 888 1316). **Open** 10am-8pm Mon-Sat; closed Sun. **No credit cards**.

Indian grocer's with an excellent range of spices, lentils, pulses and vegetables, as well as ghee and a whole row of different kinds of popadom.

Popat Store

Level -1, Galeria do Metro (21 887 1163/fax 21 886 0043). **Open** 9am-8pm Mon-Sat; closed Sun. **No credit cards**.
The shelves are stacked high with multicoloured spices, a range of chillis and exotic fresh produce. Home-made Indian sweets too.

Supermercado Chen

Level 1 (21 888 2756). **Open** 9am-8pm Mon-Sat; closed Sun. **No credit cards**.
Noodles, oyster sauce and other basic Chinese ingredients. Also grass jelly, dumplings, spring rolls, moon cakes and some home-made specialities. If you can't find what you need, there's another Chinese shop in the basement.
Branch: Poço do Borratém 23, Baixa, 1100-408 (21 886 7039).

A neighbourhood deli selling Portuguese and imported foods. Dried fruit and nuts, cheeses, wines, buckets of olives and roast chickens to take away.

Manteigaria Silva

Rua Dom Antão de Almada 1C-D, Baixa, 1100-197 (21 342 4905). Metro Rossio. **Open** 9am-7pm Mon-Fri; 9am-1pm Sat; closed Sun. **Credit** AmEx, MC, V. **Map** p311 M9.
The Portuguese have been eating *bacalhau* (salt cod) for centuries. It's sold dried and salted and the huge kite-shaped cod carcasses are stacked up whole ready for chopping to order. Alternatively, there are *caras* (faces) and *linguas* (tongues). Also stocks tinned fish and has a cheese and *presunto* (smoked ham) counter.

Manuel Tavares

Rua da Betesga 1A-B, Baixa, 1100-090 (21 342 4209). Metro Rossio. **Open** 9.30am-7.30pm Mon-Fri; 9am-1pm Sat; closed Sun. **Credit** AmEx, DC, MC, V. **Map** p311 M9.
Vast range of *chouriço* (sausage) including *morçelas* (black pudding) and *chouriço doce* (with honey and almonds). There are also smoked pig's tongues, good *presunto* (smoked ham) and Portuguese cheese, dried fruit, *bacalhau* and port.

Martins & Costa

Rua Alexandre Herculano 34, Marquês de Pombal, 1250-011 (21 314 1617). Metro Marquês de Pombal. **Open** 9am-7pm Mon-Fri; 9am-1pm Sat; closed Sun. **Credit** MC, V. **Map** p307 L7.
A mouth-watering range of Portuguese and foreign gourmet treats. Smelly cheeses, smoked meat and

Dusty vintages at **Manuel Tavares**.

fish, wines, roast chickens, pastries and cakes cooked on the premises. Imported goods include Marmite, mint sauce and specialist teas – but none of them come cheap.

Foreign delis

Despite the huge range of goods available in Lisbon's hypermarkets (*see p168*), there are some specialised food products they don't sell. For a concentration of ethnic delis, try **Centro Comerical Mouraria** (*see above*).

GB Store

Avenida Gago Coutinho Lote 4, São João do Estoril, 2765-324 (21 466 2453). Train Cais do Sodré to São João do Estoril. **Open** 9am-6pm Mon-Fri; 10am-2pm Sat; closed Sun. **Credit** AmEx, MC.

Eat, Drink, Shop

Small supermarket selling exclusively UK imports. Much frequented by homesick expats stocking up on Shreddies, PG Tips and Club biscuits. For Christmas puds, stuffing mix and Christmas crackers, get your order in before mid-November.

Supermarkets & hypermarkets

The vast hypermarket **Continente** stocks clothes, white goods and electronics as well as food, and has branches in the Centro Colombo and other shopping centres. In-town supermarket **Pingo Doce** has branches throughout the city, while **Pão de Açúcar**, in the Amoreiras centre, stocks a sophisticated product range within a manageable space.

Mercado Praça da Figueira

Praça da Figueira 10B, Rossio, 1100-241 (21 886 7464). Metro Rossio. **Open** 8.30am-8pm Mon-Fri; 8.30am-7pm Sat; closed Sun. **Credit** AmEx, MC, V. **Map** 311 M9.

Hidden away behind a deceptively tiny doorway, this is a cross between a market and a small supermarket. It's an atmospheric place to shop for your food, with Pombaline arches and original wooden beams. The saintly *azulejos* (tiles) were added later.

Tea & coffee

A Carioca

Rua da Misericórdia 9, Chiado, 1200-270 (21 346 9567). Metro Baixa-Chiado/tram 28. **Open** 9am-7pm Mon-Fri; 9am-1pm Sat; closed Sun. **No credit cards. Map** p310 L9.

Everything from the cheapest coffee at 360$00 per kilo to specialist beans costing up to 2,930$00 per kilo, with several own blends. Staff will make up an individual blend on request and grind it to suit your own coffee-maker.

Casa Pereira

Rua Garrett 38, Chiado, 1200-204 (21 342 6694). Metro Baixa-Chiado/tram 28. **Open** 9am-1pm, 3-7pm Mon, Sat; 9am-7pm Tue-Fri; closed Sun. **No credit cards. Map** p310 L9.

Old, established shop selling imported coffee from Timor, Brazil and other ex-colonies. These days it also has imported tea, biscuits and chocolates.

Cakes

Look out for *pastelarias* (cake shops) bearing the words *fábrico próprio*, which means everything's baked on the premises. Biscuits are often sold by the kilo and all *pastelarias* will box up your purchases *para levar* (to take away). See also **Confeitaria Nacional** (*p141*), **Casa Suiça** (*p140*) and **Antiga Confeitaria de Pastéis de Belém** (*see p146* **Tarts with tradition**), which offer some of the city's best takeaway cakes.

Create your own coffee blend at **A Carioca**.

Picasso

Rua Barata Salgueiro 31A, Avenida da Liberdade, 1250-042 (21 355 6625). Metro Avenida. **Open** 7am-7.30pm Mon-Fri; 7am-1pm Sat; closed Sun. **No credit cards. Map** p307 L7.

Loud, noisy café, usually packed with office workers and somewhat daunting to the uninitiated. Excellent range of cakes and pastries.

Wine & alcohol

As well as decent red and white wines, there are plenty of stronger alcoholic options, including *branca* (white) and *velha* (old) *aguardentes* (grape mash distillate). Local liqueurs include Licor Beirão (with herbs) and *ginjinha* (with morello cherries). There's also *absinto* (absinthe), though the contemporary Portuguese version lacks the hallucinatory ingredient, oil of wormwood. Local brandy comes as Macieira or Constantino, both perfectly drinkable. Vinho da Madeira (madeira) is widely available, as is vinho do Porto (port).

Garrafeira Nacional

Rua de Santa Justa 18-24, Baixa, 1100-485 (21 887 9080). Metro Baixa-Chiado/tram 12, 28. **Open** 9.30am-7.30pm Mon-Fri; 9am-1pm Sat; closed Sun. **Credit** AmEx, DC, MC, V. **Map** p311 M9.

Over 4,000 different Portuguese wines and ports. There's also a large selection of crystallised figs, limes, oranges and pears as well as dried fruits and nuts. Staff are helpful and shipping can be arranged.

Napoleão

Rua dos Fanqueiros 70, Baixa, 1100-231 (21 887 2042/www.napoleao.co.pt). Metro Baixa-Chiado/tram 12, 28. **Open** 9am-8pm Mon-Sat; closed Sun. **Credit** AmEx, MC, V. **Map** p311 M10.

Multilingual staff will show you their extensive range of Portuguese wines and ports. They do a roaring trade in shipping bottles. There's a Roman ruin under the shop visible through a glass floor. **Branches**: Rua da Misericórdia 121-123, Chiado, 1200-271 (21 342 7182); Rua Engenheiro Vieira da Silva 14 C-D, Saldanha, 1050-105 (21 314 1604); Avenida de Roma 8, Areeiro, 1000-265 (21 848 1240); Rua Luis Augusto Palmeirim, 2-D, Alvalade, 1700-274 (21 840 3679); Rua Cavaleiro de Oliveira 13-21, Arroios, 1170-086 (21 814 0841).

Solbel

Rua António Patrício 23A-C, Alvalade, 1700-047 (21 799 1050). Metro Roma. **Open** *Jan-Nov* 9am-1pm, 3-7pm Mon-Fri; closed Sat, Sun. *Dec* 9am-1pm, 3-7pm Mon-Sat; closed Sun. **No credit cards.** **Map** p304 M3.

Cheapish wine and spirits warehouse. Good range of Portuguese wines and French champagnes. Mind-numbing variety of spirits, featuring 16 different types of vodka and an excellent range of *aguardentes* and *absinto*.

Branch: Rua da Conceição da Glória 28, Avenida da Liberdade, 1250-081 (21 321 9450).

Vegetarian & health food

Celeiro

Rua 1º de Dezembro 65, Baixa, 1200-357 (21 342 2463). Metro Rossio. **Open** 8.30am-8pm Mon-Fri; 8.30am-7pm Sat; closed Sun. **Credit** AmEx, MC, V. **Map** p310 L9.

Health-food supermarket selling vegan products, cereals, beans, pulses, vitamins, herbal cures and vitamin supplements. There's a small selection of other ecological products and a range of natural health books upstairs, and a self-service restaurant in the basement.

Branches: throughout the city.

Hair & beauty

Cosmetics & perfumes

Alceste

Rua da Prata 173, Baixa, 1100-416 (21 342 7914). Metro Baixa-Chiado. **Open** 10am-7pm Mon-Sat; closed Sun. **No credit cards.** **Map** p311 M9.

The counter here is overflowing with huge, old-fashioned bottles of perfume and customers can choose fragrances to be mixed. The friendly owner also specialises in stage make-up and blends colours and oils in a back room.

Perfumes & Companhia

Edifício Grandela, Rua do Carmo 42C, Chiado, 1200-094 (21 347 9552). Metro Baixa-Chiado/tram 28. **Open** 10am-7.30pm Mon-Sat; closed Sun. **Credit** AmEx, DC, MC, V. **Map** p310 L9.

A great range of upmarket perfumes and cosmetics from the major French houses. The freely available testers mean you're likely to come out smelling like a tart's handbag.

Branches: throughout the city.

Hairdressers & barbers

Most cabeleireiros (hairdressers) will give a decent man's trim for around 1,500$00 and you'll still encounter traditional barbers where you can recline on a well-upholstered chair and enjoy a cut, shave, manicure, pedicure and shoeshine. Many salons also offer beauty

services (*instituto da beleza*). In **Centro Comercial Mouraria** (*see p166* **Mouraria – centro comercial or centro cultural**) there's a whole row of African hair salons and specialist shops.

Barbearia Campos

Largo do Chiado 4, Chiado, 1200-108 (21 342 8476). Metro Baixa-Chiado/tram 28. **Open** 10am-2pm, 4-7pm Mon-Thur; 9am-2pm, 4-7pm Fri; 9am-1pm Sat; closed Sun. **No credit cards.** **Map** p310 L9.

This barber's opened over a century ago and has changed little since then. The original marble-topped counters hold porcelain sinks and a rudely erected boiler provides hot water. There's an intriguing collection of old brushes, scissors and bottles that look as though they should be in a museum. A shave is 900$00, and a men's cut is 1,400$00.

Facto

Rua da Rosa 40-42, Bairro Alto, 1200-388 (21 347 8821). Metro Baixa-Chiado/tram 28. **Open** 12.30-11pm Mon-Sat; closed Sun. **No credit cards.** **Map** p310 L9.

Take one butcher's shop, some restored barber's chairs and a dynamic London duo – they've been known to DJ at local clubs out of hours – and you get Facto. It's usually pretty busy, so it's best to make an appointment.

Manuel João Trigo

Rua do Jasmim 16, Príncipe Real, 1200-229 (21 342 5229). Metro Rato. **Open** 10am-8pm Mon-Fri; closed Sat, Sun. **No credit cards.** **Map** p307 K8.

Trendy trims – **WIP**. *See p170.*

Eat, Drink, Shop

Trained at Vidal Sassoon in London, João speaks fluent English and French and can be trusted with cuts, dyeing and restyles. Beauty treatments include manicures, pedicures, facials and waxing. Book ahead.

WIP – Work In Progress
Rua da Bica Duarte Belo 47-49, Bica, 1200-054 (21 346 1486). Metro Baixa-Chiado/tram 28. **Open** *Shop* 2-10pm Mon-Thur; 2pm-2am Fri, Sat; closed Sun. *Hairdresser* 2-10pm Mon-Thur; 2pm-2am Fri; 3-11pm Sat; closed Sun. **Credit** MC, V. **Map** p310 L9.
A cool hairdresser and clothes shop set-up. Multinational staff and cool background tunes put it streets ahead of the competition. Definitely the place for a truly radical restyle.

Handicrafts

The Portuguese *azulejo* (tile) has been used as a wall covering for centuries (*see p37* **Where did you get that tile?**). Ornate panels decorate churches, palaces and public buildings, while the outside of old apartment blocks are routinely covered, helping to waterproof against winter rains. They're among the most popular souvenirs sought out by tourists, but among the tourist tat are plenty of fine hand-painted, contemporary and antique tiles. There are also distinctive regional ceramics and pottery, a variety of textiles from linen tablecloths to woollen blankets and *bordado* (embroidery) – the most expensive *bordado* comes from Madeira and, if genuine, carries a small seal guaranteeing authenticity.

Antiga Casa do Castelo
Rua Santa Cruz do Castelo 15, Castelo, 1100-479 (21 888 0508/antigacasa@mail.telepac.pt). Tram 12, 28/bus 37. **Open** 10am-6.30pm daily. **Credit** AmEx, DC, MC, V. **Map** p311 M9.
American-owned handicrafts shop selling tiles, ceramics, embroidery, linen, metalwork, cork and old-style Portuguese soaps. Also stocks materials to create your own picture frame or mirror with the tiles you buy.

Loja do Mundo Rural
Rua Saraiva de Carvalho 216-220, Campo de Ourique, 1250-245 (21 395 8889/ lojadomundorural@ mail.telepac.pt). Tram 25, 28/bus 9. **Open** 10am-8pm Mon-Sat; closed Sun. **No credit cards. Map** p306 H8.
Lots of earthy ceramics in subtle colours, along with metalwork and other decorative creations, and a range of handcrafted wooden toys and rag dolls, clogs, woollen jackets and rugs. Also has a deli with hams, sausages, cheeses and wines.

A Roca e o Linho
Rua da Graça 27-29, Graça, 1170 (21 812 3290). Tram 28. **Open** 10am-1pm, 3-7pm Mon-Fri; 10am-1pm Sat; closed Sun. **No credit cards. Map** p308 N8.

A council-funded initiative that has given a group of local women the chance to design and make cotton, linen and woollen textiles and clothing in more or less traditional designs. The shop also provides an outlet for others' work, with the emphasis on *azulejos*, glass and ceramics. Upstairs hosts shows by pupils of the Artes e Oficios workshop next door; pieces aren't for sale, but you can place orders.

Santos Oficios Artesanatos
Rua da Madalena 87, Baixa, 1100-319 (21 887 2031/www.santosoficios-artesanato.pt). Metro Rossio/tram 28. **Open** 10am-8pm Mon-Sat; closed Sun. **Credit** AmEx, MC, V. **Map** p311 M10.
A cut above the usual tacky tourist shops with a fine selection of handmade blankets, rugs, toys, pottery, clothes and basketry.

Tiles

Ratton
Rua Academia das Ciências 2C, São Bento, 1200-004 (21 346 0948). Tram 28. **Open** 10am-1pm, 3-7.30pm Mon-Fri; closed Sat, Sun. **No credit cards. Map** p307 K9.
Contemporary designs, created in collaboration with Portuguese and international artists such as Júlio Pomar and Paula Rego. The gallery has some temporary exhibits but most designs are in catalogues; reproductions cost around 9,000$00 for a single tile.

Sant'Ana
Rua do Alecrim 95, Chiado, 1200-015 (21 342 2537). Metro Baixa-Chiado/tram 28. **Open** 9.30am-7pm Mon-Fri; 10am-2pm Sat; closed Sun. **Credit** AmEx, DC, MC, V. **Map** p310 L10.
Sant'Ana has been producing handmade tiles since 1741 and sells copies of designs from the 17th and 18th centuries. Although some designs are aimed at the tourist market, it's worth a visit if you're thinking of retiling your bathroom or kitchen. Staff are also happy to manufacture designs to order and will ship abroad.
Factory: Calçada da Boa-Hora 96, Ajuda, 1300-096 (21 363 8292).

Solar
Rua Dom Pedro V, 68-70, Bairro Alto, 1250-093 (21 346 5522/solartiles@bigfoot.com). Metro Restauradores then Elevador da Glória. **Open** *Sept-June* 10am-7pm Mon-Fri; 10am-1pm Sat; closed Sun. *July, Aug* 10am-7pm Mon-Fri; closed Sat, Sun. **No credit cards. Map** p307 L8.
Incredible collection of over half a million antique *azulejos* from the 15th to 19th centuries, displayed chronologically. The tiles come mainly from old palaces and houses, although some were originally in churches.

Viúva Lamego
Largo do Intendente 25, Martim Moniz, 1100-285 (21 885 2408/www.viuvalamego.com). Metro Intendente. **Open** 9am-1pm, 3-7pm Mon-Fri; 9am-1pm Sat; closed Sun. **Credit** AmEx, DC, MC, V. **Map** p307 M8.

The location – bang in the middle of Lisbon's seediest area, a once pretty square that is now a downmarket red-light district – is a grim setting for this shop, which has been selling *azulejos* since 1849. Its tiles now cover most of Lisbon's metro stations (*see p37* **Where did you get that tile?**). Most of the large selection of hand-painted tiles are copies of old designs but staff can make designs to order. Tiles can be shipped worldwide.

Branch: Calçada do Sacramento 29, Chiado, 1200-393 (21 346 9692).

Herbalists

The sweet-smelling *ervanárias* (herbalists) still attract large numbers of Portuguese who discuss their ailments in hushed tones with the shopkeeper. Herbs come in 100-gram (3.5oz) bags and are then made into a tea. There's an enormous variety, used to cure everything from alcoholism to haemorrhoids, though the most common cures are for indigestion. Some herbalists also sell Brazilian incense promising luck, happiness or true love. It's easy to tell from the packaging what's being offered. A large green eye means the incense will ward off jealousy and wads of banknotes signify money.

Ervanária Eufémia Neves Almeida
Praça da Figueira 6, Baixa, 1100-240 (21 346 8855). Metro Rossio. **Open** 9.30am-12.30pm, 1.30-6.30pm Mon-Fri; 9.30am-1pm Sat; closed Sun. Closed second half Aug. **No credit cards. Map** p310 M9.
Established more than 150 years ago, this herbalist is located under a staircase and sells local and imported medicinal herbs, artificial plants and flowers, diet products and Brazilian incense.

Key-cutting

Chaves do Areeiro
Praça Francisco Sá Carneiro 10D-E, Areeiro, 1000-160 (21 848 0650/www.chavesareeiro.pt). Metro Areeiro. **Open** 9am-7pm Mon-Fri; 9am-1pm Sat; closed Sun. **No credit cards. Map** p305 N4.
Lisbon's most reputable key-cutting chain. The emergency door-opening service functions within the opening hours of the particular branch, so in evenings and weekends call one of those located in a shopping centre, which are generally open longer.
Branches: throughout the city.

Markets

Feira da Ladra
Campo de Santa Clara, São Vicente, 1100. Tram 28 to Igreja de São Vicente. **Open** approx. 6am-4pm Tue, Sat; closed Sun, Mon, Wed-Fri. **No credit cards. Map** p308 N9.
Basically a flea market with a large proportion of junk and bric-a-brac, often at highly inflated prices. Do haggle – the first price is unlikely to be the last.

Pitches are mostly laid out on the ground, with some more permanent shops along the perimeter of the square. Here you could pick up some decent semi-antique furniture but, again, prices can be off-putting. Fresh produce is available in the Mercado de Santa Clara, open between 8am and 2pm from Monday to Saturday.

Mercado da Ribeira
Avenida 24 de Julho, Cais do Sodré, 1200-479. Metro Cais do Sodré. **Open** 5am-2pm Mon-Sat; closed Sun. *Flowers only* 5am-7pm Mon-Fri; 5am-2pm Sat; closed Sun. **No credit cards. Map** p307 K10.
This imposing domed building has become purely a retail market since the recent departure of the wholesale operation. It remains a functional affair, though, so expect to dodge men carrying half a cow and women balancing baskets on their heads. The smell of coriander and coffee hang thickly in the air and *azulejos* decorate the walls. A huge variety of fresh fish is stacked up daily (except Mondays), and there's a flower market in the middle.

Mercado do Campo de Ourique
Rua Francisco Metrass/Rua Coelho da Rocha, Campo de Ourique, 1350-075 (21 396 2272). Tram 25, 28/bus 9, 18. **Open** 7am-2pm Mon-Sat; closed Sun. **No credit cards. Map** p306 H8.
Located in one of Lisbon's more affluent districts, this market offers fruit, vegetables, flowers, salted cod and meat every day except Sunday. Fresh fish is available from Tuesday to Saturday.

Praça de Espanha
Metro Praça de Espanha. **Open** 9am-7pm Mon-Sat; closed Sun. **No credit cards. Map** p304 K4.
This is the real thieves' market: watches, plastic sunglasses, car stereos and sundry other items that have fallen off the backs of lorries, displayed to the background beat from competing CD stalls, in what is essentially a large metal shed on a busy roundabout.

Militaria

Soares & Sousa
Rua da Madalena 80A, Baixa, 1100-322 (21 886 9212). Metro Rossio/tram 12, 28. **Open** 9am-1pm, 3-7pm Mon-Fri; closed Sat, Sun. Closed Aug. **No credit cards. Map** p311 M9.
Tiny shop with a great range of military paraphernalia from around the world, although Portugal and its ex-colonies dominate.

Music

See also **Fnac** (*p156*), which has an extensive collection of classical, popular and roots music.

Discoteca Amália
Rua Áurea (Rua do Ouro) 272, Baixa, 1100-066 (21 342 1485). Metro Baixa-Chiado. **Open** 9.30am-2pm, 3-7pm Mon-Fri; 9.30am-1pm Sat; closed Sun. Closed 16-25 Jan, 16-25 May, 16-25 Oct. **Credit** AmEx, MC, V. **Map** p310 L9.

A specialist in traditional Portuguese music, including fado, this shop offers old classics from the likes of Amália herself (*see p207* **Amália**) and contemporary music from artists such as Dulce Pontes and Misia. **Branch**: van on Rua do Carmo, Chiado (21 347 0276).

Discolecção
Palladium Shopping Centre, Avenida da Liberdade 7, Restauradores, 1250-139 (21 347 1486). Metro Restauradores. **Open** 1-8pm Mon-Fri; 10am-3pm Sat; closed Sun. Closed first 2wks Aug. **No credit cards. Map** p310 L8.
Variety of second-hand vinyl spanning decades, with lots more stored in a garage – ask if you're looking for something in particular. Fluent English spoken.

Discoteca Roma
Avenida de Roma 20C, Areeiro, 1000-265 (21 848 0860). Metro Roma. **Open** *Oct-May* 10am-7.30pm Mon-Fri; 10am-7pm Sat; closed Sun. *June-Sept* 10am-7.30pm Mon-Fri; 10am-1.30pm Sat; closed Sun. **Credit** AmEx, DC, MC, V. **Map** p305 N4.

Specialist in classical music, with a large, well-stocked basement area. There are also Brazilian, Portuguese, jazz and world music sections. While the rock/pop section could throw up an old favourite, don't expect the latest grooves.

Latão/V-Records
Rua do Diário de Notícias 67-69, Bairro Alto, 1200-142 (21 347 6115). Metro Baixa-Chiado/tram 28. **Open** 1pm-midnight Mon-Sat; closed Sun. **No credit cards. Map** p310 L9.
Latão sells ethnic jewellery, but the same premises are also home to V-Records – stocking a good collection of vinyl house, drum'n'bass and hip hop, plus James Brown and Aretha Franklin classics.

Valentim de Carvalho
Edifício Grandela, Rua do Carmo 28, Chiado, 1200-094 (21 324 1570/www.voxpop.pt). Metro Baixa-Chiado/tram 28. **Open** 10am-8pm Mon-Thur; 10am-9pm Fri, Sat; noon-8pm Sun. **Credit** AmEx, DC, MC, V. **Map** p310 L9.

Shopping by area

Alfama, Castelo & Graça
Antiga Casa do Castelo (Handicrafts p170); **Feira da Ladra** (Markets p171).

Avenida da Liberdade & Marquês de Pombal
Discolecção (Music p172); **Lava Neve** (Dry cleaners & laundries p159); **Livraria Buchholz** (Bookshops & newsagents p157); **Martins & Costa** (Food & drink p167); **Picasso** (Food & drink p168); Stivali (Shoes p166); **Tema** (Press & periodicals p157).

Bairro Alto & Príncipe Real
Aleksandar Protich (Fashion p162); **Agência 117** (Fashion p159); **Bad Bones** (Tattoos & body piercing p176); **Casa Varela** (Art supplies & stationery p156); **Eldorado** (Fashion p159); **Facto** (Hair & beauty p169); **Fátima Lopes** (Fashion p163); **Galeria da Arcada** (Antiques p156); **Ia** (Fashion p163); **Latão/V Records** (Music p172); **Ler Devagar** (Bookshops & newsagents p156); **Livraria Britânica** (Bookshops & newsagents p157); **Loja da Colecções** (Bookshops & newsagents p157); **Manuel João Trigo** (Hair & beauty p169); **A Outra Face da Lua** (Fashion p161); **Tom-Tom Shop** (Design & household goods p159); **Sneakers Delight** (Shoes p165); **O Velho Sapateiro** (Antiques p156).

Baixa & Rossio
Alceste (Hair & beauty p169); **Araújos** (Jewellery & accessories p161); **Azevedo Rua**

(Jewellery & accessories p161); **Casa Forra** (Repairs p174); **Casa dos Pneus** (Sports & adventure p176); **Cavalheiro & Caria** (Shoeshines & repairs p174); **Celeiro** (Food & drink p169); **Discoteca Amália** (Music p171); **Coronel Tapioca** (Sports & adventure p176); **Ervanária Eufémia Neves Almeida** (Handicrafts p171); **Filmoedas** (Numismatists p173); **Foto Sport** (Photography p174), **Garrafeira Nacional** (Food & drink p168); **GIL Oculista** (Opticians p174); **Godzilla** (Fashion p161); **Guarda-Roupa Anahory** (Costume hire p158); **Hospital das Bonecas** (Toy repairs p174); **Manteigueria Silva** (Food & drink p167); **Manuel Tavares** (Food & drink p167); **Mercado Praça da Figueira** (Food & drink p168); **Napoleão** (Food & drink p168); **Nita Cash & Carry** (Food & drink p167); **Nunes Corrêa** (Fashion p161); **Papeleria Fernandes** (Art supplies & stationery p156); **Pollux** (Design & household goods p159); **Por-fi-ri-os** (Fashion p161); **Popat Store** (Food & drink p167); **Santos Ofícios Artesanatos** (Handicrafts p170); **Soares & Sousa** (Militaria p171); **Solar** (Handicrafts p170); **Sport Zone** (Sports & adventure p176); **Supermercado Chen** (Food & drink p167); **Victorino de Sousa** (Tanners p176); **Viúva Lamego** (Handicrafts p170).

Cais do Sodré
Contacto Directo (Jewellery p163); **Mercado da Ribeira** (Markets p171).

The leading Portuguese music retailer, with a good selection of pop, rock, dance, classical, jazz, Brazilian and African CDs. This branch also has a department devoted to musical instruments, offering piano hire and selling everything from psychedelic guitars and synthesisers to woodwind, brass and grand pianos.
Branches: throughout the city.

VGM

Praça do Príncipe Real 32, Príncipe Real, 1250-184 (21 343 2592). Metro Rato. **Open** 11am-8pm Mon-Fri; 11am-7pm Sat; closed Sun. **Credit** AmEx, MC, V. **Map** p307 K8.
Specialist in classical, jazz, medieval, guitar, folk, baroque, Portuguese, African and world music.

Violino

Calçada do Sacramento 48, Chiado, 1200-394 (21 346 9355). Metro Baixa-Chiado/tram 28.
Open 9am-1pm, 3-7pm Mon-Fri; 9am-1pm Sat; closed Sun. **Credit** AmEx, MC, V. **Map** p310 L9.

This instrument shop sells traditional Portuguese guitars, along with Chinese violins and modern electric instruments, plus strings. Staff also do repairs in the back.

Numismatists

Filmoedas

Rua da Madalena 189, Baixa, 1100-319 (21 887 8317). Metro Rossio. **Open** 9.30am-1pm, 2-6.30pm Mon-Fri; closed Sat, Sun. Closed Aug. **No credit cards. Map** p311 M9.
The place for coin collectors. There are notes and coins, mainly from Portugal and the ex-colonies, including Mozambique notes from 1914 and Portuguese coins dating back to Dom Manuel I and Dom Duarte I. Other items of interest include Roman coins featuring Hadrian, Trajan and Nerva going back a couple of millennia. Numismática Notafilia Diamantino down the road at No.89 is also worth a look.

Eat, Drink, Shop

Chiado

Ana Salazar (Fashion p163); **Armazéns do Chiado** (Shopping centres p175); **Barbearia Campos** (Hair & beauty p169); **BdMania** (Bookshops p156); **A Carioca** (Food & drink p168); **Casa Alegre** (Design & household goods p158); **Casa Batalha** (Jewellery & accessories p165); **Casa Pereira** (Food & drink p168); **Caza das Vellas Loreto** (Design & household goods p158); **Cutipol** (Design & household goods p159); **Gardenia** (Fashion p159); **Engraxadoria do Chiado** (Shoeshines & repairs p174); **Fnac** (Bookshops & newsagents p156); **José António Tenente** (Fashion p163); **Luvaria Ulisses** (Jewellery & accessories p163); **O Manuscrito Histórico** (Bookshops & newsagents p158); **Mayer** (Antiques p156); **Multiopticas** (Opticians p174); **Ourivesaria Aliança** (Jewellery & accessories p165); **Pequeno Jardim** (Florists p166); **Perfumes & Companhia** (Hair & beauty p169); **Sant'Ana** (Handicrafts p170); **Seaside** (Shoes p165); **Valentim de Carvalho** (Music p172); **Violino** (Music p173); **Vista Alegre** (Design & household goods p159); **WIP – Work In Progress** (Hair & beauty p170); **Zara** (Fashion p161).

Greater Lisbon: Cascais

Galamas (Removals p174).

Greater Lisbon: Estoril

Gauntlett International (Removals p174); **GB Stores** (Food & drink p167).

Northern Lisbon

Atlantis Crystal (Design & household goods p158); **Big Video Centro** (Video rental p176); **Centro Colombo** (Shopping centres p175); **Chaves do Areeiro** (Key-cutting p171); **Colorfoto** (Photography p174); **Discoteca Roma** (Music p172); **Galerias Saldanha** (Shopping centres p176); **Horto do Campo Grande** (Florists p166); **Iznougud** (Fashion p161); **Livraria Barata** (Bookshops & newsagents p156); **Maria Gambina** (Fashion p163); **ML** (Shoes p165); **Pedra Dura** (Jewellery p163); **Praça de Espanha** (Markets p171); **Solbel** (Food & drink p169); **'Tou Aqui, 'Tou Aí** (Computers p158).

Parque das Nações

Centro Vasco da Gama (Shopping centres p176).

Rato & Amoreiras

Amoreiras (Shopping centres p175); **Blockbuster** (Video rental p176); **Charcutaria Brasil** (Food & drink p166); **Europ Assistance** (Repairs p174); **Fashion Gallery Atelier Kolovrat** (Fashion p163); **Pablo Fuster** (Shoes p165); **VGM** (Music p172).

São Bento & Campo de Ourique

Depósito da Marinha Grande (Design & household goods p159); **Loja do Mundo Rural** (Handicrafts p170); **Mercado do Campo de Ourique** (Markets p171); **Ratton** (Handicrafts p170); **Suprides** (Computers p158).

Opticians & sunglasses

GIL Oculista

Rua da Prata, 138-140, Baixa, 1100-420 (21 887 9829). Metro Baixa-Chiado/tram 12, 28. **Open** 9.30am-1.30pm, 3-7pm Mon-Fri; 9.30am-1pm Sat; closed Sun. **Credit** AmEx, MC, V. **Map** p310 M9.

One of the many smaller, older opticians, this shop was established in 1865, and offers good, personalised service and a reasonable range of glasses and and sunglasses. Barometers decorate the wall; they're for sale, too.

Multiópticas

Rua do Carmo 102, Chiado, 1249-063 (21 323 4500). Metro Baixa-Chiado. **Open** 9am-7.30pm Mon-Fri; 9am-7pm Sat; closed Sun. **Credit** AmEx, DC, MC, V. **Map** p310 L9.

Modern, efficient chain with a large range of frames and one-hour delivery. The spin-off chain, Sun Planet, specialises in sunglasses.
Branches: throughout the city.

Photography

Colorfoto

Rua Visconde de Santarém 75C, Saldanha, 1000-286 (21 312 9490). Metro Saldanha. **Open** *Oct-June* 9.30am-7.30pm Mon-Fri; 10.30am-1pm Sat; closed Sun. *July, Sept* 9.30am-7.30pm Mon-Fri; closed Sat, Sun. **Credit** AmEx. **Map** p304 M5.

Professional supplies and developing, films, spares, repairs, cameras and photographic equipment. The branch also sells second-hand cameras.
Branch: Praça de Alvalade 2D, Alvalade, 1700-035 (21 793 2475).

Foto Sport

Rua Augusta 249, Baixa, 1100-051 (21 346 3333/ www.fotosport.pt). Metro Baixa-Chiado/tram 28. **Open** 8.30am-8pm Mon-Fri; 10am-6pm Sat; closed Sun. **Credit** AmEx, MC, V. **Map** p310 M9.

Sells film, cameras and albums and offers same-day developing and framing services. Make use of the digital camera service to avoid those dodgy passport photos.
Branches: throughout the city.

Removals

The following firms offer both local and international removals (*mudanças*) and shipping, as well as packing (*embalagens*) and storage (*guarda móveis*) services. Payment is generally made by cash, cheque or bank transfer in escudos.

Galamas

Avenida Salgueiro Maia 840, Abóboda, Cascais (21 444 3021/www.galamas.pt). Correspondence: Apartado 91, Carcavelos, 2776-902. **Open** 9am-1pm, 2-6pm Mon-Fri; closed Sat, Sun.
No credit cards.

A company with a good reputation for reliable moves. ISO 9002 certified. Phone for appointment for a free estimate. An English speaker is always available.

Gauntlett International Transportes Lda.

Armazém L, Centro Empresárial Sintra-Estoril, Fase 1, Estrada de Albarraque, Estoril (21 924 2917/ www.gauntlett.com). Correspondence: PO Box 76, Estoril, 2766-901. **Open** 8am-1pm, 2-5pm Mon-Fri; closed Sat, Sun. **No credit cards.**

Established company with quality certification (ISO 9002) and membership of the international network UTS. Free estimates – telephone for an appointment. English spoken.

Repairs

Luggage repairs

Casa Forra

Poço do Borratém 32, Baixa, 1100-408 (21 888 2734). Metro Rossio. **Open** 9am-1pm, 2-7pm Mon-Fri; 9am-1pm Sat; closed Sun. **No credit cards.** **Map** p311 M9.

Downstairs is every kind of shoe and luggage accessory – it's always busy so take a ticket and wait for your number to come up. Upstairs, at the back of the shop, staff will repair or modify leather goods.

Household

Europ Assistance

Avenida Álvares Cabral 41-3º, Rato, 1250-015 (21 388 6282/www.europ-assistance.pt). Metro Rato. **Open** 9am-5pm Mon-Fri; closed Sat, Sun.
Credit MC, V. **Map** p306 J8.

Basically an insurance arrangement. This French-owned Europe-wide organisation offers, for an annual subscription of 8,621$00, assorted 24-hour household services: plumbers, electricians, glaziers, locksmiths, carpenters, appliance repairs. The company also offers policies for medical services and travel.

Shoeshines & repairs

There are any number of old cobblers who'll mend your shoes and a veritable army of shoeshiners lined up alongside Rossio Square and on busy street corners. A street shoeshine starts at around 400$00, although there's nothing to stop you giving more.

Cavalheiro & Caria

Rua do Crucifixo 50, Baixa, 1100-184 (21 342 7193). Metro Baixa-Chiado/tram 28. **Open** 8am-2pm, 3.30-7pm Mon-Fri; 8am-1pm, 2.30-6pm Sat; closed Sun. Closed Aug. **No credit cards.** **Map** p310 L10.

A cheerful shoe and leather repair service squeezed into half a hallway. A straightforward re-heeling costs 600$00.

Eat, Drink, Shop

For international chains and lots of leisure activities, head for **Centro Colombo**.

Engraxadoria do Chiado

Rua Garrett 47, Chiado, 1200-203 (21 346 1757).
Metro Baixa-Chiado/tram 28. **Open** 9am-7pm Mon-
Fri; closed Sat, Sun. Closed Aug. **No credit cards.**
Map p310 L9.
Busy shoeshine place, complete with red-leather
chairs, antique ashtrays and magazines. Costs
450$00 a time. Staff also do repairs.

Toys

Hospital das Bonecas

*Praça da Figueira 7, Baixa, 1100-240 (21 342
8574). Metro Rossio.* **Open** 10am-7pm Mon-Fri;
10am-1pm Sat; closed Sun. **No credit cards.** **Map**
p310 M9.
Surgery at this dolls' hospital takes place in a workshop upstairs, and in the ground-floor shop you can
update your doll's wardrobe. Portuguese ragdolls,
porcelain dolls and a selection of Barbies are for sale,
as well as Brazilian incense.

Shopping centres

Since the opening of the first major shopping
centre, Amoreiras, in 1987, developers have
been quick to transform the Portuguese
shopping experience into one much like
anywhere else. Extended families flock to the
homogenous centres every weekend, creating
havoc on the roads. Some go to shop, while
others go to catch the latest releases, do lunch,
work out or simply hang out. They are
typically anchored by a large supermarket or
hypermarket and contain a fair few
international chains not represented on the
high street, with extended opening hours
thrown in. For something completely different,

head for the community of ethnic shops in the
Centro Comercial Mouraria in Martim Moniz
(*see p166* **Mouraria – centro comercial or
centro cultural**).

Amoreiras

*Avenida Engenheiro Duarte Pacheco, Amoreiras,
1070-103 (21 381 0200). Metro Rato.* **Map** p306 J7.
Architect Tomás Taveira based the design for
Portugal's first shopping mall on the Brazilian concept that shopping centres should have many small
entrances making it easy to get in, but the
labyrinthine layout and poor signage in this place
make it very difficult to find your way out. The
centre has the usual international chains, a cinema
and a health club.

Armazéns do Chiado

*Rua do Carmo, Chiado, 1200-094 (21 321 0600).
Metro Baixa-Chiado/tram 28.* **Map** p310 L9.
The re-opening of this former grand department
store, recently restored together with Edifício
Grandela next door after they were ravaged by fire,
has brightened up the downtown shopping scene.
Shops inside include a Fnac superstore (*see p156*);
the top floor is dedicated to cafés and restaurants.

Centro Colombo

*Avenida Lusíada, Benfica, 1500-392 (21 711
3600/www.colombo.pt). Metro Colégio Militar-Luz.*
Lisbon's largest shopping centre, this is a leisure
complex rather than just a shopping centre, with
a multiplex cinema, a health club, golf driving
range, bowling alley, funfair and even a karting
track on the roof. Wheelchairs and pushchairs
are available free and there are kiddycars for
rent. The nursery, chapel and breakdown
service are downstairs by the car park. All the
big Portuguese chains and some foreign ones
represented, too.

Centro Vasco da Gama

*Avenida Dom João II, Parque das Nações, 1990-094
(21 893 0601). Metro Oriente.*
A popular shopping destination that can be combined with a visit to the Parque das Nações, the former Expo site. As with Expo, the oceans theme prevails. Stores are conveniently clustered by genre and you can shop 'til you drop or, if you prefer, pull up a deck-chair on the beer deck upstairs and gaze either longingly out at the Tagus or up at the water trickling calmingly in a thin film over the transparent roof.

Galerias Saldanha

*Avenida Fontes Pereira de Melo 42E, Saldanha,
1050-049 (21 351 0100/saldgaleria@mail.
telepac.pt). Metro Picoas.* **Map** p304 M5.
Fashion, jewellery and household items form the bulk of the merchandise. Downstairs there's a large food court and a cinema.

Casa dos Pneus

*Rua da Prata 124-132, Baixa, 1100-420 (21 887
7381). Metro Rossio.* **Open** 10am-7pm Mon-Fri;
10am-1pm Sat; closed Sun. **Credit** AmEx, MC, V.
Map p310 M9.
Literally 'House of Tyres', this bizarre shop sells sports and surfing gear in the front while the back is given over to hosepipes, motoring accessories, traffic cones and police sirens.

Coronel Tapioca

*Rua da Prata 67, Baixa, 1100-414 (21 342 3244/
www.coroneltapioca.com). Metro Baixa-Chiado/
tram 28.* **Open** 10am-7pm Mon-Sat; closed Sun.
Credit AmEx, MC, V. **Map** p310 M10.
Spanish chain offering all manner of survival equipment from tents, rucksacks and hiking boots to compasses, wire saws and non-rinse shampoo.
Branches: Monumental Shopping Centre, Avenida Fontes Pereira de Melo 51, Saldanha, 1050-120 (21 315 5659); Olaias Shopping Centre, Avenida Eng Arnates Oliveira, 1900 (21 840 4883); Oeiras Parque Shopping Centre, Avenida António Macedo, Paço de Arcos, 2750-560, Oeiras (21 442 2981);
CascaiShopping, Est Nacional 9, Alcabideche 2765 (21 460 1498).

Sport Zone

*Rua Áurea (Rua do Ouro) 205-207, Baixa, 1100-
062 (21 324 0511). Metro Baixa-Chiado.* **Open** 9am-
8pm daily. **Credit** AmEx, MC, V. **Map** p310 L9.
Housed in the lower floors of the refurbished Edifício Grandela, a sports department store with more than just the ubiquitous fitness gear, football shirts and balls. There's equipment for martial arts, cycling, swimming, table tennis, fishing and horse-riding. Also an extensive sports shoe section and some hiking and adventure gear.
Branches: Centro Colombo (21 711 3668); Centro Vasco da Gama (21 893 0669); CascaiShopping, Est Nacional 9, Alcabideche 2765 (21 467 9127).

Victorino de Sousa

*Rua dos Correeiros 200-202, Baixa, 1100-170 (21
342 7458). Metro Rossio.* **Open** 9am-2pm, 3-7pm
Mon-Fri; closed Sat, Sun. **Credit** AmEx, DC, MC, V.
Map p310 M9.
Established in 1921, this is now the only *correeiros* (tanner's) left on the street named after the trade, with a good stock of saddles, boots and bridles. Everything is hand-made and can be made to order.

Bad Bones

*Rua do Norte 73, Bairro Alto, 1200-284 (21 346
0888). Metro Baixa-Chiado/tram 28.* **Open** 11am-7pm
Mon-Sat; closed Sun. **No credit cards. Map** p310 L9.
You can just walk in off the street for body piercing, but tattoos are by appointment only.

Membership of local video rental shops usually requires an identity card or passport and proof of address. Most concentrate on big-budget blockbusters, albeit in the original language. For a wider selection, try one of these.

Big Video Centro

*Avenida João XXI 64A, Areeiro, 1000-304 (21 797
3463/mail@videocentro.pt). Metro Areeiro, Campo
Pequeno.* **Open** 10am-midnight daily. **Credit** AmEx,
DC, MC, V. **Map** p305 N4.
Thousands of titles, most in the original language. You can reserve in advance by phone. For membership, as well as an identity card or passport and proof of address, you will need a *número de contribuinte* (tax number), which for residents should take a matter of minutes in your local tax office.
Branches: throughout the city.

Blockbuster

*Avenida Engenheiro Duarte Pacheco 21B,
Amoreiras, 1070-100 (21 387 8755/
www.blockbuster.pt). Metro Rato.* **Open** 11am-1am
daily. **Credit** AmEx, MC, V. **Map** p306 J7.
Excellent range of over 4,500 films, mainly in the original language. To join you'll need an identity card or passport, proof of address and a tax number (although this can be waived for foreigners). Prices range from 600$00 per night for recent releases to 350$00 for older films. There are also vending machines where you can use a credit card and don't have to be a member.
Branches: Estrada de Benfica 462C, Benfica, 1500-104 (21 716 8696); Olivais Shopping Center, Rua de Cidade de Bolama, 1800-079 (21 851 9077); Hotel Cidadela, Avenida 25 de Abril 528, Cascais, 2750-511 (21 486 6480). **Vending machines**: Pingo Doce, Rua Tomás Ribeiro 97B, Picoas, 1050-227; Pingo Doce Estados Unidos da América, Rua António Patrício 13F, Alvalade 1700-047.

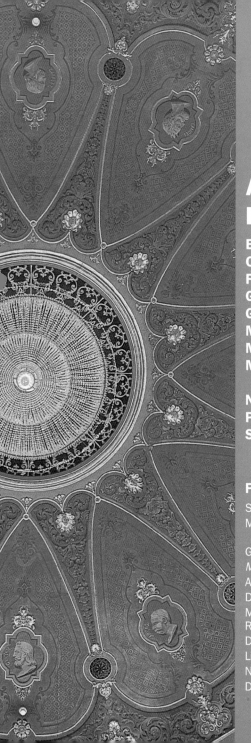

Arts & Entertainment

By Season

The saints come marching in, pretty much throughout the year, but the celebrations peak in June with the city's biggest party.

The Portuguese may be rather more reserved than their Spanish neighbours, but when it's festival time (and it often is) they love to party. *Festas* are held throughout the year – mostly celebrating saints' days – and many lisboetas are close enough to their rural roots to keep track of the festive goings-on in their ancestral village. Though religious in origin, *festas* are generally an excuse to drink, listen to bad music, set off lots of firecrackers and eat greasy doughnuts from vans that appear from nowhere. Locals indulge in some pretty unusual ideas of fun – lovers or secret admirers hand over pots of basil with corny poems attached to a paper carnation, and complete strangers might hit you over the head with giant plastic hammers or bunches of garlic.

Back in 1736, Portuguese nobleman Dom Luís da Cunha estimated that there were only 122 working days in the Portuguese year because of the number of religious festivals. Since then the country has lost a few saints' days, but added some for revolutions and workers, and every region and town finds an excuse for its own public holiday. If a holiday falls on a Thursday or Tuesday, the popular thing to do is make a *ponte* or bridge, which means awarding oneself a really long weekend by not turning up for work on the Friday or Monday. For a full list of public holidays, *see p286*.

Spring

The Portuguese countryside is at its prettiest, full of yellow mimosa and frolicking lambs. It rains a lot – locals say '*Abril, águas mil*', April being the month of a thousand waters. But as temperatures rise, lisboetas come out of hibernation. Spring also brings Easter: Portugal is a Catholic country, where the festival means more than chocolate eggs, particularly to all the old widows in black who stop scrubbing cobbles for the day. There are Holy Week processions throughout the country, although the biggest and most solemn takes place in the religious capital of Braga in the north. Easter Sunday also marks the start of the bullfighting season. In May, jacarandas bloom in the Parque Eduardo VII and along the avenue that leads up to the parliament building, and violet blossoms carpet the pavements.

Lisbon Half-Marathon

Information: Maratona Clube de Portugal (21 757 2640). **Date** late Mar.
The race starts on the south side of the Ponte 25 de Abril and ends at the Mosteiro dos Jerónimos. There's also a marathon later in the year (*see p229*).

Senhor dos Passos

Date second Sun in Lent.
A parade through Graça, on top of one of Lisbon's seven hills, in which a plaster-of-Paris bleeding Jesus is carried on a litter of violets in a tradition going back to the 16th century. Very solemn, but it is attended by leading socialites, so it's one of the few religious parades to appear in *Caras* or *Olá!* – Portugal's equivalents to *Hello!*.

Estoril Open

Estádio Nacional, Complexo Desportivo do Jamor, Praça da Maratona, Cruz Quebrada, 2765 (21 414 6041). Train from Cais do Sodré to Cruz Quebrada. **Date** 1st 2wks in Apr.
The most important tennis tournament of the year takes place around Easter and sometimes attracts a major international name or two. *See also p230*.

25 April Holiday

A day to commemorate the end of decades of fascist dictatorship by a bloodless coup on 25 April 1974. There's not much public celebrating except by nostalgic lefties, but you could always walk over the Ponte 25 de Abril to get into the mood.

Feira do Livro

Parque Eduardo VII (21 843 5180). Metro Marquês de Pombal. **Date** May/June.
Open-air stalls sell discounted and second-hand books, plus some rare and signed volumes. Stock is mostly Portuguese, of course, but there's usually also a stall or two with English-language stuff.

Marcha em Memória e Solidariedade pelas Pessoas Afectadas com o VIH/SIDA

Information: Centro Comunitário Gay e Lésbico de Lisboa, Rua de São Lázaro 88, Martim Moniz, 1150 (21 887 3918/fax 21 887 3922). **Date** mid May.
Annual march in memory of and solidarity with people affected by HIV/AIDS. *See p197*.

Queima das Fitas

Information: Universities (see chapter Resources A-Z: Study). **Date** May.
Portuguese students pin coloured ribbons to their gowns to indicate which faculty they belong to.

Saints alive!

If you ever felt the need for your very own saint, you're in the right country. Portugal has one for every eventuality, from safeguarding fishing trips or curing sick farm animals to invoking at weddings or warding off plagues. And, unlike in certain more urbanised societies, the capital's residents haven't completely discarded these rural habits.

Portugal's first ever entry in the *Guinness Book of Records* was for the fastest canonisation of a saint – **Santo António** or Saint Anthony of Padua, a Lisbon-born missionary who performed unspecified miracles in Italy, preached to the fishes and made it to sainthood within a day of his death in 1232.

The country has been adopting saints ever since. Every village has its own saint and saint's day – an excuse for a day off work and a week-long party. On *festas* or saints' days, the church and square are decorated with fairy lights and a gaudy-looking plaster-of-Paris saint is taken out of the church and paraded around on a flower-strewn litter, often followed by women bearing platters of bread on their heads. Later, a brass band will come out of the woodwork (usually from the local fire brigade), an entire shoal of sardines will be grilled and there will be dancing until late into the night. In the north, women dress in traditional costume with colourful scarves and aprons and filigree gold necklaces and men dance with sticks.

But the country's biggest party undoubtedly takes place in Lisbon in June: the Festas dos Santos Populares when the so-called Peoples' Saints – **António**, **João** (John) and **Pedro** (Peter) have their days. Liveliest of all is that for Santo António, on the night of 12-13 June. António long ago outstripped Lisbon's official patron **São Vicente** (St Vincent) in popularity. Bizarrely, he's the patron saint both of lost objects (people pray to him for their return) and of lovers.

On 12 June the mayor of Lisbon offers free weddings at the Igreja de Santo António in a big joint ceremony, which is shown live on television and followed by a reception in the gardens of the city hall.

By now, most of Lisbon's residential areas are decorated with paper lanterns, coloured lights and streamers. Each *bairro* has its own parade, and small music stages spring up everywhere. People give each other pots of basil with verses attached to a paper carnation – a kind of Portuguese Valentine's card. There is a joint parade along Avenida da Liberdade from about 10pm on the night of 12 June, at which *bairros* vie for prizes for best costumes and best song.

After the parade, the best place to head for is the old Moorish quarter of Alfama, the saint's birthplace, where locals turn front steps into sardine grills, equip the narrow streets with makeshift bars and impromptu dining tables, mix up some sangria and party all night long. There's merry-making elsewhere, too, not only in the older *bairros populares* such as Mouraria and Madragoa, but in posher parts of the city.

In Oporto, the month's celebrations peak on the night of São João, on 23 June. Locals jump over small fires while making a wish, wallop each other with bunches of garlic or leeks – or more often their modern equivalent, squeezy plastic hammers – then still get up in time for a boat race the next morning. Lisboetas just carry on partying, contemptuous of these northern customs. There's still more of the same on 29 June, St Peter's day.

When Portuguese saints are not being paraded around, they stay in chapels surrounded by lighted candles and hung with ghoulish wax effigies of body parts. These are left by people hoping for cures or showing gratitude for successful saintly intervention. You might see a wax brain, breast or pancreas. Not for nothing are the Portuguese known as superstitious people, and not only in villages in the depths of the country. Even in gentrified Cascais the launching of a humble fishing boat requires ceremonial sprinkling with holy water.

When the academic year ends in May they burn them ceremoniously, then proceed to get riotously drunk. The rowdiest celebrations are those in Coimbra (see p260), where the party lasts a week with shows by leading Portuguese groups.

Concurso de Saltos Internacional Oficial

Hipódromo do Campo Grande, Campo Grande, 1600 (21 797 9465). Metro Campo Grande. **Date** late May.
This four-day dressage event has contests such as a Nations Cup with foreign teams. *See also p229.*

Bullfights

Praça de Touros do Campo Pequeno, 1000 (21 793 2143). Metro Campo Pequeno. **Tickets** 1,000$00-12,000$00. **Date** season runs Easter-late Sept.
Bullfights every Thur eve. **No credit cards.**
The Spanish say this is not the real thing because they don't kill the bull. The Portuguese say it's better done on horseback, requiring more skill by the horse and rider, and more heart-stopping when the unmounted *forcados* then come on and wrestle the animal barehanded (see *p230* **No death in the afternoon**). Note that the city's bullring is closed for renovations in 2001.

Summer

The months of June and July are the peak period for tourism, and in recent years the city council has been organising more free outdoor events, to ensure that visitors are kept occupied. By contrast, Lisbon pretty much shuts down in August – even the swimming pools close – and most locals head south to the Algarve where it is even hotter, so this is a good time for exploring the capital without the usual traffic. An alternative is to head for northern Portugal, where it's cooler and there are lots of festivals.

Festas dos Santos Populares

Various venues. Information: Turismo de Lisboa, Palácio Foz, Praça dos Restauradores, 1250 (21 346 6307/21 352 581/www.icep.pt) or Lisboa Welcome Center, Rua do Arsenal 15, Baixa, 1100 (21 031 2700/fax 21 031 2899/www.atl-turismolisboa.pt). **Date** June.
Lisbon's biggest party, lasting almost the whole of June (see *p179* **Saints alive!**). Tradition aside, in recent years the city council has organised an ambitious series of concerts ranging from fado through pop to classical, as well as other entertainments, on stages in Praça do Comércio, Largo de São Paulo in the Cais do Sodré area, and in various squares bordering on Alfama.

Associação Portuguesa de Criadores do Cavalo Puro Sangue Lusitano

Rua Barata Salgueiro 37, Avenida da Liberdade, 1250 (21 354 1742). Metro Avenida. **Date** June.

Held at the Hipódromo, this 'showroom' for the rare Lusitano breed usually has 300 of these versatile, courageous and gentle horses taking part. *See p229.*

Arraial Gay e Lésbico de Lisboa

Information: Centro Comunitário Gay e Lésbico de Lisboa, Rua de São Lázaro 88, Martim Moniz, 1150 (21 887 3918/fax 21 887 3922). **Date** late June.
The annual Pride-like party. In 2000, with the city council's support, it took over the Praça do Município, having outgrown the Praça do Príncipe Real, but the move may not be permanent. A week-long celebration is planned for June 2001. *See p200.*

Troia International Film Festival

265 525 908/www.festroia.pt. **Date** June.
The largest film event in the region is held in the nearby town of Setúbal, south of Lisbon. *See p190.*

Sintra Music Festival

Tickets and information: Turismo, Praça da República, Sintra, 2710 (21 923 1157/fax 21 923 5176). Also available from Telecartaz (21 385 4419) and branches of Valentim de Carvalho (see p172). Train to Sintra from Rossio. **Date** mid June-July.
Classical music by international artists in the beautiful settings of the Palace of Queluz and Sintra's National Palace and Pena Palace. *See p202.*

Festival Internacional de Teatro, Almada

Tickets and information: Teatro da Almada, Rua Conde de Ferreira, Almada, 2800 (21 275 6567). **Date** 4-18 July.
Portugal's most important theatre festival, the FIT pulls in thousands of people and has spawned many new performing groups. Venues include the **Teatro da Trindade in Lisbon.** *(see p225).*

Feira Artesanato

In the park between the Casino and the Hotel Inglaterra, Estoril. Train from Cais do Sodré to Estoril. **Date** 2 July-31 Aug.
If you missed them in Lisbon in June, this is the place to eat sardines – at Bernardino's stall, listening to raucous old fishwives singing folk songs. Open every evening and worth the 250$00 entry.

Jazz on a Summer's Day

Palmela Park auditorium , behind Hotel Estoril Sol. Tickets & information: Turismo, Arcadas do Parque, Estoril, 2765 (21468 0113/fax 21 467 2280). Train from Cais do Sodré to Estoril. **Date** 1st weekend in July.
One of Portugal's oldest jazz festivals, attracting familiar faces from the jazz world.

Capuchos Music Festival

Tickets & information: turismos in Almada (21 272 4059), Palmela (21 233 2122) or Sesimbra (21 223 5743). **Date** mid July-late Aug.
Soloists of the Orquestra Gulbenkian perform in the superb clifftop setting of the Capuchos Convent and other nearby venues – mainly 20th-century music, and avant-garde and baroque pieces. *See p203.*

Feira dos Alhos

Mafra, Information: Turismo, Avenida 25 de Abril,
Mafra, 2640 (261 812 623). For transport, see
p248. **Date** 3rd Sun in July.
Beside the convent (*see p248*), this market offers
crafts, local delicacies, and wine and cheese tasting.

Música à Beira-Mar

Information: Turismo, Largo de Marinha 25-27,
Sesimbra, 2970 (21 223 5743). For transport, see
p249. **Date** weekends July-Sept.
Local musicians perform in the streets at night
in Sesimbra.

Festa do Mar

Cascais Fisherman's beach (in front of Hotel Baia).
Information: Turismo, Avenida Combatentes da
Grande Guerra, Cascais, 2750 (21 484 4086).
Train from Cais do Sodré to Cascais. **Date** late July/
early Aug.
At the Festival of the Sea, organised by Cascais
Fishermen's Association, young fishermen strut
their stuff in front of the local women. On the first
weekend in August, try, literally, to seize the bull by
the horns on the beach to win some dried codfish.
There is also fado singing, fireworks and a proces-
sion of Our Lady of the Seafarers.

Festival Sudoeste

Zambujeira do Mar, Alentejo. **Date** 1st wk in Aug.
Portugal's biggest rock festival takes place on the
Alentejo coast, a couple of hours' drive from Lisbon.
Expect to pay around 7,500$00 for a three-day ticket,
5,000$00 for one day. Numbers are limited to 25,000.
There is free camping, plus transport to the site from
local towns. The 2000 festival included Beck, Bush,
Guano Apes, Moloko, Morcheeba and, very briefly,
Oasis. In the Lisbon area, summer also sees outdoor
concerts sponsored by brewer Superbock.

Jazz em Agosto

Centro de Arte Moderna José de Azeredo Perdigão,
Rua Dr Nicolau Bettencourt, Praça de Espanha,
1050 (21 793 5131/fax 21 795 5206). Metro Praça
de Espanha. **Admission** 2,000$00. **Date** early Aug.
International and local artists in the beautiful
Gulbenkian Foundation gardens (*see p110* and
p192). Sometimes there's a big name or two.

Noites de Bailado em Setais

Sintra. Tickets and information: Turismo, Praça da
República, Sintra, 2710 (21 923 1157). Train from
Rossio to Sintra. **Date** Fri, Sat eves Aug-Sept.
Ballet companies of the stature of the Kirov dance
old favourites in the beautiful garden of the Hotel
Palácio de Seteais. Take a blanket as it can be chilly.

Autumn

Lisbon fills up again as people return from the
Algarve. In the country it's harvest time, the
fields are golden and the vineyards full of
villagers picking grapes. All very bucolic,
particularly in the Douro valley where they still

do treading. It's also hunting season, with
different days of the week allotted to the task of
shooting wild boar, hares, partridge or quail.
Chestnut sellers appear on Lisbon streets.

Avante!

Seixal. Information: Communist Party of Portugal
(PCP), Soeiro Pereira Gomes 3, Seixal, 1600 (21 793
6272). Ferry from Terreiro do Paço do Cacilhas then
Amora or Videira bus/bus from Praça de Espanha to
Seixal. **Tickets** 2,500$00. **Date** 1st weekend in Sept.
Hardly anyone votes for them any more, but the
Communists do great parties. Get the ferry across the
river for this two-day music and food extravaganza
featuring rock and folk performers – always including Billy Bragg – groups and delicacies from various
regions of Portugal.

Feast of Nossa Senhora do Cabo

Cabo Espichel. **Date** 3rd Sun in Sept.
A fishermen's festival in the wild setting of Cabo
Espichel (*see p249*), where a church and eerily
deserted monastery sit on a promontory above rocks
that have been the site of numerous shipwrecks.
Fishermen gather to pray for a good year.

Festival de Cinema Gay e Lésbico de Lisboa

Information: Centro Comunitário Gay e Lésbico de
Lisboa, Rua de São Lázaro 88, Martim Moniz, 1150
(21 887 6141/www.ilga-portugal.org/festival/index.
html). **Date** last 2wks in Sept.

Day of the Dead. *See p182.*

Arts & Entertainment

With over 100 films screened annually, and with support from the British Council, Goethe Institut and the city council, this is reckoned by some to be the largest gay film festival in Europe. *See p190.*

Encontros

Acarte, Rua Dr Nicolau Bettencourt, Praça de Espanha, 1050 (21 793 5131/fax 21 795 5206). Metro São Sebastião. **Date** Sept-Oct.

The long-running 'Encounters' festival of contemporary dance, theatre and music marks the Lisbon cultural *rentrée* after the beach season. It consistently injects new ideas and energy, by bringing in new performers, plus well-known choreographers and directors for workshops with Portuguese artists.

Republic Day

Date 5 Oct.

On the anniversary of the 1910 founding of the republic, the mayor makes a speech from the balcony of the Câmara Municipal (city hall), from where the republic was declared. It's on Praça do Município, off the north-western corner of Praça do Comércio.

Navaratri Festival

Comunidade Hindú de Portugal, Alameda Mahatma Gandhi, Lumiar, 1600 (21 757 6524). Metro Campo Grande/1, 3, 4, 36, 101 bus. **Date** Sept or Oct.

The Indian community's main annual event. Word of the Lisbon bash has spread overseas and it is growing in scale. The nine-day festival (open to non-Hindus for an admission fee of around 500$00) features traditional dancing, songs and music.

Seixal Jazz

Various venues, Seixal. Tickets: 21 222 6413. Information: Seixal Câmara Municipal (21 27 6700/ www.seixaljazz.esoterica.pt. **Date** last week in Oct.

This festival on the south side of the River Tagus attracts good musicians who are not household names – in recent years, Mark Shim, Paul Motian and Tom Harrell.

Day of the Dead

Date 1 Nov.

Florists come out in force to sell chrysanthemums for this day out at the cemetery, when families leave candles and flowers on graves.

Magusto

Date 11 Nov.

Parties are held to celebrate the opening of the first barrels of new wine, at which this *água-pé* – little more advanced than must – is consumed along with roast chestnuts. But you don't need an invitation to a private party; restaurants and fado houses often also observe the tradition, and the city council in 2000 held a public *magusto* in front of the city hall.

Maratona Cidade de Lisboa

21 364 4097/fax 21 364 3525. **Date** end Nov.

Lisbon's big road race, held for the 17th time in 2001. The programme regularly includes other events: a half-marathon and a fun run for 10- to 16-year-olds.

Festa da Música da Igreja de São Roque

Igreja de São Roque, Largo de Trindade Coelho, Bairro Alto, 1200 (21 323 5385). Metro Baixa-Chiado/28 tram. **Tickets** sold at the church 1hr before concerts. **Date** Nov-Dec.

Weekly classical concerts, sometimes with international performers. The setting is spectacular – a 16th-century church in honour of St Roch (protector against plague). *See p203.*

Winter

Lisbon is mild, but those in search of the sun head back south to the Algarve. January and February are almond blossom time.

Dia da Independência

Castelo de São Jorge, Castelo, 1100 (886 6354). Tram 12, 28/37 bus. **Date** 1 Dec.

On the eve of this public holiday celebrating liberation from the Spanish in 1640, the man who would be king if Portugal were still a monarchy joins his cronies for the *Jantar dos Conjurados*: a big dinner in the Castelo de São Jorge. Some of the people who would be his subjects gather to watch, or buy tickets for the feast, sometimes available on the door.

Moda Lisboa

Various venues. **Date** early Dec.

One of Lisbon's two fashion weeks – the other is in June – at which Portuguese designers such as Ana Salazar, Fátima Lopes and Tenente (*see p162* **Portuguese by design**) strut their stuff, occasionally with the help of a supermodel. This is a sideshow to the more important fashion week in Oporto.

Christmas

Villages try to outdo each other with the best moss-covered cribs in squares and churches. Bakeries fill with *bolo rei*, a sort of fruit bun. The person who gets the bean (and breaks a tooth) is supposed to buy the cake the next year. The main Christmas dinner of *bacalhau* is on 24 December, followed by the opening of presents and midnight mass.

New Year

Welcomed in with organised firework displays, but really no big deal.

Carnaval

Date Feb (start of Lent).

A new carnival parade was launched in downtown Lisbon a few years ago in which each ethnic community and Portuguese region has its own representative group. Traditional music and costumes feature strongly in a lively, informal parade that starts at Praça da Figueira. Otherwise, music booms from Brazilian venues around town and the Bairro Alto is as crowded on Monday night as it is normally at weekends. Outside the city, an interesting parade is the one in Torres Vedras, north of Lisbon, which has floats, and revellers wearing papier-mâché masks.

Children

All too few parks, but plenty of beaches, battlements and undubbed cartoons.

For a country that has a reputation for doting on children, remarkably little is tailored for their specific entertainment. On the plus side, restaurants fawn over kids rather than frown at them: if you can't find your waiter, it's probably because he's outside playing football with your young son. But there's the rub – your child is playing football in the street because no other distractions are laid on.

The main problem is the lack of indoor activities. Hands-on, child-oriented museum exhibits are the exception, not the rule, though things are changing as the Portuguese become wealthier and enjoy more leisure time. The legacy of the Expo 98 world's fair has been good for kids. The site, now known as **Parque das Nações**, is probably the best place in town for devoting a day to restless little ones. It has kept the famed **Oceanário** (Oceanarium) as well as an interactive science museum at the Pavilion of Knowledge and a Virtual Reality show. Also, there are plenty of energy-burning activities such as bumper boats, cycling (with bikes for hire), and monitored children's playgrounds with climbing frames and inflatable castles. Two other venues offer rainy-day relief: the **Museu das Crianças** (Children's Museum) and the **Museu do Chiado** (see p193), which occasionally offers tours made attractive for young children.

Nor is this hilly city child-friendly for sightseeing on foot, although open-topped buses, funiculars and trundling trams may both ease the pain and prove to be an attraction in themselves.

The flip side is that, in this climate and in this coastal location, there's always easy, free entertainment – the beaches. And anyway, when asked, 9½ out of every ten children said they preferred playing with sandcastles and bobbing about in the waves to sulking in museums. See chapter **Beaches**.

If all else fails in bad weather, there are the plastic pleasures of the amusement arcades at the massive **Centro Colombo** (see p175), and note that multiscreen cinemas show cartoon films in the original English as well as the dubbed version.

City-centre playgrounds are mostly the hangout of old men playing dominoes. The parks tend to be run down – sand pits are minefields of dog mess, and the ducks seem keen to pack their bags and check out of the pond. Also, there's the hazard of old women with the annoying habit of poring over young children, wondering loudly whether they're not too cold in that flimsy T-shirt.

When it comes to going to restaurants with children, it's a case of everywhere and nowhere: children are welcomed, even pampered, at most restaurants. Some have high chairs, but there are no special facilities, such as climbing frames or swings. A clever choice, however, is one of the esplanade restaurants at **Belém** alongside the broad lawns where children can happily run around.

All in all, this largely peaceful country is mostly safe for kids. Crimes against children are rare indeed and Portuguese parents confidently let children run amok. The modernisation of Portugal also means children won't want for the trappings of home life, such as pizzas, burgers or TV cartoons.

One of the few sources for information about events for children is the 'Publicozinho' section in the Saturday edition of *Público*. This information is also available on the paper's website at http://lazer.publico.pt/criancas. Children's activities are also listed in the city council's *Agenda Cultural* monthly calendar. This is available from tourist information offices (see chapter **Directory**) as well as from a fair number of cafés and bars.

Transport

Buses: Free for under-5s, then full fare.
Trains: Free for under-5s; half-price 5-11s; full fare from 12 onwards.
Metro: Free for under-5s, then full fare.
Kids under 12 are not allowed to travel in the front seat of cars. Seat belts are not obligatory in the back.

Childminding

Large hotels have babysitting services, and smaller ones will usually make an effort to find you a babysitter.

Clube dos Traquinas
(21 792 3700/96 607 2593). **No credit cards**.
The club can provide babysitters for the Lisbon, Cascais and Sintra areas costing 1,700$00 an hour up to 11pm and 2,500$00 per hour after that.

Getting to grips with **Parque das Nações**.

Sightseeing

Lisbon's topography can be torturous, especially when it's hot. Your destination always seems to be over the brow of the next hill. The 90-minute **Circuito das Colinas** (Hills Tour) run by the Lisbon public transport company, Carris, covers the seven main hills from the comfort of a refurbished old tram. The two-hour Tagus Boat Trips offer a panoramic city view with a refreshing breeze.

Slogging your way up to the **Castelo de São Jorge** (*see p79*) is a strength-sapping experience, and the smart money takes children up on trams 12 or 28, or bus 37, the only form of transport that goes all the way. It's a popular venue with energetic young 'uns, who happily scamper over the ramparts and towers.

At Belém, the **Torre de Belém** riverbank tower (*see p94*) is fun – children can run around the ramparts and watch ships coming in – as is the Padrao dos Descobrimentos, which offers an eyrie's view of the area, though smaller kids will have to be hoisted aloft to see over the rather high wall enclosing the open top. Across the road, the cloisters of the Mosteiro dos Jerónimos are enchanting, yielding the opportunity for some medieval storytelling. Take a ball or frisbee for the grassy park nearby.

And, for puppet-lovers, there's more fun to be had at the **Museu da Marioneta**, *see p114*.

Circuito das Colinas

(*21 363 2021/www.carris.pt*). **Departures** *Nov-Apr* 1.30pm, 3.30pm daily. *May, June, Oct* 11.30am, 1.30pm, 3.30pm daily. *July-Sept* hourly 10.30am-6.30pm daily. **Tickets** 3,000$00; 1,500$00 4-10s; free under-4s. **No credit cards.**
The tram tour departs from the north side of Praça do Comércio.

Carris Tour

Departures *Circuito Tejo/Zona Ocidental* Nov-Apr hourly 11am-4pm daily. May, June, July, Sept half-hourly 11am-6pm daily. Aug half-hourly 10.30am-6pm, then 7pm, 8pm, 9.30pm. *Expresso Oriente* 11.15am, 1.15pm, 3.15pm, 5.15pm daily. **Tickets** *Circuito Tejo/Zona Ocidental* 2,000$00; 1,250$00 4-10s; free under-4s. *Expresso Oriente* 2,500$00; 1,250$00 4-11s; free under-4s. **No credit cards.**
An open-topped bus departs from the north side of Praça do Comércio on a hop-on, hop-off system. There are two different circuits.

Tagus Boat Trip

(*21 322 4000*). **Departures** *Apr-Sept* 11am and 3pm daily. *Nov, Feb, Mar* 3pm daily. *Oct, Jan* closed. **Tickets** 3,000$00; 1,500$00 6-12s; free under-6s. *Nov, Feb, Mar* 2,000$00; 1,000$00 6-12s; free under-6s. **No credit cards.**
Trips by the Transtejo ferry company (www.transtejo.pt) leave from Terreiro do Paço ferry wharf and take two hours.

Museu das Crianças

Praça do Império, Belém, 1400 (21 386 2163). Tram 15/bus 27, 28, 29, 43, 49, 51/train to Belém from Cais do Sodré. **Open** 10am-5pm Sat, Sun; closed Mon-Fri. **Admission** 800$00; 550$00 children; free under-3s. **No credit cards. Map** p303 B10.
Snuggling in a single long room on the upper floor of the Museu da Marinha in Belém, this so-called children's museum is really nothing of the sort. Basically, it's a play-cum-educational area, with trained helpers who steer families around the temporary exhibits, and easily fills two empty hours.

Planetário Calouste Gulbenkian

Praça do Império, Belém, 1400 (21 362 0002). Tram 15/bus 27, 28, 29, 43, 49, 51/train to Belém from Cais do Sodré. **Admission** 500$00; 200$00 concessions; free under-6s. **Free session** (in Portuguese) 11am Sun. **No credit cards. Map** p303 B9.
The planetarium is a definite wow for children. The auditorium seats 330 and there are sessions in English at 5pm on Saturday and Sunday.

Parque das Nações

(*21 891 9898/education service 21 891 9181/ www.parquedasnacoes.pt*). Metro Oriente. **Open** *Virtual Reality Pavilion* 10am-7pm Tue, Wed, Sun; 10am-midnight Thur, Sat; closed Mon. *Pavilion of Knowledge* 10am-6pm Mon-Fri; 11am-7pm Sat, Sun; closed Mon. *Gil's Park* 2.30pm-7.30pm Mon-Fri; 10am-8pm Sat, Sun. *Music Garden* 24hrs daily. **Admission** *Virtual Reality Pavilion* 1,500$00 adults; 750$00 concessions; free under-5s. *Pavilion of Knowledge* 900$00, 500$00; 300$00 concessions; free under-3s. *Gil's Park* 350$00. *Children's Park* free. *Music Garden* free. **Credit** AmEx, V.
A series of big-budget attractions were left behind after the Expo world fair in 1998. At the Oceanário (Oceanarium, *see p103*), children can ogle sharks, stingrays, otters and outsized fish. The Virtual Reality Pavilion offers simulated trips with sights, sounds and smells. The Ciência Viva (Live Science) exhibition at the Pavilion of Knowledge offers thrilling hands-on science experiments for children

Arts & Entertainment

that can easily fill two hours. Gil's Park has inflatable castles, while the Children's Park that is part of it offers a climbing wall and climbing frames. At the Music Garden, an open space within the park, visitors can try their hand at a broad range of musical instruments, some exotic. The Parque das Nações site, whose huge expanses might prove tiring for small children, also provides bicycle hire, including tandems, from 500$00 for 30 minutes, and 30 bumper boats – a kind of watergoing dodgem car – on a stretch of water by the Oceanarium at 750$00 for 10 minutes. The park has an information centre and is well signposted. *See also p102.*

Trips out of town

Apart from the beaches, the area around Lisbon also has palaces, castles and forests, easily accessible by public transport. Frequent suburban train services from Rossio station will ferry you to Sintra for a look at the disappointing **Museu do Brinquedo** (Toy Museum, *see p113*). The mystical hilltop town also has horse-and-carriage rides and forests for picnics. On the suburban commuter train line west, Cascais has the **Marechal Carmona** park with a children's area and small open-air zoo, as well as a protected bay with beaches, while Oeiras, Estoril and Cascais have ocean pools for swimming if the sea's looking too rough. For other beaches, *see chapter* **Beaches**.

The **Vasco da Gama Aquarium** at Algés has a giant turtle pool and a frolicking family of seals, but otherwise boasts few highlights. The second floor, with its stuffed mammals, is especially missable. Perhaps most remarkable are the goldfish in the pond outside, which, stuffed for years on the leftover stumps of children's ice-creams, have ballooned to outrageous sizes.

Ogling sharks at the **Oceanário**.

Aquário Vasco da Gama

Rua Direita, Algés, 1495-718 (21 419 6337/ www.aquariovgama.pt). Train to Algés from Cais do Sodré/tram 15/bus 76. **Open** 10am-6pm daily. **Admission** 500$00; 200$00 concessions; free under-5s. **No credit cards.**

Parks & entertainment

Most parks have been strikingly neglected but there are several exceptions. The **Alto da Serafina** adventure playground in the northeast of the huge Monsanto Park is a magnet for every restless child. Also known as the Indian Park after the area of tepees, it offers an area of mock city streets for cycling around, plus climbing frames, swings, slides and other wooden structures. In the city centre, **Parque Eduardo VII** has a smaller playground near the Estufa Fria with a wooden ship for climbing. The other city centre park worth a specific visit is Estrela, which can be used as a carrot to persuade children to pop into the Basilica church across the road.

Alto da Serafina adventure playground

Monsanto Park, 1500 (21 774 3224/7). Bus 70 from Lisbon Zoo until 10.30am and from 4.30pm. **Open** *Summer* 9.30am-6pm Tue-Sun; closed Mon. *Winter* 9.30am-5pm Tue-Sat; 2-5pm Sun; closed Mon. **Admission** free.

Parque Eduardo VII playground

Metro Marquês de Pombal. **Open** 9am-5.30pm daily. **Admission** free. **Map** p307 K6.

Fairs & zoos

Feira Popular

Avenida da República, Campo Grande, 1600 (21 796 2108). Metro Campo Grande. **Open** *14 Mar-5 Oct* 7pm-1am Mon-Fri; 3pm-1am Sat, Sun. *Oct-Feb* closed. **Admission** 400$00 adults; free under-11s. **No credit cards. Map** p305 M3.

This fair can fill an evening, starting off with one of the many restaurants. It gets lively only after 9pm. For years limited to predictable dodgem cars and carousels, nowadays it has more sophisticated white-knuckle rides. The Animax section of the Lisbon Zoo (*below*) is a smaller version of the Feira Popular and more suited to younger children.

Jardim Zoológico de Lisboa

Estrada de Benfica 158-160, Sete Rios, 1500 (21 723 2910/www.zoolisboa.pt). Metro Jardim Zoológico. **Open** *Summer* 10am-8pm daily. *Winter* 10am-6pm daily. **Admission** 1,990$00; 1,500$00 3-11s (weekends); 1,300$00 3-11s (weekdays); 1,600$00 concessions; free under-3s. **Credit** V. **Map** p304 J3.

After years of decline, the money injected by sponsor companies, known as 'godfathers' (Lacoste sponsors the crocodiles, for example), has allowed the zoo

Arts & Entertainment

Wildlife at the **Jardim Zoológico**. See p185.

Centro Artístico Infantil

Fundação Calouste Gulbenkian, Rua Marquês Sá da Bandeira, Praça de Espanha, 1050 (21 782 3477/www.gulbenkian.pt). Metro Praça de Espanha. **Open** *10am-1pm, 2.30-5.30pm Mon-Fri; 2.30-5.30pm Sat, Sun.* **Admission** *free.* **Map** p304 L4.

In the gardens of the Gulbenkian Foundation, the centre has toys, musical instruments, and drawing and painting facilities, and for six-month spells has interactive exhibitions on selected themes. For children aged four to 12.

Sport

Budding surfers can learn to avoid a wipe-out, and maybe even catch a tube, at local surfing schools. The Portuguese Surfing Federation lists recommended schools, all with trained English-speaking monitors, on its website (www.fps.pt/div/schools/html).

There is one school in Cascais, the **Guincho Surf School** (96 505 9421/91 402 4400), and three others in Caparica – **Escola de Surf da Associação de Surf da Costa de Caparica** (96 291 8084/91 780 3852), **Escola de Surf da Caparica** (21 290 6082/91 963 0635), and **Escola de Surf e Bodyboard do Nucleo de Praia Nova Onda** (261 322 699). These schools offer courses of up to several hours and hire of wetsuit and boards. The **Cascais Watersports Centre** (21 483 0455), run from John David's café, at the east end of the beach by the station , has paddle boats, kayaks and rides on inflatable buoys dragged around the bay at white-knuckle speeds by a motorboat. **Cascais Yacht Club** (Clube Naval de Cascais, 21 483 0125/ www.cncascais.pt), overlooking the bay next to the fort, hires out small Optimist craft.

Nurseries & schools

St Julian's School

Quinta Nova, Carcavelos, 2777 Parede Codex (21 458 5300/www.stjulians.com). **Ages** *3-18.*

American International School of Lisbon

Central Office: Avenida António dos Reis 95, Linho, Sintra, 2710 (21 923 9800/www.ecis.org/lisbon/). **Ages** *8-17.*
Monte Estoril Campus: Avenida Faial 3, 2765 Monte Estoril (21 468 0639). **Ages** *3-7.*

Cascais International School

Rua das Faias Lote 7, Torre, 2750 Cascais (21 484 6260). **Ages** *1-6.*

St Dominic's International School

Outeiro de Polima, Arneiro, São Domingos de Rana, 2775 Parede (21 444 0434/www.e-st-dominic.rcts.pt/). **Ages** *3-18.*

---

to pull nearer to the standard of those elsewhere in western Europe. However, there are frequent rumours of continued serious financial problems. Don't miss the elephant that rings a bell if you place a coin in its trunk, or the monkey village. There is also a boating lake within the zoo grounds, plus rides for younger children.

Shows & TV

The Saturday 'Publicozinho' of *Público* lists children's entertainment over the coming week. Imported cartoon shows, mostly in their original language, are televised for several hours on weekend mornings and from 3.30pm to 6pm on weekdays on the four national channels. Cable TV is widely available and usually includes the Cartoon Network.

Multiscreen cinemas usually show both the original English and dubbed versions of Disney films. The best bets are the **Colombo** and **Amoreiras** shopping centres (for both, *see p175*).

Teatro Infantil de Lisboa

Teatro Municipal Maria Matos, Avenida Frei Miguel Contreiras 52, Campo Pequeno, 1700-081 (21 847 7853). Metro Roma. **Open** *box office 2-8pm Tue-Sun; closed Mon. Shows 3pm Sat, Sun; closed Mon-Fri.* **Admission** *varies.* **No credit cards.** **Map** p305 N4.

Stages plays, pantomimes and performances for children, mostly adaptations of well-known traditional fables, weaving in dance, song and humour. Plenty of opportunity for audience participation.

Film

Portuguese film embraces a brave new world of swish multiplexes, local blockbusters and made-for-TV movies.

A quartet of screens at **Quarteto**. *See p190.*

As in every other modern European city, Lisbon's cinema scene is now dominated by multiplexes, and the vestiges of former picture palaces are rapidly disappearing. The last surviving one, the São Jorge on Avenida da Liberdade, closed in December 2000, although there is talk of it housing a future film museum, in association with the **Cinemateca**.

Portuguese cinema has an excellent track record in terms of the main international film festivals, but such critical appreciation abroad is not mirrored at home. National film critics accuse many films of being unoriginal and repetitive, and the audience tends to shun homegrown products. This leaves room for one or two Portuguese films a year that enjoy local box-office success but that critics generally write off as trivial nonsense.

The cultural chasm between 'art cinema' and 'commercial cinema' has yawned still wider further since the beginning of 2000, as a result of an ambitious slate of 10 television movies a year from the leading private broadcaster SIC (25 per cent owned by Brazilian soap machine, Globo). SIC has also been involved in making films for the cinema, using the massive promotional machine that comes with its 50 per cent television audience share to launch Portugal's main box office hits over recent years: *Adão e Eva* (Adam and Eve), *Pesadelo Cor de Rosa* (Sweet Nightmare), *Jaime* and *Tentação* (Temptation).

Despite this onslaught of new commercial fare, traditional Portuguese 'auteur cinema' is alive and kicking. Manoel de Oliveira (*see p188* **Manoel de Oliveira – the auteur's auteur**) continues to be the main international ambassador for Portuguese cinema. Another well-known auteur is João César Monteiro, who revels in arousing controversy. He appears in the majority of his films; his recent on-screen antics include urinating into the audience in *Le Bassin de John Wayne* (The Hips of John Wayne). He also recently directed a 'black-out' version of Snow White (*Branca de Neve*), most of which has no images, and made the provocative comment that 'the Portuguese public should go screw themselves'.

There are certain common themes in Portuguese films across the spectrum from

Manoel de Oliveira – the auteur's auteur

Manoel de Oliveira, who celebrated his 90th birthday in 1998, is the only working director in Europe to have made his debut in the silent era. This Jesuit-educated former racing driver enjoyed the fast lane as a young man, but his cinematic style is characterised by silences and slow camera movements. The experience of watching a film by Oliveira is rather like entering a medieval church: suddenly removed from the rush of city life, we are confronted by echoing silences, visual tableaux and enigmatic icons. This atmosphere is typified by Oliveira's recent work *Palavra e Utopia* (Word and Utopia, 2000), based on the life of 16th-century preacher Padre António Vieira.

Oliveira has always divided opinions, even within the Portuguese intelligentsia. His 1931 debut, the silent documentary *Douro Faina Fluvial*, was greeted with stamping of feet by outraged Portuguese critics but praised by commentators abroad. Oliveira's first feature

art-house to commercial fare. In a country of bright sunshine and wide-open plains, there is a pronounced tendency to focus on dark, shadowy landscapes and claustrophobic interiors. Portuguese films are distinctly downbeat in comparison to their exuberant Spanish counterparts, and characters tend to be sarcastic, non-communicative and almost autistic in nature. Many directors come from the upper echelons of Portuguese society but like to focus on worlds of poverty and despair, thus reflecting political concerns forged in the 1974 Revolution.

Like most European countries, Portugal has experienced several different 'eras' of cinematic production. In the 1930s there was an attempt to establish a populist cinema tradition in Portugal, comparable to that being developed in Spain, Italy and Germany. The main studio,

Tobis Portuguesa, churned out a string of comedies that continue to be very popular on television and have enjoyed outstanding sales on video.

In the late 1940s a new climate of repression and censorship swept through Portugal, with the thaw only beginning in the early 1960s, as a fresh generation sought to create a 'new cinema'. Manoel de Oliveira was seen as their spiritual godfather.

In 1968, when power slipped from President Salazar's grasp (*see p22*) a new, more liberal climate emerged in Portugal. The Cinema Novo group established the Portuguese Cinema Centre with support from the Gulbenkian Foundation, while the government created the Portuguese Cinema Institute. These twin approaches – one from directors, the other from the government – still dominate Portuguese cinema today.

film, *Aniki-Bóbó* (1942, see left) met with a similar reaction, but the magical tale of a group of poor children in Oporto is now considered one of his finest works.

Oliveira was unable to direct another film until the 1960s, mainly because of Salazarist ambivalence towards cinema. He directed his third feature film, *O Passado e o Presente* (The Past and the Present, 1972) at the age of 63. For many directors of that age, this very 'theatrical' piece of film-making would have been their concluding work, but for Oliveira it was just the beginning. With the 1974 Revolution, he was elevated to the status of unofficial standard-bearer of Portuguese cinema, and was 'discovered' internationally (by French and Italian critics) through the 1978 film *Amor de Perdição* (Love of Perdition).

In the 1990s, Oliveira's critical renown has enabled him to work with some of the world's finest actors. In *O Convento* (The Convent, 1995) John Malkovich, Catherine Deneuve and Luís Miguel Cintra take part in a strange ethereal exploration of the writings of the devil, set against the luscious vegetation and medieval surroundings of the Convent de Arrábida. In *Viagem ao Princípio do Mundo* (Journey to the Beginning of the World, see above) Marcello Mastroianni performed his last film role, portraying Oliveira as an ageing film director.

In 2001, Oliveira was directing another feature film, *Vou Para Casa* (I'm Going Home), and he is also to direct a 'sequel' to his 1931 debut – a homage to the River Douro – for Oporto's stint as European Capital of Culture.

Since the Revolution, Portuguese cinema has been dominated by the auteur tradition, and has mainly lived a hand-to-mouth existence. However, the Socialist government that was elected in 1995 has tripled state funding for film, providing an important impetus to both artistic and commercial traditions. Broadcasters – principally SIC and the state-owned RTP – have increased their investment in cinema, and communications companies such as Portugal Telecom are set to start investing in this area.

SCREENING INFORMATION

The bulk of Lisbon's cinemas are in the main shopping malls and fairly easy to find. Other screens are often tucked away in odd corners of the city, and are best visited with a good map or via taxi. There is no *Time Out*-style city magazine, but comprehensive film listings can be found in the main daily and weekly

newspapers, and in magazines such as *Visão*. Online film listings and ticket sales are also available via internet sites such as www. lusomundo.net, www.iol.pt and www. publico.pt, and the larger cinema complexes (such as **Colombo**, **Monumental** and **Vasco da Gama**) have a telephone reservation service (tickets must be collected 30 minutes before the film starts). All films are subtitled except for Portuguese films and some animation pics.

Cinemas

Amoreiras

Avenida Engenheiro Duarte Pacheco, Amoreiras, 1070 (21 383 1275). Bus 11, 23, 48, 53, 58, 74, 75, 83. **Open** *Box office* noon-12.30am daily. *Last show* 12.30am. **Tickets** 900$00; 650$00 Mon; 650$00 concessions Tue, Wed, Fri. **No credit cards**. **Map** p306 J7.

Good screening conditions. Tickets are bought in a single booth, but the screens (there are ten) are dispersed across three different parts of the centre, so look at the overhead signs indicating the route to the one you need.

Cinemateca Portuguesa/ Museu de Cinema
Rua Barata Salgueiro 39, Marquês de Pombal, 1250 (21 359 6200/fax 21 352 3180/recorded information on films 21 359 6266). Metro Marquês de Pombal. **Open** *Films* 6.30pm, 9.30pm Mon-Fri; 3.30pm, 6.30pm, 9.30pm Sat; closed Sun. *Museum* 2-7.30pm Mon-Fri; closed Sat, Sun. **Tickets** *Films* 400$00; 280$00 concessions. *Museum* free.
No credit cards. Map p307 L7.
Lisbon's equivalent of London's National Film Theatre, with museum and archive attached, will be under renovation until December 2001 at the earliest. Meanwhile, films are being shown at the Palácio Foz in Praça dos Restauradores; the phone line with recorded schedule informationis still functioning. The Cinemateca provides retrospectives of classics from world cinema, with two films shown each day; free monthly programmes are provided.
The archive collection is currently housed at Rua de Dona Estefânia 175, Estefânia, 1000; it retains the normal phone number. Although not a museum in the traditional sense, the Cinemateca has had the legal status of a museum since cinephile medical doctor Felix Ribeiro convinced the government to found it in 1948. Its directors robustly defend the name, arguing that its film schedules are collections with a common theme, and, together with the archive of 1,500 publications and 19,000 books in European languages, plus posters and similar material from the history of Portuguese cinema, form a comprehensive museum of cinema. To visit the excellent libary (*biblioteca*), visitors need to leave a passport or other ID at reception and then speak to librarians Isabelle and Maria Jesus, who speak English and are very helpful. Sadly, there's no room to display the collection of antique equipment, some of it from the 1870s, which includes the camera used by Portugal's first director, Aurélio da Paz dos Reis.

Colombo
Centro Colombo, Avenida Luisada, Benfica, 1500 (21 711 3220). Metro Colégio Militar. **Open** *Box office* noon-12.35am Mon-Fri; 10.30am-12.35am Sat, Sun. *Last show* 12.30pm. **Tickets** 900$00.
Credit AmEx, MC, V.
The largest shopping centre in the Iberian peninsular with state-of-the-art equipment. Unlike Amoreiras (*above*), the ten screens are all together in a single wing of the centre. There's a ticket machine for credit-card payment.

King Triplex
Avenida Frei Miguel Contreiras 52A, Avenida de Roma, 1700 (21 848 0808). Metro Roma. **Open** *Box office* 1-10.30pm daily. *Last show* 9.30pm. **Tickets** 850$00; 600$00 Mon; 750$00 concessions Tue-Sun.
No credit cards. Map p305 N4.

Screens the best of European cinema, and many of the local films. The cinema has three screens, a café and an excellent bookshop with the most comprehensive range of film-related titles in the city.

Monumental/Saldanha Residence
Edifício Monumental, Praça Duque de Saldanha, Saldanha, 1050 (21 353 1856). Metro Saldanha. **Open** *Box office* 11am-12.30am daily. *Last show* 12.30am. **Tickets** 900$00; 650$00-800$00 concessions. **No credit cards. Map** p305 M5.
An upmarket venue for leading independent films and European art-house fare. It has excellent sound and vision, the highest audiences per screen in Lisbon and a fine café and bar offering a range of Belgian beers. A single ticket office in the Monumental shopping centre serves the four screen there, plus the four others over the road in Saldanha Residence.

Quarteto
Rua Flores do Lima 1, Campo Pequeno, 1700 (21 797 1244). Metro Roma, Entrecampos. **Open** *Box office* 1.30-12.30am daily. *Last show* 12.30am. **Tickets** 800$00; 600$00 Mon; 600$00 concessions Tue-Thur. **No credit cards. Map** p305 M3.
A key independent cinema showing US and European films. The walls are plastered with posters from cult films. Also has a small café, and sells indie video titles.

Vasco da Gama
Centro Vasco da Gama, Avenue Dom João II, Parque das Nações, 1990 (21 892 22 80). Metro Oriente. **Open** *Box office* noon-12.35am Mon-Fri; 10.30am-12.35am Sat, Sun. *Last show* 12.30am. Tickets 900$00. **No credit cards**.
This ten-screen cinema is on the top floor of the Vasco da Gama shopping centre, at the Parque das Nações.

Film festivals & events

A documentary festival – **Encontros Internacionais de Cinema Documental** – showcases international work at the Malaposta Cultural Centre (Rua Angola, Olival Basto 2675, Odivelas, 21 938 8407) in Amadora each November. Lisbon now hosts two new events: Video Lisboa (www.videolisboa.com) in February and the **Festival de Cinema Gay e Lésbico** (21 887 6141/www.ilga-portugal.org/festival/index.html) in September. The latter screens an interesting selection of 100 films, shown in locations including the British Council, the Goethe Institut and Forum Lisboa. *See also p200.*
The largest film event in the region is the **Troia International Film Festival** (26 552 5908/www.festroia.pt), held in June in Setúbal. It focuses on the work of directors from countries with an annual production of less than 21 feature films.

Galleries

Lisbon tracks global trends, but the local scene sometimes has an edge.

Portugal has never had a strong tradition in the fine arts, although artists of excellence have occasionally emerged. A noteworthy example of early Portuguese art is the Polyptych of St Vincent, attributed to Nuno Gonçalves, at the **Museu Nacional de Arte Antiga** (*see p108*).

The 19th century was characterised by the romantic, naturalist and realist movements, always strongly influenced by the art of Paris. The first manifestations of an avant-garde in the teens of the 20th century – which was, if modest, at least in step with Europe – was held in check by a dictatorship that lasted more than 40 years. The advent of modernism was handicapped if not curtailed, with the shattered pieces only picked up in the 1970s – even then in a society in some senses profoundly isolated and unable to be part of cultural changes happening abroad. Radical forms of expression did pop up throughout the authoritarian regime. But while the major styles of 20th-century art eventually made their way to Portugal, they often appeared late and seemed anachronistic. The period following the 1974 Revolution was a time of catching-up and acclimatisation.

ART GOES GLOBAL

Since the 1980s, however, there has been a heady absorption of international trends, made easier by increased travel and improved access to information. This globalisation of culture has meant that in Portugal, as elsewhere, local forms of expression have tended to give way to 'international' trends. Sometimes, the effort to keep up has worked at the expense of individual idiom, leading to work that seems derivative. At its worst, this sense that 'something is always happening somewhere else' produces cultural anxiety; at its best it gives the Portuguese scene an edge.

The three Portuguese artists best known abroad are Pedro Cabrita Reis, Julião Sarmento and Paula Rego – all with impressive international careers. Cabrita Reis (b. Lisbon 1956) uses a vast range of materials, often drawn from architecture and construction. Harnessing an impeccable and dramatic sense of place and space to a flair for the evocative potential of his materials, Cabrita Reis's installations are often site-specific and always challenging. Sarmento (b. Lisbon 1948) makes huge paintings, sculptures, and video installations: much of his work hinges around secrecy and voyeurism, and a charged erotic gaze upon the female body.

Paula Rego – perhaps the most widely acclaimed living Portuguese artist – is of an earlier generation. Born in Lisbon in 1935, she studied art at the Slade in London, settled there in 1976, and is now equally well known and popular in Britain and Portugal. Her work exudes a scarcely containable energy. Above all a storyteller, she draws from events in her own life, from children's books, folklore and myth, literature, films and the history of western painting itself. Her pictures are filled with allusions to Portuguese life and culture, particularly images harking back to her childhood, and often staged in the traditional female domain. Highlighting the familiar, the ridiculous and the grotesque, Rego's work – through many stylistic transformations – remains compelling because it taps a vein of pathos in common experience.

On the whole, contemporary art in Portugal looks much the same as anywhere else in the world today. The 1980s saw an explosion of painting, accompanying that of the trans-vanguard in Italy or neo-expressionism in Germany, and a growing need to engage with broader concepts such as postmodernism, feminism or post-colonialism. This was accompanied by a boom in the art market that has since subsided.

THE GALLERIES

The 1990s saw the beginning of an interesting phase. Galleries sprouted around town, artists began to circulate internationally and there was an increasing focus on works using installation, video and multimedia, which, unlike conventional paintings or sculptures, are not easily sold. (Artists take advantage of generous funding schemes from institutions such as the Fundação Calouste Gulbenkian.) Also, several major institutions have opened in the past decade (the **Centro Cultural de Belém** and **Culturgest** in Lisbon and the **Museu de Arte Contemporânea** in Oporto, *see p264*), widening opportunities to see contemporary art and participate in international forums.

Lisbon galleries are not centralised or clustered, but dotted all over the city and, frustratingly, opening hours vary. So take a good map, a guide and enough cash for a few cab fares. Saturday afternoon is traditionally

Arts & Entertainment

when many Lisboetas visit galleries, as traffic is easier; over the past few years, numerous galleries have been organising openings on the same Saturday afternoon, and gallery-hopping becomes also a form of people-watching.

INFORMATION

The best newspapers for information about exhibitions and events are *Público* on Saturdays (see the Mil Folhas section) and the weekly *Expresso*, which comes out on Friday (see the Cartaz section). There is also the free monthly guide *Agenda Cultural*, which provides much information, albeit sometimes frustratingly inaccurate. This can be picked up at tourist information offices and various cultural venues, cafés and bars around town.

Exhibition spaces

There are a handful of major public and private exhibition spaces, detailed below. Another venue with a wider remit is **Culturgest** (*see p202, p224*), the cultural organ of the state-owned Caixa Geral de Depósitos bank. It stages a broad spectrum of exhibitions, from monographic shows of well-known artists to polemic thematic exhibitions, as well as dance, music and theatre performances.

Casa Fernando Pessoa

Rua Coelho da Rocha 16, Campo de Ourique, 1200 (21 396 8190). Tram 25, 28/bus 9, 18, 20, 27, 38, 74. **Open** 10am-6pm Mon, Wed, Fri; 1-8pm Thur; closed Tue, Sat, Sun. **Admission** free. **No credit cards. Map** p306 H8.

In the house where Portuguese poet Fernando Pessoa spent the last 15 years of his life, this museum is dedicated to poetry in general and Pessoa in particular, and contains a library specialising in his work. Opened in 1993, the building was refurbished leaving the façade intact. Owing to the scarcity of personal belongings that survived Pessoa, the interior was not reconstructed, although the bedroom is unaltered. The house contains two other spaces where artists exhibit works. Organising poetry readings and producing several publications annually, this is always a stimulating locale, which also stages exhibitions by young artists.

Centro de Arte Moderna, Fundação Calouste Gulbenkian

Rua Dr Nicolau Bettencourt, Praça de Espanha, 1050 (21 782 3000). Metro São Sebastião. **Open** 2-6pm Tue; 10am-6pm Wed-Sun; closed Mon. **Guided tours** noon Sat, 3pm Sun. **Admission** 500$00; free concessions. Free Sun. **Credit** *shop* AmEx, MC, V. **Map** p304 K4.

The modernist building of the Centre of Modern Art skirts the beautiful park surrounding the Museu Calouste Gulbenkian (*see p110*). Light and airy, the Centre has a substantial holding of works by

The modernist **Centro de Arte Moderna**.

Portuguese artists from the early 20th century to the present, plus a small collection of works by international artists. Highlights include key works of Portuguese modernism by Amadeo de Souza-Cardoso, José de Almada Negreiros and Eduardo Viana. Look out for Almada's 1925 *Self Portrait with Group*, which depicts the artist and friends in the Café A Brasileira (*see p143*). Other works worthy of mention include those of the Portuguese surrealists António Pedro and António Dacosta and many by other notable Portuguese 20th-century artists such as Menez, Julio Pomar, Lourdes Castro, Helena Almeida and Paula Rego. A younger generation is represented by Pedro Cabrita Reis, Julião Sarmento, Pedro Proença, Rui Chafes, Rui Sanches, José Pedro Croft, Pedro Calapez and Pedro Casqueiro. The Foundation also possesses a notable collection of drawings by Armenian-born New York artist Arshile Gorky. The permanent collection rotates, and provides an essential foil to the holdings of the Museu do Chiado (*see p193*). The Centre also runs an interesting and up-to-the-moment programme of beautifully curated temporary exhibitions.

Centro de Exposições, Centro Cultural de Belém (CCB)

Praça do Império, Belém, 1400 (21 361 2400). Tram 15/train from Cais do Sodré/bus 27, 28, 29, 43, 49, 51. **Open** 11am-8pm daily (last entry 7.15pm). **Admission** varies. **Credit** AmEx, MC, V. **Map** p303 B10.

The best public art space in town. Pale and stark, the immense, grandiose building was designed by architects Vittorio Gregotti and Manuel Salgado and opened in 1993. Foiled by the 16th-century Mosteiro dos Jerónimos and Torre de Belém, it commands a magnificent view of the river. In addition to a diverse programme of music, theatre and dance, the CCB has several vast and beautiful exhibiting spaces. There is a varied programme of temporary exhibitions of the fine arts, photography and architecture. Recent exhibitions have included Donald Judd, Louise Bourgeois, and one on Portuguese architecture of the 20th century. There's a cafeteria and restaurant, a bookshop, and other shops and galleries on the premises. On summer weekends there's also an open-air programme on the concourse. *See also p38, p201 and p224.*

Fundação Arpad Szenes-Vieira da Silva

Praça das Amoreiras 56-58, Amoreiras, 1250 (21 388 0044). Metro Rato. **Open** noon-8pm Mon, Wed-Sat; 10am-6pm Sun; closed Tue. **Admission** 500$00; 250$00 concessions; free under-14s. Free Mon. **Credit** AmEx, V. **Map** p307 K7.

Unprepossessing from the outside, this foundation was set up in 1994 with the aim of exhibiting and promoting research into the work of the celebrated Portuguese modernist painter Maria Helena Vieira da Silva and her Hungarian painter husband Arpad Szenes. Although the couple lived for many years in Paris and played a central role in the School of Paris, they are iconic figures in Portuguese modernism. In addition to housing and displaying a large permanent collection of their work, the Foundation also puts on regular exhibitions of artists with affinities to da Silva and Szenes.

Museu do Chiado

Rua Serpa Pinto 4, Chiado, 1200 (21 343 2148). Metro Baixa-Chiado/tram 18. **Open** 2-6pm Tue; 10am-6pm Wed-Sun; closed Mon. **Admission** 600$00; 300$00 concessions; free under-14s; free for all 10am-2pm Sun, public holidays. **No credit cards. Map** p310 L9.

Fundação Arpad Szenes-Vieira da Silva.

Previously the Museu Nacional de Arte Contemporânea, this museum was founded in 1911 in what had once been the Convent of St Francis, and later, in the 18th century, housed the Royal Academy of Fine Arts. In the heart of the city, it now has the name of its area, which was central to Lisbon's cultural life during the 19th and early 20th centuries. After the fire that ravaged Chiado in 1988, the museum was closed for several years. Redesigned in a cool, modernist idiom by French architect Jean-Michel Wilmotte, it reopened in 1994, with an altogether more contemporary feel. The permanent collections bracket off a century of Portuguese art (1850-1950), offering a representative selection from this period, beginning with romanticism and passing through naturalism, modernism, neo-realism, surrealism and abstractionism.

Pavilhão Branco, Museu da Cidade

Campo Grande 245, Campo Grande, 1700 (21 759 1617). Metro Campo Grande. **Open** 10am-1pm, 2-6pm Tue-Sun; closed Mon. **Admission** *Pavilhão Branco* free. *Museu da Cidade* 375$00; free under-12s. **No credit cards. Map** p304 L1.

Hidden away in the Museu da Cidade gardens, the new Pavilhão Branco is one of Lisbon's most beautiful and interesting exhibition spaces. Initially, its shows of contemporary art organised by the Instituto de Arte Contemporânea, a government-funded body, were constructed around themes probing issues of broad cultural interest. Now it is funded by the city council and tends to run one-person shows of established contemporary artists.

Sintra Museu de Arte Moderna

Avenida Heliodoro Salgado, 2710 Sintra (21 924 8170). Train from Restauradores to Portela station. **Open** 10am-6pm Tue-Sun; closed Mon. **Guided tours** 11am Thur. **Admission** 600$00 adults; 300$00 students; free under-10s. Free under-18s, over-65s Thur. **Credit** AmEx, MC, V.

The Berardo Collection of contemporary art – a vast private collection without peer in Portugal – has, since 1997, been housed in the beautiful building of the old casino in Sintra. Designed by the architect Norte Júnior, the casino opened in 1924. Its refurbished grand rooms are the perfect setting for this important collection, which aims to represent the major post-World War II international art movements. Visitors are taken chronologically through the anguished late 1940s to visit the cool abstraction of minimalism, plus funky pop art, the experiments of conceptual art and Arte Povera, and the free rein of expression in the 'Return to Painting' of the 1980s, ending with the diverse uses of objects, sculpture and installation in the late 1980s, 1990s and the new millennium. In 1998, the museum made the decision also to begin acquiring pre-World War II works.

Sociedade Nacional de Belas Artes

Rua Barata Salgueiro 36, Marquês de Pombal, 1250 (21 313 8510). Metro Marquês de Pombal. **Open** 2-8pm Mon-Sat; closed Sun. **Admission** free. **No credit cards. Map** p307 L7.

The National Society of Fine Arts was founded in 1901, and has always been run by artists wishing to represent themselves. In the early 1980s it was seen as a good place to begin an exhibiting career – several notable group and individual exhibitions were held here during that time, including Depois do Modernismo (After Modernism) in 1982 and Novos Novos (the New Young) in 1984 – but by the end of the decade it had acquired a somewhat fusty image. More recently, the gallery has been revamped, and it has hosted interesting exhibitions, often with interdisciplinary themes.

Occasional spaces

Casa da Cerca – Centro de Arte Contemporânea

Rua da Cerca 2, 2800 Almada (21 272 4950). Ferry to Cacilhas from Terreiro do Paço or Cais do Sodré then Cristo-Rei bus to Almada. **Open** 10am-6pm Tue-Fri; 1-6pm Sat, Sun; closed Mon. **Admission** free. **No credit cards.**

Across the Tagus river, in Almada, on a cliff commanding a stunning view, this handsome baroque palace is one of the largest and most characteristic examples of 17th-century domestic architecture in the region. Refurbished in 1993, it is now an arts centre promoting exhibitions of contemporary art, with a particular focus on drawing. There is also a study centre devoted to the documentation of Portuguese 19th- and 20th-century art, with a particular focus on drawing.

Galeria Arte Periférica

Centro Cultural de Belém, Shop 5 & 6, Belém, 1400 (21 361 7100). Train from Cais do Sodré/ tram 15/bus 27, 28, 43, 49, 51. **Open** 10am-8pm daily. **Admission** free. **Credit** AmEx, MC, V. **Map** p303 B10.

This gallery was launched in the early 1990s in Massamá, near Queluz, with the dual aims of bringing contemporary art to the outskirts of the city (hence the gallery's name: Art on the Periphery) and expanding the range of activities to include the sale of handicrafts, postcards, picture frames and painting materials. Its new home, in the Centro Cultural de Belém, opened in 1994. Both spaces have prioritised the work of unknown Portuguese artists, often giving them their first shows, so it's a good place for bargains.

Sala do Veado, Museu de História Natural

Rua da Escola Politécnica 56-58, Príncipe Real, 1200 (21 390 4805). Metro Rato. **Open** 10am-5pm Mon-Sat; closed Sun. **Admission** free. **No credit cards.** **Map** p307 K8.

Just above the Jardim Botânico, the Sala do Veado (literally, Hall of the Stag) is a cavernous space made available by the Museu de História Natural (*see p116*) for contemporary art shows. Over the past decade, it has been the scene of many of Lisbon's more interesting exhibitions; the shadowy, stark concrete interior makes a dramatic setting for more experimental work. It's always worth looking in here to see what's on.

Museu do Chiado. *See p193.*

Arts & Entertainment

Commercial galleries

Cristina Guerra Contemporary Art

Rua Santo António à Estrela 33, 1350 (21 780 1232). Tram 28/bus 9, 22, 27, 38. **Open** 10am-8pm Tue-Sat; closed Mon, Sun. **Admission** free. **No credit cards. Map** p306 H8.

This ample space opened its doors to the public in early 2001, and promises to be one of the more high-profile art spaces in Lisbon – established trendy rather than alternative. The gallery's 'stable' boasts three generations of Portuguese artists, including Julião Sarmento, Fernando Calhau, Graça Pereira Coutinho, and the young Paulo Feliciano, Miguel Palma and Ruis Toscano.

Galeria 111

Campo Grande 113, Campo Grande, 1700 (21 797 7418). Metro Campo Grande. **Open** 10am-1pm, 3-7.30pm Mon-Sat; closed Sun. **Admission** free. **No credit cards. Map** p304 L2.

Lisbon's most high-profile and high-quality 'establishment' gallery is also one of few dating from before the 1974 Revolution. It has a huge body of work by acclaimed Portuguese artists such as Paula Rego, Alexandre Pomar and António Dacosta. It also makes forays into younger art – look out for Ana Vidigal and Fatima Mendonça. There is a fine collection of prints and drawings too, and a bookshop.
Branch: Rua Dr João Soares 5B, Campo Grande, 1600 (21 781 9909).

Galeria Diferença

Rua São Filipe Néri 42C/V, Rato, 1250 (21 383 2193). Metro Rato. **Open** 3-8pm Tue-Sat; closed Mon, Sun. **Admission** free. **No credit cards. Map** p307 K7.

An artists' initiative launched in 1979 with the aim of documenting and exhibiting work, as well as providing studios and workshops for photography and printing, and publishing the odd book. Tucked away on a side street near the Fundação Arpad Szenes (*see p193*), the pleasant gallery shows works by known and unknown artists. A smaller space is used for the exhibition and sale of prints, jewellery and objects.

Galeria João Graça

Rua de São Tiago 15A, Castelo, 1100 (21 887 4323). Tram 28, 12/bus 37. **Open** 2.30-7.30pm Mon-Sat; closed Sun. **Admission** free. **No credit cards. Map** p311 M10.

This gallery, originally housed in a tiny space near the Bairro Alto (where it was known as Galeria 1991), has now settled in to fabulous premises in the Castelo de São Jorge, with a magnificent view of the river. The gallery's main focus is on high-profile international artists, though its selection of works can be somewhat erratic.

Galeria Luís Serpa

Rua Tenente Raúl Cascais 1B, Príncipe Real, 1250 (21 397 7794/0251). Metro Rato. **Open** 2.30-7.30pm Mon-Fri; 3-7.30pm Sat; closed Sun. **Admission** free. **No credit cards. Map** p307 K8.

As Galeria Cómicos, in the 1980s, this was one of Lisbon's trendiest and classiest commercial galleries – some of the most high-profile local artists of that decade (Julião Sarmento, Cabrita Reis, Rui Sanches) showed here. Today the gallery has a 'designer' feel about it and has lost its cutting edge, but continues to be a place where interesting work by both Portuguese and international artists might be seen.

Galeria Módulo

Calçada dos Mestres 34A-B, Campolide, 1070 (21 388 5570). Bus 2. **Open** 3-8pm Mon-Sat; closed Sun. **Admission** free. **No credit cards. Map** p306 J6.

One of Lisbon's longest-surviving galleries, with one of the most interesting exhibition programmes of contemporary art, focusing on new trends. As well as bringing to light the work of unknowns, it has a stable of established Portuguese artists of the middle and younger generations, including Pedro Casqueiro, José Loureiro, Ângela Ferreira and Miguel Ângelo Rocha. It also shows the work of contemporary international artists such as Sue Williams, Karen Kilimnik, Rosângela Rennô and Allan McCollum.

Galeria Monumental

Campo Mártires da Pátria 101, Campo de Santana, 1150 (21 353 3848). Bus 23, 33, 100. **Open** 3-7.30pm Mon-Sat; closed Sun. **Admission** free. **No credit cards. Map** p307 M8.

This space started life as the initiative of a group of artists to provide a gallery, studios and workshops. The group is no longer intact and the gallery moved some years ago to these spacious premises. Fairly low-key, it focuses on one-person shows, especially by young or lesser-known artists, though it also has a stable of regulars, including Manuel San Payo, Mimi and Antônio Olaio. A mixed bag.

Galeria Pedro Cera

Rua Leite de Vasconcelos 5A, Graça 1170 (21 816 2032). Bus 12. **Open** 2.30-7.30pm Tue-Sat; closed Mon, Sun. **Admission** free. **No credit cards. Map** p308 O9.

In the clean, minimal basement space, you can see the works of interesting, offbeat contemporary artists, most of them Portuguese. The gallery has also shown the work of some interesting young Brazilian artists.

ZDB (Galeria Zé dos Bois)

Rua da Barroca 59, Bairro Alto, 1200 (21 343 0205/www.ip.pt/zedosbois). Metro Baixa-Chiado/tram 28. **Open** 5-11pm Tue-Sat; closed Mon, Sun. **Admission** free. **No credit cards. Map** p310 L9.

Lisbon wouldn't be the same without ZDB. The most experimental gallery in town: an 'alternative' cultural association that remains on the cutting edge, true to its initial aims of promoting young artists, and particularly work not tied to painting and sculpture. ZDB focuses on multimedia, and organises a biennial Festival Atlântico, dedicated to radical, multimedia activities and body arts: it has brought extreme artists like Orlan, Stelarc and Annie Sprinkle to the city.

Arts & Entertainment

Gay & Lesbian

Lisbon is busily building on its reputation as a queer destination.

Lisbon has been a gay destination for a long time, despite a history of Catholic intolerance, a grey and homophobic dictatorship that dragged on for decades, and a strongly family-oriented culture. From 18th-century writer William Beckford – who on his first visit picked up an attractive local choirboy with whom he spent the next 20 years – through the rich British and American queens who made Lisbon a regular port of call in the 1950s and '60s, to the more democratic sexual tourism of today, foreigners have always found a special allure in the city and its inhabitants. This in spite of a social climate that would seem at worst inimical and at best indifferent to queer culture.

So what is it that makes Lisbon an attractive destination? A balmy climate, handsome and available people, a pulsating and extended nightlife, plenty of leafy retreats, and sandy beaches backed by cruisey dunes might seem the obvious answers. But there's also the rather camp physical appeal of the city itself, with its pinks and pastels and baroque curlicues, plus a certain sense of relief felt by North Americans and northern Europeans at finding themselves somewhere that is somewhat politically incorrect and yet apparently welcoming. Lisbon's gay-friendly ambience also has to do with demographic changes: as a combination of ageing housing stock, high prices and traffic and parking problems drives families further from the city centre, gays have been moving in.

Portuguese culture has traditionally separated the sexes rigidly. As a result, both men and women have long found solace in the company – not necessarily sexual – of their own sex. Urban living has altered these patterns, but there is still an unabashed enjoyment of physical contact with people of the same gender.

In Lisbon, though, things are changing and a consciously political queer culture co-exists with older attitudes. The city council (run by a Socialist/Communist/Green coalition) has a declared policy of supporting lesbian and gay causes, and has joined with the private tourism

Parque do Príncipe Real – the centre of Lisbon's tiny gay and lesbian district. *See p200.*

association to actively promote the city as a gay destination. This, as one might expect, has not been uncontroversial, but it has already borne fruit: council funding for the Centro Comunitário Gay e Lesbico de Lisboa (*see below*); a gay guest house in the Bairro Alto; an annual Gay Pride gathering and an annual festival of lesbian and gay cinema; and a free (if somewhat selective) municipal guide to the city's gay and lesbian delights.

Advice and information

For more information, try publications such as *Korpus*, a Portuguese-language quarterly for men costing 1000$00 that offers history, politics, ads, gossip and lonely hearts; or for women, *Lilás* (lilas@pobox.com) or *Zona Livre* (Clube Safo, Apartado 95, 2000 Santarém). Clube Safo also organises events for women, such as camping trips.

Centro Comunitário Gay e Lesbico de Lisboa – ILGA (Portugal)

Rua de São Lazaro 88, Rossio, 1150-333 (21 887 3918/helpline 21 887 6116/ilga-portugal@ilga.org). *Metro Martim Moniz.* **Open** *Community centre* 5-9pm Mon-Sat; closed Sun. *Helpline* 9pm-midnight Mon-Thur; closed Fri-Sun. **Map** p311 M8.
Run by the Portuguese branch of international gay and lesbian association ILGA, this friendly council-funded community centre offers advice, information and counselling. It also has a bar and cyber café and organises regular social and political events.

Opus Gay

Rua da Ilha Terceira, 34, 2º, Estefânia, 1000-173 (21 315 1396/www.opusgayassociation.com). *Metro Saldanha.* **Open** 10am-1pm, 4-8 pm Mon-Fri; closed Sat, Sun. **Map** p307 M1.
Another gay centre that offers counselling and legal help, plus a laundry service, tarot readings and marriages (not legally recognised in Portugal). Tourist advice via email on opusgayturismo@hotmail.com.

Abraço

Rua da Rosa 241-3, Bairro Alto, 1200-385 (21 342 5929/AIDS helpline 800 225 115). *Metro Baixa-Chiado/tram 28.* **Open** 10am-1pm, 3-8pm Mon-Fri; closed Sat, Sun. Map p310 L9.
Charity that supports those who are HIV positive or suffering from AIDS and runs an AIDS helpline, as well as organising media campaigns and benefits. For information on other groups active in this area, contact ILGA or Opus Gay.

Websites

www.portugalgay.pt
http://supersite.sapo.pt
www.terravista.pt/ilhadomel/1339 (a very conservative site, in defence of monogamy)
www.Madeiranet.com/gaynet
www.lesbicas.homepage.com

The **Anjo Azul**, Lisbon's first gay pensão.

Accommodation

With the Lisbon scene always having been on the discreet side, the city never had any openly gay hotels – until 2000, that is, when the **Anjo Azul** (*see below*) opened its doors. There are quite a few gay-friendly hotels and *pensões*, however. The **Pensão Londres** (*see p64*), whose location between Bairro Alto and the Príncipe Real helps account for its popularity with out-of-towners, has a long tradition of welcoming gays and lesbians. **Pensão Alegria** (*see p64*) is pretty basic but well-located for both Bairro Alto and the city centre. Down in the Baixa, the gay-friendly **Pensão Florescente** (*see p63*) is in a slightly sleazy location and is not quiet, but couldn't be more central. Over in Lapa, the charming and upmarket **York House** (*see p55*) has been an ex-pat haunt for many years. (Angus Wilson used to stay here with his boyfriend in the 1960s.) Across the road, the **Pensão Janelas Verdes** (*see p50*) is in the same kind of price range but has nothing like the same charm.

Hotel Anjo Azul

Rua Luz Soriano 75, Bairro Alto, 1200-246 (21 347 8069/anjoazul@mail.telepac.pt). *Metro Baixa-Chiado/tram 28.* **Rates** 5,000$00-6,000$00 single; 6,000$00-8,000$00 double. **Credit** MC, V. **Map** p307 K9.
Gay-run *pensão* that opened in 2000 with much fanfare from the Lisbon tourism association. In a completely refurbished blue-tiled 19th-century building on the edge of Bairro Alto, the hotel has 12 smallish, simple but comfortable rooms. Clean and reasonably priced (although with no breakfast served), it's usually full, so book ahead.

Bars & clubs

Lisbon nightlife has widened its geographical spread in recent years, but the **Bairro Alto** and **Príncipe Real** are still the beating heart of the gay scene. Among the truly mixed places are **Portas Largas** (*see p151*) – an old *tasca*

Arts & Entertainment

(tavern) with marble tables and peanut-littered floor that is nominally gay but attracts all sorts, especially early in the evening. Across the street is **Frágil** (*see p217*), the old high temple of Lisbon nightlife. Although now upstaged by **Lux** (*see p222*), Manuel Reis's latest venture down by the waterfront, Frágil is still fun if you feel your look can stand it. Lux itself is more straight than gay, but is the ultimate place to see and be seen in Lisbon.

Mixed

Keops
Rua da Rosa 157, Bairro Alto, 1200 (no phone). Metro Baixa-Chiado/tram 28. **Open** 10pm-4am Mon-Sat; closed Sun. **Admission** free. **No credit cards.** **Map** p310 L9.
This cavernous bar-disco for gays and straights has been somewhat in the doldrums of late but has recently had a makeover and, at the time of writing, seems to be taking off again. The music is predominantly loud hard rock.

Mister Gay
Quinta da Silveira, Via Rápida, Monte de Caparica (96 258 6803). Bus to Caparica or Pragal Station then taxi. **Open** midnight-6am Fri, Sat. Admission minimum consumption 1,400$00. **No credit cards.**
Huge disco-bar in a converted warehouse, with drag shows and striptease. Despite its name, and a reputation as a pick-up place for suburbanites, it attracts an incredibly diverse mix of people. Bring your sister and your mum – they'll be welcome.

Mistura Fina
Rua das Gáveas 15, Bairro Alto, 1200 (21 342 0849). Metro Baixa-Chiado/tram 28. Open 4pm-2am daily. **No credit cards. Map** p310 L9.
Frequented by both sexes, this place is open late, and customers tend to spill out onto the street as the night wears on. It's also a good place to start the evening before moving on somewhere else.

Sétimo Céu
Travessa da Espera 54, Bairro Alto, 1200 (21 346 6471). Metro Baixa-Chiado/tram 28. **Open** 10pm-2am daily. **No credit cards. Map** p310 L9.
Friendly and perenially fashionable little bar with a mostly young – gay and straight – clientèle. The uptempo music includes South American and African rhythms. The place is Brazilian-run; the caipirinhas are excellent.

Trumps
Rua da Imprensa Nacional 104B, Príncipe Real, 1250 (21 397 1059). Metro Rato. **Open** 10pm-6am daily. **Admission** 1,000$00. **Credit** AmEx, DC, MC, V. **Map** p307 K8.
One of the most popular of Lisbon's mixed venues. The downstairs dance floor fills up after 2am, there are occasional drag shows and striptease, a snooker room and another, more intimate, bar upstairs.

The perennially fashionable **Sétimo Céu.**

Women

Memorial
Rua Gustavo Matos Sequeira 42A, Príncipe Real, 1200 (21 396 8891). Metro Rato. **Open** 11pm-6am Mon-Sat; 4pm-midnight Sun. **Admission** free. **No credit cards. Map** p307 K8.
Although considered Lisbon's only exclusively lesbian club, Memorial is in fact often mixed and it's not unknown for women to be hassled by men. Tiny dance floor and transvestite shows almost every night, plus Sunday matinées.

As Primas
Rua da Atalaia 154-156, Bairro Alto, 1200 (21 342 5925). Metro Baixa-Chiado/tram 28. **Open** 10pm-4am Mon-Sat; closed Sun. **No credit cards. Map** p310 L9.
A rough-looking bar with a heart of gold – noisy, unpretentious and a great place for meeting people. No dance floor but an eclectic selection of music, plus a rarity in Lisbon: a juke box! A pool table, too.

Men

An B (Água no Bico)
Rua São Marçal 170, Príncipe Real, 1200 (21 347 2830). Metro Rato. **Open** 9pm-2am daily. **No credit cards. Map** p307 K8.
One of Lisbon's oldest gay nightspots is now seeking to cater to a younger set, but still has a somewhat 1980s feel. Internet access.

Bar 106
Rua São Marçal 106, Príncipe Real, 1200 (21 342 7373). Metro Rato. **Open** 9pm-2am daily. **No credit cards. Map** p307 K8.

Another small, unpretentious bar with a rather old-fashioned feel. Back to the days of the closet: warm and safe.

Bric-a-Bar

Rua Cecílio de Sousa 82-84, Príncipe Real, 1200 (21 342 8971). Metro Rato. **Open** 9pm-4am Mon, Wed-Sun; closed Tue. **Admission** free. **Credit** DC, MC, V. **Map** p307 K8.

One of the city's longest established gay haunts. Despite endless makeovers, the ghosts of 30 years of the Lisbon gay scene linger on. Small dance floor.

Harry's

Rua São Pedro de Alcântara 57-61, Bairro Alto, 1200 (21 346 0760). Metro Baixa-Chiado/ Restauradores, then Elevador da Gloria. **Open** 10pm-6am Mon-Sat; closed Sun. **No credit cards.** **Map** p310 L9.

A real Lisbon experience. In effect a gay fado bar – pictures of Amália and other divas adorn the walls – it's also a haunt of drag queens and prostitutes.

Finalmente

Rua da Palmeira 38, Príncipe Real, 1200 (21 342 8181). Metro Rato. **Open** midnight-5.30am daily. **Admission** free. **Credit** AmEx, DC, MC, V. **Map** p307 K8.

Come too early and this place, with its peeling decor, and ageing customers (who all seem to be friends) can feel like a slow night in South Shields, circa 1972. But once it gets going, it can be fun. Tiny dance floor, rent, and drag shows.

Max

Rua São Marçal 15, Príncipe Real, 1200 (21 395 2726). Metro Rato. **Open** 8pm-2am daily. **Admission** free. **No credit cards.** **Map** p307 K8.

Despite a name change (it was formerly Tattoo), this is still the same old place – popular with 30- and 40-somethings, with the occasional drag show. Monday is Message Night – leave a message for the one you love – or whatever.

Satyro's

Calçada do Patriarcal 6-8, Príncipe Real, 1200 (21 342 1525). Metro Rato. **Open** 11pm-4am Tue-Sun; closed Mon. **No credit cards.** **Map** p307 K8.

A small bar with a reputation for danger, but it's actually quite safe. Rent. Has occasional drag shows and striptease.

Cafés

In Chiado, the touristy **A Brasileira** (*see p143*) and **Pastelaria Bénard** (*see p144*) are popular early evening meeting places. Nearby, **Café Rosso** (*see p143*) gets quite cruisey in the afternoons. Up towards Rato, there's a popular esplanade under the trees in the **Jardim de Príncipe Real**. It's not a gay café as such but a useful and pleasant meeting place on a hot summer night. It serves meals, but the waiters are pretty grumpy and the food is variable.

Café Movies

Edifício Monumental, Praça Duque de Saldanha, 1050 (21 315 0531). Metro Saldanha. **Open** noon-1.30am daily. **No credit cards.** **Map** p304 L5.

Popular pre- or post-film meeting place (attached to the Monumental cinema, *see p190*) with a big range of Belgian beers. Very mixed.

A Matilde

Rua da Barroca 31, Bairro Alto, 1200 (21 342 2900). Metro Baixa-Chiado/tram 28. **Open** 8am-10pm daily. **No credit cards.** **Map** p310 L9.

Gay-friendly *pastelaria*, serving a mixed crowd.

Restaurants

Other gay- and lesbian-friendly restaurants include **Bota Alta** (Travessa da Queimada 37, 21 342 7959), **Casa Nostra** (*see p136*), and **Pap' Açorda** (*see p122*) in Bairro Alto. Further afield, there's the long-established **Alcântara Café** (*see p121*), the recently opened **São Caetano** (*see p135*) and **Atira-te no Rio** (*see p132*).

Balões

Rua Imprensa Nacional 116, Príncipe Real, 1250 (21 397 4493) Metro Rato. **Open** 8am-midnight daily. **Credit** AmEx, DC, MC, V. **Map** p307 K8.

Horrid decor but nice ladies and cheap food. Right next to Trumps (*see p198*).

Baralto

Rua do Diário de Notícias 31, Bairro Alto, 1200 (21 342 6739). Metro Baixa-Chiado/tram 28. **Open** noon-3pm, 7pm-midnight daily. **No credit cards.** **Map** p310 L9.

Tiny space but very welcoming, with good traditional Portuguese food.

Chez DeGroot

Rua Duques de Bragança 4, Chiado, 1200 (21 347 2839), Metro Baixa-Chiado/tram 28. **Open** noon-4pm, 7.30pm-midnight Mon-Fri; 7.30pm-midnight Sat; closed Sun. **Credit** AmEx, DC, MC, V. **Map** p310 L9.

Convenient for the São Carlos opera house. It claims to offer Belgian and Portuguese food, but steaks dominate the menu.

Gran Tasca

Rua Manuel Bernardes 10, Príncipe Real, 1200 (21 395 5290). Metro Rato. **Open** 8pm-2am Mon, Wed-Sun; closed Tue. **Admission** minimum spend 2,500$00. **Credit** AmEx, DC, MC, V. **Map** p307 K8.

Opened in late 2000, this is said to be a gay fado house, although the clientele is mixed. Traditional Portuguese food; not cheap but remember you are paying for a show too.

Põe-te na Bicha

Travessa da Água da Flor 36, Bairro Alto, 1200 (21 342 5924). Metro Baixa-Chiado/tram 28. **Open** 7.30pm-midnight daily. **Credit** AmEx, DC, MC, V. **Map** p310 L9.

Good, cheap and cheerful gay-friendly tasca. The name means 'get in the queue', but the word 'bicha' is also Portuguese slang for queer.

Trivial
Rua da Palmeira 44A, Príncipe Real, 1200 (21 347 3552). Metro Rato. **Open** 8am-11.30pm Mon-Sat; closed Sun. **Credit** AmEx, DC, MC, V. **Map** p307 K8.
A gay-friendly place with a mixed clientele and good traditional Portuguese fare.

Saunas & gyms

Grecus
Rua do Telhal 77, 4º, Avenida da Liberdade, 1150 (21 346 6259). Metro Avenida. **Open** noon-midnight Mon-Sat; closed Sun. **Admission** 2,000$00. **No credit cards. Map** p307 L8.
One of the older generation of saunas – rather antiquated and cramped.

Sertório Sauna Club
Calçada da Patriarcal 34, Príncipe Real, 1200 (21 347 0335). Metro Rato. **Open** 3pm-8am Mon-Sat; 3pm-midnight Sun. **Admission** 2,000$00. **No credit cards. Map** p307 K8.
Sertório represents the new wave of Lisbon saunas – clean, safe and comfortable (the older generation tended to sleaze, fleas and squalor). Sauna, Turkish bath, bar, cinema, massage; condoms provided. Under the same ownership as the Viriato (*see below*).

Viriato Sauna Club
Rua do Telhal 4B, Avenida da Liberdade, 1150 (21 342 9436). Metro Avenida. **Open** 1pm-2am, Mon-Thurs; 1pm-5am, Fri-Sat; 1pm-midnight, Sun. **Admission** 2,000$00. **No credit cards. Map** p307 L8.
Solarium, gym, cinema, bar, Turkish bath and condoms. Recently renovated and definitely new wave. Very civilised.

Bookshop

A Esquina Cor da Rosa
Travessa do Monte do Carmo 1, Príncipe Real, 1200 (21 324 0346/esquina1@hotmail.com). Metro Rato. **Open** 3pm-midnight daily. **Credit** DC, MC, V. **Map** p307 K8.
A welcome new arrival on the scene, the 'pink corner' is a tiny shop offering Portuguese and foreign-language books and magazines of varying degrees of seriousness, including transgender material. There's also a noticeboard for events and personals.

Cruising

As in other cities, parks – with which Lisbon is unfortunately not well endowed – are the scene of most of the action. The favourites include Jardim de Príncipe Real, Praça do Império in Belém, Parque Eduardo VII and Campo Grande, although the latter two have a reputation for danger. A new, promising park recently opened

Pink publications at **Esquina Cor da Rosa**.

in Alvalade, near the airport (entrance on Avenida Gago Coutinho). There's also quite a bit going on in the station toilets along the rail line to Cascais, for example at Belém.

But the safest bets are the area in the Cidade Universitária between the Medical and Dental Faculties or the beaches. The nudist area between stops 17 and 19 on the Transpraia train from Caparica south of the Tagus is a popular beach cruising place, not least because of the dunes. Further south, Meco is an attractive mixed nudist beach, though sometimes windy. *See chapter* **Beaches**. Lisbon's largest open space, Monsanto, is not recommended as it is rife with violent crime. Unenticing as it sounds, a hot new cruising place is rumoured to be the car park of the Continente hypermarket in Amadora.

Festivals

Arraial Gay e Lésbico de Lisboa
Lisbon's Gay Pride gathering has been going since 1997. It's a good party, albeit on a small scale. In 2000, with the city council's support, it took over the Praça do Município, but the move may not be permanent. A week-long celebration is planned for the end of June in 2001.

Festival de Cinema Gay e Lésbico de Lisboa
This major festival takes place in various venues over three weeks in September. There is usually a theme and a featured director. Information from ILGA (21 887 6141) or *Agenda Cultural*, the city council's monthly guide to cultural events.

Music:
Classical & Opera

Patrons have run from a medieval troubadour king to an Armenian oil baron.

The name of a Portuguese composer may not come easily to your tongue, but don't let that fool you into thinking that there haven't been any, and of high quality. In recent years, international groups recording for big companies have taken up the early Portuguese repertoire in a big way, so you can go into your nearest record shop and find CDs of music by Dom Dinis, the medieval troubadour king and patron of the arts (*see p10*), early renaissance composers such as Pedro de Escobar and later ones such as Manuel Cardoso and João Rebelo, the 'colossal baroque' *Te Deum* of António Teixeira, the virtuoso harpsichord sonatas of Carlos Seixas or the rococo elegance of Sousa Carvalho – all performed by musicians of renown.

Dom João IV built up a music library famous throughout Europe – it was completely lost in the 1755 earthquake, but its catalogue survives to tantalise us. With gold from Brazil, Dom João V Italianised Portuguese musical taste, sending composers to study in Italy and bringing Domenico Scarlatti to Lisbon to teach music. The earthquake inevitably drastically affected artistic life in Lisbon, but Italian taste continued to dominate the capital's extensive output of sacred music. This music is now being investigated and made available for performance once more in Portugal.

Things began to change with performances of Mozart and Beethoven in the first decades of the 19th century, and the emergence of the fine composer João Domingos Bomtempo (1775-1842). The 20th century saw an explosion of composers of great imagination, from Viana da Mota (1868-1948), a pupil of Liszt, and the innovative Luís de Freitas Branco (1890-1955), to the important figures of Fernando Lopes-Graça (1906-1994), Joly Braga Santos (1924-1988), the avant-gardists Emmanuel Nunes (b 1941) and Jorge Peixinho (b 1940) and, now, a whole spectrum of younger composers working in very different styles.

Portuguese performers who have made an impact internationally include the pianists Maria João Pires, Artur Pizarro and Pedro Burmester, the singer Jennifer Smith, and the dynamic young percussionist Pedro Carneiro.

Many concerts in Lisbon take place in the attractive settings of monasteries, cathedrals, castles, old manor houses and palaces. Look out for festivals throughout the summer, some of which attract international artists. At the Gulbenkian and other venues, seasons run mostly from October to May.

Tickets & information

Information and tickets, as well as classical CDs, can be had at **Fnac** (*see p156*) and the **Valentim de Carvalho** branch at the Centro Cultural de Belém (*see p171*). Tickets can also be purchased at the following agencies:

ABEP
Praça dos Restauradores, Restauradores, 1250 (21 347 5824/21 342 5360). Metro Restauradores. **Open** 11am-9.30pm daily. **No credit cards.** **Map** p310 L9.

Agência de Bilhetes Alvalade
Alvalade Shopping, Praça de Alvalade 6B, Alvalade, 1700 (21 795 5859). Metro Alvalade. **Open** 11am-9.30pm Mon-Sat; 12.30-8.30pm Sun. **No credit cards.** **Map** p304 M2.

Venues

The **Centro Cultural de Belém** (*see p192*) has three auditoria that are all sometimes used for classical concerts. Its Grande Auditório (capacity 1,429) has excellent acoustics, but large-scale works and even opera tend to be more successful there than chamber music. The programme is usually very good and the CCB ranks with the **Gulbenkian** (*see p202*) as one of Lisbon's most important cultural venues. Annoyingly, though, the box office (21 361 2444, open 1-7.30pm daily) accepts no credit cards. Upstairs in the bar, the otherwise excellent series of free concerts by young soloists and groups (7-9pm Mon-Fri) is utterly compromised by the flat acoustics and the noise from the bar.

Coliseu dos Recreios
Rua das Portas de Santo Antão 96, Baixa, 1150 (21 324 0580). Metro Rossio. **Open** Box office 1-7.30pm Mon-Fri and 1hr before concerts. **Tickets** 1,500$00-4,500$00. **No credit cards.** **Map** p310 L8.

Lisbon's coliseum was completed in 1890 and has been both a circus venue and opera house. These days it's the stage for everything from political conventions to classic operas. Acoustics vary; some say they're best on the left side.

Culturgest

Caixa Geral de Depósitos, Portaria da Rua Arco do Cego 1, Campo Pequeno, 1000 (21 790 5454). Metro Campo Pequeno. **Open** Box office 9am-7pm Mon-Sat; 2-8pm Sun. **Tickets** vary. **Credit** MC, V. **Map** p305 M4.

Within the giant corporate headquarters of the state-owned Caixa Geral de Depósitos, Portugal's biggest bank, and sponsored by same. The largest of its two auditoria (capacity 652), which although aesthetically uninteresting has reasonable acoustics, regularly hosts music and other shows – mostly 20th-century work. No capacity for symphonic works, though. *See also p224.*

Fundação Calouste Gulbenkian

Rua Dr Nicolau Bettencourt, Praça de Espanha, 1050 (21 793 5131/fax 21 793 9294/ www.gulbenkian.pt). Metro São Sebastião. **Open** Box office 1-7pm daily. **Tickets** vary. **Credit** MC, V. **Map** p304 K4.

Unprepossessing as a building, but set in beautiful gardens, the Gulbenkian has its own orchestra, choir and ballet company, and its various concert series bring orchestras, chamber groups and soloists to Lisbon throughout the year. There are also substantial yearly festivals of contemporary music (in May) and early music (October), as well as concerts in the outdoor amphitheatre, the museum and the centre for contemporary art. *See also p192.*

Teatro Luís de Camões

Avenida Dom João II, Parque das Nações, 1998 (21 891 7725). Metro Oriente. **Open** Box office 7.30-10pm on performance nights. **Tickets** 1,000$00; 500$00 concessions. **Credit** AmEx, V.

Built for Expo 98, this big blue glass and metal cube on the riverside has a capacity of 1,000 and state-of-the-art acoustics. It has become the home for the previously stageless National Ballet. Tickets can also be bought at the São Carlos box office (*see below*).

Teatro Nacional de São Carlos

Rua Serpa Pinto 9, Chiado, 1200 (21 346 8408/21 342 7722). Metro Baixa-Chiado/tram 28. **Open** Box office 1-6pm Mon-Fri; closed Sat, Sun. **Tickets** vary. **Credit** AmEx, EC, MC, V. **Map** p310 L10.

A grand and beautifully preserved late 18th-century building inspired by La Scala. It has a wonderful rococo interior, excellent acoustics and good visibility from any seat. Operatic seasons vary greatly in quality. There has been little investment in building up a native operatic tradition, notwithstanding impressive contributions from both choir and orchestra, a superabundance of international stars and a number of real triumphs: in recent years, Bernstein's *Candide*, Ligeti's *Le Grand Macabre* and the Brazilian Carlos Gomes's *Il Guarany*. Both choir

and orchestra are active in concert work, too, and the theatre also administers the Música em Novembro festival of contemporary music, so far biennially (the most recent was in November 2000).

Orchestras

Lisbon has just one symphony orchestra – the **Orquestra Sinfônica Portuguesa** – while the **Orquestra Gulbenkian** is the only one to record for a major label or participate in international festivals.

Orquestra Gulbenkian

Portugal's oldest orchestra, founded in 1962, is the only one with its own distinctive sound, but with only 60 players it has yet to make it as a symphony orchestra. It plays mainly at the Gulbenkian's Grande Auditório. *See p203* **Gulbenkian's tuneful legacy**.

Orquestra Metropolitana de Lisboa

Founded in 1992, Lisbon's third orchestra, run by a consortium of sponsors, plays hundreds of concerts annually – not just orchestral ones but also solo performances and chamber music. Conductor is Miguel Graça Moura.

Orquestra Sinfónica Portuguesa

Based at the Teatro Nacional de São Carlos, above, though rumoured to be moving to the Teatro de Camões, the Sinfónica was founded in 1993 and remains something of a white elephant. Besides São Carlos, the OSP plays irregularly at the Centro Cultural de Belém and elsewhere in Portugal. Its repertoire includes major symphonic and operatic works that it alone among Portugal's orchestras is able to play. State-run and vulnerable to political changes, it is constantly being reformed and restructured. Chief conductor is currently the Spanish contemporary music specialist Ramón Encinar; chief guest conductor is Wolfgang Rennert.

Festivals

Sintra Music Festival

Tickets & information: Sintra Tourist Office, Praça da República, Sintra, 2710 (21 923 1157/fax 21 923 5176). Also available from Telecartaz (21 385 4419) and branches of Valentim de Carvalho. **Date** mid June-July.

Romantic works played in romantic Sintra – concerts by international artists in the beautiful settings of the Palácio Nacional de Queluz and Sintra's Palácio Nacional and Palácio de Pena. It's mostly piano recitals or chamber music, and an ideal way to see the palaces with music thrown in.

Mafra International Music Festival

Tickets & information: Palácio Nacional de Mafra (26 181 7550). Also sometimes available from Fnac Chiado, Centro Colombo and Valentim de Carvalho, CCB. **Date** Sat, Sun Oct-early Nov.

Gulbenkian's tuneful legacy

Though what was formerly a mere Secretariat for Culture has now been promoted to become a real ministry, it was the Calouste Gulbenkian Foundation that for decades kept the flag of the arts waving in Portugal. In the area of music, the Foundation remains unrivalled, maintaining its own orchestra, choir and ballet company (see p202), and running several concert series and an active music department.

Calouste Sarkis Gulbenkian himself was an Armenian Christian, born in Istanbul with British citizenship, who made millions from oil prospecting in the Middle East. When Britain seized his assets as 'enemy property' during World War II, neutral Portugal offered him asylum. After Gulbenkian's death in 1955, the Foundation was set up under the terms of his will; he left it his astonishing art collection (see p108 and p191) and made it a centre for the promotion of the performing arts.

The Gulbenkian Orchestra, the jewel in the Foundation's crown, was founded as a chamber group in 1962. It has since grown and is the only Portuguese orchestra with its own distinctive sound, but with 60 players it sits somewhat awkwardly between chamber and symphonic dimensions. This guarantees it flexibility, and its repertoire is vast, but the end result is extraordinarily variable, depending upon the inspiration provided by the conductor. Conductors change rarely and the current incumbent, Muhai Tang, has been here since 1988. But leading conductors from elsewhere are a feature of seasons that run from October to May. As in Lisbon's other orchestras, foreign membership is high, making for a cosmopolitan atmosphere backstage.

The Gulbenkian Choir, numbering around 100 members, has been in existence since 1964, but its international profile has increased greatly in recent years thanks to its work with Frans Brüggen and the Orchestra of the 18th Century, including the release of an impressive CD, produced from live performances, of Beethoven's Ninth. The chief conductor of the choir since 1969 has been the veteran Michel Corboz.

As well as overseeing the running of orchestra and choir, the Music Department organises various concert series throughout the year, including visits by orchestras from around the world and a phenomenal chamber music series. It's also responsible for the Jornadas de Música Antiga, a mini-festival devoted to early music (generally of high quality, but perhaps in need of ridding itself of its fixation with Jordi Savall) and the Encontros de Música Contemporánea, which, while bringing renowned new music specialists to Lisbon, has by and large seen fit to concentrate only on the hardline ex-avant garde. In addition, it produces scholarly editions of Portuguese music and related musicological publications.

Rarely can an offer of asylum have paid off so richly for a host country.

An innovative young festival, held annually at the bombastic Palace of Mafra (see p248), whose focus is on baroque and contemporary music (including special commissions). The basilica is sometimes used as a spectacular setting for performances, though various other of the palace's rooms – including the magnificent library – are also used. There is a strong British connection, with many young performers are brought over with British Council help.

Capuchos Music Festival

Tickets & information: tourism offices of Almada (21 272 4059), Palmela (21 233 2122) or Sesimbra (21 223 5743). **Date** mid July-late August.

Soloists of the Orquestra Gulbenkian perform in the spectacular clifftop setting of the Capuchos Convent and other nearby venues – mainly 20th-century music, and avant-garde and baroque pieces. Each year there is also a special event, such as a recent performance of 'underwater music', played in a swimming pool.

Igreja de São Roque

Largo Trindade Coelho, Bairro Alto, 1200 (21 323 5383). Metro Baixa-Chiado/tram 28. Tickets sold at the church one hour before concerts. **Date** Nov-Dec.
Weekly winter concerts in the spectacular setting of this recently restored 16th-century church. Behind the plain façade, the interior is full of beautiful tiles and makes a perfect backdrop for *música antiga*.

Music: Fado

A visit to Lisbon isn't complete without a little tuneful melancholy.

It's fair to say that you don't know Lisbon well until you've experienced fado. This musical genre is indigenous to the city, remains a lively part of its culture, and is currently making something of a comeback. Fado can be heard in a wide variety of venues, from elegant restaurants to downmarket taverns, and it's quite possible to enjoy the atmosphere and music without understanding Portuguese. While it's true that fado is often packaged as just another product for the tourist, there are still many Portuguese enthusiasts, especially in Lisbon. It's more strongly rooted here than anywhere else except Coimbra, where the style of fado – basically troubadour songs sung by male university students or alumni – is very different.

The word fado derives from the Latin *fatum*, or fate, and fado has often been regarded as an expression of the supposed national trait of fatalism. This idea has become a little tired but fado is, indeed, often about an unhappy destiny in life, and many of the more famous songs touch upon betrayal, jealousy and disappointed love – sometimes taking these themes to absurdly tragic lengths. Fado is also strongly associated with *saudade*, the notion of longing for something distant or impossible to attain.

However, fado can be upbeat in tone. In the more informal venues, the audience tends to be less reverential and sometimes interrupts the singer with repartee. Another lighter touch to fado is the *desgarrada*, basically a conversation in song, where one singer challenges another to respond, often to a satirical or caustic remark. The spontaneity of the *desgarrada* varies, but it can sound rather rehearsed.

It's the singer's voice that takes centre stage in giving expression to fado's sentimentality. Authenticity of tone is more important than technical perfection (the singers in some of the cheaper taverns can sometimes be a little harsh on the ear). The singer is usually accompanied by a *guitarra*, a 12-string Portuguese guitar, and what in Portugal is called a *viola*, an acoustic Spanish guitar. The *guitarra* is shaped like a mandolin and its strings are arranged in pairs, producing a resonant sound that at times highlights the singer's melody and at others plays solo, while the viola provides a rhythmic accompaniment to them both.

The exact origins of fado are the subject of bitter debate. A Brazilian academic recently aggrieved Portuguese sensibilities by claiming that it was introduced from Brazil in the first half of the 19th century; the earliest known reference to fado, in 1883, described it as incorporating a sensual dance, prompting some observers to link it with samba. Others see fado as a legacy of the Moors, due to similarities with North African singing styles. Most agree that it owes something to the troubadour tradition of medieval Provence.

In the mid-1800s, fado was strongly associated with Lisbon low life, and performed in the seedy taverns of the old working-class *bairros*, notably Mouraria and Alfama. But it was also taken up by members of the upper classes (*see p205* **Marialvismo**), the first in a series of transformations that extended it beyond its humble origins, while never separating it from them. Another was the interest of intellectuals; as poets began to write lyrics for fado, they added greatly to its sophistication.

A NATIONAL MUSIC

In the 20th century, thanks to radio and vinyl, fado earned its current status as the national form of music. But this doesn't mean that the average Portuguese, even in Lisbon, regularly goes to hear it live. The younger generation shares the musical preferences of its peers elsewhere in Europe and many older people are turned off by its association with the authoritarian Salazar regime, which mythologised it as an element of national identity. However, it is currently showing signs of renewed vitality; a leading Portuguese weekly recently proclaimed that fado has been 'ransomed' from its past and is poised to take up its rightful place once more.

This renewal is being carried out by a new generation of talented young *fadistas*, who vary considerably in style. Among the most acclaimed, Camané is fairly classical, while Misia mixes fado with other influences, earning her the opprobrium of purists. Watch out for other talents such as Mafalda Arnauth (chosen to sing for Bill Clinton during his state visit), Maria Ana Bobone, Cristina Branco, Ana Sofia Varela, Mariza, and Helder Moutinho, although not all of these have made recordings. Among established performers are Nuno da Câmara Pereira, Argentina Santos, Maria da Fé, Carlos

Marialvismo

Fado has always been linked with *marialvismo*, an expression to describe the romantic attraction felt by members of the upper classes for the pastimes of their social inferiors – in other words, slumming it, if elegantly. It follows from the aristocracy's traditional image of itself as empathising with *o povo*, the people, and from the love that Portuguese of all social classes shared for popular traditions such as bullfighting. In today's less class-ridden world, *marialvismo* is perhaps an outdated concept, but vestiges linger on, notably in the worlds of fado and bullfighting.

The apotheosis of *marialvismo*, and its association with fado, was the love affair between the 13th count of Vimioso and Maria Severa Onofriana, the most famous *fadista* of all time, who died in 1846 at the age of 26. Severa, as she is known, was a girl of humble origins. Before meeting the count, she had

seen her previous lover, a soldier, banished to Africa for knifing to death a rival in her affections. Vimioso was an archetypal *marialva*: a fine bullfighter and horseman, with a penchant for fado and the ladies of the underworld.

To this day, female *fadistas* typically wear a black shawl in Severa's memory, and José Malhoa's famous painting of the two lovers (left) is ubiquitous in fado venues. Vimioso's influence is still felt in the aristocratisation of fado, which proved permanent. It is still often sung by the upper classes, either professionally or informally on family occasions. In such families, fado is passed down from generation to generation. The most prominent example is the Câmara family, with several generations currently singing. One of its members, Gonçalo, recently opened a *fado vadio* venue in the heart of the Alfama – *marialvismo* personified.

---

do Carmo and João Braga. Among late greats are Alfredo Marceneiro and, of course, Amália (*see p207* **Amália**).

Venues

Fado, being an emotional affair, relies on authenticity for effect. Much depends on the audience and the atmosphere of the venue. Wherever you are, convention demands that you stop talking during the performance. There are always a number of singers, so don't worry if you don't like the first one.

In posher *casas de fado* (fado houses) – restaurants where professional musicians perform – you can generally be sure of a reasonable standard of music, but remember that people who sing (sometimes every day) for a living can sometimes get a little jaded. This doesn't happen in the downmarket taverns specialising in *fado vadio* (literally vagabond fado), where a more laid-back attitude prevails and anyone may get up and sing. Another important difference is that fado houses usually charge *consumo mínimo* (minimum consumption)

or require customers to have dinner (at prices higher than equivalent restaurants). With *fado vadio* none of this applies, and for the uninitiated or impecunious it's a good place to start. Just don't expect quality singing, or any singing, for that matter; phone ahead to check there will be fado on the evening you want to visit.

Casas de fado

Adega Machado
Rua do Norte 91, Bairro Alto, 1200-284 (21 322 4640). Metro Baixa-Chiado/tram 28. **Open** 8pm-3am Tue-Sun; closed Mon. **Admission** *Before 11pm* minimum spend 2,900$00. *After 11pm* free. **Dinner** average 6,500$00. **Credit** AmEx, DC, MC, V. **Map** p310 L9.
A folksy place – dating back to 1931 – with oil lamps, red and white checked tablecloths, black and white photos of Amália, and lots of handclapping. It's quite large and attracts tour groups for which it puts on displays of folk dancing, but it still manages to retain some atmosphere. The venue is presided over by Filipe de Araújo Machado, grandson of the original founder. House star is Fernanda Maria.

Arcadas do Faia

Rua da Barroca 54/56, Bairro Alto, 1200-050 (21 342 6742). Metro Baixa-Chiado/tram 28. **Open** 8pm-2am Mon-Sat; closed Sun. **Fado** from 9.45pm. **Admission** minimum spend 3,500$00. **Dinner** average 6,000$00. **Credit** AmEx, DC, MC, V. **Map** p310 L9.

Upmarket and slightly antiseptic venue – big and not very cosy, with stained-glass windows and stone floors – regarded as one of the best places in Lisbon to hear good-quality fado. Regular performers include Lenita Gentil and Anita Guerreiro.

Associação Concentração Musical de 24 de Agosto

Travessa do Oleiro 13, Santos, 1200-304 (21 396 6945). Tram 28. **Open** 10pm-3am Fri, Sat. **Admission** free. **Dinner** average 2,500$00. **No credit cards. Map** p307 K9.

A good place to go purely for the atmosphere – less formal and more colourful than most, while retaining reasonable musical standards. Very local and very dark, with stuffed bulls' and antelopes' heads on the wall. Friendly owner-cum-waitress Isaura gets up to sing between doling out portions of *bacalhau*. A good place to hear drunken repartee and a *desgarrada*.

A Baiuca

Rua de São Miguel 20, Alfama, 1100-544 (21 886 7284). Tram 28 to Sé, then 5mins walk. **Open** 8pm-1am Mon, Wed-Sun; closed Tue. **Admission** free. **Dinner** average 3,000$00. **No credit cards. Map** p311 N10.

This modest but charming *fado vadio* place was opened in 1998 by a former bank clerk with a love of fado and is run by his two friendly daughters. It has an unpretentious family atmosphere and matching decoration. You will not find tour groups here, as space is limited. In late 2000 it was due to close for a few months for renovations.

Café Luso

Travessa da Queimada 10, Bairro Alto, 1200-365 (21 342 2281). Metro Baixa-Chiado/tram 28. **Open** 8pm-2am Mon-Sat; closed Sun. *Traditional dance* 9-10.30pm. *Fado* 10.30pm-2am. **Admission** minimum spend 3,500$00. **Credit** AmEx, DC, JCB, MC, V. **Map** p310 L9.

Lisbon's oldest extant fado house opened in 1931, and was one of Amália's early haunts. Since then its reputation has declined. Built in the cellars and stables of the 17th-century Palácio de São Roque, it was given a 1970s makeover that added acoustic panelling and a shiny wood bar that looks decidedly kitsch. It may have lost the plot, but a planned new bar next to the restaurant could liven things up.

Clube de Fado

Rua São João da Praça 92/4, Alfama, 1100-521 (21 888 2694/21 885 2704). Tram 28. **Open** 8pm-2am daily. **Admission** 1,950$00, includes bread, broad beans and *chouriço*. **Dinner** average 6,000$00. **Credit** AmEx, MC, V. **Map** p311 M10.

Owned by affable fado guitarist Mário Pacheco, this newish club attracts all his fado friends who may get up and take a turn, and includes as regulars leading traditional *fadistas* such as Maria Armanda, Dr Fernando Machado Soares – the best Coimbra *fadista* – and Maria da Nazaré, plus new young stars such as Paulo Bragança and José da Câmara. It's a small place with a lovely atmosphere and a dining room with massive stone columns and arches.

A Fermentação

Largo de São Rafael 1, Alfama, 1100-559 (21 887 7226). Tram 28 to Sé Catedral, then 10mins walk/bus 46, 90, 35, 107. **Open** (for fado) *Winter* 8pm-midnight Fri-Sun; closed Mon-Thur. *Summer* 8pm-midnight Tue-Sun; closed Mon. **Admission** free. **Dinner** average 2,000$00. **Map** p311 N10.

Opened in summer 2000, this place is an original combination of *azulejo* gallery, restaurant and *fado vadio* venue, packed into a tiny space. The walls are hung with hand-painted tiles crafted by one of its two owners, the talented João António. House stars include Zé Mattoso and Fernando Maurício.

Grupo Excursionista 'Vai Tu'

Rua da Bica Duarte Belo 6-8, Bica, 1200-056 (tel/fax 21 346 0848). Metro Cais do Sodré or Baixa-Chiado, tram 28/bus 13, 60, 104. **Open** (for fado) *Oct-May* 7pm-midnight Sun. **Admission** free. **Dinner** average 2,000$00. **No credit cards. Map** p310 L9.

Not exactly a fado venue, but a club of the kind that proliferates in Lisbon's older *bairros*, doubling as neighbourhood meeting place and local charity. The atmosphere is friendly and informal, although a first-time visitor sticks out more than a bit. On Sundays, a host of *fadistas* come for dinner, most of whom get up to sing during the evening. The talents on show vary in quality, but with so much variety it is almost impossible not to enjoy a few of them.

Nónó

Rua do Norte 47-49, Bairro Alto 1200-283 (21 342 9989). Metro Baixa-Chiado/tram 28. **Open** 8pm-3am daily. **Fado** from 9.15pm. **Admission** minimum spend 2,000$00. **Dinner** average 5,000$00. **Credit** AmEx, DC, MC, V. **Map** p310 L9.

A cheaper and smaller restaurant than others in the Bairro Alto, where anyone can get up and sing. Don't expect top-quality singing or acoustics, but it's a friendly place. Star of the house is João Casanova.

O Forcado

Rua da Rosa 219-221, Bairro Alto, 1200-384 (21 346 8579/fax 21 347 4887). Metro Restauradores, then Elevador da Glória. **Open** 8pm-3.30am daily. Fado and folk dancing 8-11pm; fado only 11pm-1am. **Admission** minimum spend 3,000$00. **Dinner** average 7,000$00. **Credit** AmEx, DC, MC, V. **Map** p310 L9.

A vast, cavernous place that caters largely to tour groups and works on a shift system, O Forcado is not somewhere to spend an entire evening. However, its size means it attracts the better singers, and if you drop in later you avoid the folk dancing. Main

Amália

If you take the path that leads left amid mausoleums and sepulchres from the main gates of Prazeres Cemetery, the gloom beneath the cedars is suddenly lit by swathes of bright flowers and burning candles. In a simple compartment in the wall lie the mortal remains of Amália Rodrigues – no saint, but a fado singer venerated for giving voice to the passions and sorrows of ordinary people.

The impromptu shrine, created after her death in October 1999, aged 79, testifies to people's affection for a singer from a poor family whose emotional power carried fado beyond Lisbon's more down-at-heel *bairros*. Photos, plaster statuettes, handwritten poems and fado verses adorn the wall. Responding to popular sentiment, in September 2000 parliament voted that her remains be moved to the National Pantheon. For legal reasons, this can only happen five years after her death.

Amália – always known by her first name, a measure of her iconic status – was born in 1920 to a rural family that had moved to Lisbon to find work. Her singing is said to have first captivated listeners as she sold lemons on a Lisbon quayside. True or not, the anecdote is central to the Amália myth: poor girl makes good. At 19, Amália sang at the Retiro da Severa, a tavern in Mouraria. Over the next decade, she appeared in musical revues, made her first recordings and, in 1947, starred in *Capas Negras*, a film that broke box office records.

Amália was the first *fadista* to gain international recognition, singing at the Paris Olympia and appearing on Broadway. By the 1960s she was the undisputed diva of fado. She was courted by the rich and powerful, inspired some of Portugal's best poets and was herself a talented writer. *Versos*, a volume of her poetry, was published in 1997.

In keeping with her image, Amália's life and art were inseparable. 'I have so much sadness in me,' she once said. 'I am a pessimist, a nihilist. Everything that fado demands in a singer I have in me.' On stage, wrapped in a black shawl, she would throw back her head, close her eyes and hold audiences spellbound with her searing songs

of lost love, jealousy and *saudade*. She married twice, and her love affairs are said to have caused her much suffering – again, thoroughly in keeping with the spirit of fado. In later years she became, and remains, a gay icon.

Amália, and fado itself, fell out of favour after the 1974 Revolution. For a time, she was tainted by the performances she had given at the behest of the old regime. But José Saramago, Portugal's Nobel prize-winning novelist, revealed after her death that she had donated large sums to the Portuguese Communist Party.

Amália's funeral was proof that Portugal had never lost its affection for her. Thousands lined the route to Prazeres Cemetery, throwing flowers, applauding and breaking into the songs she had made famous. Politicians rushed to associate themselves with the phenomenon. 'Our country has lost its voice and part of its soul,' said Prime Minister António Guterres, suspending the general election campaign for three days of national mourning. 'No one has ever expressed better in music what it means to be Portuguese,' echoed opposition leader José Manuel Durão Barroso.

Amália, a musical based on her life, staged at the Teatro Politeama (Rua das Portas de Santo Antão 109, Rossio, 1250, 21 343 0327/8) with English subtitles, and still running as this guide went to press, failed to win critical acclaim but has been a box office hit. Her main legacy, though, is the inspiration she gave a new generation of singers such as Mísia, Dulce Pontes, Ana Sofia Varela and Teresa Salgueiro of Madredeus. Despite their diverse styles, they all draw on her work.

Amália's best recordings can be heard on *The Art of Amália* (EMI). More information can be found on the following websites, which provide links to others:
http://geocities.com/cecskater1/
www.remus.dti.ne.jp/~peanuts/amalia/

Cemitério dos Prazeres

Prada dos Prazeres, Campo de Ourique, 1350. Tram 28. **Open** *May-Oct* 9am-5.30pm daily. *Nov-Apr* 9am-4.30pm daily. **Map** p306 H8.

Arts & Entertainment

Travel back in time at the **Taverna do Embuçado**.

attractions are Fernanda Santos and Dr Frederico Vinagre, a leading exponent of the Coimbra fado.

Parreirinha de Alfama

Beco do Espírito Santo 1, Alfama, 1100-222 (21 886 8209). Bus 39 A, 104, 105. **Open** 8pm-2am daily. Fado from 9.30pm. **Admission** minimum spend 2,000$00. **Dinner** average 6,000$00. **Credit** AmEx, DC, MC, V. **Map** p311 N10.

Just off the Largo do Chafariz do Dentro and owned by fado legend Argentina Santos, although she seems ever more reluctant to sing for tourists herself. Nice atmos, though: photographs of *fadistas*, tables lit by coach lamps and a bust of Amália in a niche.

Senhor Vinho

Rua do Meio à Lapa 18, Lapa 1200-723 (21 397 7456). Tram 25. **Open** 8.30pm-2am Mon-Sat; closed Sun. Fado from 9.45pm. **Admission** minimum spend 3,000$00. **Dinner** average 8,000$00. **Credit** AmEx, DC, MC, V. **Map** p306 J9.

Opened in 1975, this is a classic among fado houses – a bit pricey but the real thing. Quite cosy and surprisingly unpompous, it boasts some of the best *fadistas*. Look out for sweet-voiced Carlos Macedo, Maria Dilar and Maria da Nazaré. Rising star Mariza occasionally sings here but is not a regular. It's owned by the grande dame of fado, Maria da Fé, who does a turn toward the end of the evening. Food is excellent; booking is essential.

Taverna do Embuçado

Beco dos Cortumes, 10, Alfama 1100-172 (21 886 5088). Bus 9, 39A, 46,104, 105. **Open** 8.30pm-2am Mon-Sat; closed Sun. **Admission** minimum spend 3,500$00. **Dinner** average 7,500$00. **Credit** AmEx, DC, MC, V. **Map** p311 N10.

Stepping into the spacious, airy and elegant Taverna do Embuçado is like travelling back in time to a glamorous corner of 1960s Lisbon. Closed for almost 20 years after 1974, it has been beautifully restored, but is yet to regain its former prestige. A prize-winning chef turns out sophisticated dishes, making this as much a place for gourmets as fado enthusiasts. The house star is Teresa Siqueiro, but look out for younger singers Mafalda Arnauth and Helder Moutinho, although they are not regulars. Just off the Rua Terreiro do Trigo.

Tasca do Chico

Rua Diário de Notícias 39, Bairro Alto 1200-141 (21 343 1040). Metro Baixa-Chiado/tram 28. **Open** (for fado) 8pm-1am Mon, Wed. **Admission** free. **No credit cards. Map** p310 L9.

A welcome alternative to other fado places in the Bairro Alto, in the sense that you can just poke your head around the door and listen in to the *fado vadio*. Frequented by a lively, mixed crowd ranging from salt-of-the-earth fado lifers to younger locals and tourists who normally inhabit the nearby trendy bars. A small place, serving snacks only, it gets very packed – arrive early if you want a seat.

Music: Rock, Roots & Jazz

Few visitors come to Lisbon for the music, but many are surprised by the variety that it has to offer.

Keep your ears open as you walk around town, day or night, and you'll soon realise that you're in a musical environment that is among the most diverse of any European city, encompassing Britpop and Brazilian samba; Lisbon fado and Cape Verdean *mornas*; chilly northern European techno and fired-up local rap. A balmy climate and a generally tolerant attitude to neighbourhood noise means that, especially in summer, all this music spills out on to the beaches of Caparica and the streets of Bairro Alto and Santos.

As for live music, there is no deep-rooted tradition of teenage wannabes playing in local bars in the hope of hitting the big time. But there are plenty of places to relax with a beer while listening to an in-house band; cover versions rule, but this is one way of getting a feel for the back catalogue of Portuguese rock and pop. And the city's status as a gateway to Europe for citizens of Portugal's former colonies means there's always a steady supply of African and Brazilian musicians.

Portugal has tended to fall off the edge of the map as far as big groups on tour are concerned. As a result, those that do visit are rewarded with a fanatical following, including Brazilian artists, who have long made a point of stopping off in Lisbon. The recent addition of the Pavilhão Atlântico (*see p210*) to the list of venues has also given Portugal more pulling power, as have the success of a handful of rock and jazz festivals (*see chapter* **By Season**).

As for Portuguese artists going in the other direction, only Madredeus (hauntingly beautiful or irritatingly vapid, depending on your musical taste) and, to a lesser extent, the talented singer Dulce Pontes have made a name for themselves abroad. Both draw on folk and fado traditions.

TICKETS AND INFORMATION

The two main dailies, *Público* and *Diário de Notícias*, both have a Friday music section with reviews and news of upcoming events. The Voxpop section of www.sapo.pt (click on música) is a good online source of information.

For tickets, the **ABEP** booth (*see p201*) and **Agência Alvalade** (*see p201*) are often a good bet. Tickets can also usually be obtained from other sources, including the Belém branch of **Valentim do Carvalho** (*see p172*) and the two **Fnac** outlets (*see p156*).

Fonoteca

Edifício Monumental, Loja 17, Praça Duque de Saldanha, 1050 (21 353 6231). Metro Saldanha. **Open** 10am-8pm Tue-Sat; closed Sun. **Admission** 300$00; annual membership 2,470$00. **Map** p304 L5.
Based on an idea imported from France, the Fonoteca record library is tucked into the basement of a shopping centre. It has more than 10,000 CDs in its collection, plus books, CD-Roms and magazines. Choose your CDs, then slide into the listening room and let an hour or two slip by. Fonoteca also hosts talks and eclectic musical performances and has resident musicologists.

Rock & pop

Initial impressions of Portuguese pop may well be negative. The *Made in Portugal* TV show on RTP1 every Sunday afternoon provides a particularly gaudy platform for *pimba*, the cheesy local version of Europop. It's the tip of an iceberg that reaches right down into rural Portugal, where bands playing boom-bang-a-bang music liven up summer fairs in villages up and down the country.

Among Portuguese musicians who aspire to be taken more seriously, veteran rock/blues guitarist and singer Rui Veloso recently celebrated the 20th anniversary of his debut album, *Ar de Rock* (literally *Rock Air*, but also a cod Portuguese pronunciation of 'hard rock'). During much of those 20 years, the likes of Veloso, hard rockers Xutos & Pontape and the poppier GNR have dominated the charts. The more folk-influenced Trovante and singer Luís Represesas have also had a good run. Other established names include Ala dos Namorados, brainchild of ex-Trovante guitarist João Gil with soaring vocals from Nuno Guerreiro, Rádio Macau and the commercial Delfins and Santos e Pecadores.

Portuguese rock has never been known for its originality, and it wasn't until the mid 1990s that Pedro Abrunhosa, who went on to record his Portuguese funk in Prince's Paisley studios, breathed some life into the scene. Newer bands include Coldfinger, who produce alternative pop with trip-hop influences; the more cabaret-style Belle Chase Hotel; the Gift, who use an orchestra for their sub-Portishead symphonic pop; the up-and-coming Ornatos Violeta; and pop-rockers Hands on Approach and Atomic Bees. Moonspell are a heavier outfit and Yellow W Van a promising hardcore band. In 1999, Silence 4 came from nowhere (or, rather, a summer festival) to dominate the charts for a lengthy spell with their earnest, REM-style rock; their second CD showed more musical diversity. Like a number of Portuguese bands, they choose to sing mainly in English.

Musicians from Lisbon's burgeoning ethnic communities do not confine themselves to African references. Those influenced by US music include General D (rap), Kika, Da Weasel and Boss AC (hip hop), Cláudia (dance music) and Rei Kuango (eclectic). Sara Tavares, whose singing style was initially mainly gospel and soul, has gone in the other direction, her recent work exposing her Cape Verdean roots.

Outdoor venues

Estádio de Alvalade
Rua Francisco Stromp, Alvalade, 1600 (21 751 4000). Metro Camp Grande.
Many of Lisbon's big concerts are held in this unprepossessing stadium. Despite the name, it's a long way from Alvalade metro station.

Praça Sony
Rua da Pimenta, Parque das Nações, 1998 (21 891 9000). Metro Oriente.
Situated at the northern end of the former Expo site, this shallow amphitheatre ringed by bars has the capacity for big concerts yet a more intimate feel than a stadium. Artists who've played here include Oasis and Brazil's Djavan.

Other major venues

A number of big concert halls in Lisbon are used for rock, as well as classical music and theatre. Among the biggest are the **Coliseu dos Recreios** (*see p201*), now used mainly for classical concerts; **Culturgest** (*see p202*), whose programming leans towards jazz; and the **Centro Cultural de Belém** (*see p192*). The latter's main auditorium is rather antiseptic, making audiences feel they should be on their best behaviour, but there are more relaxed (and free) concerts at 7pm on weekdays in the terrace bar. **Paradise Garage**

O Berro – an authentic slice of Lisbon life.

(*see p220*) is an atmospheric place to hear international bands playing everything from metal to indie-style rock.

Aula Magna
Alameda da Universidade, Cidade Universitária, 1600 (21 796 7624). Metro Alameda. **Map** p304 L2.
The main amphitheatre of the University of Lisbon. The steeply banked seating means it does not naturally lend itself to rock concerts, but it can pull them off given the right band – it was the location for a legendary Smashing Pumpkins concert, and artists as diverse as John McLaughlin and Madredeus have also performed here.

Pavilhão Atlântico
Rua Dom Fuas Roupinho, Parque das Nações, 1998 (21 891 8440). Metro Oriente.
Thanks largely to its size, this has rapidly established itself as Lisbon's premier indoor rock venue since it opened in late 1998. It kicked off with an unforgettable show by Massive Attack and has also presented Bob Dylan, REM and Alanis Morissette.

Live music bars

O Berro
Rua da Esperança 158, Santos, 1200 (21 396 5568). Train from Cais de Sodré to Santos/27, 49, 60 bus. **Open** 10pm-3am daily. *Live music* midnight-3am daily. **Admission** free. **Credit** V. **Map** p306 J9.

'The Shout' is a Lisbon fixture where friends go to relax and, like as not, sing along to the mainly acoustic covers of Portuguese pop and rock from the past 20 years. It's small and smoky and gets packed at the weekend. It never has been and never will be remotely hip, but it's an authentic slice of Lisbon life.

Jardim da Música

Rua António Patrício 118, Entrecampos, 1700 (21 793 0325). Metro Entrecampos/7, 44, 55 bus. **Open** 11.30pm-2am Tue-Thur, Sun; 11.30pm-3am Fri, Sat; closed Mon. **Admission** free. **Credit** MC, V. **Map** p305 M3.

This spacious bar successfully creates an outdoor atmosphere indoors by being decorated as if it were an esplanade. It offers a diet of Portuguese and English-language covers by mainly unplugged bands. Since a new manager took over and slashed the price of a beer to 300$00, it has attracted an 18-plus crowd from the surrounding area.

MUSIcais

Jardim do Tabaco, Avenida Dom Infante Henrique, Santa Apolónia, 1100 (21 887 7155). Bus 9, 28, 35, 46, 59, 90, 104, 105, 206, 210. **Open** *Esplanade* 11pm-1am Tue-Sat. *Bar* 1-5am Tue-Sat. Closed Mon, Sun. **Admission** *Esplanade* free. *Bar* men 1,000$00; women 5,00$00. **No credit cards. Map** p308 O9.

MUSIcais is really two bars in one, housed in a spacious riverside mall. There is unplugged music on the esplanade until 1am (inside in winter, outside in summer), then a band plays until 3am in the bar, followed by a DJ. On Wednesdays, Thursdays and Sundays, the music is Portuguese acoustic covers; on other days, it's mixed, with soul, blues, pop or rock. The place is owned and run by musician Mico da Câmara Pereira, a well-known figure in Portugal's glossy magazines.

Refúgio das Freiras

Rua Dom Carlos I 57, Loja 2, Santos, 1200 (21 395 7968). Tram 38, then 5mins walk. **Open** 11.30pm-4am daily. *Live music* 12.30-2.30am daily. **No credit cards. Map** p307 K10.

The 'Nuns' Refuge' supplies a staple diet of rock bands playing covers to an audience composed mainly of students. At 300$00 for a beer, it's one of the cheaper venues around.

Templários

Rua Flores do Lima 8A, Entrecampos, 1700 (21 797 0177). Metro Entrecampos/7, 44, 55 bus. **Open** 10.30pm-2am Mon-Thur; 10.30pm-3am Fri, Sat. *Live music* midnight-2am Mon-Thur; midnight-2.30am Fri, Sat. Closed Sun. **Admission** free. **Credit** MC, V. **Map** p304 M3.

This is a bar for all age groups, offering Portuguese and international standards.

Folk

It was a song by folk giant José Afonso on the radio that provided a musical signal for the start of the 1974 Revolution, and folk was of great importance during that period.

Sérgio Godinho, Fausto and Vitorino have repopularised many traditional songs from the Alentejo, while Júlio Perreira and bagpipers Gaiteiros de Lisboa also base their work on traditional instrumental music. In many parts of the country, such as the Minho, folk music has a very strong link to dance.

One thriving musical tradition is that of student *tuna* groups, which represent either a university or a faculty. *Tunas* perform traditional music, fado and songs of their own creation, both in university and in public spaces. Another characteristic sound is the *guitarra*, or Portuguese guitar, a crucial element of fado. Carlos Paredes was its undisputed master for many years, and António Chainho has recently won acclaim with the instrument.

For details of **O'Gilins**, a friendly venue for Irish and international folk, *see p154*.

Anos Sessenta

Largo do Terreirinho 21, Mouraria, 1100 (21 887 3444). Metro Martin Moniz/7, 8, 40 bus. **Open** 9.30pm-4am daily. **Admission** free. **Credit** AmEx, MC, V. **Map** p311 M9.

The nostalgic name ('The '60s') is a fair reflection of both the music on offer and the cosy atmosphere created by the regular patrons, typically middle-aged civil servants and professionals. It has African, folk and Brazilian evenings, but the house policy is to shift the days around periodically for variety.

Inda a noite é uma criança

Praça das Flores 8 , São Bento, 1200 (21 396 3545). Metro Rato/100 bus. **Open** 10.30pm-3am Mon-Sat. *Live music* midnight-3am Mon-Sat. Closed Sun. **Credit** V. **Admission** free. **Map** p307 K8.

'The night is but a child' is the bar's name, but the same cannot be said for its customers, who are mainly aged 30-50. Many are regulars, making for an intimate and friendly atmosphere. Bands play Portuguese folk songs from the past 25 years.

Jazz

Established Portuguese artists include the singer Maria João and her pianist Mário Laginha, whose work together involves both standard jazz songs and experimental vocal excursions more reminiscent of African music. Others, such as composer/pianist António Pinho Vargas, pianist Bernardo Sassetti, double bass player Carlos Barreto, saxophonist Carlos Martins and his group Sons de Lusofonia, and trumpet player Laurent Filipe have made their mark on the wider jazz scene.

The **Hot Clube** has an active jazz school (Escola de Jazz Luís Vilas Boas, 21 362 1740) and through this and studies abroad a new generation of jazz musicians is emerging. Look out for Nuno Ferreira (guitar), André Fernandes

Arts & Entertainment

Cool music at the **Hot Clube**.

(guitar), Filipe Melo (piano), Carlos Morena (piano), Bernardo Moreira (double bass), Tomás Pimentel (trumpet), Mário Delgado (guitar) and the school's current director, saxophonist Pedro Moreira, who is trying to get Hot Clube courses recognised by the Portuguese educational authorities as university-level studies.

Hot Clube

Praça da Alegria 39, Restauradores, 1250 (21 346 7369/www.hcp.pt). Metro Avenida. **Open** 10pm-2am Tue-Sat. *Live music* 11pm, 3am Tue-Sat. Closed Mon, Sun. **Admission** 1,000$00 when band scheduled; free jam sessions. **No credit cards. Map** p307 L8. The classic intimate, smoky jazz bar. For intimate read also poky; the ceiling is too low for the double bass to stand fully upright and the place seats a maximum of 50 (though there's also standing room and overspill on the back patio). It brings in a fair share of good jazz musicians on tour, and really is one of those places where big-name artists playing a larger venue may go to jam after their official gig.

Speakeasy

Cais das Oficinas, Armazém 115, Rocha Conde d'Obidos, Alcântara, 1350 (21 395 7308/speak easy.bar@netzero.pt). Train from Cais Sodré to Alcântara-Mar/tram 15, 18/12, 28, 32, 40, 43 bus. **Open** 10pm-4am Mon-Sat. *Live music* 11.30pm or midnight-2.30am Mon-Sat. Closed Sun. **Admission** free. **Credit** AmEx, DC, JCB, MC, V. **Map** p306 H10.

Owned by the sons of fado singer Carlos do Carmo, Speakeasy has always had the unenviable task of catering to both the Cascais jet set and jazz purists. Early in the evening it's a relatively expensive restaurant, where steak and chips plus a bottle of wine will cost at least 6,000$00. Some diners stay only for the first set; as they leave, their places are taken by a more varied crowd. Jazz can usually be heard Tuesday to Thursday, with blues and funk reserved for the busier nights, and jam sessions on Mondays. Once a month there is a more heavily promoted event featuring a well-known Portuguese artist, the main function of which seems to be to get photos of clients and bar alike into the glossies.

African

In recent years, Lisbon has built up a well-deserved reputation as a place to hear African music, with both traditional and modern styles on offer. Of the former, voice and percussion groups include Kilandokilos from Angola, Djambonda from Guinea Bissau, Txabeta from Cape Verde, Bulawê from São Tomé and Xipanipani from Mozambique. The African cultural association **Regresso das Caravelas** (21 886 1710/www.regressodascaravelas.web. pt) produces a useful catalogue of African musicians and dancers.

Cape Verdean *mornas* (as popularised by Cesária Évora) and the more uptempo *funaná* can be widely heard, alongside more modern African rhythms such as *zouk* and *kuduro*, (Afro-techno music). The most popular commercial African artists are Helder and the younger Helderzinho. Some artists try to mix the past with the present: São Tomé producer Filipe Santo, while producing much mainstream African music, also drew on the traditional healing rhythms of *puita* and *jambi* in his record *A Musa*.

Music from Portugal's former African colonies can be heard on the state-run radio station RDP-Africa (101.5 FM). It also organises free live concerts at 6.30pm most Wednesdays on the ground floor of RDP's headquarters, opposite the Amoreiras shopping centre (Avenida Duarte Pacheco 26, Amoreiras, 1070, 21 382 0000).

B.Leza

Largo Conde Barão 50-2, Santos, 1200 (21 396 3735). Train from Cais de Sodré to Santos/tram 15, 28/6, 49 bus. **Open** 11.30pm-4.30am Mon-Sat; closed Sun. **Admission** minimum spend 1,000$00 Mon-Thur; 2,000$00 Fri, Sat. **No credit cards. Map** p307 K9. Housed in a huge, crumbling 16th-century former mansion, entered through a splendid courtyard, is one of the best places to listen and dance to live Cape Verdean music. Regular performers include the excellent Dany Silva and Tito Paris. There's a strong boy-meets-girl feel to the dancefloor, and unaccompanied women wishing to remain so may find they get just a little too much attention. Cape Verdean food is served until 3.30am; a typical meal costs 2,000$00 and it's nothing special. The glass case full of trophies in the far corridor is a reminder that in another incarnation this was a sports club.

Enclave

Rua do Sol ao Rato 71A, Rato, 1250 (21 388 8738).
Metro Rato. **Open** 8.30pm-4am Tue-Sat. *Live music*
10.30pm-4am Tue-Sat. Closed Mon, Sun. **Admission**
free Tue-Thur; minimum spend (including two drinks)
2,000$00 Fri, Sat. **No credit cards. Map** p306 J7.
Cape Verdean singer Bana founded Enclave in the 1970s and it has been a Lisbon fixture ever since. It was recently refurbished and Tito Paris is now the main resident performer. There's live music upstairs in the restaurant until midnight and then downstairs, where it can get very crowded at weekends.

Brazilian

There is a fair smattering of Brazilian bars in Lisbon. A good place to find out more about them, and the city's Brazilian community, is **Casa do Brasil** (Rua São Pedro de Alcântara 63-1, Bairro Alto, 21 347 1580/www. casadobrasildelisboa.pt), an association that provides information on jobs and legal advice for Brazilians in Lisbon. It also hosts live music on Fridays from 10.30pm to 2am; the mood is very informal and floorspace is at a premium.

Bruxa Bar

Rua São Mamede ao Caldas 35A/B, Baixa, 1100 (21 886 9340). Metro Rossio or Martim Moniz. **Open**
10.30pm-3am Mon-Sat. *Live music* 11.30pm-2.30am
Mon-Sat. Closed Sun. **Admission** minimum spend
600$00. **Credit** AmEx, MC, V. **Map** p311 M9.
A well-established Brazilian bar that fills up at the weekend with a 25- to 45-year-old crowd. The resident duo (plus computerised percussion) play a variety of music to suit the evening's mood, and generally succeed in creating a party atmosphere.

Chafarica

*Calçada de São Vicente 79-81, São Vicente, 1100
(21 886 7449). Tram 28.* **Open** 10pm-3am Mon-Sat.
Live music 11.30pm-3am Mon-Sat. Closed Sun.
Admission minimum spend 600$00.
No credit cards. Map p311 N9.
A cosy bar with regulars of all ages slurping well-mixed Caipirinhas. The resident acoustic duo play melodic Brazilian music – Chico Buarque and Caetano Veloso songs – in the week and more uptempo fare at the weekend, when the place packs out but people somehow still find space to dance.

Gasoiil

Rua da Madalena 123, Baixa, 1100 (21 888 2301).
Metro Rossio or Martim Moniz. **Open** 10.30pm-4am
Mon-Sat. *Live music* 11.30pm-4am Mon-Sat. Closed
Sun. **Admission** minimum spend 600$00. **Credit**
MC, V. **Map** p311 M9.

Under the same ownership as Bruxa, and literally round the corner from it, Gasoiil caters to a mixed 18-30s crowd who dance the night away to infectious Bahian and Nordeste pop. Unlike in many of Lisbon's Brazilian bars, there's usually enough space to have a good bop, although it can get very crowded late at night.

Other venues

Bar a Barraca at the **Teatro Cinearte**
(*see p180*), **Catacumbas** (*see p148*), **Chapîto**
(*see p152*), **Ler Devagar** (*see p156*), and **ZDB**
(*see p195*), an important venue for experimental music, also host gigs. **Espaço Cabo Verde**
(*see p42*), a Cape Verdean association with a restaurant, has live music on Tuesday and Thursday lunchtimes. It can get very full.

Bugix

*Rua Dom Fuas Roupinho, Parque das Nações, 1998
(21 895 1181). Metro Oriente.* **Admission**
minimum spend 2,000$00. **Credit** AmEx, MC, V.
Part-owned by singer Luís Represas (*see p209*), this bar offers live Brazilian and Latin music on Fridays and Saturdays between 1am and 3am, followed by a DJ. The door policy is fearsome and it attracts mainly young rich kids as it's one of the most expensive places in town (a small beer costs 900$00, a whisky 1,500$00). Strictly no trainers. Nearest to the Porta Sul entrance of the Parque das Nações, if you're driving.

Dany Silva plays **B.Leza** – again. *See p212.*

Arts & Entertainment

Nightlife

Crucial clubs, big-name DJs and busy collectives – the scene is diversifying fast.

Lisbon nightlife remains a force to be reckoned with. Tens of thousands very visibly take to the streets on a weekend night – milling around the Bairro Alto before heading down to the clubs on Avenida 24 de Julho, in Alcântara or in the Docas. On any night of the week you can drink until dawn, find dance music to suit, catch a live band or scoff a late-late steak. And it's cheap, too, by western European standards.

It's one of life's little ironies, though, that just as Lisbon established its reputation as a great city to go clubbing, the scene has become more elusive. Venues once famed for their musical edginess now throb to high-street house, and it's less common for promoters to take over big spaces for sets by big-name foreign DJs.

In part, it's the stunning success of **Lux** since it opened in late 1999 that has made it tough for others to compete, except on a much smaller scale. Although a massive trance scene thrives in the sticks, these days many lisboetas are turning to lush layered soundscapes, shuffle-drum lounge beats and the wistful complexities of electronic 'nu jazz', for example at the periodic concerts at **ZDB** (*see p195*). That's not to say that Lisbon's dance culture is fading; like much here, the scene is under construction.

For its part, the Bairro Alto has confounded predictions that it would go into a steep decline after the 1999 sale of **Frágil**, the area's first and most important club, founded in the early 1980s by Lisbon nightlife guru Manuel Reis. In what is, after all, a residential area, there has long been pressure from locals and the authorities to ease noisy clubs out. Although it still has lots of late drinking dens (*see chapter* **Bars**), the number of dance clubs is much reduced.

Yet in defiance of the forecasts (and in some cases of a strict reading of the licensing laws) the odd new club still pops up here and the opening hours of existing places have stayed late – or even got later – despite the carrots dangling down by the river in the form of cheap rents, big spaces and car parking. Recent arrivals include **FL Café** and – some time soon after this book goes to press – **Carrom**, which is moving in after a successful stint in a tiny premises in Santos. One of Lisbon's most intimate and enthusiastic venues, Carrom has consistently attracted a young, multi-ethnic and bumping crowd. Regular features include warm, floor-friendly tech-house exponent DJ

Lino; an imaginative mix of tribal house, Latino house, Euro-electro and Afro-jazz fusion spun by the best local names, with international DJs every second week; and the stylish deep techno emissary Anthony Millard. Carrom's move is proof there's life in the old Bairro Alto yet.

The dockside around Santa Apolónia, home to Manuel Reis's latest, much-admired project, Lux, has otherwise seen only a couple of new restaurants and an undistinguished live music bar. In fact, the migration of nightlife eastwards reached its peak during Expo 98, when the large venues on the Expo site – now renamed Parque das Nações – offered concerts, events and general excitement that at times threatened to do away with the 2am weekend traffic jams on Avenida 24 de Julho. With a few exceptions, such as **Bugix** (*see p213*), the area's venues now tend to be patronised less by lisboaetas than by east-side out-of-towners who don't want the hassle of driving across Lisbon.

Still, the action has been trickling down towards the waterfront for a decade or so, which is also what happens in the course of the night. The Bairro Alto, which survives to meet the needs of the varous tribes that remain unimpressed with theme bars and sanitised warehouse spaces, starts closing up around 2am. From then, people who want to stay out drift down to the mostly well-established clubs and bars of Avenida 24 de Julho and the newer ones in the Docas, which are just getting going. Clubs such as **Kremlin**, Lux and those in Alcântara don't take off until even later.

Between the different areas, there are both overlaps and mutual exclusivities. Few denizens of Frágil would show their faces in Kapital, or vice versa, although Lux can bring everyone together on the dance floor. Following this psycho-geography of nightlife, we've organised our club listings according to area. We've made an exception for African dancehalls and clubs, which are dotted around town and anyway are a bit of a parallel universe. We've grouped them in a section of their own.

There's also an extremely active hip hop scene in the suburbs, but it's underground – there are no permanent venues. Unless an event is organised by a well-known bunch like Raska Sound System, this scene is strictly for insiders only. But for the incurably curious, the best starting point is **Kingsize Records** (21 887 7522/19). If you can understand Portuguese, events are also advertised on the weekly hip hop shows broadcast by Voxx FM (frequency 91.6) and Antenna 3 (from midnight to 2am on Monday and Sunday respectively).

Particularly in the Bairro Alto, there's a blurry line between bars with space to dance and discos (*see also chapter* **Bars**), but opening hours are often a good indicator of a place's true nature. Few clubs charge entrance (though some have a *consumo mínimo* or cover charge) and this raises the stakes for doormen's selection criteria, which can be unpredictable – not to say

aggressive. There was an outcry a few years ago when a young clubber died of injuries dealt him by a Kremlin bouncer, but few observers were that surprised. The incident spurred the spread of closed-circuit television cameras and other non-invasive security measures.

Bairro Alto

FL Café
Rua da Atalaia 36, Bairro Alto, 1200 (21 324 0546). Metro Baixa-Chiado/tram 28. **Open** 10.30pm-4am Tue-Sat; closed Mon, Sun. **Admission** free but restricted. **Credit** AmEx, DC, MC, V. **Map** p310 L9.

De-Lux

When **Lux** (see p222) opened its harbourside superclub in 1998, the city's club scene pounced. Proof of its continued success is given by the fact that DJ Vibe – Portugal's best-known dance emissary abroad until Rui Silva's ultra-commercial Touch Me made UK number one in early 2001 – still plays here, and even more by the list of international names it has hosted. Fortunately for Lisbon clubbers, these big names' enthusiasm for Lux has translated into regular return visits.

But if Lux has given the Lisbon nightlife its light and colour, a new breed of organiser is busily beavering away in the constantly shifting shadows. Though few such promoters have their own premises, a rash of invitations to 'animate' ailing dancefloors means that longer-running one-nighters are becoming more regular. There are incendiary hip hop nights, jazz-infused freestyle nights, reggae and ragga jams, drum 'n' bass parties, rockin' after-hours techno events and a growing number of reasonably well-attended electro sessions. Meanwhile a huge, globally significant trance scene thrives in the sticks, particularly points south.

The best places to pick up flyers about forthcoming events are the record shops **Kingsize** (Rua da Alfândega 114, 21 887 7522), **Raveman** (Travessa da Queimada 33, 21 347 1170), **Discomundo** (Calçada do Carmo 36, 21 347 8369), **Ananana** (Travessa Água da Flor 29, 21 347 4770) and the Santa Apolónia branch of **Valentim de Carvalho** (Avenida Infante Dom Henrique, Armazém B, 21 851 0403) – all with friendly DJ-ing staff. The **Good Mood Bazar** (Travessa dos Inglesinhos 13, 21 347 9095) is trance central. Otherwise ask around in bars.

Guest DJs and collectives are regularly on in Lux and **Frágil** (see p217); names to look out for include The Raska Sound System (hip hop, ragga and funk), Pedro Ricciardi (house), Fankambareggae (reggae old and new, occasionally ragga), CTC (dark drum 'n' bass), Journeys (outings in Afrobeat, broken beat, two-step garage and nu electronic dub), Anthony Millard (stylish deep techno) and two of the city's most challenging DJs: Dinis and Nuno Forte (brilliantly skewed breakbeat).

Off the club circuit, Blaast one-nighters and the annual Número Festival both bring together danceable beats and live electronica. The former, often working with promoters ZDBmüzique, usually provides an imaginative mix of upside-down pop, ear-torturing soundscapes and out-there electro weirdness, its own hyper-intense Major Eléctrico often playing support. The latter, an arts mag spin-off, has hosted a number of well-know powerbook composers, The Aphex Twin among them.

Parties organised by the Nylon label are always a treat, and may provide the chance to hear DJ-producer teams, like the Spaceboys and Shelter, play the warm and smooth flowing, deep sounding dubby grooves that are helping to give the Lisbon scene an increasingly distinctive flavour.

Arts & Entertainment

Founded by Fátima Lopes, Portugal's answer to Donatella Versace, nights inside this lilac palace feel like a film by Tim Burton. There's a brilliant but nameless house DJ whose stylish skills are masked on Saturdays by a fifth-rate tribal drummer, while shy transvestites, legless machos, wannabe pop-stars, and paralytic 'models' (from the upstairs agency) collide in the toilets downstairs. Struggling on in the most horrific outfits from the adjacent showroom, the barstaff are lovely. Other pluses: it gets going early in a city that starts late, and the doormen are friendly. But for all its ghoulish attempts to create a scene, there's nothing desperate about this place at all, except perhaps the flirty boys and girls on the pull and the fact that as of early 2001 it still doesn't have more than a provisional drinks licence. Surreal, but fun if you're in the mood.

Frágil

Rua da Atalaia 128, Bairro Alto, 1200 (21 346 9578/www.fragil.com). Metro Baixa-Chiado/tram 28. **Open** 10.30pm-4am Mon-Sat; closed Sun. **Admission** free but restricted. **No credit cards**. **Map** p310 L9.

Up until 1998 this was Lisbon's most crucial club – an institution for the cultural scene and the place that sparked the Bairro Alto clubbing boom. Never quite the same since Manuel Reis sold up and moved on to open Lux, these days it's just a club without any real crowd – and sometimes no crowd at all. Undeterred, it battles on, making the most of its fringe position. Fridays and Saturdays are strong, mostly gay nights, with pumping house, while the irrepressible Journeys collective have been busily redefining the midweek agenda, furnishing their flagship with a musical concept. Their Spectrum nights one Wednesday in the month have seen an imaginative selection of up-and-coming international names, cooking up the kind of freestyle melting-pot eclecticism that celebrates the city's club scene at its most colourful. Equally hot when residents Rui Murka (warm, jazzy, Afrobeat-inflected house), DJ Lino (floor-friendly tech-house) and Pedro Ricciardi (polished house with Latin licks and disco flashbacks) are behind the turntables. Unlikely to relive its former glory, but the cool staff and intimate feel-good factor of the tiny dancefloor make Frágil a certain survivor. Best after 1am.

Limbo

Rua do Diário de Notícias 22, Bairro Alto, 1200 (no phone). Metro Baixa-Chiado/tram 28. **Open** 11.30pm-4am Tue-Sat; closed Sun. **Admission** free-1000$00 with drink. **No credit cards**. **Map** p310 L9.

Third incarnation of a long-running club that, having hitherto occupied a recreation centre and some godforsaken dive bar, has finally come to rest in what looks like a tarted-up sleaze pit, complete with pastiche Mannerist window surrounds. But step inside and you'll realise this is as goth as it gets. Every imaginable manifestation gathers here, from rock 'n' roll ghouls with one foot in the grave,

through well-known '80s veterans to studenty metal heads in heavy mascara dancing to goth, EBM, dark-electro, sometimes black metal and the odd spot of trance. DJs Synt-Axis and Van-Acker foment the frolics around the under-lit dancefloor. Spooky.

Príncipe Real & São Bento

Rua do Século is the western boundary of the Bairro Alto, and Rua Dom Pedro V marks its northern extent. Beyond these lie São Bento and Príncipe Real. The latter is essentially an extension of the Bairro Alto, though with a pronounced gay focus (*see chapter* **Gay & Lesbian**). São Bento is a stepping stone to Santos and Avenida 24 de Julho. There are a couple of good but pricey late-night eateries in this area: **Snob** and **Café de São Bento** (for both, *see p130*).

Bar Incógnito

Rua dos Poiais de São Bento 37, São Bento, 1200 (21 380 8755). Tram 25, 28. **Open** 11pm-4am Wed-Sat; closed Mon, Tue, Sun. **Admission** free-1,000$00 with drink. **Credit** V. **Map** p307 K9.

From the outside, this 'alternative dance-bar', with its metal-plated security door and larger-than-life doorman looks as if it must be concealing something dubious. But once you get inside, eye the stylish furniture, meet the friendly bar staff and feel the positive vibe, you'll realise the only dubious thing in here might be the ever-so-slightly aimless attitude of its ageing clientele, and the owner's penchant for '80s nostalgia. That said, his taste is rather discerning. Most nights of the week it's unadulterated indie crossover, guitar-dance special – a must for cave fans. Wednesdays, by contrast, host the Journeys collective who play nu jazz, Afrobeat, salsoul grooves and dub to their regularly cool little crowd. Definitely lots of potential and poser free.

Cais do Sodré

Jamaica

Rua Nova de Carvalho 8, 1200 (21 342 1859). Metro Cais do Sodré/tram 15, 18. **Open** 11pm-4am Mon-Thur; 11pm-6am Fri, Sat; closed Sun. **Admission** minimum spend 1,000$00 for men only. **No credit cards**. **Map** p307 L10.

In a notorious red-light zone, on a road lined with seedy, neon-clad dives, Jamaica is a world unto itself. The metal-plated security door opens into a simple, bare space with a DJ desk, bar and sizeable dancefloor. The DJs may not be on the cutting edge but they really know their stuff, and unfailingly get the mixed crowd bouncing. And it is mixed. Left-wing intellectuals reputedly came here in the early 1970s to plot the Revolution between bops, and there's still a sprinkling of old bohemians in among the T-shirted students and rastas. But although the Doors always get played at some point in the evening, the music hasn't stood still; on any given night you

Mass-produced music now predominates at former factory **Indústria**.

might hear Bob Marley and veteran Portuguese blues man Rui Veloso, but also the Cure and Radio Macau, one of Portugal's few innovative bands. Tuesday is '100% reggae', and if it rocks it can go on for up to two hours later than official closing time.

Santos & Avenida 24 de Julho

Younger than the Bairro Alto, older than the Docas, the scene in Santos and along the Avenida 24 de Julho is a geographical halfway house between the happenings on the hill and waterfront goings-on, though culturally closer to the latter. This area opened up in part because cars could get along here – in the Bairro Alto there's no parking at all – and cruising the Avenida is a popular nocturnal pastime. Some of the life of this area has been sucked away since the Docas started to develop, but the Avenida 24 de Julho is still startlingly lively deep into the night. There are dozens of bars and clubs, though few we would actively recommend. Sometimes the best way to enjoy a night down here is simply to drink a few beers at the fast-food vans parked all along this stretch and watch the world sweep by.

Armazém F

Rua da Cintura, Armazém 65, Santos, 1200 (21 322 0160). **Open** *Restaurant* 7.30pm-1am Tue-Sat; closed Mon, Sun. *Bar* 7.30pm-midnight daily. *Club* 1-5am daily. **Credit** AmEx, MC, V. **Map** p307 K10.
Expensively kitted-out riverside warehouse near Cais do Sodré challenging Lux for the title of Lisbon's largest club. But its clientele could hardly be more different, with ear-splitting George Michael and Prince attracting not so much the ubiquitous Lisbon *betinho* (Sloane), complete with stripey shirt

and jumper knotted round his shoulders, as people who aspire to be *betinho*. Give the place its due, though: the restaurant has a relatively adventurous menu for Lisbon.

Indústria

Rua do Instituto Industrial 6, Santos, 1200 (21 396 4841). Tram 15, 18, 25/bus 14, 20, 28, 32, 38, 40, 43. **Open** midnight-6am Fri, Sat; closed Mon-Thur; Sun. **Admission** free. **No credit cards.** **Map** p307 K10.
The structure – a former factory – is the same and the club is run along the same free-thinking lines, but Indústria is a shadow of its former self. The original idea was great: following the model of the Oporto club of the same name from which it's a spin-off, the various bars within were to be run by different people from different crowds. The owners' interest seems to have wandered, however, and the place is currently open only at weekends and plays ever more commercial music. It's pretty much strictly for kids after 2am.

Kapital

Avenida 24 de Julho 68, Santos, 1200 (21 395 7101). Bus 14, 20, 22, 28, 32, 38, 40, 43. **Open** 10.30pm-4am Mon, Sun; 10.30pm-6am Tue-Sat. **Admission** minimum spend 10,000$00, but varies according to doormen. **Credit** AmEx, MC, V. **Map** p306 J10.
The Avenida 24 de Julho's most visible nightspot and the absolute antithesis of the Bairro Alto. It's essentially a hangout for young rich kids and poorer aspirational types but there are usually also a few students trying to negotiate the doormen's insulting criteria. They tend to get very choosy after midnight, so to stand any chance at all, dress smart. A woman alone will probably get in after a wait; a man on his own has no chance. Once into the bright, white interior, there's a strict etiquette in force. Proceed directly to the top-floor bar and terrace; then it's okay to check out the middle-floor bar; only

late-late-late is it acceptable to venture into the bottom-level dancefloor where the music crashes through jarring changes and everyone sings along to the occasional Portuguese hit. Smiling or being spontaneous is deemed a sign of social weakness. A dismal place, really. At closing time an escape route beckons behind the DJ's booth, from where a passage leads into neighbouring Kremlin. Owned by João and Gonçalo Rocha, sons of a former Sporting proprietor.

Kremlin

Rua das Escadinhas da Praia 5 , Santos 1200 Lisboa (21 395 7101). Tram 15, 18/bus 14, 20, 22, 28, 32, 38, 40, 43. **Open** midnight-7am Tue-Thur; midnight-9am Fri, Sat; closed Sun. **Admission** minimum spend 5,000$00, but can vary. **Credit** AmEx, MC, V. **Map** p306 J10.

For a time in the 1980s, Kremlin was considered by many to be the best house club in Europe. It's still fun in a whacky kind of way, but its mystique has faded; the crowds trickled to other venues, as aggressive doormen turned away both regular nightlifers and newcomers. Now, inside the monumental, chapel-like interior, deep house tunes caress a mixed crowd taking in youths eager for a legendary dance experience and gay and lesbian Bairro Altistas who head down here when their favourite bars close. At 5am, when Kapital next door shuts down, some of its revellers seep in through an internal passageway.

Alcântara

Essentially an extension of the Avenida 24 de Julho, this area saw a nucleus of clubs forming around the late lamented Alcântara-Mar (now

Meals on wheels

So, you stagger out of the club at 4am in the morning after a knee-buckling dance session, with your stomach making more noise than the loudspeakers. All the restaurants in the area are closed, so what do you do? The easiest option is look for the nearest *roulotte* (caravan) usually parked within crawling distance of bars and clubs, where Portuguese-style snacks are served to hungry clubbers. The locals' favourite is the *bifana* – a tender pork steak cooked in white wine and lard, flavoured with garlic, bay leaves and often a secret ingredient added by the *roulotte* owner. It's served in a roll, invariably with mustard.

The most popular *roulottes* are near the cluster of clubs on Avenida 24 de Julho; we recommend **Parybeb**, the first one on the right as you come out of **Kapital** (see p218). There are more in Alcântara and, elsewhere, a good one by the bullring at Campo Pequeno and two more at Praça de Espanha (by the Metro exit).

The *roulotte* phenomenon emerged in the early 1980s, when someone made the not-too-difficult discovery that clubbers got hungry after dancing, while after 11pm almost all snack bars and restaurants were closed. At first, the illegal *carros das bifanas* (*bifana* cars) were just vans into which gas bottle, stove and refrigerator had to be squeezed, leaving barely enough space to work. They were parked discreetly in alleys or empty parking lots, their only light a 60-watt bulb to avoid attracting attention. But lisboetas in the know flocked there

for a late-night snack, or to drink a last beer before going home.

As the night wore on the van's doors were kept closed when there was no custom, until someone knocked or called out the owner's name. Once in a while the police would drop by and ask to see their (non-existent) permits; after a little chat the officers would be made an offer they couldn't refuse: a couple of free *bifanas*. In exchange, the police – themselves peckish at that hour – turned a blind eye. The *carros* would stay open until 6am, or until they ran out of food or customers.

Since legalisation in 1995, the scene has been transformed. Dark, pokey vans have been replaced by big white *roulottes*, brightly lit to attract punters. They park in designated sites, where they generally open from 11pm to 6am except Sundays, when most are closed. Council officials carry out daily checks for hygiene and food quality, and the owners pay 80,000$00 a month for a permit, on top of the 300,000$00 plus it costs to buy the pitch at auction. They also now face competition from a handful of late-night snack bars catering to clubbers, such as **A Merendinha** (see p130).

Perhaps partly for that reason, *roulottes* have more varied menus nowadays, with hamburgers and hot dogs jostling for counter space. But it's not all globalisation. Another *roulotte* standard is *torresmos*, a greasy speciality from the Alentejo consisting of pork bits fried in fat and pressed into a salami-like slab. Just what the doctor ordered after a hard night's drinking.

Red-light routes

Unlike many European cities, where red-light districts tend to be well off the tourist trail, in Lisbon it's fairly easy to stumble into one by mistake. Sex clubs, too, are not always clearly distinguishable from their dance counterparts.

Intendente, near the Metro station of the same name, is one area that few visitors to Lisbon would choose to visit. It's dotted with seedy bars and peopled with some truly unsavoury characters. But you can't really avoid it if you want to make a daytime visit to buy some classy *azulejos* from the **Fábrica Viúva Lamego** (see p170); its shop window is on the busy thoroughfare, Avenida Almirante Reis, but its entrance round the back, right on the oppressively sleazy Largo do Intendente.

The police patrol this area constantly, but warn that they can't guarantee visitors' safety, especially at night. If you're after an adrenalin rush and insist on glimpsing Lisbon's seamy underbelly, then follow three rules for survival: don't go alone; don't go after dusk; and don't carry anything of value, visible or concealed.

There's a totally different scene at Rua Nova do Carvalho, near Cais do Sodré train station, where half a dozen clubs form Lisbon's would-be international circuit, bearing the names of major US and European cities. Despite their dubious appearance and nasty neon signs, the clubs themselves are pretty safe – unless you're looking for a little trouble yourself. These places often see riotous scenes as the night wears on, such as a whole crew of newly docked French sailors dancing on the tables, or dozens of bekilted Scottish football fans in town for a big match, practising their chants.

In fact, these clubs – particularly **Texas** – seem to exercise an unrivalled power of attraction over British and Irish football fans. So it's not unsurprising that some have English, Scottish and Irish banners on the walls and play British music, or even Gaelic folk songs.

Again unlike in many of Europe's red-light districts, the women in these clubs are not just mini-skirted, high-heeled professionals. Women visiting in a non-professional capacity are more than welcome and, especially when there are big events on in town, there's usually a fair balance between the sexes. One of Lisbon's longest-established and most fun discos is also in this street: **Jamaica** (see p217).

A few steps up the aspirational ladder, there is another category of clubs – the pretentiously named *boîtes* – such as **Maxime's** in Praça da Alegria, off the Avenida da Liberdade. These places are frequented by would-be high rollers who drool over blonde Ukrainian or sometimes British dancers who pretend to enjoy themselves in various stages of undress.

As in any major city, there are also pricier joints for men with big money to spend on female flesh of whatever flavour takes their fancy. Until the mid-1990s, African and Brazilian women predominated in this business. But after the Berlin Wall crumbled so did jobs for life for eastern Europeans, and sex workers from Hungary, the Czech Republic and Russia fanned out across western Europe as far as Portugal. Clubs filling this market niche cluster near the business hotels on and around Avenida Duque de Loulé and Rua Luciano Cordeiro. Two of the glitziest of such clubs are both named after pachyderms, for some reason – a reference to their lumbering customers, perhaps?

W and **Kasino**), which brought all Lisbon's tribes together under one groove in the early 1990s, and started the spread of nightlife towards the docklands. Now it's more notable for its African clubs, led by **Luanda** (*see p222*).

Paradise Garage

Rua João Oliveira Miguéis 38-48, Alcântara, 1350 (21 354 4452). Train to Alcântara Mar from Cais do Sodré/tram 15, 18. **Open** 11.30pm-4am Thur-Sat; closed Mon-Wed, Sun. *After hours sessions* 10am-4pm Sat, Sun. **Admission** 5,000$00 but can vary. *After-hours sessions* 1,500$00. **Credit** MC, V.

Housed in a converted warehouse, Paradise Garage has something of a split personality. During regular opening hours it's a lively venue for a young crowd, and stages occasional weekday gigs ranging from rock to jazz, some involving big-name foreign bands. At weekends, the after-hours daytime sessions of easy-listening garage offer relief to ravers seeking a soft dance floor to land on after a hard night.

W

Rua Maria Luisa Holstein 13, Alcântara, 1300 (21 363 6830/40). Train to Alcântara Mar from Cais do Sodré/tram 15, 18. **Open** 10pm-6am Tue-Sat; closed Mon, Sun. **Admission** varies. **Credit** AmEx, MC, V.

A lot of effort and thought has been put into this place, which takes up the larger part of the building that once housed the magnetic Alcântara Mar, sister ship to the Alcântara Café (*see p121*), which sails on unperturbed next door. The space is large, but cut across with large pillars behind which you can hide. It's all parallel lines and boxy shapes, lit by an odd mix of soft ceiling lights and candles. The music veers from funk to house to pop, and the crowd is equally mixed. Wednesday is ladies' night, and Thursdays sees a fine drum/trumpet duo accompanying the dance music. Yet to prove itself, but infinitely better than next-door Kasino, which looks as if it was cobbled together hurriedly by someone following instructions from a do-it-yourself discotheque kit.

Docas

Early in the 1990s, the city began thinking about how to open up the waterfront and the port authority decided to take the hip route. Thus began the job of docklands gentrification. The result was all the niceties of a new infrastructure: ample parking, small open-air parades for cafés or clubs, good air-conditioning, waterfront views, clean toilets – all things the Bairro Alto cannot offer. But though techie, it's also tacky. The docks are like a shopping mall of nightlife, full of theme bars and clueless clubs purveying every sound and style without one shred of authenticity. The core crowd are out-of-towners and middle-class students. Your average Bairro Altista wouldn't

be seen dead in any of these places. Still, the docks will keep developing. There are two hubs here. The Doca de Santo Amaro, to the west of the flyover by which you reach the docks, is a parade of bars and restaurants by a yachting marina. Rocha Conde d'Óbidos to the east is a row of big clubs and live venues, including **Queen's** (*see below*), bar-cum-restaurant-cum-club **Blues Café** (*see p134*) and **Indochina**.

Queen's

Rua da Cintura do Porto (Avenida Brasília), Armazém H, Rocha Conde d'Obidos, 1350 (21 395 5870). Tram 15, 18/bus 19, 28. **Open** 10pm-6am Wed-Sat; closed Mon, Tue, Sun. **Admission** free. **Credit** AmEx, MC, V. **Map** p306 H10.

A supposedly gay club – some drag queens are paid to hang around – where straight young Portuguese kids go to imagine they're being daring and decadent. The sort of place where Portugal's handful of record companies hold parties to promote their latest dance compilation. Avoidable, but in its own sweet way the best on this row of warehouse venues.

Salsa Latina

Gare Marítima de Alcântara 30, Docas, 1350 (21 395 0555). Train to Alcântara Mar from Cais do Sodré/tram 15, 18. **Open** 8pm-6am Mon-Sat; closed Sun. **Admission** minimum spend 2,000$00. **Credit** AmEx, MC, V. **Map** p306 G10.

The only major venue in town to hear salsa and merengue, in the classy setting of the modernist Gare Marítima de Alcântara (*see p92*). A well-shaken Margarita should leave you in good shape to step away from the bar and on to the dancefloor. In-house

Salsa Latina – contagious live music and Margaritas.

Arts & Entertainment

acts Sal Picante and Tequila serve up contagious live music from Thursdays to Saturdays. There's also a long elevated terrace, overlooking the river – a beautiful spot to sip your drink within earshot of the music.

Santa Apolónia

With the opening of Lux in 1999, it was thought likely that Santa Apolónia would develop as a nightlife hub. But so far there's just the crucial new pizzeria **Casanova** (*see* *p136*) and the rather less crucial Jardim do Tabaco restaurant and bar complex, another of the leisure investments that Portuguese comic Herman José makes periodically to use the vast sums he earns.

Lux

Avenida Infante Dom Henrique, Amazém A, Cais da Pedra a Santa Apolónia, 1900 (21 882 0890/ www.luxfragil.com). Bus 9, 28, 39, 46. **Open** 6pm-6am Tue-Fri; 4pm-6am Sat, Sun; closed Mon. **Admission** free but restricted. **Credit** AmEx, DC, MC, V. **Map** p308 O9.

Dismissed by some as too cool, rated by others as just a bit cooler than *Wallpaper*, either way, this is the place that has sparked the city's club life into overdrive and swung its cognoscenti around another centre. Manuel Reis, the sensitive and much-loved former owner of the legendary Frágil, has successfully lured the older in-crowd from Bairro Alto, augmented it with a sprinkling of straighter moneyed types and pulled in the capital's youth by the car load. That said, the club's size means that weeknights can be slow, and if it does get going it will only be slow when lively staff from other nightspots turn up here to unwind. The first-floor bar, with its comfy 1960s and 1970s furniture and spectacular waterfront views, is possibly best enjoyed at sunset, while the roof terrace, something of a parallel universe at night, offers a panorama of city and river – the perfect backdrop for smooching and schmoozing. Top-rate resident DJs regularly pack the large dancefloor; the revered Rui Vargas (across-the-board house), Dinis and Nuno Forte (brilliantly skewed breakbeat and jungle) are among those to watch out for. Thursday nights feature a Who's Who of heavyweights, and with the likes of Gilles Peterson and Françoise Kevorkian frequently playing full-night sets – well beyond daybreak – Lux's status as the place to go remains unrivalled.

African Clubs

African places are scattered all over Lisbon, inhabiting their own parallel universe of nightlife. Many have live music – see also **B.Leza** (*p212*) and **Enclave** (*p213*).

Luanda

Rua Rodrigues Faria 15/17, Alcântara 1300 (21 362 4459). Train to Alcântara Mar from Cais do Sodré/tram 15, 18. **Open** 11pm-4.30am Wed, Thur; 11am-7.30am Fri-Sun; closed Mon, Tue. **Admission** free for women; varies for men. **Credit** MC, V.

One of the most popular clubs among young Africans in Lisbon, the Luanda gained brief worldwide notoriety in the spring of 2000. Several people died and dozens were injured when someone threw a gas canister onto an over-crowded dance floor. Security – and safety – have since been greatly improved, but in any case the young, well-turned-out and energetic crowd seems not to have been in the least bit discouraged by the incident. As the club's name would indicate, there's a strong Angolan flavour to the music, with plenty of the Angolan Afro-techno known as kuduro, but it varies considerably. On Sunday nights Luanda is particularly well attended, as it reaches the parts that other clubs don't. It's in a building that has housed a series of late-night clubs, in an area full of nightlife places, which also helps.

Passerelle

Rua das Lusíadas 5, Centro Comercial Lusíadas, Loja 8, Alcântara, 1300 (21 363 3590). Bus 22. **Open** 11pm-5am daily. **Admission** free for women; varies for men. **Credit** AmEx, MC, V.

Close-set African club, with an accent on Angolan music and an enthusiastic young crowd. It's in the rear of a dreary shopping centre but the interior is unmistakably African, with a cosy dancefloor, stage and bar. On Mondays and Thursdays there's live music; in the past, acts here have included Bonga, Paulo Flores, Tito Paris and Dany Silva. Tuesdays it's African karaoke. Snacks are served.

Mussulo

Rua Sousa Martins 5D, Estefânia, 1050 (21 355 6872). Metro Picoas. **Open** 11pm-7.30am Wed-Sun; closed Mon, Tue. **Admission** free for women; 2,000$00-20,000$00 for men. **No credit cards.** **Map** p307 L6.

The throbbing heart of Lisbon's African club scene, yet a good deal more accessible than Luanda. A deep stairwell leads down to a spacious room filled into the dawn hours with a stylish crowd that embraces both youngsters from immigrant families and ageing *retornados*. This is one of the few clubs in Lisbon where you might see a woman in her 40s dancing with a man in his 20s. Music-wise, the deep bass and soft swing of lusophone *zouk* is dominant. But this Angolan club is also base for some of the scene's best DJs, and when they briefly up the pace with a bit of *kuduro* Afro-techno, the whole place begins to heave and grind – Sunday is the best night to catch this. On some nights trashy Brazilian pop gets thrown into the mix, but thankfully not for long. Mussulo gets going very late and can also get ludicrously crowded in the heart of the night. Don't wear trainers.

Performing Arts

Plenty of creative energy but not a lot of cash.

The performing arts in Lisbon are healthier than at almost any time in the past century, from an artistic if not from a financial point of view. State and independent theatre companies abound, producing up everything from Shakespeare and Gil Vicente, the 16th-century founding father of Portuguese drama, to Strindberg and street theatre.

Portuguese theatre has one way or another been hampered for centuries – by censorship during the Inquisition and later under Salazar, and by the prejudice of an intelligentsia suspicious of collective artistic activities. But the 1974 revolution changed everything, with young people flocking to the performing arts to see alternative groups. Theatre's contribution to events of the day was so important that critic Carlos Porto wrote: 'The revolution arrived on stage before it arrived in the streets.'

The early 1970s saw dozens of independent companies emerge, eagerly taking advantage of larger, enthusiastic audiences, more generous funding and an expanded repertoire. The momentum lasted until the end of the decade, but was followed by a financial and artistic crisis. Things improved in the 1990s, with new drama schools and major new venues. And the success of the **Festival Internacional de Teatro**, in Almada, has helped small groups to survive even in precarious circumstances.

Money remains a problem, though. Even critically acclaimed independent shows can often only afford to last a few days, and the **Teatro Nacional Dona Maria II** staggers from one financial crisis to another. With state subsidies the lifeblood even of independents, cuts to the 2001 budget of the Instituto Português das Artes do Espectáculo (IPAE), the main funding body, caused an outcry.

Bigger and better venues have meant more big-name international companies and shows, enriching the city's cultural life but eating up programmers' budgets needed for domestic groups. In the commercial theatre, production company UAU has had hits at the **Teatro Villaret** with Portuguese versions of Ben Elton's *Popcorn* and Yasmin Reza's *Art*, and more such format buying looks likely. But there are promising alternative projects, the most ambitious being **A Capital**. There is also plenty of physical theatre, where a mixing of disciplines has generated inventive shows that

Theatre takes to the streets.

are accessible to non-Portuguese speakers, by companies such as **Chapitô**, Meridional, or the more experimental Sensurround.

LISTINGS AND INFORMATION

Newspapers have listings for the big theatres and some independents: *Público* offers a cultural supplement on Fridays, *Expresso* on Saturdays. *Agenda Cultural*, a guide published monthly in Portuguese and English, is available in hotels and tourist offices, but can be elusive at the beginning of the month. The magazine *Flirt*, produced by the ZDB gallery (*see p195*) has alternative listings. The rest has to be gleaned by poster spotting, leaflet gathering and word of mouth.

Ticket agencies

The **ABEP** booth (*see p201*) in Praça dos Restauradores is a good bet for big productions, as is **Fnac** (*see p156*) and **Telecartaz**. For some shows, you can buy tickets at Multibanco (cash) machines. In general, though, people tend to buy tickets at the theatre.

Telecartaz

Rua Dom João V 13A, Rato, 1250 (21 385 4419). *Metro Rato.* **Open** 10am-1pm, 2-7pm Mon-Fri; closed Sat, Sun. **No credit cards. Map** p306 J7. Tickets for dance and theatre. English spoken.

Establishment theatres

With Lisbon's largest auditorium, another medium-sized one and a studio theatre, the **Centro Cultural de Belém** (*see p192*) has the city's best facilities. Its year-round programme of theatre and dance for adults and children brings together the best of Portuguese and foreign groups. The Grande Auditório of the **Gulbenkian Foundation** (*see p202*) is mainly used for classical concerts, but puts on ballet too. In the Foundation's performing arts centre, **Acarte** (Rua Dr Nicolau Bettencourt, 21 793 5131), the Sala Polivalente or multipurpose hall is often used for theatre and dance. Downtown, the **Teatro Nacional de São Carlos** (*see p202*) had its glory days in the mid- to late 19th century, as a venue for opera and operetta. Most other major theatres stage performances of both drama and dance, as well as music.

Culturgest
Edifício Caixa Geral de Depósitos, Rua Arco do Cego 1, Campo Pequeno, 1000 (21 790 5454/box office 21 790 5155). Metro Campo Pequeno. **Open** *Box office* 10am-7pm Mon-Fri; 2-8pm Sat, Sun. **Tickets** 2,500$00-4,000$00. **Credit** MC, V. **Map** p305 M4.
The cultural organ of the state-owned Caixa Geral de Depósitos, housed in the bank's gigantic corporate headquarters. Culturgest offers an extensive and adventurous programme of theatre, dance and music, exhibitions, conferences and workshops.

Teatro Municipal Maria Matos
Avenida Miguel Frei Contreiras 52, Avenida de Roma, 1700 (21 843 8806). Metro Roma. **Open** *Box office* open 2-8pm Tue-Sun; closed Mon. **Tickets** prices vary. **No credit cards. Map** p305 N3.

The gilded **Trindade**.

This council-run venue, with an auditorium seating 500, is home to the Teatro Infantil Lisboa (*see p186*), a children's theatre group that stages one nine-month show each year. It stands out for one thing: free baby-sitting. Occasionally stages other shows.

Teatro Municipal de São Luíz
Rua António Maria Cardoso 40, Chiado, 1200 (21 346 1260/5358/ticket office 21 342 7172). Metro Baixa-Chiado. **Open** *Box office* 2-8pm Tue-Sun; closed Mon. **No credit cards. Map** p310 L9.
Currently closed for renovation, the 1,000-seat main auditorium provides a venue for an eclectic range of events, from dance to world music.

Teatro Nacional Dona Maria II
Praça Dom Pedro IV (Rossio), 1100 (21 347 2246/ticket office 21 342 2210). Metro Rossio. **Open** *Box office* 2-9.30pm Tue-Sat; 2-5.30pm Sun; closed Mon.* **Tickets** 1,500$00-3,000$00. **No credit cards. Map** p310 M9.
Inaugurated in 1846 with the aim of 'helping civilise and improve the morality of the Portuguese nation', but lately the target of criticism for its alleged failure to fulfil the role of a national theatre – maintaining and updating a classical repertoire. Mounting debt has forced it to close for months at a time, causing the cancellation of at least one big production. Has the only theatre bookshop in town.

Teatro da Trindade
Rua Nova da Trindade 9, Bairro Alto, 1200 (21 342 3200/box office 21 342 0000). Metro Baixa-Chiado/tram 28. **Open** *Box office* 1-8pm Tue-Sat; 1-4pm Sun; closed Mon.* **Tickets** 1,000$00-3,000$00. **No credit cards. Map** p310 L9.
A turn-of-the-century gilded jewel and a favourite venue for smaller-scale, prestigious one-offs or short-run shows by prominent foreign groups. Unusually, funding seems not to be not a problem, because the Trindade is owned by Inatel, the well-endowed workers' cultural institute set up under Salazar.

Alternative theatres

A Capital
Rua do Diário de Notícias 78, Bairro Alto, 1200 (21 347 9818/artistas.unidos@mail.telepac.pt). Metro Baixa-Chiado or Restauradores then Elevador da Glória. **Open** *Box office* 5.30pm until show, Wed-Sun; closed Mon, Tue. **Tickets** 1,000$00. **No credit cards. Map** p310 L9.
This new space in Bairro Alto is the response of Jorge Silva Melo, one of Portugal's leading directors, to the lack of alternative performance spaces. Once fully renovated, the cavernous former newspaper building will house three performance spaces, three rehearsal rooms and a dance studio, plus the headquarters of choreographer João Fiadeiro. It is already home to Melo's own company, Artistas Unidos, founded to produce 'political theatre' – in the sense of attempting to be the voice of the *polis* (city). Melo organises workshops from which his texts emerge; the group also puts on plays by cutting-edge writers.

Arts & Entertainment

Chapitô

Costa do Castelo 1, 1149 (21 887 8225/21 886 1419/chapito@ip.pt). Tram 12, 28/bus 37. **Open** *Box office* 30mins before performance; phone bookings taken from 9am. **Tickets** 1,000$00; 750$00 concessions. **No credit cards. Map** p311 M9.
Home to the Companhia de Chapitô, now under the artistic direction of Brit John Mowat of London's Oddbodies theatre company, which produces inspired comic physical theatre.

Estrela Hall

Rua Saraiva de Carvalho, Estrela, 1200 (21 396 1946). Tram 28/bus 9. **Open** *Box office* varies according to performance times; book by leaving a message. **Tickets** prices vary. **No credit cards. Map** p306 J8.
Home to The Lisbon Players, the city's only well-established group to perform regularly in English, in a season lasting from October to June. Estrela Hall is also sometimes used for productions by Tagus Theatre (21 887 3789), a more professional outfit formed by leading members of the Lisbon Players. They concentrate on Portuguese texts in English and works related to Anglo-Portuguese history.

Teatro Aberto

Praça de Espanha, 1050 (21 797 0969/8898). Metro Praça de Espanha. **Open** *Box office* 2-10pm daily. **Tickets** 3,000$00; 2,500$00 concessions. **No credit cards. Map** p304 K4.
This capacious theatre puts on heavyweight plays by O Novo Grupo. Under the direction of resident playwright Vera San Payo de Lemos, a noted specialist in German literature, its repertoire is mostly Brecht and related works.

Teatro Cinearte

Largo de Santos 2, Santos, 1200 (21 396 5360). Train to Santos from Cais do Sodré/tram 15. **Open** *Box office* 7-9.30pm Tue-Sat; 2-4pm Sun; closed Mon. **Tickets** 2,000$00. **No credit cards. Map** p306 J10.
With two auditoria, the larger with 180 seats, Cinearte is big for a Lisbon alternative theatre. It's the base for the A Barraca group, directed by Maria do Céu Guerra. The upstairs café-bar has an offbeat programme of poetry readings, stand-up comedy and dance.

Teatro da Comuna

Praça de Espanha, 1050 (21 722 1770). Metro Praça de Espanha. **Open** *Box office* 3-9.30pm Mon-Sat; closed Sun. **Tickets** 2,500$00; 1,500$00 concessions. **No credit cards. Map** p304 K4.
Productions here are mainly commercially oriented, but it has staged more serious or experimental works. Has three main auditoria, each with about 150 seats, and a spacious but rarely use café-theatre.

Teatro da Cornucópia

Rua Tenente Raul Cascais 1A, Rato, 1250 (21 396 1515). Metro Rato. **Open** *Box office* 3-9.30pm Tue-Sun; closed Mon. **Tickets** 2,500$00; 1,250$00 concessions. **No credit cards. Map** p307 K8.

A well-equipped multipurpose hall with 135 seats, this theatre is a popular choice for performers but out of the financial reach of most alternative companies. Home to the Teatro do Bairro Alto group, led by Luis Miguel Cintra – an actor much used by veteran film director Manoel de Oliveira (*see p188* **Manoel de Oliveira – the auteur's auteur**).

Teatro Taborda

Costa do Castelo 75, Castelo, 1100 (21 886 0104/fax 21 888 1964). Tram 12, 28/bus 37. **Open** *Box office* 2-10pm Tue-Sun; closed Mon. **Tickets** 2,000$00; 1,300$00 concessions. **No credit cards. Map** p311 M9.
Situated below the castle with spectacular views from the cyber café and terrace at the back, this mock-up of a late 19th-century theatre is small but perfectly formed. Council-owned and used by a variety of independent groups, it has hosted a festival of youth theatre since 1999.

Teatro Villaret

Avenida Fontes Pereira de Melo 30A, 1050 (21 353 8586). Metro Picoas. **Open** *Box office* 2-9.30pm Tue-Sun; closed Mon. **Tickets** 3,500$00; 2,500$00 concessions. **No credit cards. Map** p307 L6.
A commercial theatre that has pulled in big audiences. One of the venues that periodically shows the Portuguese version of *The Complete Works of William Shakespeare (in 97 minutes)*.

Theatre & dance festivals

Encontros

Tickets and information: Acarte (Rua Dr Nicolau Bettencourt, 21 793 5131). **Date** Sep-Oct.
This long-running festival of contemporary dance, theatre and music consistently injects new ideas and energy, not least by bringing in well-known choreographers and directors to give workshops for Portuguese performers.

Festival Internacional de Dança Contemporânea/Danças na Cidade

Tickets and information 21 315 2267. **Date** summer every other year.
A biennial contemporary dance festival – 'Dances in the City' – that has become an important event on the European dance agenda. Next in May 2002.

Festival Internacional de Teatro

Tickets and information: Teatro da Almada, Rua Conde de Ferreira, 2800 Almada (21 275 6567). **Date** July.
Portugal's most important theatre festival, pulling in thousands of people to performance events. They take place at various venues, including the Teatro da Trindade (*see p224*) in Lisbon. The local council also organises a mini-festival, the Mostra de Teatro de Almada, in January.

Festival X

Tickets and information: Espaço Gingal, Rua do Cais do Gingal 53-54, Cacilhas, 2800 Almada (21 273 1532/olho@mail.telepac.pt). **Date** Nov-Dec.

A performance art festival, organised by the group Olho, at Espaço Gingal – a warehouse on the south side of the Tagus. Held for the sixth time in 2000, it embraces the new and experimental.

Lugar á Dança
Tickets and information: 21 397 0204/vo.arte@mail. teleweb.pt. **Date** early summer.
Organised by Vo'arte (*see below* **Dances in the city**), the emphasis is on dance in alternative urban spaces, with the performances often site specific.

Noites de Bailado em Seteais
Tickets and information: Sintra Tourist Office, Praça da República, Sintra, 2710 (21 923 1157/ fax 21 923 5176). **Date** Aug-Sept; Fri, Sat evenings.

Held in the gardens of the Palácio de Seteais in Sintra, the Seteais Ballet Festival is one of the highlights of the year for ballet fans. In the past it has attracted major foreign companies from Germany, Russia, the US and elsewhere.

Quinzena da Dança de Almada
Tickets & information: Companhia de Dança de Almada (21 258 3175). **Date** Nov.
An international contemporary dance festival organised by the Companhia da Dança de Almada, this annual fortnight showcases mostly Portuguese material, with some foreign groups. The events, including debates, workshops and exhibitions, take place at the Auditório Forúm Municipal Romeu Correia in Almada.

Dances in the city

What distinguishes Portuguese dance? A strong dose of African influences, a taste for the surreal but a grounding in the mundane, an irreverent attitude towards classical dance, and the use of theatrical devices.

A wealth of diverse new dance projects have sprouted in Lisbon in the last five years. **Clara Andermatt** has been working with musicians and dancers from Cape Verde in her dance group. **Companhia Olga Roriz**, formed by Roriz in 1995 after a distinguished choreographical career, has been tackling provocative social, political and religious themes. **Produções Real Pelágio**, formed by choreographer and dancer Sílvia Real and musician Sérgio Pelágio, creates humorous and inventive pieces that demand intensive collaboration from all participants, while João Fiadeiro's aptly named company, **RE.AL/Responsa Alternativa**, is big on collaborating with other groups and mixing text and theatre with dance. **Vo'arte** also branches out from its dance origins to bring theatre and music into its performances – and into the **Danças na Cidade** festival.

The darling of Portuguese dance, Vera Mantero, set up her own company – **O Rumo no Fumo** – in 1998, initially to promote her own work. It now incorporates new young choreographers such as Rafael Avarez, Teresa Prima, Miguel Pereira and Paula Castro.

Productions can involve risk-taking that doesn't always pay off, but when they succeed, it's worth it. Only a few of the companies mentioned have their own performance space – check the press, see p223, for details of performances. Below are listed more of Lisbon's finest.

Ballet Gulbenkian
Portugal's prime exponent of contemporary ballet. Since 1996, led by its Brazilian artistic director Iracity Cardoso, it has maintained its high international profile and built on the work of Cardoso's predecessor, Jorge Salavisa, by encouraging home-grown choreographers and dancers.

CEM (Centre in Motion)
This centre, at Praça de Alegria 27-2, 1250 (21 342 5422), off the Avenida da Liberdade, offers workshops for amateurs and pros, plus fortnightly experimental performance workshops, symposiums, and much-needed rehearsal space. Also commissions pieces. A good place to find out what's on elsewhere.

Companhia Nacional de Bailado
The only show in town as far as classical ballet goes. It has taken steps to broaden its repertoire with new pieces that bridge the gap between classical and modern dance. Unfortunately, 2000 saw it without an artistic director and with the same autumn programme for the third year running. Now based at the **Teatro Luís de Camões** (see p202), but on tour in Portugal much of the time.

Companhia Portuguesa de Bailado Contemporâneo
Formed in 1998 by Vasco Wellencamp, an ex-dancer and choreographer with the Gulbenkian, this company has finally found a new home. The studios and performance space (which should open some time in 2002, phone 21 412 1780 to check) will offer facilities, support and training for younger choreographers.

Sport & Fitness

Football isn't quite the only game in town – there's surfing, riding, bullfighting and roller hockey too.

Portugal's record of sporting achievement has always been poor. This is due partly to lack of infrastructure and partly to the absence of any real keep-fit culture (except for the usual periodic pre-summer and pre-beach fitness booms). This is is probably the European country where one would be least likely to run into a jogger.

For most Portuguese, sport is synonymous with football, the only team sport besides roller hockey where Portuguese sides have tasted occasional glory. Benfica won the European Cup in 1961 and 1962 and the national team (taking so much advantage of players from the colonies that some would go so far as to call it Afro-Portugal) came third in the 1966 World Cup, beating reigning champions Brazil on the way. But football has never quite risen to the same level again – until the recent spectacular exhibition of the national team which achieved an impressive third place at the latest European championship (Euro 2000), a progress only halted by the current champions, France. Also the European Championship finals will be organised and disputed on Portuguese soil in 2004 and local expectations are very high.

In contrast to the high profile of the national team, the Portuguese football league has for some years been a dull and stagnant three-club affair between Benfica, Porto and Sporting. The dullness comes largely from the fact that all their major stars end up moving to more competitive leagues in Spain, Italy and England. The foremost example is Luís Figo, former golden boy of Barcelona, now at Real de Madrid, who's achieved the iconic status of Eusébio, Benfica's Black Panther of the 1960s.

Despite the predominance of football, there is a growing interest in other sports such as basketball, volleyball and athletics. Since marathon runner Carlos Lopes won the country's first Olympic gold in 1984, Portugal has produced a few European and World athletics champions, such as Rosa Mota, Fernanda Ribeiro and Carla Sacramento. And António Pinto won the 1997 London Marathon.

Tickets

For events and venues check any one of the three sports dailies: *A Bola*, *Record* and *O Jogo*. Agencies **ABEP** and **Agência Alvalade** sell tickets for major sporting events; for details of both, *see p201*.

Major stadia

Estádio Nacional-Jamor

Complexo Desportivo do Jamor, Praça da Maratona, 1495 Cruz Quebrada (21 419 7212). Train from Cais do Sodré to Algés then bus 6 or train to Cruz Quebrada. **Open** 8am-8pm Tue-Sun; closed Mon. **Admission** free. **No credit cards**.
Opened in 1944, the national stadium was built by and for the authoritarian regime of Salazar and looks it, though the surrounding park is beautiful. Its capacity is 55.000, only filled for the 10 June Taça de Portugal football final. It's also used for athletics and as the training ground for the national football team. The lack of floodlighting limits further use, although the authorities are trying to think of other things to do with the place. At the moment it feels run-down and fusty.

Its a real marathon. *See p229.*

Lisbon strikes back

After years of grinding their teeth as FC Porto swept all before them, Lisbon football fans finally had something to cheer about when Sporting won the league title in 2000. The northerners had strung together five straight championships while Benfica, Portugal's most famous club, sank into the mire of internal wrangling.

It had been 18 years since Sporting had last won the league, and the event triggered celebrations that put New Year's Eve to shame – even if many Benfica supporters were cheering through clenched teeth.

Sporting clinched the championship at an away match in Oporto against Salgueiros, and a huge crowd almost immediately started to gather back at the team's Alvalade stadium. But before coming home to show off the cup, there were other loyalties to be rewarded. On the return journey, the team made a detour to the Café Brasil in Coimbra. There, 18 years ago, the owner had pledged that he would not raise the price of a coffee until Sporting won the league again. The promise was kept even though epic losses mounted and the owner himself died still awaiting victory. (It was his wife who sold the symbolic bica to Sporting chairman José Roquette.)

Mayor João Soares, too, was determined to make political hay. The team had to drop by at the city hall for a round of back-slapping, although by now some 50,000 *sportinguistas* were waiting at Alvalade. The team finally rolled up at around 2.30am.

As for Benfica fans, they had the choice of celebrating the long-awaited success of their neighbours or remaining bitter at their own continued trophy drought and the comic-tragic managerial farce that was being played out in

their own club. Most celebrated, but none could forget that their club remained mired in allegations and counter-allegations of corruption, bankruptcy, and non-payment of wages and transfer fees: a litany of management malpractice.

Sporting, long the butt of ridicule, had finally turned the tables. Fans still nurse a grudge over how 30 years ago Benfica snatched all-time great Eusébio away from them by slipping a contract in front of his mother as the pair got off the plane from Mozambique, supposedly on their way to Alvalade. *Sportinguistas* previously could only groan as their team lived up to tradition year after year and started slipping down the table as soon as the Christmas lights were taken down. No longer. Champions is a word that takes some getting used to. And by the time they do, the title could well have headed north again.

Below we list the homes of Benfica and Sporting, as well as Lisbon's two other clubs, which enjoy intermittent success.

Clube de Futebol Os Belenenses

Estádio do Restelo, Avenida do Restelo, Restelo, 1400 (21 301 0461). Bus 28, 49, 51. **Tickets** 2,000$00-3,500$00. **No credit cards. Map** p303 B9.
Belenenses won the league title in 1946 and are thus the only club to have broken the Benfica-Porto-Sporting monopoly.

Clube de Futebol Estrela da Amadora

Estádio José Gomes, Avenida Dom José I, Reboleira, 2720 Amadora (21 495 2732). Train from Restauradores to Amadora. **Tickets** 2,000$00-3,500$00. **No credit cards.**
A relatively young (1932) and small top-division club from the populous suburban town of Amadora.

Sporting Club de Portugal

Estádio de Alvalade, Rua Francisco Stromp, Alvalade, 1600 (21 751 4000). Metro Campo Grande. **Tickets** 3000$00-6,000$00. **No credit cards.**

Sport Lisboa e Benfica

Estádio da Luz, Avenida General Norton de Matos, Estrada da Luz, 1500 (21 726 6129). Metro Colégio Militar-Luz. **Tickets** 3000$00-5000$00. **No credit cards.**

Pavilhão Atlântico
Rua Dom Fuas Roupinho, Parque das Nações, 1998 (21 891 8409). Metro Oriente. **No credit cards.**
Built for Expo 98 to an impressive design by Regino Cruz, this UFO-shaped arena by the river Tagus is now the city's main indoor sporting venue, hosting major basketball, handball and volleyball games and for the next few years, the Tennis Masters.

Spectator sports

Athletics

Lisbon Marathon
(Information 21 361 6160/information, flights, accommodation 21 364 4097/fax 21 364 3525). **Date** last Sun in Nov.
Lisbon's big road race starts at Rossio, goes along the river to Cruz Quebrada on the Estoril coast and then back to Rossio. It has only been going a few years but is growing in popularity; more sponsorship has meant more professional participants and wider media coverage. There is also a half-marathon and, on the Saturday, a fun run for for children.

Terry Fox Run
(Information Parque das Nações 21 831 9898 or Canadian Embassy cultural department 21 352 1125/21 316 4600.) **Date** 5 May.
Held annually in remembrance of Terry Fox, a young Canadian who was diagnosed with bone cancer in his right leg, which had to be amputated. He subsequently ran across Canada, using an artificial leg, to raise funds for cancer research. The increasingly popular Lisbon run, organised by Canadian citizens at the Parque das Nações, is held in benefit of cancer charity A Liga Portuguesa Contra o Cancro.

Dressage

The Sociedade Hípica Portuguesa, founded in 1910, organises the annual Internacional Concurso Oficial de Saltos, which includes several riding contests, including a Nations Cup with foreign teams. It is held in late May at the Hipódromo do Campo Grande and lasts four days.

The other annual dressage event is the Festival Internacional do Cavalo Puro Sangue Lusitano. Held each June at the Hipódromo, it lasts three days and is the biggest 'showroom' for the rare Lusitano breed, with 300 of these versatile, courageous and gentle horses usually taking part. The Lusitano, native to southwestern Iberia, is the oldest saddlehorse in the world, used for hunting and combat for centuries. For information about riding stables, *see p233*.

Hipódromo do Campo Grande
Campo Grande, 1600 (21 797 9465). Metro Campo Grande. **Map** p304 L2.

Associação Portuguesa de Criadores do Cavalo Puro Sangue Lusitano
Rua Barata Salgueiro 37, Avenida da Liberdade, 1250-042 (21 354 1742). **Map** p307 L7.

Football

Although the Portuguese are football crazy – the three top-selling dailies are all devoted to the sport, and stories about Benfica regularly lead the evening TV news – match attendances are poor. People don't have cash for tickets and too many games are live on TV. The season runs from late August until the 10 June Cup Final at the **Estádio Nacional-Jamor** (*see p227*). Tickets for the final can be bought at the stadium (21 419 7212) or at the **Federação Portuguesa de Futebol** (21 3428207/21 3426863) but are hard to come by if one of the Lisbon clubs is a finalist, as is usually the case. For details of clubs, *see p228* **Lisbon strikes back.**

Motor sport

Autódromo Fernanda Pires da Silva
Alcabideche, on the EN9 between Estoril and Sintra, Estoril, 2750 (21 469 1462). Train from Cais do Sodré to Estoril then 'Shopping' bus. **Tickets** 500$00-18,000$00. **No credit cards.**
Still awaiting reinstatement to the Formula 1 motor racing calendar, having undergone extensive renovations to make good past safety failings. Still hosts sporadic car and bike racing, though.

Roller-hockey

The only team sport where Portugal ranks among the best, regularly splitting World or European titles with Italy, Argentina or main rivals Spain. Games in the national league are played on Saturday or Sunday afternoons and evenings. The season runs from September to June and there are also two European cups.

Clube Desportivo de Paço d'Arcos
Pavilhão Gimnodesportivo, Avenida Bonneville Franco, 2780-567 Paço d'Arcos (21 443 2238). Train from Cais do Sodré to Paço d'Arcos. **Tickets** 1,000$00. **No credit cards.**
The nicest ground, with big crowds who generate an intense atmosphere that makes life difficult for opponents.

Sport Lisboa e Benfica
Avenida General Norton de Matos, Estrada da Luz, 1500 (726 6129). Metro Colégio Militar-Luz. **Tickets** 200$00-1,000$00. **No credit cards.**
The only local team able to compete with the stronger northern clubs, Benfica were national champions in both 1997 and 1998.

Arts & Entertainment

Tennis

Estoril Open
Estádio Nacional, Complexo Desportivo do Jamor, Praça da Maratona, 1495 Cruz Quebrada (21 414 6041/tournament information 21 301 3301). **Tickets** prices vary. **No credit cards.**
Takes place around Easter and usually attracts some international names.

Activities

Bowling

Bowling Playcenter
Centro Colombo, loja A206, Avenida Lusíada, Benfica 1500 (21 711 3737). Metro Colégio Militar-Luz. **Open** noon-1am Mon-Thur, Sun; noon-3am Fri, Sat. **Admission** *One game* 650$00-850$00. *Shoes* 150$00. **Credit** V.

Ten-pin bowling with 24 alleys. In the evenings there is also 'extreme bowling', which is played in near darkness with fluorescent balls, accompanied by loud music.

Fairplay
Centro Vasco da Gama, Avenida Dom João II, lote 7.05.02, Parque das Nações, 1990 (21 895 1437). Metro Oriente. **Open** 10pm-1am daily. **Admission** *20 balls* 500$00-700$00. *Shoes* (150$00). **No credit cards.**
Large bowling alley inside the Vasco da Gama shopping centre, with noisy techno music.

Fishing
A national licence is in theory needed for fishing in Portuguese rivers, though few people bother to get one. Sea fishing is free and popular. Along the coast from Oeiras to Cascais

No death in the afternoon

Bullfighting in Portugal has long been a very different affair to that in neighbouring Spain, where matadors kill the bull with a sword after *picadors* have taunted it with with barbed spears. In traditional Portuguese *tourada*, the bull is not killed in the ring, although it is butchered out of public sight afterwards, and horsemanship is pre-eminent.

Portuguese bullfights do indeed start with a horseman in 18th-century costume sticking small spears in the bull to irk it. But instead of this being the prelude to a matador, it is followed by the *forcados* – half a dozen or so unarmed catchers on foot who must wrestle the bull to a stop after enticing it to charge.

Most Portuguese aficionados would be shocked to find bullfighting listed as 'sport'. For them this activity is pure art. For one thing, it is inseparable from the majestic Lusitano horse, which is so highly trained that it can anticipate its riders' movements and dance around the ring confident of never being caught by the bull. The Lusitano is the oldest saddle horse in the world and was prized over the centuries as a war horse. Its muscular strength, courage, acceleration, flexibility and manoeuvrability make it the ideal bullfighting mount.

For newcomers to Portuguese *tourada*, though, it is probably the second phase that is most dramatic. Here, the animal is provoked, tackled and brought to a standstill by the *forcados*, clad in brightly coloured stockings, tight breeches and woollen hats.

From the sideboards they've been watching how the bull moves, which way it swings its head. The lead *forcado* has to take the brunt of the bull's charge, and then hang on (usually to the horns, which are capped) until his colleagues can bring the beast to a stop. The arrival of reinforcements is a surprise to the bull; before it charges they hide in a long line behind their leader, shuffling sideways every time the bull moves slightly. If the lead forcado gets thrown off he stands up and tries again, and often again and again, unless he's been too badly mangled, in which case a colleague takes his place.

Among the current big names in Portuguese bullfighting are Joaquim Bastinhas, João Moura and Sónia Matias. Women fighters like Matias are gaining a foothold in this macho-dominated world and, like Christina Sanchez in Spain, have built up a faithful following.

Bullfighting in Portugal does not have the same mass appeal it once did, though. A recent opinion poll showed 12 per cent of Portuguese between 18 and 21 as fans, against 37 percent of those over 60. Yet only a small anti-bullfighting lobby exists, while some aficionados are crying out for more blood, in defiance of the 1928 law that banned lethal bullfights and prescribed gaol sentences for violators, particularly matadors.

The test case has been in the border town of Barrancos, in the Alentejo, where bulls for years have been killed with impunity by Spanish or Mexican matadors during the and up to Guincho and Cabo da Roca you can catch grey mullet, sea bream, squid and sea bass. The Tagus is improving after years of pollution and grey mullet are now returning to its waters.

Casa Diana
Rua Pascoal de Melo 62D, Estefânia, 1000 (21 355 4063). Metro Arroios. **Open** 9am-1pm, 3-7pm Mon-Fri; 9am-1pm Sat; closed Sun. **No credit cards.** **Map** p307 M6.
Well-stocked fishing shop where friendly staff will help with advice and supplies.

Direcção-Geral das Florestas
Avenida João Crisóstomo 26-28, Saldanha, 1069 (21 312 4800). Metro Saldanha. **Open** 9am-noon, 2-4pm Mon-Fri; closed Sat, Sun. **No credit cards.** **Map** p304 L5.
This is where to get your river-fishing licence. It will cost around 1,300$00.

town's summer *festa*. The authorities long turned a blind eye to the tradition, but in June 1999, in the wake of court action by animal rights campaigners to have the law applied, parliament finally moved to sort out the mess.

A new bill was tabled which, while maintaining the appearance of banning lethal bullfights, reduced the offence from a crime punishable by a lengthy prison sentence to one for which only a light fine could be imposed in cases where a tradition of killing the bull in the ring exists. The new law effectively granted Barrancos special status, but it prompted other towns and villages around Portugal to press for an outright lifting of the ban, and perhaps even paved the way for a general acceptance of Spanish-style killings.

Campo Pequeno
Praça de Touros do Campo Pequeno, 1000 (21 793 2143). Metro Campo Pequeno. **Map** p305 M4.
Built in 1892, this is one of the world's biggest bullrings, with a capacity of 8.990. The red-brick, Moorish-style arena is currently closed for repairs, to re-open only at Easter 2003. Those eager to see man meet bull will have to leave Lisbon to do it: most towns in the Alentejo has fights, and Vila Franca de Xira, a 45-minute train ride from Santa Apolónia, has a running of the bulls in early July and another in October.

Federação Portuguesa de Pesca Desportiva
Rua Eça da Queiroz 3-1, Marquês de Pombal, 1050-095 (21 356 3147). Metro Marquês de Pombal. **Open** 9am-1pm, 2-6pm Mon-Fri; closed Sat, Sun. **Map** p307 L6.
Organises championships and can give advice on fishing in Portuguese rivers or dams.

Fitness

See also p234 **Squash.**

Barriga Killer
Rua Cintura do Porto, Armazém J, Santos, 1200 (21 395 6428). Train from Cais do Sodré to Santos/15, 18 tram/32, 40 bus. **Open** 8am-10pm Mon-Fri; 11am-4pm Sat; 11am-3pm Sun. **Admission** *day pass* 3,750$00. **No credit cards.**
A club housed in a converted warehouse offering aerobics, step, powerstep, sauna, plus a Turkish bath, weights and cardiofitness training.

Ginásio Clube Português
Praça Ginásio Clube Português 1, off Rua das Amoreiras, Rato 1250 (21 384 1580/21 3872291). Metro Rato. **Open** 7am-10pm daily. **Classes** 2,250$00. **Credit cards** V. **Map** p306 J7.
Gym, aerobics, weights, swimming, tennis, shooting, archery, fencing, acrobatics, yoga, capoeira, martial arts, cardiofunk, body pump, body combat, dancing, sauna, massage and hydromassage. This 125-year-old gym is the oldest of its kind in Portugal. It now embraces virtually all the normal indoor fitness activities.

Health Club Solinca
Centro Colombo, loja A201, Avenida Lusíada, 1500 (21 711 3650). Metro Colégio Militar-Luz. **Open** 7am-1pm Mon-Fri; 10am-9pm Sat, Sun. **Admission** prices vary. **Credit** AmEx, MC, V.
Three-storey megagym at the Colombo centre. Offers squash, aerobics and hydroaerobics, hydrotherapy, massages, solarium, step, sauna, Turkish bath, weights, cardiofitness and a 25m (87ft) pool.

Super Craque
Rua Capitão Ramires 17A, Campo Pequeno, 1000 (21 792 8690). Metro Campo Pequeno. **Open** 8am-10.30pm Mon-Fri; 10am-2pm Sat, Sun. **Admission** *day pass* 2,500$00. **No credit cards.** **Map** p305 M4.
Aerobics, cardiofunk and step classes, plus massage, solarium, step, weights, yoga, stretching and fitness.

Golf

Despite an increase in the number of courses – from 17 in 1974 to 49 in 1998 – and an international reputation for facilities, golf in Portugal has remained a minority sport. Most golfers are foreigners and tourists. Conditions are excellent all year round and some courses are among the best in Europe.

Don't just lie there

Anyone visiting the crowded beaches near Lisbon on a hot summer weekend would be tempted to rule out the possibility of a casual kick-around. However, if sporting action is what you're after, you need look no further than **Carcavelos**, where an area of the wide beach is set aside for the pastime, and serious and casual sporty types alike congregate. It comes complete with football goalposts and volleyball nets that are freely available for public use, though you do have to bring your own ball. The footballers are concentrated in front of the Café Narciso (which also has table football inside), while two volleyball nets dangle from permanent wooden posts near the café Havana Club (any other nets are private). A few miles down the road, or one train stop closer to Lisbon, on the smaller Santo Amaro beach, is another volleyball net and a table tennis table. The mood here is relaxed, friendly and open.

If tournaments are your thing, on various beaches there are events ranging from high-level competitions through to the less serious, fun-day-out version. The latter usually includes a simultaneous array of any or all of football, volleyball and rugby, though be prepared for a laid-back approach to the day's timetable and also for a fairly rapid

knockout system; you may get no more than a couple of games if you lose.

Carcavelos plays host to competitions organised by the **Câmara Municipal de Cascais** (21 482 5556/www.cmcascais.pt) and open to all. The equipment is set up near the Café Narciso and you can turn up with your team on the day and enter there and then.

João Lagos Sports (21 301 3301/ www.lagossports.com), best known for prestigious tennis events like the Estoril Open, also organises beach games at a variety of locations around the country including, near Lisbon, **Praia Grande** and **Santo Amaro**. These usually include football, volleyball and rugby and, depending on the beach, there might be a surfing competition held alongside.

And for the kids? There are Easter beach games at Carcavelos, arranged by the Câmara Municipal de Cascais. They are usually on the Wednesday to Saturday leading up to Easter and provide the opportunity to try out things like aerobics, kite-flying, bodyboarding and a rowing simulator, as well as the usual team sports.

For more information on beaches in the Lisbon area, *see chapter* **Beaches**.

Golfe do Estoril

Avenida da República, 2765, Estoril (21 468 0176). **Open** 7.30am-8pm daily. **Green fee** 9,300$00. **Credit** AmEx, MC, V.
Jean Gassiat designed the first nine holes in 1929 and the rest were later completed by Mackenzie Ross. Unfortunately, the A5 motorway now crosses the course. The 16th is considered to be the best hole in Portugal. Swimming pool. The 18-hole course is open to members only at weekends; non-members can use the nine-hole course at weekends, however. To reach the course by car, take the Estoril exit on the Lisbon-Cascais A5 motorway and follow signs to Sintra. The course is on the left.

Lisbon Sports Club

Casal da Carregueira, Belas, 2605, Queluz (21 432 1213). **Open** 8am-8pm daily. **Green fee** 7,800$00. *Weekends* 9,300$00. **Credit** AmEx, MC, V.
Eighteen-hole (par 69), tricky course crossed by the River Jamor just outside Belas, near Sintra. This is the second oldest golf club in Portugal, founded in 1922 by British expatriates. Also has three tennis courts, a swimming pool and sauna. To reach the course, take A5 from Lisbon and head towards Sintra on the EN117.

Quinta da Penha Longa

Quinta da Penha Longa, Estrada da Lagoa Azul, Linhó, 2710, Sintra (21 924 9000). **Open** *Winter* 7.30am-7pm daily. *Summer* 7.30am-9pm daily. **Green fee** 14,000$00. *Weekends* 18,000$00. **Credit** AmEx, DC, MC, V.
The best 18-hole (par 72) course in the area, designed by Robert Trent Jones Jr near the Sintra hills and featuring occasional views over the Atlantic coast. There is a smaller adjacent nine-hole course costing 5,300$00 (7,000$00 at weekends). To get to Quinta da Penha Longa, take the EN9 Estoril-Sintra road; turn left at signs for Lagoa Azul.

Karting

Karting is becoming more popular, with new tracks opening opening every year.

Bugs-Kartódromo do Seixal

Quinta da Matinha, Sta Marta dos Corroios, 2855 Corroios (21 255 7979). **Open** 6.30pm-midnight Thur; 6.30pm-2am Fri, Sat; closed Mon-Wed, Sun. **Admission** *Outdoor track* from 1,000$00 (5mins) to 500$00 (30mins). *Indoor track* from 900$00 (5mins) to 4,500$00 (30mins). **No credit cards.**

This site has both indoor and outdoor tracks, which together total around 600m (2,100ft). The site is hard to reach by public transport. By car, cross the Ponte 25 de Abril, then turn left at the first junction, following signs for Cova da Piedade. When the motorway ends, turn right to Laranjeiro on the N-10. Turn right at the second roundabout and follow signs to the track.

Speed Centre

Estrada de Matos Cheirinhos, Abóboda, 2775 Cascais (21 444 6500). **Open** 6pm-1am Fri; 3pm-1am Sat; 3-11pm Sun; closed Mon-Thur. **Admission** from 2,000$00 (10mins) to 5,000$00 (30mins). **Credit** AmEx, MC, V.
Indoor 560m (1,960ft) track.

Riding

Around the Cascais coast area there are places to have riding lessons, and riding trips are available around beautiful locations such as the Sintra hills or Guincho beach.

Centro Hípico da Costa do Estoril

Estrada da Charneca, 186, 2750-530 Cascais (21 487 2064). Train from Cais do Sodré to Cascais then bus to Charneca. **Open** 9am-1pm, 3-7pm Tue-Sun; closed Mon. **Admission** *Lessons or trips* 2,500$00-4,000$00. **No credit cards.**
This riding centre in Caiscais offers rides in the Cascais-Guincho area and in the Sintra hills, as well as lessons for riders in all ability ranges, from begin-

ner to competitive level – in both dressage and show jumping. The friendly staff speak several languages and are used to dealing with tourists.

Escola de Equitação da Quinta da Marinha

Quinta da Marinha, Birre, Areia, 2750-715 Cascais (21 486 9084). Bus to Areia or Guincho. **Open** *Winter* 9am-1pm, 3-7pm Tue-Fri; 9am-noon, 3-7pm Sat, Sun; closed Mon. *Summer* 9am-1pm, 4-8pm Tue-Fri; 9am-noon, 4-8pm Sat, Sun. **Admission** *lessons or trips* 3,500$00-5,000$00. **No credit cards.**
A riding and breeding mega-complex with over 400 horses, which also includes several 'mini-schools'. Rides in the Cascais-Guincho area or in the Sintra hills are available.

Sailing

Despite the proximity of so much blue water, options are severely limited when it comes to hiring anything for a day or two's sailing.

Associação Naval de Lisboa

Doca de Belém, 1300 (21 363 7238/21 363 1865/ 21 362 0981).

Clube Naval de Lisboa

Pavilhão Náutico da Doca de Belém, 1300 (21 396 0488). **Map** p303 C10.
Both this and the Associação Naval (*see above*) run courses for beginners.

Messing about in a boat in Belém.

Arts & Entertainment

Escola de Vela da Lagoa de Óbidos

Escola de Vela, Lagoa d'Óbidos, 2500, Foz do Arelho/Nadadouro (262 978 592). **Open** *Summer* 10am-6pm daily. *Winter* 10am-6pm, Mon, Wed-Sun; closed Tue. **Admission** prices vary. **No credit cards.**

This three-year-old school was built upon the waters of the beautiful lagoon, shored up by a solid stockade. It has windsurfing, Optimist, catamaran, kayak and canoeing classes and rental. To reach the school, take the A8 towards Leiria, exiting at Foz do Arelho, then pick up the road signposted 'marginal da Lagoa'; the school is 2.5km (1.5 miles) after Rotunda da Foz.

Proiate

Rua do Ferragial 7, Cais do Sodré 1200 (21 342 6877/ laser.pro@ip.pt). Metro Cais do Sodré. **Open** 9am-12.30pm, 2-6pm Mon-Sat; closed Sun. **Credit** AmEx, MC, V.

Five yachts for rent, from the Gib'Sea and Jeanneau ranges, either in Lisbon or the Algarve (Portimão). Prices vary according to the season.

Squash

See also **Health Club Solinca** (*p231*).

Ginásio Flete

Rua Aprigio Mafra 23, Alvalade, 1700 (21 840 9074). Metro Alvalade. **Open** 10am-2pm, 4.30-11pm daily **Admission** 2,600$00 per hour (2,200$00 before noon and 2-5pm). **No credit cards.** **Map** p305 N1.

Two courts. Aerobics, martial arts and body-building are also available. Bar open till 2am.

Olaias Clube

Rua Robalo Gouveia, Encosta das Olaias, Olaias, 1900-392 (21 840 7130/squash bookings 21 847 3742). Metro Olaias. **Open** 9am-11pm Mon-Fri; 10am-7pm Sat, Sun. **Admission** 2,000$00 per hour per court. *Monthly pass* 8,000$00-16,000$00. **No credit cards.**

Portuguese national squad members train here. There are four courts, plus eight tennis courts, health club, martial arts, capoeira, massage, solarium and two swimming pools.

Swimming

In winter, the cheaper city pools can often be very crowded. Summer is quieter as everyone has decamped to the beach. Carcavelos is the closest beach for swimming but gets packed at weekends. The Caparica coast offers the best swimming conditions. *See chapter* **Beaches**.

Ateneu Comércial de Lisboa

Rua das Portas de Santo Antão 110, Baixa, 1100 (21 343 0947). Metro Restauradores. **Open** 8am-2pm, 3pm-8pm, 9pm-10pm Mon-Fri; 1.30-7pm Sat; closed Sun. **Admission** 650$00 1hr; 5,500$00 10 visits. **No credit cards.** **Map** p310 M9.

A former aristocratic residence, the Ateneu is now a sort of society/trade union for Lisbon shop assistants, founded in 1880 to provide further education and sporting activities for its members. The 25m (88ft) pool on the top of the building dates from the 1930s. It's under glass and the chlorine fumes can get a bit much on hot days.

Clube Nacional de Natação

Rua de São Bento 209, São Bento, 1250-209 (21 395 2758). Metro Rato. Bus 6, 49. **Open** *Summer* 8am-9pm daily. **Admission** 1,200$00; 100$00-500$00 concessions. **No credit cards.** **Map** p307 K8.

The club has two outdoor pools, one 50m (175ft), one 25m (88ft). It's almost certainly cheaper if you join – you pay a 1,000$00 initial fee when you become a member and then 80$00-120$00 per entry.

Piscina da Penha de França

Calçada do Poço dos Mouros 2, Penha de França, 1170-317 (21 816 1756). Metro Arroios. **Open** 12.30-9.30pm Mon-Fri; 10am-5pm Sat, Sun. **Admission** 245$00;125$00 concessions. **No credit cards.**

Municipally run, indoor, heated, 25m (88ft) pool. There's a solarium, too, but it's only open in the summer. Classes are held at various times between 8.15am and 8.15pm from Monday to Friday.

Tennis

Clube de Ténis do Estoril

Avenida Conde de Barcelona, 2765 Estoril (21 466 2770). Train from Cais do Sodré to Estoril. **Open** 8am-9pm daily. **Admission** *Mon-Fri* 1,000$00 per player per hour. *Sat, Sun* 1,250$00 per player per hours. **No credit cards.**

Upmarket but excellent facilities. Fourteen clay courts, four fast courts. Almost all floodlit (15). Swimming pool, sauna.

Estádio Nacional-Jamor

Clube de Ténis do Jamor, Praça da Maratona, 1495 Cruz Quebrada (21 414 6041). Train from Cais do Sodré to Algés or bus 76 to Faculdade de Motoricidade Humana. **Open** 8am-10pm Mon-Sat; 8am-8pm Sun. *Classes* 3pm-7pm Mon-Fri; 9am-5pm Sat. **Admission** 700$00-1,700$00 per court per hour; half-price concessions. **No credit cards.**

The stadium is the site of the Estoril Open tennis championship. It boasts 31 clay courts (including two floodlit indoor ones), plus six fast courts. Classes are also available.

Lisboa Racket Centre

Rua Alferes Malheiro, Alvalade, 1700-025 (21 846 0232). Bus 31, 44, 45, 50. **Open** 8am-10pm Mon-Sat; 9am-8pm Sun. **Admission** 1,500$00 per person per hour. **Credit** AmEx, MC, V. **Map** p305 O1.

Located in a small park, this new and friendly centre has nine courts (seven are floodlit). It also has paddle-tennis, a health club, aerobics, gym, sauna and a swimming pool.

Trips Out of Town

Getting Started

All you need to know to hit the road – or rails – and head out of the city.

By bus

Bus and coach services are usually the quickest and cheapest way of reaching an out-of-town destination, although services are sometimes organised in a rather piecemeal manner and you may have to catch your bus in somewhat out-of-the-way corners of Lisbon. National bus services were privatised a few years ago, but **Rede Expresso** (ticket office 21 354 5439/ 21 354 5863/24-hour recorded information 70 722 3344) remains dominant, followed by **Eva** (21 314 7710/7713), both based at Arco do Cego bus terminal. Bus routes are far more comprehensive than train routes and, on any other than the Lisbon–Oporto services, usually quicker too. Both Rede Expresso and Eva offer an identical discount scheme whereby children under 12 are entitled to a 50 per cent reduction in fares. Over-65s are entitled to a 20 per cent reduction. Tickets for buses are cheaper if bought in advance – ask for *pré-comprados*.

Tickets can be bought from travel agencies, but are generally more expensive than if bought directly. Agencies downtown include **Marcus & Harting** on Rossio (Praça Dom Pedro IV 45-50, 21 323 0200) and **Abreu** (Avenida da Liberdade 160, 21 347 6441), and in the Cais do Sodré area, **Cruzeiro** (Rua do Alecrim 7, 21 322 1000), and **Agência Pinto Bastos** (Praça Duque da Terceira 20, 21 346 8659/346 6911).

Arco do Cego bus terminal

Avenida Duque d'Ávila, 1050 (21 354 5439). Metro Saldanha/bus 16, 18, 26, 42. **Open** 9am-6pm daily. It's best to buy your ticket the day before travelling. Some express buses have hostess service, WC, bar, video and telephone.

By car

Portugal's road network has been improving in recent years following a wave of EU-backed investment, with upgraded highways linking Lisbon with Oporto and Spanish Galicia to the north, and with the Alentejo and central Spain to the east. Extensive improvements are also being carried out on motorways connecting the capital to the Algarve and south-western Spain.

Driving is an enjoyable way of seeing the country, but beware of the insanely cavalier Portuguese motorist (*see p272*). The quickest route is not necessarily obvious on the map – the road that might seem to take you the way the crow flies can actually turn out to be a potholed, hilly route that leads you astray for hours. Signposts, too, are notoriously lacking.

For routes east and south, we recommend taking the Ponte Vasco da Gama out of Lisbon; the Ponte 25 de Abril can get extremely congested, especially at rush hour. From the Praça Marquês de Pombal, head north-east up the Avenida Fontes Pereira de Melo, following signs for the airport. Nearer the airport you'll pick up signs for the Ponte Vasco da Gama and routes south. Once over the bridge, follow the A12 to join the A2 (IP1). When travelling to the Alentejo, the A2 leads directly on to the A20/E90 (IP7) – follow signs for Évora. When travelling to the Algarve take the A2/E1 (IP1) and follow signs for Albufeira. For routes north to Coimbra and Oporto, use the A1 E80 (A1-IP1) and follow signs to Oporto. For general information on driving in Portugal, *see p272*.

By train

The Lisbon–Oporto route is the only intercity service that could conceivably be described as efficient. Trains depart from **Santa Apolónia** station; you can also get on at the ultra-modern **Gare do Oriente** (freephone 800 201 820 or 21 8920 370) near Parque das Nações, which connects with the new Metro line. For the Algarve and some destinations in the Alentejo, first take the ferry from Terreiro do Paço to **Barreiro** rail station (21 207 4807).

Lisbon's local train network offers a regular service on existing routes – notably from Rossio (freephone 800 200 904 or 21 343 3747) to Sintra and from Cais do Sodré (freephone 800 203 067) to Cascais – and is undergoing expansion. In 1999, a new rail line literally hanging below the Ponte 25 de Abril came into operation, linking northern Lisbon to the suburbs of Almada and beyond, with buses to Caparica.

Estação de Santa Apolónia

Avenida Infante Dom Henrique, 1900 (21 881 6242). Bus 19, 28. **Open** 6am-midnight daily. If possible, tickets should be bought a day in advance at the station or at any Multibanco cash machine (the receipt serves as a ticket); they may also be bought at travel agencies, but this is often more expensive. For rail information, call freephone 800 200 904 or 21 888 4025 (8am-11pm daily).

Beaches

Most visitors to Lisbon don't know it, but the coast here is beach-bum heaven.

Mention Portuguese beaches and thoughts fly to the Algarve, where planeloads of Brits and Germans emerge blinking into the sun for the ritual roasting of flesh. But the coast around Lisbon is also blessed with beaches, and their range and dimension may surprise you: from a string of sheltered little coves on the Estoril coast to wild and windswept Guincho further west. Across the Tagus, the resort town of Caparica is the gateway to miles of dune-backed sands. Further south the beaches become more isolated. Almost everywhere you will be struck by the sands' cleanness and the coastline's beauty.

These beaches exert a strong influence on Lisbon life, revealing subtle distinctions in class, age and personal taste. The palest lisboeta in the darkest Bairro Alto dive is sure to have a favourite beach bar in summer.

STAYIN' ALIVE

The unprepared may be quite literally swept away by the power of the ocean here. It is no coincidence that Portugal is an important port of call for some of the world's most adrenaline-charged surfers and windsurfers. Every year brings several dozen drownings. The waters between Lisbon and Cascais are sheltered and calm, but care should be taken elsewhere. Note also the surprising chill of the ocean. This is particularly true to the north of Lisbon where currents seem colder. Either way, surfers will definitely want to pack their wetsuits.

Lisbon to Cascais

Catch the Cascais train from Cais do Sodré and you can be off the Lisbon streets and lying quietly on your towel in three quarters of an hour. The further down the line, the less like a capital city and the more like a holiday resort it becomes. When travelling to small stations between Cais do Sodré and Cascais, it's a good idea to have coins to buy your return ticket (or buy it before leaving), since counters at some stations close as early as 4.30pm and tickets can only be bought at automatic machines.

At Estoril – and on some other beaches along this coast – sunshades and sunloungers are rented for between 500$00 and 1,500$00. Bars and restaurants place tables and chairs along the promenade. Some also have shower facilities.

On the return leg it's hard to match the magic of Lisbon viewed at sunset from the train window.

Carcavelos

There are several working-class districts along this stretch of the railway line, which may explain why local authorities have not put more into the upkeep of this splendid beach. It's a shame, because the broad sands are unmatched elsewhere along the Cascais line and, not surprisingly, packed in summer, attracting hordes of local youngsters who swarm around footballs. The beach is also popular with surfers in winter. There is a windsurfing school, based at the **Windsurf Café** (21 457 8965), which has seen better days. Plans were afoot in early 2001 to give it a complete facelift, with a major new centre offering surfing and windsurfing lessons, jet-ski and kayak rental, and other beach-related activities.

Parede

Just a few minutes' walk from the station, the peeling promenade is ugly, but this sheltered patch of sand is sometimes quieter than Cascais and Estoril, and is good for bathing. Older Portuguese bathers flock here for the high iodine content in the waters – supposedly efficacious against rheumatism.

Cascais: sun, sea and English newspapers.

São Pedro do Estoril

An attractive beach, less frequented by foreign tourists than Cascais and Estoril, but it's popular with locals and gets crowded on summer weekends. Exit the road at the Esplanada Pizzeria sign and you'll find ample parking on the cliff top; otherwise it's an easy walk from the station. A narrow strip of sand slips into clear waters where slabs of rock create shades of blue and green. This explains the popularity of São Pedro do Estoril with the diving fraternity, but makes for a dodgy dip at low tide. The restaurants offer a good vantage above the beach. This sheltered spot is also a good place to hire a paddle boat.

São João do Estoril

There are two beaches near São João station, linked to Estoril by a promenade. Praia da Poça is a 'locals' beach that may give some respite from the crowds. **Bar Atlântico** is a particularly good spot to admire the view, and this stretch is excellent for windsurfing. The prettier and more secluded Azarujinha beach is round the headland towards Lisbon.

Estoril

With its casino and posh golf course, Estoril has an upmarket reputation, but little stuffiness has made its way on to Tamariz beach, despite it being overlooked by a crenellated holiday home owned by the royal family of Monaco. The smallish area of sand is occupied by an even mix of tourists and locals and the promenade is filled with tables from adjoining bars and restaurants. Though busy in July and August, it maintains a relaxed feel. If you want to peruse the hordes from the seclusion of a private swimming pool, the **Tamariz** club keeps the mob at bay with its 1,600$00 (weekdays) to 2,000$00 (weekends) entrance fee (open 10am-8pm, June-Sept). The beachfront also has a huddle of beachside bars that double as nightspots. **Caramba** and **Absurdo** pump out open-air music, while **Virtual** is more closed and clubby. Along the promenade towards Cascais there is another beach at Monte Estoril with its own rail station and **Bar Jonas**, a good place to snack while listening to jazz and ambient music.

Cascais

The first Cascais beach is a mere frisbee throw from the train station. Praia da Conceição is separated by a narrow strip of sand from Praia da Duquesa. Tucked in among the promenade restaurants of the latter is **John David's Snack Bar**, at the east end of the beach by the station, pandering to Anglo-Saxon palates with fried breakfasts, strong tea and English newspapers. It is also the place for water-skiing, windsurfing or pedal boats. As with other bars along here, there are showers, changing rooms and sunbeds for hire. Beyond the Hotel Albatroz is the tiny beach of Praia da Rainha. In front of Praça do 5 de Outubro, Praia da Ribeira is bigger but geared less to tourists, more to fishing.

Where to eat

In Carcavelos, **Bossa Nova** (Avenida Marginal, 21 457 0890), is a Brazilian place on the promenade that serves up spicy Bahian muquecas and BSE-free Brazilian beef. Fateixa (Estrada Marginal, 21 457 0240, main courses 2,000$00-6,500$00) is a posher fish restaurant. In Estoril, in addition to the upmarket **La Villa** (*see p243*), another notable restaurant is **Al Fresco** (Galerías do Estoril, Rua de Lisboa 5, 21 467 6770, main courses 1,150$00-3,750$00), which has friendly service and good-quality Italian food.

Getting there

By train

Trains leave Cais do Sodré for Cascais every 20mins, stopping at the destinations above. The journey to Cascais takes about 40mins, and costs 210$00. Trains in both directions run as late as 1.30am (except on Fri-Sat and Sat-Sun nights, 2.30am).

By car

Take the A5, which is well signposted around Praça de Espanha and Praça Marquês de Pombal and closes on the coast around Estoril. The N6 hugs the coastline, but is prone to traffic jams.

Guincho & the Sintra coast

The sea crashes into the rocks with a new violence once you leave Cascais behind. A kilometre along the coast road, the Boca do Inferno ('Hell's Mouth') marks the change. Great columns of water shoot up when the sea is in an angrier mood. In 1930, Aleister Crowley faked his own death at this spot.

At Guincho, cliffs suddenly give way to a great bank of sand, ringed by hills and woodland. Further north, the Sintra hills tumble down to the cliffs of Cabo da Roca, mainland Europe's westernmost point. Beyond here the beaches are smaller, tucked between dramatic headlands and linked by cliff-top trails from here as far north as Magoito.

Guincho

Six km (4 miles) from Cascais, the open sands of Guincho beach stretch back to form dunes that reach up the hillside beyond the main road. To the north, the Sintra hills form a craggy horizon, and fresh pine scents mix with the salty ocean tang. But take heed. A mere breeze in Cascais is a sign that Guincho is probably blowing a gale and it can be all a bit much when it starts lifting the sand. Bathers should also be wary of powerful waves and currents that swirl back from the beach. This all makes Guincho possibly the best windsurfing beach in Europe, host to world championships, but it's no place for beginners.

Guincho – on the wild side of Cascais.

Guincho offers good surfing too, especially in the early and late hours when the wind dies down. At the northern end, signposted from the Sintra road, **Bar do Guincho** is popular with the surf set, and offers a good selection of salads and juices. Local hotel **Estalagem do Muchaxo** (*see p61*) has an excellent restaurant overlooking the beach and its own sheltered seawater swimming pool (mid May-Sept) Non-guests pay for the privilege (1,800$00 weekdays; 2,500$00 weekends). Just south of Guincho there are two smaller beaches, offering slightly more protection from the wind. Here the **Arriba** restaurant has another salt-water pool (open Apr-Oct; info 21 487 1007).

Praia da Adraga

A road winds downhill from Almoçageme to a near-perfect beach wedged between tall cliffs, where a clean blue sea casts white-crested waves onto the sand. At one end, an arch has formed through the rocks. At low tide, you can venture around the cliff and find a string of caves uncovered. The coast is dotted with rocky stacks, and seagulls drift across the cliff tops. A beachfront bar and restaurant completes the picture. Adraga is 15km (9 miles) north of Guincho, and signposted off the Sintra road. There is little in the way of public transport, although a cliff-top trail links it with the busier Praia Grande. The narrow road down to the beach can get congested.

Praia Grande

Signposted from the Sintra road north of Adraga, this beach is less secluded than its neighbour, with a number of restaurants and bars on the promenade. At the northern end, **Hotel Arribas** boasts an Olympic-sized pool, with a view of the beach (open June-Sept; entry 1,100$00 weekdays, 1,300$00 weekends, children half-price). Praia Grande hosts various surf competitions. There are also some bars on stilts where you can eat snails. A younger crowd concentrates at its southern end, where beach sports, including rugby, are popular. A track here leads to Praia Pequena, a smaller, less crowded beach accessible from below at low tide. Steps near Bar do Fundo lead to cliff-top trails running north and south.

Praia das Maçãs

A medium-sized family beach backing on to a village with a good choice of seafood restaurants. The beach has changing rooms and showers, and there are sports facilities and a swimming pool nearby. If you're coming by public transport, the tram ride down the leafy Sintra hills is fun. This old line was reopened in 1997 and a couple of open-air traditional Lisbon trams now trundle up and down the hill from Ribeira de Sintra, 20 minutes' walk or a short bus ride from Sintra station. The tram takes 30 minutes to get to the beach, passing through the village of Colares, with its famous vineyards. As of early 2001 the council was to take over the tram line from the private company that had been running it, and timetables were not yet defined. Plans are afoot to extend the line all the way to Sintra, in which case it could open the whole year round.

Azenhas do Mar

This stunningly picturesque village clings to the cliff top over the headland from Praia das Maçãs. There is little in the way of a beach, but there is a pleasant open-air bar on the cliff top and steps lead down the cliff face to a broad swimming pool cut into the rocks and refilled every day by the tide.

Where to eat

There's an embarassment of fine fish restaurants on the coast road near Guincho, where you can divide your attention between the sunset and your fish or seafood. None is cheap and it's hard to choose between them, but **Mestre Zé** (Estrada do Guincho, 21 487 0275, main courses 1,900$00-3,500$00) is a good one. Another reliable option is **Mar do Guincho** (Estrada do Guincho, 21 485 8220, main courses 1,900$00-3,500$00.

There's no shortage of places to eat at Praia das Maçãs, but if you're after higher-quality fare, **Búzio** (Avenida Eugenio Levi 56, Colares, 21 929 2172, main courses 1,450$00-2,850$00) gets the nod. It's clean, the waiters are friendly, and it has a loyal local clientèle. A good

Trips Out of Town

alternative right on the beach is **Loureiro-Esplanada Vasco da Gama** (21 929 2442, main courses 1,800$00-2,500$00). It's a simple place serving uncomplicated Portuguese dishes, but it has a nice beach view and the owner is friendly. **Neptuno** (21 929 1222, main courses 1,870$00-3,300$00) is also right on the beach and is glass fronted, ensuring a good view whatever the weather.

Getting there

By car
Follow the Boca do Inferno road out of Cascais to Guincho, or the inland route through Birre and Areia villages. For beaches further north, take the N247 from Guincho.

By bus
The 405 and 415 buses leave Cascais station for Guincho roughly every 40mins, but are somewhat irregular. If you are relying on getting back this way, pick up a timetable from the booth across the street outside the station or call Stagecoach (21 469 9100), which offers a one day ticket for 1,250$00, convenient when planning to make several trips in this area. You can also catch a taxi (21 466 0101/21 465 9500) to Guincho, which should cost no more than 1,100$00. For beaches north of Guincho, take a train to Sintra from Rossio station and get off at Portela de Sintra. Buses leave from outside Portela de Sintra station – one stop before Sintra – for several destinations along the coast, including Praia Grande and Praia das Maçãs (bus 441), and Azenhas do Mar (bus 440, 441). To go to Portela de Sintra from Sintra, catch bus 433 in front of the tourist office in Praça da República. The 403 Cascais-Sintra bus calls at Cabo da Roca.

By bicycle
Although it is a long climb over the Sintra foothills, bicycles can be hired from Transrent, Avenida Marginal, Centro Comercial Cisne, Loja 15, 2750 Cascais (21 486 4566).

The Caparica coast

The Caparica coast begins near the mouth of the river Tagus, where an enormous maritime grain silo dominates Trafaria village. Although much of the coast is really one enormous beach, each stretch has its own feel, and there are differences in who goes where. Bars help set the tone for each section, as well as offering hearty salads, cocktails and juices.

Heading south from Caparica towards Fonte da Telha, dunes rise up a short distance from the sea, and beyond them, thickets of green reach inland to the base of a tree-crowned sandstone cliff. In spring this area is a sea of yellow flowers. The density of the beach population rises and falls in line with the popularity of individual bars. These are spaced

along the dunes, usually reached by wooden walkways from the train stops and car parks. Many have showers and first aid posts. Some are the focus of nocturnal activity, with music and dancing until late, but most are closed out of season.

São João de Caparica
Popular with the Portuguese and relatively undiscovered by tourists. It is backed by several campsites and has a large area of shaded parking. The beach has a handful of bars, some of which serve snacks and meals, and its popularity with local families is underlined by the presence of a crèche. This spot is also highly regarded by surfers and windsurfers, although the currents nearer the northern end can be treacherous.

Caparica
Not for those seeking sophistication or seclusion, but the place to get into the seaside spirit with crowds quaffing cool beer and scoffing snails. It's like a semi-tropical Morecambe. Main access to the beach is through the busy Rua dos Pescadores, where Lisbon buses unload. The approach is a predictable jumble of restaurants, ice-cream stalls and small hotels. The seafront opens up to a busy promenade where you can catch the train.

Praia Nova
The first stretches are a rag-bag of wooden beach huts and bars. There are plenty of families entrenched in the sands, but this area is also thick with local kids indulging in the time-honoured beach arts of soccer, snogging, snoozing and surfing. At train stop 5, **Bar Golfinho** is a popular hang-out, with a stoned surfy feel and live bands on summer evenings. There is also a stretch of Praia Nova that tends to be more frequented by Africans.

Praia da Mata
The true beauty of this coast reveals itself by the time you get to Praia da Mata (train stop 8). This area tends to be busy, as it is the closest point to Caparica town where you can enjoy the beauty of the landscape with nothing more than the occasional beach bar to block the view. **Bar Praia** has a good downstairs restaurant serving fish and meat dishes at reasonable prices. Nearby, a wooden footbridge leads across the dunes to the popular **Bar de Ponte**, good for sipping a long drink or juice and gazing at the sea, but with a menu limited to snacks and service that can be very slow on busy days. It steps up the pace after dark, with live bands and Brazilian/Latino music.

Praia da Riviera to Praia do Rei
This stretch attracts a younger, more middle-class crowd with their own sets of wheels. A hip alternative along here is **Praia Vermelha** bar. Adorned with the red and green national colours of Portugal, it has a cool surfed-out feel. The salads, shots and cocktails here are more than a match for the larger

Clapboard houses line the **Caparica** coast south of Lisbon.

Praia da Riviera (stop 9) and **Praia do Castelo** (stop 11) bars. **Rouxinhol** bar (stop 11) has Warsteiner beer and Brasileira coffee.

Praia do Rei to Praia da Sereia

At Praia do Rei (stop 13) the eponymous eaterie offers good fish and seafood options. On Praia da Morena (stop 14), the **Hula Hula** bar attracts a younger crowd, with a cool cane interior and an outside patio. It serves all the salads, sangria, juices and tropical cocktails you would expect from a Caparica bar, as does the nearby **Borda D'Água** (stop 14). At Praia da Sereia (stop 15), the perennially busy **Bar Wai KiKi** is the place where good-looking young poseurs go to see and be seen. The bar lays on the tropical imagery with its beach shack decor, serves a good selection of cocktails and snacks, and booms dance music out onto the sands. Sometimes there are live bands and DJs. Drinks are also served to sun loungers on the beach.

Nova Vaga to Fonte da Telha

The sands are less crowded from Nova Vaga (stop 16). After Bela Vista (stop 17) the beach bars disappear. The final 3km (2-mile) stretch down to Fonte da Telha is a male nudist domain and the site for much gay cruising – the dunes are particularly active, though the beach remains fairly quiet. If this isn't your scene, there are plenty of peaceful spots on the fringes of the nudist zone.

Fonte da Telha

The Transpraia train line ends just before the village at Bar Terminal, where you can eat or drink with an excellent view. The beach is busier again

here, with the ubiquitous wood cabin beach bars pulling in the younger customers. A walk up the road to the hilltop reveals more stunning views of the sea, as well as walks along the wooded cliff top. The village has its own bus link with the Cacilhas ferry terminal.

Where to eat

In Fonte da Telha, **O Camões** (Avenida 1º de Maio 94, 21 296 3865, main courses 1,200$00-1,800$00) is probably the most established local restaurant. The fish is caught by the owners, so you know it's fresh. **Beira Mar** (Avenida 1º de Maio C-105, 21 297 2636, main courses 1,800$00-3,950$00), with its wooden terrace and fine sea view, is a relative newcomer but has already built up a good reputation.

In Caparica, there are some good seafood restaurants along the promenade, notably the bustly **O Barbas** (Praia da Vila 26, 21 290 0163, main courses 1,300$00-1,500$00) – if you can deal with the live music. In the town itself, **O Capote** (Rua dos Pescadores 40-B, 21 290 1274, main courses 1,950$00-2,700$00) is a pricier option, with a more varied menu and nice atmosphere.

At Transpraia train stop 12, the **Cabana do Pescador** (Praia do Pescador, 212 962 152, main courses 1,500$00-1,700$00) is a popular restaurant, offering an excellent choice of fresh fish and dishes and attracting lunch crowds even in winter.

Getting there

By car

You can get from Lisbon to anywhere on the Caparica coast in less than 60mins, provided you avoid rush hour on the Ponte 25 de Abril. Follow signs to Caparica. From there the coast road gives access to 12km (7.5 miles) of beaches as far as Fonte da Telha. These are signposted off the road along dusty tracks; each has its own parking. Alternatively, you can continue down the A2 after crossing the bridge, before taking the N378 Sesimbra road.

By bus

The service from Lisbon is reasonable, but limited at the southern end of the peninsula. Catch a Caparica bus from Praça de Espanha, which drops you in Caparica town, a 5-min walk from the beach and the little open-air Transpraia train that scoots between the dunes as far as Fonte da Telha. Ring the bell to stop at the beach of your choice; stops are numbered. The highest price you'll pay if going to the second of the two zones is 360$00 single and 620$00 return. The service runs from Easter-Oct; the last train leaves Fonte da Telha at 7.30pm. Another option is to catch bus 75 either at Campo Grande metro station, where it starts, or at another stop on the route such as Marquês de Pombal. The bus runs from the first weekend in June to the last in Sept. (Tickets are 520$00 return; combined ticket with the Transpraia train: 700$00 return to the end of zone 1 – Praia da Riviera – or 900$00 return if you're going further).

By train

The new rail line that crosses the Ponte 25 de Abril starts at Entrecampos and links Lisbon's northern rail line to the suburbs of Almada and buses to Caparica and further south. Get off at Pragal and from there catch a bus to Caparica. Transpraia trains leave at 6- to 15-minute intervals depending on the day and time. Last train to Entrecampos, 12.36am from Fogueteiro; to Fogueteiro, 1.28am. Ticket price 530$00 return.

By boat

Catch a boat from Cais do Sodré to Cacilhas and then a bus to Costa de Caparica. A fun alternative – provided you prefer to be always rolling, even if it's slowly, than to be stuck in a traffic jam – is the ferry between Belém and Trafaria. It leaves at 15min to 1hr intervals depending on the day and time (the boat is used by commuters). From there you can catch the bus to Caparica or hop off at São João.

Lagoa de Albufeira & Meco

South of Fonte da Telha, there is a long stretch of beach without any access from the road. Walking this way you are unlikely to see a soul other than an occasional misanthropic nudist. It's just you, flocks of gulls and the deep blue sea. This sense of isolation increases the further south you go, although there are points with access from the road running to the village of Meco, including the Albufeira lagoon, another

windsurfer's paradise. Everything seems to intensify on these final unspoilt stretches. The sea seems bluer, the cliff-top shrubbery greener, and the air even more fresh.

Lagoa de Albufeira

A tree-lined lagoon winds its way inland, cut off from the sea by a thin bar of sand. The constant breeze and smooth waters make this a perfect location for windsurfers not yet ready for the perils of the open sea, and there's a local windsurfing school to help out. There's a beach bar serving food, and another simple restaurant by the lake.

Meco

A kilometre or so south of Lagoa de Albufeira, a big sandstone rock marks a place known as **Praia da Tramagueira**. Here there is a restaurant and a couple of beach bars and, thanks to the road link with Meco village, more people. The final stretch is nudist and if ever there was a beach to bare your butt, this is it. The sea here is clean and refreshing, and the coarse-grained sand defies the breeze. Don't be alarmed if mud-caked natives sway into view, all genitals and eye-whites. Fresh, non-drinkable water trickling down the cliff side forms a clay that makes an ideal all-over mud pack. Bake in it for a while, then jump into the sea, and marvel at how good your skin feels. Walking around the cliff headland at low tide gets you to **Praia das Bicas**, which has a seafood restaurant and a large campsite on the cliff tops. Nearby Meco village has several bars and restaurants for late afternoon snacks.

Where to eat

O Peralta (Aldeia do Meco, 21 268 3696, main courses 1,800$00-3,800$00) is a Meco institution – although it can be a bit pricey, depending on what you're eating. It's just outside the village, at the corner where you turn down to the beach. In the village itself, **Mequinhu's** (Rua Central, 21 268 3648, main courses 1,100$00-2,000$00) is a cheaper alternative; it specialises in delicious tapas-type dishes that are large enough to satisfy most appetites.

Getting there

By car

Follow the A5 from the Ponte 25 de Abril, take the N378 Sesimbra road, and then the backroads to Lagoa de Albufeira and Meco. Minor roads give access to several points along these beaches.

By bus

Day-tripping here by public transport is challenging. Buses run to Sesimbra from Praça de Espanha or Cacilhas. Get off at Santana. From Santana around 8 buses daily run to Meco village. Ask the bus driver for a timetable if you don't want to get stranded coming home.

Around Lisbon

Fishing ports and resorts, extravagant palaces – and glorious Sintra.

Located near an Atlantic coastline studded with fine beaches and capes, and surrounded by small towns boasting fantastical abbeys and palaces, the Lisbon region offers a wealth of things to see and do on a day trip.

Queluz is to the capital what Versailles is to Paris – on a smaller scale – but **Sintra** is the area's only must-see, even if you're only around for a weekend.

West of Lisbon

Estoril

The train from Lisbon to Estoril follows the Tagus and then the seafront, with views of golden sands and old forts (sit on the left-hand side). Estoril, once a grand resort for titled Europeans, is now fading somewhat – though the Grimaldis of Monaco maintain a castle-like holiday home on the seafront.

During World War II Portugal remained neutral, and Estoril became an important listening post for both sides, attracting spies, writers and exiled royals (*see p56* **The spies who stayed in the sun**). Kings Umberto of Italy and Juan Carlos of Spain lived here, while Graham Greene and Ian Fleming were among the intelligence officers-turned-writers who were to later draw inspiration from wartime experiences at Estoril. These days the only royal-in-residence is the Queen Mother of Bulgaria, and the tourist office is reduced to boasting that Bryan Adams grew up here.

The Casino – which in its 1940s heyday attracted pearl- and fur-clad society ladies and tux-wearing gents – was the inspiration for Ian Fleming's *Casino Royale*. Fleming was tracking a Yugoslav spy, who he found to be gambling with the cash he was couriering. Nowadays, it's full of slot-machine addicts, but it still has an over-the-top nightly floorshow, gives out the biggest weekly prizes in Europe, and has been renovated by its current owner, Macao-based gambling tycoon Stanley Ho.

Where to eat

Through the shady palm-fringed Casino gardens towards the sea, turn left by the post office to reach **Garrett** (Avenida de Nice 54,

21 468 0365, closed Tue), a charming old café for coffee and cakes. Even the waitresses seem stuck in the 1930s. In the Casino, **Estoril Mandarin** (21 466 7270, main courses 2,500$00, closed Tue) is reputed to be the best Chinese restaurant in the Lisbon region, but if you're going to push the *barco* out we recommend **La Villa** (Praia do Tamariz 3, 21 468 0033, main courses 3,000$00).

Getting there

By bus
Stagecoach bus 498 runs from the airport to Estoril and Cascais, taking 45mins. The 1,200$00 ticket includes unlimited travel for one day on Stagecoach buses, serving the whole Sintra region. (21 469 9100). From Lisbon, the train is the best means of transport.

By train
There are four trains per hour (5.30am to 2.30am) from Cais do Sodré station (fewer at night). Journey time: 35mins; 210$00.

Tourist information

Turismo
Estoril station, 2765 Estoril (21 466 3813).
Open 9am-7pm Mon-Sat; 10am-6pm Sun.

Beaches and faded grandeur at **Estoril**.

Cascais – once a fishing port, now a resort.

Cascais

Another once-fashionable resort, Cascais is an important fishing port and a busy town full of shops, bars and British expats and tourists. On the seafront by Praia dos Pescadores (Fisherman's Beach) you can see lobster pots and painted boats as well as old fishermen discussing football and politics. The day's catch is auctioned every evening around 5pm.

The former seaside home of the Count of Guimarães, now the **Museu Conde de Castro Guimarães** is worth a look. When he and his wife died childless, both in 1892, they bequeathed to the state an eclectic jumble of Indo-Portuguese furniture, oil paintings, tiles, porcelain and antique books.

A free road-train chugs around town and out to **Boca do Inferno** (Hell's Mouth) where, as the name suggests, the sea smashes against the rocks with a vengeance at high tide. It was here, in 1930, that Aleister Crowley faked his own death. En route you pass the palace where the Duke of Windsor and Mrs Simpson stayed after the abdication.

Museu Conde de Castro Guimarães

Avenida Rei Humberto II de Itália, 2750 Cascais (21 482 5407). Train from Cais do Sodré to Cascais then free mini-train to museum. **Open** *Summer* 11am-6pm Tue-Sun. *Winter* 10am-5pm Tue-Sun. **Admission** 260$00; free children, students, over-65s. **No credit cards.**

Where to eat & drink

The **Tagarela Tearoom** in the Rua Luís Xavier Palmeirim (up the steps on the right on the way round the bay to the fort; 21 486 7242) is a great place for tea and scones with a

spectacular view over the bay, or you can catch an English football match and sup a pint at **Beefeater Bar** (Rus Visconde da Luz 1A, 21 484 0696). For food, **Dom Manolo** (Avenida Combatentes da Grande Guerra 13, 21 483 1126, main courses 1,000$00) on the road often known as the Avenida Marginal, offers good, cheap grilled chicken and chips, while **Pimentão** (Rua das Flores 16, 21 484 0994, main courses 2,500$00) does great fresh fish. Or, if you want to splash out, go round the coast beyond Boca do Inferno to **Furnas** (Estrada do Guincho, 21 486 9243, main courses 7,000$00) and try the superb fish baked in salt, while watching the sea crash on the rocks below. The even fancier **Porto de Santa Maria** (*see p122*) is on the same road; don't forget your Gold Card.

Getting there

Train from Cais do Sodré station. Cascais is an additional 5min on the train (or a 20min walk along the seafront) from Estoril (*see p243*).

Tourist information

Turismo

Avenida Combatentes da Grande Guerra, 2750 Cascais (21 484 4086/21 846 8204). **Open** 9am-7pm Mon-Sat; 10am-6pm Sun.

Cabo da Roca

Although you can take the bus, it's worth renting a car to drive along the coastal road west from Cascais, often compared to California's Highway One (except it only takes 15 minutes from start to finish). The road rolls past rocky bays, wild dunes and vast sandy beaches, such as windswept Guincho – the

Cabo de Roca – the edge of Europe.

windsurfers' favourite – and up over craggy
cliffs, eventually reaching Cabo da Roca,
continental Europe's westernmost point and
scene of many shipwrecks.

If you can stand up in the wind, walk around
the point – Promontorium Magnum to the
Romans – and for a moment everyone else in
Europe will be to the east of you. This spot is at
its most beautiful when it's blooming with pink
and white flowers.

Getting there

Stagecoach bus 403 from Cascais station every hour.
Journey time: 30mins; 300$00.

Sintra

'Glorious Eden' was Lord Byron's description,
and if you take one day trip from Lisbon, this
should be it. A Unesco World Heritage Site,
Sintra is a magical place of lush forests and
palaces with neo-Gothic towers and Disneyland
turrets, often shrouded in mist. Always several
degrees cooler (and rather wetter) than Lisbon,
it was once the royal family's summer retreat.

A ticket for the Stagecoach special tourist
bus from Sintra station allows you to get on and
off at all the main attractions. Alternatively,
rent a horse-drawn carriage and head first for
the Moorish **castle** ruins, with its dragontooth
walls creeping over the hills (known to the
Romans as the Mountains of the Moon). It's a
lovely spot to sit in a turret and read a book, or
just absorb the atmosphere.

On a clear day there are spectacular views to
the sea and the pink and yellow **Palácio da
Pena** on the next hill. Built by the German
Dom Ferdinand II in the 19th century at the
height of the Romantic movement (when such
follies were fashionable), the palace is a
pastiche of various architectural styles. Its
lavish exterior is covered with gargoyles and
boasts an incredible bay window, held up by a
massive stone Triton. The palace is entered
through an impressive portcullis and set in
acres of rolling gardens – a wonderful place to
walk and picnic, particularly by the swan lake.
The palace's interior is, alas, a disappointment.

The other highlight in Sintra is the **Palácio
Nacional** – the building with the two massive
white chimneys in the centre of the old town. It
was built in the 14th century by Dom João I,
who lived here with his wife Philippa of
Lancaster, daughter of John of Gaunt. The tiled
Arab room is stunning, as is the Swan room.
The hexagonal Sala dos Brasões is also walled
with blue and white *azulejos*, while its domed
ceilings are painted with the coats of arms of
nobles of the court. It has fabulous views. One

Disneyland? No, it's the **Palácio da Pena**.

of the palace's oldest rooms is the Magpie room,
painted with 136 of the birds, each bearing a
rose and a scroll marked 'Por bem'. The story
goes that the wandering hands of Dom João I
proffered a rose to one of the ladies-in-waiting
when Queen Philippa wasn't looking and a
magpie snatched it. The king excused himself
by saying 'Por bem' – all to the good. A less
colourful version has it that the king ordered
the panels painted to rebuke the women of the
court for gossiping like magpies.

If you feel hungry, pop over the road to
Periquita (Rua Consiglieri Pedroso, 21 923
0626, closed Wed) for a local *queijada* – another
cake with a secret recipe (Sintra has three
bakeries claiming to make the best). Dotted
around are pricey antiques and lace shops.

Further along the road is the newly
renovated **Lawrence's Hotel** (21 910 5500),
where Byron started writing *Childe Harolde's
Pilgrimage*. Past that is **Quinta da Regaleira**
(21 910 6650), an exotic neo-Manueline fantasy
with a mystic past linked to Freemasonry, a
garden full of grottos and a secret passage
from a well. There are several guided tours a
day, but it's best to book ahead (during office
hours, weekdays only) as there is a maximum
of 30 people on each tour. Even further along
the road is the **Palácio de Seteais** (21 923
3200), a luxury hotel and a swish place to
take tea or cocktails.

The commercial centre of Sintra (past the
station in the other direction) has little to
recommend it apart from the excellent **Sintra**

Trips Out of Town

Duas Linhas de História

Two Lines of History ● Dos líneas de ferrocarril con Historia.

Lisbo

Pelas Linhas de Cascais e Sintra poderá percorrer caminhos da História e da Cultura Portuguesas. Viaje com toda a segurança e rapidez de comboio e descubra o prazer de ser turista na região de Lisboa.

Cascai

Take the train along the Cascais and Sintra lines on a journey through Portuguese history and culture. Enjoy your holiday to the full in the safety and comfort offered by Portuguese Railways.

Sintr

Por las líneas de ferrocarril de Cascais y Sintra podrá recorrer caminos de la Historia y de la Cultura Portuguesa. Viaje con toda a seguridad y rapidez en tren descubra el placer de ser turista en a región de Lisboa.

Gabinete de Apoio ao Cliente
Customer Assistance Service

Linha de Cascais: 800 203 067
Linha de Sintra: 800 200 904
Linha de Azambuja: 800 201 820

UNIDADE DE SUBURBANOS DA GRANDE LISBOA

Caminhos de Ferro Portugueses, EP

Museu de Arte Moderna (*see p193*), in a restored casino building.

Near Sintra is the village of **São Pedro de Sintra**, which has better curio and antique shops than Sintra itself, and hosts a bustling market full of food, wickerwork, ceramics and small animals on the second and fourth Sunday of the month. Ask for maps at the Turismo – Sintra is a walker's paradise.

Palácio da Pena
Estrada de Pena (21 910 5340). **Open** *Winter* 10am-5pm (last entry 4.30pm) Tue-Sun; closed Mon. *Summer* 10am-6.30pm (last entry 6pm) Tue-Sun; closed Mon. **Admission** 600$00. **No credit cards**.

Palácio Nacional
Largo da Rainha Dona Amélia (21 910 6840). **Open** 10am-5.30pm (last entry 5pm) Mon, Tue, Thur-Sun; closed Wed. **Admission** 600$00. **No credit cards**.

Where to eat

There's no shortage of over-priced touristy cafés and restaurants, so you only really get value for money if you go upmarket. During the week the set lunches at **Toca do Javali** in São Pedro de Sintra (Rua 1 de Dezembro, 21 923 3503, main courses 2,200$00) are a bargain. The restaurant at **Quinta da Regaleira** (see above, 21 923 1671, main courses 2,800$00, closed Mon, lunch Sun) has lately built up a good reputation for Portuguese and French traditional and nouvelle cuisine.

Getting there

By bus
From Estoril, Stagecoach bus 418; from Cascais, 413 or 417. Journey time: 30mins; price 480$00. Tickets pre-purchased from the Stagecoach stand at Cascais station offer discounts.

By train
From Rossio station. Every 20mins, 6am to 1.30am. Journey time: 45mins; 210$00.

Tourist information

Turismo
Praça da República, 2710 Sintra (21 923 1157/fax 21 923 5176). **Open** *Oct-May* 9am-7pm daily. *June-Sept* 9am-8pm daily.

Queluz

The only thing to see in the otherwise shabby town of Queluz is the palace, a sort of mini-Versailles, but it's definitely worth a half-day trip. The pink 18th-century edifice started life as a royal hunting lodge until, in 1747, Prince Dom Pedro decided he fancied it as a home and

The madly baroque **Palácio de Queluz.**

had it extended and converted into a rococo palace. In 1760, when he married his niece, the future Queen Maria I, he organised operas and chamber concerts for her in the music room. But in 1788, after their son José died of smallpox, she went mad, wandering the corridors tearing her hair and shrieking.

Queluz seemed to attract strange royal women. When the Palácio da Ajuda in Lisbon burned down, the royal family moved here, and interior decoration was taken over by Carlota Joaquina, the grotesquely ugly Spanish wife of Dom João VI. A dwarf, Carlota wandered the corridors wearing a green cloth coat embroidered with gold frogs, her dirty hair entwined with pearls and diamonds, and plotted intrigues. On hot days, she would paddle in the fountains of the formal gardens, full of *azulejos*, topiary and statues.

When the royal family fled to Brazil to escape the French invasion of 1807, they took most of the furniture with them, but the palace has been refurbished to give a fair picture of aristocratic life in the late 18th century. One wing is used to accommodate visiting heads of state and the music room, with its superb acoustics, is often used for concerts as part of the **Sintra Music Festival** (*see p202*).

Palácio de Queluz
2745 Queluz (21 435 0039). **Open** 10am-5pm Wed-Mon. **Admission** 600$00; 300$00 concessions; free under-14s. **No credit cards**.

Where to eat

Cozinha Velha, a privately-run restaurant in the palace's old kitchens (21 435 0232, main courses 3,500$00), serves fine food to the accompaniment of a tinkling harp. The café

Trips Out of Town

inside the palace entrance is less welcoming, but there are a couple of *tascas* across the square at the start of the road into Queluz.

Getting there

By bus
Vimeca (21 435 4210) bus 107 from Marquês de Pombal, journey time 45mins; 340$00; or buses 101, 105 or 163 from Colégio Militar Metro station, journey time 30mins.

By train
From Rossio station, journey time 25mins, then a 15min walk; 170$00.

North of Lisbon

Mafra

The enormous pink marble **Palácio-Convento de Mafra** was begun in 1717 by Dom João V, and paid for with gold from Brazil. The project became ever more elaborate and extravagant as it proceeded, taking 38 years to finish and employing more than 50,000 builders.

Standing 68 metres (234 feet) high and 220 metres (722 feet) long, its 880 rooms and 300 monks' cells have been restored to their original glory. The dome is one of the world's largest,

Vertiginous views of **Sesimbra**. *See p249.*

and the stunning rococo library has a chequered marble floor and over 35,000 leather-bound books (which, unfortunately, rats have been feasting upon).

Many of the other rooms are rather dull, though the monks' pharmacy is quaint with its old medicine jars and bizarre medical instruments. The basilica has 114 bells – the world's largest assemblage – and is famous for its carillon concerts on Sunday afternoons in summer (ask at the Turismo). The monastery was abandoned in 1834 after the dissolution of all religious orders, and the palace closed in 1910 when Portugal's last king, Dom Manuel II, escaped his republican persecutors from here. The adjoining *tapada* (hunting grounds) are worth a visit and include an interesting wolf conservation project, but there's little else of interest to see in town.

Palácio-Convento de Mafra
(261 817 550). **Open** 10am-5pm (last entry 4.30pm) Mon, Wed-Sun; closed Tue. **Admission** 600$00; 300$00 concessions; free under-14s. **Credit** AmEx, MC, V.

Where to eat

The café opposite the palace has local cakes and sandwiches made from Mafra bread. But if you have a car, consider driving to the village of **Negrais**, famed for its *leitão* – suckling pig. It has several restaurants turning out hundreds of the creatures lying snout-first on trays (ask to see the kitchens if you're not squeamish), but locals favour **Caneira** (Avenida General Barnabe, 21 967 0853, main courses 2,000$00; closed Mon), where they eat the ears for starters and wash it all down with fizzy house wine. Or you can drive on to the increasingly touristy fishing village of **Ericeira** for fresh fish; the best restaurants are tucked away in sidestreets.

Getting there

By bus
Mafrense (261 816 159) bus travels to Mafra from Campo Grande bus station in Lisbon. Journey time: 1hr 45mins; 540$00. Or from Sintra bus station; journey time: 45mins; 400$00.

By train
Rossio to Cacém, changing as for Óbidos. Journey time: 1hr 30mins; 350$00.

Tourist information

Turismo
Avenida 25 de Abril, 2640 Mafra (261 812 623). **Open** 9.30am-6pm Mon-Fri; 9.30am-1pm, 2.30-6pm Sat, Sun.

Óbidos

Picture-postcard perfect, this whitewashed village on a hill was a wedding gift from Dom Dinis to his bride Isabel of Aragon in 1282, and remained the personal property of Portugal's queens until 1834.

Beautifully preserved inside the old castle walls, Óbidos is full of pink bougainvillea and window boxes of geraniums, and its houses all have terracotta roofs and trademark ochre or blue bands painted around their base. Though touristy, it is still inhabited by old widows in black scrubbing cobbles, wringing washing or chasing cats away with brooms, and is full of evocative imagery for budding photographers.

The village's five cobbled streets house the old pillory with the town's arms – a fishing net with a drowned person inside (Isabel and Dinis's son was drowned in the Tagus and fished out in a net) – and the Igreja de Santa Maria, where ten-year-old Dom Alfonso V married his eight-year-old wife in 1444. The church has some 17th-century tilework, wooden painted ceilings and panels by Josefa de Óbidos, a Spanish-born artist (1634-84) who moved to the village, and whose dark still lifes are enjoying an international revival. She is buried in the Igreja de São Pedro; some of her works can be seen in the museum. The castle is now a *pousada* but you can walk the walls and try to spot the sea in the distance – Óbidos used to be a port.

Where to eat

The café by the beautifully tiled town gate Porta da Vila serves local pastries. For a first-rate but pricey meal, head for **Alcaide** (Rua Direita, 262 959 220, average 1,900$00, closed Mon); in summer, you may need to book.

Getting there

By bus
Rede Expresso bus from Arco do Cego terminal to Caldas da Rainha. Journey time: 1hr 15mins; 1,050$00.

By train
From Rossio to Cacém (on the Sintra line) then change for slow train to Óbidos (on the Caldas da Rainha line). Journey time: about 2hrs; 850$00.

Tourist information

Turismo
Booth by Porta da Vila, Óbidos (262 959 231). **Open** 9.30am-6pm Mon-Fri; 10am-1pm, 2-6pm Sat, Sun.

South of Lisbon

Sesimbra

Overlooked by a fairytale castle, Sesimbra is a busy fishing village-cum-resort with whitewashed streets leading up from the harbour, where old men in caps and checked shirts gather on the seafront, playing draughts.

Sesimbra is reached by crossing Lisbon's Ponte 25 de Abril and then traversing the Serra da Arrábida. This is a beautiful protected area of towering sandy coves and limestone cliffs covered with pines and thickets of green Mediterranean-style vegetation, which thrive thanks to Arrábida's microclimate.

From Sesimbra you can get a boat to one of the beaches or drive to the sheltered Praia do Portinho da Arrábida where the water is relatively warm and much favoured by snorkellers. If you have time on the way to or from Sesimbra, visit the **Convento da Arrábida** (21 218 0520), a 16th-century Franciscan monastery perched up on the hills with spectacular views, though you must phone ahead to book.

If you are driving, stop on the way back at **Cabo Espichel**, an abandoned convent on a windswept cliff, used by German director Wim Wenders as a location in his *Lisbon Story*. There are plans to turn it into a *pousada*. The 18th-century church is open and full of candles lit by fishermen in front of their favourite saints. Just to add to the eeriness of the place, dinosaur footprints were found on the beach below.

Getting there

By bus
Transportes Sul do Tejo bus (21 275 0064) from Praça de Espanha. Journey time: about 1hr (depending on traffic over bridge); 570$00.

Where to eat

Not surprisingly for a village that supplies fresh fish to posh Lisbon eateries, there are some great seafood restaurants here – try **O Farol** just off the main square (Largo de Marinha, 21 223 3356, main courses 2,600$00, closed Tue).

Tourist information

Turismo
Largo de Marinha 25-27, 2970 Sesimbra (21 223 5743). **Open** *June-Sept* 9am-8pm daily. *Oct-May* 9am-12.30pm, 2-5.30pm daily.

The Alentejo

Forests of cork, ancient stone circles, Portugal's prettiest mountain villages and lots of things to do with stale bread.

After the bustle of the capital or the mayhem of the Algarve, the Alentejo is an almost startlingly restful place to be. This region 'beyond the Tejo', east and south of Lisbon, covers almost a third of Portugal and is one of the poorest and least populated parts of the country. It's divided into two segments: Baixo Alentejo to the south, where there's not much to see at all, and Alto Alentejo to the north, which is studded with interesting things. The central attraction is Évora, the region's capital and a Unesco World Heritage Site. To the east are the 'marble towns' of Estremoz, Borba and Vila Viçosa. Over near the Spanish border are the spectacular fortified hill villages of Marvão and Monsaraz. And dotted here and there, particularly around Évora and Monsaraz, are lots of prehistoric monuments.

Coming from Lisbon, the first thing that hits home is how empty it all is. Roads are clear. The sky is big. The countryside, mostly planted with cork oak, rolls gently for miles. Ancient olive trees growing amid boulders piled just as when the fields were first cleared hint at how long people have worked this land – agriculture arrived in Portugal around 5,000-4,000 BC.

Alentejan red wines are fruity and full-bodied, thanks to the Romans, who first brought vines here – along with olives and irrigation schemes. Julius Caesar colonised Évora in 60 BC and set up huge estates, called *latifúndios*, to make the most of poor soil and scant water. Like the ancient piles of boulders, these estates still exist today.

The Moors arrived in the eighth century and brought with them citrus fruits, rice, cotton and crop rotation. The Alentejo remained under their control a century longer than most of Portugal, but by 1279 they'd been pushed out and Dom Dinis (*see p10*) started building fortresses on the frontier with Spain – such as those at Marvão, Monsaraz, Castelo de Vide and Estremoz. But the Alentejo was to remain a backward area – particularly after the Discoveries turned Portugal's attention out to sea and away from the interior. Only Évora flourished, and that only until Philip II of Spain took control in 1581.

Alentejans carried on working the land on the *latifúndios*, generation after generation, and history pretty much passed them by. This at least gave them time to develop a distinctive regional cuisine, mostly based on the use of pork, garlic, coriander and stale bread. Vegetable soups are common, such as *açorda* – a sort of porridge made with olive oil, garlic and coriander, thickened with stale bread and served with a poached egg on top – or *gaspacho alentejano*, more like a drowned salad than its puréed Spanish cousin. It has stale bread in it too, as does *migas à alentejana*, where the bread is fried and rolled and served with a stew of pork and peppers. *Carne de porco à alentejana* – effectively the region's 'national' dish – is marinated pork stewed with clams. Meals are finished with a sweet, invariably made from almonds, sugar and egg yolks.

In the 1974 Revolution, peasants, tired of what was still essentially feudalism and very possibly also fed up with stale bread, seized the land from its owners and many *latifúndios* were collectivised. Few succeeded as cooperatives, however, and most are now back with their original owners. Meanwhile, droughts, job losses through mechanisation of agriculture and better work opportunities elsewhere have caused many to migrate to Lisbon or abroad. The population has shrunk by nearly half in the last few decades. A backwater the Alentejo always was, and a backwater it remains. That, in a way, is its appeal.

The area is fiercely hot in summer and fearfully cold in winter, but in spring the fields are full of wild flowers and the autumn is mild. These are the best times to visit.

Getting there

By bus

Rede Expresso buses serving major towns in the Alentejo depart from Arco do Cego terminal. Journey time to Évora is 1hr 45mins, the price 1,650$00. For Marvão, bus to Santo António das Areias, then local bus; total journey time 4hrs 15mins, price 2,200$00. For Castelo de Vide, journey time 4hrs 15mins, price 2,100$00. Estremoz: journey time 2hrs, price 1,650$00. Vila Viçosa: journey time 2hrs 40mins, price 1,650$00. For Monsaraz, there are just two direct buses on weekdays to Reguengos, where you change to a local bus; total journey time 2hrs 40mins, price 1,700$00. Most people bussing it to Reguengos go to Évora and then change. A network of local buses run between destinations.

By car

Cross the Ponte 25 de Abril onto the A2 (IP1), which soon mutates into the A6 (IP7), taking you to Évora in an hour if traffic is thin. Alternatively, cross the Ponte Vasco da Gama; the A12 meets the A2 after a few miles. For Monsaraz, follow signs to Beja on the Évora ring road, then bear left after 14km (9 miles) towards Reguengos; Monsaraz is a few miles further on. For Estremoz, Vila Viçosa, Castelo de Vide and Marvão, either pick up the N18 from the Évora ring road, or turn off the A2 earler, outside Montemor-o-Novo, picking up the N4 (IC10) to Estremoz. The N4 continues to Borba, from where it's a short hop to Vila Viçosa; for Castelo de Vide and Marvão take the N18 north from Estremoz to just outside Portalegre, then follow signs.

By train

For Marvão and Castelo de Vide, trains depart Santa Apolónia station for Abrantes, where you change. Total journey time three hours; price first class 2,500$00, second class 1,550$00. For other destinations, catch a ferry from Terreiro do Paço to Barreiro rail station, cost 195$00, then train to Évora, from where local buses go to Estremoz, Vila Viçosa and Monsaraz. Journey time to Évora three hours; price first class 1,450$00, second 990$00.

Évora

The regional capital is the kind of place that strikes fear into the heart of the tourist – so many sights, so little time. A Unesco World Heritage Site, Évora has more listed buildings than anywhere in Portugal, bar Lisbon. Apart from the emblematic Templo Romano, there are warrenous Moorish alleys, medieval city walls, the Romanesque **Sé** (cathedral), a 16th-century aqueduct, lots of Renaissance palaces, some very curious churches, a 19th-century neo-classical theatre, a scattering of significant neolithic sites and plenty of lesser sights.

It's not a big place (population 54,000); most of the action is within a compact and ancient town centre, defined by walls that are in part built over first-century Roman fortifications.

The area was a centre of neolithic activity. The **Cromeleque dos Almendres**, an irregular oval of some 95 stones, is worth a detour – head west on the Lisbon road, turn south for Guadaloupe and follow signs. Other signs point to the equally impressive **Dolmen of Zambujeiro**, Europe's largest.

But it's the **Templo Romano**'s 14 surviving pillars that are the city's icon. They stand on Largo do Conde de Vila Flor in the upper end of the town centre, flanked by the imposing 12th-century Sé, where the flags of Vasco da Gama's ships were blessed in 1497; the former archbishop's palace that now houses the archeological objects and Portuguese and Flemish paintings of the **Museu de Évora**

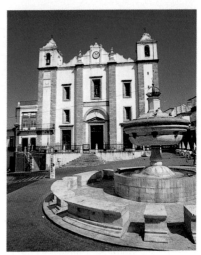

Praça do Giraldo: centre of Évora life.

(Largo Cone Vilaflor, 266 702 604, closed Mon, Tue morning); and the 15th-century Convento dos Lóios – now a top-notch *pousada*.

Downhill from here, past narrow streets with cafés, restaurants and craft shops, is the **Praça do Giraldo,** modern hub of Évora. From here you can strike out to explore the former **Judiaria,** or to witness the arches of the **Aqueduto da Água de Prata** stooping to meet street level in the northern part of town. Or nip over to see the macabre Capela dos Ossos in the **Igreja de São Francisco** (Largo 1° de Maio, 266 704 521), intriguingly constructed from the bones of 5,000 dead monks labelled cheerily in Portuguese: 'We bones here are waiting for yours.' The local Turismo can supply a glossy folder of 'Historical Itineries', organised by period and relentlessly featuring every last thing to see, as well as booking you on tours of neolithic sites.

Where to stay & eat

When it gets too dark to see more sights, head for one of Évora's many restaurants. There are cheap eats on Rua de Pedro Simões, the best being the one with no name save a clockface indicating a quarter to nine (try the *sopa de beldroegas* made from a weed that grows in irrigation channels). But if you have some money to spare, it would be a shame not to visit **O Fialho** (Travessa do Mascarenhas 16, 266 703 079, main courses 4,250$00, closed Mon), whose reputation for traditional Portuguese cuisine is such that people drive all the way

Trips Out of Town

Marvellous **Marvão** – one of Portugal's most picturesque villages.

from Lisbon for dinner. After dinner, there are
a few late bars, such as the **Diplomata Pub**
(Rua do Apóstolo 4, 266 705 675, closed Mon)
or the **Club Dezasseis** round the corner
(Rua do Escrivão da Câmara 16, 266 708 806).

There's no shortage of hotels in Évora,
and the Turismo (*see below*) can help finding
accommodation. If the luxurious **Pousada dos
Lóios** (Largo do Conde de Vilaflor, 266 704 051,
rates 24,500$00-35,300$00) is beyond your
budget, there's the cheaper but charming **Solar
Monfalim** (Largo de Misericórdia 1, 266 750
000/fax 266 742 367, 10,000$00-15,000$00), in a
former palace. It's very central, as is the even
cheaper **Pensão Policarpo**, in an interesting
16th-century townhouse at Rua da Freiria de
Baixo 16 (266 741 176, rates 6,000$00-15,000$00).

Tourist information

Turismo
Praça do Giraldo 73 (266 702 671). **Open** *Nov-Mar*
9am-12.30pm, 2-5.30pm daily. *Apr-Oct* 9am-12.30pm,
2-7pm Mon-Fri; 9am-12.30pm, 2-5.30pm Sat, Sun.

Marvão

Approaching Marvão from the direction of
Évora, emerging from cork forest to catch a
glimpse of the fortifications in the distance,
perched on a huge cliff, it's hard to believe the
place is real. Once inside the walls, the peace
and tidiness of this small village (population
under 1,000) seem equally surreal. It was first
inhabited by Romans, and the forbidding castle
– only taken once, and then through a secret
gate – was built by Dom Dinis in 1229 to beef
up the border against Spain. The views are
extraordinary: rocky slopes tumbling down

savagely below the walls and leagues of
faintly wild country fading into the horizons.

By day tourists clatter round the castle,
inspect the **Museu Municipal** (Largo de Santa
Maria, 245 909 132) and its small ragbag of
historical remnants, and then set off back down
the hill. It's from dusk onwards that this place
is most atmospheric – an eerily silent eyrie,
surrounded by an immense dark.

Where to stay & eat

There are a couple of restaurants and a
convivial bar on the western side of the village.
However, the **Pousada de Santa Maria** (Rua
24 de Janeiro 7, 245 993 201/2, rates 15,300$00-
25,100$00) offers Marvão's one serious dining
option, but at 4,500$00 for a full meal it's pricey,
even given the view. Cheaper, though hardly
bargain, rooms can be had at the comfortable
Pensão Dom Dinis (245 993 236, rates
7,500$00-9,000$00) on Rua Dr Matos
Magalhães. Otherwise, ask at the Turismo
about private rooms.

Tourist information

Marvão Turismo
Largo de Santa Maria (245 993 886). **Open** 9am-
12.30pm, 2-5.30pm daily.

Castelo de Vide

Neither as wildly situated nor as postcard-
perfect as its near neighbour, Castelo de Vide is
Marvão's ever-so-slightly plainer sister. But
what she lacks in looks, this ancient spa town
more than makes up for in character. It spreads
over the slopes below a 14th-century castle, and

has plenty of life – such as a Friday market in Praça Dom Pedro V, mainly selling cooking pots, textiles and unexceptional clothes.

The town's centrepiece is the square containing the 16th-century **Fonte da Vila**, from which locals still fill containers with springwater. The nearby *termas* (spa) is open in summer for treatment of diabetic, kidney and blood-pressure problems. From here, steep cobbled alleys flanked by whitewashed cottages with gothic doorways lead up to the town's 13th-century **Judiaria**. The tiny **synagogue** on the corner of Rua da Fonte and Rua da Judiaria is Portugal's oldest. This medieval enclave is much more interesting than the plain, bulky **castelo**, though the neighbourhood inside it is cute, and contains the **Ramo D'Oliveira** (Rua Direita do Castelo 27, 919 186 125) – a more-interesting-than-usual craft shop owned by Englishwoman Christine Schreck, housed in what was the town jail until 1967.

Where to stay & eat

There are assorted cafés and restaurants on Rua de Bartolomeu Álvares da Santa. **Marino's** (Praça Dom Pedro V, 245 901 408, main courses 3,000$00) offers Italian food. For more traditional Portuguese fare, and a reasonably priced bed for the night, try the well-equipped **Casa do Parque** (Avenida da Aramenha 37, 245 901 250, rates 4,500$00-10,000$00, main courses 1,300$00, restaurant closed Tue).

Tourist information

Castelo de Vide Turismo
Rua Bartolomeu Álvares da Santa (245 901 361). **Open** *Oct-June* 9am-12.30pm, 2-5.30pm daily. *July-Sept* 9am-12.30pm, 2-7pm daily.

Estremoz

The centre of Estremoz, largest of the Alentejo's 'marble towns', is a giant square. The Rossio Marquês de Pombal might as well have been dropped in here from Moscow; it's so big that its lively Saturday morning market – goat's cheese, baby ducks, watermelons, sheepskin slippers, peasants in flat caps – seems to huddle in one corner to keep warm. Around the edges are dotted: an 18th-century town hall; a **Museu Rural** full of folk costumes, cork products and tiny figures and furniture made by shepherds as thank-you presents for doctors; and a **Museu de Ciências da Terra** (information 268 339 214) where marble-quarrying paraphernalia clutters a 16th-century cloister.

The palace on the fortified hill at the town's western extremity was once a palace of Dom

Dinis. Then it was an ammunition dump for 350 years until the contents blew up and destroyed most of it. Dom João V restored it for use as an armoury. And now it's the **Pousada Rainha Santa Isabel** (*see below*), a hotel so grand as to be pompous, though non-guests can still peer around and climb the 27-metre tower.

Where to stay & eat

On a normal night there's a bit of life in the cafés and tascas along the western side of Rossio – the **Águias d'Ouro** (268 337 030, main courses 3,500$00) is a good spot to dine – and along Rua do Almeida. The **Adega do Isaias** at No.21 (268 322 318, main courses 3,000$00, closed Sun) specialises in hearty outdoor grills, big communal tables and brimming jugs of wine.

At the **Pousada Rainha Santa Isabel** (Largo de Dom Dinis, 268 332 075, rates 24,900$00-36,400$00) one may quite literally live like a king. In striking contrast, the **Pensão Estremoz** at Rossio 14 (268 322 326, rates 3,000$00-10,000$00) offers tatty but cheap rooms overlooking the square. **Pensão Restaurante Mateus** (268 322 226, rates 3,500$00-7,000$00) at Rua do Almeida 39/41 is a slightly smarter option, with a restaurant.

Tourist information

Turismo
Largo da República 26 (268 333 541). **Open** 9.30am-12.30pm, 2-6pm daily.

Vila Viçosa

This is marble country, and the road from Estremoz through **Borba** and its many antique shops to Vila Viçosa passes several quarries. They're worth a look. The marble is cut out in huge blocks, leaving gaping cubist holes in the ground, while all around red earth contrasts with an indigo sky.

Marble can be made into whitewash, slapped annually on houses across the Alentejo. Colours are created by adding oxides. Blue is supposed to keep flies away, yellow holds fever at bay. Most of the small, white houses in Vila Viçosa are detailed in one powdery hue or the other. Windows and doorways are framed in marble, and wrought-iron balconies are de rigueur.

An equestrian statue of Dom João IV stands in the broad square, Praça da República, before the **Paço Ducal** (268 980 659, closed Mon). The guided tour of this 16th-century pile costs 1,000$00, lasts one hour and is in Portuguese only. To see the Armoury (500$00), the collection of carriages (300$00) or Treasury

Trips Out of Town

Marble town: **Estremoz**. *See p253.*

(500$00) costs extra time and money. Most of this stuff is pretty dull. The Dukes of Braganza once lived here, having moved from Dom Dinis' **castelo** up the road. That's free to see – if you don't bother with the Museu da Caça (Hunting Museum) – and has the 15th-century Igreja de Nossa Senhora da Conceição and a few inhabited streets within its walls. From the top of these you can look north over the 2,000-hectare royal hunting ground where most of the museum's exhibits were bagged.

Where to stay & eat

Within a short of stroll of the Paço Ducal, both **O Forno** (Rua Cristovão Brito Pereira 13, 268 999 797, main courses 1,200$00, closed Sun) and **A Restauração** (Praça da República, 268 980 256, main courses 1,400$00, closed Mon) offer traditional Alentejo food. Cheapish rooms may be found in the Praça at No.25 in the **Hospedaria Dom Carlos** (268 980 318, rates 4,000$00-7,000$00). Apart from private rooms – ask at the Turismo (*see below*) – most of the other accommodation here is upmarket: the **Casa de Peixinhos** on the road out to Borba (268 980 472, rates 14,000$00-17,500$00) is a 17th-century manor house; and next door to the Paço Ducal, the **Pousada de Dom João IV** (268 980 742, rates 18,800$000-31,900$00) in the former Convento das Chagas.

Tourist information

Turismo
Praça da República 34 (268 881 101). **Open** 9am-5.30pm daily.

Sometimes referred to as the Ninho das Águias or Eagle's Nest, Monsaraz (not to be confused with the nearby but more prosaic Reguengos de Monsaraz) vies with Marvão for the title of Portugal's most picturesque fortified village. It

perches on the top of a hill in the middle of a plain, and is visible for miles around, looming over a landscape that is dotted with cork oaks, olive trees and neolithic standing stones. There were Iron Age settlements round here too, and the Romans, Visigoths and Moors all had their turn before crusader Geraldo sem Pavor (Fearless Gerald) took the town in 1167. Monsaraz was given to the Knights Templar in 1232 and the **castle** was built in 1310 by Dom Dinis, as were most of the fortifications in this ancient border zone.

The village, most of which can be seen in half an hour, sits entirely within the mid-17th-century walls. The **Igreja Matriz de Santa Maria do Castelo** dominates the main square, while the castle anchors the south-western end.

Signposted on the road from Telheiro to Onteiro is the neolithic **Menhir de Bulhoa**, and the **Cromeleque do Xarêz**, a small stone 'circle' (actually a rectangle) is on the right, about five kilometres downhill from Monsaraz on the Mourão road. Off the Reguengos road, the **Anta do Olival da Pega**, a 3,000-year-old dolmen surrounded by old olive trees, is also signposted. Ask at the Turismo (*see below*) for details of other Stone Age sites.

Where to stay & eat

Lumumba (Rua Direita 12, 266 557 121, main courses 1,600$00) is one of the town's few restaurants. Despite the African-sounding name, its speciality is a very Portuguese lamb stew (*sopa de borrego*). For an unexpectedly classy dining option head down the hill in the direction of Reguengos to the nearby village of Telheiro. In an old olive oil factory, with a genial bar and cosmopolitan staff, **Sem Fim** (Rua das Flores 6, Telheiro, 266 557 471, main courses 2,000$00, closed Mon-Wed) is probably the only restaurant in the entire region with vegetarian choices among the Alentejan specialities.

The best accommodation in the area is also down on the plain. The **Turismo de Habitação Monte Saraz** (266 557 385, rate 19,000$00) is a group of beautifully converted farmhouses with self-catering apartments and a small swimming pool, signposted from the Reguengos road. Up in the village, the main drag is strewn with *pensões*, such as the one run by **Dona Antónia** (Rua Direita 25, 266 557 142, rate 6,000$00); the Turismo can supply information about private rooms.

Tourist information

Turismo
Praça Dom Nuno Álvares Pereira 5 (266 557 136). **Open** 10am-1pm, 2-5.30pm daily.

The Algarve

Busy beaches, secluded coves, and an awful lot of golfing.

The Algarve's allure goes a lot further than the delights of sun and sand or sweating through a paperback by the pool. Much of this allure stems from the Algarve's location. A compact, 150-kilometre (95-mile) long, south-facing amphitheatre tucked into the extreme southwest corner of the continent, it is profoundly influenced by North Africa as well as Europe, and by the Mediterranean as well as the Atlantic.

The Algarve has a Mediterranean-type climate. Over 3,000 hours of annual sunshine is a statistic the local tourist board likes to trot out. What that actually means is wall-to-wall blue skies for much of the year. Even in winter, technically the wet season, there are often prolonged periods of gloriously sunny weather. In midsummer, Atlantic breezes keep the thermometer from rising to the oven temperatures common in neighbouring Andalusia. It is because of the Atlantic that the Algarve's spectacular beaches are so sandy and it is the open Atlantic, not the almost tideless Mediterranean, that washes them clean. But it is from the Mediterranean basin that most of the Algarve's human influences have come – until the late-20th century invasion of northern European tourists, that is.

Neolithic cultures infiltrated from the flatlands of Spain to the east, rather than across the northern hills that separate the Algarve from the rest of Portugal and still represent a cultural divide of sorts. By about 600 BC, the indigenous Celto-Iberians were joined from the far end of the Med by seafaring Phoenicians who set up trading settlements. Ancient Greeks also came to compete for local raw materials until both Phoenicians and Greeks lost out to the Carthaginians. Then came the Romans, bringing with them a new religion and a new language, which survived, albeit in it a somewhat adapted form, the next great wave of foreigners: the Moors who occupied the Algarve from the eighth to the 12th centuries.

The name Algarve is a derivation of the Arabic 'Al-Gharb' meaning 'the west'. Al-Gharb was an outpost west of the western Islamic capital, Córdoba. The Moorish legacy in the Algarve well outlasted the medieval Christian reconquest and indeed much remains today, visible in village alleyways and castle ruins.

During Portugal's most illustrious period, the 15th-century Age of Discovery, the Algarve played a central role. Many of those who manned Henry the Navigator's vessels on their voyages into the unknown were Algarvians, the leathery likes of whom you see every day mending nets on the Algarve's beaches.

There is remarkable diversity in this small region. Charmingly simple villages remain unhumbled by seriously sophisticated resorts. The opulent villas and manicured greens of the exclusive golf estates west of Faro seem light years away from the north-eastern hill region, one of Portugal's most sparsely populated areas, where modernisation has had little impact; but it's actually less than an hour's drive along winding roads. Back at the coast, at last count golfers had the choice of 16 golf complexes, offering a challenge to all level of players. Most are pricey yet busy, especially during the main golfing season, which is from October to May.

The Algarve qualifies as an all-year-round destination. Spring starts in January and February, when the gently sloping land between the coast and the hills is awash with almond blossom and the carousels at Faro international airport are full of golf bags. In March and April, migrating birds flock in from Africa. The first flurry of human summer visitors arrives at Easter, mostly from chilly northern Europe. The invasion steadily grows to reach its peak in July, when the schools in the UK break up, and in August, when Lisbon and the cities of the north of Portugal disgorge their office and factory workers onto the southern shores. Mind you, even in August it remains possible to find patches of sand big enough to swing a cat without scratching bare boobs – there are just so many beaches, ranging from vast expanses of exposed sand to intimate coves. The tempo begins to subside in September – not before time for the tour reps and waiters who are starting to look as frazzled as the countryside. The first revitalising rains come in the mild month of October. In November, many shutters come down and the Algarve has a brief period of repose – until almond blossom time.

TOURIST INFORMATION

There are tourist information offices (*turismos*) in all the main Algarve towns, but they do not have uniform open hours. Most are open 9.30am-1pm and 2pm-5pm from September to April, closing two hours later in summer.

Getting there

By bus

Rede Expresso (21 354 5439) and Eva Turismo (21 314 7710) run regular, comfortable services from Lisbon every day. Travel times vary, but it is about four hours by bus to Albufeira, five or more to the other main towns. Buses leave from the Arco do Cego bus station at Avenida Duque de Ávila.

By car

The quickest way by car is on the A2 and IC1 past Grândola and Ourique. After about 275km you emerge just north of Albufeira and have the choice of turning east on to the Via do Infante motorway to Faro (295km/183 miles) and Tavira (320km/198 miles), or west to Portimão (280km/174 miles), Lagos (300km/186 miles) and Sagres (340km/211 miles).

By train

Catch a **ferry** from Terreiro do Paço to Barreiro rail station, cost 195$00. There are daily train services (21 888 4025) from Barreiro station (on the other side of the Tagus from Lisbon) to Tunes, a junction roughly midway between Faro and Portimão. That connects with the trans-Algarve line running from the Spanish border town of Vila Real de Santo António to Lagos.

By plane

The Algarve is an easy place to reach at any time of the year. TAP Air Portugal (flight information 21 354 5439) has daily services from Lisbon to Faro.

Tavira

Situated on the banks of Gilhão river in the eastern Algarve, Tavira has a history that stretches back to well before Roman times. Its heyday was the 15th and 16th centuries, when it rose in importance as a commercial port, exporting salt, wine and dried fish to Africa and north-western Europe. Since then, however, Tavira has repeatedly lost out.

A bubonic plague epidemic in 1665 wiped out much of the population. The great earthquake of 1755 destroyed most of its buildings. The gradual silting up of the Gilhão estuary closed the port to merchant ships. It continued to flourish as a major tuna fishing centre, but then the great shoals of migrating tuna disappeared from Tavira waters. The local canning industry collapsed. By then tourism was starting to take over from fishing and farming along the Algarve, but nearly all the development was to the west of Faro, not to the east. Tavira had lost out yet again. That is what makes it such a placid and picturesque place to visit today.

Places worth a look include the seven-arch Roman bridge spanning the river and the **Igreja de Santa Maria do Castelo** (Largo Dr Jorge Correia). The neighbouring castle ruins have views over the town's 36 other churches

and its characteristic four-sided rooftops to the salt pans and the port that once was. Beyond lies Ilha de Tavira (Tavira Island), a long sand-spit with an attractive beach on the open sea side.

Where to stay & eat

The four-star **Hotel Vila Galé Albacora** (Rua Quatro Águas, 281 380 800, rates 8,700$00-37,300$00), a ten-minute drive from the town centre, faces Ilha de Tavira. A cheaper and more central option is **Residencial Máres** (Rua José Pires Padinha 134-140, 281 325 815, rates 5,000$00-16,000$00). **Restaurante Bica** (Rua Almirante Cândido dos Reis 22, 281 323 843) has a good reputation among locals as well as tourists for inexpensive traditional food.

Tourist information

Turismo

Rua da Galeria 9 (281 322 511).

Faro

Faro is the capital of the Algarve and the gateway for all travellers arriving by air. A glimpse through the cabin window as the plane comes into land is all most foreign visitors ever see of it. The international airport is just west of the town. Further west along the coast is where most arriving holidaymakers are heading. The only thing to draw them back into the city is the old, walled section of an otherwise ordinary provincial centre.

The old city is best entered through the **Arco da Vila**, an Italian renaissance archway next to the tourist information office in a corner of the square at Faro's little harbour. The Romanesque-Gothic **Sé** (Largo da Sé) was originally built in 1251, probably on the site of a Roman temple and a Moorish mosque, and had to be extensively rebuilt after the great earthquake of 1755. The nearby Convento de Nossa Senhora da Assunção was occupied by nuns for 300 years from the 16th century. For many years thereafter it functioned as a cork factory. At present it houses the clumsily named **Museu Arqueólogica e Lapidar Infante Dom Henrique** (Prince Henry Archaeological and Lapidary Museum, Largo Dom Afonso III, 289 870 870) the largest and most interesting museum in the Algarve.

The old city sits next to the Ria Formosa nature reserve, a network of low-lying islets and sand spits in shallow, lagoon waters, which harbours enormous numbers of breeding, wintering and migrating birds.

Albufeira – the onetime fishing village is now a magnet for package tourists.

Where to stay & eat

Hotel Eva (Avenida da República, 289 803 354, rates 14,900$00-25,500$00), next to the harbour, has the best view in town. Just a short walk away but at the other end of the price range is the **Residencial Madalena** (Rua Conselheiro Bivar 109, 289 805 806, rates 4,500$00-9,000$00). **Restaurante Baia** (Largo Silva Nobre 7, closed Sun) has a wide choice of inexpensive dishes, including seafood. The charmingly old-fashioned **Café Aliança** (Praça Francisco Dom Gomes, 289 820 810) is good for light refreshments.

Tourist information

Turismo

Rua da Misericórdia 8, (289 803 604/289 800 400). This and its branch in the airport arrivals hall (289 818 582) are open every day, with no lunch break.

Albufeira

You love it or hate it. The Algarve's most tourist-intensive town, with its piled-up acres of whitewashed holiday apartments overlooking a long sandy beach, welcomes package holidaymakers with open arms. There are restaurants, cafés, bars and discos galore. There is Bass, Boddington's Bitter, Newcastle Brown, Beamish, Budweiser, burgers and butties – all

at competitive prices. There are jugs of sangria for those who are under the impression that the Algarve is a Spanish island. Where better to watch English football live on the giant screen? Happy hours, karaoke, quiz nights, free entry passes for the girls, triple measures of shorts, shots, shooters and slammers for the boys. And fear not: there are full English breakfasts to help with the hangovers, for those able to get up in the morning.

Lest you think that anything less than the full Monty of holiday naff is on offer, hear this: near a stretch of road known locally as 'the Strip', bullfights and bingo share the same premises. Much of the after-dark action is along the aforementioned 'Strip' or in the vicinity of the main square in the old section of town. Both places are no further than a Frisbee throw from Albufeira's most central and popular beaches, the venues for much of the daytime action. For those with wheels who would prefer less crowded conditions, the choice includes several kilometres of uninterrupted sand known as **Praia da Falésia** to the east, or more than half a dozen bays and coves, ideal for swimming, snorkelling or scuba diving, to the west.

The main Lisbon-Algarve highway joins the trans-Algarve motorway just north of Albufeira, which is almost exactly midway along Portugal's south coast. So, whether you love it or hate it, it's an easy place to get to and just as easy to leave.

Where to stay & eat

The **Cerro Alagoa** (Rua do Município, 289 583 100, rates 11,100$00-29,350$00) is the best centrally located hotel. **Pensão Silva** (Rua 5 de Outubro, 289 512 669, rates 5,000$00-14,000$00) is near the centre of the old town and the beach. A **Lagosteira** (289 501 679) near the Sheraton Hotel in Açoteias, and A **Ruina** (289 512 094) right next to Fishermen's beach are better (and a bit pricier) than the many run-of-the-mill restaurants.

Tourist information

Turismo
Rua 5 de Outubro 8 (289 585 279).
This office is open daily, but closes for lunch 12.30-1.30pm from September until April, and closes at 12.30pm at weekends.

Silves & Portimão

Silves, nowadays a quiet market town surrounded by orange orchards, was the venue for medieval sieges and pitched battles between Moors and crusaders. They took place in and around the red sandstone **castelo** that hangs over the town looking neat enough to grace a chocolate box lid. The rowdiest event in modern times is the annual Silves beer festival, held in July. Even that has now been banished from the castle grounds after years of complaints.

The castle, and the modest **Sé** (cathedral) next to it where several crusaders are buried, are the town's buildings of historical interest. From the battlements you have a view of the surrounding countryside. It was from here that the Moors watched as a fleet of ships full of crusaders sailed up the Arade river in 1189.

Only low-draught sightseeing boats make it all the way up to Silves from **Portimão** at the mouth of the Arade nowadays. Portimão, the Algarve's second-largest town, can be recommended as a place to shop. It is not an attractive town, though the municipal authorities are now tarting up the riverfront. One of its few attractions are the fish restaurants strung out along and just behind the quayside by the old iron bridge across the river. The massive beach at **Praia da Rocha**, a suburb of Portimão, is a 15- or 20-minute drive from Silves, as are an assortment of beaches in the vicinity of **Carvoeiro**, one of the Algarve's most popular villa holiday neighbourhoods.

A drive northwards from Silves up into the hills forested with pine, eucalyptus and cork oak, will take you in less than an hour to the spa village of **Caldas**, the market town of **Monchique**, and the Algarve's highest point,

Fóia, from where on a clear day you can survey the coastline stretching all the way from Sagres to Albufeira.

Where to stay & eat

The only hotel in Silves is the **Colina dos Mouros** (Pocinho Santo, 282 440 420, rates 6,250$00-18,500$00) on the south side of the river. A cheap alternative is **Residencial Sousa** (Rua Samora Barros 17, 282 442 502, rates 2,500$00-6,000$00). Easily the best-known restaurant in Silves is **Marisqueira Rui** (Rua Comendador Vilarinho, 282 442 682, closed Tue), near the Turismo. It's famous for its shellfish and always busy.

Tourist information

Turismo
Rua 25 de Abril (282 442 255).

Lagos

Discerning visitors like Lagos because it embraces tourism without compromising too much on its traditional character and reputation as a place of historic importance. It is a picturesque, easygoing place where nothing moves too fast. The only new-fangled thing about it is its marina.

Lagos has been big on seafaring ever since Prince Henry the Navigator had ships built and victualled here for voyages of discovery to the Atlantic islands and down the west coast of Africa in the 15th century. There is a statue of him in one of the main squares – Lagos is big on statues.

Men in marble are not the only ones hanging around the town centre. There is a good choice of street cafés by day and bars and restaurants by night. The best place for lolling about on the sand is not the long, golden strand sweeping around the east side of the bay, nor on the little beach by the fort at the entrance to the harbour. It is on **Praia D'Ana** or **Porto de Mós**, beaches on either side of the spectacular Ponta da Piedade headland just south of the town, only a short drive or sightseeing boat ride away.

Lagos (pronounced lahgosh, not laygos) is big on cultural events, too; the **Centro Cultural** (Rua Lançarote de Freitas 7, 282 770 450) has a lively calendar of musical performances. The **Museu Municipal** (Rua General Alberto da Silveira, 282 762 310) houses an eclectic jumble of items dating from Roman times to the fairly recent past. A tour of the museum has an unexpected and brilliant ending – you emerge into the adjacent

Lagos – resisting erosion.

Igreja de António and an astonishing display of gold-leaf baroque gone barmy.

If you want a break from all this excitement, head west to **Luz**, **Burgau** or **Salema**, villages with family beaches, or on to the wild west coast where some of the most stunning beaches are surprisingly accessible.

Where to stay & eat

It is wise to book well in advance for any type of accommodation in the Lagos area, especially in centrally located places like the four-star **Hotel Lagos** (Rua António Crisogono dos Santos, 282 769 967, rates 7,440$00-28,815$00), or **Pensão Caravela** (8 Rua 25 de Abril, 282 763361, rates 3,500$00-6,500$00). Rua 25 de Abril is one of the main streets for bars and restaurants, but for a special night out savour the international fare in the British-run **O Trovador** (282 761 792, main courses 4,500$00, closed Mon, Sun), near the Hotel Lagos.

Tourist information

Turismo
Rua Vasco da Gama (282 763 031).
Open daily in summer, but closed at weekends from November until April.

Sagres

A steady stream of travellers from around the globe come to the tacky village of Sagres and on to the sturdy lighthouse at **Cabo de São Vincent** (Cape St Vincent) because their location, at the extreme southwest corner of Portugal and Europe, used to be regarded as literally the edge of the earth. It was here that Prince Henry the Navigator came in 1419, at the age of 25, to devote his life to pushing back the frontiers of the known world. Long before him the Romans had called this Promitorium Sacrum, the sacred cape. Too bad the Portuguese authorities do not show more respect for the place today.

Henry was by all accounts a zealot who surrounded himself with some of the most gifted technical and scientific brains of his era. He is said to have had a 'school of navigation' in the vicinity of Sagres, which legend places within the much renovated ramparts of the **Fortaleza de Sagres**. Having come this far (there is a fairly frequent bus service from Lagos, the last at 7.30pm), a visit to the Fortaleza is almost mandatory. Unfortunately, apart from the spectacular view of the mighty arc of cliffs linking the two headlands and a starkly simple little chapel, there is not much here that Henry would recognise. Cabo de São Vicente is a six-kilometre (three-and-a-half-mile) walk or drive from Sagres; the trip ends at the lighthouse, one of most powerful and best-known in Europe.

Where to stay & eat

The top spot is the **Pousada do Infante** (Ponte de Atalaia, 282 624 222, rates 16,300$00-26,900$00), but if you are on a tight budget you can get a room in a private house for 3,000$00-6,000$00 (from Turinfo, Praça da República, 282 620 003). For a reasonably priced restaurant with a view, there is none better than **A Tasca** (Rua das Naus, 282 624 177, closed Sat) down by the harbour.

Tourist information

Turismo
Rua Comandante Matoso (282 624 873).
This office is closed on Monday.

Coimbra

Roman ruins, a medieval university, and one of the world's great love stories.

The Romans built the settlement from which Coimbra takes its name, but the town is best known for its medieval university. Much of the academic quarter was flattened by the Salazar regime and replaced by fascist bombast, but architectural gems remain. Like most university towns, Coimbra has a split personality. In term time it's abuzz, above all during the mayhem of May's Queima das Fitas celebrations, when students burn their faculty ribbons to mark the end of the academic year. But at weekends, when the students have gone home to their parents, it has an air of sleepy provincialism.

Coimbra changed hands several times during the Reconquest. But when Afonso Henriques was proclaimed king in 1139, it became the capital of the new kingdom (until 1385). Work soon began on what is now the **Sé Velha**. The Romanesque portal dates from this period; in the cloisters Gothic predominates. The **Igreja de Santa Cruz** is older, founded in 1131, but much of it was built later, including the 16th-century west front and cloisters.

Coimbra was the setting for what became one of the world's most celebrated love stories. Inês de Castro, a Spanish noblewoman, arrived after her cousin Constanza married the crown prince, later Dom Pedro I, in 1340. The prince fell for Inês and, though his father Dom Afonso I exiled her, when Constanza died in 1345 Pedro recalled Inês. She bore him several children out of wedlock – though he later claimed they had married in secret – but there was constant scheming against her by nobles. In 1355 she was murdered, reputedly in the garden of the Quinta das Lágrimas (Estate of Tears), near the **Igreja de Santa Clara-a-Velha** (just across the bridge from town), where she was later buried. When Pedro became king, he had her killers executed and enthroned her disinterred corpse, forcing his court to pay homage. Her remains were later moved to the monastery of Alcobaça; Pedro's tomb was built facing hers so that the first thing they would see at the Resurrection would be each other.

The story adds to the romantic aura of Santa Clara-a-Velha. The church, with its beautiful rose window, is all that remains of a 13th-century convent that is disappearing into silt borne by the Mondego river. Things were so bad by the 17th century that Santa Clara-a-Nova was built up the hill.

Meanwhile, Portugal's only **university** had arrived (founded in 1290 in Lisbon but moved in 1308). The old buildings frame the quadrangle that you enter through the iron gate on Largo Porta Férrea. Worth a visit are the **Sala dos Capelos** with its wooden ceiling panels and the **Capela Universitária** with its 17th-century *azulejos*. Best of all is the **Biblioteca Joanina** (ring the bell to enter), whose baroque gilt decor is evidence of the rich Brazil trade.

The university soon became a bastion of conservatism and later a seat of the Inquisition. Under the Marquês de Pombal, the local bishop was arrested and education reformed. He also founded the delightful **Jardim Botânico** (botanical gardens).

The university was reformed again in the 1830s, but remained as a brake on change, its graduates opposing mass education. Alumni include poet Luís de Camões and Nobel Prize-winning medic Egas Moniz, but most famous is future dictator António Oliveira Salazar, who taught here before becoming a minister in 1928.

Today, the university is far exceeded by Lisbon in terms of student numbers and often quality, but Coimbra remains one of a handful of towns that provide a cultural counterweight to the capital. Another unique feature is its own style of fado, sung solely by male students or alumni. Ask at the *turismo* where it's on.

Among other sights, the **Museu Nacional Machado de Castro**, in a former archbishop's palace, is one of the country's most important museums., with Portuguese and Flemish art from the 15th to 18th century, ceramics from the 17th to 19th century, 18th-century architects' drawings and *azulejos*, gold- and silverwork, and embroidered vestments. Don't miss the Roman *cryptoporticus* – underground passages with Visigothic and Roman artefacts on show.

Conímbriga, Portugal's largest Roman site, is 16 kilometres (10 miles) from the modern town. An on-site museum provides information.

In Coimbra, the *turismo* organises themed walking tours in town on the last Sunday of the month from March to December. You can take boat trips on the Mondego all year round with **Basófias** (Parque Dr Manuel Braga, 239 826 815). In summer, boats depart at 3pm, 4.30pm and 6pm Tuesday to Sunday, with trips lasting one hour, 15 minutes.

Trips Out of Town

Conímbriga

(Museu Monográfico 239 941 177). **Open** *Site* Mar-Sept 9am-8pm daily. Oct-Feb 9am-6pm daily.
Museum Mar-Sept 10am-8pm Tue-Sun; closed Mon; Oct-Feb 10am-6pm Tue-Sun; closed Mon. **Admission** museum 600$00; 260$00-300$00 concessions; free under-14s. **No credit cards.**

Jardim Botânico

(239 822 897/fax 239 820 780). **Open** *Oct-Mar* 9am-5.30pm daily. *Apr-Sept* 9am-8pm daily. **Admission** *Garden* free. *Greenhouses* 300$00; 150$00 concessions; free under-6s. *Guided tours* (book in advance by fax) 400$00; 200$00 concessions. **No credit cards.**

Museu Nacional Machado de Castro

Largo Dr José Rodrigues (239 823 727). **Open** 9.30am-noon, 2-5pm Tue-Sun; closed Mon. Partly closed for renovation from the end of 2001. **Admission** 350$00; 250$00 concession; free under-14s; free for all Sun mornings. **No credit cards.**

Sé Velha

(239 825 273). **Open** 10am-6pm Mon-Thur, Sat; 2-6pm Fri; closed Sun. **Admission** *Sé* free. *Cloisters* 150$00; 100$00 concessions. **No credit cards.**

Velha Universidade

(239 859 800). **Open** 9.30am-noon, 2-5pm daily. **Admission** 500$00; 250$00 concessions; free teachers and students. **Admission** per building 250$00; 125$00 concessions. **No credit cards.**

Where to eat

On Largo da Portagem, **Café Montanha** (239 823 475) has snacks but **Briosa** (239 824 238) is best for regional pastries. By the river, **Pistrina** (Avenida Emídio Navarro 44, 239 822 444) has a good afternoon vibe. At weekends the Solum area near the municipal stadium is lively. Whole families gather on the esplanade of the **Bar São José** (Centro Girassolum, 239 402 190).

There are lots of cheap eateries in the Baixa, in Rua Direita. A step up is **Zé Manel dos Ossos** (Beco do Forno 12, 239 823 790, main courses 1,500$00, closed dinner Sat, all Sun). For a swisher setting, **Dom Pedro** (Avenida Emídio Navarro 58, 239 829 108, main courses 2,700$00), serves fondue, steak and lobster.

For something different, **Toscana** (Avenida Conego Urbano Duarte 6, 239 405 792, main courses 1,350$00, closed Sun), has 19 kinds of pizza plus vegetarian specials. By the Botanical Gardens, **A Taberna** (Rua dos Combatentes da Grande Guerra 86, 239 716 265, main courses 2,800$00, closed Sat) is famed for hearty dishes such as roast kid. There are several good places on Rua do Brasil. **A Pharmácia** at No.96 (239 404 609, main courses 1,550$00, closed Tue) also has fado after 11pm, as does its branch at

No.81. In Solum **Piscinas** (Rua Dom Manuel I, 239 717 013, main courses 1,850$00, closed Mon) offers steak and seafood. Opposite Santa Clara-a-Velha, **O Alfredo** (Avenida João das Regras 32, 239 441 522, main courses 1,600$00) also does meat and fish.

For a nightcap, the hip **Galeria-Bar Santa Clara** (Rua António Augusto Gonçalves 67, 239 441 657), overlooks Santa Clara-a-Velha.

Where to stay

The **Astória** (Avenida Emídio Navarro 21, 239 853 020, rates 13,000$00-26,000$00) is a classy riverfront option. A little cheaper are **Pensão Residencial Jardim** (No. 65, 239 825 204, rate 7,500$00), **Hotel Ibis** (No. 70, 239 852 130, rates 7,300$00-8,900$00) and **Residencia Coimbra** (Rua das Azeiteiras 55, 239 837 996/, rates 5,000$00-8,000$00). Among the cheapies, all rooms at the **Dómus** (Rua Adelino Veiga 62, 239 828 584, rates 3,500$00-7,500$00) and the nearby **Moderna** (No. 49, 239 825 413, rates 4,000$00-9,000$00) have heating/AC. But the **Flôr de Coimbra** (Rua do Poço 5, 239 823 865, rates 3,000$00-7,000$00) is the best value. Its owners are doing up the tatty rooms and serve meals (1,000$00), with a daily vegetarian option.

Getting there

By bus

Several companies run express services from Lisbon. Rodoviário de Lisboa (21 354 5439) has several daily services from Arco Cego terminal, taking 2hrs 20mins. AVIC Mondego (239 823 769) runs buses direct to **Conímbriga** at 9.05am and 9.35am Mon-Fri, 9.35am Sat, Sun, from the Centro Comercial Arnado on Rua Manuel Rodrigues, near Coimbra A rail station. To return, buses leave Conímbriga at 1pm and 6pm Mon-Sat; 6pm Sun.

By car

From Lisbon, take the A1 (Auto-Estrada do Norte) toll road. Signs clearly indicate Coimbra exit.

By train

Half a dozen Alfa or Intercidades express services daily from Lisbon's Santa Apolónia or Gare do Oriente to Coimbra B. Change platforms and wait for a local train to Coimbra A; no new ticket needed.

Tourist information

Região de Turismo do Centro

Largo da Portagem (239 855 930/fax 239 825 576/www.turismo-centro.pt). **Open** 9am-12.30pm, 2-5.30pm Mon-Fri; 10am-1pm, 2.30-5.30pm Sat, Sun.

Posto Municipal de Turismo

Largo Dom Dinis (239 832 591). **Open** 9am-6pm Mon-Fri, 9am-12.30pm, 2-5.30pm Sat, Sun. **Branch**: Praça da República (239 833 202).

Trips Out of Town

Oporto

Port, football, and lots of alleys to explore – Oporto isn't just a load of old tripe.

A millennium or two ago, there was a Lusitanian settlement called Cale on the left bank of the river Douro – an important crossing-point on the road between Lisbon and Braga – and later another called Portus on the opposite bank. Portus-Cale became capital of the county of Portucalia, and it was from here that Alfonso Henriques launched the Christian reconquest of what became known as Portugal. So in many ways Oporto is the cradle of the nation.

Today, little love is lost between Lisbon and Oporto. There's precious little to-ing and fro-ing and vile slurs are exchanged. Lisboetas traditionally diss the citizens of Oporto as tripeiros – tripe-eaters – while doing their best to forget that for five years until 2000 FC Porto prevented Sporting or Benfica from winning a league title. Portuenses return the compliment by referring to lisboetas as *alfacinhas* or lettuce nibblers, and southerners in general as mouros or Moors. Oporto's 2001 stint as European Capital of Culture is an undisguised bid to catch up with the capital in terms of infrastructure, but it's gone a little askew. The cultural programme is impressive but much of the city centre will be a building site until well into 2002 as the Metro and other projects are completed.

Sightseeing

In bare essentials Oporto doesn't sound radically different from Lisbon: a hilly city centred on the north bank of a river spanned by famous bridges, its western outskirts stretching downstream to seaside towns at the river mouth. But it doesn't take much more than a glance at the splendid view of Oporto afforded from the left side of the train as it sweeps in from Lisbon to see that Portugal's second city is a somewhat different proposition.

For a start, it is much smaller – the population is around 325,000. The river is in a narrow gorge rather than a vast estuary, spanned by an assortment of bridges including the extraordinary two-level **Ponte de Dom Luís I**, built in 1886, and the Eiffel-designed railway bridge, **Ponte de Maria Pia**. Then, whereas Lisbon's city centre includes both flat bits and hills, Oporto is one big, steep slope with streets that seem to tumble down to the riverfront.

There is hardly, you quickly realise, a horizontal street in the whole town. For anyone who hasn't already limbered up by hoofing it around Lisbon's hills for a few days, Oporto can be very hard going indeed, particularly in hot weather. This is not a city for faint-hearts or cyclists. Nor for motorists, really, given narrow thoroughfares, labyrinthine street layouts, arcane one-way systems and a notable lack of parking space.

Most trains from Lisbon arrive at Campanhã station, two kilometres from the city centre. From there it's possible to catch another train for the short hop to the much more central São Bento station. Once deposited in the steeply gradiented maze that is the city centre, it can be hard to get your bearings, and decent maps are not easy to come by – with an even more unremitting regularity than in Lisbon, somewhere that appears on the page but a few blocks distant turns out to involve a dispiriting 500-foot ascent. The simplest way to suss the lie of the land is to visit the **Torre dos Clérigos**, a short haul up the Rua dos Clérigos from São Bento.

It's around 240 steps to the top of this 18th-century tower, designed by Italian architect Nicolau Nasoni for the church of which it is part. The view is worth the hike (and the 100$00 entrance fee), taking in everything from the Romanesque Sé (cathedral) in the east to the pier and the polluted beach at Foz do Douro where the river runs into the Atlantic (*foz* literally means river-mouth).

On a hilltop overlooking Vila Nova de Gaia on the south bank, the **Mosteiro da Serra do Pilar** stands at the upper level of the Ponte Dom Luís I, while down below, between the tower and the Ribeira district, beyond a patchwork of red rooftops, is the neo-classical **Palácio da Bolsa**.

Completed in 1842, this glass-domed former stock exchange is a monument to money, and includes a particularly over-the-top neo-Moorish ballroom that took 18 years to build and was gilded with 18 kilograms of gold. Regular guided tours gloat over the cost of every item, in keeping with Oporto's image of itself. It has always been Portugal's commercial and manufacturing centre and takes pride in being a hard-working, money-making, no-nonsense kind of place.

Back down at street level, trade and commerce are carried on in a brisk but still

Barrels of Oporto's most famous export bob in boats on the River Douro.

old-fashioned way. Compared to Lisbon, Oporto is relatively un-postmodernised. The big exception is the shiny new **Via Catarina** shopping centre in Rua de Santa Catarina (No.312, 22 207 5600); behind a classical façade is a plethora of big-name shops and, on the top floor, kitsch mockups of traditional house- and shopfronts. Elsewhere, though, gorgeous old signage survives and familiar retail chains are mainly noticeable by their absence. People make calls from the kind of old red telephone boxes that have almost completely disappeared in the UK. It's easy to imagine yourself a decade or two back in the past.

Dom João I married Philippa of Lancaster at the Oporto Sé in 1387, and their son Henry (later famed as Prince Henry the Navigator, *see p10*) was born here in 1394, supposedly at the **Casa do Infante** (22 205 6025; closed Sat, Sun) on Rua da Alfândega in the Ribeira, now an historical archive and exhibition hall. The **Sé**, overlooking the river on a hill above São Bento, is more like a fortress than a cathedral. Founded in the early 12th century, rebuilt in the 13th and then again in the 18th century, it's an ugly, unappealing place but offers great views both from the chapterhouse – reached by another Nasoni-designed set of stairs – and from the courtyard outside.

The streets cascading from here down to the waterfront are fantastic: narrow, steep and almost medieval in feel. Locals sit around on doorsteps or chatter in small squares. These insalubrious alleys – known locally as *ilhas* or islands – dip dankly below scaffolding where

renovation of derelict structures is going on, or twist and turn past unannounced shops: grocers, wineries, cafés, cobblers, and workshops of one kind or another. They reach the waterfront at the **Ribeira** district, where lanes dotted with bars and restaurants spread east and west from Praça da Ribeira.

Vila Nova da Gaia is a separate municipality. There would be little to lure the visitor across there if it wasn't for all the port lodges, but that's where they are and no visit is really complete without a look around one and a few free samples. There had been English traders in Oporto since the 13th century, but Portugal's most famous export only took off in the mid-17th century when a cross-Channel squabble stopped English imports of French wine. Companies like Taylor's, Croft's and Warre's were established in the early 1700s. Later, the Marquês de Pombal (*see p16*) set up the Companhia Velha to control the trade and the Alto Douro, the upper reaches of the river, became the world's first demarcated wine region. Today, it is the French who consume the most port, and few lodges are still controlled by the Anglo families whose names they bear.

The local **tourist office**, on the waterfront near Sandeman, can provide a rough map showing which lodges are open for tours and when, as can the tourist offices over in Oporto (*see p265*). Of the lodges, **Sandeman** (Largo Miguel Bombarda 3, 22 374 0500; closed Sat, Sun in winter) is the most visible, and has a museum, but charges a 500$00 entrance fee (later deducted from the cost of any wine you buy). The others are free. We'd recommend the beautiful **Taylor's** lodge (Rua Barâo de Forrester 406, 22 370 8255) – family-owned since 1692 and a strenuous 10-minute walk up Rua do Choupelo – or the more coherent tour at **Graham's** (Rua Rei Ramiro 514, 22 377 6330, closed Sat, Sun in winter), at the western end of town.

In all of them, the drill is pretty much the same: a stroll around cool old storage rooms full of enormous casks and barrels, a brief explanatory talk from a guide who'll try and imply that all the grape-crushing is still done by foot (it isn't), and finally a few free glasses of whatever it is on offer. You can then buy bottles, but there's no pressure to do so. A couple of these tours will make for a pleasantly light-headed walk back to your hotel.

If you're in town for a few days, you're unlikely to venture beyond the areas described – except perhaps out to Avenida da Boavista to visit the gleaming new **Museu de Arte Contemporânea**, set in the delightful gardens of the Fundação Serralves. Designed by Portugal's star architect, Álvaro Siza Vieira (*see p38*), this cleanly beautiful building stands accused of attempting to eclipse its contents: a permanent collection of post-1960s art and temporary shows of works by contemporary, mainly Portuguese, artists.

Torre dos Clérigos

Rua dos Clérigos (22 200 1729). **Open** *Church* 10am-noon, 2-5pm Mon-Sat; 10am-1pm, 8-11pm Sun. *Tower* 10am-noon, 2-5pm daily. **Admission** *Tower* 200$00. **No credit cards.**

Palácio da Bolsa

Rua Ferreira Borges (22 339 9000). **Open** 9am-12.30pm, 2-5.30pm daily. **Admission** 800$00; 500$00 concessions. **Credit** DC, MC, V.

Sé

Terreiro da Sé (22 205 9028). **Open** 9am-12.30pm, 2.30-5.30pm Mon-Sat; 2.30-5.30pm Sun. **Admission** 250$00. **No credit cards.**

Museu de Arte Contemporânea

Rua Dom João de Castro 210 (22 615 6500 or freephone 808 200 543 from Portugal). **Open** 10am-7pm Tue, Wed, Fri-Sun; 10am-10pm Thur. **Admission** 800$00; 400$00 concessions; free under-13s. **No credit cards.**

Where to eat & drink

There's a real café culture in Oporto; despite their reputation as hard workers, *tripeiros* find time for endless chats over a *cimbalino*, as they call it (after the Italian machines), or a *francesinha*, a grotesque local speciality consisting of layers of meat in a double-decker sandwich drenched in a spicy sauce. Oporto's most famous café is the **Majestic** (Rua de Santa Catarina 112,

22 200 3887, closed Sun), where uniformed waiters serve set breakfasts or afternoon teas against a backdrop of cherubs and gilded woodwork. Out at Foz, the trendy **Bar da Praia do Ourigo** (Esplanada do Castelo, 22 618 9593) serves drinks and snacks – it calls itself a 'tapas and wine bar'. It's right on the beach, and has a terrace protected from the wind. At 200$00 for a coffee, though, you have to wonder how the students who pore over their books here undisturbed by the waiters can afford to come.

When meal-time comes, the **Adega do Olho** (Rua Afonso Martins Alho 6, 22 205 7745, main courses 900$00, closed Sun), next to São Bento station, is as *típico* as it gets – full of local characters scoffing simple fare. The sign above the door, complete with a huge painted blue eye, is an Oporto landmark. There are several places in the Mercado do Bolhão, the old market in Rua Sá de Bandeira, where traditional dishes such as tripe go for a song. For the people of Oporto really are tripe-eaters. Legend has it that this gastronomic peculiarity dates back to 1415, when a Portuguese fleet was setting off to conquer Ceuta. Oporto's patriotic citizens sent it their best meat, leaving themselves only offal.

Most places along the touristy Cais da Ribeira are a little pricier. At no. 40, the **Filha da Mão Preta** (22 205 5515, main courses 1,800$00, closed Sun) is as good a place as any to try Oporto dishes. Some locals go to the swanky **Dom Tonho** upstairs at No.13 (22 200 4307, main courses, 2,400$00) because it's owned by veteran Portuguese bluesman Rui Veloso. Someone should tell Rui his staff are sulky and the building needs heating in winter, but even so the food – which is excellent for the price – and the views of the river and the towering Ponte Dom Luís I make it worth a visit. Nearby, **Chez Lapin** (Rua dos Canastreiros 40, 22 200 6418, main courses 2,500$00) is tucked away under the arches, but sought out by locals and discerning visitors alike for its fish, in particular. Another place near the water that serves very fine grilled fish indeed is **Peixes e Companhia** (Rua do Ouro 133, 22 618 5655, main courses 2,400$00, closed Sun).

Nightlife

The Ribeira district is the heart of Oporto nightlife, although the big clubs are mostly located out in the 'burbs: Matosinhos, where you'll find the enormous new **Tomate** (Rua Manuel Pinto de Azevedo 15, 22 616 8435, closed Sun); Massarelos, home to **River Café** (Calçada João do Carmo 31, 22 617 1124, closed Mon, Tue, Sun), or Foz, whose **Indústria** (Avenida Brasil 843, 22 617 6806, closed Mon-Thur, Sun) is the parent of the Lisbon version. But the only club in Oporto open every night is **Swing** (Praceta Engenheiro Amaro da Costa 766, 22 609 0019), a classic mixed disco known locally (without irony) as the Babylon of Boavista, and a laugh if you're in the right mood.

Nevertheless, Oporto really is workaholic. The sort of places that in Lisbon would close at 5am or 6am even during the week, here start winding up by 2am. When the bars around Praça da Ribeira begin to close, those who don't have to get up in the morning wander up Rua de São João, where there are a clutch of late bars. But **Aniki-Bóbó** (Rua da Fonte Taurina 36, 22 332 4619, closed Sun) remains the most radical downtown option, filling up around 1am and playing acid jazz, house and drum 'n' bass until 4am. Whoever survives that troops back down to Praça da Ribeira, where **Meia Cave** at No.6 (22 332 3214, closed Sun) keeps going until 7am. There are usually a few guys fishing all night down here too, watching the dark water sweep under the Ponte de Dom Luís I while the neon signs of the port wine lodges over the river in Vila Nova da Gaia cast a disembodied glow.

Where to stay

Booking ahead is essential in fancier hotels during 2001, because of the extra demand created by Oporto's stint as European Capital of Culture. Among our favourites, the **Hotel Infante de Sagres** (Praça Dona Filipa de Lencastre 62, 22 339 85 00, rates 29,000$00-31,000$00), in the heart of the old town, has antique furniture, spacious bathrooms and a splendid inner courtyard. It was recently joined in its class by the **Porto Carlton** (Praça da Ribeira 1, 22 340 2300, rates 20,500$00-42,000$00), housed in a gorgeously converted former market right on the main riverside square. Its tastefully decorated rooms (most of them with a river view) feature exposed bits of the Muralha Fernandinha, the medieval city wall that forms part of the building's structure.

The conveniently located **Residencial dos Aliados** (Rua Elisio de Melo 27, 22 200 4853/4, rates 6,500$00-10,000$00), is a once tatty mid-market favourite whose owners have upgraded it in time for Porto 2001. The sitting room is positively plush and all 41 rooms have heating/air-conditioning and refurbished bathrooms. The views from those that look out on the Avenida dos Aliados, dominated by the town hall, are as breathtaking as ever. It's a good place for families, as some rooms take up to five beds. The similarly-priced **Hotel Tuela** (Rua Arquitecto Marques da Silva 200, 22 600 4747, rates 6,500$00-14,000$00), in the business district near Praça de Mousinho de Albuquerque

(generally known as Praça da Boavista because it's in the middle of that Avenida), has parking, a laundry service and a huge restaurant.

Out at Foz, the friendly **Residencial Porto Foz** (Rua do Farol 155, 22 617 2357, rates 9,000$00-14,000$00) is the pick of the bunch; it has a comfy bar, restaurant and lounge, and spacious rooms – some with fireplaces and many with great views. And cheap digs can be found at the well-equipped **Pousada da Juventude** (Rua Paulo da Gama 551, 22 617 7257, rates 2,500$00-6,000$00), which has an excellent reputation and fine views of the Douro estuary and sea.

The area around São Bento and Praça da Batalha has many cheap and mid-range hotels.

Getting there

By bus
Several companies run services from Lisbon to Oporto. Rede Expressos has 10 or more departures daily from Lisbon's Arco do Cego bus station at Avenida Duque d'Ávila; journey time about 3hr30min.

By car
From Lisbon, it's straight up the A1 Auto-Estrada do Norte, but you pay a 3,000$00-plus toll.

By train
Three types of train depart from Lisbon's Santa Apolónia station for Porto Campanhã. The Alfa Pendular is the most comfortable, taking 3hrs, 15mins; price 5,700$00 first class, 3,700$00 second class. The Intercidade takes five minutes longer and costs 4,250$00 or 2,650$00. The normal train costs just 3,190$00 or 2,150$00, but takes 4hrs, 20mins. From Porto Campanhã, switch to a local train to São Bento (5mins), or take bus 35 or 80.

Tourist information

Turismo Nacional
Praça Dom João I 43 (22 205 7514/fax 22 205 3212). **Open** *Oct-June* 9am-5.30pm Mon-Fri; 9.30am-3.30pm Sat, Sun. *June-Sept* 9am-7.30pm daily.
Helpful office that can provide maps and leaflets of themed walking tours (medieval Oporto, for example), information on visits to port wine cellars, and help with accommodation. The airport branch stays open until 11pm.
Branch: Airport (22 941 2534/fax 22 941 2543).

Turismo Municipal
Rua Clube dos Fenianos 25 (22 339 3472). **Open** *Oct-June* 9am-5.30pm Mon-Fri; 9.30am-4.30pm Sat, Sun. *July-Sept* 9am-7pm Mon-Fri; 9-30am-4.30pm Sat, Sun.
Branch: Rua Infante Dom Henrique 63 (22 200 9770).

Turismo Vila Nova de Gaia
Avenida Diogo Leite 242 (22 375 1902). **Open** 10am-12.30pm, 2-6pm Mon-Fri; 2-6pm Sat; closed Sun.

>> If you're looking
for enchantment,
visit the new Lisbon.

Here in Parque das Nações
a new Lisbon is being born.
Boasting Portugal's most
recent national monuments,
breathtaking contemporary
architecture, thematic riverside
gardens, Europe's largest
Oceanarium, floating restaurants,
the largest national bowling alley
and a wide array of shows and
exhibitions – it's well worth a visit.

**Come and enjoy yourself
in the Invented City.**

PARQUE DAS NAÇÕE

Directory

Directory

Getting Around

By air

Portela, Lisbon's main international airport, lies on the north-eastern fringes of the city, within sight of the Ponte Vasco da Gama. An airport shuttle bus departs every 20 minutes until 9pm, taking passengers via Praça do Comércio to Cais do Sodré for 460$00 – less if you have a Lisboa Card (*see p286* **Tourist information**). A cheaper alternative is to take the 5 bus to Areeiro, where you can catch the Metro; the 8 or 22 bus to Martim Moniz; or the 44 or 45 bus to Rossio. Maps are available at the tourist information office at the airport. By car, it's a short drive into town down the Avenida Almirante Gago Coutinho and Avenida Almirante Reis. A taxi downtown should not cost much more than 1,500$00, with a 300$00 charge for luggage added on to the basic fare. Some of the city's dodgiest operators work this route, so watch the meter.

Mindful of the impression that such bad apples were giving visitors, the authorities have introduced a system of vouchers whereby newly arrived travellers can pay for their trip into town in advance and then use the voucher in any taxi that has joined the scheme (identifiable by a window sticker). There are a variety of fare formats and options; for destinations in central Lisbon, you pay 2,800$00 during daytime, 3,360$00 between 10pm and 6am. Information and vouchers can be had at the Turismo de Lisboa booth in the arrivals hall. You may end up paying slightly more (although the cost of the voucher includes tip and baggage fee) but it gives peace of mind.

Another trick is to head upstairs to departures, where there's a taxi rank over the road outside the entrance. Drivers here haven't usually been waiting so long for a fare and tend to be less grumpy if you want to go only a short distance and also less likely to fleece you. It's best not to try this if you have a lot of luggage, though; not only is it a pain to lug it around the airport but some taxi drivers may balk at such evident deviousness.

The airport has a 24-hour telephone information service (21 841 3700), and there are both automated and staffed bureau de change services.

By rail

Trains from Spain, France or the north of Portugal end at Santa Apolónia (21 888 4025); ticket office open 6am-11.30pm daily). The station is beside the river half a mile from the central Praça do Comércio. It has its own tourist information booth and bureau de change. There is a taxi rank outside and a range of bus services. A Metro station was due to open here by 2000, though after part of Praça do Comércio caved in due to construction work it's a moving target.

Trains to Santa Apolónia also call at the showcase Gare do Oriente station at the Parque das Nações, the former Expo site. Passengers alighting here can take the Metro into town.

Trains from the south of Portugal arrive on the south bank of the Tagus in the working-class town of Barreiro. The ferry across to Lisbon offers wonderful views and is surely one of the most stunning ways to arrive in any city. Barreiro has nothing in the way of tourist information but the station staff are helpful enough.

By road

There are a variety of routes to Lisbon from Spain. From up north, there's the E8 European route from Salamanca, which turns into the Portuguese IP-5 at Vilar Formoso. The IP-5 continues on past Viseu to eventually meet the A1 Oporto-to-Lisbon motorway. This route is best avoided, however; the sharp twists and steep inclines of the IP-5 have resulted in an astronomic accident rate and the deathly nickname *Estrada da Morte*.

A safer option is the new direct motorway from Madrid via Badajoz, the E4 Euro-route. Once in Portugal, you'll be on the A6. This road forges through the Alentejo, past Évora and on to Palmela, about 35km (20 miles) south of Lisbon (by which time the motorway has metamorphosed into the A2). Just before Palmela, you have a choice of staying on the same road and entering Lisbon via the Ponte 25 de Abril, a suspension bridge, or taking the A12 and crossing the newer Ponte

Get streetwise

Wandering around the warren of Alfama, or blitzed in the Bairro Alto, it's easy to get lost in Lisbon. But surely that shouldn't be a problem? You'd just consult a map...

Well, perhaps – or perhaps not, for here in the Portuguese capital, maps often only compound the problem. It's not just the general indecipherability of all those narrow little twisty streets with insanely long names. It's that some of these narrow little twisty streets have more than one insanely long name. Or else no name at all.

To take only the most central and obvious example, nobody but nobody ever calls Rossio by its official name. It's Rossio, and has been since the Middle Ages, but look on a map and you'll find Praça Dom Pedro IV. And then leading off it to the south there's Rua do Ouro. Or is it Rua Aurea? The answer is, it's both.

Try telling a taxi driver to Largo Trindade Coelho. A simple enough destination, you surmise, because there's a taxi rank there, right outside the Igreja de São Roque. But for some reason the driver takes you to Rua Nova da Trindade, or the Largo do Carmo, or some such undesired destination. Why? Because Largo Trindade Coelho is only the name on the street sign. Everyone actually calls it Largo da Misericórdia.

Meanwhile, Praça do Comércio is often called by its old, 18th-century name, Terreiro do Paço. The confusion multiplies when you try to get to the nearby ferry terminal. Is it the Estação Fluvial Praça do Comércio? Or the Estação Fluvial Terreiro do Paço? Or even Cais da Alfandêga? The answer is: all three. And don't forget that the Jardim da Estrela is actually called the Jardim Guerra Junqueiro. Is that clear?

Maddest of all is the road that runs east from the Baixa up past the Sé to the *miradouros* overlooking the Alfama. There's not one person in Libson who knows the name of this street. In one 500-metre stretch it runs through a boggling array of nomenclature, changing from Largo da Madalena to Rua de Santo António to Largo de Santo António da Sé to Largo da Sé to Rua Augusto Rosa to Largo de São Martinho to Largo do Limoeiro to Rua do Limoeiro to Largo de Santa Luzia and finally to Largo das Portas do Sol.

In fact it changes names so many times that it effectively has no name at all. The 12 and 28 trams run along here, and so locals refer to it as the 'Rua do Eléctrico da Sé' – the street of the tram of the cathedral. But don't try looking that up on a map.

Aware of the limitations of cartography? Well, go ahead and buy a map. From a generally sorry clutch, we'd recommend the **Falkplan**, available at most bookshops (*see* chapter **Shops & Services**).

Vasco da Gama, a 17km (10 mile) pontoon bridge. Both routes offer arriving traffic a fine introduction to the city's breathtaking topography.

Public transport

Lisbon is well served by a comprehensive and growing network of trains, ferries, buses, trams and funiculars. The state-owned **Metro** has undergone a major expansion, and the city now has a highly efficient and modern underground system which is a pleasure to use. The developers are also to be congratulated on architecturally pleasing new stations, which add to, rather than detract from, Lisbon's charms (*see p104* **Underground art**). The trams and funiculars are fun to use but are not the quickest way of getting around. These, and the bus service, are run by **Carris**, another state-owned company.

Information

Maps of both the bus and tram system and the Metro are normally available at Carris booths (*see p270* **Buses**) and major Metro stations respectively.

Fares & tickets

Lisbon's tourist pass (Lisboa Card) allows unlimited travel on metro, buses and trams. It costs 1,760$00 for four days and 2,490$00 for seven days and is available from Carris kiosks or metro stations; you must carry ID with you.

There are also monthly 'L' passes covering the whole Lisbon area, including Belém. They cost 4,040$00, plus the cost of getting a photocard made (160$00).

See also the following sections for fares for each means of transport.

Metro

The speediest way to travel in Lisbon is via the greatly improved Metro system. Travel cards are sold in the following stations: Campo Grande, Entre

Campos, Saldanha, Marquês de Pombal, Restauradores, Cais do Sodré, Arroios, Areeiro, Jardim Zoológico, Colégio Militar and Pontinha.

The Metro runs from 6.30am to 1am daily and trains leave every two minutes during rush hours and every five minutes during the rest of the day. **Tickets** are sold in the station ticket offices and vending machines. Validate the ticket by inserting it into the small boxes next to the barriers until it engages. The fine for not having a valid ticket is 8,500$00 (plus the cost of the fare) though inspectors are fairly thin on the ground.

A single ticket costs 100$00, a daily ticket 270$00 and a *caderneta* of ten tickets 850$00. Better value for frequent travellers is the seven-day pass, costing 940$00 or the one-month pass, at 2,160$00.

There are public telephones in all Metro stations and a lost and found office at Marquês de Pombal.

The Metro has four lines:

LINHA GAIVOTA (SEAGULL LINE)

The blue line runs from Pontinha to Baixa-Chiado. It is being extended along the river to Santa Apolónia.

LINHA GIRASSOL (SUNFLOWER LINE)

The yellow line runs from Rato to Campo Grande, but there are plans to extend it as far north as Lumiar.

LINHA CARAVELA (CARAVEL LINE)

The green line runs from Cais do Sodré to Campo Grande. It is to be extended as far as Telheiras.

LINHA ORIENTE (ORIENT LINE)

The red line runs from Alameda to Oriente. The plan is to extend it as far west as Campolide, and as far east as Moscavide.

Buses

Lisbon's orange buses provide good services way out into the suburbs. There are some night buses, but since taxis are relatively cheap, most late revellers will prefer this option. Information on buses can be obtained from Carris's administrative headquarters at Santo Amaro 21 361 3000. There are smaller information offices and ticket booths all over the city, including at: Praça da Figueira, Areeiro, Alcântara, Cais do Sodré (near the train station), Campo Pequeno, Santa Apolónia, Santa Justa, Alvalade and Campo Grande.

Tickets can be bought from the driver and cost 165$00 per trip. A two-trip ticket bought from a Carris kiosk before you travel allows two journeys for 175$00, and is valid on both trams and buses. Punch tickets in the machine to validate each journey you make.

Carris booths also sell travel cards allowing unlimited travel: 460$00 for one day; 1,080$00 for three-days. *See also p269* for details of Carris-Metro combined passes.

Other companies operate bus routes beyond Lisbon. These include **Stagecoach** (21 483 2055) along the Estoril coast and across to Sintra, and **Transporte Sul do Tejo** (21 726 2740), which operates routes south of the river. Key stops include Areeiro, Praça de Espanha, Cacilhas and the central bus station on Avenida Duque d'Ávila in Arco Cego, near Saldanha.

Trams

This is undoubtedly the most charming form of public transport in Lisbon, albeit not the most efficient. Coming into operation in 1901, these old trams used to be the main form of transport. Many of the older ones were built in the United States and later refitted in England and Germany. In recent decades swelling traffic flows, and buses, have forced the closure of several less scenic lines. As with the buses, you have to get on at the front, and get off at the back. Today, the more traditional trams, like the 12, 18, 25 and 28 routes, have been joined by the ultra-modern rapid transit models built by Siemens, notably the 15 that links Praça da Figueira with Algés. Tram fares are integrated with the bus system.

Funiculars

Three funicular trams negotiate the steeper slopes of the city, again for 165$00; Carris passes may also be used. The Elevador de Santa Justa is a lift, rather than a funicular, but also integrated with the bus system. The viaduct connecting the top end to the Largo do Carmo has been closed for years, meaning that the lift is only useful for catching the view from the top, where there's a café.

ELEVADOR DA BICA

From Bairro Alto (Calçada do Combro) to Santos (Rua de São Paulo). 7am-10.45pm Mon-Sat; 9am-10.45pm Sun & holidays.

ELEVADOR DO LAVRA

From Avenida da Liberdade (Largo da Anunciada) to Campo de Santana (Rua Câmara Pestana). 7am-10.45pm Mon-Sat; 9am-10.45pm Sun & holidays

ELEVADOR DA GLORIA

From Avenida da Liberdade (Restauradores) to Bairro Alto (São Pedro de Alcântara). 7am-12.55am daily.

ELEVADOR DE SANTA JUSTA

From Baixa (Rua do Ouro (Áurea) to Bairro Alto (Largo do Carmo). 7am-11.45pm daily.

Off their trolleys

One of Lisbon's most enduring images is that of the brightly painted tram clanking its way around narrow cobbled streets. Inside, a uniformed driver pulls on his levers, all the while exchanging gruff pleasantries with the pensioners who clamber aboard. Groups of tourists peer out of the open windows, fascinated and delighted to have found such an authentic Lisbon experience.

But behind these sedate – nay, idyllic – images lies some gritty urban etiquette.

First rule: never jump the queue. Even if the carriage is empty as it pulls up in front of you and the old-timer who is your only tram-stop companion, an attempt to board out of turn will trigger a finger-wagging lecture about the nature of civilised society. And unless you want to blare your tourist origins, remember that though you get on at the front, you get off at the back.

Second: hold tight. Lisbon's trams have a knack of producing savage angled jerks at the very moment the passenger is adjusting his or her balance. All too often, poorly attached pensioners fly across the boards, landing with a sickening thud before being pulled to their feet – remarkably undamaged – by tut-tutting fellow passengers.

Third: don't try to imitate the locals. You will notice impish packs hanging off the back of the trams. These mucky-faced free riders are tolerated and ignored by the driver. Try it yourself and you will certainly leave your kneecap on a sudden Graça street corner.

Fourth: watch your pockets and your bags. Small bands of pickpockets make light work of fat German wallets here.

Fifth: be nice to the driver. Paid a wage to wander beloved streets in this classic piece of engineering, surely his lot is a happy one? Look closer and you might notice the clenched jaw, the wild stare and the disturbed muttering as he aims ironic jibes at the cars cutting across his path.

Our blue-blazered friend has to contend with some of Europe's most ill-mannered, impatient and downright incompetent motorists. And rarely does a journey go by without the protruding wing of a badly parked vehicle bringing everything to a grinding halt, quickly triggering a cacophony of hooting from without and complaining voices from within. Down the line impatient passengers are already working themselves into up into a lather, and preparing harsh tirades for our tardy driver's ears. Meanwhile, hordes of guide-book clutching tourists will further fray his nerves with linguistic challenges and a complete lack of small change.

So it should come as no surprise to learn that the stoical public servants who steer us around in their charming clanking machines have in fact been identified as some of Lisbon's likeliest victims of occupation-linked mental health problems.

Still want to be a tram driver when you grow up, sonny?

Rail services

Local train services, run by national railway **Caminhos de Ferro Portugueses** (CP) are improving. Trains run along the Estoril line from Cais de Sodré station as far as Cascais every 20 minutes during the day for a fare of 190$00. Escape to the beach is easy, thanks to the existence of the Cais de Sodré Metro station. Another busy rail line links Queluz and Sintra to Rossio station. The network has been under expansion, with a new link built between the Lisbon-Sintra line and the Gare do Oriente and a line

suspended under the Ponte 25 de Abril. This, along with the immense Ponte Vasco da Gama, is providing more options for crossing the river Tagus. However, ever-growing transport needs mean the sight of commuters streaming off the orange ferry boats is unlikely to disappear from the Lisbon cityscape.

Ferries

Ferry services link various points of Lisbon with the southern bank of the River Tagus. They are usually packed during rush hour as people commute over the river

from neighbourhoods such as Almada and Barreiro.

From the Lisbon side, the boats link Terreiro do Paço to Barreiro, Montijo and Seixal. From the neighbouring Alfândega boat station, ferries normally leave for Cacilhas, which is a hub for buses to the Caparica coast and beyond. However, this ferry service was suspended in late 2000 after a road near it collapsed, so for the time being ferries for Cacilhas depart only from Cais do Sodré. Other boats leave Belém for the picturesque towns of Porto Brandão and Trafaria, at the mouth of the Tagus.

Ferries are run by the **Transtejo** company. Each station has an information office. Fares range between 100$00 and 300$00.

Taxis

Taxis in Lisbon are thick on the ground and inexpensive. Newer cabs are cream coloured, the older variety are black with a green roof.

The standing charge is 320$00 from 6am to 10pm and 380$00 from 10pm to 6am, and the fare is supposed to be 10$00 per 158 metres (171 yards), and each 28 seconds when stopped. At night, from 10pm to 6am, and on weekends and holidays, the rate is for every 130 metres (141 yards).

Tipping is optional and a moderate amount will be appreciated. It must be said, however, that many taxi drivers have a serious attitude problem, and can be all too ready to take out their frustrations – heavy traffic and poor wages – on the customer. Sometimes this is just a matter of gruffness, and can be easily ignored or soothed away. But they can also be downright rude.

In the early hours and when it's raining, taxis are hard to come by, but you are rarely very far from a taxi stand.

Some of the busiest and most reliable are those at Rossio, Largo do Chiado and Largo de Trindade Coelho (known as Largo da Misericórdia) in the Bairro Alto.

There are 24-hour dial-a-cab services on 21 811 9000 (**Radio Taxis de Lisboa**), 21 793 2756 (**Autocoope**) and 21 811 1100 (**Teletaxis**). You pay an extra 150$00 if you order one.

Driving

Lisbon is not the easiest city to negotiate by car. Traffic is chaotic and many of the streets are narrow, winding and frequently one-way. Even worse, the Portuguese leave their fabled manners behind when they get behind the wheel. Drivers are aggressive and any vacillation on your part will attract a cacophony of honking and abuse. Outside of Lisbon it is even worse. The Portuguese drive too fast and enjoy overtaking on blind bends. As reward, they often top the EU table for road deaths (and are second to South Korea in the world league).

Rush hour in Lisbon is between 8am and 10am and 5pm and 7pm. The worst black spot is the Ponte 25 de Abril, which often jams up. The problem has not noticeably eased since the rail line under the bridge started functioning. The Praça Marquês de Pombal roundabout at the top of the Avenida da Liberdade is also hell at rush hour.

Note also that police are empowered to issue on-the-spot fines for minor driving offences. Don't argue.

Speed limits are apparently 60 kilometres an hour in built-up areas, 90 elsewhere and 120 on the gleaming new EU-funded highways, but few people take any notice.

All Portugal's motorways, or *auto-estradas*, are toll roads (*portagens*) – costing approximately 3,500$00-5,000$00 from Lisbon to Oporto – and are prefixed with the initial A on maps. Those prefixed with an E are cross-continental European routes. IP on maps stands for itinerário principal, or main road. IC stands for *itinerário complementar*, or subsidiary road. Other two-lane roads have the prefix N on some maps – but sometimes not. Confusingly, on some maps highways can also change prefixes along their route. *See also p269* **Get streetwise**.

Seat belts are obligatory in both front and back. Note also: the legal limit for alcohol in the blood is very low at 0.05 per cent – so drinking and driving is not an option.

ACCIDENTS AND BREAKDOWNS

If you are involved in an accident on a main road, use the orange SOS phone to call for help. In collisions, leave the car exactly where it is (regardless of the disruption this causes) and wait for the police to arrive to document the situation.

In cases of breakdown drivers can call **Automóvel Clube de Portugal** for help (21 942 9103). This is affiliated all over Europe, and membership of a foreign automobile association is likely to result in entitlement to reimbursement of the service charges, providing this is within the conditions of the drivers' own membership.

Alternatively, look in the Yellow Pages under *Reboques*. Some of the companies listed offer a 24-hour service.

Automóvel Clube de Portugal

Rua Rosa Araújo 24, Marquês de Pombal, 1250 (21 318 0100). Metro Marquês de Pombal. **Open** 9am-5.30pm daily. **Map** p307 L7.

Portilavauto

Rua Fernando Palha, 44-48, Moscavide, 1900 (21 861 0600). **Open** 24 hours daily.

FUEL STATIONS

There are plenty of petrol stations around Lisbon, most of which will accept credit cards, but check first. Petrol (*gasolina*) comes in several forms: with additive to replace lead (although your hire car won't use that) is *com aditivo*; unleaded is *sem chumbo*, which comes in two grades – 95 and 98. Diesel is *gasóleo*.

To ask the pump attendant to fill the tank you say *cheio, por favor*; a small tip is appreciated. There are various 24-hour filling stations, many of them placed close to the main access roads into Lisbon. Otherwise filling station hours are as follows: BP 7am-midnight, Shell 24 hours, Galp 7am-midnight, all daily.

Hitch-hiking

Hitch-hiking in Portugal is not at all common and anyone sticking their thumb out will have to be very patient indeed. Women on their own should take great care.

Parking

Parking in Lisbon can be a trying task. In older bairros, cars are crammed nose to bumper along the pavements, reflecting a lack of private garages (tuck the mirror in on your rental car). A building boom gave developers the chance to equip newer buildings with spacious underground parking facilities. The council is also backing the construction of numerous underground car parks, which has meant upheaval as the city's squares are dug up. It is not hard to find space in such lots, but some are expensive. They are clearly signposted with the usual white P on a blue background. Much of downtown Lisbon is now covered by a meter system, for which you will need some coins handy. Be warned that parking illegally will often result in a heavy fine or the vehicle being towed away.

In downtown areas drivers will also be met by young people who wave you toward a parking place. These are the *arrumadores* – roughly translatable as 'fixers' – who haunt downtown Lisbon in their hundreds and jealously guard their own patch of street. They will expect an advance tip of at least 100$00 for this unsolicited service: refusing to pay may trigger some unfriendly muttering.

The *arrumadores* are there to watch your car and keep it from harm. The vast majority also happen to be funding a heavy-duty drug heroin habit, and the drug dealer's pocket is the most likely destination for any tip you choose to give.

Drivers ill-inclined to pay for an unsolicited service may worry about the consequences to their vehicle. However, local tales of wilful damage to cars are greatly exaggerated, as testified by the uneasy truce between the *arrumadores* and the police.

Car hire

To rent a car in Portugal you must be over 21 and have had a driving licence for more than one year.

All the major rental companies have locations in Lisbon, although it often works out cheaper to arrange a deal through your travel agent or airline at home.

Avis
Avenida Praia da Vitória 12-C, Saldanha, 1050 (21 351 4560/ www.avis.com/reservations 800 201002 freephone). **Map** p305 M5. **Branches:** Airport (21 843 5550); Santa Apolónia train station (21 881 0469); Hotel Ritz (21 381 3499).

Budget
Rua Castilho 167B, Marquês de Pombal, 1250 (21 386 0516/fax 21 383 0978/www.budget.com/ reservations 21 994 0443). **Map** p307 K7. **Branch:** Airport (21 849 5523).

Europcar
Aeroporto de Lisboa (Airport), Portela, 1700 (21 840 1176/fax 21 847 3180/www.europcar.com/ reservations 21 940 7790). **Map** p305 O3.

Hertz
Rua Castilho 72 A-B-C, Marquês de Pombal, 1250 (21 381 2430/fax 21 387 4164/www.hertz.com/ reservations 21 942 6300 0490/800 238238/800 201231 freephone). **Map** p307 K7. **Branches:** Airport (21 843 8660); Avenida Visconde Seabra 10 (21 797 2944/fax 21 797 0371); Hotel Atlântico Estoril (21 486 3486).

Iperrent
Avenida 5° Outubro 54C, Saldanha, 1050 (21 317 2160). **Map** p304 L5.

Cycling

Lisbon's streets are unfriendly to cyclists. Slippery cobbles, tyre-trapping tram lines and inconsiderate drivers make it dangerous going.

Bicycles may be taken on the Metro at weekends, but there is a near-blanket ban on the railways. The best bet is to go out to Cascais and arrange bike hire there. The Estoril and Sintra areas offers the best in scenic cycling.

For rental, try the following:

Tip Tours
Avenida da Costa Pinto 91A, 2750 Cascais (21 484 2055). Train from Cais do Sodré to Cascais. **Open** 9.30am-1pm, 2.30-6.30pm Mon-Fri.

John David's snack bar
Praia da Duquesa, 2750 Cascais (21 483 0455). Train from Cais do Sodré to Cascais. **Open** *Mar-Nov* 10am-7pm daily. Closed Dec-Feb.

Walking

Lisbon's many hills (there are certainly more than seven!) make it challenging terrain for even energetic walkers, especially on a hot day. But 20 minutes spent steaming up an incline is often rewarded with a view that takes away what breath you have left (*see p75* **Best miradouros**).

The exhausting nature of the whole business may be why there is such a scarcity of outfits offering guided walking tours. The following is an honourable exception.

Walking Around Lisbon
Rua São João de Mata 5-3, Lapa, 1200-846 (21 395 0699/mobile 96 908 6602/fax 21 390 6149/jcabdo@ip.pt). **Map** p306 J9. Three-hour walking tours around Alfama/Castelo/Chiado/Bairro Alto arranged for a minimum of 15,000$00 (about 2,500$00 per person). Specialist tours on Saturdays include Legendary Lisbon and visits to sites connected with Fernando Pessoa, Eça de Queiróz and Almeida Garrett.

Directory

Resources A-Z

Business

Portugal's economy was one of the fastest growing in the European Union during the 1990s, thanks partly to unprecedented flows of EU aid for infrastructure projects. As burgeoning revenues helped narrow the deficit and ensure membership in economic and monetary union (EMU) from the start of 1999, a virtuous circle ensued whereby interest rates fell to record lows, further boosting growth. Fast-growing consumer demand has made Lisbon in particular an attractive market for companies in services such as retail and catering.

Growth is slowing, though, and inflation rose from a record low of 1.7 per cent in 1997 to more than 2.5 per cent in late 2000. The economy now lags behind the EU average.

The common European currency was met with enthusiasm in Portugal. The government has opted for a 'big bang' switch to euro notes and coins in 2002, with all cash machines to change over by 15 January and the escudo ceasing to be legal tender on 1 March (*see p282*).

In policy terms, the Socialist government is little different from its Social Democrat predecessor. Prime Minister António Guterres talks fluently of social justice while keeping an eye on financial markets. Privatisations accelerated after he took office in 1995. The liberalisation of the telecoms and other markets is, as elsewhere, bringing in new players and price competition.

It is becoming easier all the time to do business in Portugal. Since the mid-1980s there has been a sustained assault on bureaucratic hurdles. Recent reforms include the lifting of the requirement for foreign companies to seek permission to invest (now they just have to register for statistical purposes) and the removal of exchange controls. The tax system is being reformed, with mixed results; corporate tax rates have fallen but tax breaks have been repeatedly changed, generating paperwork and confusion.

Regulations also change frequently and the official you first speak to may well give you false information about what documents you need for any given purpose. Positive helpfulness is rare in government departments, except for ICEP (*see p276*). Use common sense and take every bit of paper you might need – the original and two copies. Make sure you always use the same signature as on your passport, to avoid having to resubmit applications. Never write anything in red ink, as it is seen as insulting. For advice in your own language, try the commercial section of your embassy (*see p277*).

Agencies such as **Bureaucratic Help Service** and **Documédia** (for both, *see p287*) can be a great help in navigating government agencies, although at a price.

You may set up as a sole trader with unlimited or limited liability – the former is Empresário em Nome Individual while the latter is Estabelecimento Individual de Responsibilidade Limitada (EIRL) – or as a general partnership – Sociedade em Nome Colectivo (SNC). Or you can set up a limited company. This can take the form of a Sociedade Anónima (SA) and a Sociedade por Quotas (Limitada or Lda, for short), which can have just one shareholder (Sociedade Unipessoal por Quotas). For either kind you need to have the name approved and registered at the national Registry of Collective Persons. That should take a few days, but make sure you submit as many alternative names as are allowed, so that you don't have to start from scratch if it is rejected. You must then have a notary draw up an incorporation deed, get a tax number, arrange publication in the *Diário da República* and register with social security and a series of other bodies within 30 days of starting operations. All of this you can arrange at the **Centro da Formalidade de Empresas** (*see p276*), where the relevant organisations are represented. You can open a company bank account without a tax number for the purpose of depositing the share capital where required, but must provide full documentation before making any transactions.

While Portugal's legal framework is creaky, it is being overhauled, and contracts are in any case secure. However, enforcement of copyrights is weak. *See also p280* **Legal help.**

The Portuguese appear laid back in their business dealings. All but the most manic investment bankers love long lunches with no siesta. Even top executives can be engagingly informal.

The Portuguese usually address each other formally, using '*Doutor*' for anyone who has been to university. Businesspeople tend to dress smartly and conservatively. Matters are more fluid when it comes to appointments; unless you have already met the person, it's best to write to request a meeting and then follow up with phone calls until you have a firm answer. It isn't unusual to be kept

The thin end of the wedge

A relatively small population, and one that spent half of the 20th century turned in on itself, is bound to throw up some odd cultural characteristics. *Cunha* – literally 'wedge' but in fact a term even more untranslatable than *saudade* (see p31) – is one of these.

Nepotism is the nearest equivalent concept, except that *cunha* isn't just about 'a job for the boys' – a borrowed English phrase frequently heard these days in Portuguese politics. *Cunha* applies equally to those occasions when you know someone at the *Câmara* (town hall) who promises to get your request for planning permission through unscathed; or when your cousin at the gas company makes sure that you get your pipes fixed before other impatient and infuriated customers.

Of course, it is partly a class phenomenon – Portuguese society is highly stratified and the upper crust inevitably has the best *cunha* – but it also goes much further. In fact, *cunha*

works at each respective social level through humdrum but incessant networking. It may bring one-off benefits for the individual, but it's also the flipside of the fact that there is still little opportunity for the vast majority of people to move beyond their immediate social grouping.

At the Lisbon offices of one multinational bank, for example, almost every one of the administrative support staff comes from the same couple of blocks in a distant Lisbon suburb. Similarly, the Universidade Aberta, Portugal's answer to the Open University, is run by two intermingled families and the postal service's central sorting office is disproportionately staffed by people from the distant rural region of Beira Baixa. Word is passed: 'Head for the smoke and slot letters for big bucks – third-uncle Mário can get you in'. If asked how they got the job, the honest answer for many workers in Lisbon would be: '*Foi uma cunha.*'

---

waiting in reception for an hour or more, if the person they are meeting is high up the Portuguese pecking order.

Women may have to contend with patronising attitudes, at least until they have made clear (not too aggressively, mind) that they mean business. While doing lunch is fine, they would do well to avoid one-on-one business dinners as these are invariably misinterpreted.

Conventions & office hire

Some of the business centres listed below may be able to help with the organisation of larger events, as will most major hotels.

Centro Luxor

Rua da Misericórdia 76, Chiado, 1200-273 (21 321 0100/fax 21 321 0299). Metro Baixa-Chiado/tram 28. **Open** *Office staff* 9am-midnight Mon-Fri; closed Sat, Sun. *Reception* 9am-midnight Mon-Fri; 9am-6pm Sat; closed Sun. **No credit cards**. **Map** p310 L9.
Furnished offices with secretarial support. Also hire of meeting rooms.

Feira Internacional de Lisboa (FIL) – Centro de Reuniões

Parque das Nações, Rua do Bojador, 1998-010 (21 892 1721/fax 21 892 1722/www.fil.pt). Metro Oriente. **Open** 9am-6pm Mon-Fri; closed Sat, Sun. **Credit** AmEx, MC, V.
On the former Expo site, the Lisbon International Exhibition Centre's conference centre has three auditoria (including a 500-seater) plus four meeting rooms housing up to 50 people. Handy for the airport.

Forum Telecom

Avenida Fontes Pereira de Melo 38C, Saldanha, 1050-123 (21 311 7000/fax 21 354 6175). Metro Picoas. **Open** 9am-6pm Mon-Fri; closed Sat, Sun. **No credit cards**. **Map** p307 L6.
Also known as Forum Picoas, a central site for meetings. On offer are an exhibition space, a 500-seater auditorium and meeting rooms with capacity from two to 250.

Intess

Rua de São Julião 62-1, Baixa, 1100-526 (21 888 2506/fax 21 887 1820). Metro Baixa-Chiado/tram 28. **Open** 9am-1pm, 2.30-5.30pm Mon-Fri; closed Sat, Sun. **No credit cards**. **Map** p310 M10.
Conference and congress organisers with interpreters on tap if necessary.

Regus Business Centre

Avenida da Liberdade 110, 1269-046 (21 340 4500/fax 21 340 4575/www.regus.com). Metro Avenida. **Open** 9am-6.30pm Mon-Fri; closed Sat, Sun. **Credit** AmEx, MC, V. **Map** p307 L8.
Air-conditioned, well-staffed serviced offices.

São José Business Centre

Edifício São José, 5°, Alameda dos Combatentes da Grande Guerra 247, Cascais, 2750-326 (21 483 8500/fax 21 483 8533). Cascais train from Cais do Sodré. **Open** 9am-6pm Mon-Fri; closed Sat, Sun. **No credit cards**.
Similar to Regus, but in Cascais.

Couriers & shippers

For moderately urgent packages, EMS, the courier arm of the state postal service, is usually satisfactory. Sending a document up to 250g to the UK costs 4,622$00, to the US it would be 6,126$00.

DHL

Rua da Cidade de Liverpool 16, Anjos, 1170-097 (21 810 0099/fax 21 815 5495/www.dhl.pt). **Open** 8.30am-10.30pm Mon-Fri, 9am-6pm Sat; closed Sun. **No credit cards**.

Phone for pick-ups until 10.30pm.
Cost of sending a document weighing
200g or less: 5,920$00 for London (24
hours), 5,810$00 for the US (48 hours).
Branch: Rua C, Edificio 124, Lisbon
Airport (21 849 0070)

Jet Worldwide Portugal

*Avenida Infante Dom Henrique,
Lote 10, Olivais, 1849-003 (21 854
6060/fax 21 854 6061).* **Open** 9am-
12.30pm, 2-6pm Mon-Fri; closed Sat,
Sun. **No credit cards**.
A package of 200g or less to London
costs 6,200$00, to New York
6,600$00. Pickups until 11pm.

TNT

*Rua C, Edificio 77, Aeroporto de
Lisboa, 1749-104 (21 854 5050/fax
21 840 3080/www.tnt.com/pt).*
Open 8am-7pm Mon-Fri; closed
Sat, Sun. **Credit** AmEx, MC, V.
Sending a 200g package to London
costs 8,050$00, to New York 8,875$00.

UPS

*Quinto do Figo Maduro, Rua 1a Rua
Particular, Prior Velho, Sacavém,
2685-312 (freephone 800 205020/
www.ups.com/europe/pt).* **Open**
8.30am-6.30pm Mon-Fri; closed Sat,
Sun. **Credit** AmEx, MC, V.
An envelope sent Express (arrival by
10.30 the following day) costs
5,316$00 to London or 5,569$00 to
New York. Express delivery for a
package up to 500g to London is
6,379$00, to New York, 7,695$00.
Branch: Avenida da República 44,
Saldanha, 1050-194 (21 794 1664).

Secretarial services

Egor Portugal

*Rua Castilho 75-7, Marquês de
Pombal, 1250-068 (21 389 6306/
fax 21 389 6301/www.egor.pt).
Metro Marquês de Pombal.*
Open 9am-6pm Mon-Fri; closed
Sat, Sun. **Map** p307 K7.
Recruitment of professional,
technical and administrative staff.

Randstad

*Rua Braamcamp 13-1, Marquês de
Pombal, 1250-049 (21 319 4900/fax
21 330 4555/www.pt.randstad.com).
Metro Marquês de Pombal.*
Open 9am-7pm; closed Sat, Sun.
Map p307 K7.
Provision of temporary staff,
primarily office and administrative.

Vedior Psicoemprego

*Rua Castilho 75-5, Marquês de
Pombal, 1250-068 (21 382 3200/fax
21 382 3290/www.vedior.pt). Metro
Marquês de Pombal.* **Open** 9am-1pm,
2-6pm Mon-Fri; closed Sat, Sun.
Map p307 K7.

Dutch-Portuguese combination
providing temporary office,
industrial and catering staff. Sister
company Vedior Psicoforma (Rua
Castilho 75-5, 21 382 3200) does
recruitment and selection.

Translation & interpreters

The **British Council** (Rua de São
Marçal 174, Principe Real, 1200-423,
21 347 6141) can provide a list of
English/Portuguese translators.

AIP-Assistentes Intérpretes de Portugal

*Avenida da República 41-3,
Saldanha, 1050-187 (21 799
4360/fax 21 799 4369). Metro
Saldanha.* **Open** 10am-1pm, 2.30-
6pm, Mon-Fri; closed Sat, Sun.
Map p305 M5.
Official and legal translations. Also
simultaneous translations.

Traducta

*Rua Rodrigo da Fonseca 127-1,
Marquês de Pombal, 1070-240 (21
388 3384/fax 21 385 7886/
www.traducta.pt). Metro
Marquês de Pombal.* **Open** 9am-1pm,
2-6pm Mon-Fri; closed Sat, Sun.
No credit cards. Map p307 K7.
Established company offering
translations and interpreter services
in a range of languages.

Other services

Simple photocopying jobs can be
done by most small newsagents. For
bulk, colour or anything more
complex, try **Papelaria Fernandes**
(*see p156*) or one of the specialist
one-stop shops below which provide
a range of office support services.

Mail Boxes Etc

*Avenida de Paris 24, Areeiro, 1000-
229 (21 846 2757/www.pt.mbe.com).
Metro Areeiro.* **Open** 9.30am-7.30pm
Mon-Fri; closed Sat, Sun. **Credit**
AmEx. **Map** p305 N4.
You can rent a mail box with 24-hour
access, and the company will receive
registered deliveries. There are also
photocopying, fax and internet
services and office supplies; national
and international courier delivery
can be arranged.
Branches: throughout the city.

PostNet

*Rua Braamcamp 9, Marquês de
Pombal, 1250-048 (21 351
1050/www.postnet.pt). Metro
Marquês de Pombal.* **Open** 8am-8pm
Mon-Fri; 9am-2pm Sat; closed Sun.
Credit MC, V. **Map** p307 K7.

This US franchise is the only place
in town that offers photocopying
discounts for students and teachers.
It also has a wide range of business
and communications services,
including internet, design and
printing of business cards and
invitations, mailings, translations,
secretarial support and even key-
cutting. Rental of mail boxes also
available, with access during
opening hours.
Branches: throughout the city.

Useful organisations

Centro da Formalidade de Empresas

*Avenida Columbano Bordalo
Pinheiro 86, Praça de Espanha,
1070-065 (21 723 2300/fax 21
723 2323/www. cfe.iapmei.pt).
Metro Praça de Espanha.* **Open**
9am-6pm Mon-Fri; closed Sat, Sun.
Map p304 K4.
A one-stop shop for setting up a
Portuguese company (*sociedade*). On
location are representatives from
each of the relevant government
bodies. There's limited capacity for
handling the processes in any one
day, so to be sure of being seen
either show up early or call to make
an appointment.
Branch: Rua da Junqueira 39-39A,
Santo Amaro, 1300-342 (21 361
5400/fax 21 361 5423).

Banco de Portugal

*Rua do Comércio 148, Baixa, 1100-
150 (21 321 3200/www.bportugal.
pt). Metro Baixa-Chiado/28 tram.*
Open 8.30-noon, 1-4.30pm Mon-Fri;
closed Sat, Sun. **Map** p310 L10.
The Portuguese central bank has
various departments at several
locations but the switchboard here is
the best place to start.

Fundo de Turismo

*Rua I. Silva, Lote 6, Campo Pequeno,
1050-124 (21 781 0000/fax 21 793
7521). Metro Campo Pequeno.* **Open**
9am-12.30pm, 2-5pm Mon-Fri; closed
Sat, Sun. **Map** p304 M4.
The main body for evaluating and
granting funds in the tourism sector.

ICEP Portugal – Investimentos, Comércio e Turismo

*Avenida 5° de Outubro 101, Campo
Pequeno, 1050-051 (21 790
9500/fax 21 795 0961/www.icep.pt).
Metro Campo Pequeno.* **Open** 9am-
5.30pm Mon-Fri; closed Sat, Sun.
Map p304 L5.
The Portuguese Investment, Trade
and Tourism Institute is the nearest
thing to a one-stop shop for people
wishing to do business in Portugal.
Plenty of English speakers.

Instituto de Apoio às Pequenas e Médias Empresas e ao Investimento (IAPMEI)

Rua Rodrigo Fonseca 73/73A, Marquês de Pombal, 1269-158 (21 383 6000/fax 21 383 6283/www. iapmei.pt). Metro Marquês de Pombal. **Open** 9am-6pm Mon-Fri; closed Sat, Sun. **Map** p307 K7.

The Institute for Small and Medium-Sized Enterprises and Investment doles out most of the government business grants, not just those aimed at small business.

Ministério das Finanças

Avenida Infante D. Henrique 1, Baixa, 1194-009 (21 881 6800/www.min-financas.pt). Metro Baixa-Chiado/28 tram. **Open** 9am-12.30pm, 2-5.30pm Mon-Fri; closed Sat, Sun. **Map** p311 M10.

Finance Ministry hours can vary depending on the department.

Chambers of commerce

For a full list of bi-lateral Chambers of Commerce look in the Yellow Pages under *Câmaras de Comércio*.

British-Portuguese Chamber of Commerce

Rua da Estrela 8, Estrela, 1200-669 (21 394 2020/fax 21 394 2029/ www.bpcc.pt). Tram 25, 28/9, 20, 27, 38 bus. **Open** 9am-5pm Mon-Fri; closed Sat, Sun. **Map** p306 J8.

Câmara de Comércio Americana em Portugal

Rua da Dona Estefânia 155, Estefânia, 1000-154 (21 357 2561/fax 21 357 2580). Metro Saldanha. **Open** 9.30am-1pm, 2-5pm, Mon-Fri; closed Sat, Sun. **Map** p307 M6.

The US Chamber of Commerce.

Consumer

Consumer rights are not very well protected in Portugal, although there is a secretary of state for consumer affairs. The most active campaigning organisation is Deco, which can also offer advice.

Deco

Rua Artilharia Um 79-4, Marquês de Pombal 1250-038 (21 371 0200/fax 21 371 0299/www.deco.proteste.pt).

Disabled

Lisbon is spread over several hills, the roads and pavements are narrow, pitted and often paved with cobblestones and flights of steps are frequent. This is not the easiest city for disabled travellers to negotiate. The Portuguese word for disabled, *deficiente*, is indicative of unenlightened local attitudes, although recent legislation has tightened up the rules for new buildings.

In museums, hotels and shopping centres, facilities for the disabled are becoming more common, as are assigned parking spots. The recent wave of construction has also seen a sharp increase in the number of ramps and such. These facilities are evident on newer Metro stations.

Cooperativo Nacional de Apoi a Deficientes

Praça Dr Fernando Amado 566-E, Chelas, 1900 (tel/fax 21 859 5332/cnad_sede@clix.pt). Metro Chelas. **Open** 10am-1pm, 2.30-6pm Mon-Fri; closed Sat, Sun.

This has a department providing advice and information about tourism services for the disabled, including equipment and vehicles.

Adapt Car

Rua Pascoal de Melo 3-3, Sala 3.4, Saldanha, 1170 (21 812 3526/fax 21 812 3516). Metro Estefânia. **Map** p307 M6.

This company will hire (and deliver) adapted vehicles.

Drugs

As a European capital and a busy port, it's not surprising that Lisbon has its share of drug problems. Consumption and possession are against the law, but from July 2001 no longer a crime punishable by imprisonment. In any case, enforcement is low-key and small-time users may get away with a caution. Clubs and bars are rarely raided. Dealing, by contrast, will be taken very seriously indeed, and is likely to result in imprisonment.

Ecstasy use has risen sharply in the past couple of years, while cocaine remains fairly widespread. Signs of a serious smack problem are not hard to detect.

Addiction support

Centro de Apoio a Toxicodependentes (CAT) do Restelo

Avenida do Restelo 36, Restelo, 1400 (21 303 0600). Bus 51. **Open** 9am-6pm Mon-Fri; closed Sat, Sun. **Map** p303 B9.

CAT das Taipas

Rua das Taipas 20, Avenida da Liberdade, 1250 (213240870). Metro Avenida. **Open** 9am-7pm Mon; 2pm-8pm Tue; 9am-8pm Wed; 9am-6pm Thur, Fri.

Gabinete de Dependência Química

Rua Epifânio Dias 44, Alvalade, 1700 (21 842 1670). Metro Alvalade/Bus 7, 21, 33, 35, 55. **Open** 10am-6pm daily. **Map** p305 M2.

This is the main non-government funded centre for the treatment of drug addiction in Lisbon.

Electricity

Electricity in Portugal runs on 220V. Plugs have two round pins. To use UK appliances, simply change the plug or use an adaptor (available at UK electrical shops, but hard to find in Lisbon). American appliances run on 110V and require a converter, available at larger specialist electricity stores in Lisbon.

Embassies & consulates

For a complete list of embassies and consulates look in the yellow pages (*Páginas Amarelas*) under *Embaixadas, Consulados e Legações*.

Australian Embassy

Rua do Marquês de Sá da Bandeira 8, Praça de Espanha, 1300 (21 353 0750). Metro São Sebastião. **Open** 9am-4pm Mon-Fri; closed Sat, Sun. **Map** p304 L5.

Directory

British Embassy

*Rua de São Marçal 174, Príncipe
Real, 1200 (21 392 9440/www.uk-
embassy.pt). Metro Rato.* **Open** 9am-
11.30am, 2-4pm Mon-Fri; closed Sat,
Sun. **Map** p307 K8.
**British Consulate and
Commercial Section**
*Rua São Bernardo 33, Estrela, 1249-
082 (21 392 4000/fax 21 392 4186).
Metro Rato.* **Open** 9am-1pm, 2.30-
5.30pm Mon-Fri; closed Sat, Sun.
Map p306 J8.

Canadian Embassy

*Edifício Vitória, Avenida da
Liberdade 196/200-3, 1269 (21 316
4600/commercial section 21 316
4600/fax 21 316 4695). Metro
Avenida.* **Open** 8.30am-12.30pm,
1.30-5pm Mon-Fri; closed Sat, Sun.
Map 307 L8.

Irish Embassy

*Rua da Imprensa à Estrela 1,
Estrela, 1200 (21 392 9440). Tram
28.* **Open** 9am-12.30pm, 2-4pm Mon-
Fri; closed Sat, Sun. **Map** p306 J8.

US Embassy

*Avenida das Forças Armadas,
Sete Rios, 1600-081 (21 727
3300/www.american-embassy.pt/
commercial section 21 7700
2525/fax 21 726 8914). Metro
Jardim Zoológico/32, 54, 55 bus.*
Open *Visas* 8-10am Mon-Fri; closed
Sat, Sun. *Information* 11.30am-
4.30pm Mon-Fri; closed Sat, Sun.
Commercial section 2-5pm Mon-Fri;
closed Sat, Sun. **Map** p304 J3.
The commercial section's library is
generally open to the public at the
same hours, but it's best to call first.

Emergencies

For emergency services call
112, and specify either *polícia,
ambulância* or *bombeiros* (fire
brigade). *See also below*
Health, *p279* **Helplines** and
p283 **Police stations**.

Health

There are no special threats
to health in Portugal, though,
for children especially, a
strong sun cream and hats
should be kept handy.

Portugal's public health
system is poor by EU
standards. Once you reach the
specialists, standards are
reasonable, but GPs are
underfunded, burdened with
bureaucracy and inefficient.

EU visitors who do not
make social security payments
in Portugal are entitled to
reimbursement only on
emergency treatment.

Those who have health
insurance will be better off
taking advantage of a strong
private sector. A mere visit to
a private doctor will cost you
around 12,000$00, but the
service is good.

Complementary medicine

Portugal does not have a culture of
alternative medicine, apart from the
use of traditional herbal remedies.
However, there is a growing interest
in holistic and homoeopathic
remedies, and there is a reasonable
choice in the Yellow Pages under
Homeopatia.

Sociedade de Homeopatia

*Rua Andrade Corvo 16, Picoas,
1050 (21 315 3355). Metro Picoas.*
Open 9am-7pm Mon-Fri; closed Sat,
Sun. **Map** p307 L6.

Contraception & abortion

Condoms are easily available in
pharmacies, supermarkets or
dispensing machines. An attempt
a few years ago to liberalise the
country's strict abortion laws
failed to mobilise the population,
so termination is still only allowed in
strictly defined circumstances.There
are a number of reputable clinics in
Portugal that quietly defy the law,
but there are also horror stories
about some unlawful establishments.

Hospital de Santa Maria

*Avenida Professor Egas Moniz,
Campo Grande, 1600 (21 797
5171/21 790 1330). Metro Cidade
Universitária/bus 32, 54, 55.*
Open 8am-no more patients
Mon-Fri. **Map** p304 K2.

Maternity Hospital Doutor Alfredo da Costa

*Rua Pedro Nunes, Saldanha, 1050
(21 318 4077/21 318 4000). Metro
Picoas.* **Open** 8am-no more patients
Mon-Fri. **Map** p304 L5.
Has family planning clinic and
provides counselling services.
Call in advance for appointment.

Dentists

Public health dentists are available
for a nominal fee, but standards are
patchy. If you can't wait until you
get home,we advise you to splash
out on private treatment. Look under
Dentistas in the Yellow Pages. Some
we can recommend:

António Rebocho Machado

*Rua Dom João V 4, Rato, 1250
(21 388 5063). Metro Rato.*
Open 9.30am-1pm, 2-6pm Mon-Fri.
No credit cards. Map p306 J7.

Clínica Dentária e Ortodôntica

*Avenida Combatentes da Grande
Guerra 130, Algés, 1495 (21 410
3999/3815). Tram 15/train to
Algés.* **Open** 9.30-11.30am, 2.30-
6pm Mon-Fri; closed Sat, Sun.
No credit cards.

Manuel João Patricio Alves

*Avenida Estados Unidos da América
103, Alvalade, 1700 (21 796 8540).
Metro Roma.* **Open** 9am-noon
Tue, Wed; 2.30-7pm Thur; closed
Mon, Fri-Sun. **No credit cards.**
Map p305 M3.

Thomas Schreiner

*Rua Pascoal de Melo 60, Arroios,
1150 (21 355 9424/ 8471). Metro
Arroios.* **Open** 9am-8pm Mon-Fri;
closed Sat, Sun. **No credit cards.**
Map p308 N6.

Doctors

Dr João Sá

*Rua Martens Ferrão 26, Picoas,
1050 (21 314 6253). Metro Picoas.*
Map p307 L6.

Dr António Alvim

*Rua Ivens 26, Chiado, 1200 (21
342 5626). Metro Baixa-Chiado.*
Map p310 L9.

Dra Vera Horta e Costa

*Avenida Luís Bívar, 93, Saldanha,
1050 (21 315 7908). Metro
Saldanha/bus 16, 18, 26, 42.* **Open**
11am-6pm Wed, Fri. **Map** p304 L5.
A gynaecologist.

The International Health Centre

*Rua do Regimento XIX 67, 2750
Cascais (21 484 5317). Train from
Cais do Sodré to Cascais.*
Offers a 24-hour service and
home visits by British and English-
speaking Portuguese doctors
and nurses.

Directory

Hospitals: public

For a complete list of hospitals in and around Lisbon, consult the Yellow Pages (*Páginas Amarelas*) under *Hospitais*. Hospitals with emergency wards (*serviço de urgência*) open 24 hours daily include Lisbon's largest, the Hospital de Santa Maria (*see p278*) and:

Hospital Curry Cabral

Rua da Beneficência 8, Praça de Espanha, 1069 (21 792 4200/2).
Metro Praça de Espanha/bus 16, 21, 26, 36, 44, 45, 56. **Map** p304 L4.

Hospital Miguel Bombarda

Rua Dr Almada Amaral, Campo de Santana, 1199 (21 317 7400).
Bus 58. **Open** 24-hours daily.
Map p307 M7.
Psychiatric help.

Hospital São Francisco Xavier

Estrada Forte Alto do Duque, Restelo, 1400 21 300 0300/21 301 7351). Bus 23, 51. **Map** p303 A8.

Hospitals: private

Hospital da Cuf

Travessa Castro 3, Avenida Infante Santo, Alcântara, 1350 (21 392 6100/15). Bus 13, 14, 20, 28, 32, 38, 40, 43. **Map** p306 G9.

Hospital Inglês

Rua Saraiva de Carvalho 46, Estrela, 1269 (21 395 5067/ 21 397 6329/4066). Tram 25, 28/9, 20, 27, 38 bus. **Open** 9am-9pm Mon-Fri; 9am-noon Sat; closed Sun. **Map** p306 J8.

Hospital Particular de Lisboa

Avenida Luís Bívar 30, Saldanha, 1050 (21 358 6200). Metro Saldanha/12, 20, 22, 23, 27, 32, 53 bus. **Map** p304 L5.

Hospital São José

Rua José António Serrano, Campo dos Mártires da Pátria, Campo de Santana, 1150 (21 881 0475). Bus 23, 30, 33, 100. **Map** p307 M8.

Anjos da Noite

Rua Francisco Franco 5-1E, 1700 (21 796 3609).
Open *head office* 9am-1pm, 2-6pm daily. **Map** p305 O2.
Members of 'Night Angels' pay a fee of 1,400$00 a month. Offers a range of medical services with clinics and a visiting service. Contact head office (above) for more information.

Opticians

See chapter **Shops & Services**

Pharmacies

Lisbon's plentiful pharmacies are identified by a green cross. Many drugs are available without a prescription and you can get some basic advice on the spot. Out of office hours there is at least one pharmacy open in each neighbourhood. Look in pharmacy windows for the rota.

STDs, HIV & Aids

For most problems, see a GP, or use the emergency service of a hospital. Aids has been aggravated by high levels of needle use among heroin users, but the authorities have introduced some enlightened policies in recent years. English is spoken at the following HIV/AIDS helplines:

Abraço

(21 342 5929). **Open** 24hrs daily.
(21 343 2499). **Open** 10am-1pm, 3-8pm Mon-Fri; closed Sat, Sun.

SOS-Sida Information, Orientation, Support

(freephone 800 201 040). **Open** 6-10pm daily.

Helplines

Alcoólicos Anónimos

21 716 2969.

Centro SOS Voz Amiga

(21 354 4545/freephone 800 202669). **Open** 5pm-7am daily.
Freephone number 9pm-midnight daily.
Helplines for sufferers of loneliness and depression.

Linha Vida

(freephone 800 255255). **Open** 10am-midnight Mon-Fri; closed Fri, Sat.
Advice in case of overdoses.

Narcóticos Anónimos

freephone 800 202013.

According to Portuguese law, you're supposed to carry ID with you at all times, which for British and non-EU nationals mean a passport. In practice you're unlikely to be asked for it unless you get into trouble.

The Departamento Legalização de Viaturas of the Automóvel Clube de Portugal (*see p272* **Accidents and breakdowns**) can help with paperwork for importing, registering and insuring a car in Portugal – but you have to join. For household insurance and services, **Europassistance** (*see p174*) offers a package for residents. *See also p278* **Health**.

Young Portuguese in particular have taken to the internet in a big way, although economic factors limit the spread of PCs. Most major companies (and many mid-sized service companies) now have websites or at least email.

Internet access

For a short visit, try one of the cybercafés listed below, or **Telepac** (*see p280*). *See also p280* **Libraries** and **Mail Boxes Etc** and **PostNet**, (for both, *see p275*).

Café.com

Costa do Castelo 7, Castelo, 1100 (21 886 5786/21 887 8225/21 886 1419). Tram 12, 28/37 bus. **Open** 6pm-2am. **Map** p311 M9.
Publicly funded outfit within trendy bar-restaurant Chapitô. It has nine computers, available for 500$00 an hour; 350$00 for under-21s.

Ciber Chiado

Centro Nacional de Cultura, Largo do Picadeiro 10, Chiado, 1200 (21 346 6722/www.cnc.pt). Metro Baixa-Chiado/tram 28. **Open** 4-7.30pm Mon-Fri, 8.30pm-midnight Sat; closed Sun. **Internet use** 600$00 per hour. **No credit cards.** **Map** p310 L9.

Cyberbica

Rua Duques de Bragança 7, Chiado, 1200 (21 322 5004/www.cyberbica. com). Metro Baixa-Chiado/28 tram. **Open** noon-2pm Mon-Fri, 7pm-2am Sat; closed Sun. **Internet use** 600$00 per hour or 150$00 per 15min block. **No credit cards.** **Map** p310 L9.
Six terminals with internet access.

Web Café

Rua Diário Notícias 126, Bairro Alto, 1200-145 (21 342 1181/

Directory

*web1@mail.esoterica.pt). Metro
Baixa-Chiado/28 tram.* **Open** 4pm-
2am daily. **Credit** AmEx, MC, V.
Map p310 L9.
Snug bar with computers making it
a fun place to log on. It costs 800$00
per hour, but with a sliding scale for
smaller blocks of time: 500$00 per
half-hour and 300$00 per 15mins.

Online services

If you don't have an internet account
and are not sure you'll be in Lisbon
for more than a month or two,
there are a number of free internet
providers you might consider.
Theyinclude **NetSapo** (www.
netsapo.pt), Teleweb's **Easynet**
(www.easynet.pt) and **Netfamily**
(www.netfamily.pt), **Oninet**
(www.oninet.pt), **Clix** (www.clix.pt)
and IOL (www.iol.pt). Or you can pay
for a higher priority service such as
the **Netpac** package offered by
local internet provider Telepac
or the **NetPlus** and **NetMaster**
packages from Teleweb.

Telepac

*Forum Picoas, Avenida Fontes
Pereira de Melo 38-40, Picoas, 1050-
123 (21 314 2527/freephone 800
200079/www.telepac.pt/www.cidadevi
rtual.pt/netpac). Metro Picoas.* **Open**
9am-7pm Mon-Fri; closed Sat, Sun.
No credit cards. Map p307 L6.
With Telepac, for 6,950$00 you get a
CD-Rom with access software; user
name, password and two e-mail
address, plus 40 hours of internet
use. You also get a code that you
need to recharge your account at
ATMs, at a cost of 5,000$00 for a
further 40 hours. Telepac has one
access number for all Portugal, so is
a good option if you are travelling a
lot. There's also off-the-street internet
access at Forum Picoas, with 24
computers available for internet and
outgoing email at a competitive
400$00 per hour (with a minimum
half-hour charge). You can print in
black and white for 25$00 per page
or in colour for 70$00.

Teleweb

*Avenida Defensores de Chaves
73, Saldanha, 1000-114 (21 780
1318/www.teleweb.pt). Metro
Saldanha.* **Open** 9am-11pm
Mon-Fri; 9am-8pm Sat; closed Sun.
No credit cards. Map p304 M5.
The NetPlus package costs
5,950$00 which includes one
month of unlimited internet use;
monthly recharges are for either 20
hours (1,950$00) or unlimited hours
(2,950$00). The top-priority package,
NetMaster, costs 6,950$00 including
one unlimited month, with further
monthly costs of 3,450$00 for
unlimited hours.

Language

For Portuguese words and
phrases, *see p288*, and for
language courses, *see p284*. If
you plan to speak the language
during your stay in Lisbon but
picked it up in Brazil, you'll
find that adapting to local
ways will be appreciated.

Left luggage

Airports

The Depósito de bagagem (21 841
3500) is in the arrivals hall. Cost is
according to weight, with 310$00 per
day forup to 10kg, 520$00 per day for
between 10kg and 30kg and 1,040$00
for 30kg to 60kg. Theoretically, there
is no limit on the number of days that
you may leave luggage.

Legal help

If you get into legal difficulties,
the British Embassy or any
other (*see p277*), can provide a
list of English-speaking
lawyers in Lisbon on request,
or look on the US Embassy
website. For a fuller list, look
in the Yellow Pages (*Páginas
Amarelas*) under *Advogados*.
Most big firms have English-
speaking lawyers.

Ordem dos Advogados

*Largo de São Domingos 14-1,
Rossio, 1160 (21 882 3550).*
Open 9.30am-12.30pm, 2-6pm
Mon-Fri; closed Sat, Sun.
The professional body for lawyers
will put you in touch with an
English-speaking lawyer.

Centro de Apoio para
Estrangeiros

*Centro Comercial de Queluz, Avenida
António Enes 31, 2745 Queluz (21
435 3810/fax 21 436 6483). Train
to Sintra from Restauradores
(Queluz-Belas station).* **Open** 9am-
10pm Mon-Fri, 2-8pm Sat.
Help specifically for foreigners.

Abreu & Marques e
Associados

*Rua Filipe Folque 2-4, São Sebastião
de Pedreira, 1069-121 (21 330
7100/fax 21 314 7491/amadvog
@mail.telepac.pt). Metro Parque.*
Open 9am-7pm Mon-Fri; closed Sat,
Sun. **Map** p307 L7.
Established company specialising in
business; has an office in London.

Marques Bom e
Associados

*Rua Castilho 65, Marquês de
Pombal, 1250-068 (21 384 1540/
fax 21 388 6462/mba.adv@
mail.telepac.pt). Metro Marquês de
Pombal.* **Open** 10am-7pm Mon-Fri;
closed Sat, Sun. **Map** p307 K7.
Wide experience with franchises and
business contracts.

Libraries

Specialist libraries are listed in
Agenda Cultural.

Biblioteca do Instituto
Británico

*Rua de São Marçal 174, Príncipe
Real, 1249 (21 347 6141). Metro
Rato/15, 58, 100 bus.* **Open** 2-8pm
Mon; 10am-8pm Tue; noon-8pm Wed;
10am-7.30pm Thur; noon-7pm Fri;
closed Sat, Sun. **Map** p307 K8.
The British Library offers free access
for reference purposes. Use of the
lending service requires membership.
Students and other concessionary
groups pay an annual fee of 2,500$00.
Others pay 3,000$00.

Biblioteca Municipal
Palácio Galveias

*Palácio Galveias, Campo Pequeno,
1000 (21 797 1326). Metro Campo
Pequeno.* **Open** 10am-8pm Mon, Tue;
10am-6pm Wed-Fri; 11am-5pm Sat;
closed Sun. **Map** p304 M4.
This is the main municipal lending
library (for branches, see the Yellow
Pages). Present ID for access, and
proof of residency for borrowing.
Also has free internet access.

Biblioteca Nacional

*Campo Grande 83, Campo Grande,
1700 (21 798 2000). Metro Entre
Campos.* **Open** 9.30am-7.30pm Mon-
Fri. 9.30am-5.30pm Sat; closed Sun.
Map p304 L2.
Portugal's national library. Use
is restricted to over 18s. Non-EU
citizens must show a passport, EU
citizens ID. Annuity: 1,000$00. Holds
interesting documentary exhibitions.

Lost or stolen
property

For lost or stolen property, try
the lost and found section of
the Lisbon police, the PSP (*see
below*). But don't hope too hard.
Theft should be reported at
any police station, in person.
For lost or stolen credit cards,
contact your bank.

Airport

If your luggage has gone astray, go to the desk in arrivals set up for this purpose. Anything lost in the airport building and handed in goes to the police, the PSP, which also has a desk in the arrivals hall (21 853 5403).

Public transport

For buses and trams, contact the Carris headquarters in Santo Amaro on 21 361 3000. There is a lost and found office at Marquês de Pombal Metro station.

Taxis

If you leave something in a taxi, you will have to phone the company. If you have a receipt with the car's number on it, all the better. If you can't remember the name of the company, and your ride was in central Lisbon, there's a fair chance it will be Rádio Taxis de Lisboa, the biggest company (21 811 9000).

Media

The hexagonal green newspaper kiosk remains a symbol of old Lisbon, though most have been replaced by standard-issue grey cubicles. Despite an illiteracy rate of around 10 per cent (higher among the older generation and in rural areas) and a limited public appetite for hard news, the print market is in a phase of expansion. There has been a wave of mergers of late, with even major magnates Francisco Pinto Balsemão (a former prime minister) – who owns *Expresso*, a clutch of magazines and SIC TV – and retailer-industrialist Belmiro de Azevedo – who owns *Público* – jumping into bed together. Sports are the prime concern everwhere in the media, driven by the obsession with football.

Magazines

If you can read Portuguese, magazines worth looking at include *Grande Reportagem*, a news monthly that goes deeper than its glossy appearance suggests. Travel mags such as *Volta ao Mundo* and *Evasões* are good for tips on hotels and tourist spots off the beaten track. *Visão* is a news weekly that tends to recycle *Time* and *Newsweek*'s take on

international news but gives concise summaries of Portuguese happenings with the odd amusing feature.

Newspapers

Público

Comprehensive, quality coverage; good on international events. Has a number of special sections, including a Friday guide to the arts.

Diário de Notícias/ Jornal de Notícias

The somewhat old-fashioned Oporto-based *Jornal de Notícias* – whose big selling-point is the local sections it produces for pretty well all parts of the country – remains the biggest-selling news daily. Its sister paper, by contrast, has been losing ground to *Público* since the latter slashed its price to 100$00. Good classifieds.

Diário Económico

Daily business paper that covers international finance as well as local stories and market coverage – albeit in a very inconsistent fashion.

Expresso

A bulky weekly that has to be served in a plastic bag, it has so many sections. It once set the agenda, but has never been the same since feisty rival *O Independente* knocked it off its perch in the 1980s before itself going downhill. Now *Expresso* tends to summarise the events of the past week. Still leads on political analysis, though. Its cultural listings are good.

Tal e Qual

A tongue-in-cheek tabloid that's about as lowbrow as you can go. Staples are celebrity romance, tax evasion exposés, astrology and readers' letters. It's always amusing, and lots of people read it on the sly.

A Bola/Record/O Jogo

These three football papers are the country's most popular daily read, respectively biased towards Benfica, Sporting and Porto. Lots of pictures and graphics – 90 per cent football, though other sports do squeeze in.

English-language

Anglo-Portuguese News

This amateurish weekly that looks like a parish handout has its own niche of devoted readers and is known fondly as the APN. Covering the British community and published in the expat heartland of Estoril, it offers warmed-over local and foreign newsbriefs, listings and classified ads.

Here, bargains are often to be had when diplomats sell off their goods before leaving for the next posting.

The News

This Algarve-based weekly is better for news, though with similar listings and small ads. Hard to find in Lisbon.

People and Business

Slick property and business monthly, providing an overview of investment and culture for travellers and expats. It is distributed free at many hotels.

Foreign newspapers

These can be found at some kiosks and shops in Restauradores and Rossio, and in shopping malls. Note that the fact that a kiosk's awning has the name of a major international newspaper emblazoned on it does not mean the publication is on sale there. Downtown, **Tema** has the best selection. Delivery of British tabloids is regular, as the *Sun, Mirror, Mail* and *Express* print in Spain for the expat community, but quality dailies only turn up late in the afternoon, the next day, or sometimes not at all.

Tema

Avenida da Liberdade 9, Baixa, 1250 (342 0140). Metro Restauradores. **Open** 9am-9pm daily. **Credit** MC, V. **Map** p310 L8. Wide-ranging stock includes specialist titles and trade mags. Can order in. **Branch:** Centro Colombo (21 716 6890).

Radio

Apart from football, traffic and one news station, the airwaves are filled with music. **Rádio Cidade** (107.2FM) is the liveliest (or most irritating) station, with screaming Brazilian DJs and a dance-pop mix. Church-owned **Rádio Renascença** has various stations, one as staid as the next, and the biggest combined audience. Its morning talk shows are popular with housewives. **TSF** (89.5FM) is news radio 24 hours a day, with a few gaps filled with pop, live football and ads. State-run **Antena 1** (95.9 FM) is also a good news and football source.

French speakers can tune to **Rádio Paris Lisboa** (90.4FM), while the **BBC World Service** is on short wave on various frequencies; schedules are printed regularly in the *Anglo-Portuguese News*.

Television

Some of the most creative reporting is now on television, where social dramas are played out. The seamy underbelly of society – prostitution, drug abuse – is a favourite theme. This is part of a general downmarket tendency, a direct result of opening up two channels to the private sector. Balsemão led the way with **SIC's** diet of *telenovelas* – Brazilian soaps, titillating docudramas and absurd game shows, although news is a flagship, as evidenced by the 2001 launch of **SIC Notícias**, a cable TV news channel. The Catholic Church launched **TVI** – only to lose control after ratings slipped, making further cash injections necessary. TVI now often beats SIC at its own game, as evidenced by its success in securing the Portuguese rights to *Big Brother* – and ensuring it was a massive hit.

State TV saw which way the wind was blowing: **RTP1** started its own dumbing-down process, leaving **RTP2** to hold the fort with overtly cultural, public-service image with good movies, classical music and high-quality imported sitcoms. As with movies, these are not dubbed.

With reporters in all the country's former colonies (and in parts of the world with large Portuguese communities) and close ties, Portuguese media consistently lead the rest of the West in coverage of parts of Africa, not to mention East Timor. RTP has its own satellite TV channel dedicated to African coverage, **RTP África**. This is available as part of the cable TV packages to which many Lisbon hotels subscribe, as are **CNN International** and **BBC World**.

Money

Portugal is proud to be in the first wave of countries participating in the European Monetary Union. The Portuguese escudo remains the sole currency in use until the end of 2001; for two months thereafter the two units will co-exist as legal tender, after which the escudo will be withdrawn. As with all other countries in the euro zone, the conversion rate is already fixed, in this case at 200.482 escudos to the euro.

How smoothly the changeover will go is anyone's guess, though the evidence suggests that many companies were unprepared well into the countdown to E day, especially in Portugal, where small, family-run businesses dominate. To avoid the feared

cash drought after the escudo is phased out, banks will give retailers advance access to euros and Portugal's huge network of cash machines will be converted and filled – how efficiently this is done is expected to be a key factor.

The euro (€) is divided into 100 cents (¢). Notes come in denominations of five, ten, 20, 50, 100, 200 and 500 euros; coins in one and two euros and one, two, five, ten, 20 and 50 cents.

The escudo is denoted by the symbol $00. Coins in use are 5$00, 10$00, 20$00, 50$00, 100$00 and 200$00. Notes come in denominations of 500$00, 1,000$00, 2,000$00, 5,000$00 and 10,000$00.

For a euro/escudo conversion chart, *see p3*.

Cash machines

Portugal's Multibanco system links all the country's cash machines (ATMs), allows locals direct debit payments almost everywhere and permits payment of bills in the blink of an eye. You're never far from a Multibanco in Lisbon. Debit cards compatible with all cash machines are widely used, often in the tiniest cafés and shops, and electronic money is also fairly common. Many ATMs and in-store machines accept Mastercard, Visa and other major cards, including Maestro and Cirrus, making this the best way to spend or transfer small amounts, given the relatively good exchange rates used.

Banks

Little more than a decade ago Portugal's banks were fusty state-controlled institutions. An aggressive privatisation programme and heavy investment has changed all this. Banks generally open from 8.30am to 3pm. Most have a small number of branches that stay open until 6pm.

Most of the head offices listed here have a branch on the premises; where this is not the case, a downtown one has been listed.

Banco Bilbao Vizcaya e Argentaria (BBVA)
Avenida da Liberdade 222, 1250-148 (21 311 7200/www. bbvbportugal.pt). Metro Avenida. **Open** 8.30am-4pm Mon-Fri; closed Sat, Sun. **Map** p307 L8.

Branch: Rua Áurea (Rua do Ouro) 40-48, Baixa, 1100 (21 321 8500).

Banco BPI
Largo Jean Monnet 1-9º, Rua do Salitre, Avenida de Liberdade, 1269-067 (21 310 1000/www.bancobpi.pt). Metro Rato. **Open** 8.30am-3pm Mon-Fri; closed Sat, Sun. **Map** p307 L8. *Branch*: Avenida da Liberdade 9A, 1250-139 (21 342 1068).

Banco Comercial Português
Avenida José Malhoa, Lote 1686, Praça de Espanha, 1099-010 (21 721 8000/www.bcp.pt). Metro Praça de Espanha. **Open** 8.30am-3pm Mon-Fri; closed Sat, Sun. **Map** p304 J4. **Branch**: Rua Augusta 62, Baixa, 1149-023 (21 321 1000).

Banco Espírito Santo
Avenida da Liberdade 195, 1250-142 (21 315 8331/ www.bes.pt). Metro Avenida. **Open** 8.30am-3pm Mon-Fri; closed Sat, Sun. **Map** p307 L7. The retail branch is next door.

Banco Mello
Rua Alexandre Herculano 50, Marquês de Pombal, 1269-055 (21 312 5000). Metro Marquês de Pombal. **Open** 8.30am-3pm Mon-Fri; closed Sat, Sun. **Map** p307 K7. **Branch**: Rua Áurea (Rua do Ouro) 95, Baixa, 1100-060 (21 347 0491).

Banco Nacional Ultramarino
Avenida 5º de Outubro 175, Campo Pequeno, 1050-053 (21 791 8000/www.bnu.pt). Metro Campo Pequeno. **Open** 8.30am-2.45pm Mon-Fri; closed Sat, Sun. **Map** p304 L4. **Branch**: Rua Augusta 24, Baixa, 1100-053 (21 346 9981).

Banco Pinto & Sotto Mayor
Rua Áurea (Rua do Ouro) 28, Baixa, 1100-063 (21 340 2929/www. bpsm.pt). Metro Baixa-Chiado/tram 28. **Open** 8.30am-3pm Mon-Fri; closed Sat, Sun. **Map** p310 M10.

Banco Português do Atlântico
Rua Áurea (Rua do Ouro) 110, Baixa, 1100-063 (21 323 1172/7/8/9/www.bpa.pt). Metro Baixa-Chiado/tram 28. **Open** 8.30am-3pm Mon-Fri; closed Sat, Sun. **Map** p310 M10.

Banco Santander
Praça Marquês de Pombal 2, 1250-161 (21 317 2560/www.santander. pt). Metro Marquês de Pombal. **Open** 8.30am-3pm Mon-Fri; closed Sat, Sun. **Map** p307 K7.

Banco Totta & Açores

Rua Áurea (Rua do Ouro) 88, Baixa, 1100-063 (21 321 1500/www.bta.pt). Metro Baixa-Chiado/tram 28. **Open** 8.30am-3pm Mon-Fri; closed Sat, Sun. **Map** p310 M10.

Barclays Bank

Avenida da República 50, Campo Pequeno, 1050-185 (21 791 1100/www.barclays.pt). Metro Campo Pequeno. **Open** 8.30am-3.30pm Mon-Fri; closed Sat, Sun. **Map** p305 M4.

Caixa Geral de Depósitos

Avenida João XXI 63, Campo Pequeno, 1000-300 (21 790 5000/www.cgd.pt). Metro Campo Pequeno. **Open** 8.30am-3pm Mon-Fri; closed Sat, Sun. **Map** p305 M4. The branch in Centro Colombo (21 716 6354) is open from 10am to 4.30pm and the Baixa branch has cash and money-changing machines open after hours. **Branch:** Rua Áurea (Rua do Ouro) 49, Baixa, 1100-060 (21 340 5000).

Bureaux de change

There are clusters of these around Rossio and Praça da Figueira. They differ little from banks in terms of cost, but are often faster. They also have a wider range of currencies on tap. The main Baixa branch of Caixa Geral de Depósitos (*see above*) has a money-changing machine, one of a handful dotted around the centre.

Credit cards

American Express, MasterCard and Visa are by far the most widespread cards, but are not accepted in many shops, cafés and restaurants.

Tax

Residents of EU member states may not claim back any value-added tax on purchases. US residents may do so if they buy goods at shops that adhere to the Tax-free scheme; they will have a sticker displayed in the window. Claims are made by filling in a form available at the Tax-free counter at the airport (21 846 8813), near Departures. There's also an information line (21 846 3025).

Though the 1755 Lisbon earthquake proved earth-shaking enough for shocked European commentators of the time to question the existence of a benevolent God, there hasn't been another big one since then. Unlike the Azores, where tremors are relatively common, the very occasional ones in Lisbon are tiny. Otherwise, aside from fierce Atlantic waves, Portugal is free of natural hazards.

Opening hours

Shops are normally open from 9am to 1pm and 3pm to 6pm or 7pm, although some high-street shops remain open during lunch. Most supermarkets stay open until about 8pm. In shopping centres, hours tend to be from 10am until 10pm or even midnight in the case of some shops in Centro Colombo and Centro Vasco da Gama (*see p175*). Banks usually open from 8.30am-3pm, weekdays only, and downtown post offices (*correios*) from 9am-6pm, also weekdays only (smaller branches may close for lunch).

Police stations

Lisbon police have a relaxed air, but as is typical in former dictatorships, Portugal's law enforcers are only gradually regaining the trust of the population. Old authoritarian attitudes can still be detected, and, when pushed, Portuguese police can still act with brutality. Training and image have improved, however, and you will usually find them polite and capable of helping you out. But do not try to resist or argue if you get into bother. Quiet diplomacy is easily the best way to avoid a sore head. There is a special police station for tourists in Palácio Foz on Praça dos Restauradores.

Postal services

First class mail is Correio Azul (Blue Mail). Costing a minimum 350$00, it should get anywhere in Europe in under four days, and to the US in no more than six. For domestic letters under 20 grams (7oz) second class or normal post costs 53$00, or 50$00. The rate for other EU countries is 90$00 for Spain and 105$00 for all other EU countries. The rate for outside the EU is 140$00.

Stamps are sold at all post office counters and at machines there or on the street, from which they cost a few escudos less. Mailing boxes offer two routes: red for regular post, blue for *correio azul*.

Main post office

Praça dos Restauradores 58, 1150 (21 323 8971/21 347 8400). Metro Restauradores. **Open** 8.30am-10pm Mon-Fri; 9am-6pm Sat, Sun. **Map** p310 L8. There is also a 24-hour post office at the airport (21 843 5050).

Poste restante

This should be addressed 'Poste restante' and to a particular post office. It can be collected from the office on Praça dos Restauradores.

Religion

Portugal is a Roman Catholic country, and you are never far from a church. Check on the church doors for service times.

Anglican

St George's Church *Rua São Jorge, Jardim da Estrela, 1200 (for details call the English Cemetery 21 390 6248). Bus 9, 20, 22, 27, 38.* **Mass** 11.30am Sun, 1.30pm Tue. **Map** p306 J8.

Baptist

Igreja Evangélica Baptista da Graça *Rua Capitão Humberto Ataíde 28, Santa Apolónia, 1170 (21 813 2889). Bus 18, 42.* **Services** 10am Sun; 3pm Wed. **Map** p308 O8.

Buddhist

Budismo Tibetano Nyingma *Rua do Salitre 117, Avenida da Liberdade, 1250 (21 314 2038). Metro Rato.* **Open** 9am-9.30pm Mon-Fri; closed Sat, Sun. **Map** p307 L8. Also has a vegetarian restaurant and yoga centre.

Catholic

Basílica da Estrela *Largo da Estrela, Estrela, 1200 (21 396 0915). Bus 13, 14, 20, 22, 27,*

28, 32, 38, 40, 43, 49, 60. **Open**
8am-1pm, 3-8pm daily. **Map** 306 J8.

Sé Catedral
Largo da Sé, 1100 (21 886 6752).
Tram 12, 28. **Open** 9am-5pm daily.
Map p311 M10.

Hindu
Comunidade Hindú de Portugal
Alameda Mahatama Gandhi,
Lumiar, 1600 (21 757 6524).
Metro Campo Grande/1, 3, 4, 36,
101 bus. **Open** 9am-7pm Mon-Fri;
closed Sat, Sun.

Ismaeli
Centro Cultural Ismaelita
Rua Abranches Ferrão, Laranjeiras,
1600 (21 722 9000). Metro
Laranjeiras. **Open** 9am-7pm
daily. **Map** p304 J3.
This beautiful modern mosque and
cultural centre was opened by the
Aga Khan in 1999.

Islamic
Mesquita Central de Lisboa
Avenida José Malhôa, Praça de
Espanha, 1070 (21 387 4142/2220).
Metro Praça de Espanha. **Open**
7am-7pm daily. **Map** p304 K4.

Jewish
Comunidade Israelita de Lisboa
Rua Alexandre Herculano 59, Rato,
1250 (21 385 8604). Metro Rato.
Open 10am-1pm, 3-5pm Mon-Thur;
10am-1pm Fri. **Map** 307 K7.

Safety & security

Lisbon is a relatively
safe town, but be aware of
pickpockets among crowds.
Skilful groups of them work in
twos and threes, especially on
trams. Lisbon's narrow streets
and dimly lit alleys offer an
ideal environment for street
crime, but incidents are rare.
Basic safety rules apply: do
not carry too much cash on
you; avoid dark and deserted
places, and be careful with
valuables. Be alert when
visiting tourist areas such as
Bairro Alto, Cais do Sodré and
the lower Alfama. There is
heavier drug-related crime in
the poorest neighbourhoods
and peripheral shanty towns,
but visitors are unlikely to
come into contact with this.
Car crime is common and
the usual precautions should
always be taken when leaving
vehicles unattended.

Smoking

There are well-stocked
tobacconists all over town.
Most bars and cafés have
vending machines, but you
can't always count on this.
News kiosks do not normally
sell cigarettes. Smoking is not
permitted on public transport
or in museums. Elsewhere,
there are relatively few
restrictions and not many
restaurants have no-smoking
areas, although they are
becoming more common. Many
of the more modern hotels are
also starting to introduce
smoke-free floors.

Study

Language classes

The following offer courses in
Portuguese.

Cambridge School
Avenida da Liberdade 173, 1250 (21
352 7474). Metro Avenida. Fees
Classes of three to six students:
94,400$00 plus 7,900$00 enrolment.
Individual classes 228,800$00.
Map p307 L8.
Five levels. Classes begin each
month, from Monday to Friday.
Each course consists of a total of
40 lessons, two lessons per day.

Cial
Departamento de Português
para Estrangeiros, Avenida da
República 41, Saldanha, 1050
(21 794 0448). Metro Saldanha.
Open 9am-5.30pm Mon-Fri;
closed Sat, Sun. **Map** p304 M5.
Four-week course, with a
maximum six students, for three
hours a day cost 155,000$00,
including all necessary materials.
Individual tuition totalling 60 hours
per month is 5,500$00 per hour, or
5,000$00 per hour if you do more
than 60 hours per month.

International House
Rua Marquês Sá da Bandeira
16, São Sebastião, 1050 (21 315
1496). Metro São Sebastião.
Open 9am-9pm Mon-Fri;
closed Sat, Sun. **Map** p304 L5.
A four-week intensive course, three
hours a day Mon-Fri, including 12
guided tours around Lisbon, costs
135.000$00. Individual tuition in an
intensive course, 80 or 120 hours over
four weeks, costs 608,000$00 and
846,000$00 respectively.

Linguacoop
Avenida Manuel da Maia 46, Praça
de Londres, 1000 (21 840 9777).
Metro Alameda. **Open** 10am-8pm
Mon-Fri; closed Sat, Sun. Fees
Individual classes 10 lessons
46,300$00; 20-lessons 88,200$00.
Intensive classes 40 lessons – price
by arrangement. **Map** p305 N4.

Universidade de Lisboa
Alameda da Universidade, Cidade
Universitária, 1649 (21 792 0000).
Metro Cidade Universitária. **Fees**
100,000$00 per term, plus an annual
fee of 25,000$00. **Map** p304 K2.
Courses usually begin in October and
finish in May. The final date for
registration is 12 October.

Universities

Lisbon has a total of 58 universities.
Public universities are government-
funded, but top-up fees were recently
introduced, triggering a major
protest campaign on the campuses.
Private universities are not cheap,
costing around 40,000$00 per
month. Portuguese educational
establishments can produce areas
of brilliance, but the wider system
has a lot of catching up to do.

Universidade de Lisboa
Alameda da Universidade,
Cidade Universitária, 1649
(21 796 7624/fax 21793 3624/
www.ul.pt). Metro Campo
Grande. **Map** p304 L2.
The university was founded around
1288 by Dom Dinis. In 1911, it was
re-organised as four colleges: the
College of Languages and Literature
(Curso Superior de Letras), the
Medical College (Escola Médico-
Cirúrgica), the Polytechnic College
and the Pharmaceutical College.
More institutions were subsequently
integrated, including the Museu
de História Natural, the Jardim
Botânico, the Museu do Instituto
Geológico e Mineiro and the Museu
da Ciência. *See chapter* **Museums**.

Universidade Técnica de Lisboa
Alameda de Santa António dos
Capuchos 1, Campo de Santana,
1100 (21 885 2434/fax 21 357
1140/ www.utl.pt). Bus 23, 30, 33,
100. **Map** p307 M7.
This was created from four
existing colleges in 1931 – College
of Agronomy (Escola Superior de
Agronomia), College of Economical
and Financial Sciences (Escola
Superior de Ciências Econômicas e
Financeiras), College of Veterinarian
Medicine (Escola Superior de

Directory

Medicina Veterinária), College of
Engineering (Instituto Superior
Técnico). It later took on board social
and political sciences, physical
education and architecture faculties.

Universidade Nova de Lisboa

*Praça do Príncipe Real 26, Príncipe
Real, 1269 (21 342 2100]/fax 21
346 1924/www.unl.pt). Metro Rato.*
Map p307 K8.
Founded in 1973, the New
University's aim was to integrate
a technological perspective with
humanities, social sciences and
medicine. It is strong on research and
develops projects with the EU and
Portuguese-speaking countries.

Universidade Católica

*Campus de Palma de Cima, Praça de
Espanha, 1600 (21 721 4000/fax 21
727 0256/www.ucp.pt). Metro Praça
de Espanha.* **Map** p304 K3.
The UC was created by the Holy See
in 1967 on request of the Portuguese
Bishops Conference. Its first college
was the College of Philosophy in
Braga. In 1968 it expanded to Lisbon
where it now has its largest campus.

Universidade Lusíada

*Rua da Junqueira 188-198, Belém,
1349 (21 361 1500/fax 363
8307/www.ulusiada.pt). Bus 14, 27,
43, 49, 51.* **Map** 303 D10.
Founded in 1986, as 12 Centres of
Study and Research and eight
Institutes, which develop their
specific activities in different
scientific and cultural areas.

Information

CIREP

*Avenida 5° de Outubro 107,
Saldanha, 1050 (21 799 5470/
www.desup.min-edu.pt). Metro
Saldanha.* **Open** 9am-7pm Mon-Fri;
closed Sat, Sun. **Map** 304 L5.
Education Ministry service providing
information about all levels of the
eduation system and courses offered.

Telephones

Dialling & codes

To call Lisbon from overseas, first
dial your international access code
(0011 from Australia, 011 from
Canada or the US, 00 from New
Zealand and the UK) followed by 351
for Portugal. There are now no city
codes; Lisbon numbers all start with
21, but these digits form part of the
number. (If you want to call an old
seven-digit number, adding 21 at the
front should work; this replaces the
old city code, 01.)

Making a call

To dial another part of Portugal
from Lisbon, simply dial the number,
which invariably starts with 2.
There are no longer any area codes in
Portugal. If you have an old, pre-2000
number together with an area code
starting with zero, replacing the zero
with a 2 may do the trick. In some
towns, however, an extra digit was
added somewhere in the number to
bring it up to the full eight digits.
  To make an international call from
Portugal dial 00, followed by the
country code, the area code and then
the number. Useful country codes
are: Australia 61, Canada and the
US 1, New Zealand 64, the UK 44
(drop the initial zero of the area code).
Various cards are available but deals
are constantly changing so look out
for leaflets (almost always in English
as well as Portuguese) at kiosks and
in shops selling phone cards.

Operator services

For directory enquiries, dial 118.
International directory enquiries
is 177/9 but it's pricey; less well
publicised is freephone 800 201520.

Public phones

Portugal has coin-operated booths
and phone card kiosks, a handful
of which are of the old red variety,
dating back to the days when they
were maintained by the British
company. Phone cards are available
from news kiosks or post offices.
Older coin-operated booths are
less reliable and impractical for
international calls. Phoning from
hotels is expensive. Phone calls
between 9pm and 9am are cheaper,
as are weekends and holidays. There
is a large Portugal Telecom booth
with several phones on the north-
eastern corner of Rossio.

Telephone directories

The ordinary white-page directory
for Lisbon covers the Greater Lisbon
area, including Sintra and Cascais.
The *Páginas Amarelas* – Yellow
Pages – is now also online at
www.paginasamarelas.pt. However,
the usefulness of these publications
is compromised by the fact that
businesses such as shops and
restaurants are more often than not
listed under the owner's name.

Mobile phones

The Portuguese love their mobile
phones, and there are three domestic
operators: Optimus, Telecel and

TMN. All have good coverage in the
city, but it's worth checking out the
deals offered by all three before
subscribing. New users often buy
phones as part of a promotional pack
at very competitive rates.

Óptimus

*Edifício Green Park, Avenida dos
Combatentes 43-13, Sete Rios, 1600
(21 723 3600). Metro Sete Rios.*
Open 10am-7pm Mon-Sat; closed
Sun. **Credit** V. **Map** p304 K3.
Subscription pack 9,000$00-
53,000$00.

Telecel

*Centro Empresarial Torres de
Lisboa, Rua Tomás da Fonseca
Torre A 14, Benfica, 1600 (21 722
5000/722 4000). Bus 26, 41, 68.*
Open 9am-7pm Mon-Fri; closed
Sat, Sun. **Credit** MC, V.
Subscription pack 9,900$00-
170,000$00.

TMN

*Edifício Santa Maria, Avenida
Álvaro Pais 2, Entrecampos, 1649
(21 791 4400). Metro Entre Campos,
Campo Pequeno.* **Open** 8.30am-
7.30pm Mon-Fri; closed Sat, Sun.
Credit MC, V. **Map** 304 L3.
Subscription pack 26,600$00-
70,000$00.

Faxes

Faxes may be received and sent from
all large hotels (sometimes free) and
some smaller ones (at varying costs).

Time

Portuguese time is always
the same as British time. It's
in line with GMT in winter
and advances by one hour
in summertime. The 24-hour
clock is often used in everyday
situations.

Tipping

In restaurants and cafés a
tip of up to ten per cent is
normal. Tipping in bars is
less common, although
meagre wages often warrant
it. Tipping taxi drivers is less
common and frankly few of
them deserve it. We would
encourage tipping those
worthy few who actually
manage to take you to your
destination without whingeing,
griping or snapping.

Directory

Toilets

Lisbon is not particularly well blessed with public toilets (*sanitários* or *casas de banho*). Bar owners are not too fussy about people wandering in off the street, but your senses may be abused by the putrescence of some of the facilities. Museums, restaurants and shopping centres have the cleanest rest rooms. Men's are usually marked with an H for *homens*, women's with an S for *senhoras*.

Tourist information

Information in English on all Portugal can be had on freephone 800 296296. The best one-stop shop is the Turismo in Praça dos Restauradores (*see below*). In summer, the Lisbon tourist authorities set up 'Ask Me' booths around the city, which have helpful staff and lots of leaflets.

Turismo

Palácio Foz, Praça dos Restauradores, Baixa, 1250 (21 346 6307/21 352 5810/www.icep.pt). Metro Restauradores. **Open** 9am-8pm daily. **Map** p310 L8.
Run by the national tourist board, ICEP, this office can provide information about all Portugal. City tourist officials also have a desk here, and from them you can buy a Lisboa Card that offers up to three days unlimited travel on public transport, plus a range of discounts on cultural activities and entertainment. There is also a booth at Santa Apolónia train station (21 882 1604). At the airport there are both an ICEP desk (21 849 4323) and a Turismo de Lisboa booth (21 845 0660), where you can buy the Lisboa Card and taxi vouchers.

Lisboa Welcome Center

Rua do Arsenal 15, Baixa, 1100 (21 031 2700/fax 21 031 2899/www.atl-turismolisboa.pt). Metro Baixa-Chiado/15, 18, 28 tram. **Open** 9am-9pm daily. **Map** p310 L10.
A walk-in space recently opened by the public-private Associação de Turismo de Lisboa (ATL) in the same building as the association's new headquarters on the corner of Praça do Comércio. As well as an information desk, where you can buy the Lisboa Card and arrange accommodation, there is a tourism documentation centre, an upmarket Portuguese restaurant and grocery, a space to showcase the work of Lisbon's fashion designers, a newsagent's/tobacconist's and a café. It also houses a gallery and a 160-seater auditorium.

Visas & immigration

Standard EU immigration law applies. That means that EU citizens planning to stay more than six months will need to apply for a residence permit, but are otherwise free to come and go. Nationals of Australia and New Zealand are entitled to stay up to 90 days without a visa, but US and Canadian citizens must apply for a 60-day visa before entering. Applications for extensions should be made at least a week before the expiry of the previous leave to stay.

There are number of agencies in Lisbon that deal with residence and work permits, documentation for cars and the like. They include **Documédia** and **Bureaucratic Help Service** (for both, *see p287*).

Weights & measures

Portugal uses the metric system (kilometres, metres and centimetres, kilograms and grams, litres and millilitres).

What to take

Light, loose clothing is good for the height of summer, although the proximity of the sea means that Lisbon temperatures rarely get into the high 30s. In winter, a lack of heating in some cheap *pensões* (and many houses) and the tendency for café and restaurant owners to leave their doors open means warm clothing is essential. In winter, an umbrella is also useful, although hustlers selling cheap brollies spring from nowhere and around Metro station exits whenever it rains.

All day-to-day medical supplies are available, but bring good supplies of any prescription medicines.

Other useful things to take include photocopies of documents, high-factor sun cream in summer, and an electrical adaptor if necessary (*see p277* **Electricity**).

When to go

Accommodation prices are lower during the winter, unsurprisingly, but the rates of hotels oriented to business travellers often don't vary.

At Easter, Lisbon is overrun by visitors from Spain, who have enough days off at this time to make a long weekend worthwhile. At New Year, Italian tourists are common.

Climate

Lisbon has long, dry summers lasting from June to October and a mild winter, limited to a period of wetter and cooler weather between December and February. Autumn (October and November) and spring (March to May) are mild, but sometimes damp. May is a particularly beautiful month. Summer temperatures can reach 40°C, but outside the July-August period the nights can be cool, and there is often a wind-chill factor to contend with. On sunny days, a protective cream is a must for most skin types. In winter, the temperature rarely goes below 10°C.

Public holidays

Most shops close on public holidays, except for shopping malls and big supermarkets. Restaurants, cafés and cinemas tend not to close either, but museums do. Public holidays are: New Year's Day (1 Jan); Good Friday, Revolution Day (25 Apr); Labour Day (1 May); Corpus Christi (6 June); Camões Day (10 June); Assumption (15 Aug); Republic Day (5 Oct); All Saints Day (1 Nov); Independence Day (1 Dec); Immaculate Conception Day (8 Dec); Christmas Day (25 Dec).

Women

Like much in modern Portuguese society, recent dramatic changes in the status of women have their origins in the 1974 Revolution.

Practice lags far behind theory, however. Unequal pay is the norm, and the social status of women remains complex. The birth rate is above the EU average, even after years of decline, yet female participation in the job market is higher than anywhere in the EU except Scandinavia and the UK. That is partly because it is so tough here to support a family on one wage, but it has also altered women's social status.

The fiasco of the 1998 referendum on legalising abortion – less than a third of the electorate voted after a bitter campaign that pitted self-styled progressives against the influential Catholic Church – led some observers to wonder whether the gains of the Revolution had come too easily. In any case, a situation of profound hypocrisy remains, with the police and society at large tolerating what are conservatively estimated as 200,000 illegal abortions a year.

Like people's opinions on even such emotive issues, Portuguese machismo is far from clear-cut. Most men are positively shy and retiring compared to some Italians or Spaniards. A woman will find dodgy-looking types making lewd comments, and then mumbling and looking at their feet if she confronts them.

Facilities dedicated to women are limited; there are no bookshops or women's centres open to the general public. The organisations listed below are mostly documentation centres with an academic bent, helplines or lobbying groups, mainly state-funded. Many have no permanent premises.

Associação Portuguesa de Mulheres Empresárias

Praça das Indústrias, Edifício FIL, Santo Amaro, 1300 (21 362 3044/fax 21 362 3043). Tram 15/14, 27, 43, 49, 51, 56 bus. **Open** 9.30am-1pm, 2-6.30pm Mon-Fri; closed Sat, Sun. **Map** p305 D10.
The Portuguese Association of Businesswomen aims are to lobby for 'women's dignity in the workplace'; promote equality of opportunities through training and other means; and provide an information network.

Comissão para a Igualdade e para os Direitos das Mulheres

Avenida da República 32-1, Saldanha, 1050 (tel/fax 21 798 3098). Metro Saldanha. **Open** 10am-5pm Mon-Fri; closed Sat, Sun. **Map** p304 M5.
The government's Commission for Equality and Women's Rights is the best information source for women's issues and organisations. The library (pre-arranged visits only) is a good source of information on the history of the women's movement here.

International Women of Portugal

Apartado 1060, Cascais, 2070 (21 482 0385).
International social and support group that uses English as its common language. Annual membership 7,000$00.

Intervenção Feminina

Rua Luciano Cordeiro 24, Estefânia, 1150 (21 354 6831/21 314 2514). Metro Marquês de Pombal, Picoas. **Map** p307 L6.
Arranges seminars and conferences on various themes. Its aim is the promotion of women's participation in every area of political, cultural and social life, and the development of 'feminine bonds of solidarity' with other women's organisations.

União de Mulheres Alternativa e Resposta

Rua de São Lázaro 111, Martim Moniz, 1150 (21 886 4845/7096/fax 21 888 4086). Metro Martim Moniz. **Open** 10am-1pm, 2-6pm Mon-Fri; closed Sat, Sun. **Map** p311 M8.
UMAR, the Alternative Union of Women, is one of Portugal's most militant and famous organisations, with an unashamedly left-wing agenda. It has generated piles of important documentation, which is finally being organised and archived. Its activities nowadays tend to be practical, focusing on employment rights and the welfare of women from disadvantaged groups.

Working in Lisbon

Work permits

EU citizens are free to work in Portugal, although if they intend to stay for more than six months they will need a residence permit.

For non-EU nationals wishing to reside in Portugal, permits may be issued to students or workers filling a gap in the labour market, but this is not easily arranged. Portugal's recent construction boom has triggered several initiatives under which illegal immigrant workers – mainly African and South Asian – were permitted to apply for residence permits, but, with the boom slowing, the government is unlikely to have any more such amnesties (*see p42* **Eastern exposure**), and it may get harder to get a permit There are even fears that existing permits will not be renewed, raising the spectre of deportations.

For more information on immigration issues, contact the Portuguese embassy or consulate in your home country.

Useful addresses

Serviço de Estrangeiros e Fronteiras

Avenida António Augusto de Aguiar 20, Marquês de Pombal, 1069-119 (21 358 5500/www.sef.pt). Metro Parque. **Open** 9am-3pm Mon-Fri; closed Sat, Sun. **Map** p307 L6.
Either you or your *despachante* (agent) must queue at the Foreigners Registration Office if you intend to get a residence permit. Take a ticket from each dispenser as you are bound to be in the wrong line. **Branch**: Rua da Bela Vista 84, Cascais 2750-304 (21 484 6217).

Bureaucratic Help Service

Centro Comercial Charneca, Loja 13, Rua das Lapas, Cascais, 2750-772 (21 485 8233/fax 21 485 8238/bhs@mail.telepac.pt). Train from Cais do Sodré. **Open** 9am-6pm Mon-Fri. **No credit cards.**
Handles problems ranging from residence permits and tax numbers through driver's licenses, car legalisation and official translations.

Documédia

Rua Alexandre Herculano 19, 2°, Room 4, Rato, 1250-008 (tel/fax 21 357 0306). Metro Rato. **Open** 9am-6pm Mon-Fri; closed Sat, Sun. **No credit cards.** **Map** p307 K7.
Deals with most official documents, including tax numbers and the paperwork for starting a business.

Directory

Vocabulary

On first contact, the Portuguese language can seem unsettlingly difficult. Here, on the western fringes of Latin Europe, one might expect something closer to the resonant rattle of Spanish or the Romantic cadences of Italian. Instead, the closed vowels and insistently shushing consonants could fool the linguistically challenged into believing they have been transported somewhere east of Prague, throwing many visitors off the scent.

In fact speakers of other Romance languages are in better shape than they might first think – particularly with written Portuguese. A glance at the nearest road sign will provide an immediate, and sometimes amusing, sense of familiarity. It doesn't take too much linguistic intuition to realise that *modera a sua velocidade* means 'reduce your speed'. Conversations, too, quickly become less inpenetrable.

Equally encouraging is the fact that the Portuguese are themselves excellent linguistics. For decades millions of them have packed their bags to try their luck elsewhere. Even people with little formal education are likely to have picked up foreign language skills while working abroad.

Pronunciation

Pronunciation follows some clear rules. Once you get the hang of it, the sshh is one of the more pleasing sounds to play with. However, there are one or two awkward rules to its use. The s always takes the sh sound at the end of words. Elsewhere, it becomes sshh only when followed by t or c. Watch the latter, however. Cascais is 'Kashkaish', whereas *piscina* is 'pisheena'. Try this: *há uma piscina em Cascais* – 'There is a swimming pool in Cascais'. Another feature is the nh and lh consanants, which are similar to the Spanish ñ and ll. Thus Saldanha is pronounced 'Saldanya', and *bacalhau* is 'bakalyow'. The c is soft before e and i, but hard elsewhere. Thus *comércio* is 'commersio'. Note also that m takes on a nasal tone at the end of words. Thus *sim*, for yes, actually sounds closer to the spanish *sí* than it looks on paper.

Vowels are tricky, and it is the closed, truncated way of expressing them that makes locals difficult to follow. Accents usually denote a stressed syllable, although the tilde and the ^ also give the vowel a more nasal or more elongated sound. The ão is the Portuguese specialty that most famously trips up foreign mouths. A highly nasal and truncated 'oww' is the best description we can offer. Thus *informação* is 'informasow', with a nasal yelp on the last syllable.

The e is silent at the end of the word, unless it has an accent. So *saudade* is pronounced 'sowdad', whereas café is 'kaffay'.
More pronunciation tips:
ç – like the 's' in song
sh – like the sh in ship
j – like the s in treasure
g – is like j, except when it comes before an a, o or u when it is hard.
q – is like k in English
x – is like the sh in Welsh
ei – like the ay in hay
ou – like the or in sorted

Useful phrases

Yes *Sim*
No *Não*
Maybe *Talvéz (se calhar)*
Hello *Olá*
Good day/evening/night *Bom dia/boa tarde/boa noite*
Goodbye *Adeus* (formal)/**ciao** (informal)
See you later *até logo*
How are you? *Como está? Como estás?* (more informal) *Tudo bem?* (more informal still)
I'm fine *Estou bem*
Thanks *Obrigado* (masc) *Obrigada* (fem)
You're welcome *De nada. Não tem de qué*
Please *Por favor/Se faz favor*
Excuse me *Com licença*
Sorry *Desculpe/Desculpa* (informal)
That's/It's okay *Está bem*
Today *Hoje*
Tomorrow *Amanhã*
I'd like *Queria*
Where is (a fixed thing). *Onde fica?*
Where is (a movable thing or person) *Onde está?*
Where is the toilet? *Onde fica a casa de banho?*
Men's *Homens/Senhores*
Women's *Mulheres/Senhoras*
There is/There are *Há*
There is/aren't *Não há*
Why *Porquê*
When *Quando*
Who is it? *Quem é?*
Very *Muito*
Near *Perto*
Far *Longe*
Big *Grande*
Hot *Quente*
Cold *Frio*
Small *Pequeno*
Now *Agora*
Later *Mais tarde*
Before *Antes*

Is there a good restaurant around here? *Há um bom restaurante por aqui?*
With/Without *Com/Sem*
Is it cheap/expensive? *É barato/caro?*
How much is it/are they? *Quanto é/quanto são?*
Buy *Comprar*
Rent *Alugar*
Open *Aberto*
Closed *Fechado*
Entrance *Entrada*
Exit *Saída*
Good *Bom/boa*
Bad *Mau/má*
I like... *Gosto de...*
I don't like... *Não gosto de...*
I don't speak Portuguese *Não falo Português*
Do you speak English? *Fala inglês?* (formal) *Falas inglês?* (informal)
I don't understand *Não entendo*
Speak more slowly please. *Fale mais devagar, por favor*
What is your name? *Como se chama* (formal) *Como te chamas* (informal)
My name is *Chamo-me*
I am English/American *Sou inglês/norte-americano* (masc). *Sou inglesa/norte-americana* (fem)
Airport *Aeroporto*
Railway station *Estacão de comboios*
Bus station *Rodoviário*
Do you know the way to... *Sabe o caminho para…*
Left *Esquerda*
Right *Direita*
Straight on *Sempre em frente*
Until the end of the street. *Até ao final da rua*
Bus stop *Paragem de autocarros*
Petrol *Gasolina*
Diesel *Gasóeo*
Ticket office *Bilheteira*
Single *Ida*
Return *Ida e volta*
I'd like to go to... *Queria ir á...*
When does the train to/from Oporto leave/arrive? *A que horas sai/chega o comboio para Oporto?*
One/two/three o'clock *Uma/duas/tres Horas*
Do you have a single/double room for tonight? *Tem um quarto individuo/duplo para hoje?*
Bathroom *Casa de banho*
Bed *Cama*
Bath *Banheira*
Shower *Chuveiro/Ducha*
I feel ill *Sinto-me mal*
Doctor *Médico*
Pharmacy *Farmácia*
Hospital *Hospital*
Ambulance *Ambulância*
Police *Polícia*

Directory

You what?

'You' for the Portuguese is like 'snow' for the Inuit: a simple, one-word concept for most of the world, but for them a complex phenomenon requiring its own intricate lexicon.

In Portugal, deference has been elevated to an art form. A natural Latin tendency for the ornate, magnified by social history, resulted in elaborate forms of address that translate into English like lines from a Restoration comedy. Buying groceries can become a courtly dance of manners; introductions a social minefield. Foreigners are excused compliance with the more arcane nuances, but a little awareness can lend depth to the simplest encounters.

Speculative explanations abound. Did the Salazar regime freeze social manners in the 1930s, when Portugal was essentially still a 19th-century society? Did an oligarchy run by a few powerful families insist on excessive hierarchical respect? Could an awareness of a huge network of petty political informers have even made formality a defensive strategem?

Certainly, limited access to higher education has long entitled anyone with a degree to special esteem. Graduating elevates you to Senhor Doutor, Senhor Engenheiro, Senhor Arquitecto or the feminine equivalents. These are everyday forms not reserved for letterheads or award ceremonies. 'I'm afraid Madam Doctor is in a meeting,' says a secretary. 'Would Sir Engineer like to see the menu?' a waiter asks.

Mastery of other Latin languages is no guide: the Portuguese contrive to be more formal than the French, more elaborate than the Italians. Spaniards, though sticklers for etiquette, are more straightforward in this respect. True, the Portuguese indulge foreigners' mistakes, but inappropriate use of *tu*, the familiar second-person singular, even if you are stumbling with your first phrases, could cause embarrassment.

Nuances abound even in close relationships. Parents always use *tu* to address their children, and most sons and daughters reciprocate. But in many families that consider themselves well bred, the children will use the more formal third-person singular form. Asking Mum a question such as: 'Is Mother going to the hairdresser's today?' instantly marks you out as posh.

Third-person singular is the rule when it might be wrong to be familiar. *O senhor* or *a senhora* serve when nothing specific is known about the addressee. 'Is Madam being served?' a shop assistant will ask. Safety can usually be found by using the third-person singular of the verb, with no subject. *Você*, meaning you, with the third-person singular verb, is a Brazilian usage adopted by some Portuguese. But it is looked down on as vulgar by the well mannered.

When you know someone a little, though, you can start bandying about their first name, for example asking your business acquaintance Claudia: 'When is Claudia taking her holidays?'

The *tu* form is for family, friends, children and animals. But it is also good for insults. When berating a driver who has mangled your bumper, always use *tu*. Professional solidarity is also conveyed by the familiar form. Journalists, for example, always call each other *tu*, even if they have never met, and regardless of seniority.

The Portuguese themselves are never quite free from the pitfalls and often smooth the way for each other. 'Is it all right to call you *tu*?' is a common query as people get acquainted.

Raised in all these subtleties, it is perhaps not surprising that the Portuguese excel at diplomacy, trade and negotiation.

Days of the week	**five** *cinco*	**eighteen** *dezoito*
Sunday *domingo*	**six** *seis*	**nineteen** *dezanove*
Monday *segunda-feira*	**seven** *sete*	**twenty** *vinte*
Tuesday *terça-feira*	**eight** *oito*	**twenty one** *vinte e um*
Wednesday *quarta-feira*	**nine** *nove*	**thirty** *trinta*
Thursday *quinta-feira*	**ten** *dez*	**forty** *quarenta*
Friday *sexta-feira*	**eleven** *onze*	**fifty** *cinquenta*
Saturday *sábado*	**twelve** *doze*	**sixty** *sessenta*
Numbers	**thirteen** *treze*	**seventy** *setenta*
one *um/uma*	**fourteen** *quatorze*	**eighty** *oitenta*
two *dois/duas*	**fifteen** *quinze*	**ninety** *noventa*
three *três*	**sixteen** *dezasseis*	**hundred** *cem*
four *quatro*	**seventeen** *dezassete*	**one thousand** *mil*

Directory

Further Reference

Books

Literature & fiction

Camões, Luís Vaz *The Lusiads*
This is Portugal's national work of
literature – an epic poem chronicling
the adventures of Vasco da Gama
during the Discoveries. If you can't
read Portuguese, bad luck – it's all
but unreadable in English.

**Lisboa, Eugénio & Macedo,
Helder (eds)** *The Dedalus Book of
Portuguese Fantasy*
Portuguese fantasy: a wonderful
collection of stories from famous
Portuguese writers.

Lisboa, Eugénio (ed) *The
Anarchist Banker and Other
Portuguese Stories: Volume I*
Excellent Portuguese lit primer -
short stories by Pessoa, Eça de
Queiróz and others.

Lisboa, Eugénio (ed) *Professor
Pfiglzz and His Strange Companion
and Other Portuguese Stories:
Volume II*
More short stories from lusophone
literary luminaries.

Pires, José Cardoso *Ballad of
Dog's Beach*
This detective story is set in the
Salazar years, and based on a real-
life murder that happened during
those years.

José Saramago

'*O prémio Nobel*' (the Nobel Prize), they call
him – Portuguese makes no distinction
between prize and the prizewinner. And
indeed, in the eyes of many of his proud
compatriots, José Saramago is
indistinguishable from the great prize,
awarded for the first time to a Portuguese
writer and thus, many feel, to a small country
with a large but little-known literature.

Saramago himself, a 78-year-old man of
humble beginnings, wags his finger at them
from podiums across the country, warning
that humanism is being suffocated by global
capitalism and materialistic desires.

Since his first major success, with
Balthazar and Blimunda (*Memorial do
Convento* in the original) in 1982, and even
more so since his 1998 Nobel Prize,
Saramago travels a great deal to meet his
readers, in circumstances large and small.
'Because they invite me,' he explains, 'and if
people want to listen to me, to be with me, I
would find it very difficult to turn them down'.
Or, more succinctly, 'because they like me'.

Rather than talking about his books on
these occasions, Saramago often uses the
platform to expound his view of the world and
its ills, although he does this with a humour
that alleviates the deep pessimism that
underlies it. Nevertheless, the moralising of
this long-time Communist Party member can
sometimes seem simplistic, in contrast to
his writing, where the delivery of the same
world view is much more polyphonic and open
to fruitful interpretation.

Saramago's style of writing is an obstacle
to many readers. His refusal to use any
punctuation other than commas and the
occasional full stop, or to divide the text into
paragraphs, is near legendary. His late, great
translator into English, Giovanni Pontiero,

always dedicated much of his preface to
explaining the author's grounds for this: that
the text should be regarded as a narrative in
the old sense, as a story told by a speaker,
and that speakers don't use punctuation.

That is arguable. Speakers have many ways
of indicating nuance – intonation, rhythm,
facial expressions and gestures – that
writers couldn't match with any amount of
punctuation. But once you get into Saramago,
that hardly matters. The beauty of his style,
which is comparable to both Joyce and Jack
Kerouac, is that the reader provides the
punctuation. As with much great music, the
rapturous listener/reader predicts the next
change, be it of key, rhythm or reasoning, an
instant before it happens – or so it seems.
And those trailing dialogues in Saramago's
work, where you lose track of who's saying
what, are no reason to despair. You don't
always need to know who's talking; it's
actually the author's interior dialogue, as
he may soon remind you in one of those
occasional asides to the reader.

There is a deeper meaning to this.
Saramago's books have become darker
since the relative playfulness of *Balthazar
and Blimunda*, *The Stone Raft* (*A Jangada
de Pedra*) or *The History of the Siege of
Lisbon* (*História do Cerco de Lisboa*).
He has described his latest three books,
Blindness (*Ensaio Sobre a Cegueira*), *All
the Names* (*Todos os Nomes*) and *The
Cave* (*A Caverna*) as an involuntary trilogy,
as if he wanted to get further under the skin
of what he had previously described: 'As if
I wanted to get inside the individual.' His
journeys on the inside are no joyride, for
sure, but there is plenty of dry humour,
practical philosophy and everyday heroism
to dampen that hollow echo at the core.

Pessoa, Fernando *The Book of Disquietude*
The savagely solipsistic 'factless autobiography' of Bernardo Soares, now available in Richard Zenith's translation.

Pessoa, Fernando *A Centenary Pessoa*
Excellent introduction to Pessoa. An anthology of Pessoa's poetry and prose also containing some critical commentary, a 'life and times' chronology as well as two 'posthumous interviews'.

Pessoa, Fernando *Selected Poems*
A slim Penguin Modern Classic.

Queiróz, Eça de *Cousin Bazilia*
From Portugal's premier 19th-century novelist, the story of an affair between a bored bourgeois Principe Real housewife and her dashing cousin.

Remarque, Erich Maria *The Night in Lisbon*
The author of *All Quiet on the Western Front* sets an adventure and love story in neutral Lisbon during World War II, as enemies of the Third Reich try to flee the continent.

Saramago, José *Balthazar and Blimunda*
The book that made the name of the 1998 Nobel prize winner for literature, an almost magically realist adventure set in Lisbon and Mafra about a priest who wanted to make a flying machine.

Saramago, José *The Year of the Death of Ricardo Reis*
Saramago gets to grips with a Pessoa heteronym – Reis returns from Brazil to Lisbon under Salazar, and meets the ghost of his creator.

Tabucchi, Antonio *Declares Perreira*
A newspaperman questions his life in the face of state censorship. A novel that illuminates the oppressive nature of the Salazar years.

Zimler, Richard *The Last Cabbalist of Lisbon*
Essentially a detective story, set in the anti-Jewish riots of 1506. Readable and involving.

History

Boorstin, Daniel J *The Discoverers*
Substantial, standard text on the era of maritime exploration.

Boxer, CR *The Portuguese Seaborne Empire (1415-1825)*
The classic account of Portugal's glory days and maritime empire.

Figueiredo, António de *Portugal: Fifty Years of Dictatorship*
From the 1926 military coup to the 1974 Revolution – a more than serviceable account of fascism in Portugal.

Saraiva, José Hermano *Portugal: A Companion History*
Decent, short, no-nonsense history of Portugal, complete with chronology, gazetteer and historical maps.

Travel & memoir

Kaplan, Marion *The Portuguese: The Land and its People*
Updated and revised in 1998, the best single-volume introduction to Portugal and the Portuguese.

Macaulay, Rose *They Came to Portugal*
An account of British travellers in Portugal from the Crusaders to Byron and Beckford, adding up to an oblique anecdotal history.

Pessoa, Fernando *Lisbon: What The Tourist Should See*
Apart from everything else, Lisbon's iconic poet also wrote a guide book. Sadly, it covers only the obvious sights, but it's a nice volume with fold-out map.

Pinto, Fernão Mendes *Peregrinations*
A huge and no-holds-barred account of 20 years of rape, pillage and adventuring from Portugal to Japan during the era of the Discoveries – written after Pinto returned home and became a priest. Lots of fun.

Food & drink

Mayson, Richard *Portugal's Wine and Wine-Makers: Port, Madeira and Regional Wines*
A hefty coffee-table book with history, breakdown of wine regions, and pretty much everything else you might need to know.

Vieira, Edite *The Taste of Portugal*
Loads of recipes, combined with snippets of history and Portuguese lit. Well written in a hearty kind of way.

Film

Although there are relatively few Portuguese films compared to the production of most European countries, even those there are can be quite difficult to see. Classics sometimes show up at the Cinemateca (*see p190*). Otherwise there are specialist video collections on imprints such as Atalanta and Costa do Castelo. Here we list ten landmark Portuguese films.

A Cançao de Lisboa
(*Lisbon Song*, 1933) Cottinelli Telmo
Portugal's first sound film, which heralded a series of classic comedies. Vasco is living the high life on the money sent by his aunts to pursue his studies. Everything is wonderful until one day his aunts decide to visit.

Pai Tirano
(*The Tyrannical Father*, 1941) António Lopes Ribeiro
One of Portugal's finest comedies. A young girl who works in a drugstore and adores the movies is torn between the charms of a budding actor and a veteran seducer.

Aniki-Bóbó
(1943) Manoel de Oliveira.
A band of children in the streets of Oporto. They are poor, free and live in a magical world of adventure.

Verdes Anos
(*Green Years*, 1963) Paulo Rocha
The start of the Portuguese New Wave. A young man from the provinces travels to Lisbon to try his luck as a cobbler. A vision of Lisbon as a claustrophobic labyrinth, filled with cul-de-sacs.

Trás os Montes
(1976) Antonio Reis and Margarida Cordeiro
A masterpiece capturing the world 'beyond the mountains', that seems to be a land where time stands still.

Recordações de Casa Amarela
(*Memories of the Madhouse*, 1989) João César Monteiro
Monteiro himself stars as João de Deus in this idiosyncratic tale of transgression and madness in a popular neighbourhood of Lisbon.

Viagem até o Princípio do Mundo
(*Journey to the Beginning of the World*, 1997) Manoel de Oliveira
A moving auto-biographical portrait in which Manoel de Oliveira (portrayed by Marcello Mastroianni) returns to his roots in northern Portugal.

Ossos
(*Bones*, 1997) Pedro Costa
A dark journey, with breathtaking cinematography, into Lisbon's underbelly, performed by non-professional actors.

Tentação
(*Temptation*, 1997) Joaquim Leitão
Starring Joaquim d'Almeida, Temptation is the all-time biggest box office hit among Portuguese-made films. A Catholic priest succumbs to the twin temptations of the needle and the flesh.

Os Capitães de Abril
(*Captains of April*, 2000) Maria de Medeiros
A story based on the key events of the 1974 Revolution, that successfully recreates the 'flower-power' atmosphere of the Carnation Revolution.

Websites

Information on tourism and cultural events can be found on:
www.portugal.hpv.pt/lisboa/agenda
www.maisturismo.pt
portugalvirtual.pt.

Index

Figures in **bold** indicate sections containing
key information. *Italics* indicate photographs.

Advertisers' Index

Please refer to the relevant pages for
addresses and telephone numbers.

Place of Interest and/or Entertainment	
Railway Stations	
Tube Stations	
Parks	
Hospitals	
Steps	
Churches	✚
Area Name	CHIADO

Maps

Portugal

Ourense

VIGO

Bragança

Chaves

Braga

Vila Real

Torre de Moncorvo

OPORTO

Lamego

Vilar Formoso

Aveiro

Viseu

Guarda

Figueira da Foz

Coimbra

Covilhã

S P A I N

Leiria

Tomar

Castelo Branco

Peniche

Torres Novas

Castelo de Vide

Marvão

Santarém

P O R T U G A L

Tejo

Badajoz

see page 301

Estremoz

Cascais

LISBON

Vila Viçosa

Setúbal

Évora

Monsaraz

Baia de Setúbal

Grândola

Beja

Serpa

A T L A N T I C

O C E A N

Odemira

SEVILLE

Silves

Vila Real de Santo António

Lagos

Albufeira

Portimão

Tavira

Golfo de Cádiz

Cabo de San Vincente

Sagres

Faro

0   30 miles

0   40 km

© Copyright Time Out Group 2001

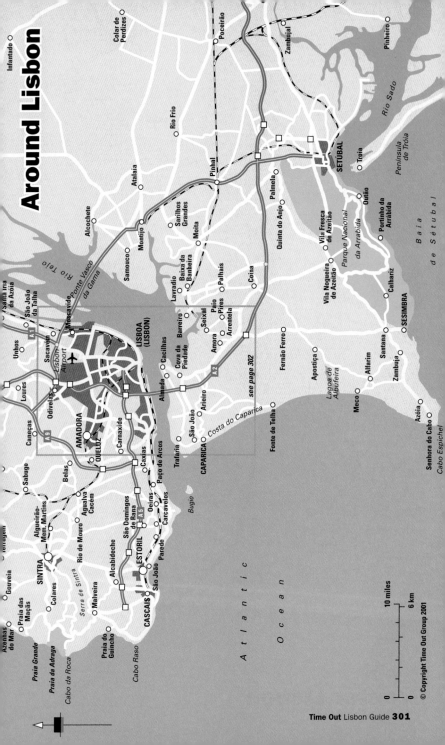

Around Lisbon

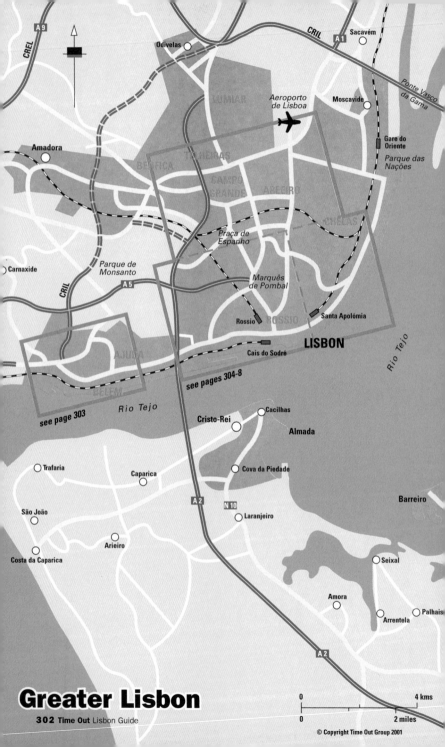

Greater Lisbon

© Copyright Time Out Group 2001

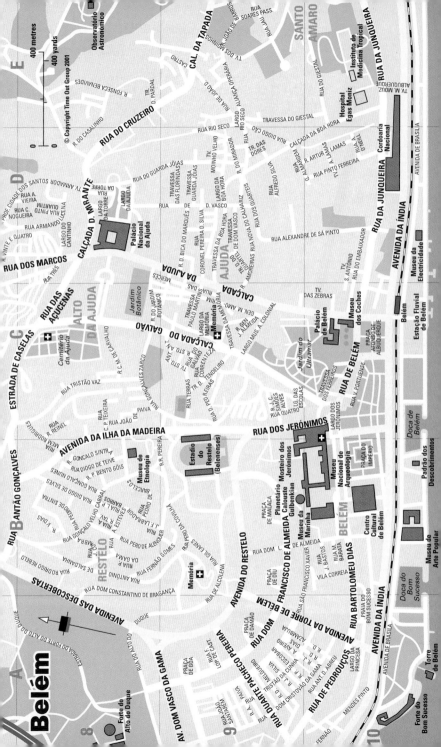

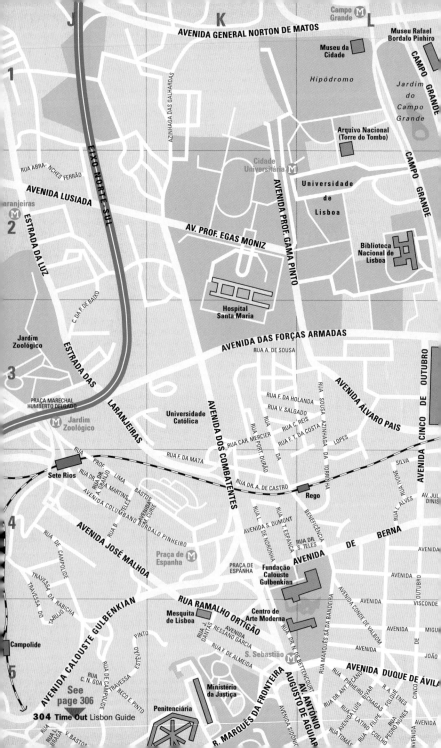

AVENIDA GENERAL NORTON DE MATOS

Campo Grade

Museu Rafael Bordalo Pinheiro

Museu da Cidade

Hipódromo

Jardim do Campo Grande

Arquivo Nacional (Torre do Tombo)

CAMPO GRANDE

RUA ABRA- NCHES FERRÃO

AVENIDA LUSIADA

aranjeiras

ESTRADA DA LUZ

Cidade Universitária

Universidade de Lisboa

AV. PROF. EGAS MONIZ

AVENIDA PROF. GAMA PINTO

AZINHAGA DAS GALHARDAS

EIXO-NORTE-SUL

C. DA DE BAIXO

Biblioteca Nacional de Lisboa

Hospital Santa Maria

Jardim Zoológico

ESTRADA DAS

AVENIDA DAS FORÇAS ARMADAS

RUA A. DE SOUSA

PRAÇA MARECHAL HUMBERTO DELGADO

Jardim Zoológico

LARANJEIRAS

Universidade Católica

AVENIDA DOS COMBATENTES

RUA F. DA HOLANDA

RUA V. SALGADO

RUA C. REIS

RUA F. T. DA COSTA

AVENIDA ÁLVARO PAIS

AVENIDA CINCO DE OUTUBRO

RUA SOUSA

RUA CAR. MERCIER

RUA PORT. DURÃO

AZINHAGA DA TORRINHA

LOPES

RUA F. DA MATA

RUA DR. A. DE CASTRO

DA

SILVA

RUA L. IVONE

Sete Rios

RUA PROF. LIMA BASTOS

RUA DR. GAMA MARTINS

AVENIDA COLUMBANO BORDALO PINHEIRO

Rego

BENEFICÊNCIA

RUA A. DE NORONHA

AVENIDA S. DUMONT

RUA DR. S. TELES

RUA S. T. ESPANÇA

RUA L. ALVES

AV. JUL. DINIS

BERNA

DE

AVENIDA JOSÉ MALHOA

RUA DE CAMPOLIDE

TRAVESSA DA RABICHA

TRAVESSA DO TARUJO

Praça de Espanha

PRAÇA DE ESPANHA

AVENIDA

RUA MARQUÊS SÁ DA BANDEIRA

AVENIDA CONDE DE VALBOM

VISCONDE

OUTUBRO

Campolide

RUA RAMALHO ORTIGÃO

Mesquita de Lisboa

Centro de Arte Moderna

Fundação Calouste Gulbenkian

AVENIDA CALOUSTE GULBENKIAN

See page 306

RUA C. N. GOA

RUA DE CAMPOLIDE

PINTO

ESTÊVÃO

TRAVESSA

BECO E PINTO

RUA J. DANTAS

RESSANO GARCIA

RUA F. DE ALMEIDA

AVENIDA

S. Sebastião

AVENIDA DUQUE DE ÁVILA

RUA PINHEIRO CHAGAS

RUA CONDE DE REDONDO

MIGUEL

JOÃO

AVENIDA

AVENIDA ANTÓNIO AUGUSTO DE AGUIAR

AV. ANTÓNIO

RUA DR. N. BETTENCOURT

Ministério da Justiça

Penitenciária

R. MARQUÊS DA FRONTEIRA

AVENIDA SIDÓNIO

AVENIDA DUQUE DE ÁVILA

RUA TOMÁS

RUA LUÍS

RUA PEDRO NUNES

M

N

O

Lisbon
Airport

0
400 metres

0
400 yards

1

© Copyright Time Out Group 2001

Hospital
Julio de Matos

AVENIDA DO BRASIL

RUA A. MAFRA

RUA J. SARAIVA

RUA DO C. CULTURAL

RUA R. JORGE

RUA A. FERREIRA

RUA ALFERES
MALHEIRO

RUA A. DE PAIVA

RUA L. A. PALMEIRIM

RUA C. MAYER

AVE. S. JOANA A PRINCESA

Alvalade

AVENIDA DA IGREJA

AVENIDA DO RIO DE JANEIRO

RUA CONDE DE FICALHO

AVENIDA D. RODRIGO DA CUNHA

RUA FRANCISCO FRANCO

2

ALVALADE

RUA AFONSO

LOPEZ VIEIRA

CAMPO GRANDE

RUA F. PESSOA

RUA M. A. VAZ DE CARVALHO

RUA C. M. DIAS

RUA VIANA DA MOTA

Entrecampos

RUA ANTÓNIO PATRICIO

AVENIDA ESTADOS UNIDOS

AVENIDA DA AMÉRICA

RUA S. E. ALBUQUERQUE

RUA A. R. COLAÇO

RUA F. M. CARDOSO

RUA EPIFÂNIO DIAS

RUA D. BONTEMPO

RUA DUARTE LOBO

RUA E. DE NORONHA

AVENIDA ALMIRANTE GAGO COUTINHO

Parque
da Bela Vista

3

Feira
Popular

RUA DE ENTRECAMPOS

RUA J. F. VASCONCELOS

RUA FLORES DO LIMA

RUA F. FERREIRA

RUA F. TOMÉ DE JESUS

DA

ROMA

Roma

RUA C. BENTO

RUA DR. GAMA BARROS

ROMA

AV. ESTRADOS

AVENIDA UNIDOS DA AMERICA

RUA G. SUGGIA

RUA F. A. ARRAIS

T.H. CARDOSO

Entrecampos

AVENIDA FREI MIGUEL CONTREIRAS

Areeiro

REPÚBLICA

AV. ANTÓNIO
SERPA CAMPO

CAMPO
PEQUENO

DA

PRAÇA
DE TOUROS

PEQUENO

RUA CAPITÃO RAMIRES

RUA ÓSCAR M. TORRES

AVENIDA DE MADRID

4

Campo
Pequeno

Palácio
Galveias
(Biblioteca
Municipal)

AVENIDA

R. ARCO DO CEGO

Caixa Geral
de Depósiteos

AVENIDA MARCONI

JOÃO XXI

PRAÇA FRANCISCO
SA CARNEIRO

AVENIDA DE PARIS

RUA SARMENTO DE BEIRES

AVENIDA AFONSO COSTA

BARBOSA

DU

BOCAGE

AVENIDA

ARCO
DO
GEGO

PRAÇA DE
LONDRES

PRAÇA
PASTÉUR

RUA A. VIRGINIA

Areeiro

AVENIDA ALMIRANTE REIS

OLAIAS

Olaias

5

AVENIDAS

ELIAS

CHAVES

GARCIA

DE

DE

VALMOR

AVDA. MÉXICO

AVDA. GUERRA JUNQUEIRO

PRAÇA JOÃO
DO RIO

RUA P. L. DO CARMO

RUA CARLOS

RUA L. DO CARMO

RUA MARDEL

RUA ISIDORO

RUA A.

RUA ABADE

RUA A. J. ROSA

RUA EGAS MONIZ

RUA BARTO

RUA FARIA

ROTUNDA
DAS OLAIAS

NOVAS

BOMBARDA

CRISÓSTOMO

AVENIDA DOS DEFENSORES

RUA D. FILIPA DE VILHENA

REDOL

AVENIDA A. JOSÉ DE ALMEIDA

Instituto
Superior
Técnico

AVENIDA DE MAIA

ALAMEDA

DOM

RUA V. SARMENTO

RUA JOSÉ NEVES

RUA DE MENEZES

RUA AUG. MACHADO

RUA CARLOS

RUA A.

AVE. ENG.

Saldanha

See
page 307

AV. ROVISCO PAIS

AVENIDA MANUEL DE MAIA

AFONSO

See
page 308

HENRIQUES

Alameda

ALTO DO PINA

RUA C. FALCÃO

RUA AD. MACHADO

R. PROF. MIR
FERNANDES

RAÇA DUQUE

PRAIA VITORIA

E SALDANHA

V. SANTARÉM

TRAVESSA
DAS FREIRAS

Q. DA FONSECA

RUA F.
SILVA

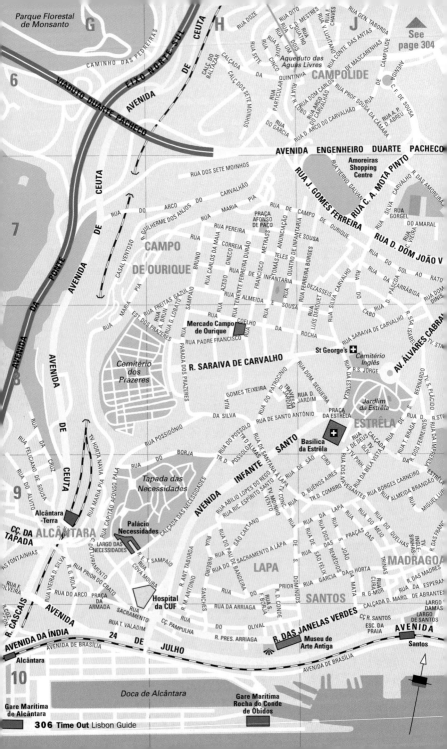

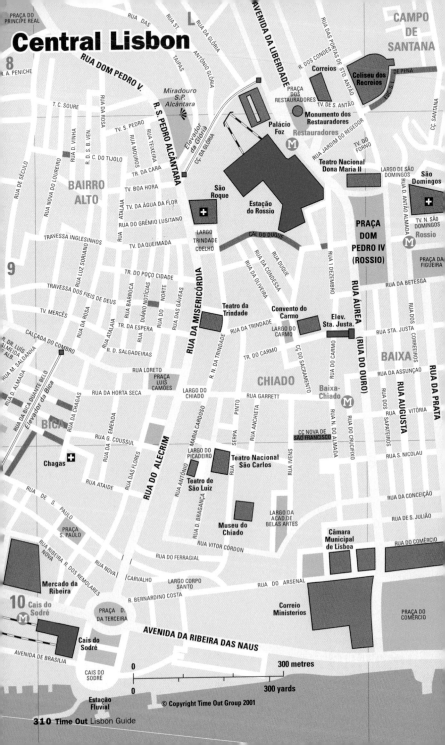

Central Lisbon

© Copyright Time Out Group 2001

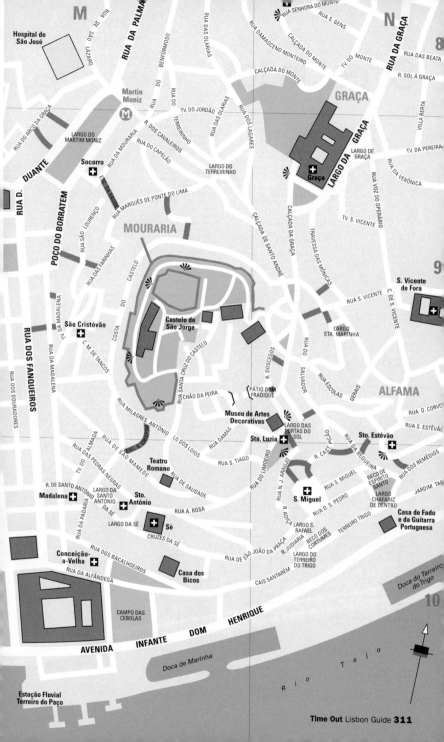

Street Index

Metro

Diagrama da rede

Odivelas

Senhor Roubado

Ameixoeira

Lumiar

Quinta das Mouras

Telheiras   Campo Grande |

Pontinha

Carnide

Colégio Militar/Luz   Cidade Universitária   Alvalade

Alto dos Moinhos   Entre Campos | Roma

Laranjeiras

Jardim Zoológico   Campo Pequeno   Areeiro |

Praça de Espanha   Saldanha   Alameda

S. Sebastião   Picoas   Arroios

Parque   Anjos

Marquês de Pombal   Intendente

Avenida   Martim Moniz

Rato   Restauradores   Rossio

Baixa–Chiado

Cais do Sodré   Terreiro do Paço | Santa Apolónia |

Oriente

Cabo Ruivo

Olivais

Chelas

Bela Vista

Olaias

Legenda

Interface com caminho de ferro

Interface com autocarros suburbanos

Interface com barcos

Em construção